Spirituality and Communion in the Orthodox Liturgy

Dumitru Staniloae

Spirituality and Communion in the Orthodox Liturgy

Translated and Edited by
Ioan Ionita

Foreword by
Radu Bordeianu

HOLY CROSS
ORTHODOX PRESS
Brookline, Massachusetts

© 2025 Ioan Ionita
Published by Holy Cross Orthodox Press
Hellenic College, Inc.
50 Goddard Avenue
Brookline, MA 02445

ISBN: 978-1-960613-08-0 ePub -- 978-1-960613-10-3

All rights reserved. No part of this publication may be reproduced in any form, by print, microfilm, microfiche, mechanical recording, photocopying or by any other means, known or yet invented, for any purpose except brief quotations in reviews without the prior written permission of the publisher.

On the cover: Paten with the Communion of the Apostles, Byzantine, 6th century. Dumbarton Oaks collection.

Publisher's Cataloging-in-Publication
(Provided by Cassidy Cataloguing Services, Inc.)

Names: Stăniloae, Dumitru, author. | Ioniță, Ioan, editor, translator. | Bordeianu, Radu, writer of foreword.
Title: Spirituality and communion in the Orthodox liturgy / Dumitry Staniloae ; translated and edited by Ioan Ionita ; foreword by Radu Bordeianu.
Other titles: Spiritualitate și comuniune in liturghia ortodoxă. English
Description: Brookline, MA : Holy Cross Orthodox Presss, [2025]
Identifiers: ISBN: 9781960613080
Subjects: LCSH: Orthodox Eastern Church--Liturgy. | Spiritual life--Orthodox Eastern Church. | Orthodox Eastern Church--Doctrines. | Lord's Supper--Orthodox Eastern Church. | Sacraments--Orthodox Eastern Church.
Classification: LCC BX350.A5 S7313 2025 | DDC: 264/.019--dc23

Contents

FOREWORD vii
INTRODUCTION xiii

PREAMBLE

A. The church building: image of cosmic and human creation 1
   1. The meaning of cosmic creation as a potential developing Church 8
   2. The human being as church and the human person as priest within the church 11
B. The church building proper: heaven on earth or the liturgical center of creation 18
   1. The holiness of the church building 19
   2. The church building: the space consecrated by God's very presence and by His descent within it 22
   3. Ascension toward God symbolized and aided by the architecture of the Orthodox church building 29
   4. Through its consecration the church receives God within it as the One who fulfills His saving work 40
C. Holy icons in the Orthodox worship 51
   1. Justification of holy icons 51
   2. The purpose of holy icons in the Orthodox Church 67
   3. Placement of holy icons in the church 78
D. The modes of Christ's presence in the worship of the Church 85

ON THE HOLY LITURGY

CHAPTER ONE
   Proskomedia or the service of the pre-offering of the gifts for Christ's holy sacrifice 117

CHAPTER TWO
   The Liturgy proper: the joint progress within the kingdom of the Holy Trinity 149

1. The Liturgy of the catechumens or of the calling
   and teaching — 149
2. The praise of the promised Kingdom of the Holy Trinity
   as an exhortation for and a beginning of one's progress
   toward it — 151
3. The threefold series of fervent supplications (litanies) — 185
4. The small entrance or Christ's coming out to preach
   and the praise of God's holiness — 210
5. Christ's preaching: the reading of the Epistle
   and of the Gospel — 225
6. The litany after the reading of the Gospel and the prayers
   for the deceased and for the catechumens — 236

CHAPTER THREE
The Liturgy of the faithful or of the Sacrifice and of Holy Communion
1. The litanies for the faithful and the two prayers of the priest as
   preparation for the offering and the transformation of the gifts
   of the faithful into the unbloody Sacrifice — 261
   a. The first litany and prayer for the faithful — 261
   b. The second litany and prayer for the faithful — 268
2. The prayer of the priest in which he asks directly to be
   deemed worthy of offering Christ Himself as sacrifice — 271
3. The Great Entrance — 272
4. The litany and prayer of the priest before the Creed — 285
5. The love among the faithful and the recitation of the Creed — 292
6. Anamnesis as preparation for the presentation of the gifts
   to God and for their sanctification — 306
   a. Introduction to the anamnesis that prepares
      the gifts for the transformation — 306
   b. The two parts of the anamnesis — 315
   c. The offering of the gifts of bread and wine — 339
   d. Epiklesis (the invocation of the Holy Spirit) and
      the transformation of the gifts into the body
      and blood of Christ in a state of sacrifice — 345
7. The supplications addressed to God after the transformation — 368
8. The preparation of the Holy Gifts for Holy Communion — 409
9. Holy Communion for eternal life — 413
10. Praises, thanksgivings and the new supplications addressed to
    God after Holy Communion — 462

CONCLUSIONS — 483

NOTES — 487

Foreword

Who is the greatest Orthodox theologian of the twentieth century? Some might answer, Sergei Bulgakov, due to the originality of his Sophiology and pioneering exploration of the most-discussed topics of twentieth century Orthodox theology, such as the relationship between person and nature, the Church and the human being as communion, and pneumatology. Others might advocate for Nicholas Afanasiev given his influential eucharistic ecclesiology and attention to the local church. Some might say that George Florovsky's neo-patristic synthesis has motivated the resurgence of patrological studies in the East. Still others might argue that no Orthodox theologian had a greater influence on liturgical life and frequent communion than Alexander Schmemann. Similar arguments could be made for Ioannis Zizioulas and Kallistos Ware. The twentieth century clearly knew a plethora of Orthodox theologians who had a dramatic impact on Christian theology in general and Eastern thought in particular; any of those mentioned above could claim the title, "the greatest Orthodox theologian of the twentieth century."

What is Dumitru Staniloae's place among these theologians? He was certainly the most prolific of them: he published over 1,200 books, articles, and journalistic works. These achievements are even more impressive considering the incessant opposition from a communist regime that censured his publications and incarcerated him for five years. Staniloae is a modern-day martyr, therefore the Romanian Orthodox Church canonized him as a confessor saint. He is also undoubtedly the greatest, most influential Romanian theologian of all time. Most contemporary

Romanian theological works, conference presentations, and curricula build on his contributions. As Staniloae's works are being translated into Western languages, his influence grows throughout the theological world—Orthodox and beyond.

Staniloae's thought is particularly appreciated for his balanced understanding of the relationship between person and nature, Christology and Pneumatology—themes that have been debated ardently within Orthodox theology. While some theologians mentioned earlier attempt to present a balanced understanding between these elements, they inevitably prioritize one over the other, but Staniloae avoids these shortcomings.

Moreover, Staniloae's ecumenical openness is astonishing given his isolation behind the Iron Curtain and the pressure of the communist regime to write with an anti-Western bias in line with the state's ideological opposition to capitalist countries. And yet, he regarded ecumenism as a sacred duty and the cause of Christian unity as an obligation for the Orthodox Church. Staniloae used Western scholarly research (particularly in Patrology) and admired theologians such as Karl Barth. Later, when the regime allowed him to travel abroad as a delegate to ecumenical dialogues, he also gained an admiration for the positive developments in Protestant and Catholic theologies in the second half of the twentieth century. In the present volume, he shows remarkable ecumenical receptivity by considering the terminological debates about transubstantiation as secondary to the truth that Catholics and Orthodox share in common regarding the Eucharist as the Body and Blood of Christ. Moreover, he affirms that the Catholic Church has preserved the faith in the Trinity and Christ, even if it has added to the Church's ancient faith the teachings on papal primacy, papal infallibility, the Filioque, and purgatory. Among these, only the dogmas of papal primacy and infallibility are obstacles for communion or church-dividing, but not the Filioque and purgatory.

Last but not least, Staniloae's contribution to patristic studies cannot be exaggerated: he translated and analyzed (sometimes with footnotes more ample than the translated text) the works of numerous Church Fathers, including Gregory Palamas before he was rediscovered by the rest of the Christian world, Maximus the Confessor (his favorite saint), and an enlarged version of *The Philokalia* in twelve volumes—the largest such collection in the Orthodox world.

Perhaps the question of who is the greatest Orthodox theologian of the twentieth century is unanswerable, similar to the twelfth-century controversy that arose in Constantinople where the supporters of Sts. John Chrysostom, Basil the Great, and Gregory the Theologian argued for each of them as being the first; in response, the Church decided to honor the Three Hierarchs with a common feast on January 30. Or, based on these briefly-outlined considerations, one could argue that Dumitru Staniloae was the greatest Orthodox theologian of the twentieth century.

The English-speaking public now has access to Staniloae's most important works. His *Teologia Dogmatică Ortodoxă* (1978) appeared in the six-volume series, *The Experience of God: Orthodox Dogmatic Theology*,[1] which is actually part of a trilogy focused on dogmatic theology, spirituality, and Liturgy. *Spiritualitatea Ortodoxă*—published in 1981 and based on an earlier course on Asceticism and Mysticism—is also available in its English translation entitled, *Orthodox Spirituality*. Thanks to the sacrificial love and tireless work of the foremost translator from Romanian, Fr. Ioan Ionita, *Spirituality and Communion in the Orthodox Liturgy* (*Spiritualitate și comuniune în Liturghia Ortodoxă*, original 1986) now completes Staniloae's trilogy for the English-speaking public.

Besides offering a fuller representation of Staniloae's thought, this volume fills a significant lacuna in recent Orthodox theology, namely an extensive commentary on the Liturgy. The twentieth century obviously produced its share of liturgical commentaries and the list discussed below is by no means exhaustive. Robert Taft's *A History of the Liturgy of St. John Chrysostom* remains the definitive study on the stages of the liturgical rite, its expansions, abridgments, variants in different places, eras, authors, manuscripts, and its reception. But the Liturgy is more than its text and its rubrics. It is, above all, the work of God through the work of the people that these external aspects occasion invisibly, mystically. Staniloae's intention is not to provide a study of liturgiology, but a theological and spiritual interpretation of the Liturgy.

Alexander Schmemann embarked on a similar project, although he was not able to bring it to completion. His collaborators published posthumously *The Eucharist* based on his earlier studies and drafts. Although smaller in size and less theological than Staniloae's, Schmemann's com-

---

1 In Romanian, the term "dogmatic" does not carry the negative connotations that its English equivalent does.

mentary undoubtedly had the greatest impact on the liturgical life of twentieth-century Orthodoxy.

Emmanuel Hatzidakis' *The Heavenly Banquet: Understanding the Divine Liturgy* provides a line-by-line commentary for a popular readership and is well researched. Staniloae's commentary could equally be used in catechetical settings with (more) guidance from a learned teacher, but his commentary delves deeper into the Liturgy as a source for theology and spirituality.

Hieromonk Gregorios' *The Divine Liturgy: A Commentary in Light of the Fathers* gathers patristic analyses of the Liturgy, providing an excellent introductory source. Staniloae's use of commentaries, however, is not merely a compilation of patristic texts with brief introductions by an author whose voice is only secondary (something that Hieromonk Gregorios would undoubtedly regard as a compliment). *Spirituality and Communion* is an original work that uses many theological sources besides patristic commentaries on the Liturgy, showing how the entire Orthodox spiritual and theological traditions are integrated.

Now that it is translated into English, Staniloae's book should complement and supplement these notable commentaries. The twenty-first century has not yet produced a work comparable to those of our predecessors, so the present volume remains the most thorough theological, spiritual, biblical, patrological, philosophical, dialogical, and pastoral commentary on the Liturgy in recent history.

In the "Introduction" to his *Dogmatics*, Staniloae expressed his hope to depart from scholastic treatments of dogmas as abstract propositions meant to satisfy our theoretical curiosity and instead show the spiritual significance of dogmas—truths that bring the soul in communion with God and neighbor—and the contemporary relevance of the Fathers by writing as they would have written today. Here, in *Spirituality and Communion*, he continues to present the liturgical life of the Church as a spiritual experience that deepens our communion with God and neighbor.

Staniloae argues that the worshipping Church is raised into the Trinity and the Eucharist is the Kingdom of the Trinity. The Church is a union sharing in the love between the Father, Son, and Holy Spirit. As adopted children of the Father, those who are united with Christ through faith, Baptism, and the Eucharist, experience this filial relationship in the Church. More specifically, in the Eucharist we discover our quality as members of the Body of Christ. When we partake of the eucharistic sacrifice, Christ empowers us to present ourselves as spiritual sacrifices to the Father, united with the Son's sacrifice. As the Church—the Body of Christ—is sacrificed to the Father, we, its members, grow into the likeness of Christ, are clothed with grace, and the love of the Father descends upon us. In Christ, we find ourselves in the presence of the Father because of the presence of the Holy Spirit in the Eucharist and the irradiation of the Holy Spirit from the sacrament, having the Holy Spirit rest upon us. As we are raised in the Trinity, we also progress in our union with the other members of the Church. This ecclesiastical communion needs to be taken to the rest of humankind, so that the Church may transform human society into the image of trinitarian communion. Beyond humanity, as God descends to us through the gift of creation and we lift the world up to God, all members of the Church—ordained and not ordained alike—exercise their sacred, priestly ministry within cosmic creation.

Having established the place of Staniloae among Orthodox theologians and of the present volume among similar works, it is important to conclude by observing that, as a priest serving at the altar, Staniloae's own spirituality radiates through every page of *Spirituality and Communion in the Orthodox Liturgy*. His lived experience of Orthodox theology, spirituality, and liturgy were foundational arguments for his canonization in 2024. Moreover, he was a confessor martyr, imprisoned and tortured by the Communist persecutors who harassed and forced him to live in poverty for decades after his incarceration. Despite (or because of) his suffering, he remained serene, loving, generous, and continuously immersed in the Jesus prayer. Besides these official reasons for Staniloae's canonization, several other aspects of his life and work were canonized, albeit implicitly: ecumenical openness, intellectual inquisitiveness (especially important in our age of fideism), elite academic work, theological creativity, married life, and surviving the trauma of losing two young children. He was a saint who looked, dressed, and lived like most of us, thus being a relatable model of holiness for today's Church. It is, therefore, providential that the present work is now available in English translation, helping us experience the spirituality and profound sense of communion that St. Confessor Priest Dumitru Staniloae drew from the Orthodox Liturgy.

Radu Bordeianu

Introduction

In the book titled *Orthodox Spirituality*[1] we described the growth in the spiritual life of the Christian seen as an individual person. It is clear in that book that this implies, at least up to a point, his relationship with others, because the Christian's cleansing of passions and his growth in virtues as a basis for pure prayer cannot be achieved except in the loving relationship with his neighbors.

The purpose of this book is to go further and to show that the constant prayer of the Christian as an individual person presupposes his preliminary and often repeated warming-up through his prayer offered in common with others.

Generally speaking, true spirituality is a living spirituality that engages the human person as a whole. As such, this spirituality is nourished by communication through prayer and by the manifestation of the identity of faith among many persons. It is this communication alone that warms up everyone's spiritual life. A spirituality developed in isolation cools off, dries up and becomes increasingly a theoretical thinking that engages only the mind and once in a while at that. Communion necessarily belongs to spirituality. Everyone's life is enriched in relationship with others, a richness that comes from others. This living spirituality, which encompasses the whole human being and is nourished by the communication with others thus creating communion, is maintained in Christianity through the Holy Liturgy. It receives in the Orthodox Liturgy a unique seal.

If spirituality is understood to be the content of faith experienced in an active way, the Orthodox Liturgy does this in a distinctly emphasized manner. This is also seen in the following fact: spirituality provides for the Christian a path which he is to walk on toward a more complete experience of the content of faith or of God, which means it also leads him toward a goal. Through spirituality the Orthodox Christian approaches the target of his perfection, as it is understood through his faith. One can also say that it is on this perfection and deepening in the faith that his communion with other Christians and, thus, the creation of an increasingly stronger community among themselves, is based. No one can perfect and deepen his faith without the help of others and without proving that his advance toward perfection is made in relationship with others.

The Orthodox Liturgy fulfills this need in a very special way by nourishing the spiritual communion among the faithful with the deep and rich content of the Christian faith. Even if there is an individual ascent of the faithful toward God through the cleansing of passions, through the gaining of virtues and through the contemplation of the logoi (inner reasons) of creation, this ascent would not be possible if it were not aided by a liturgical ascent toward God, which is achieved individually with the help of other faithful. It is the risen Christ united with the faithful through the Holy Eucharist who sustains this ascent. But the union with Christ in the Holy Eucharist unites the faithful gathered together in Christ with the Holy Trinity as well. This strengthens their quality as co-heirs with Christ of the Kingdom of the Father, having the Holy Spirit resting upon them.

Certainly, the risen Christ with whom we are united is also the Christ who sacrificed Himself for us, a way in which He manifested Himself as being free of any egoism and in which He strengthened us in this endeavor. Therefore, in uniting ourselves with Him we are to manifest ourselves free of egoism as truly living sacrifices, holy and well pleasing to God (Rom 12:1). This is shown in the active love toward our fellow human beings. That is why Christ calls those who fed the hungry, clothed the naked, visited the sick, etc. (Mt 25:34ff) to inherit the Kingdom of His Father. In this way we advance into the communion between us and God, as the Kingdom of the Holy Trinity. We would not be able to do this without our union, through the Holy Eucharist, with Christ who is in a state of sacrifice.

Consequently, the Holy Liturgy could also be considered as a means for human persons of transcending from the life enclosed in a state of egoism here on earth to the life of communion with and in God, viewed as His Kingdom. The prayers indicate such a transcendence or an exit of the human person closed off within his egoism toward the God in Trinity, the God of love, even when we ask in those prayers for material things necessary for life on earth, as conditions for preparing ourselves for the Kingdom of God. For the awareness that these material things are given to us by God for the strengthening of our community in Him, is in itself a transcending or an advancement from the egoism closed off in itself here on earth to the God of Trinity, the ambiance and the source of communion. This is what we derive from the Holy Liturgy: our transcendence or ascension above our egoistical and bodily concerns that binds us to this world and our union in a spirit of sacrifice with Christ and, through Him, with the Father in the Holy Spirit. And when we all gather together in the ambiance of communion that exists within the Holy Trinity, we strengthen the communion among ourselves. That is why we ask this collectively for all.

The communion realized among the faithful in the ambiance of the Holy Trinity is one and the same with the Kingdom of the Holy Trinity where there are no masters and subjects, but all are brothers among themselves because they are children of the heavenly Father and brothers of His Son made man for eternity and united with them as He is the one who sacrificed Himself for them.

The Church is the ship on which the believers advance toward this state as children of the heavenly Father and as brothers of the Son made man and sacrificed for them. She is the anticipated Kingdom of the Holy Trinity. And the Holy Liturgy is the place where this foretasted Kingdom of the Holy Trinity is strengthened. The Holy Liturgy is the fountain that quenches believers' thirst for the life of communion with the Holy Trinity and among themselves. It is in the Holy Liturgy that the Holy Trinity most descends to believers, and they experience as a foretaste the encounter with it and the joy of this encounter in the enthusiastic praises they offer. All the exclamations of the priest represent praise offered to the Holy Trinity. The believers are most united with the Holy Trinity through their union with the Father's Son made man, sacrificed and risen for them in the Holy Spirit.

These exclamations represent a continuation of the praises offered to the Holy Trinity in the New Testament. In the spiritual atmosphere of the Holy Liturgy the atmosphere of the New Testament is extended, the one experienced by the Holy Apostles around the Savior. Salvation is identified both in the Liturgy and in the New Testament with the quality as members of the Kingdom of the Holy Trinity. He who remains in isolation and does not live in the communion of the Kingdom, which takes the form of the Church and is experienced to the utmost degree in the Liturgy, has no part of salvation. In the same way, the kind of humanity scattered and troubled by all kinds of conflicts is not a saved humanity. That is why at the end of the Liturgy, in the prayer before the ambon, the priest prays both for the salvation of the people and for the blessing of God's inheritance, namely of His Kingdom. In the Liturgy the believer experiences the relationship of a dialogue with the Holy Trinity and thus a certain presence of the Trinity.

Thus, in all his prayers the priest asks for the salvation of the faithful but he concludes them by praising the Holy Trinity. The faithful do the same at the urging of the priest. Everything is a collective doxology to the Trinity and a supplication for salvation. In the Liturgy the priest has the position of the one who prays for the congregation that, at his request, accompanies him. His role is to offer unto God the prayers and gifts of the faithful, being a visible instrument for the transformation of the gifts into the body and blood of Christ and the one who transmits God's blessings to the faithful. Consequently, his role is not to show that the people have no relation with the Holy Trinity, but that he is a visible instrument of Christ the High Priest. Christ Himself prays with the priest for the faithful, He addresses them and gathers the prayers and gifts of the faithful by uniting them with His own. Through the priest Christ teaches in the Gospel, transforms the gifts of the faithful into His body and blood and unites the faithful with Him in the Holy Eucharist so that He may present them to the Father as children filled with the Holy Spirit. If the priest did not have this role as intercessor, neither would Christ be present with His role as intercessor between them and the Father. The priest is a sort of transparent person of Christ. Without the priest there would be no one to gather the community together and, more broadly, to make possible the fulfillment and safeguarding of the Church in Christ.

The dependence of one's participation in the Kingdom of God on one's partaking of Christ is shown by the priest in the second prayer for the faithful. When the priest places the gifts on the altar to be transformed into the body and blood of Christ so that the faithful may partake of them, he asks that God remember in His Kingdom all categories of believers. The priest prays for the transformation of the gifts into the body and blood of the Lord "that they may be to those who partake thereof for the forgiveness of sins, for communion with the Holy Spirit, for the fulfillment of the Kingdom of Heaven, for boldness towards You." In a prayer after the transformation the priest, accompanied by the faithful, asks the same thing.

The fact that the priest is accompanied in his prayers and in everything he does by the prayers of the faithful shows that, even if on the one hand the hierarchy is essential in the Church in order to realize and maintain the unity of the Church, on the other hand, the hierarchy must act in the Church not as a factor of mastership, but of sustaining the cohesion through love according to the example of Christ who became man and was sacrificed for us. Every priest and bishop must follow this not only through his teaching, but also through the example of his sacrificial life. Only in this way is the Church a pledge of the Heavenly Kingdom in which the Father remains as Father toward all human persons and the Son remains as their Brother who does not exercise any authority over them in a worldly manner.

Let us give a few examples regarding the identity of the praises offered by the priest to the Holy Trinity and its Kingdom with those in the New Testament.

In Revelation 4:8 the four living creatures (the Seraphim) sing unceasingly: "Holy, holy, holy, Lord God Almighty." Through this they "give glory and honor and thanks to Him who sits on the throne, who lives forever and ever" (Rev 4:9). This is being done in the Trisagion hymn and in the exclamation after the first litany of the Liturgy of the catechumens as well as in the first litany of the Liturgy of the faithful. Similar praises, to which the remembrance of the civil authorities and of the Kingdom of God are added, are often repeated in the book of Revelation. St. Peter the Apostle also says: "To Him be the glory and the dominion forever and ever. Amen" (1 Pt 5:11). This is mentioned in the Liturgy in the exclamation following the second litany. St. Paul offers "to the King eternal . . . honor and glory forever and ever. Amen" (1 Tim 1:17).

We have seen that Christ promises the Kingdom of the Father to those who help the poor and the persecuted (Mt 25:34), while the unmerciful are sent to the eternal fire that belongs to the evil and the selfish ones, a fire for which they prepared themselves through their egoism (Mt 25:41). This latter state is neither like that of the Kingdom nor a state of communion, but one of loneliness. That is why "it is hard for a rich man to enter the kingdom of heaven" (Mt 19:23), which is a loving communion. In that Kingdom those who left everything and followed Christ and His example of service and sacrifice (Mt 19:28) will enjoy a special glory. These will "reign forever and ever" (Rev 22:5). The Savior urges us to seek this Kingdom and its righteousness first and foremost, for everything else will be added to us (Mt 6:33). Upon heeding this exhortation we seek this Kingdom first of all in the Holy Liturgy. Together with that Kingdom will be added to us especially the glory of being children of the eternal King and brothers of His Only Begotten Son (St. Cyril of Alexandria, *Adoration in Spirit and in Truth*, book X).

When the priest begins the Holy Liturgy, blessing the Kingdom of the Holy Trinity, he makes known to the faithful the assurance given by St. Peter the Apostle: "For so an entrance will be supplied to you abundantly into the everlasting kingdom of our Lord and Savior Jesus Christ" (2 Pt 1:11). The priest follows the advice of the Apostle: "For this reason I will not be negligent to remind you always of these things" (2 Pt 1:12).

Thus, only by detaching ourselves from the narrow life of egoism are we filled with the Holy Trinity's infinite life of communion. The Church has expressed this paradox by viewing Christ's death as "life giving," contrary to any egoism. Christ's sacrificed body is "the living bread" given "for the life of the world," as the Lord Himself said (John 6:51), because in Him this state of being detached from egoism in view of the wide communion with all is long lasting. By immersing His body in God through death within the infinite breadth of life in a supreme transcendence of the self, Christ has filled it with the undying and always loving life of the Holy Trinity. He who dedicates himself out of love, together with Christ, enters into a relationship and is filled with the living waters of the triune godhead which is love and, therefore, unending life.

By establishing this relationship with the life of the Holy Trinity, the believer does not cause his person to disappear. The person who immerses himself out of love in another person, even if that person is infinite, is not dissolved in that person. Two persons united through love cannot sustain their love except by remaining aware of each other and rejoicing one in the other. Because love is the greatest joy a person has regarding another person, one of its essential characteristics is the union without confusion of those who love each other.

In the union with God, the Christian remains an unconfused person just as God, in the Christian teaching, is a Trinity of persons where the unity is so much greater even as the unconfused preservation of the person is just as real. By uniting himself with God, the Christian maintains his awareness of the Father as being distinct from the Son with Whom being also united he feels the filial affection the Son has toward the special affection of the Father. Thus, the Christian is also aware that the Son is distinct from the Father and he experiences his filial affection toward the Father from and together with the Son's affection toward the Father without being confused with the Son. The Christian feels that his affection toward the Father does not come from within himself, but from the Son's affection toward the Father as from a special and inexhaustible source. In like manner, he is aware that the Holy Spirit is distinct from the Father and the Son because through the Spirit the Christian unites himself with both the Father and the Son as a distinct person with distinct Persons, because the Spirit who gives him the impulse for this union is also a distinct Person. Because of the fact that the three divine Persons are unconfused, the human person cannot be confused with God either. For that to happen, God Himself would have to become impersonal, devoid of any personal interest in every human being as a distinct person. When the child experiences the joint but also distinct love of both his parents toward him as a distinct person, he cannot be confused with them.

The liturgical ascent experienced by the believers as an increasing joint union with the God in Trinity—that is to say as an experience of God's love, of the intimate relationship with the living God—is distinct from theology, which in the best case is a reflection upon this experience. In the Holy Liturgy something happens between God and the human persons. It is not a purely subjective experience. The Holy Liturgy is the continual actualization of the Gospel, the actualized relationship with the Christ of the Gospel, a relationship that is continuously experienced by believers. When the theologian conveys this experience as his own, then his theology is genuine as well, even if not as genuine as the experience itself. When the theologian reflects upon someone else's experience, his theology is dead. But even when the theologian himself goes through the experience, it is one thing to sing within the ecstatic enthusiasm of your own experience of the Holy Trinity together with others and it is another thing to reflect upon that experience. Sometimes the reflection does not follow the experience or does not lead to it (in the case when this happens to the theologian), but it can also accompany it. Then his reflection is even warmer and deeper. Therefore, something good happens in the succession or the simultaneous union between the experience of the God in Trinity during prayer at the Liturgy and theological reflection. Theology deepens the experience of what happens in the Holy Liturgy and the meaning discovered therein, while the experience of God in Trinity gives life to theology and deepens it.

The fact that the Holy Liturgy is experienced by believers collectively as an ascent or advancement into the ambiance of communion with the Holy Trinity makes it the most effective means of creating, maintaining and strengthening the fellowship among people, as anticipation of the Kingdom of the Holy Trinity. The believers who regularly go together to the Holy Liturgy in the same church feel as gathered together more and more in the God of triune love and, thus, they increase their communion as well. No other kinds of associations, gatherings or connections are able to create such a deep communion between human persons as does the Holy Liturgy. This is so because those kinds of associations do not bring them together in God who is above them and who makes them overcome their fleeting interests that cannot all be identical, or because they do not feel helped by each other in resolving the various interests. But the Liturgy becomes a unifying means even for the other kinds of associations and gatherings because it establishes a common foundation to their lives within the visible diversity.

Even members of the same family strengthen their communion when they gather together on a regular basis for the Holy Liturgy. Their fellowship is then nourished from the supreme common source of love and of everlasting life, which may decrease the problems between them caused by fleeting interests.

In the Greek language, the Holy Liturgy means collective service. It gathers persons in a collective service offered to God in Trinity who is the God of communion. It is, therefore, the greatest power that creates the community. It gathers all more and more into the Kingdom of the Holy Trinity's endless love.

Christianity is distinct from other religions and philosophies through the fact that it is the religion of love. But love means to affirm the eternity of the person and the belief in it. Only in this way is the light of meaning projected upon existence. We experience this light to the highest degree in the Liturgy, the light that is projected forth from the Son of God made man for eternity. In the Holy Liturgy every person is illumined as a mystery of existence with an inexhaustible value. Because the person is a source of inexhaustible light, at the same time it is the greatest mystery, thirsty for eternity and capable of giving other persons eternal joys with which those persons are never completely filled.

If there is no person, there is no love. Only a person can love and a person can only love another person. If there exists a person who loves another person and who is loved by that person, they want to be immortal for an ever-fuller love. I want to be loved forever and I want to love another person forever in a union ever more perfect. Persons, love and immortality toward a more complete union belong together. These give full meaning to existence. What meaning would the world have without these? A person without love does not have the worth or the meaning he seeks. A person without love is weakened and lives a tormenting life. Persons and love without immortality lack worth and full meaning. Suffering is mingled with their love. In its turn, love cannot exist without the person. And the immortality of persons without love is hell; it is the spiritual death of persons. Similarly, immortality without a continuous progress in union through loves becomes monotonous. In the absence of these four, existence plunges into nonsense or into darkness.

If I do not love other persons and are not loved by them, my life becomes poor and I become bored with myself to the point of being unable to tolerate myself. Some resort to suicide on this account. But once the human person receives his existence from God, he cannot end his own life except in its form here on earth. Once God has given it to him, He does not take it away. Thus, the human person remains bored and self-tormented forever if he does not grow accustomed to love and does not become worthy of being loved during life on earth. God thereby shows us that He did not create human persons for a transitory existence, but for the eternal existence. Their fullness of life depends on their love, which in turn depends on their freedom. Even through their tormented existence in the eternal hell, persons give testimony to the eternal value God bestowed on them as free human beings.

Christian faith affirms that the Holy Trinity is the eternal foundation of human persons and the model of happiness in the unity of love. God created human beings as persons to love as Father and as Brother. When through their freedom they fell from love, God sent His own Son to become their full Brother by assuming human nature through the Incarnation and to offer His love toward them up to His self-sacrifice, thus assuring their eternity through His resurrection. In this way He manifested an even greater love toward them after they fell from love into sin. In the Holy Liturgy this love is permanently shown, proven and communicated to us by the Holy Trinity, by the Son who was incarnate, sacrificed and risen in order to thereby lead us to the perfect love of the Kingdom of the Holy Trinity.

Only this eternal union in love between persons gives meaning to existence, a union founded on the Holy Trinity, sustained by the Son of God through incarnation up to His self-sacrifice for us and assured for eternity through the resurrection. Otherwise everything would be meaningless. Without sacrifice, the world would be exclusively a theater of war on account of wild egoisms; without resurrection, the birth of human beings would have no logic. Existence itself would be altogether inexplicable. Only resurrection fills everything with meaning and light.

The world has its origin in the love of the Holy Trinity. The Holy Trinity sanctioned earthly existence as a path for human persons to grow in love whose end will be eternal and ecstatic love in perfect union with the Holy Trinity and among themselves. The Holy Liturgy is the central place where human beings grow in this love and union through the joint partaking of the Son of God who was crucified and rose for them. In this way they learn and take strength to love each other up to the point of sacrifice and thereby to advance toward the resurrection with Him in the everlasting life. Had sin not intervened, we would have grown in love just through mutual self-offering. But the sin of egoism made necessary the form of self-offering as a sacrifice united with the pain implied in the separation from the habit of egoism's false and transitory sweetness.

Sin causes the diminution of the person; it brings about physical death. And if existence continues in the next life it will be a tormented existence, an eternal spiritual death that begins here on earth.

Christ conquered death because He has conquered through His sacrifice on the cross the sin of lovelessness. He has reestablished the person within the normal characteristics of love and immortality. He has thus reactivated the communion among persons. In the Holy Liturgy the believers experience and grow accustomed to increase their love and their never-ending union with the sacrificed and risen Christ and among themselves. They activate love as an attribute of persons and have, as a pledge, a foretaste of the eternal life after resurrection, which is the happy life in the ever-increasing communion that is nourished from Christ and the Holy Trinity. Thus they experience in anticipation the full meaning of existence, a meaning indicated by the candles that are lit for the entire duration of the Holy Liturgy.

In the communion begun with the Holy Trinity through their Eucharistic union with Christ and thus through their adoption that makes them akin to the Son, the believers live, if they so wish, in anticipation as heirs of the Kingdom of the Holy Trinity or as partakers in it. And the communion of the Holy Trinity is the supreme and inexhaustible source of the three highest values of existence: person, love and their eternity. These values are communicated to us by the Son of God who became man, was crucified, rose again and ascended, not so that He may no longer be with us or to remain just a memory and a hope that He will also raise us up, but in order to remain with us, to dwell within us through the Sacraments as sacrificed and risen and to strengthen in us the love toward resurrection and eternal life. To this end He unites Himself with us most completely through the Holy Eucharist in the Holy Liturgy as the One who was sacrificed and risen. That is why the Holy Liturgy represents *par excellence* the life in the sacrificed and risen Christ so that we may strengthen within us the spirit of love that leads to sacrifice, contrary to egoism. Thus we advance toward the resurrection in the kingdom of the Holy Trinity's eternal love.

The Kingdom of the Holy Trinity or the communion in it is experienced in the Holy Liturgy not only among those present, but also with all who are devoted to Christ and to the Church, whether they are living or departed. Love as an attribute of the person sees the departed continuing to live their life in eternity. Those present at the Holy Liturgy also manifest their love toward the departed as well as their faith in their immortality, which was made happy through their love and through their frequent remembrances of them in prayer. In this way those present show not only their faith in the everlasting existence of the loved ones, but also the consciousness of their responsibility for the happy eternity of the loved ones. Where there is no faith in the eternity of the person, the responsibility of one for the other is diminished. This responsibility reaches incalculable proportions there where one knows that the eternal happiness to which our fellow humans are called depends on our deeds toward them while still living and on our prayers for them after their death. Only such a responsibility, grown out of a boundless love, does raise the quality of the human person to stages of indescribable heights.

PREAMBLE

A. The Church Building: Image of Cosmic and Human Creation

The idea that the church building is an image of the cosmic creation and of the human person, as potential developing churches, has been strongly affirmed by St. Maximos the Confessor.[2]

As the church building keeps in unity the laity in the nave and the clergy in the altar who all together advance toward union with God[3] and toward a greater union among themselves, so cosmic creation keeps in unity the multitude of visible and invisible beings who advance ever more toward God and thus toward a more intense union among themselves. Likewise, the human being is a unity made up of body and soul which advance ever more toward God and thus toward their more complete union.

One cannot say that the church building and the cosmic and human creations are three units independent of each other, even if cosmic creation and human creation have an initial dual unity and a movement toward God as well as toward their own greater unity. For cosmic creation, at least in its visible aspect, and the human person, at least in his condition after the fall, have no clear consciousness of their progress toward God. Only the community of believers (the church in its quality as their community) has the consciousness of this progress toward God, thus giving the church building where they gather for liturgical service the characteristic of an actualized church. The progress of the cosmic and human creations toward God is different from the liturgical progress—in the strict sense of the word—within the church building proper. Cosmic creation and the human being are church dwellings in a different sense, that is in a larger sense than the church building proper, and their progress toward God is distinct from the liturgical movement in the strict sense within the church building proper. However, they complete each other.

Therefore, only in solidarity with the church building proper or with the community of believers gathered there could cosmic creation — in its visible aspect — attain to and remain in the state of actualized church or as an extended church. The same is true for the human person. On the one hand, the actualized church is, properly speaking, a part of the visible cosmos and of the human community in general; on the other hand, it is like a yeast that permeates the entire cosmos and the entire human community, tending to help toward the actualization of their characteristic as churches, certainly in a different sense than that of the church proper. God exerts His enticing work in this part of the cosmic creation and of the human community, in the sense of their union with Him and among themselves, in a more effective way after the incarnation and resurrection of His Son as man and after the sending of His Holy Spirit on the day of Pentecost. This is done not to separate this part of the cosmic and human creation from the rest, but to thereby attract the latter altogether in an even closer union with Him.

Thus, since one can speak of neither a separation nor an identification but about a correlation between the Church proper and cosmic and human creation—which are also objectively connected to God—one can say that cosmic and human creation, objectively united with God, not only have a similarity with the Church, but take an active part to a certain degree within the Church, just as the Church actively participates in the cosmic creation and in humanity. Through this both the Church and the cosmic and human creation together with the human being are interpenetrated and at the same time are called to an ever more accentuated interpenetration. In this sense one can say that creation is a different kind of Church, undeveloped[4] or not completely actualized, having the Church within itself like a yeast that helps it to develop toward the status of actualized church albeit in a way proper to it. Just as the yeast has the potential to make the flour rise and the flour the capacity to be leavened and to become bread, so does the Church tend to penetrate creation and creation has the tendency to allow itself to be penetrated and transfigured by the Church. Because the Church activates the Spirit of the incarnate Word through whom the world was created.[5]

Therefore one cannot say that there are three parallel Churches or one within the other, but only one whole Church with three aspects. The Church proper has the entire cosmic creation and the entire humanity partly connected to her, like an immense courtyard, and a great multitude of human beings who have not explicitly and fully assimilated in their proper way the characteristic as Church. However, they are called to assimilate that characteristic through their positive response to the work of that part of creation and of humanity that has explicitly and fully become church. But the fact that this cosmic courtyard and this human multitude have within their nature a motion toward their complete unification, when they will be filled with a more perfect spiritual content and with a greater beauty, and that this motion is sometimes very powerful even if there is no awareness of its true path and objective—for which reason failure often occurs—gives magnitude and complexity to the Church; this shows that they too have a certain characteristic as churches, the Church proper being their icon as model.

But only when cosmic creation and the human being obtain the clear awareness that the goal of their progress is God, in whom they find true perfection, can their motion avoid ambiguous forms — in part good and in part bad—and they can be called churches in an actualized sense. In this case they are imprinted with the clear form of the Church and thus they become aspects of the unique Church or a specific kind of organic parts of the unique Church or, further yet, forms through which the Church is manifested.

It is worth noting that St. Maximos does not include God in his definition of the Church as the building of the liturgical community of believers and as image of cosmic creation and of the human being. St. Maximos considers God as being above the Church in His quality as uncreated. But he implicitly affirms His relation with the Church when he views God in His relation with creation as similar to the relation between the Church and creation.

We will include the presence of God in the definition of the Church in her three aspects. For even if God as uncreated transcends any cosmic or human creation, objectively He is in such a strong relation with it that the Church does not exist in her three aspects without His presence.

In the church building of the liturgical community God is at the highest place, which is the holy table in the altar, in the body and blood of Christ. At the peak of cosmic creation God is the One from whom all things originate and He sustains them all. In the human being He is the foundation and the infinite horizon that can be felt in connection with the heart.

In addition to this we mention that St. Maximos views the angelic beings as the invisible part of the Church — cosmic creation. Without contesting that cosmic creation as the Church also has this aspect in its own way, we will concentrate our attention on the reasons (inner principles) of things as superior part of the cosmic Church. We are able to see God in this Church in a strong relation with these reasons. Moreover, the human being is not viewed as separated from this cosmic Church. Even if the angelic beings could also be a kind of priesthood of the visible cosmic creation, because they praise God for the marvelous order of the cosmos, the most proper priest of the cosmos is the human person or the human community in its totality. The human being or the human community all together cannot be, in their own way, fully actualized as Church without the cosmic creation and vice versa. For the movement of cosmic creation toward God, or generally toward higher and well-ordered stages, cannot be achieved without the human being; neither can the human being advance toward God or toward a superior life without the help of cosmic creation.

Thus the cosmic courtyard that stretches around the church building, with the potential of becoming Church in its own way, is filled with the multitude of human beings, and their progress is a combined motion either toward their actualized participation in the Church proper through their explicit progress toward God, or toward a weakened and ambiguous state of this characteristic as Church through their progress toward beings that are not truly good.

Furthermore, we should also mention that the human being normally fulfills his function as priest of the cosmic creation inasmuch as he discovers the unseen reasons (inner principles) of created things and makes those reasons become efficient in their proper and true content within visible creation. Once the human being rises to this knowledge, he also sees the angels working toward uncovering these reasons and toward the fulfillment of their purpose as means of approaching God through the visible creation. In this case the angels make God more evident within cosmic creation for the human being and make more effective the service to God by the human person in this cosmic creation.

In addition to these reflections, which partly retain St. Maximos's vision about the three component aspects of the Church and partly complete their significance, we find worth mentioning another characteristic from St. Maximos's vision on the Church in order to highlight its importance and to further clarify its meaning.

In the church building St. Maximos views the category of the laity represented by the nave and that of the clergy represented by the altar reserved for them not as set in their status, but he views the category of the laity as a prospective priesthood and that of the priesthood as the category of the laity that has actualized its potential priestly calling. "Thus, the nave is the sanctuary in potency by being consecrated by the relationship of the sacrament toward its end, and in turn the sanctuary is the nave in act by possessing the principle of its own sacrament."[6]

But just as the visible part of cosmic creation does not become an angelic world, regardless of how transparent the latter becomes through the first, so the category of laity is not confused with that of the clergy, regardless of how much they are imprinted upon each other; they become one unit in such a way that they are not confounded. However, one should keep in mind the idea of the laity being imprinted with the status of priesthood and of the potential presence of the priestly status within it, and vice versa, which occurs not through the lowering of the priestly status to that of the laity but through the leading of the laity by the clergy toward union with God, namely toward their unification in God.[7]

In this vision one can see the deeper foundation of the laity's universal priesthood and the duty of the sacramental priesthood to not distance itself from the laity, but to bring them closer by helping them to advance together toward union with God and together to advance in God.[8]

Furthermore, the universal priesthood of the laity, whose activity helps the sacramental priesthood in exercising its function, manifests itself in the fact that the believer becomes a priest in the church of his own being, and also in the fact that he discovers the unseen reasons/inner principles of things, thereby contributing to the discovering and promotion of the cosmic creation's characteristic as Church as well as that of his own being.

When human beings discover the images of divine reasons in created things, they know that the angelic minds comprise in them the reasons of all perceptible realities as increasingly higher stages toward God up to their origins in God in an ever stronger solidarity among themselves, just as the minds of human beings gradually comprise those reasons at an inferior level. By comprising the reasons of created things, the angels make human minds sensible of the presence of those reasons as perceptible images in which they are materialized. Thus they help human beings to have a clearer knowledge of the reasons of created things and to exercise their activity over them as materialized images of those reasons in a more efficient and better organized way, or to present in the form of works of art the transparent, beautiful and mystical depths of created things.

But once raised to the vision of divine reasons and to the sensing of the angelic beings who shine forth through the visible images of these reasons—after the detachment from the passionate clinging to the visible aspect of things considered as the ultimate reality that produces sensible pleasures and concerns—the human mind sees God through them. While St. Maximos had seen in the invisible aspect of the cosmic Church the angels more than anything else, Kallistos Angelikoudes sees in that aspect the reasons of created things. We believe, however, that these are only two stages in the human person's spiritual ascent. It is known how much St. Maximos insisted on the reasons of created things. In any case, both of them perceive—the first through angels and the latter through the reasons of things—the One God. Here are the words of Kallistos Angelikoudes: "Through divine grace, I am filled up from the depths of my heart with sacred light through the inextinguishable guiding-torch of the Spirit (if I may say so). And so I am guided into the *logoi* of all things, all united in one mystical *Logos*, and I see the words of the Scriptures all culminating in that Word (Logos)."[9]

Kallistos Kataphygiotes introduces a different idea regarding the invisible aspect of the cosmic Church. For him this aspect is constituted of the saving energies, or through them as well. In this way he sees God in a more intimate relationship with the world. But the human mind can also rise through the reasons of created things to union with the One

God. In the first case, God works more efficiently our salvation for He works through the very Spirit of Christ. While the knowledge of the reasons of created things is also proper to natural reason, the knowledge of the uncreated energies occurs through an experience of the human person endowed with grace. Such priesthood is achieved by a person working in the world on the basis of a natural knowledge of the reasons of created things. Here are the words of Kallistos Kataphygiotes in this regard: "Although the many come from the One,[10] each of them comes from the One in a different manner, since realities proceed from the first Unity in various modes. Some of these 'many' have a beginning and are created, while others are uncreated and outside of the principle of beginning in time. Now, the One beyond reality is the Cause of absolutely all of these realities, but It is the Cause of the former according to the mode of creation and of the latter according to the mode of nature. And for this reason we ought not to approach and engage with all these realities in the same way or to an equal extent, but the things that exist under the principle of beginning and creaturehood should be approached for the sake of something else and not for their own sake, as in the way we approach a mirror not for the mirror's sake, but to see the form and image reflected by it. In fact, we can receive no fulfillment by approaching creation for any other reason than for the sake of the ultimate One manifested within it. On the other hand, we approach the beginningless and natural [properties] of God not for the sake of something else, but both for their own sake and for the sake of the One from whom they proceed. For these are the realities that should truly be approached for their own sake, and the supreme One belongs to them in an immediate and natural mode; or rather, they belong to the ultimate and supreme One in an immediate and, again, natural mode. . . . Hence, when we examine aright the caused realities that are created, we are naturally drawn to raise our intellects in contemplation to the reflection of the One and to unite them to the undifferentiated perception of the transcendent One in an absolute and simple manner; that is, of course, as long as our intellect contemplates them properly. In the case of those realities that come naturally from the Cause, when the intellect operates in accordance with them for the sake of the Cause, or conform to their likeness, it can be united through them with That which is truly One in Itself."[11] For such a person the cosmos has become truly Church in which the One God is transparent.

Let us now continue with the presentation of the three aspects of the Church.

1. *The Meaning of Cosmic Creation As a Potential Developing Church*

St. Maximos considers the angelic beings as an invisible, thus priestly, aspect of creation as Church. There is some truth to this idea because the angels praise God for His wisdom and might manifested in creation and they help to lead creation to God. Here we are interested not in the priestly service of angels, but in the role the human being plays in creation. In fact, when St. Maximos specifies that visible creation is composed of "visible beings," we believe he understands by this not created things or animals, but human beings. In this case human persons are all laymen in relation to angels as priests. But a sort of laymen in motion toward the state of the angels or of the superior priests of cosmic creation, certainly according to their service, not their essence. However, in order to reach the level of the priestly calling of angels, human beings must continually practice a service proper to them as priests within the cosmic creation of things and animals. The general sense in which St. Maximos views laymen as nave in their quality as visible beings and the angels as priests allows us to consider angels as priests not so much of the material and animal order of creation as of human beings.

The fact that human beings have the quality as subjects capable of free initiatives and acts within inanimate cosmic creation offers us the understanding that St. Maximos considers angels as using human persons for leading both material and animal cosmic creation toward God. This is shown by the very fact that St. Maximos considers human beings as potential priests. Consequently, in the visible creation as nave we are to distinguish as a special category the human subjects as potential priests who, by serving God, open up the world for a more efficient work of God within it.[12]

Since our concern here is not so much created things or animals but human beings, more emphasis will be placed on the latter in their role as priests called to transfigure the sensible aspect of cosmic creation, making it possible to see God more clearly through this aspect as the One in whom all will be united. This action or movement of human beings must encounter the forces planted in nature and actualize all the potentials of these forces in harmony among them and with the harmonized needs of human beings.

God gave us all these forces as gifts imprinted with complementary reasons that allow themselves to be either organized for our own benefit or revealed in their varied and still unitary rationality and beauty. It is human movement that reveals this rationality through scientific activity: our work organizes the forces of nature in conformity with their reasons for our benefit, and art puts in bold relief their harmonious beauty. Through all these the human being fulfills a service of praise offered to God, a service full of gratitude for the benefit that comes from the gifts of creation through which he can advance toward God.

But God granted us all the gifts so that we may offer them as gifts and use them as gifts among us after having enhanced and organized them through our work. This is the sacred or priestly service we were destined for within the framework of cosmic creation. The act of partaking of these gifts with gratitude toward God is an image of the Eucharist. Through all things we partake of the "body" of the Word.

The real union of all in the unique Giver from whom everything comes is achieved through love. And love is manifested through gifts. We must respond to God's gift, or to His love, with our gift. But our gift can only be His gift developed through our work and offered as a sign of our love by returning to Him everything that He gave us. We have to also manifest our love among us through the same gifts we give each other from God's gifts. And just as the gifts we give each other are the result of our love for God, so too does the force of our love for each other take its strength from God's love toward us.

Work and dedication—up to one's own being—are the two aspects of human destiny and together they comprise our liturgical service, in the broad sense of the word, as progress toward our union with God and among ourselves within the framework of cosmic creation. This is the cosmic liturgy of which St. Maximos the Confessor speaks as our progress toward God and as a growing union among us through our advancement in God.

In this cosmic liturgy that leads us toward God and toward our increasingly stronger union among us in Him is included the work of parents in bringing up their children and their sacrifice for them, as well as the work of all who contribute selflessly to a more friendly way of life within human communities. So is the search to discover the divine inner principles of creative forces, the work of writers and other creators of art who make human co-inhabitation more beautiful and brighter. This work and its sweat have changed from condemnation into service to God and neighbors, a means of exultation for the human person. The sweat has changed into holy water, as Patriarch Athenagoras of Constantinople once said during a visit to Romania.

When this work is avoided or when the literary and philosophical works as well as the artistic creation are used to stimulate the passions and to advance evil tendencies and all kinds of conflicts, one understands that the characteristic of cosmic creation as Church is not developed. Those who do this are not fulfilling their liturgical and holy service and the cosmic creation is treated as a place and occasion for battle and discord. Those who make use of work in such a way do not lead creation toward God and toward strengthening unity among humans, but toward increasing the forces of evil and hatred in the world.

However, we should not forget that since the God toward whom the human person advances within cosmic creation is the crucified Christ, the human person must also share in His cross. This is why in this advance the human person faces hardships, afflictions and, ultimately, death. If these are accepted as participation in the cross of Christ, the human person attains resurrection through them and becomes sensitive to the good and to spiritual progress. The human person also develops the habit of self-renunciation and of gradually renouncing physical pleasures and even earthly life, and he repents on account of those hardships and afflictions and cleanses himself of sins through them. Thus they are transformed from punishment for the original sin into a means of increasing the spiritual life and a path toward eternal life with the risen Christ. The prime example for the first case is Job, and for the second case is the thief on the cross at the right hand of Christ.

If the human person revolts because of all afflictions, he finds no meaning in them. Some accuse God for them as being unjust, or they consider Him powerless, forgetting that in this way they question His attributes as true God, which means that they deny Him; others link them to the processes of nature, contradicting their affirmation of the perfection and rationality which, in their opinion, nature must have as its supreme reality.

The purpose of the gathering of human beings in the church building proper is to help them fulfill their liturgy, in the broader sense, in the cosmic nave through the liturgy officiated in the church in the direct and explicit sense of the word.

2. *The Human Being as Church and the Human Person as Priest within the Church*

The gathering of human persons in the church proper helps them to fulfill their priestly function within cosmic creation, because through the Liturgy in the church they realize in their own beings an explicit and conscious progress toward God who is on the Holy Table in the sanctuary and a spiritual advance toward each other. But it is not enough for the believer to advance only in the church toward Christ who is in the altar, but he must become himself a church and a priest of this church, advancing—as St. Maximos says—in the church building proper toward the priestly condition. Thus he can serve God in this quality as a priest within the cosmic creation.

The believer must develop in his being the quality as church that has God in its center, as well as his quality as priest who serves God who is found in the altar of his heart.[13] Because his profound heart where God abides from Baptism is like an altar on which is found the same God Who is also found in the hearts of other believers and at the basis of creation as well as on the altar of the church. The hearts filled with God encounter each other as they open up toward the same divine infinitude and bathe in His loving light without being blended in each other and in Him. They meet in the same infinitude that is also the all-powerful foundation of creation and the infinitude toward which the altar or the high place of the church is open.[14]

God is found in the most concrete way on the altar of the church because it is there that He is invisibly found as the Son of God Who came to us by taking on our body and whom God offers to us filled with the Holy Spirit after He gave Him to death for us and then He has risen together with us. In this way we are united with Him and among ourselves, and He facilitates the visible realization of our union because He communicates Himself to all of us under the elements of bread and wine visible to all. We know all these clearly and all of us gathered in the church accept them through the unity of faith.

St. Mark the Ascetic wrote very clearly about the human person as church. The believer is an actualized church according to the measure of his faith, a church in which he himself offers his gifts to Christ. The remarkable fact is that St. Mark the Ascetic sees the human person's priesthood as strongly connected to and dependent upon the central high priesthood of Christ. It is exactly what takes place in the Liturgy officiated in the church building where the one Who offers Himself as sacrifice to be partaken of through the priest by those present is Christ, the unseen high priest. And we must see this fact also in the cosmic Liturgy in which Christ, Who is the source of all gifts we offer to God, has also become—after His incarnation—the high priest who offers them and us to the Father as gifts transformed into His sacrifice or included in His sacrifice, given that after He gave us the goods of nature as gifts and ourselves as gifts to each other we neglected our duty to offer them to God as well as to offer ourselves to God and to each other.

St. Cyril of Alexandria stressed the fact that we cannot enter into the presence of the Father, therefore we cannot be saved, except in a state of pure sacrifice by overcoming any kind of egoism. But we cannot obtain this state except in Christ, Who accepted the cross for us by denying Himself. He takes us into Himself and presents us to the Father as a pure sacrifice, freed from egoism, through His state of pure sacrifice — source of all love. It is understood that He does not take us into Himself as objects, but we also have to offer ourselves through our own will in the act by which Christ offers us or He gives us the power to offer ourselves together with Him. "After He rose from the dead, Emmanuel, the new imperishable fruit of humanity, has ascended into heaven in order to now appear before God the Father for us (Heb 9:24), certainly not to bring Himself into the Father's view [for He is always with Him and as God is never without the Father], but rather in order to bring us in Him into the Father's view, we who were out of His view and under His wrath on account of our disobedience.... Thus, in Christ we obtain the possibility of appearing before God, for He makes us now worthy of receiving God as ones who are sanctified."[15]

Thus, in the act by which Christ takes us with Him in His sacrifice we obtained, through Christ's quality as sacrifice and as high priest of His sacrifice as well as source of power for our sacrifice, the quality and the power for total sacrifice not outside our own freedom, therefore not outside our quality as priests of our sacrifice. "For our sacrifice is accepted by and pleasing to God because of Christ's saving passion. And I believe that this is what the Lord Himself said: 'for without Me you can do nothing' (Jn 15:5). Therefore, in our sweet fragrance [the sweet fragrance of our sacrifice by which we overcome out of love our egoism] is mingled the sweet fragrance of Christ's sacrifice, as He rises with it to the Father. For we are not otherwise accepted except through Christ."[16]

But this offering and sacrifice of ours to Christ, as the High Priest who offers us to the Father thus establishing, sustaining and making fully efficient our priesthood through His high priesthood, is also done within us. Within our being there is Christ as High Priest of our intimate church and we are priests in it together with Him. St. Mark the Ascetic says this by declaring that we offer to Christ, who is found within our heart as an altar, all our thoughts from the moment of their inception, before the beast of passion or of anger bites them. Through these thoughts we live an inner life dedicated to Christ but connected to the outside world, consequently a life not without a sanctifying effect upon this outside world.

Since St. Mark the Ascetic regards the sacrifices we offer to Christ on the altar of our heart not only as an offering of our being but also of all our thoughts and feelings, he shows that we are not to renounce our life in the world but to dedicate it along with everything it produces in the world as gifts to Christ.

In other words St. Mark the Ascetic links our inner priesthood, operating in the church of our being, to our activity in the world which contributes to its sanctification or to our priestly action in the outward creation. However, St. Mark the Ascetic declares that Christ burns up "in the divine fire these firstborn thoughts, thus unbitten by the beast of sin's temptation, namely He makes us pass through these thoughts beyond them into union with God."[17]

St. Mark recommends that we offer to Christ on the altar of the heart not the outer things, because we cannot do that, but our thoughts by which we start to commit actions directed toward things and persons around us.

Here are St. Mark the Ascetic's words: "The [personal] temple is the holy house built by God. And the altar is the table of hope placed within this temple. On this table the mind brings forth the firstborn thought of every thing or circumstance we arrive at, like a firstborn animal as sacrifice of purification for the offerer, if he offers it without stain. This temple has a place behind the iconostasis, where Jesus entered for us as Forerunner (Heb 6:20), dwelling in us since Baptism, if we are not unworthy Christians (2 Cor 13:5). This place is within the innermost, the most hidden, the purest chamber of the heart. If this chamber does not open up through God and through rational and intelligible hope, we cannot know for certain the One who dwells in it and we cannot know if our sacrifices of thoughts were accepted or not. As the faithful heart opens up through the hope mentioned, the heavenly High Priest accepts the firstborn thoughts of the mind and burns them up in the divine fire of which He said: 'I came to send fire on the earth, and how I wish it were already kindled' (Lk 12:49)."[18]

Through this inner liturgy a unification of all motions and tendencies of the believer is achieved in the church of his being as well as between him and God. In its turn that inner liturgy helps toward the unification of every human being with all others in God in his activity within cosmic creation, thus intensifying the liturgy from within the church building in the strict sense, liturgy that is his support. For a person lacking unification within himself—something that can only be fulfilled in God—cannot be unified with others either.

At the same time when we bring to Christ our thoughts about things, we return them pure and with thanksgiving to the One from whom all the reasons of created things originate, thus unifying them with Him as well as us together with them: "Thine own of Thine own." St. Maximos the Confessor affirmed the maintaining of the inner principles of things in the purity in which God created them by offering them to God. In this way we keep ourselves pure and do not add to them our passion. Regarding the need to separate passion from the simple understanding of things St. Maximos says: "An impassioned conceptual image is a thought compounded of passion and a conceptual image. If we separate the passion from the conceptual image, what remains is the passion-free thought. We can make this separation by means of spiritual love and self-control, if only we have the will."[19] St. Maximos also says about the purification of the soul itself by separating the passions from the simple understanding of things: "Impurity of soul lies in its not functioning in accordance with nature. It is because of this that impassioned thoughts are produced in the intellect. The soul functions in accordance with nature when its passible aspects—that is, its incensive power and its desire—remain dispassionate in the face of provocations both from things and from conceptual images of these things."[20]

Just as Mark the Ascetic sees the burning of pure thoughts as they are offered to Christ, so St. Maximos calls for the raising of the mind beyond the simple reasons of things as it is surrendered to Christ: "The virtues separate the intellect from the passions; spiritual contemplation separates it from its passion-free conceptual images of things; pure prayer brings it into the presence of God Himself."²¹

The high-priestly activity of Christ in our heart is not restricted only to the reception of our thoughts and our being, but it is also manifested in our partaking of Him. This because in any true love there takes place a mutual surrendering. The act of partaking is one of mutual love between the believer and Christ. St. Symeon the New Theologian and the hesychasts who attained the climax of union with Christ shining forth as the light within their own being, speak of both Christ's surrendering to them and of their surrendering to Christ. It is in this that the human person experiences the most indescribable mystery.

In this sense Kallistos Kataphygiotes says: "When, from the fathomless depths of the fountain of divine and noetic contemplation, spiritual power springs forth bursting from the heart, then naturally there has come the time to be silent. For then the intellect wordlessly conducts the worship and adoration of God in Spirit and in truth (Jn 4:24)."²²

Kallistos Angelikoudes speaks even more directly about this inner partaking: "When the intellect sets its gaze solely upon the divine truth in Christ, then it is a time to be silent (Ecc 3:7). For then is a time to drink of the divine nectar, a time for jubilation and spiritual exultation; a time for mystical visions and the enjoyment of spiritual goods. For it is then that the intellect clearly sees the cup full of unmixed wine in the Lord's hand [the divinity and humanity united but not mixed in Christ's person, thus in His blood as well], and when the Lord tilts it from side to side [Christ's pouring of Himself within us], the intellect manifestly beholds and fully realizes that it has not been emptied to the dregs (Ps 74:9). For the last draught of the divine goodness poured out for us (which is to say the depth of the wealth and the extent of His grace) is never shown to be empty in the present life, indeed even if one attains the highest ascent toward God and deification. For the end and the 'perfect' are reserved for all to enjoy in the age to come."²³

Christ offers Himself to us not in a simple way, but with His blood shed on Golgotha for us, with the blood that preserves the disposition in which Christ surrendered Himself to the Father for us. For when He offered Himself for us He did this so that we may offer ourselves together with Him to the Father, but we have not yet opened ourselves to receive Him. Now by opening ourselves to Him, He offers Himself specifically and effectively to each of us. Just as when someone gives his blood to someone else he gives him of his life with everything that is proper to the latter, so does Christ give us His life by giving us His blood. And because His blood is free of any (spiritual) passion He gives us at the same time with this pure blood His pure life that is eternally lasting and united to that of the Father, saving our life from every disease of sin and strengthening us physically during our existence on earth (1 Cor 11:30).

Our partaking of God is always accompanied by the feeling that what is received, no matter how rich it might be, is only a small part of the infinite richness of divine life. St. Symeon the New Theologian described extensively this experience that we in fact also have in the partaking of knowing the created reality or through loving union with another human being: "In my opinion, it is the whole recapitulated that one sees not indeed by essence, but by participation. In reality, you light fire with fire, it is the whole fire that you take and yet the fire remains undivided without having lost anything."[24]

Neither in the human abode of God, nor in the cosmic one, nor in the liturgical one proper can the partaking of God reach the end. In all these abodes of God when we partake of Him we experience His infinitude. In all of them we encounter infinitude, for when we partake of Him we realize that His life surpasses infinitely what we are able to receive. It is this that maintains our thirst to receive more and more of Him.

St. Symeon again says: "When I drink, I thirst again . . . . I desire to hold the whole and to drink, if it is possible, all the abyss at once. But, as that is impossible, I tell you that I always thirst, although in my mouth there always is some water which flows, which brims over and runs down. But when I see the abysses, I believe not to drink at all because I desire to possess the whole, although I possess with abundance the entire water entirely in my hand; I am always a beggar when I really possess the whole united with the tiny bit."[25]

This is what sustains our growth, unending but always in Christ. It is a growth sustained not only by receiving Christ but also by our offering to Him. And this is what it means to grow through love and in the love that is never satisfied. We grow in love by giving and receiving. We receive to the extent that we give and vice versa. But we give only from the power of what we receive from Him.

If the progress of creation as a whole toward perfection at the present time is not very clear in the Christian teaching, given the end we have to go through in order to reach perfection in God, or the progress toward a total deterioration in one's distancing from God, the very same teaching presents most clearly our perfection in the life to come. At the same time a fact clear and verifiable through experience is the progress toward spiritual perfection of certain believers. Christian spirituality is able to describe the phases of this progress of the individual believer. He travels the road of purification so that he may later reach an ever more intensified union with Christ.

On the other hand, the individual believer does not effectuate this progress, or this personal liturgy, apart from cosmic creation and from the human community. The believer effectuates the phase of cleansing the passions and gaining the virtues—which culminates in love—and of the knowledge of God from creation, from within himself and from his fellow human beings not only through his relationship with God through faith and prayer, but also by fulfilling his duties toward his fellow human beings through his work upon creation.

The first place between the individual believer and cosmic creation and his fellow human persons is occupied by his family. For progress toward God is not the exclusive prerogative of the monks (who, in fact, also have the monastic community instead of their family). Thus the human person has the duty to make of his own house a place of God through which he may advance toward union with Christ in a service or in a liturgy that takes him increasingly closer to Christ.

To this end the members of a family are called to help each other first of all. They are called to forgive each other the mistakes they make as human beings, to encourage each other by word and by example to avoid evil things, to help each other in good things, to take care of each other and to exhort each other to prayer by their own example. In doing this they feel how they advance toward Christ. Or they may experience that without Christ it is very difficult to lead a life in peace and understanding that is without grave sins or quarrels. In this way they are also strengthened for fulfilling their duties to those outside the family by giving an example of honest living and of fulfilling duties through their actions for the benefit of society. Both the exhortation and the example are duties belonging especially to those who have a greater responsibility by the position they have in the family either by age or through a more advanced spiritual stage. Thus the members of the family may come to see Christ Himself working in each of them.

They strengthen their relationship with Christ and their progress together with Him in the family life by maintaining the relationship with Christ from His Eucharistic abode. There they can clearly know and can better take to heart the exhortation always offered to them for peace and for mutual spiritual and material help, or they can feel how the gift of peace and understanding is strengthened in them especially through the words of the priest addressed to them as he raises the cross: "Peace be to you all!" As they constantly look at the cross through which Christ gave up His earthly life out of love for them and as they partake of His crucified body and of His blood shed for them they receive, as members of the family, the power to overcome their egoism and to live their life in peace, abstaining from all bad tendencies and quarrels that make family life difficult, and thus they increase the love and self-sacrifice among them.

B. The Church Building Proper: Heaven on Earth or the Liturgical Center of Creation

In the church building Christ continues to perform in the most direct way His entire saving or sanctifying activity. Through this activity Christ unites with Himself and among themselves those who believe in Him, strengthening them in the work of their general priesthood within their own being and within cosmic creation. In this way God leads creation toward its perfect and triune unity, something that is being done through the offering of creation in Christ to God as well as through God's offering in Christ to us. The church building is the liturgical center of creation, or the central place where Christ's saving power is active and from where the same power spreads over the entire creation through His Spirit or through His uncreated energies. Thus the progress of creation toward its most complete unity is being encouraged. It is a unity imbued with the triune unity owing to a more accentuated penetration of creation by the Holy Trinity or by its power that unites persons in love without confounding them.

The church building is the central space of Christ's saving work; for the heart of the Liturgy officiated there is the Divine Eucharist, which consists of the Mystery of the transformation of the bread and wine into the body and blood of the Lord and the partaking of them by the faithful. A large part of the other services officiated therein is made up of the other Sacraments. In the Sacraments the believers receive through the prayers and visible acts of the priests or bishops the grace of God, which—as an uncreated work springing up from God's being—is not separated from the loving presence of God; in this work is present the very One who works.

When in the church building during the Holy Liturgy the body and blood of Christ are present through transformation on the altar table so that the faithful may partake of them, there takes place the encounter between the faithful and Christ and His Holy Spirit, who has actually transformed the bread and wine into the Lord's body and blood and filled them with His presence. The encounter with Christ in the church is not experienced by the faithful as isolated persons, but within the community, thus strengthening the unity among them without which there is no salvation.

Therefore, the church is not only a house of prayer of the faithful who would take from within themselves the power to unite with God and among themselves, but a house in which God works, better said Christ Himself through His Holy Spirit, unseparated from the Father. The Holy Trinity unites the believers in the church without confusing them, just as the divine persons are united. The believers do not gather in church to pray together to a God who remains distant or to listen to a sermon about Him. The church building is also a place of the Triune God's presence and work. Just as it is in heaven, so is the Holy Trinity in the church, or the heaven is present in the church. The Triune God listens not only from the faraway heaven to the prayers of the faithful, but He answers their call with His presence and work. This encounter culminates especially in the eating of the body of the crucified and risen Son of God and in the drinking of His blood poured out for us out of His boundless love, so that we too may be filled with a similar love by which we may respond to Him and through which we encounter each other.

This general substance of the Orthodox worship, especially of the Holy Liturgy officiated in the church, is seen in several of its characteristics which are presented below with special reference to the Holy Liturgy.

1. *The Holiness of the Church Building*

The Holy Liturgy and the other Mysteries officiated in the church are experienced by the faithful as sacred events solemnized in the world, but they originate beyond the world and transfigure a part of it, having as their purpose the transfiguration of the entire world. This is what envelops the church building with the characteristic of holiness.

Western Christianity has made from ancient times a distinction between the notions of holy (*sanctus*) and sacred (*sacer*). *Sanctus* refers to God as person; the believers who reached perfection are also called in the Roman Catholic Church sometimes saints, but in recent times they are more often called *beati*, being proclaimed as such through an act of beatification. For the church building, for the acts of worship and its objects and for everything that the believers experience in the church, the notion of "sacred" is used, which is something less than holy. This is why even the Mysteries are called sacraments or sacred actions. If we add to this the fact that the grace given through the sacraments is considered in Catholicism as created, we realize that the sacred falls within the category of what is created. Not to mention Protestantism and the denominations arisen from it which no longer know the reality of the sacred but consider only God as holy Who is transcendent to any experience and does not produce any kind of transformation in the lives of the believers.

We believe that in this distinction between sacred and holy in Catholic Christianity is implied the lack of knowledge of God's uncreated operation. This operation itself being holy like God, its Subject, makes all the acts officiated in the Orthodox Church, all persons and objects touched by that operation, regarded as "holy" because all are "sanctified" by it. Orthodox Christians speak of "the sanctification of the water," "the sanctification of priestly vestments," of icons, of homes, of the "sanctification" of the person being ordained as priest. For them the cross is "holy," the icons are "holy," the church and the objects in it are "holy." They do not consider God Who is holy as separated from these.

If one can say that in the distinction Catholicism makes between "holy" and "sacred" is implied the teaching about the created character of grace that God uses to produce certain transformations in the ecclesiastical arena, but not certain imprints of God's powers, the fact that in the Orthodox Church there is no knowledge of the distinction and separation between "holy" and "sacred" implies the knowledge that God Himself is present personally in His uncreated operations as regards those raised within the plane of church life.

In this regard the Orthodox Church follows the example of the Holy Scriptures where the name "holy" is given not only to God and to the persons who enter into a relationship with Him, but also to the objects used for His work, objects that cannot be conceived of except in connection with the person of God or with human persons—blessed through God's operation. In Exodus 3:5 we read: "The place where you stand [where the burning bush appeared] is holy ground." Exodus 29:37: "The altar shall be most holy." Leviticus 10:10: "That you may distinguish between holy and unholy, and between unclean and clean." Ezekiel 40:23: the priests "shall teach My people the difference between the holy and the profane, and cause them to discern between the unclean and the clean." Jonah 2:5, 8: the temple is called "holy." Habakkuk 2:20: "But the Lord is in His holy temple." Psalm 95:9: "Worship the Lord in His holy court."

In a few passages of the Old Testament the French translation uses the expression "sacred" for the object of worship. But the Romanian translation uses the expression "holy" throughout. Here is the text in the French translation: "Then you shall make a sacred garment for Aaron" (Ex 28:2). "And on the turban, on its front, he put the golden plate, the sacred crown" (Lv 8:9). "Phinehas the son of Eleazar the priest with the sacred vessels" (Nm 31:6). But the Romanian translation uses in all these places the expression "holy," and even the French translation uses this expression in the great majority of places,[26] for at the basis of both French words is the Hebrew *kadosh*.

In the New Testament the term "holy" (αγιοξ) is used not only for God but also for persons consecrated for His service and even for all Christians, namely for the Church constituted by them (Eph 5:22). St. Paul the Apostle asks us to present our bodies as "a living sacrifice, holy, acceptable to God" (Rom 12:1), and he calls the woman who cares about the things of the Lord "holy both in body and in spirit" (1 Cor 7:34). The Savior calls the temple and the altar inside "holy" and even the gold and the gift placed on the altar (Mt 23:17). It is true that for the foods eaten in the temple sometimes the New Testament uses the term "sanctified" (ιερα) (1 Cor 9:13), translated in Latin as "sacred." But the fact that both terms, holy (αγιον) and sacred (ιερον), are used in the New Testament for the temple shows that there is no strict distinction between these two terms. The Romanian language renders this fact very well when God is called holy as the One who has holiness in Himself while the persons and things partaking in God's holiness are sometimes called holy and other times sanctified (ιερα). This is justified in the Romanian language by the fact that even if human persons and certain objects are considered only as partakers of holiness, consequently only sanctified, not holy in and of themselves, the uncreated power of the same God—the source of holiness—has descended upon and dwells in them, which means that they have not received a created grace that maintains a separation between them and God.

2. The Church Building: the Space Consecrated by God's Very Presence and by His Descent within It

Thus, far from profaning everything, as some Protestant theologians have said recently, through His incarnation and the sending of His Holy Spirit, the Son of God has brought about the possibility for all who receive Him with faith to be clothed with holiness. For Christ "became for us wisdom from God—and righteousness and sanctification and redemption" (1 Cor 1:30). He no longer asks us to become holy more through our efforts, but He makes us holy through His dwelling and that of the Holy Spirit in us (Gal 2:20; Eph 2:9; 3:24).

As regards the holiness of places and things, no longer is there a single holy temple in which to offer sacrifices to God, but God accepts worship everywhere as long as it is offered "in spirit and in truth" (Jn 4:24). But as there is a gradation of holiness in persons, so is there a gradation of holiness in places. Places, or better said the buildings in which believers gather with a common effort of thoughts and special feelings in order to attend and participate in holy acts, have a special holiness. They gather together in them with such feelings, thoughts and intentions because they know that God dwells there in a more special way.

Since the time of the Apostles certain rooms were reserved for the gathering of the faithful, for prayer and for officiating the Mysteries, as well as for listening to the word of God. St. Paul the Apostle writes to Timothy "so that you may know how you ought to conduct yourself in the house of God" (1 Tim 3:15). So this house was not considered only as a place of prayer addressed to an absent God, but God Himself was considered to have dwelled in it. The fact that St. Paul continues: "which is the church of the living God, the pillar and ground of the truth" (1 Tim 3:15), shows that he saw a strong connection between the house of worship and the church community (*ecclesia*) gathered there. Indeed, a house for praising God in which the believers no longer gather is no longer a living place or a place of God experienced as active, therefore living.

It is no less true that a simple house without God being present in it together with the community of believers, therefore a house for a simple gathering of believers, would no longer be "the pillar and ground of the truth." This is why the Holy Fathers gathered in Councils, when deciding on the formula of an enduring truth of the Church, saw themselves as being united, as representatives of their local churches, with the Holy Spirit: "For it seemed good to the Holy Spirit and to us" (Acts 15:28). One must remember that the meetings of Councils were usually held in the church. It is said of the Fourth Ecumenical Council that the bishops placed next to the relics of the martyr Euphemia in the church of Chalcedon of which she was the patron, two papers with the two formulas on which the members of the Synod were divided ("in two natures" and "of two natures") and they realized that the latter formula was thrown away from the relics, but the first remained there. The Council, therefore, approved the first one. The saints, thus, participate in establishing Christ's truth, as they are in a special way instruments of the Holy Spirit and members of the Church.

This shows how strong is the Church as the body of Christ linked to the church as dwelling in which the community of believers experiences to the utmost its characteristic as the body of Christ. The sobornicity of the Church as the body of Christ cannot be maintained without the communities gathered in church dwellings so that all may partake of the same body and blood of Christ through the priests ordained by the bishops who are in communion. The gathering of the Church's believers for the offering of the Holy Eucharist gives proof to the unity of the body of the Church. We do not gather in church to pray individually, but to manifest and maintain the mystery of the one Church through the prayer filled with the same Christ and by partaking of Him.[27] And the Church fulfills her sanctifying work upon cosmic creation or, rather, works toward its unification through the communities of believers gathered in church dwellings.

The "churches" mentioned in the Acts of the Apostles and in the epistles of St. Paul must have had this characteristic as houses of God, but also as places for gathering of the faithful. Thus, the book of Acts mentions the "church" in Jerusalem that was praying fervently in the form of litanies for Peter while he was in prison (Acts 12:5). Here the word "church" is again used for both the gathering of the faithful and for the place of the gathering.[28] St. Paul the Apostle mentions twice the church in the house of Aquilla and Priscilla (Rom 16:3, 5; 1 Cor 16:19). In another place he mentions "Nymphas and the church that is in his house," which he distinguishes from the "brethren" in the same city of Laodicea, showing that it is about a house and not the Church as a body of Christ's believers (Col 4:15). Certainly, it is in this church dwelling that St. Paul asks for his epistle to the Colossians to be read. It seems that this meaning is given to the "churches of Asia" following which St. Paul mentions "Aquilla and Priscilla... with the church that is in their house" (1 Cor 16:19). This meaning can also be given to all "the churches of Christ" (Rom 16:16).

This meaning of the "church" as dwelling is also confirmed by the distinction St. Paul makes between the "church" in which the believers partake of the Lord's body and blood and their own houses in which they satisfy their thirst and hunger. "Do you not have houses to eat and drink in? Or do you despise the church of God and shame those who have nothing?" (1 Cor 11:22). If in 1 Timothy 3:15 the church building is called "the house of God," here it is called "the church of God," thus showing in these two names that these houses are not simply houses of prayer devoid of God's presence, but houses in which God is actively present.

In those houses there was also an altar (1 Cor 11:13), which should be seen as the table on which the transformation of the bread and wine into the Lord's body and blood is officiated for the communion of the faithful (1 Cor 11:27). Christian worship places could not have appeared as public places at the beginning of Christianity when the number of believers was very small. Therefore, they had to be located in the houses of Christian families. In Greece, the custom has prevailed until now that in each house or near the house a room is reserved as a church in which the priest comes once a year to celebrate the Holy Liturgy. But these home churches received a public character when the number of Christians increased and especially when they were no longer persecuted. However, even in these home churches it was a community that gathered. Christianity could not have lasted without the gathering of Christians in houses where they strengthened each other's faith through "psalms and spiritual songs" (Eph 5:19) and where they also had faith in the presence and work of God, culminating in Christ's presence on the altar under the form of bread and wine following the "breaking of bread" and the "blessing of the cup" (Acts 2:42; Didache of the Twelve Apostles). This conviction based on the experience of God's work is clearly attested to by the Apostles. St. Paul the Apostle says: "For our gospel did not come to you in word only, but also in power, and in the Holy Spirit and in much assurance" (1 Th 1:5). Or: "For this reason we also thank God without ceasing, because when you received the word of God which you heard from us, you welcomed it not as the word of men, but as it is in truth, the word of God, which also effectively works in you who believe" (1 Th 2:13).

We learn from the time of Clement of Rome, toward the end of the first century, that the service officiated by the community in these "houses" was called Liturgy[29] and that it was officiated under the leadership of the Hierarch surrounded by priests and deacons, the Hierarch being the one who broke the bread and blessed the cup. This was done in obedience to the Savior's commandment, at specific times and in specific places.

This indissoluble union between building, community and Christ's presence for the communion of the faithful, or in general for receiving the uncreated graces and gifts, has been integrally preserved up to the present time in the conviction and practice of the Orthodox Church.

It is very likely that even from the first centuries of Christianity there appeared public places of worship at times and in places where persecution subsided. It is known that such public worship places appeared in the second century in Syria and Smyrna. They were called *basilica*, a name passed on to the Christianized Traco- and Daco-Romans from the Balkan Peninsula and Northern Danube, especially after the retreat of the Roman authorities and thus of the cessation of the persecutions of Christians. But to the Daco-Roman Christians the meaning of these public worship places has evolved into that of *houses of God the King*. The beginning of the Liturgy with the words "Blessed is the Kingdom of the Father and of the Son and of the Holy Spirit" has also influenced this modification very early. Thus, this meaning of the church building underlined even more its link to God's presence in it, or with the encounter of the faithful on earth with God and with the saints in the same Kingdom of God especially in the Holy Liturgy. In fact, the name King used for God, especially in the mentioned places, for the church and in the beginning words of the Liturgy, has been, together with other elements, taken into the Christian worship from the Judaic worship at the inception of their separation.[30] We see this name applied to God first by St. Paul the Apostle in the context of a sentence that sounds almost like a liturgical hymn. In naming God "the King of Kings," St. Paul concludes:

"to whom be honor and everlasting power. Amen" (1 Tim 6:16).[31] We have here one of the likely hymns recited in the "churches" even in the apostolic times. The name King is given to God also in Revelation 15:3.[32]

The name "biserica-basilica" (church) preserved until today in Romania shows how old its Christianity is.

As mentioned above, Orthodoxy has preserved the feeling of holiness for the church building as well as the teaching that it is the house of God and thus within it the faithful encounter God in a special way. Consequently, they also should gather together in order to receive in communion with each other His power and even the body and blood of Christ.

In defining the church building, St. Symeon of Thessalonica says that it is "the house of God and even if it is made of inanimate things, it is sanctified by the grace of God and through the priestly prayers. It is not like other houses, but it is built for God and it is God who dwells in it and His glory, power and grace are found in there.... Therefore, we call it not just a house, but holy, as it is sanctified by the Holy Father with the All-Holy Son through the Holy Spirit, being the dwelling of the Holy Trinity."[33] Thus, its consecration means that God dwells in it, or better said it is the dwelling of the Triune God of one and undivided essence. Patriarch Germanos of Constantinople from the eighth century says: "The church is the temple of God, a holy place, a house of prayer, the assembly of the people, the body of Christ. It is called the bride of Christ . . . . The church is an earthly heaven in which the supercelestial God dwells and walks about. It represents the crucifixion, burial, and resurrection of Christ . . . . The holy table corresponds to the spot in the tomb where Christ was placed. On it lies the true and heavenly bread, the mystical and unbloody sacrifice. Christ sacrifices His flesh and blood and offers it to the faithful as food for eternal life."[34]

The church envelops in itself all heavenly and earthly things and offers the means for the continuation of Christ's saving work until the end of time.

Therefore, whoever enters the church or passes in front of it makes the sign of the cross because he or she enters in or passes by the place where the Holy Trinity dwells and performs the saving works that are for our eternal deification. When passing in front of the church, the believer knows that he or she passes in front of God in Trinity out of which one Person was crucified for us. That is why he or she makes the sign of the cross, remembering both the Holy Trinity and Christ's sacrifice and sensing the work of the Trinity and of Christ crucified for him or her.

The fact that the believer knows that in the prayer and even more so in the Liturgy officiated in the church it is not only him or the community of faithful but also God that is active, gives him or her the feeling of coming out of the usual earthly life, a feeling of exaltation but also of lowliness before the divine greatness. Archimandrite Vasileios, the Abbot of Stavronikita Monastery of Mount Athos, writes about this feeling experienced in the church and in the Liturgy officiated in the church:

> It composes and holds together everything in and around us. It embodies the invisible and uncreated and brings it near us and into us, tangible and open to our consciousness. It transfigures and sanctifies what is visible and insignificant. We experience the unconfused interpenetration of created and uncreated, of life and death, of movement and motionlessness, of mystery and rational thought, of miracle and law, of freedom and nature. Things invisible are seen in an invisible way. Things that cannot be spoken are expressed ineffably. Things that cannot be approached, that are far beyond us, dwell among us. And we ourselves are something infinitesimal, even non-existent, which contains something unlimited and unattainable. The more we advance voluntarily toward diminishing, finally becoming so small that we vanish, the more the glory that cannot be approached shines, realizing and bringing from non-being into existence endless new creations and joys.
>
> In the end, one cannot tell if things invisible are more perceptible than created things, or if the latter are more holy than the former.[35]

"In his *Poem on the Holy Wisdom of Edessa*, St. Maximos the Confessor described the church in these words: 'It is the most admirable thing that a small church can be like the vast universe. . . . Its raised dome is like the heaven of heavens . . . and rests solidly on its lower part. Its arches represent the four corners of the earth.'"[36] "Each church therefore is an *omphalos*, a cosmic center. . . . The church reproduces the internal structure of the universe . . . . The Heavenly Jerusalem shows precisely the interaction of the circle and the square (Rev. 21:16). The nave (from *navis* meaning "ship") is an eschatological ship on which is set the spherical form of the dome. We therefore have the union of the circle and the square, the measure and number of heaven and of the Kingdom." This gives it measure with all the suggestion of the infinite. "St. Isaac the Syrian felt that "measure made everything beautiful."[37] "The square or the cube represents unshakable immutability and the stability of the accomplished plan, and inside, the circular dynamism of services and rites take place."[38] It is the movement within stability of the epektases of which St. Gregory of Nyssa spoke. "The development of liturgical space proceeds along a vertical plane. This is the direction of prayer symbolized by the rising of incense . . . . The raised hands of the priest, the movement of the invocation of the Holy Spirit, and of the elevation of the holy gifts are also an indication of this vertical plane."[39]

This preservation of the human being so fragile and its being filled with the infinite greatness of the uncreated is explained by the fact that God is personal. If He were impersonal, He would crush it, as it is so small. Here is why the experience of God's holiness that permeates everything in the church, is not an experience by which the human person feels shocked, threatened or crushed, but it is similar to the experience of a child in the parental bosom, in the bosom of an all-comprehending and all-loving parent.

Perhaps it was the weakening of feeling of the relationship between God's holiness and His characteristic as a person who loves humankind, a feeling experienced in Orthodoxy, and the replacement of this feeling with the feeling of sacred experienced in the West as something impersonal that caused Rudolf Otto to define in his renowned book *Das Heilige* this sacred with impersonal terms that indicate a reality producing certain feelings that lack love: "Das Numinose" (the divine in neutral gender, impersonal), "mysterium tremendum" (the mystery that makes one tremble), "das ganz Andere" (something other). This "sacred" is experienced as an overwhelming but vague greatness, since it does manifest a will that can benevolently adapt itself to the ability of the human being to communicate; it is something of which you are afraid as of a discretionary or impersonal force, of an essence not only completely different than ours, but also one that bewilders and threatens us.[40]

This feeling of a huge but impersonal force is also produced in the Western churches through the playing of the organ, while in the Eastern Christendom the singing by the human voices produces the feeling that the human person remains before God or that he enters within a familiar communion with God who is also personal.

3. *Ascension toward God Symbolized and Aided by the Architecture of the Orthodox Church Building*

Perhaps in this experience of the sacred in the writings of Rudolph Otto is felt the influence of Calvin's conception of God who had predestined some, of whom the believer has no knowledge, and consequently he may be among those who suffer eternally with no rational cause and with no mercy. In any case, this sentiment of the sacred in the sense of something terrifying has an architectonic parallel in the dark angles of the ceilings of Gothic churches in which God is hiding, or in the decorations of their exterior walls with monstrous images that have no human sentiment in them. These close off the human person within a created immanent order at the discretion of certain human powers. This is also suggested by the rectangular ceiling of churches with roman style that lacks the presence of mystery, which is benevolent and luminous. In this is shown that aspect of God's separation from His relationship with creation, the separation of which the Catholic theologian H. Mühlen speaks.

In Eastern Christianity the sentiment of holiness, as that of the all-good God's personal attribute of love toward mankind and as an attribute of a perfect person, has as an architectural parallel the church's central cupola and other smaller cupolas, which express God's descent at various levels with great loving care toward believers. One can see in the embracing aspect of these cupolas God's descent toward the community gathered in the church, manifesting both His love and the will to cause the members of that community to gather ever more in His love and embrace. This lowered cupola indicates not "a descending (anonymous) transcendent" (according to Lucian Blaga's expression) so to deviate creation's élan for ascension, but the personal God Who embraces with love the community in order to attract it to His life by deifying it; He persuades it to unite itself with Him Who protects it as the All-Sustaining (the Pantokrator painted on the central cupola). Even the Moldavian churches, influenced by the Gothic style, have inside them one or more cupolas. The cupola arched above the community of believers conveys the fact that the Son of God Himself descended from heaven and continues to remain with those who believe in Him and form His body, not out of inner necessity but out of love for us humans and for our salvation, which He effectuates for our benefit especially in churches.

Still, we also have to advance toward Him through our own efforts of purification and through a continually intensifying prayer. This is an advancing with a double meaning: both through the ascension of our soul toward Christ at the top of the cupola, and advancing toward living a purer life that brings us closer to Him Who is on the altar table. That is why the church has Christ both as Pantokrator at the top of the cupola in the center of the church, and as a living sacrifice on the altar table toward which we are to advance so that we may become worthy at the end of the Liturgy of His state of sacrifice and of resurrection. Thus, the Liturgy is a movement with both of these meanings toward Christ.

While the "Almighty" of the West is distant and discretionary, the Pantokrator or the All-sustaining Christ is God close to us and all-concerned for our life, Who is mentioned in Revelation 11:17, 15:3, 21:22 and in the writings of the Holy Fathers. This quality of His concurs with His quality as sacrifice on the altar. For it is where God is a Father or a close Brother that the community feels like a family in which neither the angels nor the saints as members or unseen brothers of the family are strangers.

This does not mean that the Pantokrator, who descends to us and lovingly listens to our prayers, is totally comprehensible or that He is not full of glory, or He does not inspire in us the sentiment of mystery, or He is not infinitely beyond our understanding. His incomprehensible mystery does not mean remoteness, coldness, separation, but is the mystery of Him who came to us and sacrificed Himself. He does not elude us into the incomprehensible boundlessness, as the Catholic theologian H. Mühlen says ("entzieht Sich uns unbegreiflich als Grenzenlose [eludes us as the incomprehensible boundlessness]").[41] He is here with His incomprehensible infinitude because it is an infinitude full of His love's warmth and He offers Himself to us as sacrifice. It is the infinitude of love and the mystery of love, not the mystery of remoteness, of emptiness and of darkness. It is similar to the mystery of a parent for a child, a parent who holds the child in his arms with strength but also full of delicate and compassionate care. This closeness and love are felt by those whose conscience is not burdened by sins and who have decided to repent and to ask for His forgiveness. "No one enslaved by passions and pleasures of the flesh is worthy to come, to approach and to serve Thee, the King of glory" (prayer recited by the priest during the Cherubic hymn).

Archimandrite Vasileios calls this inexpressible mystery of the One who, though unlimited in His power, is still close to us through love, "apophatic theology" which he sees expressed in the hymn "It is meet and right to sing of Thee, to bless Thee, to praise Thee, to give thanks to Thee, to worship Thee. For Thou art God ineffable, incomprehensible, invisible, inconceivable; Thou art from everlasting and art ever the same"[42]

St. Gregory of Nazianzus regarded the cupola of the octagon built in his father's memory as a "dwelling of light." "On the eight equally long columns the nave returns to itself. Through the cupola it enlightens from above, as if it were truly a dwelling of light."[43] The infinite God is distinct from the world, has life in Himself, but light irradiates from Him; He has no need to come out of Himself, since He is infinite in Himself. If He still comes out of Himself, He does it out of love for us. His Light manifested to us is the light of love that gives meaning to our life and to the entire existence.

"The early basilica was in a certain way the image of heaven, to be sure less by imitation (of the cosmic heaven) than through the palpable rendering, as a house, of the holy community (called ecclesia) as the property of Christ, the Basileios, and the throne chamber of God." Especially St. Sophia, built at the order of Justinian, has become an ideal model for the later Byzantine churches, "with its large cupola floating over the crown of windows as an imitation of heaven and with its entire space seen as a cosmos dominated by heaven and hierarchically ordered, which makes the liturgy a participation through imitation or a direct participation in the heavenly liturgy of angels."[44]

The symbolism of heaven and of light is overwhelmingly felt in the architecture of St. Sophia. Procopius describes it the following way in his book about Justinian's buildings: "The huge round dome offers a distinctly beautiful view. It does not seem to be placed on a firm foundation, but it covers the space as if hanging by a chain."[45] "It is full of light" and of the sun's brightness; it can be said that space is not limited on the outside through the solar light, but it has its own shining; that's how much overwhelming light overflows within the church."[46] God has become part of the church's interior. One feels that He is not beyond it. "The one who prays, whose spirit is lifted to the heavenly heights, knows that God is not far off, but He is willing to be in this place because He Himself has chosen it."[47]

In this architecture of the church it is shown that the church being "heaven on earth," "its purpose is not to escape the world. God keeps it connected to Him until through the church the entire creation becomes heaven."[48] The dome arched over the community and over the world, having Christ the Pantokrator in its highest center, shows us God at the supreme peak, Who looks toward us and embraces us in a fatherly way. At the same time He is drawing us into Himself as in the supreme One where we can all be united and can have everything.

"The cathedrals of former times were charged with a supernatural force and intensity. Their dynamism can even today make one breathless and lead to ecstasy. In the Gothic cathedrals, the vertical line and the mass of stone are violently launched toward the infinite and pull man's spirit along with them. In contrast, in Hagia Sophia, everything is ordered around a central axis and crowned by the dome's majesty; beauty is expressed in a more esoteric manner. This beauty comes from a mysterious depth and an unlimited height and descends on man and fills him with a transcendent peace. . . . By its lines, the dome gives visible form to the descending movement of divine love, and its spherical shape unites all men in an assembly, in a body. Under the dome, we feel protected and saved from the Pascalian anxiety of infinite spaces."[49] The dome suggests an infinity of the loving heart, not of the exterior heights that are cold and limitless.

God who observes us and embraces us from the dome is above all, but He encompasses all and is in all with His personal love. He is near all and still above all. He is above all but not detached from all, nor is He closed in on Himself, but He comprises, protects and guides all. He is both familiar and infinite in His mystery. It is the mystery that surrounds us and sustains us, not the mystery hidden from us. We do not imagine that He is somewhere, but we feel His embrace in the church. It is not an imagined mystery, but the visible and felt mystery that sustains us. It is a mystery we love, not fear.

H. I. Schulz, who used the previous quotes from Procopius, sums up the ideas from those quotes in these three impressions: "The dome does not seem to belong to the earthly and overwhelming matter, but it seems to stand in a direct link with the heaven whose copy it is. The dome is just like the cosmic heaven, the source and the dwelling place of light that flows from there unto the nave and as it rises up it also lifts up into the heavenly height the spirit of those who pray... The light that descends within the church from one level to another is an imitation of the enlightening grace that, according to Dionysius, is imparted to the church hierarchies by means of the heavenly hierarchies."[50]

Wulff observes that, while the Roman churches lead us through their large halls to the opposite end and while through their flat ceiling any progress of our vision beyond the world is impeded (they were buildings inspired by the non-Christian Roman halls), and the Gothic domes call us forward and also attract our vision toward a height without finding its rest in transcendence, the domed churches in the Byzantine style enable our advance toward Christ as well as our ascension from now toward heaven, a heaven which embraces us and from which the light eternally shines forth.[51] After quoting from St. Gregory of Nazianzus and Procopius, Wulff quotes from the Ekfrasis of Photius about the Nea church at the royal palace in Constantinople: "As soon as one leaves the pre-nave and entered the nave, what an enchantment and at the same time what emotion and wonder is one filled with! It is as if one entered heaven without any hindrance and from all sides one is engulfed by many kinds of beauty as if by stars."[52] Stars are understood as signifying the icons. Photius speaks about the experience of motion rather than that of rest. It is a motion within the fullness of the same infinitude. Everything seems to be in motion. The nave seems to be in a circular motion. It is the experience of the same fullness, unitary and complex, that is also suggested by icons and is lived in the Liturgy where the same Christ-God continuously offers Himself to us in ever-new ways, but wholly and with the entire plenitude of life and of saving works. One does not expect the experience of plenitude only in the eschatological future, nor does one imagine it as being hidden in an unapproachable height in this life. This would weaken the effect and perception of Christ's incarnation and resurrection, or would consider Him entirely ascended from us after having paid for our sins, as is the case in the West. In Orthodoxy one has the conviction and the feeling that Christ continues to be with us and to work upon us through His Holy Spirit. Wulff himself concludes his article with the words: These churches appeal to us "with the voice of a conception based on the belief in the incarnation of God and in an unshaken saving plan."[53]

As we mentioned above, in addition to the central dome there are other domes as well; they represent God's descents closer to us through actions linked to the incarnation of His Son. Evdokimov sees in them symbols of the candles and of the prayers raised toward heaven: "Churches built on a central plan, sometimes even veritable towers, with their cupolas like golden flames, call to mind the Easter candles; they sing the Resurrection . . . a church with several cupolas is like a chandelier ablaze with flames."[54]

Aside from the central dome and from the other domes all churches, including those in the West, have the space for the altar [sanctuary], which is curved in almost all of them. This means that the community is oriented toward unity with God, the origin of all, in Whom all find their rest and salvation. In the East this meaning is highlighted by the fact that this place began to be separated, as we know, in the Hagia Sophia church of Emperor Justinian, suggesting the divine mystery toward which the faithful advance.

Schulz sees in this separation only the separation between laity and hierarchy, in accordance with the vision of Dionysius the Areopagite understood by Schulz in a rigid and non-dynamic sense.[55] But the fact that through the open altar doors one can see the rays of light from the altar table flickering from the mystical plane shows that in this separation we have an illustration of the distinction between the incommunicable divine essence and its energies that shine forth and are at work in creation. And in the fact that the priest oftentimes comes out in the nave being surrounded and touched by the people in the most familiar way shows that the emphasis is not placed on an authoritarian placement of the priest above the people, but on the mystery of God's transcendence Who still descends full of love among the faithful. In the Orthodox churches there is no great distance between the faithful and the place where the priests serve around the altar table, as is the case in the West, which points to a God accessible to rational speculation but incommunicable through His energies.

P. Evdokimov refers the separation of the altar from the nave through the icon screen but still in communication with the faithful through the doors to Christ ascended from us but still communicating with us. We cannot comprehend Christ, but we experience His love because we feel His beneficial works.

One can also say that the separation of the altar from the nave through the icon screen shows that the life on earth of the Church's members is distinct from the life in the heavenly Kingdom, being oriented toward that life. "We have no lasting city here, but we walk toward the future one without reaching it before death. This co-traveling of the faithful takes its strength from and is shown especially in the Eucharistic synaxis. The divine Eucharist is for the Holy Fathers a holy 'syn-odos,' a co-traveling of those here on earth toward heaven, or of the human persons toward angels, of the visible world toward the invisible one."[56] It is at the same time a certain encounter between things on earth and those in heaven, something that must increase continuously.

> This transparent wall of intercession receives and amplifies the prayer of the heart: "Lord Jesus Christ, Son of God, have mercy on me a sinner." It also undergoes the violence of the saints who take hold of the Kingdom and under their pressure, following Christ, the royal doors open wide and allow us to see the vision of heaven.
>
> The commentaries on the liturgy naturally explain the immediate symbolism of the door as the image of Christ "through whom you will see the heavens opened up" (Jn 1:51).
>
> The symbolism of the sanctuary carries us even further. Christ the door opens up the way into himself; the royal doors open up unto the altar, the high place of the *Opus Dei* and the center around which the sacred action of the liturgy takes place. St. Germanus said that the altar was "heaven descended on earth, the heaven where the triune God moves." (PG 98, 384)
>
> The altar, anointed with the "oil of gladness," "radiates with the perfect joy of love," unlike anything else here below. Only Christ is the Lover who magnetizes love and introduces himself to us so that we can begin to live again in him. St. Nicholas Cabasilas stated what is simply and clearly evident: "The human soul is hungry for the infinite. The eye was created for light and the ear for sounds. All things have their reason for being, and the soul's desire is to launch itself toward Christ."
>
> In his third homily on Jeremiah, Origen attributed the following saying to Jesus: "Whoever is near me is near fire." Is not this saying a beautiful illustration of the mystical interiorization of the "Door" which opens onto God's heart?
>
> Fr. Sergius Bulgakov made reference to the ineffable quality of passing through Christ the Fire on the occasion of his ordination: "The whole consecration was fiery. The most overwhelming thing about it was the first time I went through the royal doors

toward the altar. I literally went through a wall of fire, burning, illuminating, and renewing; I entered into another age, I entered into the Kingdom."[57]

We have seen that St. Mark the Ascetic also said that Christ receives the thoughts we offer Him on the altar of the heart. The believer who feels the closeness of Christ experiences Him as a fire not only on the church altar, but also on the altar of his being.

In any case, both in the West and in the East this orientation of the liturgical space toward the East shows the characteristic of the earthly journey toward the eschatological encounter with God. The Orthodox Church, in addition to this orientation of the curved altar toward the East, also has one toward the central dome as well as toward the others. This shows again that already in this earthly life we have in part Christ the Pantokrator as guide and sustainer and also as a foretaste of our union with Him in the life to come. This aspect has been lost in Western architecture because it has been lost in Western theology, especially in the Protestant one. A further step in this direction of eliminating this significance in Western churches is the fact of placing the altar in the middle of the congregation, thus eliminating any sentiment of mystery and entirely closing the community in the immanent.

About the orientation of churches in Moldavia toward the East, also a generally common characteristic of all churches until recently in the West, Wilhelm Nyssen wrote: "The churches in Moldavia are churches that suggest the life to come. They call for a journey from West to East, which is precisely contrary to [we believe that is not contrary, but in combination with] the usual Byzantine dome placed in the middle even in the small churches. The axial orientation of the space from West to East is common to the churches in Moldavia and to many churches from the Balkan countries, but this can bring to mind the early constructions that appeared during the migration of the northern people, especially the Visigoth buildings preserved in Spain or in the wooden architecture of the North."[58] In addition to this, it is known that these buildings symbolize the ships that sail through time toward the haven of the life to come. "An important example for the symbolism of the ship is the church of Dragomirna Monastery as well as those of Moldovita and Sucevita."[59] The lateral apses near the altar, specific to most Orthodox churches, give the faithful or the liturgical community the conviction that they are gathered within the Cross of Christ or incorporated in the crucified

Christ, advancing through Him toward the resurrection with Him. For if it is true that the Church or the community is the body of Christ, then it is the body of the crucified Christ and together with Him it travels the road toward His risen state. This would be in conformity with the fact that in the center of the Liturgy or of the fundamental event of the Liturgy officiated in the church stands the partaking of the crucified Christ, of Christ as sacrifice, and also with the fact that He remains permanently on the altar with His body and blood. Therefore, Archimandrite Vasileios from the Holy Mountain rightly says: "The unseen presence of the Lord lights and reveals everything [in the church]."[60] In regards to this we note that the church building and its form as well as the vessels and all services officiated in it are not simply symbols, in the sense of metaphors of certain spiritual actions separated from them, but they are rational means through which those actions are produced as they are filled with and penetrated by those spiritual actions. As the believer advances in the spiritual life, he experiences the fact that by being in the church he is within the Cross of Christ, of the sacrificed Christ who embraces us all, or furthermore of the Christ who, although risen, continues to travel the road of sacrifice or of the Cross toward resurrection. Additionally, the believer, being led by Christ the Pantokrator, travels the road toward full union with Him in the Eucharist and in the life to come, but not without the cross during this earthly life.

St Maximos the Confessor explained in the most profound way the meaning of the church that was architectonically realized in Hagia Sophia on the one hand as a cosmos partly unified with God, and on the other hand advancing toward full unification with Christ under His leadership.

While the churches in the West suggest the advance toward God of a community uninterested in the transfiguration of cosmic creation, the cupola of the Eastern churches with the Pantokrator at the top calls the community and every believer, also considered as a mobile church, to preoccupation with the entire creation. Having Christ within it as the Pantokrator, the church is at the same time "the image" of God at work in the world for its return within Him.

Thus Christ does not fulfill through the Church a work separated from the one He fulfills as Pantokrator in the world, but He is also concerned with the world, starting from a small circle of men with the intention of extending His perfecting work to the entire creation.[61]

Certainly, in the understanding of the church as image of the cosmos under the care of the Pantokrator, or as tending to extend itself upon creation and to comprise it, is also implied the will of the faithful who participate at the Liturgy in the church to take with them outside the church the spirit of union with God and of their union in Him. They go out as personal churches amidst the outside world. "As Orthodox, when we speak of the liturgical life we do not mean our liturgical devotion of a few hours in the church, but our entire life, which starting from the liturgical acts in the church becomes liturgical and dedicated to God. The Orthodox Christian is not schizophrenic. He does not live a liturgical life in the church and a non-liturgical life outside the church. He devotes as much as possible a few hours in church [at the Liturgy or other services] so that he can live outside the church closer to the spirit, the atmosphere and the moral exhortation of the Divine Liturgy."[62] It should not be in vain that the believer promises at the Holy Liturgy: "Let us offer all our life to Christ, our God."

If creation advances through the church toward unity between its sensible and intelligible parts and toward their unity in God, the human person advances toward unification between his body and soul and toward their unification in God, but not apart from his work upon creation. The bond between the parts of creation and of the human person will endure and progress—in those who have the will for that—until the one supreme personal Reason who connects them will cause them to reach fulfillment through a more mysterious bond in the life to come. At that time the cosmos of visible things will die, just like the human body, and will be raised again fully renewed from its old state, just as the human person will be raised again as part of the whole or as a small world together with the big world. This bond will be sustained by the divine power that will be manifested in all things in a clearly and fully efficient manner. Through the fully realized union between body and soul and between sensible things and intelligible realities, this divine power will enable the vision of God through all things. For all things will be encompassed by God Who is Spirit *par excellence*.[63]

St. Symeon of Thessalonica takes up and develops the ideas of Dionysius the Areopagite, Procopius and St. Maximos the Confessor, showing that this understanding of the church building is not connected to temporality, but has a permanent validity. He says: "By its double aspect of things inexplicable (the altar) and of those outside, the church signifies Christ himself in His duality as God and man, visible in one part and invisible in the other. It also signifies the human person who is made up of body and soul. It further signifies the mystery of the Holy Trinity that is unapproachable in its essence but known in its providence and its operations [uncreated energies]. It also signifies this world itself: the heaven through the Holy Altar and things on earth through the nave. In a different sense, the entire divine church proves to be threefold: the pre-nave, the nave and the altar, which signify the Trinity and the hosts on high with their threefold order and the groups of orthodox believers who are divided in three: those ordained, those on their way to perfection and those in a state of penitence; likewise those on earth, in heaven and above the heavens. For the pre-nave signifies those on earth, the nave signifies the heaven and the Holy Altar signifies those above the heavens."[64]

These meanings of the church building can be considered not as alternatives, but as all being comprised in each other. The Holy Trinity is not separated from the world of angels or from the world on earth and from the human person, but It is found in all and all are found in It. The believers are united among themselves and with the cosmic creation as well as with the world of angels and with the Trinity. Only the sinner is willingly separated from all. The believer is united with all.

Archimandrite Vasileios says:

> The Church also knows and is familiar with all things through God. It has the One "who, as the ultimate source, knows and holds together all things," and thus it has everything. Through its God-like organization it knows God in itself, and all creation and its needs, and transmits life-giving grace.
>
> Within the Church, man too can know all things once he knows himself truly, as the image of God. He comes into an immediate ontological relationship and contact with everything. "To him who knows himself is given knowledge of all things. For knowing yourself is the fulfillment of the knowledge of all things . . . . At the point where humility is paramount in your conduct, your soul becomes subject to you, and with it all things will be subject to you." [Abba Isaac, Logos 16].
>
> Either one understands the "one thing" and therefore all things, or one becomes alienated from everything in the attempt to know things "from a human point of view" and to gather them together, piling them up and dragging them off for oneself."[65]

If Christ comprises everything in Himself even from the womb or the arms of His Mother, all the more does He comprise everything from the church building, and those united with Him also comprise everything or are united with all things. Thus, by having the Pantokrator within it, the church, no matter how small it is, comprises virtually all things: "When Christ dwelled in the womb of His Mother, all created things were dwelling within Him.... He was whole within the body of His Mother and at the same time whole in all things."[66] By carrying Him, His Mother was carrying all things. In like manner, the believer carries within himself all things and the church that comprises Him.

4. *Through Its Consecration the Church Receives God within It As the One Who Fulfills His Saving Work*

The church building does not keep the services officiated there locked inside. It is the place from where Christ extends his work upon creation. This means that the liturgical acts cannot be considered as representations or images of Christ's saving work, as are the rituals from the ancient mystery cults. They are to be considered as forms that express the saving work manifested in the church, not as images to be looked at. They are palpable forms in which the invisible work of Christ is fulfilled. It is in them that Christ, present and working through the Spirit, manifests Himself in the faith of the believer.[67]

The consecration of the church building makes it, in fact, the place of the Holy Trinity in which the believers encounter one another and thus they encounter heaven or Christ in His saving work, not just a place where certain symbolic acts take place. The consecration transfigures this space from where God's light and operation are projected upon the entire creation. In the church the believers live on another level of reality and in an ambiance different from that of the natural world. Just as the one who loves sees in the loved one a transfigured being and is himself transfigured, that transfiguration being projected upon the entire world, so does the believer see the consecrated church as a space filled with a divine light that is spread upon the whole world. In the church the past is not separated from the present or from the eschatological future; there is no longer a separation between heaven and earth. The created realm is no longer closed off in itself but is transfigured by the uncreated one. The tribulation of life in the world is overcome within the calm of another life.[68] In the interpretation of St. John Chrysostom, there exists not only an identity of purpose and offerer between the Mystical Supper and the Eucharistic partaking, but also an identity of space: "This table is the same as that, and hath nothing less. For it is not so that Christ wrought that, and man this, but He doth this too. This is that upper chamber, where they were then; and hence they went forth unto the mount of Olives."[69]

Even from the setting of the church's foundation, the hierarch himself, having censed and blessed the construction materials, recites a prayer at the place where the Holy Table will stand and places the foundation stone in the shape of the cross, thus showing that the foundation is Christ Himself who was crucified, the cornerstone. At the same time, Christ Himself is, according to St. Symeon of Thessalonica, the One who selects the place of His saving work at this moment.[70]

Once the construction of the church is completed it becomes the place for Christ's dwelling and sanctifying work. The consecration is officiated by the hierarch, thus showing that Christ Himself establishes His abode in it and begins there His saving work. The hierarch enters the church vested in all the hierarchical vestments, which shows the fruition by Christ through the hierarch of His incarnation and sacrifice through which He established the Church and in which He continues His saving work as High Priest. On top of his vestments the hierarch puts on a shroud that symbolizes Christ reliving His being placed in the tomb from which life came forth, since there will take place the consecration of the altar that represents the tomb mystically containing Christ[71] as an uninterrupted sacrifice offered on our behalf to the Father, the tomb from where the life of resurrection will ceaselessly spring forth.

The Holy Table is the tomb from where we are shown Christ's sacrificed body and blood in the form of bread and wine. It is also the table of the Mystical Supper and the heavenly throne on which the sacrificed Christ is placed as a slaughtered lamb. The glory is not contrary to sacrifice, but in sacrifice there is the true glory (Rev 5:13). The sacrifice is implied in Christ's incarnation as man. This is why the Holy Table is also a manger. Christ is on the Holy Table with all His recapitulated saving works. For only in this way does He save us.

"The holy table corresponds to the spot in the tomb," says St. Germanus, "where Christ was placed. On it lies the true and heavenly bread, the mystical and unbloody sacrifice. Christ sacrifices His flesh and blood and offers it to the faithful as food for eternal life. The holy table is the throne of God, on which, borne by the Cherubim, He rested in the body. At that table, at His mystical supper, Christ sat among His disciples and, taking bread and wine, said to His disciples and apostles: 'Take, eat, and drink of it; this is my body and my blood' (cf. Mt 26:26–28). The altar corresponds to the holy tomb of Christ. On it Christ brought Himself as a sacrifice to [His] God and Father through the offering of His body, as a sacrificial lamb, and as high priest and Son of Man, offering and being offered as a mystical bloodless sacrifice, and appointing for the faithful reasonable worship, through which we have become sharers in eternal and immortal life . . . . The altar is and is called the heavenly and spiritual altar, where the earthly and material priests who always assist and serve the Lord represent the spiritual, serving, and hierarchical powers of the immaterial and celestial Powers, for they also must be as a burning fire."[72] St. Maximos the Confessor had this idea that the angels are like priests through whom Christ is offered as a sacrifice and is given for communion. They, the angels, are internally present for the priests.

The tabernacle [ciborium] on the altar "represents here the place where Christ was crucified; for the place where He was buried was nearby."[73] The perpetual presence of the Eucharist in the tabernacle shows the abiding presence of Christ in a state of sacrifice to be partaken of by the faithful. Never will there be a moment without Christ's disposition for sacrifice and for being partaken of as sacrifice.

Just as under the heavenly altar there are the souls of the martyrs who followed Christ, reaping to the maximum the fruits of His sacrifice, the souls of those "who have been slain for the word of God and for the testimony which they bore, and they cried out with a loud voice, saying, 'How long, O Lord, holy and true, until You judge and avenge our blood on those who dwell on earth? . . . and it was said to them that they should rest a little while longer, until both the number of their fellow servants and their brethren, who would be killed as they were, was completed" (Rev 6:9–11), so in the holy table of the visible altar on which is found the sacrificed Lamb (Agnetz) in the form of the bread as nourishment for eternal life, there are the relics of the martyrs and thus the martyrs themselves in an invisible manner, just like under the Throne-altar on which the sacrificed Lamb is found. Their supplication after the last judgment and the promise that it will come when the number of those who will give testimony for Christ is completed shows the eschatological orientation of the Holy Liturgy of the visible Church. The martyrs are in expectation and the Lamb on the altar assures them that its fulfillment will come. Holy Liturgy is a preparation for the life to come through the sacrifice of the Lamb, of the martyrs and through the invisible presence of all the saints "as a cloud of witnesses," showing us the height they have reached, urging us through their self-offering, and helping us through their prayers to advance through a similar self-offering up to self-sacrifice for spiritual perfection and for unity among ourselves, through which we will gain eternal life.

Inside the church this paradox continually takes place: through the cross to resurrection, through the tomb to life, through the present partaking of the Eucharist to the union with Him Who through sacrifice had ascended to glory. This because the cross and the sacrifice we partake of have as subject the Son of God, the Source of life, Who became man in order to destroy death, to which man is subjected, by taking it upon Himself; to destroy it first in Himself and then in those who partake of Him; to destroy the death that appeared through the separation of man from God—the source of life. As God, He unites in Himself first the global humanity and then the humanity that reached its fulfillment in those who receive Him. This is why in the church the resurrection of Christ is praised while making the sign of the cross, thus expressing the paradox of destroying human death by being assumed by the Son of God together with our human nature. The church is thus Christ's place of death and of His invisible resurrection as well as that of the descent of His Holy Spirit, which means also the place of our anticipated resurrection together with Him. The created being's death in God is like a submersion into the source of life in which the dead one returns to a new and sanctified life. It is like a baptism in water and the Spirit. For it is out of water and the Spirit that every life comes to be. Everyone who avoids this submersion in God through the death of the life weakened by sin will lose his life by remaining within an existence mixed with nothingness. The person whose origin is in God, the infinite but personal source of life, does not die, but passes to the true life. For by accepting death with faith in Him, as a self-offering to God, he will find life in Him and will forever strengthen his identity. The personal God, as the source or the root of all personal identities, never gives up the manifestation of His love in His relationships with the innumerable personal identities. Only if he were a part of nature would the human person dissolve his identity in the unconscious processes of nature that produces other and other monotonous forms. The martyrs represent examples for us of this entrance and eternal preservation as well as deepening into their personal identity through their death with and for Christ.

Christ, who is eternally in a state of sacrifice in order to offer Himself to us—surrounded by the martyrs, who continually preserve this state of their martyrdom for Christ, and by the angels through whom the heavenly High Priest continually offers His sacrifice—carries on an uninterrupted heavenly liturgy. Together with this liturgy and from its strength or that of the sacrifice offered in heaven to the Father, there takes place the liturgy of the community that represents the visible creation gathered before the altar or the throne of the same Lamb slain in order to overwhelm by the partaking of Him any trace of the beast and to be imprinted with the Lamb's features. This makes possible the peaceful and pleasing co-habitation among human beings. "And every creature which is in heaven and on the earth and under the earth and such as are in the sea, and all that are in them, I heard saying: 'Blessing and honor and glory and power be to Him who sits on the throne, and to the Lamb, forever and ever!'" (Rev 5:13). The "revenge" asked for by Christ's martyrs is not one in the worldly sense of the word, but their desire to emphasize for those on earth the value of their sacrifice for Christ, the value of the imitation of the slain Lamb, so that peace and good will may be established among human beings and that they may advance in their true unity toward the eternal life through the strengthening in the same spirit of sacrifice.

During the consecration of the church the lay people stay outside, because the consecration of the church, or of the place where people receive sanctification, does not come from them but from Christ, symbolized by the hierarch surrounded by priests and by invisible angels. The lay people are to enter the church that is already consecrated. They approach Christ and receive salvation from Him after His resurrection and after He is preached by the Apostles upon whom descended Christ's Holy Spirit who sanctifies. The consecration of the church signifies the descent of Christ's Holy Spirit upon the Apostles gathered in the upper room, which became the first church through the descent of the Holy Spirit.

Similarly, when the church is consecrated every movable thing, namely everything that is transitory, is taken out and only what belongs to its wholeness remains, for the church begins with Christ, abides through Him as its source of holiness and through the Holy Spirit who sends the Apostles and their successors to preach and to consecrate creation. Only after that those who will bless and those who will be blessed gather around Him. "Thus the doors are closed, for the church becomes then a heaven and the power of the Holy Spirit comes upon it. This is why there must be present only those who are heaven's, namely those ordained, and no one else must see because only the holy ones must see the holy things until they are completed."[74] The consecration of the church is a renewed Pentecost. The Holy Spirit descended upon the community of the Apostles in the form of tongues of fire, imparting to each one in that community the power to begin preaching the risen Christ. In this way they represented the first church community, not an isolated individual. "But Peter standing up with the eleven, raised his voice and spoke to them [to those who had gathered at the place where the sound produced by the descent of the Holy Spirit occurred]" (Acts 2:14).

The prayers and actions of the hierarch at the consecration of the church express in a great variety of forms the same fact of Christ's dwelling, He who conquers death by death. He is present together with the Father and from His eyes irradiates the unlimited quantity of gifts through the Church over all the earth.

We mention a few more acts from the consecration of the church: the table proper is attached to the pillars of stone with a mixture of wax, frankincense, aloe and other ingredients, "all of them signifying the burial of the Savior."[75] These, by their adhesive quality, "signify the unity with us and the love that Christ had toward us until death."[76] They also signify Christ's remaining with us in a state of loving sacrifice, with the power of the resurrection penetrated by the same love.

The holy table is then washed with water, mystically representing Christ's Baptism before He began His saving activity. In this way "He who was baptized in the Jordan river is invoked for the blessing of this water and for the consecration of the altar table."[77]

This cluster of meanings regarding the church, the altar, and the liturgical acts are based on the fact that Christ's saving works awake in us a real recollection (anamnesis) of His entire life starting with the Incarnation. This also means that all the ensuing saving works are virtually present in every moment of Christ's life starting with the Incarnation, and these works remain in Him as living and efficient traces in view of their being reflected in us. The Fathers of the Synod of Trullo saw in every icon of Christ the anamnesis of His entire saving work.⁷⁸ If they saw Christ's entire work in His icon, "much more so"—says Schulz—"must this be valid for the Liturgy, which is not a simple icon, but comprises the reality of Christ's life."⁷⁹ St. Athanasius said: "When the Word descended into the Holy Virgin there also came into her the Holy Spirit, and the Word formed His body in the Holy Spirit with the intention of gathering creation into Himself and of bringing it to the Father to be again reconciled in Him" (Ad. Serap. I, 31, PG 26, 605). The Logos or the Word, as the heart of reasons or of words, gathers all reasons of created beings in Himself by the power of the Spirit Who also fashioned the Word's body within the Holy Virgin. The entire economy of salvation is potentially contained in the Incarnation.

Therefore, the holy table is also the Jordan River in which He was baptized in order to begin His preaching that was crowned with His resurrection. According to St. Ephrem the Syrian, the Jordan River in which Christ is immersed to be baptized is also a bosom from which He is born again as man. In Baptism He experiences again His birth, but He also anticipates His death and resurrection. The human person's existence in God is a continual death and birth or resurrection. "The river in which (Christ) was baptized had again symbolically conceived Him. The moist bosom of the water conceived Him in purity, gave birth to Him in light and made Him appear in glory."⁸⁰

The concomitance of the presence in Christ of all saving moments lived by Him beforehand has an analogy in the fact that even when I remember what really happened in my life or someone else's life, those occurrences do not remain as a simple remembrance with no effect upon my life, but they are in reality relived. This means that the occurrences that I remember from my life are still effective within me and irradiate upon others as well.

In an icon of the Lord's Nativity dating back to the middle of the fourth century "the manger of the incarnation is shown as the altar of the world from which the bread of the Word of God is offered as food to the peoples of the world; in the mystery of Christmas is seen and glorified the entire salvation. The child himself is the image of the One who offers an inexpressible sacrifice."⁸¹ For when we behold the child in the manger in His present state after the resurrection and in His present activity toward us, we see in His state as a Child everything He would do for our salvation. Even before His incarnation He intended to do all these. This is why we see His resurrection in His state as a child and we see the child in His state of the resurrection. It is in this sense that we are to understand what is said of Peter, bishop of Alexandria, who was beheaded in 311 by Emperor Maximin, that while he was in prison Christ appeared to him as a twelve-year-old child with his clothes torn who inspired compassion. When Peter asked, "Lord, who torn your robe?" Christ answered: "Arius has torn it, but be mindful not to accept him to communion... Also tell the priests Aquila and Alexander, who after your death will shepherd the Church for which I became a small child and died—living eternally—not to receive him."[82]

After the holy table is washed with water and soap and wiped off, it is washed with wine and rose water. These signify the divine Myrrh in honor of Christ's burial, as Christ said about the washing of His feet by the sinful woman (Mt 26:12).

Up until this moment the holy table is not the Lord's tomb, but the chair on which He sat in the house of Simon the leper where He allowed His feet to be washed in view of His burial.

Then follows the anointing of the holy table with Holy Myrrh. "Thus the hierarch makes three crosses with the Holy Myrrh on the Holy Table: in the middle and on both sides. The Holy Table is anointed with these three crosses while Alleluia is being sung. Through the Holy Myrrh the Holy Spirit descends upon the Holy Table and the coming of God in Trinity is announced by the song Alleluia." The triple anointing with the sign of the cross shows that the Holy Spirit is not separated from the other two divine Persons and that He comes together with the Christ crucified for us and Who is now buried in the Holy Table as in a tomb from where His pure life is continuously spread. "For the poured myrrh represents the name of Christ, our God. And the Holy Table, which shows Him buried in it, becomes entirely myrrh through the anointing with myrrh. For the table itself receives the gift of the Spirit," Who is active in it as the Holy Eucharist is officiated on it and also the Holy Gospel is placed on it, both of them representing Christ who never comes or is present without the Holy Spirit. "Truly this table is the altar of Christ, the throne of glory, God's dwelling place, Christ's tomb and rest."[83]

The icons of the four Evangelists are placed in the four corners of the Holy Table, showing that upon Christ, the cornerstone, are placed the Apostles as foundation and as the first beginning of the building of the church upon Him, and that He is made known through the Holy Gospels in the four corners of the world. The Holy Table, which represents Christ, is then covered with a cloth representing Christ's shroud. On top of it is placed a white sheet that represents Christ's robe of glory and light. On top of that is placed the Holy antimension, which represents the burial of Christ. In it are sewn the relics of a particular saint, which means that the Church is founded on Christ's sacrifice, but it is also sustained through the added sacrifice from its power of those who believe in Him and give testimony with the price of their life for Him. The reason for this is that all believers may learn to be rooted in the Church, namely in the body of Christ, or in the loving communion between them and Christ, through their sacrifice or through a life permeated with the spirit of sacrifice from the power of Christ's sacrifice. Only the one who sacrifices the earthly and transitory things by detaching himself from them is able to forget himself through sacrifice, and rises to the heavenly and eternal things, to loving unity with Christ and through Him with all his fellow human beings.

The antimension is given to each church by the hierarch, for the Church, first established by Christ through the Holy Spirit in Jerusalem, is extended also by Him, through the hierarchs as His representatives, in the local Churches that are in unity through the bishops as successors of the Apostles, the bishops themselves remaining in unity. Relics are placed in the antimension, which is washed, anointed with Holy Myrrh and consecrated just like the Holy Table because it can replace the Holy Table in exceptional circumstances.

On top of the antimension is placed the Holy Gospel because it is through the Gospel that everything accomplished by Christ with an eternal value is preached; it is through the Gospel that the hearts of those who want to be part of Christ's body are opened and by keeping the commandments contained in it are maintained and grow into the unity with Christ represented by the Gospel. The Gospel is Christ in His activity in the world, on the basis of His descent on earth, into the grave and of His coming out of the grave to the life of the resurrection.

Afterwards, the bishop censes the church and one of the priests following him anoints with Holy Myrrh the entire church: "Since the Holy Myrrh sanctified the Holy Table and rendered it perfect, from it as from a ripened fruit and from a beginning of holiness the entire house is sanctified, just like Christ sanctified with the divine gift of the incarnation our entire nature. The Apostles, having partaken of this gift, shared it with the whole world." Then the hierarch comes back into the Holy Altar, kneels in front of the Holy Table, recites one prayer and concludes with the following prayer in which is shown that the descent of the Holy Spirit and the consecration of this particular church is a true Pentecost, as was the one in which the Apostles rejoiced: "We thank you, O Lord, that the grace You poured upon Your Apostles You have also poured upon us sinners. Therefore, we pray You that the offerings which will be brought herein be transformed into the sacred body and blood of Your only begotten Son for the salvation of all and of our unworthiness."[84] The Holy Spirit descends not because Christ remains in heaven, but in order that Christ may come upon the Holy Table with His body and blood in the form of bread and wine that, filled with the Holy Spirit, will be distributed to the faithful. The Pentecost and the Eucharist are strongly united, as the Pentecost and all the sacraments of the Church are united and through them we are united with Christ. Christ sends the Holy Spirit so that the Spirit may bring Him and may open up the created things to Him.

After taking off the white robe and keeping on the hierarchical vestments, the hierarch goes in procession to the old church and brings from there the holy relics of the martyrs, carrying them on his head, and places them in the Holy Table, as the souls of those who died for Christ are under the heavenly altar (Rev 6:9–10).

The martyrs are, together with the Apostles, "the foundation of the Church,"[85] on account of the testimony they gave to the resurrection of Christ with the price of their life, with the example and the power they give us so that we too may give this testimony and may offer ourselves, as transitory beings, "living sacrifices" to God in order to gain the eternal life of the resurrection.

The relics are brought from the old church, which shows that as the gift of the same Christ is transmitted through the Apostles and through hierarchs as their successors through the uninterrupted succession of ordinations, in the same way it is transmitted from the old churches to the new ones. This is the living tradition of the saving and sanctifying power and of its reception by faith. Tradition is not only the transmission of a theoretical teaching, but of faith filled with the power of Christ capable of continual living sacrifice and also, in certain circumstances, of dying for Christ. Tradition is the power of Christ that persists uninterruptedly through faith in Him united with sacrifice.

When the hierarch arrives in front of the door of the new church, which is closed, he says: "Lift up your gates and be lifted up," for the relics he carries represent Christ who rose from the dead, whose power was manifested in the martyrs and is shown in their relics, while the church represents the heaven and its gates—the angels—who bar the entrance of the person unworthy of heaven or of union with God after falling into sin. But just as Christ Who as man can, through His sacrifice as a total offering to God, enter after the resurrection before the Father above all the heavenly levels, so can the martyrs enter, united in sacrifice with Christ. St. Cyril of Alexandria says that only in a state of pure sacrifice, obtained by us in union with Christ, are we able to enter before the Father. The entrance of the martyrs into the church—entrance before the Father—is the entrance of Christ or accompanies the entrance of Christ with His sacrifice.

This is why after the hierarch who consecrated the church, or after Christ who has opened the consecrated place before the Father, there also enter the laity or the community that has decided by faith to follow Christ.

We enter the consecrated church, where God truly is, to participate at the Liturgy as a common service to God, to partake of Christ's sacrifice and to assume His state of sacrifice so that we may enter before the Father.

"But Christ came as High Priest of the good things to come . . . . Not with the blood of goats and calves, but with His own blood He entered the Most Holy Place once for all, having obtained eternal redemption. For if the blood of bulls and goats and the ashes of a heifer, sprinkling the unclean, sanctifies for the purifying of the flesh, how much more shall the blood of Christ, who through the eternal Spirit offered Himself without spot to God, cleanse your conscience from dead works to serve the living God? And for this reason He is the Mediator of the new covenant, by means of death, for the redemption of the transgressions under the first covenant, that those who are called may receive the promise of the eternal inheritance" (Heb 9:11–15).

Once Christ has established His dwelling in the church building, which coincides with its consecration by Him through the visible hierarch, the first Liturgy is officiated in it as Christ's saving work.

If the church building is the place where the believers gather, helping them to advance together through prayers, praises to God, efforts to cleanse themselves of sins, enmities, egoism and through self-offering toward Christ, and since full union with Him is achieved through the partaking of His body and blood found on the Holy Table, then between the church building and the Liturgy officiated therein, whose climax is the Holy Eucharist, there is a strong connection. "The serious theologians begin to increasingly understand the fact that it is not possible to speak of the church without first mentioning the divine Eucharist and the very strong connection between Eucharist and the church."[86]

As we mentioned above, from the church building, as the space for Christ's sanctifying work, Christ extends the power of this work outside this space as well. Christ departs from here with those who have partaken of Him and He accompanies them everywhere, helping them to pray and to fulfill the good works of helping others. Thus, Christ continues to be everywhere with the person of each believer; He is present amidst those who speak of Him or who help each other out of their faith in Him, out of responsibility toward Him. He is in every place where there are Christians or families with a life more or less holy, in every place where the priest goes, as the visible organ of Christ's priesthood, taking there the light and work of Christ through his services, exhortations, counseling and pastoral work.

Christ extends His sanctifying work especially from the Sacraments that are usually officiated in the church and from the priest's preaching about Him in a more regular way in the church.

To the extent to which the Christians go to church more often, thus knowing Him better and partaking more often of His power, they increasingly spread through their life His power in the world.

The church buildings are like flowers that, although they grow in certain places, spread their aroma to great distances wherever there are human beings capable of sensing it.[87]

C. Holy Icons in Orthodox Worship

1. *Justification of Holy Icons*

We also worship the Lord Jesus Christ and venerate the Mother of the Lord and the saints through the icons that represent them.

In the final analysis we honor the Mother of God and the saints because Christ shines in them and because Christ's image has been imprinted in them. Thus we honor their icons because they represent those who are the pneumatized dwellings of Christ, whose humanity is perfectly pneumatized through the Holy Spirit, who is united by essence with the hypostasis of this humanity.

The basic justification of the icons of the Mother of God and of the saints is therefore implied in the justification for the icon of Christ.

But what is the basis for the justification of the icon of Christ? In the Old Testament there were no icons of God. There existed only sacred symbols: the Paschal lamb, Aaron's staff, the holy tabernacle, the ark of the law, etc.

In admitting sacred symbols, the Old Testament forbids images and resemblances of God (Ex 21:4, Dt 5:18-19). What is the distinction between the admitted symbol and the forbidden idol in the Old Testament? The sacred symbol is a tangible sign of the presence of God, an object in which God has shown and continues to show His power. God can work through all created beings as His creations and in fact He does work through all things. But He has shown and is showing that He works in a most accentuated way through some of them. This means that He works supernaturally and not simply naturally. This distinction made in the Old Testament between natural symbols and sacred ones, indicated through Supernatural Revelation and introduced in worship, was meant to prevent the people of Israel from confusing God with nature in a pantheistic way. Once this distinction is made and by clarifying through the object chosen supernaturally by God, as a place of His special activity, the fact that He is not confounded with nature, the Old Testament does not avoid saying that the glory of God is visible through all things ("heaven and earth are full of His glory").

The idol worshipers no longer made this distinction between nature and God. They manufactured or chose by themselves certain objects and worshiped them, without a God distinct from nature manifesting Himself through a supernatural act that He is specially present in those objects called idols. They were simply "carved" or chosen by a human decision, not presented by God through an act of supernatural power as dwellings of His presence and activity.

The idol was a simple piece of nature or a man-made object. It was especially in this quality that it was identified with God. Inasmuch as it represented, as part of nature, the entire nature or a certain force of nature, was the idol considered, as such, to be essentially identical with God.

However, the Jewish people, on the basis of the revelation of the Old Testament, made a distinction between symbol and God, whether a natural symbol or one chosen by a special act of God, a supernatural act. From this we conclude that it was not the recognition of a work of God in natural objects and especially in sacred symbols, indicated by God in a supernatural way, that was forbidden in the Old Testament, but their identification with God Himself.

This is the reason why the Old Testament has forbidden the idol, but it recommends the vision of God's glory in all things and especially in certain objects in which God has shown through a supernatural act that He has worked and continues to work, that is in the sacred symbols used in worship. Through idols one loses the awareness of the distinction between God and nature. The awareness of this distinction was maintained through natural and sacred symbol. Through the idol the people of Israel would have lost the awareness of God as superior to nature, therefore conscious, personal, superior to nature and distinct and free from it. Through symbol they maintained faith in the God distinct from the world and transcendent to it, and they experienced a concrete relationship with Him through adoration, worship and prayer on the basis of the belief that this God was capable of protecting them even against the hardships of nature and its implacable laws. Through symbol they saw the entire world in a dependence on this personal God, superior in power to nature, almighty compared to it and provider for it and especially for human beings.

In all cases, through its sacred symbols and also through all of nature seen as symbol, the Old Testament confesses faith in the communicability of God through tangible symbols, but also His distinction from these means. In this sense the symbols represent an anticipation of icons, just as the Old Testament is an anticipation of Christ.

The icon is not an idol that identifies a piece of nature, whether manmade or not, and thereby the entire nature or its various forces with God, nor is it a symbol that attests to the presence of God in it, although it affirms God's distinction from it. Rather the icon is the representation of God Himself become the personal hypostasis of human nature, neither identifying Himself with this nature nor being confounded with it. The icon preserves the distinction between creature and God, just like the symbol, but it perceives in a created human face the divine hypostasis Himself who became its Subject. Through the spirit pertaining to it, human nature is distinctly suited to become the proper nature of the divine hypostasis—a medium of direct manifestation of the divine Person. Olivier Clement has drawn special attention to the unfathomable mystery which the human face reveals, because it is a revelation of the spirit within the human person that is oriented toward the infinite.[88] The face of the human person reveals an indescribable infinitude. If it is bright, it is happily anchored in the comforting infinitude of God-Person. But if it is dark and tragically sad, it is terrified of the infinite emptiness opening up within the mind of human consciousness. One knew about the human face anchored in the infinitude of God through the spirit visible through it in the Old Testament, when it is said that there was so much shining on the face of Moses that the Jews could not look at it, and that is why Moses had to cover it with a cloth that moderated its brightness. The believers of the Old Testament could not behold this glory on the face of Moses because they were not prepared to understand that God could reveal Himself through the face of the human person, or maybe because they could consider Moses as God Himself, without that being so. But when Jesus Christ came, through whose face the very God was looking, the cloth was no longer necessary because the revelation of God, on the one hand totally perfect, on the other hand this very perfection in which he was manifesting Himself gave His face a pure meekness and humility that never has been seen among human beings. The face of Christ convinced the Apostles that it is the face of God Himself, but of a God who does not terrify, for His maximum closeness to human beings is that of His infinite love and goodness in human form.

Thus, those who remain attached to the letter of the Old Testament know "the image of God's glory" shining on Mount Sinai (Ex 24:18) and shining in general on sacred objects on the basis of the fact that God can do this with certain objects and places in nature (sacred symbols) because they are all part of His creation, that is, His symbols in a general and natural way. They also realize that "the image of God's glory" shone on Moses's face in a very intense manner but hidden at the same time, because they are scandalized at the idea that God could take on a human face as His own. "But when they return to God (namely when they acknowledge that Christ is truly the incarnate God) the cover from their hearts will be removed" and they will acknowledge that the face of the Lord Jesus Christ is God's most perfect "image."[89]

But if the sacred symbols of the Old Testament, as places and objects in which God's power was manifested in a special way, were preserved for worship until the direct appearance of God through the human face—and even the entire creation could, for all times, be considered as an assembly of natural symbols of God's presence and work—would God not want to also afford us a way of preserving both the consciousness and the sentiment of the presence of His human face as His full manifestation until it will be openly revealed at the end of time? Did God not afford us the possibility of keeping alive the consciousness of the presence of His face, especially that in reality He preserves this face until the end of time, although physically invisible but then visible in eternity in a spiritualized manner?

This manner of preserving the consciousness of the perpetuation of God's presence among us with His human face from His invisible realm was given to us by God through His icon. If the incarnate Son of God continues to be among us until the end of time through all divine powers by means of His body, why would He not continue to be present and active among us also through His face in a way in which to make us aware of this presence with His face? If we cannot comprehend that the Lord activates in us His powers without the means of His deified body, how can we think that He is not present also with the face of His body through which His intimacy and communicability with us are most fully manifested? This is also the divine infinitude of love in the form of the human face which, more than all the objects of nature and more than the members of the human body, is the expression of infinity or of the human person's connection with infinity. If we partake of the Lord's body and blood, which are the source or the human means of the partaking of Christ's all divine powers, why would not there exist a certain partaking of His face as well? Is not the Lord there in the Eucharist with His face but only with a body and a blood without a face? And if we preserve the "images" of His body and blood in the Eucharist, in the form of bread and wine, could we not also preserve a certain presence of His face, definitely without His invisible face being transformed into a visible face as with the transformation in the Eucharist?

God has various ways in which to make us aware of His presence, namely to help us preserve the consciousness of His presence among us.

It is significant that the rejection of icons is proper to those who reject in general any kind of communication of Christ with us form the invisible realm through a certain power, except of a certain communication of power through word. Those who rely on word as the sole means of Christ's communication with us say that the other means are chosen and organized by the human person. But is not the word spoken in the name of Christ chosen and organized by the human person? Is there any sermon given only by repeating the Lord's words from the Scripture? There are numerous proofs that the Lord's communication through the word was subjected to most personal human interpretations more than all other communications, something that contributed greatly to the breaking of the unity of faith where only the word was used. Only there where the word was associated with the Sacraments and with the veneration of icons was the unity of faith preserved and, through their identity at all times, they were the means by which the word was kept within the framework of Tradition begun from the Apostles.

One can go even further along this line of proving the justification of icons.

The human face in and of itself is the means of communication among persons. The face is not given to the human person to have an isolated individualistic existence. In this respect there is a great similarity of roles between face and word. They are both given to a person in order to communicate with others. They are given to the human being as a person, namely to a communicable subject, a subject for other subjects. The human being as a person exists not only for himself, but also for others or makes progress in communication with others. In his face and word is reflected and realized the consciousness that he exists for others and that he cannot advance except in communion with others. The face of the human person reflects all the traces of his encounters and conversations with others. His words are richer on account of his conversation with others as he learns from them and from their words whether spoken or written. In everyone's face and words are preserved the traces and vibrations of the feelings caused by others or the feelings nurtured and expressed toward others.

The human person is an interpersonal being; we Christians say that he is a tri-personal being after the image of the Holy Trinity, because two people who speak to each other always have in view a third person or that person multiplied. They are preoccupied by things only as objects in which they have a common interest, objects that they either want to give or to take.

The face is proper to the human person because he exists for others and through the face he shows the need to be with them, to show an interest in them and for others to know about this. The face does not belong to someone in isolation. The face is the inevitable projection of one individual toward others. It belongs to him because he belongs to others.

This is why the Son of God took on the human face. In this way He showed His interest toward us and His will to communicate with us.

On the one hand, the human being is the expression of the infinite meaning toward which the human spirit is oriented; in the case that the spirit believes it is the expression of its comforting connection with the personal, divine infinitude. On the other hand, it shows the will to communicate this experienced infinitude to other fellow human beings. By taking a human face, the Son of God took to the extreme the anchoring of this face in the divine infinitude and, on the other hand, its tendency to communicate with other human persons this experience of the humanity He assumed into the divinity's infinity of life and love. If He took the human face in order to communicate through it to His human brethren the experience of divine life lived by Him, why would He not continue to maintain His communication with us? If He wants His word to be permanently communicated to people, as expression of His experience as man into the depth of divinity, why would He not want this communication to be made continuously also through His face, which comprises in a concentrated manner all His words and which communicates more than the word not only meaning, but also power and life?

The believers want to have not only the word of Christ until the end of time, but also His human face and through it the "Face" of divinity as the source of all human faces including the face assumed by Christ; in other words, the divine "Face" as a form above forms of His eternal, tri-personal existence as intra-Trinitarian expressivity—the source of every created interpersonal expressivity and communication. And if the Son of God took the human face in order to be in a maximum communication with all of His brothers in humanity, why would He not satisfy His will and their thirst for maximum communication between Him and them through the face He assumed?

His word would seem to them as lacking the maximum intimacy and warmth if they did not feel that it started from His face in which is concentrated all intimacy and warmth toward human persons. It would seem to them as a word coming from afar, from a hidden, distant God who after the ascension retreated into His transcendence. They would like to know not only theoretically or through historical memory that these words were once spoken by Christ, but also that He speaks to them now and that His face is the unique, permanent and living point of His relationship with them.

This face of Christ is in fact the inexhaustible and living plenitude of His words. They are rays that start from the deep and infinite life expressed through His face, and also from His love that is expressed through the face in a more plenary way than the words, since it is the subsistent and hypostatic expression of His love, which intends to be communicated and which did not come to be as the face of God the Word except that He wants to endlessly communicate Himself through it.

This is why He wants His face which He assumed to continue to be with us through the icon also after His ascension into heaven; He wants His very face to speak to us about Him. Through the icon He Himself speaks more plenary and livelier than in the words separated from Him. It has been said that icons are the Bible of those who cannot read, which today can mean: for those who do not have time to read or to listen to the words about Him. In addition to this, one can say that the icon of Christ in a way places Christ Himself before us, or it gives us the consciousness of His presence with His very face before us in the invisible plane. In a way the icon makes Christ Himself transparent to us, just as He can be seen through a transparent fabric on which His image is projected. Thus the icon of Christ helped not only to preserve the precise meaning of Christ and His teaching, presenting Him to us throughout the history of the Church as the same Christ, the author of His saving works, but it also had an important role in enlivening the faith by maintaining in the faithful the consciousness of Christ's presence as Subject of the words spoken by Him or about Him.

In addition to this, the Orthodox icon of Christ, represented in the same way as He was represented in the entire tradition of the Church since the first centuries, has preserved Christ in the integrity of the characteristics of His pneumatic life, as model and directive for the believers to strive for a more spiritual life, after the image of Christ. If Christ asks the faithful to imprint His image in themselves, or to grow according to His image, how would they succeed in imprinting in themselves the authentic image of Christ if they had only His words or the words about

Him, which every theologian or preacher could interpret as he wished? Therefore, the icon of Christ, preserved from the first centuries until now with His pneumatized countenance, has constituted along with the spiritual literature of the Holy Fathers an important guide for the spiritual formation of Orthodox believers after the authentic image of Christ. The icon of Christ in Orthodoxy has been not only a Christological icon, but also a pneumatological one, considering the fact that Christ has been filled with the Holy Spirit Whom He granted to the faithful who saw Him as a determining power toward holiness.

The saints were the ones who more than others formed themselves in this way; in their icons is reflected this pneumatic life of Christ and on their faces shines forth the purity and presence of Christ's sanctifying Spirit. The Byzantine style of icons maintains to this day the same old and elevated spirituality superior within the framework of Christian iconography. Nowadays this style begins to again be appreciated, not because it is the style of the Byzantine era, but because it is the style of true pneumatic finesse and delicacy that cannot be replaced by another. This pneumaticity, in addition to the fact that it represents Christ together with His unique saving works, is the only "objective" mode in which can be suggested the "un-circumscribed" spirituality of Christ's divinity in the human circumscribed form, suggesting the abyssal divine depths through the features of a human face physically circumscribed, but through the spirit that it reflects by suggesting what cannot be circumscribed.

Undoubtedly, the talented iconographers are able to give a more accentuated profoundness to this pneumaticity of Christ's divine presence.

Let us return to the communication realized between believers and Christ through the icon.

The believers know that the icon does more than just speak to them about Christ and show them the path on which to walk in life toward sanctification in order to become more and more like Christ. They are convinced first of all that through the icon they enter into a real communication with Christ.

Thus, the key issue for the theological explanation of the meaning of the icon in Orthodoxy is: what is the real, living and present relationship between the living Person of Christ and His icon or, better said, between Christ and the believer who prays before His icon? And in what mode is this relationship established?

The easiest answer would be that Christ responds to every word of prayer addressed to Him by the believer, since Christ is alive as man. For there is no word addressed by one person to another to which the latter would not have to respond, on the basis of the dialogical-ontological unity that exists between persons and especially between human persons among whom the Word of God was well-pleased to dwell, the Word of God who is the sustainer of all words and of the relationship between those who speak to each other. The Christian is challenged in an especially pressing way to think of Christ and to address Him in prayer while beholding His icon. Just as the face of our fellow human being provokes us to address him, or as while we address him our face strongly provokes him to respond, so are we to consider that countenance of Christ's face provokes us in an especially pressing way to address Him, and our presence before His icon determines Him to respond to our words.

The answer to the above question can also be based on explanations from authoritative texts of the ecclesiastical tradition.

The definition of the Seventh Ecumenical Council affirms that our veneration of the icon "passes" or "ascends" to the person being represented, or to the prototype, the living model of the icon. This expression is usually interpreted as a willing "transition" of our thought from the icon to the prototype, as from the image to living reality of Christ on the basis of an association made. However, this "transition" has a deeper meaning. The believer in Christ cannot but make this transition from the icon of Christ to His living reality. In this necessity that the thought pass from the icon of Christ to His living reality is also implied Christ's action upon the person beholding the icon. If all existing things are materialized words of God addressed to us, all the more is the icon of Christ a word, an exhortation addressed to us by Christ. Thus, just as a specific word about Christ is also a word of Christ that provokes in the person hearing it the thought about Christ and a response to His word, likewise this materialized and concentrated word about Christ or of Christ, which is His icon, provokes in the one beholding (which is also a type of hearing) it the compulsion to think of Christ and to respond to Him through prayer and prostration.

There is an ontological connection (connection through essence) between a representation and the reality depicted, similar to the one that exists between what is or has been spoken by word and the content or even the person who has spoken the word and, even further, between that person and those who hear or have heard the word. If through the word of Christ spoken two thousand years ago, or the word about Christ, that is repeated now in my hearing, a relationship is established between Christ and me, why would a relationship not be established between Christ and me through His icon, which is a word given material form that contains His entire Person? This relationship between me, who hears the word or sees someone's image or the image about someone, and that word or image is established with the subject of the word or of the image because there is, first of all, an ontological relationship between what is said about someone or by someone and that particular someone, or between His image and His very Person.

There is no person who does not have intrinsically his image or the word about him or his word if that person is a conscious reality. For example, the word about me or my image are implied within me because I exist for the other. That is why it is impossible that I would not be interested in the necessary reaction that these provoke in others or that I would not seek to provoke certain reactions in others. In fact, through the word and the image linked to a person in order to communicate through them with others, that very person exerts an action upon them, thereby reaching realization of his own self.

St. Theodore the Studite expresses this idea as follows: "If every body is inseparably followed by its own shadow, and no one in his right mind could say that a body is shadowless, but rather we can see in the body the shadow which follows, and in the shadow the body which precedes; thus no one could say that Christ is imageless, if indeed He has a body with its characteristic form, but rather we can see in Christ His image existing by implication and in the image plainly visible as its prototype. From the simultaneous existence of both, it follows that when Christ is seen, then His image is also potentially seen, and consequently is transferred by imprint into any material whatever."[90] In the same sense, St. Theodore the Studite continues: "Even if the natural is not simultaneous with the arbitrary, as Christ with His image, nevertheless by its potential existence even before its artistic production we can always see the image in Christ; just as, for example, we can see the shadow always potentially accompanying the body, even if it is not given form by the radiation of light. In this manner it is not unreasonable to reckon Christ and His image among things which are simultaneous."[91]

One should notice that by affirming that the prototype and the image are simultaneous, St. Theodore the Studite does not confound them. They are connected, but not identical. While in the prototype, the image is not distinguished from it. But when the image is shown, it is distinguished but not separated from the prototype. Just as the prototype cannot exist without having a virtual shadow or image, neither can the image or the shadow exist outside of a connection with the prototype. The image continues to have its foundation in the prototype even if it is something other than the prototype itself.

This is what we would explain with the example of the relationship between the word and the person who speaks the word. As long as the word is not spoken, it cannot be perceived as distinct from the person. Once it is spoken, the word is noticed as being distinct from the person. Still, it cannot be explained without the person who uttered it. The word does not have a full effect without considering its connection with the person uttering it. Just as there is no person without words, so there cannot exist words without a person. This is also valid for the relationship between person and image. But just as the word is detached from a person only when another person is present to listen, so it is with the image: it is detached from within for someone desiring to know it, in the case of Christ for a worshiper. The fact that someone's image cannot be separated from the person representing it is shown in the need of the beholder to think of that particular person, just as once you hear the word uttered by a person you, at the same time, must think of the person who uttered it.

Certainly, the multiple words circulating among people cannot be identified with their respective authors, because they can belong to anyone. But the words of Christ belong exclusively to Him for their uniqueness. This is why when you hear them, you necessarily must think of Him, and apart from Him you cannot grasp them nor can you attribute them to another person.

So it is with His icon. When you behold it you can only think of Christ's Person and it is impossible not to think of Him. Even if the icon had only this purpose, it would have a great significance for the life of Christians.

As we have seen, this relationship that we must subjectively establish between the icon of Christ and His Person has an ontological basis beyond our subjectivity.

One can proceed even further. If the shiny shadow proves to be connected to its body through certain rays emanating from it, the image of a person proves to be connected to the reality of that person through spiritual rays as well, through which that person necessarily projects his specific image into the souls of others. The image of a person says something of a spiritual nature to others; it says what is characteristic about that person. All the more does the icon of Christ say not only what is characteristic especially about Him as man, but it also portrays Him as the unique Savior. When we behold His icon, we necessarily think of Him as of our unique Savior. And this motivates people to believe, pray and give thanks.

Thanks to this fact, the Person of Christ necessarily and uniquely provokes the believers through His icon to think of Him. In this way He attracts them to Him. St. Theodore the Studite says this again when he insists upon the concomitance between beholding the icon and thinking of its prototype: "The prototype and the image belong to the category of related things, like the double and the half. For the prototype always implies the image of which it is the prototype, and the double always implies the half in relation to which it is called double. For there would not be a prototype if there were no image; there would not even be any double, if some half were not understood. But since these things exist simultaneously, they are understood and subsist together. Therefore, since no time intervenes between them, the one does not have a different veneration from the other, but both have one and the same."[92]

One notes St. Theodore the Studite's affirmation that there is no interval between icon and Christ as its prototype and also his comparing them with two halves that cannot be separated either in thought or in reality. We must mention, however, that the ontology of the image is in the prototype, a fact that cannot be reversed. The icon as half has its foundation in the prototype, but not vice versa. The icon exists from the ontology of the prototype, but the prototype manifests His entire ontological reality in the fact that He also has an image. If He did not have His image implied in Him as a potentiality, He would not have a true reality. He who does not have a shadow does not exist; the same with he who does not have the potentiality of his image or of his word. He who is not for others, is not for himself either. In this sense, the shadow or the potentiality of the image or of the word is the condition for the ontology of the prototype.

Hence the full justification of the believer's conviction that when he beholds the icon he speaks with Christ and by venerating the icon he does this before Christ. If he venerated the icon with a veneration different than that of Christ, he would make the icon a kind of idol in itself, even if he accorded the icon a lesser power than to Christ. In fact, the power manifested through the miracle-working icons is the power of Christ, not of the icon itself.

When the believer prays before the icon, he prays to Christ, not to the icon. When beholding it, his sight is spiritually directed toward Christ, just as the mother looking at her child's picture speaks to him even if she does not confuse the picture with the child himself. She forgets about the picture, just as the believer forgets about the icon. The mother smiles at the child, the believer prays to Christ before the icon while beholding it. The icon and the prototype are beheld at the same time through thought and feeling without being confounded. Or better said, the icon is forgotten because the believer experiences properly the relationship with the prototype. St. Theodore the Studite wants to specify this directly.

To the accusation that he divinizes the icon by combining in a single veneration the icon and Christ, he responds: "There is no such thing in my epistle, but that the icon of Christ should not be adored. This is an idolatrous thought and only the Holy Trinity is to be adored. Christ adored in the icon is adored together with the Father and the Holy Spirit while the icon is given a relative veneration."[93]

The defenders of icons did not have yet the knowledge about the uncreated energies brought into creation by the Holy Spirit. This would have made it possible for them to explain the relationship between Christ and His icon, a relationship that they affirmed without sufficiently explaining it. Since they did not sufficiently explain the meaning of the terms "relative veneration" or "veneration that passes to the prototype," they did not explain that the transition from icon to the prototype does not mean a separation between Christ and His icon or a distance between them. That is why they affirm both one and the other (namely the transition and the relationship between them) but without a unitary explanation in synthesis. In this way some have maintained only the idea of separation while others only the idea of co-existence of the icon and of Christ, without confounding them.

A clearer explanation of this relationship is given in the prayer for the blessing of Christ's icon contained in the Euchologion of the Orthodox

Church. This explanation is manifested also in in the piety of the people. The prayer mentions the touching of Abgar's cloth to the face of Jesus who, together with His image, imprinted on it His power that healed the prince of Edessa who sent it. This confirmed what has been said, that someone's image and word are linked to that someone's subject through a radiation of power from him. One asks in the prayer: "Do Thou look down with mercy upon us and upon this Icon, and . . . send down upon it Thy heavenly blessing and the grace of the Most-holy Spirit, and bless and sanctify it; and grant it the power that heals and dispels all diabolical snares; and fill it with the blessing and strength which that other holy Icon Not-Made-by-Hands richly acquired from the touching of the holy and most-pure Face of Thy Beloved Son, whereby, through its powers and miracles, it may act for the confirmation of the Orthodox Faith and the salvation of Thy faithful people."[94]

The prayer asks that the icon being blessed share in the power of the icon not made by hands by the touching of Christ's face with the cloth, and thus to extend the power of that icon to the icon being blessed. This is how the living face of Christ, which He eternally preserves, acts with its power in the icon of His face that remains present invisibly in His icons through that power. Therefore, we always have the face of Christ, or better said its divine power, through the features of the faces painted in its likeness. In this way it is through the icon of Christ that His real face full of love looks at us, works in us and remains in communication with us.

The prayer concludes with the affirmation that before the icon one offers adoration to God in Trinity: "Whereby all that are bowing down in worship before them to Thee and Thine Only-begotten Son, and the Most-holy Spirit, earnestly praying and calling upon [Thee] in faith, might be heard."[95]

In response to the prayer addressed before the icon, the Holy Trinity pours out its power upon those who behold the icon, urging them to worship the Trinity and to ask for its help by calling it to turn its face toward them.

Let us recap: most of the time the idol had a monstrous image that conveyed the disordered forces of nature that were not understood. By venerating the idol, the human being's face, which reflected the consciousness of the relationship with the personal God and the source of order, subjected itself to the inferior nature conceived as a complexity of disordered forces. That was considered as the ultimate reality, and the human person resigned himself to support its whims, without having the consciousness of his incomparable superiority and being able, through the spirit reflected by him, to control nature as God asked him to do.

Through sacred symbol, which implies the recognition of the entire nature as subjected to the bright or personal spirit of God, man worshiped God as distinct from nature, himself growing into the communion with this infinite, personal God. But this God still remained at a certain distance from man. The potential intimacy that exists between the personal God and the person and therefore the human face was not known. This was the superior phase of the Old Testament vis-à-vis naturalistic religions. In the glory that rested on the face of Moses one could guess this special relation that the personal God could have with the human being as person; one could guess the special brightness that God, or the relation with Him, gives the human face. But this glory manifested from a certain distance more the power of God rather than His love, such as in the sacred symbols taken from nature the power of God is reflected more than His love as the most proper characteristic of the person. This is why the Jews could not look at the uncovered face of Moses.

The full humanity between the human face or the human person and the personal, loving characteristic of God is shown when God the Word makes the human face His own in order to enter into a visible relationship with all His brethren in humanity. Human persons are no longer afraid to behold the incarnate God's human face full of divine glory; on the contrary they feel attracted by it, are eager to behold it unceasingly and to regard it as the model for the perfection of their own faces. A relationship of avid affection is established between the human face become God's face and those who recognize in Christ the God of supreme love for human persons as well as the fulfillment of human aspirations for perfection through love. The divine glory of Christ's human face is so proper to them and so dear that it also spreads upon their faces through their communication with Him. "But we all—says St. Paul—with unveiled face, beholding as in a mirror [namely through Christ's human face] the glory of the Lord, are being transformed into the same image from glory to glory [namely more and more from day to day], just as by the Spirit of the Lord [it is something that happens through the work of the Holy Spirit]" (2 Cor 3:18).

But in order for this glory to increase, or for God's light on our faces according to the likeness of the glory on the face of Christ that reflects the depths of love and purity, one understands that one must continuously behold the face of Christ. But how can we behold it if we do not have Christ's icon? To believe in Christ but to not behold His face's glory through His icon means to be deprived of the possibility of partaking of the glory of His face and of growing spiritually through Him. It means to reduce enormously the efficiency of Christ's work on the believer and to fail to appreciate the value Christ placed on the human face as a means and object of spiritualization. It also diminishes the importance of the fact that God took upon Himself the human face for eternity as the most concentrated manifestation of human spirituality toward nature.

2. The Purpose of Holy Icons in the Orthodox Church

Just as the Holy Liturgy cannot be officiated without prayers, neither can it be officiated without icons. If exceptionally it is officiated in a place outside the church, there must be present at least the antimension on which the icon of Christ's burial is painted, an icon of Christ on the right side and an icon of the Mother of God on the left toward which the believers look.

The primary function of the holy icons is to guide towards and strengthen the right faith. St. Basil the Great said: "What the word brings to the ear, the same does the painting for the eyes."[96] They imprint on the minds and memories of believers the teaching on the triune God, the saving works of Christ, the place of the Mother of God in the economy of the Son of God's incarnation, the fruits of faith in Christ and in the saints as encouragement for our spiritualization.

The Holy Fathers, who speak about the teaching role of the holy icons, also speak of the emotional way in which they implant in us the teachings of faith and the examples of how the saints fulfilled them. St. Gregory of Nyssa beholds with a deep awe an icon of Isaac's sacrifice.[97]

St. Basil the Great offered the formula that was also adopted by the Seventh Ecumenical Council: "The veneration of the image passes to the one depicted" (Commentary on Isaiah the Prophet, ch. 13). The transition of the veneration to the model of the image is done naturally. Bishop Hypathius of Ephesus writes: "We allow decorations in churches because each group of believers is elevated to God in a way proper to that group and some are elevated from this decoration to a spiritual beauty as well as from the multiple lights within the church to a spiritual and immaterial light."98

More than this, through the holy icons those depicted in them become present in the church. Thus, in the Epistle to the Hebrews, after many righteous persons from the Old Testament were mentioned (and perhaps also from the era of the New Testament before the epistle was written), it is said: "Therefore we also, since we are surrounded by so great a cloud of witnesses, let us lay aside every weight, and the sin which so easily ensnares us, and let us run with endurance the race that is set before us" (Heb 12:1). The saints from before remained alive even after death. Moreover, they surround the faithful, especially when these are gathered together for prayer and when Christ offers Himself from their midst as sacrifice to the Father. The saints cannot be absent from around Christ since Christ Himself promised: "and lo, I am with you always, even to the end of the age" (Mt 28:20). But Christ is with them when they open themselves to Him through prayer and by listening to His words. When He hears that His words are listened to, He Himself is present, repeating these words in a spiritual manner and rejoicing when these words are listened to and fulfilled. And He also sees Himself present there where He sees His image beheld with faith and with love. This is why we can say that through icons there is given an additional presence and saving work, or an additional amount of gifts is poured forth over the faithful gathered in the church building.

"The Seventh Ecumenical Council stated very explicitly: 'Whether it be by the contemplation of the Scriptures or by the representation of the icon... we remember all the prototypes and *we are introduced into their presence.*' [*Mansi* XIII, 482] The Council of 860 affirmed the same thing: 'What the Gospel says to us in words, the icon announces to us in colors and *makes it present to us.*' (*Mansi*, XVI, 400)."99

Especially by being consecrated by the priest, after he has verified its conformity with the content of the Christian faith, the icon becomes a wonderful helper, or a "channel of grace and sanctifying virtue."100 "The icon is a witness to the saint's presence and expresses his ministry of intercession and communion. It is certainly true that the icon has no reality of its own. In itself, it is only a wooden board. The icon gets all its theophanic value from its *participation* in the Wholly Other; the icon is a mirror of the Wholly Other. It can therefore contain nothing in itself but becomes rather a grid, a structure through which the

Other shines forth . . . . The icon thus expresses an energetic presence which is not localized nor enclosed but which shines out from a point of condensation."[101]

The veneration that passes from the icon to its living prototype is not a passing from one defined space to another, but the passing from the defined to the supra-defined space, to a space of a different order but neither distant nor detached from the link with the defined space. This passing from the icon to its living prototype is thereby an entrance into contact with the presence of the unseen, spiritual prototype. But the orientation of the venerating soul toward the prototype of the unseen image also draws the attention of the one being venerated. And when looking at the venerator, the saint looks as if filled with the power of the Holy Spirit, a power that shines forth from the saint. The service of the consecration of the icon, in which the Holy Spirit is called upon to come over it, is a confirmation of this fact. By strengthening the believer's trust in the power that irradiates from the prototype upon him through the icon, this service intensifies the thought full of faith of the venerator toward the prototype of the image and it also asks the prototype to turn more attentively toward the one who venerates it. The calling upon the prototype by name with faith and with the conviction that in the prototype Christ is present and from Him irradiates the Holy Spirit, is like an epiklesis addressed to the Holy Spirit found in the prototype. According to St. John of Damascus, the icons are "filled with the working power of God and with grace, for the name of the one portrayed is called over them in a kind of epiklesis (invocation)."[102]

Summing up the ideas from the writings against Emperor Constantine V Kopronimos by John of Jerusalem, the sinkelos of Patriarch Theodore of Antioch, H. I. Schulz says: "By beholding it with faith, the icon leads to the spiritual contemplation of and the mystical encounter with holy persons and the saving works it represents . . . . This presumes that the encounter through grace with the one portrayed is not just a simple, subjective opinion, but one based on an objective presence of the one represented in the image."[103]

This descent of the prototype toward the one venerating the icon takes place whenever a believer venerates the icon upon entering the church. Moreover, this also takes place even when the icon is venerated at home or other places. But more accentuated is this descent of God in Trinity, of the Lord Jesus Christ, of the Holy Birthgiver of God, of the saints and angels during the Holy Liturgy when they are invoked through the priest's prayers together with the entire community. For the priest exhorts the community at the end of every litany not without a reason: "Remembering our most holy, pure, most blessed and glorious Lady, the Birthgiver of God and ever-virgin Mary with all the saints," to which the congregation responds: "Most Holy Birthgiver of God have mercy on us."

We mentioned that where Christ is present His holy Mother is also present together with all the angels and the saints. They are present not individually or in isolation, but all of them are focused on the saving action of Christ which He performs in the Holy Liturgy. This is why when we address the Lord's Mother or one of the saints before their icons, at the same time we address Christ and find ourselves within a continuous progress in this solidarity and in the work of the Holy Trinity and of Christ the Savior exerted upon us.

On the other hand, we place ourselves in relationship with Christ not only by listening with faith to His words and beholding His image, or His words incorporated and realized in the saints, but also when we speak those words ourselves. All His words spoken by us are comprised in a condensed way in His name and those incorporated in the saints are comprised in their names. Through the name we distinguish, on the one hand, one person from another and, on the other hand, we comprise all the deeds of that person. Therefore, all the deeds of a person with that person's specific characteristics are comprised even in a single deed, because it is imprinted with the seal of all his/her deeds as a unique person. But when the name is spoken we specifically call that person or draw our attention and enter into a direct relation. This is why Evdokimov rightly says that "God's Name is his oral icon. We do not 'take the Lord's Name in vain,' for God is present in his Name"[104] or in the one who pronounces His name. This is why the icon becomes important for believers from the fact that when is sanctified it is given a name, just as a person is given a name at baptism.[105] And the name is proper to a person, for only the person is conscious that it is called by name and thereby distinguished from others. This is why when beholding the icon of Christ, of the Birthgiver of God and of the saints the believers encounter them also because they address them by name. The believer challenges the divine persons or those of the saints to be present precisely by calling upon them by name with faith.[106]

PREAMBLE

Within the Holy Liturgy, the mystical encounter with the persons portrayed in icons is a sort of preparation for a more complete encounter with Christ in the sacrament of Holy Eucharist, such as are in fact the prayers of the priest and those of the community guided by the priest. Both are, on the one hand, means of being strengthened in the right faith, on the other hand they are means of encounter with Christ the Savior surrounded by angels and saints. For it is both in the word and in the images portrayed in icons that God the Incarnate Word is mystically present, the Subject of all the words and of the saving, deifying deeds. Together with Him are present, as most faithfully incorporated words, His Most-holy Mother, the angels and the saints who surround Him as the hypostasized words fulfilled in an exemplary way that communicate most beneficially and effectively. But the increase of this encounter with Christ through the prayers of the Holy Liturgy and through the icons in the church advances toward the supreme encounter in the Eucharist.

If the Liturgy represents our progress with Christ, who leads us through His saving works to the transformation of the bread and wine into His crucified and risen body and blood and to our partaking of them, then both He and His works must dominate the principal space of the church building, surrounded by angels or having nearby His All-pure Mother. Only a bit farther should be painted certain categories of saints, each one in a separate icon. The main and most-represented theme of icons is a Christological one, or rather the saving work of Christ which began with His historical acts and continues to be realized now as it is extended throughout the Liturgy so that it can also be applied to those who believe and come to encounter Christ in the church. The saints show us the effects of Christ's saving work in the past, but they also open up for us the perspective of our deification similar to theirs, and they exhort us to strive as they did for the fulfillment of accomplishing the program of spiritualization from the power of Christ. They further assure us of their prayerful help through their invisible presence represented in icons. The prayers of the community to Christ alternate at times with their prayers to the saints. The community feels that their supplications and hymns of praise toward God are accompanied and intensified by the prayers of angels, saints and especially of the Birthgiver of God. The Christ in the church is not an isolated Christ, as in the Protestant world, nor is He a master hidden in a transcendence totally separated from the world of those who are saved, from the saints and from us who are in church. The transcendence has descended and is descending through the entire universe of persons who were saved in the past, is present and at work in the angelic world that surrounds us as it surrounds Him, it is further present in His Holy Mother and in all the saints shining forth through them upon us. The heaven of the saints, of the angels, a heaven that means the presence of Christ and of the Holy Trinity in them, is united with the earth for the transfiguration of the visible creation. Their prayers united with those of the faithful rise together toward Christ Who is above them but also in them, and Who receives them and presents them to the Father in the heaven of heavens, in the most heavenly altar, culminating with His sacrifice. Christ Himself also fills them all with the power of His Holy Spirit. To a certain degree, Christ is even now wholly in all who believe and advance toward Him. This unity of theirs through His presence in them advances toward the Eucharistic partaking of Him and then toward the eternal, eschatological life when the unity of all will be perfected (1 Cor 15:28). The prayer and chanting of the faithful, in which the Spirit of Christ is not absent, are strengthened by beholding the icons that determine the thought to rise beyond them to Christ Himself surrounded by angels and His saints.

This experience of God, of the Mother of God and the relation with the saints by looking at their icons and by calling upon their names is beyond what one can define as rational. It is apophatic. That is why the icon itself is apophatic, because it offers the opportunity for the relation of the one beholding it through contemplation with the living and mystical reality of God beyond senses, or the reality of saints also filled with God Who cannot be defined.[107] The icon is apophatic as is the entire Liturgy. It is apophatic because it unites the past with the present and with the eschatological, eternal future. "The icon is an image of eternity. It allows us to overcome time and to foresee the future age in the trembling mirror of images."[108] To Florensky's characterization we can add that the icon is an image of the living eternity because through it transpires the One who has neither beginning nor end nor boundary in His powers. It is an image through which transpires God's infinity.

But the eternity and the infinity of life toward which the icon opens the door belong to the divine hypostasis who became man out of love, and to the human hypostases in whom the incarnate divine hypostasis dwells and together with Him the entire Trinity. This is why the icons are named after persons. It is not an eternal and infinite essence that flickers through them, but a divine person who implies a communion with others through the human faces that have a personal characteristic. It is an eternity and an infinity which speak to us and with which we speak, with which we are in dialogue and which pour into us their helping, loving, guiding and sanctifying eternity and infinity. This eternity that transpires through icons and is poured into the body lifts up the body to eternal life through the resurrection of the body assumed by the Son of God. Through the fact that it shows us both personal eternity and the eternalization of the body, "iconography is the metaphysics of concrete existence,"[109] which at the same time is the concrete metaphysics of life.

According to St. John of Damascus, the holy icon has its beginning in the Incarnation of the Son of God, thus in the beginning of the descent out of love of the Son of God to us in view of our salvation. It is the proof of the saving and loving God's love for us. Behind the rejection of icons is hidden doubt of the love of God coming down to us. The icon proves the fact that the One without beginning, above existence, has been manifested in human form and has taken on a human mode of existence, even though in this mode of human existence transpires the entire mystery of the One above existence. This is why only above the icon of Christ the words "He who is" (Ο ΩΝ) are written. Human existence has discovered in Him its depth hidden in the divine infinity that is above existence. At the same time, the icon is the crowning of the Son of God's work along the line of our salvation, showing in Himself our risen and eternalized humanity. The icon is a praise offered to God, not to a God whose greatness would hinder him from approaching us, but to a God Who out of love for us became man in order to deify the human person. "God is great in His saints," incomparably greater than a God who remains in a plane totally separated and hidden from us and who has no benevolence toward us. The icon thus materializes in itself God's greatness and the greatness imparted to the human person. It concentrates in itself the incarnation of the Son of God and the assumed humanity's resurrection out of His power that proves efficient and loving at the same time.

The fact that the Son of God takes on a human face and can eternalize it through resurrection, making it a medium for communicating the divine glory, or the fact that His divinity can transpire through the human face, show that God Himself has the potentiality of the human face in which is concentrated the entire spirituality of human nature. It further shows that God created the human person after the image of His spirituality and capable of communicating with the divine spirituality. "The dogmatic conscience of the church has affirmed the truth of the icon in relation to the Incarnation [that is fulfilled in the resurrection], but the Incarnation itself is conditioned by man's creation 'in the image of God' and by the iconic structure of the human person. Christ did not become incarnate in a foreign and utterly element, but he found in man his own heavenly and archetypical image,"[110] or the image whose archetype is Himself. An animal cannot be the subject of an icon, for through it there cannot transpire the conscious spirituality of the person in communication with the infinite spirituality of the personal God. In Christ the human image and the divine archetype are united in a unique hypostasis. The Apostles who beheld the face of Christ could distinguish between what was human and what was divine in it. Through Christ's image in the icon transpires the divine archetype and both are to be regarded in their unity. In the icon of Christ the divine hypostasis was actualized in His human image, or the supreme prototype in His own image; *humanum capax divini* means that God can assume, by purifying at maximum, the thought, feeling, will, namely the entire complexity of human life present in the body that finds its entire expressivity in the face.

"In opposition to an excessive spiritualism, we affirm that God's fullness would be diminished if he did not have his image [the archetype of images, especially the human one]. God is the form of all forms, the Icon of all icons; he is the all-containing archetype. The apophatic approach is not a pure denial or negation. It rather affirms that God is a Meta-Icon, in the words of Pseudo-Dionysius, a Hyper-Icon. The iconoclasts showed a strange insensitivity to the sacred realism of being, a docetic rupture between the spiritual and the incarnate."[111] God cannot be regarded as condemned to an eternal state that is vague or chaotic.

Christianity does not regard everything as a unique, pantheistic essence, subjected involuntarily to certain cyclic processes, nor does it keep God separated from the world He created, incapable of giving it certain forms that correspond to His potentials full of meaning. But it sees God as One Who gives potential, deepens and renders sensitive through His powers, His will and His eternal, infinite love for certain non-uniform persons the powers, the life and the love of the created being, increasing its beauty with His incomprehensible and infinite beauty.

If God is the light in which there is no trace of darkness (1 Tim 6:16), this light cannot be chaos, a total indefinite, but the harmony that is above any harmony of all positive meanings, of powers of life and of loving feelings. Only nothingness lacks interior structure. Every existence is by itself structured.[112] Supreme existence is the unitary bosom of all structures that is actualized, certainly on an infinitely inferior plane, in their variety in the limited exigencies, but connected among them and capable of being filled by and increasingly reflecting the supreme harmony. All created things are lights, because all have an organized, interior structure. But the human person comprises them potentially and is called to comprise all of them actually and to be stamped by all. Because the human person is the image of God, in his reasonable light are unitarily comprised and revealed all created lights or all harmonized meanings. Each person is a light distinct from others but in relation to them, each one understanding exclusively all but in solidarity with all. This is why the person has a proper name, unlike things. In the name of that person we express his distinct mode of being and of comprising all and of organizing all in harmony with the modes of other persons of seeing and organizing all things. Thus, through the name itself we express a rational light, or rather this light expresses itself for another rational light and indicates itself to be an exclusive rational light for other rational lights. Interpersonal relations as conscious lights are sustained through names and are expressed in a concentrated manner through names. "The light of the icon does not open up to an impersonal ocean, but it represents the content and the super-abundance of communion"[113] among persons.

But it is in Christ that the human person gains the capacity to comprise all in a manner that is unitarily organized and in the depth of complete light not covered by darkness or distorted. In Christ the image of God is fully restored since it is intimately penetrated by the divine archetype.

By creating the human person as a conscious being limited in powers, God the Word cannot but give him an image actualized up to a certain degree. For the image is the organized form of rationality proper to the human person as a crowning image in cosmos destined to imprint his image upon the entire cosmos and in all the things he does by organizing them in conformity with his reason and, therefore, indirectly in conformity with the supreme Reason toward which the human person's reason tends, constantly returning to the previous forms in which he organized his things and deeds. Being in harmony with the divine Logos as archetype, this image is, on the other hand, connected with the infinite divine archetype and is called upon to imprint himself in all things in an ever perfect manner and to comprise all things, just like his archetype and in greater conformity with that Archetype. The image of God in the human person, having its foundation in his soul, is reflected or extended in his body as well and especially in his face. The archetype that penetrates Christ's image is also reflected in His human face. This is also true to a certain extent for the faces of those who are united through faith and life with Christ, which shows us how to organize our life and our relations with our fellow human beings and with creation in an ever more perfect manner.

In this way the human face regains all its light and all its depth and it gathers all the senses of creation in a correct and harmonious manner. "According to nature the human person remains entirely human; according to grace and participation, after the old man has been crucified and likeness is regained, he becomes entirely god in his soul and body, having the uncreated grace and the crystal shining of heavenly glory and of the light of the God-man Jesus Christ's face, which unites him with the glory of the Father and of the Son and of the Holy Spirit. This is why the holy icons depict the saints similar according to grace and participation with the One who, being wholly God, fills them wholly with Him and leaves no space in them without His presence. Through the deified nature of the human person in which all things are recapitulated, God Himself becomes all in all."[114] "For Orthodoxy the human person and the creation that God has made are theological existences, one being in the other, each and all participating according to the proper measure in the uncreated energies of God. They were all created in Christ and they participate at the center of the world which is Christ."[115] All creation participates at the center of light, which at the same time is the fiery center of love that is Christ.

The gathering of all the saints accomplished in heaven and the one intended on earth by the faithful in Christ is orally affirmed through the words at the end of every litany: "Commemorating our most holy, pure, most blessed and glorious Lady the Birthgiver of God and ever-virgin

Mary with all the saints, let us offer ourselves and one another and all our life unto Christ our God." We should live our life as they did so that we may arrive in Christ at the full union with Him.

But "the light of the icon is not of this world. It does not come from the exterior to temporarily illumine it, but it comes directly from the icon, from the faces of the saints. It is from the changed creation that the light pours forth, a light that is clear, comforting, gracious, uncreated and unfading as a gift and grace of the Holy Spirit. Icons depicting events that took place during the day are no more luminous than those depicting events that took place during the night. The icons of the Mystical Supper and the prayer in Gethsemane garden are not darker than the icons depicting the conversation with the Samaritan woman at Jacob's well, the resurrection or Pentecost. It is not the day that illumines the scenery of the icon or the night that darkens it . . . . The icon has no need of the day and does not fear the night. Both the night and the day need the transfiguring power and the grace of the icon . . . . All created things are filled with the uncreated light... We are in the antechamber of heaven and of the new earth, outside the created light, and of the enclosed spirit of the world that spread all over the natural world."[116]

"The icon of the Transfiguration is no more luminous than the icon of the Crucifixion. The Lord's face does not 'shine' more at the Transfiguration than in any other of His icons. The Transfiguration depicted in an icon is not an isolated and separated fact, but grace and mystical light that fills and enlivens all created things. The entire iconography is a transfigured space... It is the transfigured world, the world of uncreated illumination . . . . All things have penetrated each other; they are everywhere and nowhere,"[117] in the natural space.

Olivier Clement also says: "The light of the icon symbolizes the uncreated divine glory, veiled precisely through its profundity and pointing to its supra-essential source. This is why in an icon the light does not come from a focus situated within the cosmos and provoking the phenomenon of shadow or expressing man's opacity and division... The iconographers call the background of the icon light . . . . All colors in this art are defined as many refractions of the light of lights, a vibrant white that sums up all and opens up to the transcendent through touchups of a solar gold."[118]

In church we find ourselves in the divine horizon that is all light, but a light that, even though it originates in Christ, does not confound with Him the persons of the saints who remain as lights filled with His light. The church space is a space of the supra-essential light, of the plenary and eternal meaning of existence. The community preparing for the Holy Liturgy sings: "Glory to You Who has shown us the light." "Let us honor the Birthgiver of God and the Mother of Light in hymns" is sung at Matins, thus showing Christ as light not only in His divinity, but also in the humanity saved from the darkness of sin that He received from the Holy Birthgiver of God so that He may fill the world with that light.

Man's face is revealed in its true reality in communion through the fact that it is illumined, showing that it is the image of the communion of the triune Persons. The icon is luminous because it depicts Christ's face within the triune communion as well as the faces of the saints in communion with God, among themselves and full of benevolent attention toward us. St. Gregory Palamas says: "Thus one must offer to God the passionate part of the soul, alive and active, that it may be a living sacrifice . . . . How can this be done? Our eyes must acquire a gentle glance, attractive to others, and conveying the mercy from on high (for it is written, 'He who has a gentle look will receive grace' Pr. 12:15)."[119]

"The face of the saint in an icon is luminous because it is lovingly open to God and to the faithful and thus it is happy. The icon suggests the fulfillment of the prototype through the double and simultaneous opening to the transcendent and to the neighbor. It shows an exteriority–interiority, a presence of the unknowable in which transcendence offers itself while it remains inaccessible."[120] "The good face of the glance is maintained, silence nourishes the promise of a word."[121] The light of the loving face says more than any word. Because the saint beholds the infinite, loving transcendence, "his icon is unmoved and silent, which is the silence of a call. But it is not thereby static. It presents at times the balance of the most extreme tension."[122]

3. *Placement of Holy Icons in the Church*

Through the order in which the icons are placed in it the church presents the recapitulation of all in Christ, the recapitulation realized to a certain extent in the saints and to be realized in us by advancing into the likeness of Christ and by approaching Him until complete union with Him. Even if not all saints are depicted in the church, those who are depicted represent all, just as, even if not all living believers are present in church, or in a single church, those who are present in a church represent all. The saints and the believers on earth partake of the same Christ, the latter in the form of bread and wine as well as in other modes before that and the former in a spiritual manner.

Christ the Pantokrator views and embraces all from the central cupola of the church: the angels and the saints who departed this life—the latter being generally placed in a register inferior to that of the angels—and the living believers in the church. Patriarch Photius, in his discourse at the consecration of the Nea church on May 1, 881, built by Emperor Basil I, says when describing the frescos: "In the cupola there is an image that represents Christ. One could say that He looks over the earth and is preoccupied with its order and supervision, so fittingly did the iconographer depict in a colored image the providence of the Creator toward us. In lower, circular registers there is depicted a great number of angels who move serving the common Lord."[123] On the pendentives of the cupola one finds the icons of the four evangelists, who through their writings inspired by God united heaven with the earth, and represent the entire teaching by which Christ leads us toward Him and which tells us that the Pantokrator was incarnate for our salvation and union with Him. Further down on the lateral walls are the saints who approached Christ during their life on earth and more so in their life after death. The images of the saints themselves in the nave are arranged in the order used in the Nea church: "While the cupola is the place of the heavenly church [of the angels around the Pantokrator], the lower area represents the image of the church on earth . . . . The patriarchs, church teachers and priests have their places in the nave, near the main apse, or in the niches placed immediately under the cupola. The martyrs grouped in a certain order cover the main arches of the cupola, the walls, the columns and the vaults of the nave, while the ascetics, the pious men and the local saints occupy the spaces on the west part of the church close to the entrance."[124] But Christ the Pantokrator leads us in this life through angels and saints toward the life to come to the union with Him. They call us to partake of Him who is found, or who has come to meet us, on the Holy Table in the altar. But in relation with the Pantokrator, the angels and the saints, we have even in this life a foretaste of the life to come. This helps us to advance toward a more complete foretaste of that life through Holy Communion with the sacrificed and risen Christ on the altar.

"The apse of the altar calls for a representation which should have a special relation to our salvation... If Christ's image has a privileged place in the cupola . . . the second rank after Him can only be given to the image of the Birthgiver of God. The work of salvation, the actualization of which concludes on the altar, begins from His incarnation within the bosom of His Mother depicted in the apse of the altar. The most expressive representation of this image is the later Byzantine image of Platitera (more comprehensive than the heavens), of the Birthgiver upon whose chest is resting the incarnate Word, floating in a halo. In the Nea church, Mary is depicted in the old form of the Prayer (Oranta) with the hands stretched toward her Son on His right hand, and on His left is St. John the Baptist. Photius presents her as the great intercessor and as the defender of the kingdom, just as she is praised in the Akathist hymn."[125]

The two large churches dedicated to the divine Wisdom, after the model of Hagia Sophia in Constantinople, namely St. Sophia in Kiev (1037) and the one in Ohrid (1050), take further the representation of the Lord's saving work officiated in the Liturgy, thus opening the way for the following phase of themes and of the iconographical order of the Byzantine churches.[126] The cathedral in Kiev places the Eucharistic partaking of the Apostles in the apse of the altar space and on the lower level the images of the great hierarchs of the Church: St. Athanasius, St. Basil the Great, St. John Chrysostom, St. Gregory the Theologian and St. Cyril of Alexandria, as models of officiators of the Holy Liturgy and as models of Christ the High-Priest who communes the Apostles on a higher level and the priests and faithful during the Liturgy that is officiated in the church. On the walls of the altar area in the cathedral of Ohrid are painted the sacrifice of Jacob and other scenes related to the Holy Eucharist.[127]

The church of the New Monastery in Chios (middle of the eleventh century) has an enlarged cycle of scenes that show eight of Christ's main acts related to salvation, through which the believers are led toward the union with Christ found on the altar table. They are in the niches between the altar area and the nave and they represent: The Annunciation, the Nativity, Presentation into the Temple, the Transfiguration, the Crucifixion, Taking down from the Cross and the Resurrection. In the church of Daphne there are twelve scenes in these niches, among which the Nativity of the Holy Virgin.[128] What is represented in them is not only the number of royal feast days, but also the mystery of Christ in its entirety as it is actualized in the liturgical-sacramental life of the Church and during the ecclesiastical year, but concentrated especially in the officiating of the Eucharist, in the Holy Communion and in the preaching of the Gospel.

"Thus in their own way, the icons emphasize the fact that the church is the place of the saving presence of Christ's mystery and by doing this they themselves contribute to its actualization."[129] The twelve royal feasts are also represented in the icons on the first row of the iconostasis, above which the Apostles are placed, then the prophets, and at the top the cross which dominates everything as a parallel of the Pantokrator, since "through the cross salvation has come to the whole world." In the self-sacrifice of Christ for us and in our sacrifice for God and among ourselves lies the entire salvation or the entire "liturgy."

The icons represent in images what is expressed in words, in prayers, through the officiating of the Sacrament of the Holy Eucharist and through the partaking of it. As alternate means of the direct reflection of Christ's power and also through His Holy Mother, through angels and saints, the icons also contribute to the believers' reception of Christ's gifts and to the experience of the saving action performed by Christ in the Holy Liturgy.

The believer is introduced to or prepared for this participation and experience of Christ's work by looking in the narthex at the judgment of Christ, at the eternal happiness and eternal torments awaiting those who do or do not fulfill His commandments, those who advance in union with Christ by conforming their will with His or those who resist this advancement.

We mentioned that the church building, as liturgical space, represents for the believers another world or a created world that is transfigured or in the process of being transfigured, a world in which the separation between past, present and the eschatological future, between heaven and earth, between created and uncreated, is surpassed. To a great extent, the icons in the church contribute to this characteristic of the church building. Archimandrite Vasileios, the abbot of Stavronikita Monastery in Mount Athos, describes in words of subtle observation and full of poetry the atmosphere irradiating from icons: "A religious picture is an altogether different thing from a liturgical icon. The one is the creation of someone's artistic talent, the other the flower and reflection of liturgical life. The one is of this world. It speaks of this world and leaves you in this world. The other brings you a simple, peaceful and life-giving message, coming down from above. It speaks to you of something which has gone beyond the categories of yesterday and today, here and there, mine and thine . . . . Through the icon, an everlasting and unchanging reality speaks without words; a reality which, in the clarity of silence and in tranquility, rises up from the deepest level, that which unites everything in man."[130] "What we have in the icon is not a neutral, faithful historical representation, but a dynamic liturgical transformation. In iconography, the events of salvation are not interpreted historically but expressed mystically and embodied liturgically; . . . the door to the Mystical Supper has not been closed. The refreshment of Pentecost is not past . . . . Being baptized into the joy of the new creation, they [the faithful] enter into the iconographic and liturgical world where they find the Lord and the saints alive. They come into immediate contact and communion with life."[131]

In the world of the icons liberated from changes non-confusion and tranquility prevail; "the breeze of the Spirit blows . . . . Here is to be found the true keeping of the Sabbath, which alleviates pain and satisfies our longing for life. We find ourselves in a state beyond any trials: in the eighth day, in the land of Paradise."[132]

The unchangeable and rich eternity of life in God is affirmed in the Orthodox icons through the great variety of colors combined with the stability of forms. The Catholic theologian Tomáš Špidlík has observed this when he wrote: "Russian [we would say Orthodox] icons show a surprisingly rich combination of colors, and the register of feelings which they evoke varies greatly, while the lines and forms are almost always unchanging, as the iconographic canon demands. For a Western artist, to grow and become more skilled means to respond to the irresistible impulse to invent new forms, to 'restructure'. By contrast, the icon painter is happy to find unchangeable prototypes, an art form well protected against all individual expressions of personality."[133] The Orthodox icons convey the "mobile rest" or the "stable motion" of spiritual life, of life in the same infinite and unchangeable God of whom the Eastern Fathers speak (St. Gregory of Nyssa, St. Maximos the Confessor, etc.). The life of the saint is not outside God, does not cross over to something else or go beyond Christ, because God is infinite and outside Him, therefore outside Christ who became man to make the human person eternal as he in fact is in his infinite potentiality, there is nothing higher.

In the world depicted by the icon everything is paradoxical. There is a union of the opposites, namely a union of all aspects of reality in abundant peace. The body of Christ from the icon "bears the marks of the nails and cannot now be harmed by any nail or death. We find ourselves participating in the mystical experience and the lively equilibrium of the saints, in 'sober drunkenness,' in the fervor of life throbbing in the midst of infinite and undisturbed calm."[134] We find both humility and magnificence in the supreme degree accessible to the human person, the plenitude of life that "wells up behind an outward appearance of motionless, and there is a 'hidden beauty.' . . . Nothing shows an inconsolable misery that brings death . . . and everything is expressed with the calm and joy of contrite devotion."[135] All this can be seen in the space of the church. "The unity of the faith and the communion of the Holy Spirit is present throughout this liturgical world as it lives, prays, builds, paints and sings. Everything is free and reconciled, like brothers and kinsfolk... There is no disturbance from the present age, though the whole of creation is present, interwoven with incorruption and filled with sweetness by the light . . . . The same eight tones in the liturgical chant express the pain and suffering of Holy Week and the joy of the Resurrection and of Pentecost . . . . Sorrow in the context of the Liturgy does not end in disappointment and rejection of God . . . . Everything is mingled with the hope that gives consolation, with the Spirit, the Comforter. Joyful sorrow reigns during the period of the Triodion of repentance, and the same attitude of contrition will shine out, reverent and priestly, with the light of the Resurrection, with the victory of God who is also man."[136]

Regarding the experience of overcoming the separation between the visible and the invisible worlds, a fact that strengthens this experience in the Liturgy, H. I. Schulz says: "the specific of this iconography lies in the precise fact that the boundaries between visible and invisible, between time and eternity, between symbol and reality are overcome and they express the enduring unity expressed in both."[137]

Even if the icons depict Christ and the saints as being immersed in eternity, they look toward us and send their powers to us. The Pantokrator is not only serious in preserving the world within its general order, but also attentive to each of us by helping and comforting each of us. Our life is both personal and communitarian in the ambiance of Christ and the saints. In addition to the icon of Christ the Pantokrator there also appeared very early the icon of "Christ the Merciful," "the Philantropos" or "the Benefactor," on the basis of a tradition from the first centuries of Christianity.[138] The icons suggest to us the living presence of Christ and of His saints in the church building. They facilitate the dialogue of the faithful with the Holy Trinity, with the Mother of the Lord and with the saints.

Eastern iconography is an overflowing of the merciful eternity upon the earthly life and it sweetens the latter with the hopeful serenity of eternity.

N. Ozoline made the remark that the icons are not only a visual representation of the invisible plane of Christ's saving works that have been fulfilled and are fulfilled in the Holy Liturgy and which have shown their full efficiency within saints, but they also have a complementary role. It consists, on the one hand, in the intensification of the faithful's encounter with Christ and with the saints during the Holy Liturgy and, on the other hand, in emphasizing the wider significance of the saving events. This is why one cannot officiate the Liturgy without certain icons, for example without the icon of Christ on the right side of the royal doors and that of the Lord's Mother on the left side, or of the image of the Lord's burial painted on the antimension. The priest is to venerate before them while celebrating certain acts and saying certain words and also at various times to kiss them. On the other hand, in an icon from St. Catherine's Monastery on Mount Sinai from the seventh century, the central place among the Apostles is empty. It is the place of the Holy Spirit. In this way there is represented the apostolic plenitude of the Church, which cannot be without the Holy Spirit. In the same icon St. Paul the Apostle stands before St. Peter, which does not correspond to history. Thus there is again represented the apostolic plenitude of the Church, which cannot be conceived of without St. Paul the Apostle.

From the seventh century onward one begins to depict the Lord who is transfigured on Mount Tabor in mandorla, which shows the uncreated glory enveloping Him. This puts into an even bolder relief the transcendence of Christ who is enveloped in glory, the transcendence that does not obstruct the irradiation of that glory upon the Apostles and through them upon the entire Church.[139]

D. The Modes of Christ's Presence in the Worship of the Church

The Orthodox Church is aware of Christ's presence in its worship in the following ways: a) in the Eucharistic sacrifice; b) in the other Sacraments; c) in sacramentals, other church services (Praises), in the prayers and blessings of the priest; d) in the words of the Holy Scripture read by the priest in the church; e) in the preaching of the priest; f) in the prayers recited and sung by the faithful and in the dialogue carried on between them and the priest during worship; g) in the readings of the faithful from the Holy Scripture outside the church building, in their prayers as well as in other readings from Orthodox spiritual writings; h) in the conversations of the faithful about God carried on with faith and in their good and pure deeds done out of faith.[140] In this way the entire life of the faithful is a worship offered to God, or a liturgy in the broad sense of the word.

Before reflecting on some of these modes of Christ's presence in worship and on the means whereby the various modes of Christ's presence are obtained, one should mention that all the modes of Christ's presence presume a group of believers who, together with the priests and the hierarchs, form a constitutive part of the Church, herself having as a specific foundation the various modes of Christ's presence. On the one hand, the Church is constituted and maintained through the Holy Mysteries and through the other means of obtaining and maintaining Christ's presence. On the other hand, the premise of all these means is the Church. Christ comes in the Church, which He extends through all her forms of prayer, preaching and fulfilling His will. However, He is in the Church through His Holy Spirit, making the prayers, preaching and good deeds of the believers means of His continually renewed coming, all these being necessary for every believer.

Speaking about the Liturgy especially in this strict sense, Romano Guardini says: "The Liturgy is not officiated by a single believer, but by the totality of believers. But this community is not made up only by the people who are in the church: it is not the gathered 'community.' It extends farther beyond the respective space and comprises the believers from all over the earth. It also extends beyond the boundaries of time, since the praying community on earth knows itself to be one with the departed for whom time no longer exists, but they are in the eternal realm. Thus, the fact of general inclusion does not exhaust the notion of liturgical community. The I that carries on the activity of liturgical prayer is not only the counting together of all right-believing individuals. As such, their unity is something more than the gathering of those who constitute their totality . . . . The believers are connected through a real and common fundament of life. This is the real Christ; His life is ours and we are incorporated in Him. We are His 'mystical' body. The power that sustains this great unity, which causes the individual person to participate in its life, plants and sustains him in it, is Christ's Spirit, the Holy Spirit. Each believer in particular is a cell of this unity of life, a member of this body . . . . In the Liturgy, within the framework of which the individual is most intensely conscious of this unity that includes him, he does not feel as a separate being standing before God, but as a member of this unity."[141]

If in this book we sometime call the faithful people "community," we thereby understand a community united with all communities or with the Church as a whole, which has Christ within, the foundation of unity both among the members of the community gathered in the same church building and between them and the members of the Church from everywhere. A certain unity is realized or exists among all people who are connected through something in common apart from their human nature: in their families, nations, etc. But the deepest unity is achieved in the Church.

This unity shows that the human beings gathered in one place are not simply uniform individuals put together. Arithmetic cannot capture this inner relationship among those counted who are not entirely identical. In arithmetic the numbers represent simply uniform units put together, a fact that does not exist in reality. The four operations do not open the real plan in which the numbers do not indicate uniform units and in which among those counted there is achieved a certain unity without being melted in that unity. In arithmetic or mathematics, as a science, this truly real plan remains closed, for it operates with uniform, separate and abstract units so that it can execute its general operations, which are valid up to a point. All exact sciences are the same in that general and abstract plan outside the concrete plan of the real human life, while only by separating or uniting the uniform elements in comingling them, can it make exact or only generally valid affirmations.

Thus, the mystery of community remains inaccessible to mathematics, given that the community is neither a simple unity nor a simple gathering of units.

Its form is perfectly given in the Holy Trinity, where there is neither separation nor fusion, but a union of non-uniform and non-confused units.

There is another mystery strongly linked to this one: a large human community cannot originate from the numbers that constitute it as units, or from their union of essence. For we see how much the human community is divided when it is founded only on human units that constitute it, or on their union of essence. Only the community of faith manages to overcome these divisions by relating itself to the One who is above and transcendent but not outside the relationship with this community. In the immanent, human universe we cannot find a One that could have so much force as to keep us with our consent in a loving and happy union, or to lead us ever deeper into that union. But since this One does not lead us into a union that might confuse us, He Himself must be a "One" in whom the Persons are maintained without being confused or identical. By itself, the universe of human consciences exists in a state of continuous division. On the subhuman and material plane the constitution of the wholes alternates with their decomposition, and within and among wholes, as long as they exist, one cannot find a conscience of union or the promoting of union with their consent.

This compels us to think that there exists a "One" that is transcendent to the immanent universe, but in relationship with it, from whom it can willingly receive power toward more union, a "One" who does not exclude, but implies the form of a perfect union. This is the Holy Trinity. Efficiency compels us to think that from Him the immanent universe has its origin and duration, and especially human beings, together with their power to maintain themselves and grow in union; not by force, but willingly and without being ever confused among themselves, something that would mean the loss of their varied identities. On the other hand, this "One" would not cause human individuals to willingly grow in their union were He to remain transcendent to them. His unifying efficiency is exercised more forcefully by the fact that He also makes Himself for them an immanent center. This is Jesus Christ through Whom the unifying force among humans is exercised from within them, but at the same time it comes from above them. The restoration and promotion of their union is due to His presence, willingly accepted by them, in various degrees and modes that correspond to certain means they use.

If we take a closer look at these means through which Christ becomes present for us in various modes, we realize that among them the word and the prayer are especially most visible. Through them Christ is active in the believers and they are themselves active toward the strengthening of His presence within and among them. In some Mysteries, in addition to prayer one also uses certain matter or gesture, or matter combined with gesture, which are fundamentally incorporated words.

But there exists a gradation in words and prayers. The gradation of the word consists in the measure in which the word is united with prayer. For between word and prayer there exists a very fluid boundary. Christ's presence that comes and is maintained through word is much more felt and efficient as the word is less separated from prayer. Both of these become much more efficient in obtaining Christ's presence as they are increasingly the work of the church community officiated through the priest and through the people visibly united around the priest as a visible representative of Christ—the community's invisible but felt center.

The word and the prayer are means which bring Christ, because they connect the thought of those who recite or hear them with Christ and through this thought they also place themselves in relationship with Christ. In this way even in the hearts of those who pray Christ is present and active through His Holy Spirit (Rom 8:26), as well as in those who preach Christ (Mt 10:20; Acts 4:8; 6:31). This is so because in the state of prayer and preaching, full of faith in Christ's saving power, the human person experiences fully the opening to Christ and the entire fragility of his own being, taken in itself, as well as the strengthening and assurance that come from the One who is prayed to and about Whom one speaks or is spoken to.

The first form of the word that makes Christ present is the word about Christ or about God spoken with faith. Since the relationship with the real and whole Christ cannot be established except through thinking about the real and whole Christ Who is made known by the Church through the priest as an authorized servant of her word about Christ, the word preached by the priest is the first means through which Christ's presence is established. This is why first there was Peter's preaching or that of Philip and then those who heard the preaching and were moved in their hearts asked to be baptized (Acts 2:37–38; 8:35–36).

But the word preached by the priest makes Christ's presence more efficient if it is filled with the spirit of prayer and received in the same spirit by those who hear it and in a spirit of repentance for sins and desire for salvation. Therefore, a higher level of the word preached by the priest is represented by his various prayers for the benefit of the faithful, as prayers in which he asks God to bless them or the environment in which they live in certain situations. The prayers bring a more active presence of Christ upon them, a presence that reestablishes or strengthens the health of believers, helps them in their needs and increases in them the spiritual life.

Following Boris Bobrinskoy,[142] Fairy von Lilienfeld says: "These prayers for blessing accompany the entire life of the faithful even outside the liturgical and sacramental life, from birth to death, both family life and professional life." Through them the whole life of the faithful is accompanied by Christ's work, by His care and help. Then Fairy von Lilienfeld cites from Bobrinskoy: "Nothing is unworthy of the heavenly grace, nothing is indifferent. All the works of human hands are meant for the glory of God. God helps the human person and the human person, being helped by God to grow, thereby glorifies God." And Fairy von Lilienfeld continues: "The Church blesses houses, boats, fields, seeds, beehives, trees and fruits, salt, flocks, etc. She asks for blessings needed for the beginning of every activity, for every good work, for the beginning of a new year, for the beginning of study or every work, for the healing of the sick, for comforting the unhappy, for travelers, for those in captivity... for defense against enemies, against earthquakes, drought, etc."[143] Through the prayers for blessing one expresses faith "in the divine power manifested in the growth, strengthening and maintaining of everything that is useful against evils in the world."[144] God's activity extends upon request to all things in the cosmos and makes them useful for the faithful. One asks for granting of good children, for good harvest, for increasing the number of cattle. If one sees God's activity in everything, how could one not see Christ as active during the entire course of the Liturgy, which is the prolonged prayer or a number of prayers?

But the highest level of the Church's prayer offered through the priest is the one through which certain Mysteries are performed by the coming of the grace proper to them, and above all the Eucharistic epiklesis.

Christ's working presence in various degrees and modes is not produced in the faithful if they are not open through faith to the word, which has a greater effect if it is filled with the spirit of prayer. And the prayers of the faithful also must rise in correspondence with the prayers for blessing, for consecration and calling upon the Holy Spirit in Mysteries, being aligned in their content with the content of the word preached by the priest and of his prayers. The aligning of the faithful's prayers with the content of the priest's word and prayers signifies a true confession of their belief in what the priest says in his word and prayers. The believers also make this confession formally before receiving one sacrament or another. By listening together to the preaching of the word by the priest as an authorized representative of the Church and by praying and singing together in consonance with the content of the priest's preaching and prayers, the believers introduce themselves into and grow into the knowledge and unity of the faith in the true and the whole Christ, or are filled together with the presence of the same Christ.

The link between word and prayer is so strong that the word is present in the prayer and the prayer is present in the word. Nevertheless, the word itself is necessary so as to show the meanings contained in prayer, and also the prayer so that the mind of the believers may not forget to pray, not only to think, upon hearing the word. When either of them is neglected in its true form, the spiritual life of believers does not develop integrally or it no longer develops in general.

The strong link between word and prayer was neglected in the West perhaps to the detriment of prayer, and in the East during the last few centuries that link was neglected to the detriment of the word. In early and Byzantine Christianity, the more prayer was practiced the more reflection on the prayer was produced. All the Eastern spiritual writings are proof of that.

Lately there have begun to appear profound reflections on prayer in Orthodoxy. Some of these reflections and analyses of the meanings contained in the prayers of the Church were published under the name of the great Russian theologian Pavel Florensky. Below are some of his analyses referring to prayer, after which we will present new details regarding the link between word and prayer within Orthodox worship and specifically in the Holy Liturgy.

Pavel Florensky gives first the general framework of the prayers through which the priest asks for the blessing and sanctification of believers and of their goods. Here is the framework:

1. Addressing God: Lord, the Good One.
2. Remembering God's acts in the past from the Old Testament or the New Testament similar to those that the priest (followed by the faithful) intends to ask on their behalf.
3. The supplication itself.
4. The praising of God, usually the One in Trinity.
5. The confirmation of this praise through the word; "Amen."[145]

And he gives other examples, such as the prayer for the blessing at the digging of a well: "1. O Lord, our God, ... 2. Who, from a dry rock did grant flowing streams of water and did satisfy Thy thirsty people, 3. Do Thy Thyself now also, O Master of All, hearken unto the supplication of us, Thine unworthy servants, and grant unto us water in this place—sweet and tasty . . . . 4. that in this way we may glorify Thy most-holy and magnificent Name: of the Father, and of the Son, and of the Holy Spirit, now and ever, and unto the ages of ages. 5. Amen."[146]

As a prayer following this framework, one can also present from the Holy Liturgy the one recited by the priest while the community sings the thrice-holy hymn:

"1. O, Holy God . . . 2. Who has brought all things out of non-existence into existence; Who has created man in Thine own image and likeness . . . 3. Thou, O Master, accept the thrice-holy hymn from the mouths of us sinners and visit us in Thy goodness. Forgive us every transgression, voluntary and involuntary . . . 4. For holy art Thou, O our God, and unto Thee we send up glory, to the Father and to the Son and to the Holy Spirit, now and ever and unto the ages of ages. 5. Amen."

One can see that in his prayers from the Liturgy the priest asks on behalf of the people more spiritual good things, which shows that the Liturgy is a ladder of spiritual ascent.

But going beyond this distinction, the prayer offered by the priest in the name of the Church—his supplication for us being based on the creative act of God or on similar help given to others in the Old and New Testaments—is raised from our arbitrary subjectivism and is included in the objectivity of creation willed by God through its being created and sustained in existence by Him. We ask, and through the priest the

Church herself asks on our behalf, something that is in conformity with the sustaining of creation by God, or we conform our will to God's will.[147] "My wish at the beginning is a subjective impulse, but at the basis of this subjective motion something objective is being shown; at the basis of my wish lays the divine care for creation. Through this is shown that what is subjective is objective." Thus, my wish is shown as being "according to God's will." "I act through the power of God, or through my medium it is the power of God that acts." I acknowledge in prayer that at the basis of all powers and motions in the world, as well as of my powers and acts, is the power of God, and God utilizes it in the most beneficial way for me at my appeal. Toward this end He also strengthens my power and adapts the powers of the creations of my works for the purpose sought. Prayer is not only a supplication for God's work for my benefit, thus strengthening my work and adapting for it the natural powers and the works of my fellow human beings, but also my offering to become a voluntary instrument of God's work, the expression of my will to become a coworker of God. Prayer implies the synergy between God and me. The powers within creation and within my being do not move alone for my benefit, but with God's help and through my work strengthened by Him. That is why prayer is also a sacrifice of my being offered to God, which I express through words, a "reasonable sacrifice"[148] through which I place my own body (Rom 12:1) at the service of God. But I would not be able to offer this sacrifice without calling on God in advance and without the gift of the Holy Spirit. "For of Him and through Him and to Him are all things, [even the power to pray and to offer ourselves as sacrifice] to whom be glory forever. Amen" (Rom 11:36).

But Florensky dedicates the most profound analyses to the calling on God's name at the beginning of prayer. "When we address God by name through an act of our will, we open up our solitude to the One we call upon, we recognize ourselves as existences of the second degree, we see before us someone higher than us and we come out of being closed in our subjectivity. The appeal [to Him for help] means my acknowledgment that I do not exist alone and by myself and that I am not the foundation of the entire existence." In every appeal I come out spiritually and existentially from myself, and the one called upon comes out of himself and enters spiritually and existentially within me; this occurs more intensely in the appeal we address to God and in His appeal to us in our conscience. In fact, even in my fellow human being's appeal for my help and when I am called by name I feel, in the unconditional obligation to respond, God's appeal. Thus, the name given to us at Baptism is not only for the purpose of being called by our neighbors, but also to feel in their appeal God's appeal.

But in prayer we call God directly, not only indirectly as it happens when we call others by name. When we call God means that we open ourselves in a more complete way, it means

> the opening up of our hidden being, the crossing (direct and conscious) of the boundary found between the human person and God, or between human persons, eliminating the barriers in the communication of the depths of our being with the One named in prayer . . . It is an act of "the will to communicate." But we willingly commit this act because we have the conscience that we are able to cross the boundary between God and us, or that God is willing to open Himself to us. "In this moment God has ceased to be a god of the philosophers; He became a living God, of Abraham, of Isaac and of Jacob."
>
> Before our eyes there is a thick cloud and when we look at it we see many interesting forms, but we do not know that it is not only a cloud and it is up to us whether we remain in our illusions and explain the cloud through its forms, namely to explain this or that form of the cloud one way or another. But lo, we rose above the cloud and we see the starry heaven or the shining sun. And now we know that this is something we did not produce, but something beyond any doubt.
>
> The calling through prayer is precisely this rising above our subjectivity, above our subjective interpretation of our own spiritual motions . . . . Anyone knows how the cloudy heaven opens up when God is called and how infinitely different in quality is the sensation of our being enclosed within from this encounter face to face with our Father in heaven, and how powerful, clear and diamantine does the foundation appear under our personal existence and under everything occurring around us.[149]

Certainly, this calling through prayer presupposes faith in God, even if Florensky does not say it. 'So then faith comes by hearing, and hearing by the words of God" (Rom 10:17).

This is why the Catholic theologian B. Langemeyer, OFM rightly sees Christ's mode of His presence through faith as the fundament of all His modes of presence in the Church. According to him, Christ is present in our faith taken not as feeling or as a subjective state of the will, but as a real presence of the risen Christ come through the Holy Spirit following the preaching of the word about Him. "Christ continues to live [after His resurrection and ascension] and makes Himself present in the world through the faith He produces."[150] And Christ works out this presence primarily through His word or through the word about Him. It is a presence in the Church in general, for throughout the whole Church His word or the word about Him is heard. But once His word that was heard produces faith in certain people, who thus become members of the Church, they see the word of Christ even in the things and persons in the world as well as in the circumstances of their life lived among the things of the world and in relation with other persons. The objective presence of Christ is in all, but subjectively it is perceived through faith, which is produced first of all by the word of Christ or by the word about Him.

The word of Christ or the word about Christ is not only information about the past saving acts of Christ, but it produces an assurance about His actual saving work in the one who believes and a gradual growth of eternal life in him. In the saving work experienced in a real way is exercised Christ's transforming power upon the one who believes. Thus, it Christ Himself that works in him.

"The whole person is enveloped by the transforming Spirit through faith in the One who produces it. The entire raising of the human being to faith is thus carried and produced by Christ's presence. Although transcendent to faith, Christ is present within faith. Since He is present within faith, as the One granting it—namely as the One granting the Holy Spirit—He is present as origin of faith and within faith. This formulation avoids any indication to the understanding of Christ's presence as a subjective product; it eliminates the idea that this presence would be produced or assured subjectively by faith. On the contrary, it is the risen One Himself Who makes Himself constantly present, since He everlastingly produces faith in His presence."[151]

Faith, as a sign of Christ's working and transforming presence in the human person, receives its existence and is maintained in the Church. This is so because the human person cannot come to faith by himself and he cannot maintain and invigorate it except in a relationship with other human persons who believe, who already have Christ within them and who speak about Him. Faith is born, maintained and invigorated in the human person from a faith—or from Christ—that moves and is manifested around him, from a relationship with Christ through other believers.

It follows that "the duration of His presence in the world does not depend on the loyalty in faith of isolated individuals. When one of these rejects the faith or falls from it, Christ remains present in the faith of others, which He produced or is producing. In other words, the faith through and in which Christ remains present in the world is the faith of the community, the faith of the Church."[152]

This fact, or more precisely, the fact that in faith as act or status of the believer and of the community Christ is present as the One who has operated and continues to operate His saving acts within the Church, causes faith as act or as status to be nourished from faith as content, from faith in the totality of Christ's presence and work. "Christ's transcendent presence, which makes possible the act of faith and its content, comprises the whole reality of the risen Christ."[153]

But the nature of the word itself explains the connection in which Christ's word places us with His person in the form of faith, when the one speaking the word communicates to us, through the faith with which he utters it, the energy of his being which is filled with the experience of Christ, and the one hearing the word opens himself up to this energy with his utmost attention. The word is the incorporation of the energy through which a person gains access within the being of the person who is addressed. The Savior compared the word with the seed. And this means, firstly, that the one speaking penetrates with his energy the person being addressed; secondly, this energy starts from within his person, namely it carries something from his person to the one he addresses, shaping him after his model to the extent to which he speaks more and more and is listened to with increasing attention. Even if he speaks to another about various things, he introduces to that other one a specific way of seeing, therefore a passion of his own being. We observe this regularly in the words people communicate to each other. In the necessity of and the capacity for communicating through words, human persons show that they are not closed monads complete from the start, but they are made for a continuous movement of reciprocal interpenetration and formation, or of a continuous enrichment and spiritual relation. From this comes also the fact that the word used by some who are distorted by selfish interests having an eloquent appearance of truth, also deceive and distort others who are not experienced in the ability of using the word deceptively. Another consequence of this deceptive way of using the word could be reciprocal dishonesty among people, which could go as far as no longer trusting each other, or the words themselves having no value, something that leads to total isolation. This is the hell in which the human person alters, through the lack of trust in the word, the communitarian functionality and suffers from this alteration.

Human persons can avoid or be healed of this alteration only by the conscience that the words originate in the supreme Word and in the responsibility that their conscience maintains in using the words, in the responsibility to be maintained as human beings who communicate sincerely through words as authentic reasonable beings.

But some can falsify even Christ's words or their meaning. The root cause of that is the human person's pride. The medicine against this disease is the reception and transmission of Christ's words and the words about Him just as they were recorded in the tradition coming from the Apostles, that is not one individual or another, but the entire ecclesiastical community. This is the correct word of Christ or about Christ. Only this correct word of Christ or about Christ, preserved by the ecclesiastical community, has the authority to also keep all who receive it in the unity of the correct living wished by Christ. Otherwise, when everyone states as correct what he thinks is correct, there consequently follow various ways of living, contrary to one another. For those who do not receive the words as coming from God and do not receive as correct those that the apostolic tradition guarantees as coming from Him, any personal opinion is justifiable. In this case anything is permissible. For everyone considers personal opinions as the ultimate basis of his deeds.

But if the word about Christ enters the being of those who receive it with faith, their word of prayer causes the reverse to happen: that person enters before God, closing the circuit between God or between Christ and believers.

If the characteristic of reasonable human beings shows that they are created in order to pervade and open up reciprocally, the extremely impressive power of the divine word over them and the tendency toward the word of prayer show that they exist to be imbued with God and for them to enter before God, to be penetrated to the deepest fundament of their being and also to penetrate the deepest fundament of existence in order to be united with God through interpenetration. Only this dialogical interpenetration, that is also interpersonal, with the ultimate fundament of existence that guarantees their full existence explains the necessity for their personal interpenetration with their fellow human beings for their preservation in existence. For the inevitable need to speak and to respond to other persons shows that words, as means of personal interpenetration, have their ultimate origin in God. He is the supreme reasonable Word who addresses us through all persons who are created reasonable words. Otherwise we would not feel the unconditional need to respond to them.

The fact that the word is connected to the human person's being, necessarily communitarian, the person's dependence on the spoken words of his neighbor and the response to them, indicate the word's transcendental source which is personal and communitarian. When this is not acknowledged and the word is disconnected from its purpose of sustaining the community, each individual manipulates it for the deepening of social breakdown and for justifying any behavior that produces division. Only faith in the transcendental source and in the unifying purpose of the word, followed by fulfilling the divine Word's will, can sustain a correct and harmonious living among people. For this faith is confirmed through fulfilling the divine Word's will in deeds. In this way the word manifests its complete efficacy. The word bearing fruit in deed shows a faith that is more powerful and the word itself is more convincing. In the works of faith one feels more strongly the work of the Holy Spirit. This is why in the lives of saints Christ's presence is manifested in a totally efficient manner. Their lives are uninterrupted words of faith carried to the ultimate intensity. This is why they also produce in us a faith more powerful and a more accentuated perception of Christ's presence. To the extent to which we try harder to translate the faith into action, we increasingly feel Christ's presence within us. Christ's presence is imprinted so much in us that we cannot separate our life from Christ's life. "It is no longer I who live, but Christ lives in me" (Gal 2:20).

But this life, transformed by Christ and configured after His life, is not born nor is it strengthened in us from a word unaccompanied by prayer and not producing prayer in the one who hears it. The Apostles, and together with them the first Christians, alternated the preaching and reception of the word with prayer (Acts 2:42, 47). Prayer as dialogue with Christ indicates an acute conscience of His presence. St. Paul the Apostle inserts between words of teaching in his epistles supplications, hymns of praise and thanks to God, or he concludes them with such praises, also urging his listeners to pray (Rom 16:17; 2 Cor 13:7, 13; Col 3:16; Eph 1:16, 18–19, 23–24; Php 4:6, 19–20, 25; 1 Th 5:17, 23, 25, 28).

The word of preaching is the word of God toward us and prayer is our word toward God, but nourished through the word of God toward us and by His working power within us. For prayer as a response to God's word has in it, as any other response, the power from the word that requires a response. In prayer we manifest our faith toward God, which came to be through His word. In prayer we show the courage given to us by His word or the word about Him to ask for what He assures us through His word. If God has entered into dialogue with us through the word, it is in prayer that we also enter into dialogue with Him. In prayer God has asked us to trust Him and also in prayer we respond to Him showing our trust and calling upon Him. Without prayer we would not be able to show the trust He asks from us. In prayer we feel closer to God than as a He about whom the priest talks: we feel Him as a Thou with whom we enter into a direct relationship. Without prayer it would seem that we avoided this relationship, which He seeks. Florensky described very impressively in the quotations mentioned above this experience of the direct presence of God in prayer.

But when a priest (or even a believer) speaks about God in God's name, having the experience of God's presence or in the spirit of responding to His commandment, which is the spirit of prayer, then the one hearing the word feels that through this word he is called by God or by Christ Himself.

Such a word is already a word intended for prayer. Through this word God also speaks to and through the one uttering it, but the person uttering the word toward God also speaks. However, in this case the word of God has preeminence. In any case, first God calls someone through the word, and then he calls God through prayer. Florensky did not mention this. If the human person is not called by God, faith is not awakened, neither is the tendency to address God born in him. God first calls Samuel, then He gives him the gift of knowing the future of the priest Eli and of power in all his words (1 Kg 3:18) together with the spirit of prayer. No one can keep the word of prayer unceasingly or of remembering God unless one feels intensely His presence and call, namely His Spirit. Only the one who is constantly compelled by the conscience that he is called by God can live his life as a service to Him. If I do not feel that I am first called as a "you" vis-à-vis God through His word, neither does He become a "Thou" of mine in prayer. I can only call "you" the one who also calls me "you," or I feel encouraged to enter the familiarity he offers me when I ask for something. If my desire to also call upon him did not originate through God's call through the priest or through someone else in the Church, this is a sign that faith was not yet born in me. In the prayer I address to God once He originates in me the faith through His word, I have the initiative. In true prayer I feel that God has awaited my prayer and He responds to it, filling me with joy, peace and the assurance of fulfilling my supplication. This is why oftentimes when I begin to pray, I feel that I am called beforehand, attracted and encouraged by God to address Him. He calls me to prayer and I have to respond to His call. He causes us to address Him with the sentiment and trust of the children for their father: "The Spirit Himself bears witness with our spirit that we are children of God" (Rom 8:16). And if, attracted by the fatherly love of God, we begin to pray, it is the Spirit who comes to our help in prayer. "Likewise the Spirit also helps in our weaknesses. For we do not know what we should pray for as we ought, but the Spirit Himself makes intercession for us with groanings which cannot be uttered" (Rom 8:26). God responds to my supplication, on the one hand, immediately, and on the other hand, later. God calls me to Supper when I also show my desire to partake of it and He offers me the goods of the Supper (Lk 14:16–24). The word of God addressed to me (sometimes through the preaching or the prayer of others, but sometimes in a direct manner) and my prayer to Him are immediately linked in a dialogue. The initiative of the dialogue in word belongs to God; in prayer it is usually mine. In God's word addressed to me I feel first of all as a "you" vis-à-vis God and I feel Him as a "Thou" addressing me; but at once I become "I" and God becomes for me a "Thou." The distance between my quality as "you" vis-à-vis God and the quality as "I" addressing Him, therefore the distance between His quality as "I" addressing me and as "Thou" whom I address, is so short that these qualities appear simultaneously, as in fact they do in all conversations.

This occurs both when the word begins and when the prayer begins. When I ascend to God through a supplication, He comes to meet me by responding to it. I at once pass from my quality as "I" who calls upon God to the sentiment as "you" toward whom God descends, so that I have simultaneously these two qualities, just as God becomes immediately from my "Thou" an "I" vis-à-vis me and I am filled with His grace.

The relation I-Thou between me and God, which can be at the same time or can immediately become the relation "I-you" between God and me, or the relation between me and God, is so strong and so intimate that it can also be called a "perichoresis" between me and Him, a reciprocal interiority, a come-and-go between God and me, being at the same time giver and receiver of love, God certainly being the first source of this reciprocal exchange.

Generally, I cannot be "I" without a "you," or a "you" without an "I" which means that my existence implies, as its fundament, God as my supreme and original "You" or "I" which constitutes me as "I" and as "you," qualities without which I cannot exist. Since my "you" exists as an "I" that speaks to me and I exist as an "I" that speaks to him, or as a "you' who must listen to his word and he as a "you" who listens to my word, the word is the inevitable expression of this dual reality in which I am encompassed, of this perichoretic relationship.

At the basis of my word there is the need to respond as a "you" to the divine "I." I cannot exist without word because I do not exist alone, independent of my existence or all by myself. In my need to speak and to respond there is proof of God's existence as the supreme "I" Who brought me into existence and Who maintains my relationship with Him by speaking to me and me responding to Him as to an "I." I am permanently called by an "I" on whom I depend absolutely. But I become more clearly aware of this dependence in prayer in which I must call upon God as my supreme "I."

In God's word toward us His love for us is made known and felt, but not without our love for Him being awakened. In prayer we express our dependence on and our affection for Him, but not without feeling the response of His love to that prayer. Through both of these we enter the spiral of the ever-ascending motion in the communication between God and us. For prayer itself, as a response to the word of God, is also His gift as well as our response to His word and gift. In prayer we show that we are not passive to the gift of faith awakened through word. In prayer is shown that the word of God toward us has brought forth fruit and keeps working in us through His Holy Spirit. In and through prayer our thanks and trust resulting from His word and from His Holy Spirit return to Him, but also new gifts from God for us are poured forth as through outstretched hands toward Him. For when we raise our hands and heads in prayer toward Him, we raise our being that is open to Him and detached from all that is foreign to Him, not only to offer ourselves to Him but also to receive from Him the gifts He pours forth on us.

But just as the faith of the individual is weakened when it is for too long outside the relation with the faith of the church community or away from Christ who speaks through many others who believe, so is his prayer when it is not strengthened by communal prayer or by the prayer of others, even if after he has advanced much in the power of prayer, he may attain in his personal prayer deeper levels in his immersion into the relationship with God. The most efficient union between the prayer rising toward God and the descent of the Holy Spirit is achieved in Mysteries, when the prayer is offered by the priest in the name of the Church for those who come with a conscientious preparation for accepting this descent.

Through the Mysteries Christ's presence finds abode in those who receive them, permanently in certain Mysteries and long-lasting in others. In this instance the priest's prayer is the prayer of the entire Church. Through this prayer there is also manifested the desire of those who want to receive the Mysteries to offer or sacrifice themselves totally to God, and through the descent of the Holy Spirit the sacrifice is accepted and sanctified, for the descending Spirit is the Spirit of the sacrificed Christ Who wants to make us like Him, if we also want that.

In order for us to better understand the more intense and more durable presence of Christ established as a sacrifice and placing ourselves as sacrifices in the Mysteries through the prayer of the Church and also our own prayer, we should analyze further the relation between the word calling us to unity with the sacrificed Christ and prayer as our sacrificial offering in the assembly of the community of believers as sacrifices.

As we stated above, even though prayer is a means of a more deeply felt experience of the sacrificed Christ's presence and work, it cannot happen without the word. Prayer is the fire that kindles and takes up to heaven our sacrificed being, but this fire is the flame that bursts out from the warmth of faith brought into the soul by the Holy Spirit through the word. By maintaining faith, the word continuously gives more impulses for the outburst of the flame of prayer. For the word is inspired from or describes the loving works of Christ as God incarnate, works that become a content of a more inflammable knowledge that produces an increasingly hotter flame in the form of prayer in which our being is offered as a sacrifice to God together with Christ, His Son who became man and unites Himself with us through the word. The word places in increasingly brighter reliefs that produce more warmth the limitless goodness of God manifested in Christ, and prayer kindles our desire to offer our being to Him as thanksgiving for this goodness, in the likeness and from the power of Christ. Prayer is more apophatic than the word, for in its warmth the effect of the word has reached its climax as well as God's love that kindled our love. It is the flame that is kindled in the bosom of our being, but the coals were lit by the word about the works of Christ pervading us with the warmth of the Holy Spirit. In the word, God is experienced as soliciting or claiming our love on the basis of the revelation of His love toward us. This is why in prayer the love with which we respond to God is felt not only as our deed, but also as the fruit of God's love.

On the other hand, being the expression of our love and trust in God, prayer has also the function of deepening the content of faith or of the experience of God Who is infinite love.

Prayer follows the word, but the word also follows prayer, which enriches and brings warmth to the word, for in prayer one experiences God more deeply, and also Christ's love manifested in His incarnation, sacrifice, resurrection and ascension as well as in His coming to us through His Holy Spirit. Prayer is kindled more and more by means of the word and the word is increasingly and more deeply illumined by prayer. This role of prayer of bringing to fruition and of illuminating the word determines St. John Chrysostom to place prayer first and then the word, certainly for those who are already members of the Church, though not for those who do not yet know of Christ; or rather for those who, even being part of the Church, are colder and do not know much about Christ and do not ask through prayer to understand more from the words about Him: "Prayer stands in the first place; then comes the word of instruction. And that is what the apostles said: 'Let us devote ourselves to prayer and the ministry of the word' (Acts 6:4). Paul does this when he prays at the beginnings of his epistles so that, like the light of a lamp, the light of prayer may prepare the way for the word. If you accustom yourselves to pray fervently, you will not need instruction from your fellow servants because God himself, with no intermediary, enlightens your mind."[154]

Corresponding to these words, during the Holy Liturgy a candle holder (the candle of prayer) is carried before the Gospel book and the priest prays before the reading of the Gospel: "Illumine our hearts, O Master, the lover of mankind, with the pure light of Thy divine knowledge and open the eyes of our mind to the understanding of the teachings of Thy Holy Gospel." Based on the knowledge of the Gospel, in the same prayer one asks for a purer life. Thus, it is not only the prayer that precedes the word, but also the word of the Gospel strengthens the prayer. These two meet reciprocally more fully when they are performed in the church, in the community, not in an individualistic isolation.

In any case, the word and the prayer complement each other. Moreover, each must have something from the other.

This is why preaching must not be absent in the Church, just as the spirit of prayer in preaching must not be absent either, but they should always be together. St. Paul the Apostle says: "Take heed to yourself and to the doctrine. Continue in them, for in doing this you will save both yourself and those who hear you" (1 Tim 4:16). This is about a word intended to help others to be saved, a word conveyed "in love, in spirit, in faith, in purity" (1 Tim 4:13), from the priest's conscience to have been called through grace to preach. It is about a word that irradiates the conviction of the preacher that salvation came through Christ. Or, "Preach the word! Be ready in season and out of season. Convince, rebuke, exhort, with all longsuffering and teaching" (2 Tim 4:2). St. Paul the Apostle also says: "Pray without ceasing" (1 Th 5:17).

Thus, the reading of God's word from the Gospel and the epistles of the Apostles is an integral part of the Holy Liturgy. Even the content of prayers from the Liturgy comes from the Holy Scripture. They are the word of God assimilated within the faithful's being and used as foundation for prayer.[155] The word of Scripture itself is interwoven with the prayer. For when God communicates it, the human person is so impressed by it that he often passes from the communication of God's word, or from God's works, to prayer of thanksgiving, of praise and of supplication toward God.

But the Holy Fathers were not content only with the reading of the words from the Scripture during the Holy Liturgy, but they always preached to interpret, to apply and to discover the endless depths of God's word, but also to warm up the prayers of the Liturgy by explaining the word and also to kindle even more the prayers of the liturgical community. This is why the priest must always preach within the frame of the Liturgy. When the preached word is offered un-falsified and conveys the whole Christ found in the Church, "the same Spirit speaks through the mouth of the Apostles in the Holy Scripture and of their successors when they preach."[156]

According to St. Symeon of Thessalonica, "the priest or the hierarch who preaches the word is the mouth of God and worthy of Christ doing an exceptional thing, more obligatory than all others."[157] "The word of teaching, obligatory and needed, is the work of the spirit entrusted to the hierarch. In the prayer from the ordination of a priest and of a hierarch one asks that they preach the Gospel of the Kingdom and officiate the holy service (*ierourgein*) of the word of truth." For, if in the prayer of the priest and in his actions of officiating the Mysteries, Christ Himself prays and works, in the same manner the priest's words are those spoken by Christ. If during the hostile olden times, when the priests did not have a theological education and candidates for priesthood learned only to officiate the worship services and to read the prayers associated with them, why do they nowadays study theology if not to communicate by word Christ's teaching to the faithful? Why would they keep to themselves or forget the education they received? In the awe experienced by the priest out of his conscience that through him Christ communicates His word is shown, on the one hand, that he is different than Christ and, on the other hand, that he must place himself with all his responsibility at Christ's disposal as a serving instrument for communicating His word. He lives as a "you" of Christ, called to preach and he experiences Christ as "I" who himself preaches, but he also lives as an "I" who asks from Christ the power to preach Him with saving effect. If the priest is aware that he speaks in the name of Christ, he would not boast with the power irradiating from his word, for where the name of the Lord is mentioned He is also present as the One who preaches; the priest thus feels responsible as an efficient and authentic instrument of Christ's word and power. The more humble the priest, the more effective is he in his word, for he shows that he experiences Christ Himself as operating in him. Precisely in the priest's awe full of humility toward Christ, Who is experienced as operating in him as an instrument, the faithful realize that the priest feels that it is Christ Who speaks through him, something that is transmitted to them as well.

It is worth mentioning the strong connection between the sermon and the Holy Liturgy, as well as its characteristic as holy. The preaching of the sermon in church during the Holy Liturgy contributes to this characteristic, as well as to the quality as priest, or as being consecrated, of the one preaching.[158]

"One must especially put in bold relief the mystagogical character of the sermon. This consists not only in remembering the Scriptures, but also in the fact that it helps to introduce the faithful to the sacred, mystical acts that are officiated."[159]

But the inner connection between word and prayer is shown not only in the fact that the word accompanies the prayer, but also in the characteristic as word of prayer itself. And the highest form of prayer is the epikleptic one. Generally, prayer produces a more accentuated and more affective feeling of God than the word. And the prayer that produces the highest degree of feeling God's presence is the epikleptic prayer (of invoking the Holy Spirit) through which the grace of a certain Mystery descends on certain matter, through the priest's gestures, or it transforms the bread and wine into the body and blood of the Lord.

The Greek professor Phountoulēs, considering this other mode of using the word of God in the Liturgy as the third (in addition to the word from Scripture and from the sermon; we consider it as the fourth, after the one from Scripture, from the sermon and from prayer in general), affirms that this shows the creative power of the divine word. "Its specific characteristic lies precisely in the creative power of the divine word."[160]

We consider important this gradation of the divine word up to the form of prayer, which reaches the highest degree in the epiklesis prayer. But, on the other hand, it seems that he makes too great a distinction between the preached word and the word as prayer, especially as epiklesis prayer. For he says: "There [in its other modes] the human person hears the word as it was spoken and as it worked in the past. Here the Word activates directly at the present time. Now the salvation of the people is worked out through the word."[161] This power of the word through the Mysteries produces the indelible (*anaphairetos*) sanctification of persons—as it is the one of those who believe through Baptism, of priests through ordination, of monks through the service of tonsure, and of those who marry through the service of marriage—and of matter—as it is that of the bread and wine in the divine Eucharist, of water in Baptism, of chrism and oil from the Holy Unction, of the consecration of churches, of vessels, of vestments, of holy icons."[162] "For whatsoever the Holy Spirit has touched, is surely sanctified and changed."[163]

Prof. Phountoulēs considers that the almost exclusive emphasis in the East on the work of the Holy Spirit in the Mysteries was born out of the Holy Fathers' effort from the second half of the fourth century to defend the divinity of the Holy Spirit against the pneumatomachi. In fact, he says that the affirmation of the work of the Holy Spirit is implied in the work of the Word.[164]

Prof. Phountoulēs sees in the activities of consecration and transformation an extension of the acts performed by the Savior while He was on earth. "This work of the Word in the Mysteries is compared by the Fathers with the two of the sacred actions of the Word of God known from history: on the one hand, the creation of the world and, on the other hand, the incarnation of the Word from the Virgin through the word of the angel, concomitant with the coming of the Holy Spirit."[165] Just as the words at creation "let there be light" are continually fulfilled, but not without a process of nature, and as the words "grow and multiply" are continually fulfilled, but not without the union between a man and a woman in marriage, so do the words of Christ from the Mystical Supper: "Do this in remembrance of Me" extend their power to the Eucharistic transformation, but only through the operation of the priest. This is what Nicholas Cabasilas says.[166]

"According to this interpretation, the entire performing activity of the Mysteries has in itself the power springing up from the words and acts of the Savior Himself; but it is completed in every holy act separately in its extension through the priest's word by which God the Word Himself speaks and acts. Thus, at ordination, the Lord Himself ordains the priests through the ordaining hands of the successors of the Apostles; at Baptism, the Word Himself offers new birth; at Confession, Christ Himself gives forgiveness; at the Holy Unction, through the words of the priest, Christ Himself heals the sick through the blessed oil; at Marriage, the true Word Himself who has established the earth blesses and strengthens through the words of the priest the conjugal union."[167]

What we would like to point out first is that Christ also performs a certain operation through the words and prayers before the act of officiating the Mysteries. These words and prayers represent not just the human prayer of the faithful for the understanding of the Mysteries to be officiated and to be received by bringing to mind those things said and done by Christ while He was on earth. "The sacramental of the word" which is spoken of as the priest's responsibility at his ordination, is more than a simple remembrance of those things spoken and done back then by the Savior. Prof. Phountoulēs has said this as well.

Between the words of the Lord and the prayers before the transformation at the Liturgy—to dwell a bit more on this—and the act of the Eucharistic transformation, we are to see the distinction that we also see between the presence of someone speaking to us and his gestures toward us in a direct way or through things that he touches first; or between the presence of someone appearing to us on the horizon as he approaches and our embracing of him. There is a gradation, not a discontinuity between these two. Christ Who speaks to us invisibly through the priest or to Whom we speak when we pray to Him—not without the help of His Holy Spirit—is not only a Christ of remembrance, but One who is present in various degrees of intensity, even active in us in a certain way. This takes place in the relationships among people as well.

We feel a certain power within us of the one speaking to us as a power that produces either consolation, strength and joy, or sadness, pain, unpleasantness and courage toward good deeds before us or controlling the tendencies toward evil. And when we ask for something, we either thank the one constantly showing his love or we praise him, and we feel in him a benevolent opening and a certain joy. In no case do we feel totally separated from him.

Much more so does this occur when Christ speaks to us through the priest, or when we ask Him something, or when we thank and praise Him through the hymns of the Liturgy, listening to the exhortations of the priest or joining him in prayers.

But not only when someone speaks to us, but also when someone touches us in a friendly manner, or embraces us, or gives us something prepared especially for us, do we feel that a greater intimacy has been established between that person and us. Verbal communication leaves a distance between the one who speaks and us; that distance or space needs to be filled with a greater closeness. Similarly, the request, the thanks or the praise we offer them, which strengthens the communication on our part, leaves room for a greater approach. In such a greater intimacy Christ communicates to us a much greater power when He touches us through the priest in the Mysteries, either through the priest's hands or through the matter which the power of His pure Person penetrates, thus purifying and sanctifying it while He envelops us in it. The first case takes place in the Mysteries of Confession, Marriage and Ordination, while the second one in the Mysteries of Baptism, Chrismation and Holy Unction.

But in the Mystery of the Holy Eucharist, Christ imprints in matter not only His purifying, sanctifying and strengthening power in order for Him to communicate with us through it, but He transforms the bread and the wine into His very body and blood, the source of all His power, fully overwhelming them with His presence in order to give them to us to eat and drink and to appropriate them.

Thus, through His words and through our prayer, the power He communicates to us works fully only at the moment of communication or of prayer. But the power He imprints in us with His touch through the priest or through the matters that He penetrates, or through His body and blood, is more durable. If we confess our sins frequently asking for forgiveness, it is because we have committed other sins than the ones already forgiven, and broken the communion with Him. And if we partake frequently of His body and blood, it is because we want to increasingly unite ourselves with Him.

However, the word or Christ's presence through the word remains also in the acts by which He offers Himself more efficiently, but not just as word with an instructing power, but as word that explains and deepens spiritually the communion by touching the believing persons either through the priest or through the sanctified matters or through His body and blood. The union of Christ with the believers is more fully accomplished through His contacts with them through the priest; but the word accompanying those contacts more effectively makes understandable what Christ wants from us and what He accomplishes in us through them. When I embrace someone, I am more united with him than when I just speak to him. But if I also speak to him words of love explaining the feeling shown through the act of embracing, this increases the evidence of my love for him or makes more transparent the act of embracing by explaining my feeling attached to it. Only the revealing word of the other opens to me the originality and uniqueness of his way of being and of manifesting himself: his person. Through this revelation in word his presence becomes transparent. His countenance, gesture and action are illumined through the inner word by which he appears as what he really is: an expression of the way in which a person as a distinct existence becomes present in the relationship with me.[168] Only the word of that person proves that he treats me as a distinct and understanding person with whom he communicates.

The person makes himself present differently and offers himself differently in his visible manifestation, in word, in gesture and in his gift. The degrees of intensity in which he becomes present are also different according to the forms of expression and manifestation. For example, a festive dinner represents the most intensive degree of the way for the community to become present (actual) in celebration. In the Liturgy there are Mysteries and sacramentals, there is the word of the Scripture and the confession of the Apostolic faith, but also their explanation through the sermon, prayers and hymns with various contents. All the forms of expression are complementary ways for the Church to become present and active, or rather for her Head to be present and active within the Church. If one part is removed from the whole in favor of another, even if it be the most intensive, the reality of Christ's presence and work is weakened. This was clearly seen in the fixation of Christ's presence in the Church too exclusively in the eucharistic images, as was the case in the counter-Reformation piety, as the Catholic theologian quoted above stated with regret.[169]

In this sense, another Catholic theologian, Walter Kasper, pleads for acknowledging the word as a means to communicate Christ's power and to take the Mysteries out of the narrowness of magical-juridical formalism. He sees in the combination between the words of the priest and his gestures in the Mysteries a more efficient closeness of God in the concrete situation of the human person, among which the crucial situations receive a more efficacious help through the Mysteries in the strict sense of the word. He says: "Word and Sacrament make up between them one unity and one whole. One cannot begin to define their relationship from their distinction, but the unity comprising them must be understood as two phases of one whole . . . . This unity can also be seen within the framework of the traditional teaching on the Sacraments. According to this, the word is sacramental, it is *sacramentum audibile*."[170] The Mystery is the visible word, *verbum visibile*.

"Just as the sacrament is *signum efficax* (effective sign) so the word is *verbum efficax*. All that can be essentially said about the sacrament can also be said about the word: each one is an operative memory of Christ's saving work as its extension and anticipation of the eschaton. Just as the word is sacrament, so the opposite is true: the sacrament is verbally structured. The word is the soul (the form, the forming power) of the sacrament and as such has the function to imprint and to bring into bold relief the meaning of the sacrament and thus the function of consecration. Therefore, the sacrament is a different form of preaching the word"[171] (1 Cor 11:26).

However, this does not mean that the word can be replaced with the Mystery and vice versa. "It is more correct to say that there is a reciprocal perichoresis between word and sacrament. Essentially, both refer to each other and are strengthened reciprocally. The word refers to a human situation that finds its ultimate fulfillment in the sacrament... They both form a wholeness .... The sacrament must have a verbal characteristic [*worhaft*] and the word must be strengthened [rendered in a concrete form] through the sacrament .... Normally, the sacrament involves the human person entirely and more fully in his corporeal-concrete being, in his communitarian relationship than the simple word .... The ministry of the Church by the Church through word and sacrament must again become more humane .... The ministry of salvation on behalf of the Church must be detached from the obsolete and incomprehensible formulas and from the sacrosanct rigidity."[172] Just as God descended through the biblical revelation not only to the human understanding in general, but also to everyone's way of speaking and thinking, so should the Church now approach more and more the people of today and their needs. The seven Mysteries are there to help the human person during the crucial situations of his life, but one must not make a separation between them and the need for help in every situation of his life. "Since the characteristic of the entire human and Christian life is one of opportunity and of visible sign in which one can offer a divine help, the proper forms of the sacraments receive their whole meaning."[173] For if the body is a visible sign and a means of getting into the soul and of its manifestation, any act with a sanctifying intention and power that touches the body has a characteristic as Mystery or sacramental that pervades the entire being of the human person.

The word of God, the word spoken in the name of the Lord, and the very name of the triune Persons when spoken with faith are means of God's work; they are even much more so when they are supplemented with gestures as signs of love for God's love and closeness to human beings. But these gestures are made even more transparent and more efficient in their loving significance through the words that explain them. Or rather the words render the gestures more humane just as the gestures make the words more humane. Only together do they render God's incarnation and His saving works (crucifixion, resurrection) more comprehensible and more felt as He wants to show through them His permanent closeness and help toward human beings.

While the Reformation accorded an almost exclusive efficiency to the word, and Catholicism has separated too much the word and the prayer from the Mysteries as well as the Eucharist from the entire Liturgy, from this point of view Orthodoxy has maintained a balance. The believers benefit from the Holy Liturgy even if they do not partake [of the Holy Eucharist]. And not just a didactic or sentimental benefit, but they also benefit from Christ's operation in it as they encounter Him through His word or the word about Him, through prayers, hymns and through the transmission of His power, especially at the moment of the transformation as well as from His presence on the altar after the transformation.[174]

Christ's work in the Liturgy is not separated from the work of the Holy Spirit. Western denominations see almost exclusively Christ alone, the Protestants through the word of the sermon and the Catholics through the act of transubstantiation of the bread and wine by the simple repetition of Christ's words of institution.

In fact, Christ is present and working in the entire Liturgy in various degrees and modes together with the Holy Spirit. Where not only the word of Christ or about Him is present, but also His operation in the hearts of believers for their sanctification, the Holy Spirit is also present. The word belongs to Christ, but His power penetrates hearts, moves, sanctifies and warms them toward prayer through the Holy Spirit. When a Mystery is officiated one does not only repeat Christ's words, but one also invokes the Holy Spirit through prayer. For when a human person prays, the Holy Spirit is in that person as well. Generally, everything is asked from the Holy Trinity, which is always praised. The worthiness to stand before the Holy Table in the Altar and to offer to God the unbloody sacrifice is considered by the priest as coming from Christ, or from the Father through the Holy Spirit. The Holy Spirit is considered as the One through whom Christ works in the priest or in the believers, for it is through the Holy Spirit that Christ actualizes His saving work operated in the course of time.

Even from the beginning of the Liturgy the priest asks for the help of the Holy Spirit through the prayer "O, Heavenly King." The Holy Spirit is invoked more directly as the Liturgy progresses toward the act of Christ's sacrifice. In the prayer after the entrance with the Holy gifts, the priest prays: "that the Holy Spirit may come down upon us, upon these gifts here offered and upon Thy people." Even before that, once the gifts are placed on the Holy Table, the priest says at the prompting of the deacon: "The Holy Spirit may come down upon you and the power of the Most High may overshadow you," and the deacon responds: "May the same Spirit work together with us all the days of our life." They ask for the Holy Spirit not just for some transitory effects in them, but for His operation in them during their whole life.

During the epiklesis (in the invocation of the Spirit for the transformation of bread and wine into the body and blood of the Lord), the priest asks from the Father to send the Holy Spirit as the One through whom the Father Himself transforms the bread and the wine into the body and blood of His Christ. The transformation is not just Christ's work, even if the bread and the wine are transformed into His body and blood, just as He became incarnate not without the work of the Spirit within the Virgin. The act of transformation begins with the Father Himself, but the Father accomplishes it through the Spirit, just as the creation began and was accomplished. The Father and the Spirit are not unaware of what happens with the body and blood of Christ, or with the bread and the wine set forth for transformation. The work of salvation achieved through the incarnation of the Son of God, through His crucifixion and resurrection and through its being transmitted into our being, is a joint work of the Holy Trinity. Each Person of the Trinity plays its distinct part in this work, but as a whole it is a joint operation. The Son does not accomplish our salvation alone. When the Son accepts the kenosis by becoming like us so to achieve salvation on our behalf, He implicitly accepts a certain willing passivity, which reaches its climax in accepting the state of sacrifice extended into the eucharistic transformation. This is implied in the state as Lamb which He accepts. The cause of our sin lies in our will to solve everything by ourselves, as if everything would depend on us. Full communion cannot be realized where everyone believes that there is no need of someone else in order to reach happiness. The Son becomes man because the Father asks Him and in order to fulfill the Father's will; and He becomes incarnate in cooperation with the Spirit. The Son remains obedient to the Father in the entire work for our salvation in order to make all of us the Father's children. At the same time He has within Himself the Holy Spirit who keeps Him as Son united with the Father, so that the Son may give us the Spirit who makes us feel as adoptive children of the Father. The Father has the initiative not only of His Son's incarnation, but also of the continuous transformation of the bread and wine into His body and blood, because He sent Him to appropriate them. He does this through the Holy Spirit so that by this He may also give us the Spirit as children together with His Son. The Son accepts permanently this transposition of His in a state of sacrifice that fulfills His destiny as perfect man vis-à-vis God and so that He may instill that state in us.

The Son Himself spoke even before His incarnation about His obedience to the Father in all the saving work for us through the words of the Psalmist, as St. Paul the Apostle says: "Therefore, when He came into the world, He said: 'Sacrifice and offering You did not desire, but a body You have prepared for Me. In burnt offerings and sacrifices for sin You had no pleasure. Then I said, 'Behold, I have come to do Your will, O God'" (Heb 10:5–7; Ps 39:9). Along the same line, St. Paul the Apostle says: "Though He was a Son, yet He learned obedience by the things which He suffered" (Heb 5:8), in order to make us perfect by learning from Him the obedience of children. There cannot be perfection where there is no obedience, since in that case there is no love either. Therefore, even though He was the Son of God, Christ did not take on His own the office of High Priest, which as an office of self-sacrifice is also combined with true glory, but He received it from the Father. "And no man takes this honor to himself, but he who is called by God, just as Aaron was. So also Christ did not glorify Himself to become High Priest, but it was also said to Him: 'You are My Son, today I have begotten You.' As He says in another place: 'You are a priest forever according to the order of Melchizedek'" (Heb 5:4–6). But the calling of Christ as a High Priest and His glorification as man is done through the Spirit (Jn 7:39).

As the most accentuated act of sanctifying particular material objects deemed worthy of becoming the body and blood of the incarnate Son of God so that we may also be sanctified through the partaking of them, it is natural that the transformation be made through the

Holy Spirit. The Holy Spirit transforms the bread into a pneumatized body in which the senses are entirely spiritualized, even deified, without ceasing to be human. When the priest places the particle with the initials IS from the lamb transformed into the Lord's body into the chalice containing the Lord's blood, he says: "The fullness of the Holy Spirit." The presence of the Holy Spirit found in Christ's body intensifies up to plenitude the presence of the Spirit found in the blood. When the warm water is placed in the chalice, the priests says: "The warmth of the Holy Spirit." By partaking from the chalice, the believers will receive along with the Lord's body and blood the Holy Spirit who will warm up their faith. There is a special connection between the Holy Spirit and faith. The Holy Spirit is a real Person of the Holy Trinity, thus having an objective reality. But His objective reality produces the deepest subjective sensibility. Even though the Lord's body and blood are an objective reality, their objectivity is a factor that generates faith and irradiates from them the Holy Spirit. God and all things that He fills with the Holy Spirit represent the strongest objectivity irradiating the most accentuated sensibility, both being manifested in faith. The more fervent someone's faith is, the more certain one is of God's presence through the Holy Spirit. This is why after the transformation the priest prays for those who will partake of the Lord's body and blood that they may be unto them "for communion with the Holy Spirit" Who is in them.

The power of the Holy Spirit that transforms the bread and wine into the Lord's body and blood is found in them even before their transformation. In this sense, Christ, who is filled with the Holy Spirit in His body and blood, also operates at the transformation of the bread and wine into them.

Christ, with whom the priest in solidarity with the community is in a dialogue in which Christ communicates His power and the priest together with the community open themselves up through their prayer filled with faith and the sentiment that comes from it, is throughout the entire Liturgy the Christ who sacrificed Himself to the Father and rose with His body filled with the Holy Spirit. He now advances toward being placed again on the Holy Table in this permanent state of sacrifice offered to the Father, so that when the believers share in it they may also offer themselves to the Father as sacrifices purified through Christ's body and blood that are filled or transfigured by the Spirit through the resurrection.

In conclusion, we could sum up the modes of Christ's presence in the Liturgy, perceived by those who believe and not perceived by those who do not believe, as follows:

1. Through personal activities and circumstances of life. This is a presence through words given material forms, a presence through the power placed in these words as they are materialized and maintained in existence.

2. Through Christ's words from the Gospel, or through those spoken by the priest, received in faith through the prayers of praise, thanksgiving and supplication of the believers recited individually or sung by the community. This is also a presence through power albeit through a more direct power, because the priest's conscience as well as that of the believers is directed more specifically and with more feeling toward Christ as in a real dialogue.

3. Through the words and gestures of the priest spoken and made as sacramentals and Mysteries. It is a more accentuated and enduring presence through gifts and graces. Through them Christ's work in creation is strengthened. The faith through which the believers ask and receive these gifts is manifested through prayer.

The presence through works resulting from the words of prayers has various degrees, according to the concentration and persistence in prayer. In addition, in the prayers of the Liturgy the degrees of Christ's presence increase according to the advance of the priest and of the faithful people within the ambiance of prayers and of Christ's approaching the moment of transformation.

It must also be mentioned that Christ, present and active through the prayers and appeals for the Holy Spirit in Mysteries and sacramentals, has imprinted in Himself the saving works effected by Him up to the resurrection and ascension so that He may also transmit them to us in various degrees.

4. The presence with His body and blood in the form of bread and wine is one in which Christ is actually most emphatically as a Person together with the Father and the Holy Spirit, because He offers us not just an operation through His body, but His very Body sacrificed and risen, as it is now entreated. Christ, who acted through the Liturgy through His word and through the prayers of the priest and of the community, is intensifying now to the extreme through the irradiation of

the Holy Spirit His efficiency upon the matter of the bread and wine in order to offer Himself under their species in an act of supreme and overwhelming love that transforms them, with His own Body and Blood as sacrifice both to the Father and to the faithful so that these may also offer themselves together with Him and from His power to the Father and to each other.

Being aware of this supreme offering of Christ to the Father through the Spirit and at the same time to the faithful in this act, the priest specifically asks the Father to send the Holy Spirit through the epiklesis to transform the bread and the wine into the body and blood of "His Christ."

ON THE HOLY LITURGY

CHAPTER ONE

Proskomedia or the Service of the Pre-Offering of the Gifts for Christ's Holy Sacrifice

The gifts that will be transformed into the body and blood of the Lord together with their specific offering to God toward the end of the Holy Liturgy, are brought beforehand by the faithful and are prepared through a special service before the Liturgy of the catechumens.

Beginning from the middle of the nineteenth century the opinion was that the Proskomedia was developed as a distinct part of the Holy Liturgy, after the institution of the catechumenate was dissolved, when a brief preparation of the gifts for the transformation, before the Great Entrance, was moved from the beginning of the Liturgy of the faithful to the beginning of the Liturgy in general. In connection with this, the opinion was that until this change the brief service of the Proskomedia contained only the sacrifice of the Lamb. Only after this change, as the idea that the Liturgy is also a representation of the Savior's course of life was born, the theme of His birth and thereby that of the sacrifice of the Child was introduced.[175]

But Robert Taft presented arguments, considered decisive by Felmy, that such a shift of the Proskomedia did not take place and the commemoration of the Savior's birth has been connected with the commemoration of the Lamb's sacrifice.[176] Among other arguments, Taft also presents the one that in the East when the believers brought the gifts (the prosphora) their names were written down. Jerome already said this in the fourth century. But this writing down of the names could not take place except at the beginning of the Liturgy. (Today, the names of the living and the dead are brought by the believers themselves.)

Regarding the antiquity of the theme of the Lord's Nativity and thus of the sacrificed Child, Felmy presents the apophthegmata 7 and 8 from the Paterikon, where one finds the story of how the sacrificed Child is shown to an old man who doubted the transformation. These apophthegmata, found under the name of Abba Daniel, date back to the fifth–sixth century.[177]

Felmy sees this combination between the theme of the Child and that of the sacrificed Lamb as based in Isaiah 53, where the Savior is foreseen as a Child, but as a Child who allows himself to be sacrificed like a silent Lamb. Another reason for the presentation of Jesus as being sacrificed at the age of a child and not of man is the text from Genesis 22 about the sacrifice of Isaac by Abraham who agrees, as an image of the heavenly Father, to sacrifice his son whom God allows to be replaced with a lamb.[178] One can add that the combination between the incarnation of Jesus and the sacrificed lamb in the Proskomedia is verified by even older information.

First we mention an image of Jesus's birth in a reliquary brought to Rome from Bethlehem and kept there, dating from the sixth century. In this image Christ is depicted in the manger as a sacrifice. Wilhelm Nyssen says about this image: "Under the vault of the cave the manger of the Child resembles the architecture of an altar. The Child himself has the image of an indescribable sacrifice that is offered... The early Church affirms not only through her icons but also through the words of St. Paul the Apostle that the particular moments of salvation that occurred on earth always comprise the whole of salvation, namely the coming of the Lord into the world and the changing of the world through His coming."[179]

Nyssen quotes a text from St. Irenaeus (end of the second century) in which St. Irenaeus sees the sacrifice of Christ implied in His birth: "The disobedience of the forefather Adam threw us all into the bonds of death. This is why it was necessary and right that the bonds of death be destroyed through the One who became man. Since death had dominion over the body, it was necessary and right that it be subjected also through the body and thus man might be liberated from its slavery. The Word became incarnate so that the body, through which sin came to dominate and subjugate, might become itself again. This is why God took the same body as that of Adam, so that He can fight for humans and through Adam's body might conquer the one through whom Adam was defeated."[180]

For the implication in the past of the sacrifice of Jesus as Lamb in His birth there is also evidence in the hymns of St. Ephrem the Syrian from the fourth century. Speaking about the Lord's birth, St. Ephrem sees implied in it the reconciliation through the cross and our being nourished with His body sacrificed in the Eucharist: "Your day is the intermediary and guarantee of peace.... Your day has reconciled heaven with the earth, for in it heaven descended to the things of earth... Your birthday can reconcile the Just One who was aggrieved on account of our sins.... Your day has forgiven us thousands of sins, for with it came Your mercy upon sinners.... The early ripe grape is this day in which the cup of salvation was hidden.... Joseph filled numerous chambers with wheat, but they were emptied during the famine. But the bread yielded one true ear, the heavenly and eternal bread... The bread which the First-born had broken in the desert was consumed and did not last even though He multiplied it.... But He broke a new bread which all the nations and generations will not finish... The seven breads which He broke were consumed and finished as were the five breads. But the one bread which He broke overcame creation for no matter how much is divided, it keeps on multiplying.... He has filled the jars with much wine that was drunk and finished. But the power of the drinking from the cup which He gave, however little, is huge and interminable. It is a cup that receives in it all the wines and still its symbol is the same... The one bread which He broke has no boundary; and the cup that He mixed cannot be limited."[181]

These hymns of St. Ephrem can offer an explanation as to why Jesus is presented at the Proskomedia as sacrificed at the age of a child: since the Son of God was incarnate in order to save us through His sacrifice, His forthcoming sacrifice was implied in Him from the very moment of His birth as a man. The righteous Simeon saw this spiritually and this is why he told the Holy Virgin: "Yes, a sword will pierce through your own soul also" (Lk 2:35). And this is why the eyes of the Virgin gaze into the distance with unending pain to the death that the baby in her arms would suffer.

The reason why St. Ephrem insists on the quality as bread of the Child being born is that Christ declared Himself "the bread that came down from heaven" in relation to the promise that He would give His body to be partaken of. It is the bread that gives eternal life, contrary to the food that does not offer immortality (Jn 6:58). It is thus proper that even from His birth or from His descent on earth in the body, Christ be seen by the Church as the bread that came down from heaven, which is seen in the body as in a visible bread that came to nourish human beings in its quality as heavenly bread through His body as visible bread, full of His divinity as invisible bread. His body is precisely the means by which He offers Himself as the heavenly bread, and it was natural that this body be given to us in the form of bread so that it might most fittingly represent the heavenly bread.

In a special way, after Christ's sacrifice has been accomplished, His disciples and all Christians see imprinted in the Child Jesus everything that He would do for our salvation. They see that He was incarnate for the precise purpose of sacrificing Himself for us and offering Himself to us as heavenly bread through His body, as visible bread — the agent for the invisible one. They see that in His birth are potentially given His resurrection and the partaking of His body. In the manger of Bethlehem they see implied Golgotha and the upper room of the Mystical Supper. They also understand that Christ was born in Bethlehem since it means "the House of Bread," of the eucharistic bread that would be offered to us as body sacrificed on the cross.[182] This is why St. Paul the Apostle sees death on the cross as a continuation of the incarnation, which means that he sees implied in the incarnation the fulfillment of the model man through perfect obedience all the way to death: Christ "made Himself of no reputation, taking the form of bondservant, and coming in the likeness of men. And being found in appearance as a man, He humbled Himself and became obedient to the point of death, even the death on the cross" (Php 2:7–8).

Thus, if the Holy Liturgy is for us an actualization of Christ's saving work, which begins with the birth and ends with the death followed by the resurrection, it is natural that, once we know that Christ has gone through all these and that He makes them actual as the One in whom all these are imprinted, the Liturgy begins with His birth, but showing that it also implies His sacrifice.

The Church sees in Christ who is born not only the Lamb to be sacrificed, but also the One who conquered death through the death on the cross and was raised to the divine throne. Therefore, as the bread that came down from heaven, He bears on the bottom side of the Agnets the cut of the cross and on the upper side His name together with the word NIKA: Jesus Christ conquers. He forever conquers through the cross that remains imprinted within the depth of His being. Through the incarnation, the Son of God became for us the bread of life through the fact that He accepted the cross, but He also conquered it. All things are concentrated in Christ. Through the spear the agnets is not just separated from the prosphora as from the body of the Virgin, but also the death on the cross is thus prefigured. In the same way, the piercing of His side on the cross is prefigured.

As we now think of Christ or as we enter into relationship with Him, after He completed all His saving acts so that we may receive the power of all those acts, we begin with His birth, which we know potentially contains the cross and the resurrection.

Here are a few more hymns of St. Ephrem the Syrian that offer a new reason why the theme of the Nativity is linked from the beginning with that of Christ's sacrifice: "The most high became a Child and in him was hidden the treasure of wisdom, large enough to be sufficient for all."[183]

Thus we can see, as another reason for the theme of the Child depicted as sacrificed even in the Proskomedia, the will to be shown that from the Son of God's greatest humility — the humility of a Child — there begins the salvation of all or the power for the salvation of all. The humblest and most innocent one in his sacrifice was able to offer salvation to all. This is so because the saving powers did not come from Him as man, but from His divinity that is also present in the Eucharist.

We also mention that the theme of the sacrificed Child appears in the life of St. Gregory of Decapolis (beginning of the ninth century), who converts a Saracen after he has seen a sacrificed child both at the Proskomedia and during the Great Entrance as well as during the communion of the faithful.[184]

In connection with the theme of the Lord's Nativity at the Proskomedia, we can add that Christ is present in the Holy Liturgy not only from the moment of the transformation of the bread and wine in His body and blood. From this moment there begins His presence as the One who unites Himself with us, after He completed His saving work on earth and ascended into heaven, in the form of bread and wine. But until this union He somehow makes us His contemporaries on the path He completed on earth for us. Or rather He makes Himself our contemporary on this path that He covered. This journey together with us has in itself a certain mystical reality.

When a person has completed many acts, that person cannot be seen afterwards, if he is still alive, apart from all those acts. All of them are concentrated in that person and from them the actual identity of that person is known. There is no separation between the person and his events from the past. But when they are remembered they become in a certain way present to those who remember them. The past is somehow present, a fact that is characteristic of the Holy Liturgy, as has been specified in some of the older explanations. Thus, the Proskomedia is not only a preparation of the gifts that will be transformed into Christ's sacrifice, but also a certain pre-offering or pre-presence of the sacrificed Christ.

Nicholas Cabasilas specified more than any other commentator on the Holy Liturgy before him the distinction between Christ's presence before the transformation of the bread and wine into His body and blood and that which begins at this moment: "When these words have been said, . . . the splendid Victim, the Divine oblation, slain for the salvation of the world, lies upon the altar. For it is no longer the bread, which until now has represented the Lord's body, nor is it a simple offering, bearing the likeness of the true offering, carrying as if engraved on it the symbols of the Savior's Passion; it is the true Victim, the most holy Body of the Lord, which really suffered the outrages, insults and blows; which was crucified and slain, which under Pontius Pilate bore such splendid witness; . . . It is that Body and Blood formed by the Holy Spirit, born of the Virgin Mary, which was buried, which rose again on the third day, which ascended into heaven and sits on the right hand of the Father."[185]

However, one should not deduce from this that Nicholas Cabasilas thinks that at the Proskomedia there is only a "prefiguration and foretelling of Christ as in the Old Testament."[186] The "type" and "icon" of Christ at the Proskomedia are something else than His "type" in the Old Testament. In fact, even in the Old Testament there is a certain presence of the Word. St. Maximos the Confessor says that, before the visible coming in the flesh, the Word of God "was coming spiritually to the Patriarchs and the Prophets." The "prefiguration" in the Old Testament does not mean that there only His "image" exists, but that in the image He was there Himself.

The Proskomedia is officiated on the basis of the accomplished fact of Christ's incarnation and crucifixion and this incarnate and crucified Christ continues to be with those who believe in Him. When the priest thinks of this Christ a certain presence of Him is triggered, namely a presence through Christ's special work even in the Proskomedia, a work which does not produce the transformation of the bread and wine into His body and blood. If a simple prayer toward Christ puts us in a kind of relationship with Him, even more so do the acts of the Proskomedia. But if even in the icon there is a certain working presence of Christ, even more so must there be in the Proskomedia, which is also called "image" or "icon" of Christ. This is a certain presence of Christ who was born of the Virgin, was crucified and rose again. At the least, the Proskomedia has the characteristic of a sacramental or of a holy act of preparing the Sacrament of the Eucharist.

Nicholas Cabasilas says: "The consecration of the elements—the sacrifice itself—commemorates the death, resurrection, and ascension of the Savior, since it transforms these precious gifts into the very Body of the Lord, that Body which was the central figure in all these mysteries, which was crucified, which rose from the dead, which ascended into heaven. The ceremonies which precede the act of sacrifice symbolize the events which occurred before the death of Christ: his coming on earth, his first appearance and his perfect manifestation. Those which follow the act of sacrifice recall 'the promise of the Father', as the Savior himself called it: that is, the descent of the Holy Spirit upon the apostles, the conversion of the nations which they brought about, and their divine society. The whole celebration of the mystery is like a unique portrayal of a single body, which is the work of the Savior; it places before us the several members of this body, from beginning to end, in their order and harmony. That is why the psalmody, as well as the opening chants, and before them all that is done at the preparation of the offerings, symbolize the first period of the scheme of redemption. That which comes after the psalms—readings from the Holy Scriptures and so on—symbolizes the period which follows."[187] Only the work of Christ through the Holy Spirit can sanctify the believers.

Thus, the Proskomedia officiated by the priest out of the people's view represents Christ before His coming out to preach and to perform His saving acts. But it represents Christ who relives His private birth and life with a view toward His crucifixion. Therefore, even though He is not seen during this period portrayed at the Proskomedia, He is still active in the world and His work is felt by the priest who represents the inner circle of His family, of the righteous Simeon who sees Him as born but also as the One who will consent to be crucified; also the limited circle of Anne the prophetess, who sees Him as Savior, and of those close to His family who realized that "the child increased in wisdom and stature, and in favor with God and men" (Lk 2:52). Now His bodily organs were growing along with His human faculties so that they could serve as means of communication of His divine wisdom, and He increased His human experiences so they could capture and render in understandable human language the mystery of His divinity, as well as to show what stature can be reached by the human nature that has God as its hypostasis.

The fact that the priest's gestures during the Proskomedia symbolize Christ, Who by being born was going to be crucified, is also shown by His image as a Child in the chalice above the table of the Proskomedia, an image based on the vision of Alexander, the Patriarch of Alexandria. We, who already know Christ as crucified, are able to see Him as crucified in the Child being born. In Him these acts are no longer distant, but they constitute the plenitude of His Person accomplished as man. The acts from the past are concentrated in Him, swallowing up the temporal distances. The temporal acts are not lost in eternity, but they become co-eternal with eternity and their temporal order is changed into the order of value. Christ's sacrifice on the cross takes first place in the eternal dimension in which Christ lives after the resurrection, because it is the most valuable and most efficient communitarian and saving act. Nevertheless, the Proskomedia is distinct from the Holy Liturgy in that it has a less accentuated intensity of Christ's working presence.[188] This fact allows for the understanding of the procession with the Gospel and of its reading as Jesus Christ's coming out to preach even today.

Since Christ's birth and crucifixion constitute the basis of His permanent activity, including also within the Proskomedia and the Holy Liturgy, one may consider that Jesus is actually present with His entire activity both through the acts of the Proskomedia and those of the Holy Liturgy in various degrees. These two degrees of presence and of activity succeed each other, but sometime they overlap. In the eternal Christ the past, the present and the future are active, the distance between them having disappeared. The past, the present and the future are condensed, not separated. This fact is experienced by the faithful. They can experience all of Christ's acts both as present and as in the future. They can worship Christ who was crucified in the past as well as the Christ who is now crucified, and they can concentrate their gaze first upon the risen Christ, then upon Christ who is born and crucified. Christ's eternity is not empty of the acts performed by Him in time, but it is full of them, and they can be reversed according to the will and the experience of the faithful.

Just as in the Eucharistic transformation there is shown not only a past moment from the life of Christ, but also a present act, so in the preparation of the agnetz as an image of Christ who is born and crucified there is shown not only Christ's life unknown before His coming out to preach, namely not only this past period from His life is indicated, but also the actual characteristic of that period. The entire Holy Liturgy is not just a history of what Christ has done in the past, but also a presence of Christ who is working even now. In the Holy Liturgy everything is present, without the past being annulled. The separation between past and present is overcome. Christ is the same yesterday and today. Being in heaven, He is above the separations that are proper to time. In a spiritually advanced life, we ourselves do not live a present separated from the past and from the future. The more we grow older and spiritually advanced, the more our past acts done without realizing their significance and consequences become increasingly present and we dwell on them more. Within the present, the past is experienced even more fully and the future becomes present more powerfully as a warning and a hope. In other words, the future does not escape our sight with its efficiency projected on us. From here we have begun to enter the realm of eternity.

Even more so is Christ present in the form of the Agnetz, active in the present but full of experience from the past and prepared for future activity. Alongside Him is the Lord's Mother, together with all the departed with faith in Him, experiencing again the past and working full of hope for our salvation, and even all those who believe in Christ who are still alive. As they become more spiritually mature, all of them have a taste of Christ's eternity full of His past saving works that are also present in their activity All remember His birth and crucifixion and live with Him in the present the movement of His acts from the past as they advance toward their future effects on themselves. The mystery of the human being is also grounded in the fact that he is not closed off in the successive, interrupted and separated moments of time, but belongs more and more to eternity.

This will be seen in the following pages as we explain in their order the words and gestures of the priest during the Proskomedia.

The priest stands in the middle of the church facing the Sanctuary and asks God "to extend Your hand from the height of Your dwelling place to strengthen me for the service ahead of me so that by standing in front of the Holy Table I may be able without condemnation to offer the unbloody sacrifice." Thus the working power of God comes from this moment upon the priest and within his being. Then, upon entering the Sanctuary he makes three prostrations before the Holy Table, kisses the Holy Gospel, the Holy Cross and the Holy Table. The prostration is always three-fold, because God is Triune, and accompanied by the sign of the cross because the remembrance of Christ's cross must be with us every time we think of God. And the Holy Gospel, the Holy Cross and the Holy Table represent Christ who taught, was crucified and continues to offer until the end of the world the sacrifice for us (the sacrifice that is shown in the form of bread and wine on the Holy Table) before "the true tabernacle" (Heb 8:2) where "He always lives to make intercessions for us" (Heb 7:25).

Everything points to heaven's descent on earth. "The Lord's hand" descends from heaven upon the priest; by standing before the Holy Table that is seen, the priest stands in a real way before the unseen one in heaven where the eternally slain Lamb stands between the throne and the four living creatures and the elders (Rev 5:6).

The priest's three prostrations holding the vestments while saying the words "O, God cleanse me a sinner," and then again at the beginning of the Proskomedia as well as before the great Entrance and before the transformation, show how the degrees of the Holy Trinity's presence increase, and primarily that of Christ, as well as the priest's conscience of this fact which increasingly fills him with the feeling of his sinfulness.

Then the priest puts on the priestly vestments which raise him from the plane of ordinary life and show him adorned with grace's vestments of purity and light through which he will perform the acts of salvation, will gird himself with power and will activate the grace of his priesthood for the fulfillment of this service.

After that he washes his hands and prays that this visible washing may be accompanied by the invisible washing of his soul from all foreign thoughts and immersing it in purity, so that by standing around the altar on which our Lord Himself is offered as sacrifice through him, he may be able to hear the voice of praise sung by the angels and, further, he may be able to announce with comprehension and saving effect the Lord's saving miracles. For the Lord performs miracles through His sacrifice, and a miracle is the descent of the Almighty to the state of sacrifice in order to raise us to His meekness and sacrificial offering to which our salvation is tied. Aware of his lowliness vis-à-vis the sacred action which he begins and through which he mediates Christ's sacrifice on the Holy Table, the priest continues to pray: "O, Lord, cleanse me and have mercy on me."

While coming then to the preparation table after making again three prostrations saying: "O, Lord, cleanse me a sinner," the priest shows that he does not officiate just a symbol empty of Christ's presence, but that in what he is about to do Christ's presence through action will be even more emphasized.

After this bowing, the priest raises the prosphora with his two hands up to his forehead showing that he begins the preparation of Christ's saving sacrifice by remembering the economy of salvation, the foundation of which Christ has laid through the crucifixion and by the pouring of His blood from His side pierced with the lance, blood through which the source of human beings' immortality came about. The prosphora together with the lance represent and has to a certain degree Christ who, on the one hand was crucified, and on the other hand will be crucified, an event filled with memory and its continuation in His being. Christ connects the past with the future through the present with the intention of keeping it within Him and making it efficient until the end of the world. Christ's blood once poured out will grant immortality until the end of the world to all who will drink it in the Mystery of the Eucharist, for in it is the very divinity of Christ as well as the immortal life, unlike the blood received through the parents of those born from Adam. But in order to be continuously available for drinking to those who believe in Him, this blood must be always ready to be offered.

After this preamble, the priest blesses again the prosphora with the lance by making the sign of the cross, remembering, prefiguring and actualizing to a certain degree the crucifixion of Christ's body, reciting the words from the beginning of every liturgy or service: "Blessed is our God always now and ever and unto the ages of ages." May God be eternally blessed by us, that we, too, may have the occasion to eternally bless Him who benevolently wanted His Son to become man out of inestimable love for us; also that the heavenly bread of life may become a human body to be sacrificed for us and to be given to us in the form of bread that nourishes our life as bread for the eternal life of our body.

Through our word of praise addressed to God made possible through our body, we show that the word was given to us to be used first of all for praising and blessing God, to respond with our praise to His gifts and to His words that He is speaking to us, first through all the things and blessings He has given us and continues to give us. For all things have their ultimate and unitary origin in the divine hypostatic Word. In the first place we are to offer for God's praise every word of ours that has its origin in Him, specifically when we are about to receive His gifts and especially the gifts of our salvation through His incarnate Son. All our words have their beginning in the divine hypostatic Word and they must be a response to His words. Our initial word blesses God the Word (and inclusively the Father and the Spirit), but the sign of the cross is made over the prosphora, namely over the bread given to us, as a means of sustenance and as an image of our body out of which His Son will take His body in order to sacrifice it to the Father for us and as an example for us. Only through a sacrificed body can someone be purely united with his fellow human beings. Only a sacrificed body forgets about itself and is purified of the carnal pleasure of egoism that lacks any perspective. Only a sacrificed body is a spiritualized body that gives life to others. It is Christ who manifests this through His sacrificed body.

Since the word implies the communitarian and rational soul, the human body and the bread, it forms the three components or principal gifts of the reality of our life. The bread sustains our body, making it when it is filled with spiritual life a means of sensing and uttering the divine Word. The body nourished with bread makes possible our word, which must be addressed with love first of all to God and then to our fellow human beings. This is why the Son of God can offer us eternal life through His body by sacrificing Himself or giving Himself to us as food in the form of earthly bread that sustains our earthly life, during which we prepare ourselves for the eternal, heavenly life. The word of the fellow human being, as attention toward us and as an expression of the meanings experienced by him and communicated to us, nourishes us because it is itself nourished from the word of the perfect love that contains all the meanings found in the divine Word. The divine Word who shows His supreme love in sacrificing His body is for us the bread of our eternal life. He also includes in Himself the bread of our earthly life. He unites Himself with our body just as our word is united with our body that is nourished with the bread and assimilates it, as it is a rational body. Thus, the more our body is united with the divine Word, the more it is filled through the word with a spiritual content and with spiritual life. Our body assumed by the divine Word is thus transformed into the bread of life that begins to be actualized toward our eternal life and for which the priest, in the name of the community, blesses God in Trinity.

We note that "prosphora" means "offering," that is offering of the bread as sustenance of our life and thus the offering of ourselves to God. But since we offer what we have from God, it is also an offering of His Son who became incarnate on our behalf. This is why the prosphora is imprinted with a seal in the form of the cross which has on the two upper parts the letters IS and HS, and on the two lower parts the letters NI and KA, which put together mean: *Jesus Christ conquers*. Henceforth, only this part represents the body of Christ. The whole prosphora out of which this part is taken represents the Lord's Mother, who in her turn represents the entire humanity offering itself to God through her.[189] This bread which represents the body of Christ bears from the beginning the conquering cross, the cross that remains imprinted eternally in Him, that is even after He suffered it. But through the cross Christ has conquered death because He conquered the sin of selfish affirmation, which is the cause of death. The cross conquers death because it conquers the pleasure of sin and because it is the self-sacrifice offered to God by the sinless Christ, thereby eliminating the sin that separates the human person from God, the source of life.

In the Romanian Liturgy book this part is called "agnetz" (from the Slavonic word that means lamb and has the common origin with the Latin word *agnus*). In the Greek Liturgy book it is called only: "holy bread," or "the seal."[190] But the fact that when the priest cuts this part from the right and left sides he says the word "lamb" shows that it is not wrong to call it "agnetz."

Next the priest makes the sign of the cross three times with the lance over the prosphora saying each time: "In remembrance of our Lord and God and Savior Jesus Christ." At this time he no longer blesses God in general, but he commemorates especially Christ the Savior. His attention is concentrated on the person of Christ and on everything He has done for our salvation. And at once the priest cuts with the lance the part of the prosphora with the seal on its right side saying: "Like a lamb that is led to the slaughter has He been offered." Then on the left side he says: "and like a sheep that before its shearers is dumb, so He opened not His mouth."[191]

Although this cut represents the beginning of the separation of the Lord's body from the Virgin, namely His birth, still the thought is directed to the Lamb who sacrifices Himself, namely to the crucifixion. This also means to say that even in birth, the crucifixion is implied. The coming into the world from the Virgin Mary implies the advance toward crucifixion. In fact, we think of Christ together with everything He has gone through: the birth and the crucifixion, or the birth accepted in view of the crucifixion.

The symbol of the visible bread is united with the symbol of the Lamb who is invisible but is spoken of. The gesture of cutting combines in itself the remembrance that has a certain actualization of Christ's birth and crucifixion as well as the Lamb who sacrifices Himself for us. The one who is born is the Lamb who will sacrifice Himself, the only one sacrificed. He is born as a sacrificial Lamb. But He is also born with a body that is given to be consumed and will be given forever.

By Lamb one indicates more emphatically that Christ is the living bread and the Lamb who sacrifices Himself. The bread is made to be eaten and the Lamb is to be sacrificed. Christ is the Bread, conscious that it will be given for eating and the conscious Lamb who willingly sacrifices Himself. He is now called "the silent Lamb" to show that He suffered pain through crucifixion and that, at the same time, He accepted this pain in all meekness, without protesting or complaining. He who protests and complains is weak. Christ was weak as man, but He was strong in bearing the pain because He was also God.

This is the amazing greatness of God revealed in Christ: God makes Himself a sacrificial Lamb without complaint, a Lamb who controls the pain with the power of meekness, able to appease those tempted toward quarrels, hatred, protests and grievances. He has done this so as to transform human beings from beasts into lambs who do not protect their own interests through hatred, quarrels and protests. He who was able to speak with a voice stronger than any thunder consents to receive death without complaining. He is silent even though He could plead His innocence better than any lawyer. Humility and innocence are stronger in silence than in manifestation through words. St. Ephrem the Syrian says: "Mary was carrying the silent child in whom all words were hidden… He was silent as a little child while giving at the same time His commandments to all created beings."[192] He who is silent on account of wisdom has in himself not only meekness, but also the humility that does not want to impose itself, for he is not afraid of being ignored; he also possesses all the meanings and all the words or reasons/inner principles of things that cannot be clearly expressed. In meekness there is awareness of the infinite power and the all-comprehending and all-encompassing wisdom. The meek one is self-confident in this wisdom. St. Ephrem the Syrian also says: "The conqueror came down to be conquered, not by Satan, because He has conquered and drowned him. He was conquered by the Jews who crucified Him. But He had conquered through His righteousness and at the same time He was conquered by His goodness."[193] He was victorious because He allowed Himself to be willingly conquered out of goodness. He conquered because He let Himself be conquered. "He had conquered the strong and was conquered by the weak. They crucified Him because He gave Himself up to them. He allowed Himself to be conquered in order to conquer. He conquered through the sufferings willingly accepted. He conquered through His mercy."[194]

Only this Lamb can save, for only He can ennoble human persons by imprinting on them the sense of the Lamb. If in the state of sin the human person is *homini lupus*, in Christ one can attain the state of *homo homini agnus*. From His sacrifice, those who believe in Him can receive the power of a death that implies the supreme power of the Spirit, that eliminates the death of the Spirit in the human person through the Spirit Who can conquer death. Those in the Old Testament had vaguely felt—through the revelation of that time—that through His meekness the Lamb represented the saved humanity. But only the Son of God was able to accomplish in Himself this beginning of the true humanity, of both the saving and the saved humanity. The Paschal Lamb of the Old Testament had vaguely showed the aspiration of humanity to "pass" from the slavery of sin to the freedom of dominion over sin and of loving communion with the Almighty vis-à-vis sin. The incarnate Son of God, the true Lamb, truly transports us to this freedom, for He is also as man united with the Father whose almighty freedom is not dominated by anything.

He manifested His non-weakened freedom by accepting the cross. For the self-offering up to death out of love, without objection, is manifested in the greatest freedom and power.

Only in breaking the limits of our egoistic selves can we connect with Him, the source of life and of freedom. St. Ephrem the Syrian says: "Forced by this Lamb of life, death has given up the righteous who came out of their tombs. Between lamb and Lamb there were the Apostles. They ate the paschal lamb but also the true Lamb. The Apostles stood between symbol and reality. They witnessed how the symbol disappeared and how the reality appeared."[195]

It can also be said that just as Christ as the true and meek Lamb has eliminated through His strength of conscience and love the insensible lamb as symbol, so has the true Bread that is transformed into His body as bread voluntarily offered out of love eliminated the symbol of the unleavened bread. Following Christ's words (Jn 6:58), St. Ephrem says: "Through the bread that the Lord broke for us has disappeared the unleavened bread the consumers of which were dying."[196] St. Symeon of Thessalonica says: "By taking from the center of the prosphora that particle of the leavened bread the priest shows how out of our nature, not from another being, the Savior became incarnate from a blessed and holy woman, the ever-virgin."[197] The living bread of His body comes from the living bread of His Mother's body.

The placing of what the priest officiated at the Proskomedia in the continuous present, without ignoring that he does this based on the past, is shown not only in the emotion manifested by the priest during these acts, but also in the dialogue between the deacon and the priest. In fact, the priest uses the past tense only in the words of the prophet Isaiah 53:7, which show that Isaiah sees their future in the past, and through the priest Christ's saving activity is perpetuated in the present on the basis of the past sacrifice. This is why, after the priest removes the agnetz from the prosphora the deacon says to him in the present tense: *Father, pierce!* Then the priest pierces crosswise or cuts in the form of the cross the divine Lamb who is identical with the Child who came out of the Virgin's body and says: *Sacrificed is the Lamb of God, Who takes away the sin of the world for the life of the world and its salvation.*

The crosswise piercing is done after the agnetz is placed face down, showing that Christ's incarnation and sacrifice occurred for those down on earth, for their benefit, and that the premise of the complete sacrifice of Christ is His total humility up to the total concealing of His face in which divinity was shimmering. This is shown by the priest even a little earlier, saying further the following words, according to Isaiah, when cutting the upper part of the agnetz, thus indicating Christ's coming from above: "In His humility His judgment was taken away" (Is 53:8), namely in His humility was shown the wisdom of His high judgment, the criterion for the true judgment of human deeds. He who does not humble himself, does not exalt himself as a human person in his judgment. This humility or kenosis is so great, for He who assumed it is from a supreme generation or source that no one can declare, a fact expressed by the priest according to Isaiah: "and who will declare His generation?" (Is 53:8). No one can declare His unknown generation, that, after so much humility, is again raised to the supreme height from where He came. His generation is above word. But neither can His generation from below be declared, for He does not have a father to be connected with a generation.

The priest says this directly in what follows: when the deacon prompts the priest in the present tense, "Take up, Father," a fact that indicates again a present actuality both of Christ's birth and death as well as His ascension, the priest takes the agnetz completely out of the bread, using the lance on the right side, saying with the implication of all three meanings: "For His life is taken from the earth" (Is 53:8). The taking out of the agnetz means at the same time His birth from the Virgin, but also His departure and ascension from humans through death.[198]

A certain presence based on the past of Christ's sacrifice is expressed in the dialogue between the deacon and the priest when the priest, after placing the agnetz face down on the paten and at the prompting of the deacon "Pierce, Father," cuts it in the form of the cross, showing Christ's death, but not the dissolution of His hypostasis. With its face down, the agnetz is partly cut in the form of the cross, thus showing that Christ suffered a true breaking of His body through death with His face toward humans, or for their benefit, without destroying the unity in His person.

After He accepted death, Christ's face turns upward showing that His death accepted for human beings is the sacrifice offered to His Father. Thus, His death becomes a source of strength. His real death as well as

His power manifested after death are shown in the fact that out of His side came forth the pure blood and water filled with the Holy Spirit, the blood that will give immortal life to those who will drink it and the water which will wash away the sins of those who will be baptized in the name of the Holy Trinity. Even His blood, which those who believe in Holy Communion will drink, also has water, for not only the blood but also the water is the principle of life for the human body. Our body advances toward eternity when it cleanses its blood and water from the tendency toward sin and it is filled with the Holy Spirit through the all-pure blood and water that came out of Christ's side.

This is why the priest, after piercing with the lance under the initials IS, that is in the man Jesus, who is turned with His face toward the Father through His sacrifice in the name of humanity, a face that the Father loves in every human person (as St. Cyril of Alexandria says in *Adoration in Spirit and in Truth*), pours at once in the chalice wine and water saying the words: "But one of the soldiers pierced His side with a spear, and immediately blood and water came out. And he who has seen has testified, and his testimony is true" (Jn 19:34–35).

Just as the bread is the potential body, so the wine and the water are the potential blood of Christ. Just as the bread will be transformed into the body, so will the wine and the water will be transformed into the blood that will flow from Christ's sacrificed body. St. Cyprian insists on the detail from the Gospel of St. John (19:34–35) that out of Christ's side blood and water came out, and he affirms that even at the Mystical Supper Jesus mingled the wine with water. He also says that the water represents Christ's union with the believers (*Epistle LXIII to Caecilius*, 13). Later on it has been affirmed against the Armenians that the water is the symbol of human nature united with the divine nature in the hypostasis of the Word (St. Symeon of Thessalonika, *On the Holy Liturgy*, ch. 92). In a Romanian icon painted on glass, Christ is represented as sitting on a bench with the cross in the back, and out of Him there grows a vine from whose grapes He squeezes the wine into the chalice. In the same way, in His representation as a Child in the chalice above the table of the Proskomedia, a vine grows out of Him. The wine flowing out of Him is His blood, or rather the blood flowing out of Him is the wine transformed into blood. This is the overcoming of the distance between two phases of His life. Nature [as in essence] is destined to personification in the human person, on account of his body, but then it also becomes Christ-like on account of the body that Christ appropriated. His representation as vine who gives us to drink the strength-giving drink of His life follows His words: "I am the true vine" (Jn 15:1).

The blessing given by the priest to the mingling of the water and wine in the chalice shows once again that the power of Christ who shed His blood for us begins to be perceived to a certain degree, although at the same time they [the blood and the water] represent our gift. The words of the blessing are: *Blessed is the mingling of Your holy things, always now and ever and unto the ages of ages. Amen.*[199] From this moment they are God's and they are blessed, for they are both offered to God and they prefigure the human blood of His Son given to His Father for us, the blood in which are found both the wine and the water that are transformed; they are God's and they are blessed, because being given to us by God for the sustenance of earthly life, we are returning them through Christ Who appropriated them fully purified and blessed through the transformation into His body and blood.

Then the priest covers the chalice with the designated cover. But the paten with the agnetz remains uncovered, because next to the agnetz will be placed the particles in commemoration of the saints as well as of the living and the departed; however, no wine will be poured into the chalice for them because they were not crucified for the life of the world. The chalice is covered, because the blood is also fully covered in the body while the body is uncovered, albeit clothed, and in some sense in communication with others.

The agnetz has the shape of a square because Christ the man represents the whole humanity dispersed in the four directions in which the human person, or humanity, moves without being infinite in its being and in its continuous actualization.

After this the priest takes out a large particle in the shape of a triangle for the Lord's Mother, then smaller particles in the same shape for the saints. The conscious beings that have their basis in the general creation ascend toward God with the mind or the refined point of their person. While he cuts and places the particle for the Lord's Mother on the right side of the agnetz the priest says: "In honor and memory of our most blessed and glorious Lady Theotokos and Ever-virgin Mary. Through her prayers, O, Lord, accept this sacrifice upon the altar in the highest heaven." Nicholas Cabasilas instead of "in honor" uses the words "for the glory." Christ's sacrifice and the preparation of the transformation as His sacrifice in the Holy Liturgy is also for the glory of His Mother. For in this sacrifice has been and will be shown for what great outcome the Son of God was born of her. But the agnetz not yet transformed is still the sacrifice of the community. This is why the priest prays that through the prayers of the Lord's Mother Christ may accept the sacrifice of the community onto the altar in the highest heaven, so that He may transform it into the sacrifice of His body that will thus include in it the sacrifice of the community.

These words have an additional meaning. The Lord's Mother's pure life of prayer made it possible for the Lord to take His body from hers in order to be offered as sacrifice for our salvation. At this moment, being represented next to the agnetz or next to the image of her Son's body as well as a particle of humanity which is concentrated in the prosphora as in the image of the body of the Lord's Mother, she again prays before the entire community so that this agnetz may be accepted upon the altar in the highest heaven to be transformed into the sacrificed body of her Son. Once taken out of the prosphora or from the bread offered by the community and especially from the image of her body, He will represent the sacrifice of the community and of the Lord's Mother herself. The entire community is represented by the bread offered to God so that He may accept it upon the altar in the highest heaven and transform it through the Holy Spirit into Christ's body. But the Lord Himself will transform the bread offered in His body in order to continuously offer it for us and to be given to human persons. He does this not before a passive humanity that does not rejoice in what is being officiated, or rather does not wish it, does not expect it and does not pray for this transformation and offering as Christ's sacrifice for humanity. The transformation and the Lord's offering for humans can efficiently operate upon them only with their will. If through the partaking of the Lord's body and blood our sanctification is being sought, Cabasilas says that "in order to obtain the effects of the divine mysteries we must approach them in a state of grace and properly prepared."[200] We can reach this state through prayers, psalms and everything that is said and officiated piously in the Holy Liturgy. These acts sanctify us and make us fit, on the one hand, to receive these holy gifts and, on the other hand, to offer our contribution so that the Lord's sacrifice may be accepted also as our sacrifice upon the altar in the highest heaven.

The Lord's Mother unites her prayers with the prayers of the community for the Agnetz to be received and transformed into the sacrificed body of the Lord upon the altar in the highest heaven, through the working of the Holy Spirit. This is why we magnify her.

Just as Christ was not separated from humanity when He became incarnate but mediated between humanity and God, so the Lord's Mother did not separate herself from this relationship or from the transformation of the bread into His sacrificed body. She prays to Him so that her sacrifice may be accepted, which is represented by her particle and that of the Agnetz that prefigures His body taken from her, as His real body that was sacrificed and received "upon the altar in the highest heaven."

"The altar in the highest heaven" is the spiritual height before the Father where Christ has entered with His sacrifice on Golgotha and where He remains permanently, transforming into this sacrificed body the sacrifice of bread of the community that is also approaching this supreme height where He is found in a state of sacrifice. "But this Man, after He had offered one sacrifice for sins forever, sat down at the right hand of God . . . . and having a High Priest over the house of God, let us draw near with a true heart in full assurance of faith, having our hearts sprinkled from an evil conscience" (Heb 10:12, 22).

The Lord's Mother is up there at the right hand of her sacrificed Son, making use of His sacrifice as she is filled with His Spirit of sacrifice and of His glory on account of her position. This fact is stated by the priest when he places the particle of the Lord's Mother at the right side of the Agnetz: "At the right hand stood the Queen, arrayed in golden robes, all glorious." She sits at His right hand as she stood next to Him on Golgotha. She sits at this supreme height of glory immediately after that of the Son, still praying to Him to transform our gifts into His sacrificed body and blood. Her "commemoration" does not imply our prayer for an even greater elevation of her—although the transformation of our gifts into the sacrificed body of the Son and our being drawn into an ever greater union with Him also makes her glory ever more evident—but an additional praise offered to her.[201]

The particles for angels, prophets, apostles, hierarchs, venerable martyrs (monks), unmercenary doctors (great benefactors in general), Joachim and Anna and all the saints, St. John Chrysostom or St. Basil the Great are placed on the left side of the Agnetz at the same level, thus showing that they, too, rejoice in the glory of the crucified and resurrected Lord, but they are not in the same intimacy with the glorified Christ as His Mother. The particles that represent them are taken out while saying the words: *In honor and memory* . . . . They are asked to pray for those in the church, but these prayers are not called "intercessions," nor does one ask that through them the Agnetz may be accepted in heaven for the transformation into the Lord's body and blood, but they are simply called prayers for the visitation and support of the faithful. Nevertheless, the offering of the gifts that will be transformed into the Lord's body and blood is also done "in their honor" because when the faithful receive Christ they also praise the saints who received Christ and made Him known through their testimony and life. It is in this sense that their commemoration is made, not that they be forgiven for their sins. One does not pray to them for the transformation into the Lord's sacrificed body, for they did not play any role in the incarnation of the Lord, nor did they remain next to Him praying or suffering on Golgotha. Even though they pray to Christ for us from the height where they are near Him, they do not contribute to the continuation of the Lord's state of sacrifice or to the completion of the transformation.

In any case, the transformation of the bread into Christ's body and the partaking of Him by the faithful in the Eucharist and in any sacrament is only achieved in the prayerful presence that is full of conscious joy of the whole Church in heaven.

Contrary to the Greek Liturgikon, in the Romanian Liturgikon of 1956 the particle for angels is missing and the number of nine particles is obtained by separating that of St. John the Baptist from the other prophets. This seems to be unnatural. The expression "in honor of" shows that the Lord's sacrifice has for the saints the role of placing into bold relief their honor or glory, as that of those who believed in Christ. This role also applies to angels. The whole Church in heaven is glorified in the Eucharistic transformation. The angels, too, have an increased understanding of God's love after they know that He gave His Son to death for the human beings. ". . . The fellowship of the mystery, which from the beginning of the ages has been hidden in God who created all things through Jesus Christ to the intent that now the manifold wisdom of God might be made known by the church to the principalities and powers in the heavenly places" (Eph 3:9–10). In addition to this, their joy has increased as they entered into their communion, in the increased communion between those who praise God and human beings, that is the other category of conscious creatures. In a certain spiritual sense, all those in heaven partake even more of Christ;

through the Holy Liturgy a greater union between those in heaven and those on earth is achieved.

However, around Christ is achieved not only the solidarity of the Church in heaven with the one on earth but also the solidarity on earth. For after the priest has placed the particles for the saints and the departed he also takes out the particles for the living. In this way it is shown that they also participate even in this life in Christ's eternal life. Those who present prayer lists for their relatives and acquaintances feel that their life in Christ would not be without certain shadows of egoism if they did not share in it together with them, just as their joy of partaking of Christ would not be full if they did not partake of Him together with their relatives, friends and acquaintances, living or departed with faith in the Lord.

Just as when we commemorate the saving works of Christ, or when we implore Him, in a certain way we bring about His presence, likewise by commemorating the saints and all those departed we enter into a certain relationship with them. If here on earth the intense thinking of someone is sometimes provoked by that someone and this thought determines that person to think of us through a mysterious spiritual relationship, likewise this can happen when we commemorate the departed. This because they are not totally dead. This relationship is achieved especially through the fact that by commemorating them simultaneously with the prayers addressed to the living Christ with maximum intensity, He Himself commemorates them and brings them into a certain relationship with Him and, thus, into a greater relationship with us. For being in a relationship with Christ through our prayers addressed to Him, we encounter next to Him the departed whom we commemorate.

If a spiritual closeness can be achieved among those of us here on earth separated by a distance, why cannot a similar closeness be achieved through thought and through "commemoration"? In this is also shown everyone's endless responsibility toward their fellow human beings and, thus, their eternal existence.

The Russian theologian Sergius Bulgakov has attempted to capture in the significance of the name the basis for the fact that by pronouncing someone's name we make a connection with that person. He sees in someone's name an existential incarnation of the word and a connection between this incarnation and the incarnation of the divine Word. According to him, the name is not just a concentrated expression of the attributes of a person, but an expression of its unique core, beyond its deeds and partial attributes; that core is really at their basis as an essential, unitary and unique incarnation of the attributes. When we utter the name of a person we make that person vibrate because we have touched that person in its concrete, existing uniqueness, while when we state someone's attribute it can be anyone's attribute and nobody vibrates at the mentioning of this attribute.

> A name is . . . in a certain sense as **I**, with the difference that a name is a concrete, qualified, individual **I**, whereas the latter is individual only by the power of a mystical indicative gesture. ... But a name speaks about being, not about quality; . . . Here is not a predicative idea alone but being, an idea that has become reality, a point in the cosmos.
>
> Therefore, a name gives a general, although dull, undifferentiated sensation of being. For those who understand and accept the ideal roots of being, a name is an ideal concrete, an individuality in its nonrepeatability but hence also inexpressibility through attributes . . . . The answer about the inner core of a name can only be this: a name is a power, an energy, an incarnate word. Here the completely particular *ensarkosis* [incarnation] of a word takes place, the mystery of which is incomprehensible as is every mystery of embryonic life, fulfilling the command *let there be*. But the consequences are clear: the word became flesh, the ideal became the real, the idea was converted into energy, yearning for its entelechy, and name entered the cosmos of the names of being.
>
> . . . The incarnation of the word supposes and at the same time postulates the incarnation of words. The source of the word in the world is the Divine Word by which the heavens were made firm. If the Lord was pleased to be incarnated and become a human being, with an individuality and a Name, this presupposes human individuality and name as the general form of life. The divine incarnation presupposes human name-incarnation... The Lord has two natures, two wills, but one Hypostasis and therefore one Name. His Name does not revoke the general law of name-incarnation but fulfills it, makes use of it. Human naming and name-incarnation exist in the image and likeness of divine God-incarnation and naming. In general, the image and like-

ness of God in the human being, by virtue of which alone the incarnation of God became possible, presupposes a full human Godlikeness, and in particular in what concerns naming as the incarnation of a name.[202]

This determines us to point out specifically that the name is proven to express a real existence and not just features in the abstract, insofar as every time it is pronounced it touches this real, individualized existence. For the real existence is so alive, so full of radiant energy and so definite in its being that once it is touched by the name, it sends its energy toward the person naming it, thus its name pronounced by another person produces an impulse for reaction.

One can say that the name indicates that existence which reacts at the pronouncing of its name. This proves that the name expresses the existence that is alive and conscious to the fullest. The name expresses the unique core of each person, that core that reacts every time it is uttered. Only a conscious person reacts when its name is pronounced and this because it understands the appeal to its uniqueness. Only a person who has a name and thus can receive a response is able to speak to another person by name. All other words circulate among persons who have names. The names of two persons form the basis of all the words they exchange, because all the words they exchange indicate their characteristics, deeds and intentions past or future, or rather the things that connect them through which they enter and remain in a relationship. Therefore, all things exist in order to be named by persons so that the persons may reveal through them their will by way of the words they address to each other. Each person addresses words to another person in order to receive words, for every person is able to transmit and receive words. Things do not consciously react to our words, which is why they do not have names. This shows that the person bearing a name does not remain passive nor does it react passively or only physically to our words. When this happens with human persons it means that they exist according to the image of a communion of supreme persons. This is why when we address God with a name that can only be given to Him, He certainly reacts in the most real way and, in our turn, we react to His call addressed to us by name. We speak with each other because that is how we were created. We were created as having a name through which we are obligated to respond, to call each other and to be called by God, to call Him and to respond to Him, thus strengthening our uniqueness in communion. As we come into the world capable of bearing a name and being obligated to respond when we are called by name, our origin can only be in a supreme being bearing a name, thus having to respond to the call of that supreme being and to the call of all our fellow human beings bearing a name.

Just as a certain presence of Christ at the Proskomedia is achieved not only through the words of the prayers and by uttering His name, but also through the Agnetz taken out of the prosphora and by making the sign of the cross over it, likewise the presence of the departed with the faith in Christ is achieved not only be mentioning their names, but also through the particles of bread taken out of the prosphora and placed next to the Agnetz which represents Christ.

The bread is the creation, concentrated and fully useful, given by God for our sustenance. But, as that which represents the sustaining power of life in the body, the bread also represents us. And when we connect it with a certain person, it also represents that person. This is why, by taking out a particle from the bread for a person commemorated by name, we represent especially that person. The Agnetz represents not only a human person, whoever that might be, but the Person who, by becoming man like us, has become the central Man around whom all gravitate, since He remained God as well, who is the origin and the foundation of the entire creation.

The particle of bread taken out for each human person distinguishes those for whom it is taken out, but it also brings them closer to Christ and among themselves, thus showing them as being of the same nature with Christ and with each other. But Christ is in the center, being at the same time God and representing the entire creation and humanity. The bread is a specific human nutrition, because only the human person can prepare it. This is why Christ as man is represented by the Agnetz. And indicating the name of each person for each particle shows that particular person's eternal distinction within the solidarity with those of the same nature.

This is why we do not partake of the particles representing the persons, not only because they are not the source of our life, but also because we want to assert their unmixed and even eternal existence. This is the reason why at memorial services we pray God to grant them memory eternal. For only those who are commemorated exist in a plenary way through the attention given to them by God and by other human persons. Those who do not have the attention of others and especially of God are drowned into an extremely tormenting minus of existence.

We partake of Christ and this is why the Agnetz is transformed into His body, for His existence assured by Him endures even if we partake of Him. Moreover, through His divinity united with His body He is the foundation and the source of power for the entire creation and especially for us, human beings. By partaking of Him we show our willingness to reestablish and increase through our will, too, our union with this personal foundation of all, with which we will not be confused precisely because we take out a distinctive particle that remains distinct for each of us. All of us are united with Christ through communion, but we also remain distinct from Him or next to Him through the particles of which nobody partakes.

But the lasting distinction of those commemorated and represented by the particles is united with the offering of their lives to Christ through the bread that sustains them. Each believer offers himself to Christ, but each one also offers all their loved ones and acquaintances, knowing that in this way they will exist eternally. "Let us offer ourselves and each other and all our life unto Christ, our God." It is not only Christ who offers Himself to the Father for us and to us in a state of sacrifice, but we too offer ourselves together with Him to the Father and to Him from the power of His offering so that we may truly exist. Love is mutual self-offering, a continuous gift and counter-gift. This is how it is with God, this is how it is among human persons. This mutual offering shows that at the basis of life there is the loving communion of certain supreme Persons and this extends to the plane of creation. Life in its fullness is manifested and maintained in love. This is shown at the Proskomedia through Christ's will to sacrifice Himself. But we also come alongside Him, being attracted by His self-offering love, and we bring others along with us. We offer them as well so that we may continue to have them with us even more. If we wanted to keep them for ourselves, or if we did not want them to be offered, we would neither have them with us fully nor would they have the plenary life that can only come to them from Christ, the source of life, as they offer themselves to Him. On the other hand, creation is the multiple word of the divine Word, and the bread is the word in which is shown most clearly and effectively the Word's love for human beings.

If in the Agnetz is shown most clearly the loving will of the Word, who intends to communicate to us His will for our perpetuation and salvation through sacrifice, then in the particles that represent us we respond to Him with our word of thanksgiving and with our devotion. As our words and gifts are placed through the particles next to the Word, they represent our response to the Word and to the supreme gift of the One who speaks to us and offers Himself to us with love. Through our word we also respond and offer ourselves with our love, and we determine all our loved ones to do the same. A dialogue takes place on the paten between us and the divine Word for our becoming eternal.

Nicholas Cabasilas makes the following distinction between the service of the Proskomedia and that of the Liturgy: at the Proskomedia Christ is offered to God as the first fruit of creation, or as a gift presented to the Father from when He took our body from the Virgin, therefore before He was crucified; this is why the holy gifts are not placed on the altar from the beginning. "At the end of his mortal life he became a victim when he was sacrificed to give glory to his Father. Also, he was dedicated to God from the beginning; in the eyes of the Father he was a precious gift; he was acceptable both as first fruit of the human race, and also by reason of the Law, because he was the firstborn."[203]

But as, by the will of God, Christ pre-offers Himself through the bread as a fully developed body even before He is crucified, so do we pre-offer ourselves together with Him. It is for this purpose that He became incarnate and pre-offers Himself as gift to the Father so that we, too, may pre-offer ourselves together with Him, thus preparing ourselves for a true death of the old man with Christ in order to rise together with Him.

Christ pre-offered Himself as gift to the Father so that we, too, may pre-offer ourselves together with Him; having life and the entire creation as the gift of God, this gift calls for our response with a counter-gift. Nicholas Cabasilas reverses the positions: he makes us the beginners in the process of offering. But he admits that God has established this change. So, He still has the initiative. Cabasilas says: "For what reason must we offer these oblations to God as first fruits of human life? The reason is that God gives us life in exchange for these gifts. Now it is fitting that the gift should have something in common with the reward, and not be utterly removed from it. Since the reward is life, then the offering should to some extent be life also; especially since he who prescribes the gift is also the Giver of Life, . . . it is he who gives us in return the Living Bread, the chalice of eternal life . . . so that we may receive life for life, eternity for temporality."[204] The first Giver was God, giving us earthly life and the bread for its sustenance; but wanting to later give us the superior gift of eternal life nourished by the risen body of the Word, overfilled with the Spirit, He raises us up to this gift under the condition that we, too, make a gift out of the primary gift given to us by God, out of the bread that represents and sustains the body or our earthly life. And we do this by following the example of the incarnate Word.

But even before God gives us the body and blood of Christ, in exchange for the gifts of bread and wine which represent our earthly life, He gives us the gift of the Holy Spirit. The priest says this when he censes the gifts prepared at the Proskomedia. "We offer You incense, O Christ our God, as a sweet spiritual fragrance. Receive it upon Your heavenly altar, and send down upon us in return the grace of Your All-Holy Spirit." The gifts were sent to the Father as the herald of Christ's love and of our love toward Him; namely, they are permeated even now with the Father's benevolence. It remains for us to complete the supreme calling upon the Spirit (epiklesis) so that they may be transformed into the body of the Lord and that we may partake of Him or to feel Him in our proximity as such.

At the Proskomedia the dialogue between us and God begins as an ascension of gifts. As we climb the ladder of the exchange of gifts toward the Kingdom of God, we increasingly transcend ourselves.

After the gifts are prepared and censed, the star is placed on the paten on which they are. The star comes over the manger where Christ was born or is born for us. The entire cosmos comes, with its roundness, to cover Him, worshiping Him and also covering Him until the beginning of His public activity. It is the state of kenosis in which divinity is covered by using the cosmos precisely for this kenosis. "And the star came and stood over the place where the young child was." Those who want to see, like the Magi, are able to perceive Christ's divinity through the transparent shining of the cosmos and also of Christ's body and of His earthly life. Through the star and through the astronomic cosmos we can see Christ even today. On the one hand, this cosmos covers Him, on the other hand it leads us to the incarnate Word. It covers Him in a way that leaves Him transparent for those able to see Him. The Proskomedia represents not only Christ's state of kenosis (humility) from His earthly life, but also Christ Himself with all the stages He went through, namely also Christ who is now in glory. This can be seen from the fact that the Agnetz is cut not only in the form of the cross, but it also has imprinted on it the word NIKA, namely He who is victorious; He is now victorious from heaven over the enemies of the good, but in an invisible way. This is why on the paten the things on earth are together with the things in heaven; the entire creation is found on the paten around Christ, the creation of the living and of those who have passed away into the afterlife. This union of all is even better represented by the placing over them of the semi-circle that has a star at the top, namely Christ. Heaven, or Christ Himself, forms a cupola over those who have been or are on earth and those who are in the afterlife. It is a union between heaven and earth, between the incarnate, crucified and risen God and His creation. The entire creation culminates and attains its highest level in Christ.

Then the body of Christ or the paten is covered with the prescribed cover. And over the paten and the chalice, also covered, another cover is placed. According to Nicholas Cabasilas this means that "the power of the Incarnate God was veiled up to the time of his miracles and the witness from heaven."[205]

To keep something covered shows that there is something special waiting to be uncovered. Thus, being represented by the priest, those who know what is under the covers have the feeling that the power of Christ pervades through those very covers. This is why they cover Him, but they also reveal Him. The priest says this: "The Lord is King. He is robed in majesty; the Lord is robed, He is girded with strength.... Your virtue has covered the heavens, O Christ, and the earth is full of Your praise." The priest says this referring to Christ in His glory and to the Lamb found on the altar on high that is represented by the Agnetz. Through the covers, namely through humility but also through the cosmos that covers Him and makes His glory transparent, His virtue (power), the praise of His power, spreads over the earth. The virtue of the Lord as man has overwhelmed the virtue of angels. We also ask to be covered by this power and, through it, to drive away all enemies, to be filled with peace and for all the world to be filled with His saving mercy.

The covers are His invisible wings. Through them He protects and covers us and chases away the enemy; through them He has mercy on us and on the entire cosmos and He saves us: "Cover us with the shelter of Your wings, and drive away from us every foe and adversary. Give peace to our lives, O Lord, have mercy on us and on Your world, and save our souls, for You are good and love mankind."

The Proskomedia now acquires a Christological and cosmological sense, representing Christ in His glory, Who invisibly covers and leads our souls and the world to salvation.

The Lord is covered together with us; He is covered with us so that He may cover us against enemies and keep us close to Him; He goes deep within Himself in order to attract us into His invisible depth which is the source of life. It is there that the concentration of power is found, from where we set out to manifest our visible life in our deeds together with Him, and to fly carried by Him toward the summits of life.

CHAPTER TWO

The Liturgy Proper: the Joint Progress within the Kingdom of the Holy Trinity

1. *The Liturgy of the Catechumens or of the Calling and Teaching*

In olden times, there were many being called to Christ [the catechumens] who decided to become Christians, and before being baptized they spent some time being taught the catechism. They were allowed to attend the Holy Liturgy until the beginning of the prayers for the transformation of the bread and wine into the body and blood of Christ and for communion. At that time they were asked to leave: "Catechumens, depart." There began a mystery for which they were not prepared. Nowadays, those desiring to become Christians or members of the Orthodox Church but not yet baptized are not so many, at least in the Christianized communities or those entirely Orthodox. Still, this part of the Holy Liturgy continues to be called as such even in these regions. Also, in fully Orthodox regions even "the faithful" participate in this part of the Liturgy as in the early times. This is even more evident as the members of the Orthodox Church have increased and they have little knowledge of the Christian teaching or are indifferent to it or even spiritually estranged from it. These can benefit from this part of the Holy Liturgy dedicated to teaching. Moreover, this part should be expounded.

Those who do not receive Holy Communion for various reasons can remain until the end of the Holy Liturgy so that they may know even better the content of the Christian teaching.

Therefore, just like the non-Christians or the non-Orthodox and the indifferent can benefit from the entire Liturgy so, too, the regular and diligent members of the Church can be continuously called to an increasing progress into the knowledge of the Christian teaching and, thereby, to a life more conformed to it. St. Paul the Apostle considered that he had not yet reached the goal and was in a continuous race (Phil

3:14); he urged the believers in Corinth to run as in a stadium (1 Cor 11:24). He considered this race a response given to "Him who calls you" (Gal 5:8). The continuous race is a response to a continuous call.

In a strict sense, the called and the catechumens are those who have not yet joined the Orthodox Church, but in a broad sense all believers are constantly called. Perhaps this is why the original name of the Church in Greek is that of Ekklesia, or the community of those who are called, of those constantly called. On the other hand, it is significant that while in the Greek language the first part of the Holy Liturgy is called the Liturgy of the Catechumens, in Romanian is called the Liturgy of those called. Couldn't the reason for that be that the Romanian translators wanted to place in bold relief the quality of the believers as being called, which in the Greek language gave the Church the name Ekklesia?

One should explain how the idea that all believers are, in a broad sense, continuously called can be reconciled with the fact that at the end of the first part of the Liturgy one says: "Those who are called depart... so none of those who are called remain." Or how can these words have significance today for the faithful present in church? They can be understood as an invitation addressed to the faithful to not remain in the state they are, but to come out of it by advancing toward the state of believers worthy of participating at the offering of the eucharistic sacrifice, in the sense in which St. Gregory of Nyssa regards the entire life of Christians as a sequence of "epektases," of exits from the previous states and of advances toward superior stages, a sense taken from St. Paul the Apostle (Php 3:13). St. Gregory of Nyssa specified that this means a series of "exits" and of "entries," of exits from lower stages and of entries into higher stages.

But the Liturgy of the catechumens, concluded with the words "Catechumens depart," has, according to St. Maximos the Confessor, an always current sense also because they represent those who, though called, do not pass over to the state of true believers and that is why at the Last Judgment they will be separated from those who believed.[206] "For many are called, but few are chosen" (Mt 22:14). Thus, the words that conclude this part of the Liturgy are a beneficial exhortation for those who come to church so that they may no longer remain in the state of being called, but pass over (or exit) to the state of true believers.

2. The Praise of the Promised Kingdom of the Holy Trinity As an Exhortation for and a Beginning of One's Progress toward It

The priest begins not only the Liturgy of the catechumens but the entire Liturgy with the words: *Blessed is the Kingdom of the Father and of the Son and of the Holy Spirit, now and ever and unto the ages of ages.* As he says these words he makes the sign of the cross with the Gospel over the antimension on the altar table. When the faithful together with the priest bless God, they will themselves be blessed by God as well. They know this from the end of previous Liturgies when the priest said as he addressed God: "O Lord, Who bless those who bless You... save Your people and bless Your inheritance" by making them members of Your Kingdom. He who blesses God does this because he feels His goodness and thereby he feels God's grace upon him. St. Paul the Apostle says: "Blessed be the God and Father of our Lord Jesus Christ, who has blessed us with every spiritual blessing in the heavenly places in Christ" (Eph 1:3). Thus, through these words we also express the hope that we will be part of the heavenly Kingdom. But when blessing the Kingdom of the Holy Trinity we ask for the blessing of all those who are or will be part of it, including our blessing as well.

We mention six out of the many meanings contained in these words:

a. The praise of the Holy Trinity implies in it the will of the community to advance toward it, for he who praises something wishes to partake of that which is praised.

b. This Kingdom is the Kingdom of the loving heavenly Father, of the Son who, through incarnation, became our most loving Brother, and of the Holy Spirit who cleanses our sins and liberates us from the passions that control us as multiple forms of egoism.

c. Being the Kingdom of love, it has the meaning as a communion of those who are part of it, which increases continuously in every Holy Liturgy so as to reach perfection in the life to come.

d. The Kingdom will endure forever, so we will also be eternally happy and part of it; as such, it opens up for us the eschatological perspective and gives us the assurance that our existence will not end through death; this is why both the priest and the faithful look toward the East, toward the eternal God from whom everything comes; they advance from the world of egoistical divisions behind them toward their unity in the Holy Trinity as toward their final, eternal goal beyond which there is no other, for it will be our happy rest, without end, in the communion of eternal love.

e. This Kingdom has been opened for us through and in the Son of God Who, by conquering death forever—through the cross suffered for us—for our humanity which He assumed, has also conquered it for us; thus He showed us both the eternal love of God in Trinity and the manner in which we can also enter into that Kingdom in which there is no longer death, a manner that consists in overcoming through sacrifice our sinful egoism.

f. By showing us such a great meaning of existence that consists in our eternal life in the endless joy of the communion of all, the Liturgy is a true feast, full of light and opposite to darkness in which nothing can be seen. This is why candles are lit on the altar table and in the nave, this is why the priest prays before the reading of the Gospel, saying: "Illumine our hearts . . . with the pure light of Your divine knowledge" and this is why the faithful say after receiving the Holy Communion: "We have seen the true light." Christ is "the light of the world" (Jn 8:12), as the One who is the eternal Son become man forever has shown us through the resurrection our eternal existence as children of the heavenly Father. The Liturgy is the feast of the resurrection in a special way. This is why at the head of a dying person a candle is lit, showing that the one who apparently has entered the darkness of non-existence and everything is without meaning, enters into the eternal life of Christ and his existence does have a meaning. The meaning of existence has been most illumined through Christ's resurrection. At the resurrection "all things have been filled with light."

These six meanings contained in the praise of the Kingdom of the Holy Trinity are inherently united. Therefore, we will not treat them completely separately, but as whole. First, a few preliminary considerations.

Through His incarnation, teaching and saving works, Christ has made it clearly known as being a Trinity of Persons, a community of love between the Father, the Son and the Holy Spirit. This distinguishes the Christian faith about God, clearly present in the New Testament, from any other religion. The Kingdom of heaven was thus specified as the Kingdom of a God who is not a solitary Person, but an eternally loving

Father of an eternal Son Whom He sent to become man so as to make Him our brother and thus to extend His fatherly love toward us, too, who have been created for this purpose. An eternally solitary person is not even a person because it lacks love. And if that person creates other persons, it does so out of the need to be completed, in which case it is not free. Properly speaking, this god is not God, and the pantheistic understanding of that god is inevitable, being one with the world.

God the Father is King from eternity, namely He has absolute power, not being reigned over by anybody and having nothing from anybody; the Son is also King; the Holy Spirit is King, too, for the Trinity is never ruled by any law above it or by any necessity, having all the happiness in its life and love. It is perfectly free, being a communion of Persons in perfect love, thus possessing everything. For where a law or a passion for something else rules, there is no happiness in perfect love, therefore there is no perfect communion of perfect Persons.

Christians knew from the beginning, from Christ and the Apostles, that not only the Father is King, but also His Son is King. They knew that, in His quality as the Son of the Father, Christ is King from eternity, but through incarnation, through the sacrifice for us, through resurrection and ascension He became King also as man and that together with Him— as His brothers and as children of the heavenly Father—will inherit the Kingdom all those who adhere to Him through faith and become like Him through their liberation from the egoism of passions (Lk 22:29-30; Mt 25:34-40; Mk 14:62; Jn 18:36; Lk 23:3, 42-43; Rev 1:5-6). They knew from St. Paul the Apostle that the Son was "bringing many sons to glory" (Heb 2:10). It was proper for the Son to make others children and partakers of His glory. But the Son does this by fulfilling the Father's will and by becoming incarnate as man and suffering death for them, so as to destroy the sins and the death in their nature and thus to give them an example of His glory as basis for their glory. St. Paul the Apostle says: "that you would walk worthy of God who calls you into His own kingdom and glory" (1 Th 2:12).

Explaining the words of the Psalmist: "Therefore God, Your God, anointed You with the oil of gladness" (Ps 44:8; Heb 1:8). St. Athanasius of Alexandria says that the Son was King from eternity together with the Father and the Holy Spirit, and this is why by becoming man He also became King as man and thus He made us, too, kings in Himself: "And therefore He is here 'anointed' not that He may become God, for He was so even before; nor that He may become King, for He had the Kingdom eternally, existing as God's Image... but in our behalf is this written, as before. For the Israelitish kings, upon their being anointed, then became kings, not being so before;... but the Savior on the contrary, being God and ever ruling in the Father's Kingdom, and being Himself He that supplies the Holy Ghost, nevertheless is here said to be anointed, that as before, being said as man to be anointed with the Spirit, He might provide for us men, not only exaltation and resurrection, but the indwelling and intimacy of the Spirit."[207]

It is of this promise that the priest thinks, together with the faithful, when he utters the words: "Blessed is the Kingdom of the Father and of the Son and of the Holy Spirit." But they also think of the condition for receiving this Kingdom mentioned by St. Peter the Apostle: "Therefore, brethren, be even more diligent to make your call and election sure" (1 Pt 1:10), who then specifies that it is about their call and election for the heavenly Kingdom (1 Pt 1:11).

Christ has promised this Kingdom to those who believe in the Holy Trinity that, out of love and willing to raise them to the status of children of the Father, sent the Son to become man, to be crucified for them, to rise again and to ascend as man and to sit at the right hand of the Father so as to attract them, too, to this summit. In this is shown that it is a Kingdom of love between God and us and among ourselves, not of a god desiring to reign over, or of human beings who compete to be superior over each other. It is the Kingdom of the loving Trinity, given that the Father's beloved and loving Son from eternity also became, as man, King together with the Father, and thereby has also raised us who believe in Him to the dignity of kings, unchained from any slavery to the egoistic passions. Christ has raised us through His Holy Spirit to perfect freedom from passions, from sins with tendencies toward gaining dominance, for where the Spirit who sanctifies is, there is liberty (2 Cor 3:17). In this Kingdom all will be kings, namely free, once we are children of the Father King and brothers of the Son King, without being controlled by any passion and, therefore, by each other. It will be a true Kingdom because there will be no egoistic passion to control its members, nor will there be any division among them, for it will be the Kingdom of love and of perfect communion, which at the same time is perfect liberty. Those who love each other have no desire to control each other nor are they forced to submit to each other. But they all have the greatest joy to offer themselves to each other and to mutually enrich each other spiritually, which means that they do this in the most perfect freedom. That Kingdom will be the perfect union in freedom, in the freedom of love. Its members will rejoice in "the glorious liberty of the children of God" (Rom 8:21). But this being the true freedom, they will "not using liberty as a cloak [mask] for vice" (1 Pt 2:16).

This Kingdom has been extended to us through the Savior, but its coming was announced by St. John the Baptist, and Joseph of Arimathea, among many others, was waiting for it (Mk 15:43). This waiting was mentioned in the Mosaic worship. But the Savior specified that God whose Kingdom He was preaching was His Father and our Father (the Lord's Prayer, the Sermon on the Mount). As the Son of the Father, the Savior also presents Himself as King (before Pilate). St. Gregory of Nyssa, on the basis of many old manuscripts, says that "Luke, who, when he desires the Kingdom to come, implores the help of the Holy Spirit. For he says in his Gospel [11:2]; instead of *Thy Kingdom come* it reads 'May Thy Holy Spirit come upon us and purify us.'"[208] Thus, the Holy Spirit as being of the same essence with the Father and the Son is also King, or He is the One who opens for us the Holy Trinity's Kingdom of love. This is why we, too, address the Holy Spirit, calling Him "Heavenly King" and the priest recites the prayer "O, Heavenly King" before he begins the Holy Liturgy with the blessing of the Holy Trinity.

On the basis of the revelation of the Kingdom of heaven as the Kingdom of the Trinity, the Christian community, as it began its own worship, replaced the blessing of the Kingdom of heaven or of God in general in the Mosaic worship with the blessing of the Kingdom of the Father and of the Son and of the Holy Spirit.

Clement of Alexandria says, soon after the middle of the second century: "And do Thou Thyself cause that all of us... may be wafted in calm by Thy Holy Spirit,... by night and day to the perfect day; and giving thanks may praise, and praising thank the Alone Father and Son, Son and Father, the Son, Instructor and Teacher, and the Holy Spirit, all in One, in whom is all, for whom all is One, for whom is eternity, whose members we all are, whose glory the aeons are; for the All-good, All lovely, All-wise, All-just One. To whom be glory both now and for ever. Amen."[209]

This Kingdom is an extension of the love of the Holy Trinity toward us, and it falls to us to respond with our love for the Holy Trinity and also among ourselves. Only in this way do we prove that we truly want to be part of it.

This is shown by the priest in the name of all when, after pronouncing the blessing of the Kingdom of the Holy Trinity, he kisses the Holy Table as the throne of the Holy Trinity and as the tomb of Christ who has next to Him the relics of the saints; he also kisses the Holy Gospel or Christ and His cross. Before that, the faithful themselves kissed the Gospel in the nave, for Christ is also with them.

Upon hearing the blessing of the Holy Trinity by the priest, the faithful give their assent with the word *Amen—Let it be so*, thus they, too, bless this Kingdom in all the meanings mentioned above and show their desire to be part of it. Its blessing by the priest is its proclamation, which gives joy to the faithful, for what is given to them now and for the hope of inheriting it fully in the life to come.

The proclamation of the Kingdom on behalf of the faithful is shown by the priest when, prior to that, he opens the royal doors and soon after that he closes them but without closing the curtain. This means that the Kingdom of the Holy Trinity, the Kingdom of eternal love, was made known by Christ and the people are invited to enter and to advance in it; but in the earthly life, before the full union with Christ, it is not fully experienced. It shines forth in this life, but it is not entirely given to us. This is shown by the fact that the inside of the altar is not completely covered through the drawn curtain behind the royal doors, but through an intense flashing of its light through the space above the royal doors, only a part of this light is filtered through. During the Holy Liturgy the royal doors will be opened again at the Small Entrance, when the thrice holy hymn is sung, during the reading of the Apostle, the Gospel and the Creed. Then, from the communion of the faithful onward they will remain open until the end of the Holy Liturgy, symbolizing that through the Holy Communion they have fully entered the Kingdom of the Trinity.

Thus the Holy Liturgy offers the occasion for the anticipated experience, by way of guarantee, of the heavenly Kingdom and the prefiguration of fully attaining it after a gradual progress toward it in the earthly life. This liturgical ascent from the partial experience to the full experience in the Kingdom of the Holy Trinity is represented in the Holy Liturgy as an ascent toward union with the sacrificed and risen Christ, not of the single believer, but of the community that is increasingly filled with the irradiation of His presence, energized by His saving offering to the Father and to them, so that He may prepare them to offer themselves united among themselves and together with Him to the Father at the end of time, when the Father will be all in all and in all things, without the disappearance of the Son and of the adopted human persons (1 Cor 15:28).

In this *Amen* of the community there is a joy that anticipates the one which its members will have when they will receive it in its fullness, when all those who are saved will cry out with a loud voice: "Alleluia! Salvation and glory and honor and power belong to the Lord our God" (Rev 19:1). St. John the Apostle sees and hears in advance that joy: "And I heard, as it were, the voice of a great multitude, as the sound of many waters and as the sound of mighty thunderings, saying, 'Alleluia! For the Lord God Omnipotent reigns!'" (Rev 19:6). At that time the glory of Christ the King made man will be manifested in all its brightness. But at the same time will also be shown the glory of those with whom He united Himself as the Lamb who was slain for humans as well as the glory He clothed them with, similar to the glory with which the groom clothes his bride. For the Apostle John hears the multitude continuing to say: "Let us be glad and rejoice and give Him glory, for the marriage of the Lamb has come, and His wife has made herself ready" (Rev 19:7).

The word *Amen* was taken even by the first Christians from the Mosaic worship. But Christians say it on the basis of the fact that in Christ the Kingdom of the loving Trinity has been truly revealed, that through Him this Kingdom has been truly established and promised. St. Paul the Apostle says that we say every *Amen* for the glory of God in Christ, because in Christ have been fulfilled, on the one hand, all of God's promises, and on the other hand, their future fulfillment for those who believe (2 Cor 1:20) has been assured. Therefore, it is especially of Christ that we think when we say *Amen*. Only Christians can say for certain *Amen—let it be so—*for only they know about the present and future fulfillment of God's promises in Christ for us and only they have the hope of salvation founded in Him.[210] Only through Christ do we know that godhead is not an infinity without form or unipersonal, lacking love, but it is full of love; within that infinity there is a loving Father and a loving Son, a life that is not morally indifferent, but a holy life. Through Christ we know that the Kingdom of God is the Kingdom of eternal love, that its glory, reign and power belong to a Triune God and thus a God of love. Through Him we know that if we believe, the Spirit will make us its members for eternity.

Happy forever will be those who will become its members. Thus, the word *Amen* expresses also the conviction of the members of the community that they will be a part of this Kingdom, or their hope that they, too, will be worthy of the happiness found in it.

Firmly based on the hope of the Kingdom into whose anticipated ambiance the faithful enter from the beginning of the Holy Liturgy, they remember the condition set by the Savior for those who want to attain its fullness in the life to come: care for the needy and persecuted, because in this they become like the Son who was close to them, the Son who became like them and who said: "Come, you blessed of My Father, inherit the kingdom prepared for you from the foundation of the world: for I was hungry and you gave Me food," etc. (Mt 25:34-35). That Kingdom is not of those who are powerful in a worldly sense, but of those who are humble and brethren in humility. The hope for that Kingdom is also given to those who committed evil deeds during their earthly life, but have repented in the last hour like the thief on the right side who prayed to Jesus: "Lord, remember me when You come into Your Kingdom" (Lk 23:42).

This Kingdom is the union of those who believe in the Holy Trinity, through the marriage of the faithful humanity with the Son of the heavenly King followed by the banquet of eternal love (Mt 22:1, 14). One enters into this Kingdom through the Holy Mysteries of Baptism and Chrismation; after the fall from it one re-enters through the Mystery of Confession, and one maintains one's life in it through Holy Communion. This is why the Holy Liturgy begins with an unbroken promise for this union with the Holy Trinity and for this eternal banquet of love toward which the faithful advance through Holy Communion as union with Christ.

In the full union with the sacrificed Christ, as we become one body and blood with Him, we ascend as a community so that its members may offer themselves together with Him to the Father and to each other, so that the Father may be all things in all. But the ascent toward the sacrificed Christ consists in their being totally filled with the inclination for sacrifice or for dedication to God and to each other, which comes from the power irradiating from the sacrificed Christ who approaches them more and more according to their preparation so that He may fully offer Himself to them.

Thus the entire Holy Liturgy is the movement of the community in the spirit of Christ's sacrifice toward full union with the sacrificed and risen Christ, as well as the mutual offering among themselves from the power of His sacrifice. This is one and the same with the ascent within the fullness of love. It is equivalent with the entrance into and advance in the Kingdom of the Trinity. This places a seal of sacrifice out of love upon the entire Christian life, as all of it becomes a Liturgy in the broad sense. This sense of the Liturgy is shown by the fact that the priest accompanies the blessing of the Kingdom with the sign of the cross, which he makes with the Gospel over the Holy Antimension, representing Christ's death for us and having near Him the relics of the martyrs who gave us the best example of their appropriation of Christ's spirit of sacrifice. But he also makes the same sign over the Holy Table which, on the one hand, represents the throne of the Holy Trinity, and on the other hand, the tomb of Christ or the table of sacrifice before the Father on which Christ sits forever in a state of sacrifice for us so that we, too, may receive the power to sacrifice ourselves. In fact, the Kingdom has been revealed and established by the Holy Trinity through the incarnate, sacrificed and risen Son so that He may unite through sacrifice on both sides the Trinity with the creation, because Christ's sacrifice has not been regarded with indifference by the Father and the Holy Spirit. The all-merciful Father also suffered together with the Son who was offering Himself as sacrifice for us, and the Holy Spirit strengthened the Son as man in the offering of this sacrifice. The state of the Son's permanent sacrifice being His attention toward us, it also indicates the attention of the entire Trinity.

Thus, by blessing the Trinity we offer thanks for what It has done so that It could make us part of Its Kingdom, and at the same time with the gratitude and the joy we show we also resolve to walk the path which Christ showed us through His sacrifice while the Father and the Holy Spirit agreed on the sacrifice of the Son for our salvation. This is the path imitated to the highest degree by so many martyrs and devotees to the service of others, a path by which we will also, to the extent to which we imitate it, attain the resurrection of happiness.

But he who offers a sacrifice is also a priest. The Christians who offer themselves as sacrifice by abstaining from the passions of egoism and thus sacrificing themselves for others become not only kings, but also priests. Christ is the universal High Priest and the source of the high priesthood for those who offer themselves as sacrifice for the reason that

He is also the source of the power for sacrifice for all. We become priests by appropriating Christ's power for sacrifice, personally assimilating His state of sacrifice. But we also become children of the eternal King since we become siblings of His Son.

The identity of the status as king and priest of Him who sacrifices Himself is shown in the book of Revelation and by St. Peter the Apostle. In the book of Revelation Christ is called, on the one hand, the Lamb: "in the midst of the throne and of the four living creatures, and in the midst of the elders, stood a Lamb as though it had been slain" (Rev 5:6). On the other hand, He is praised by the four creatures and the elders with the words: "You are worthy to take the scroll, and to open its seals [history], for You were slain and have redeemed us to God by Your blood out of every tribe... and have made us kings and priests to our God and we shall reign on the earth" (Rev 5:9–10). The slain Lamb is the Son of God who became man and who liberated us from slavery to sinful passions, death and the devil through His sacrifice. Thus He became King as man, too, and He made us co-kings with Him or He established a knew Kingdom for us, for both He and we became and are kings through His sacrifice. Therefore, just as He became High Priest and King, so we, too, became priests and kings together with Him. The twenty-four elders manifest this quality by carrying bowls full of incense, which symbolize the prayers of the saints rising up to the Father as a sweet-smelling fragrance and as a good behavior in obedience that is pleasing to the Father. In this way one makes a distinction between the ordained priests and other Christians priests in general, whose prayers are offered by the presbyters. All believers are priests and pray, but their prayers are gathered in unity by the ordained priest so that they rise as a unitary wave, pure and well-pleasing to God. Because they are priests who offer as a sacrifice their prayers, they are also kings reigning over the passions and called to resurrection as victory over death, once they became brothers with Christ, the only begotten Son of the Father, through the union with Him in Holy Communion and through the appropriation of His spirit of sacrifice.

But it is not only the twenty-four elders who praise the Lamb who made those who believe in Him priests in a broad sense, but also the billions of angels who surround them, showing that closer to the Lamb who reigns through His sacrifice are His priests and the saints whose prayers they gather. This is because Christ became a High Priest and a sacrifice for human beings and they were able to appropriate especially through their bodies the status as sacrifice and as priests: "Then I looked, and I heard the voice of many angels around the throne, the living creatures, and the elders; and the number of them was ten thousand times ten thousand, and thousands of thousands, saying with a loud voice: Worthy is the Lamb who was slain to receive power and riches and wisdom, and strength and honor and glory and blessing" (Rev 5:11–12). It is again understood that He accepts this as man, thus He became king as man, too, so that we may also become kings. As man, He accepts the glory and the power so that we, too, may receive them.

St. Peter the Apostle unites the quality as priests and kings of the believers into a single one: "royal priesthood." The believers have this dual quality on account of Christ's sacrifice as they bring to fruition Christ's power of sacrifice in their spiritual sacrifices. Through them, on the one hand, they serve God as priests and, on the other hand, they, as kings, liberate themselves from passions and from death. Thus, those who liberate themselves from passions through sacrifices make up a royal priesthood or a closely knit community that advances within the bosom of the Holy Trinity. However, St. Peter the Apostle does not call this a kingdom, but "His own special people" (1 Pt 2:9), or the "spiritual house" made of living stones built on the foundation stone, which is Christ: "You also as living stones, are being built up a spiritual house, a holy priesthood, to offer up spiritual sacrifices acceptable to God through Jesus Christ" (1 Pt 2:5).

The faithful are called to transcend attachment to the world and being closed off in the passing time toward the plane of the eternal Kingdom of the Trinity, of the unique God in Trinity from whom all things come and in whom we all are to rise, achieving unity by fulfilling His will. This Kingdom has an eschatological characteristic. It begins as a different life plan even during our earthly existence, but it will be revealed in all its fullness in the life to come. It is to the quality as members for eternity of that Kingdom that we are also called. We are called to appropriate this transcending from the power of the incarnate, sacrificed and risen Christ, a power which He has because He is also God. A God who is not transcendent to this world, subjected to laws and affections would not be a true God. That God would also be subjected to the law of emanation and evolution toward no goal, without any meaning. If He did not have in Himself a life of love, self-sufficient, and if He were not a Father who has a Son born of His essence and distinct from the world created out of nothing, not appearing as a result of the evolution of an essence identical with the essence of the world, He would not be able to raise us from the existence subjected to the same laws of the appearance and death of all in a senseless succession.

The sacrifice itself represents such a free transcending. It shows the human person's capacity to rise over a world subjected to certain laws that recognize only a senseless succession. This shows that sacrifice itself gives meaning to life. A mother does not see the meaning of life outside of sacrificial service to her children. But service to other persons would not be imposed as an unconditional commandment if it were not for the absolute value of the persons who are helped and them being regarded as destined for eternity, for an eternity whose happiness also depends on the service I offer. I cannot believe in their eternity unless I believe in God, the personal source of eternity. Service toward human persons has its unconditional importance only if I experience it as the fulfillment of a commandment of the personal God, who assures the eternity of the persons He created out of love so that He may love them forever. Service toward human beings is thus included in service toward God. God has given so much value to human beings that He made His own Son their servant (Mt 20:28). By accepting death as sacrifice for them, but accepting it out of such a limitless love, He also conquered it. Thus, He gave a positive meaning to death itself which, outside of Christ, places upon existence the seal of the greatest absurdity and tragedy.

Pascal said:

> We know that life, and especially the life of Christians, is a continuous sacrifice, which cannot end except in death; we know that Jesus Christ by coming into the world considered Himself and has offered Himself to God as a complete holocaust and as a true gift of sacrifice; that His birth, His life, His death, His resurrection, His ascension, His eternal sitting at the right hand of His Father and His presence in the Eucharist are but one single and unique sacrifice; we know that what took place in Christ must take place in all His members; Let us, therefore, regard life as a sacrifice and think that the accidents of our life have no significance for the spirit of Christians except to the extent to which they interrupt or complete this sacrifice. We do not call evil except what makes the gift of sacrifice destined to God a victim of the devil . . . . If we do not cross over to God through the

Mediator Christ, we find nothing in us except true afflictions or condemnable pleasures. But if we view all things in Christ, we will find complete consolation, complete contentment and our complete spiritual growth.

Let us, therefore, view death in Christ and not outside of Him. Without Jesus Christ it is horrible, detestable, it is a horror of nature. In Jesus Christ death is worth loving, it is sacred, it is the joy of the believer. Everything in Christ is sweet, even death. This is why He suffered and died, so as to sanctify death and suffering.[211]

Thus, through Christ's cross appropriated by us we pass over into the Kingdom of heaven, into the Holy Trinity's Kingdom of love. "For He Himself is our peace, who has made both one, and has broken down the middle wall of separation, having abolished in His flesh the enmity,... so as to create in Himself one new man from the two, thus making peace, and that He might reconcile them both to God in one body through the cross, thereby putting to death the enmity... For through Him we both have access by one Spirit to the Father. Now, therefore, you are no longer strangers and foreigners, but fellow citizens with the saints and members of the household of God" (Eph 2:14-16, 18-19).

Through His Son become man, the Trinity came to us forever, and It raised us to Itself, for through Christ's sacrifice the human person has abolished the wall of egoism and come before the Father. In the person of Christ the path toward the Holy Trinity has been opened for us through the cross on which, by accepting it from Him, we come out of the egoistical separation from God and among ourselves. For only through sacrifice can we open the gate of God and the gate of our neighbor.

The Kingdom of heaven, which was announced by St. John the Baptist as being at hand, has become in Christ a reality and has been defined as the Kingdom of the loving Trinity that manifested Its love through the Son, become man like us and crucified for us so that He may determine us to respond to Its love and to manifest our love among ourselves.

Jesus Christ has shown us that God is love, because He is not a single person, but a Trinity of persons in a relationship between Father, Son and Holy Spirit, and has proven through His incarnation and sacrifice for us that He extends His love toward us as well. For this purpose He made use of the human body, showing its value and our value as bodily beings. He resurrected His body to an eternal life, showing that our body, too, is destined for eternity. He has also shown that God's unity is not an abstract unity, but one that is alive and loving. And He wants us to have this unity as well. We achieve this unity in the Church that is "filled with the Trinity." Christ has shown us that the Trinity is alive and loving through the very fact that He, One of the Trinity, became man and sacrificed Himself for us, offering Himself to the Father and to us so that we, too, may offer ourselves, from His power, to the Father and to each other, so that being filled with the Trinity we may be in the image of the Trinity: a loving unity of unconfused human persons, extremely precious to each other. For God's unchangeability is not one of rigidity, but an unchangeability of mobile love.

These things are beautifully stated by Archimandrite Vasileios of Stavronikita Monastery from Mount Athos: "With the Incarnation of the Word, the way to reconciliation is opened. With the creation of the Church we have 'the dwelling of God . . . with men' (Rev 21:3). The Church has a mission to bear witness to unity, because in it God is known not simply as sole ruler, but as a perfect communion of three persons. Furthermore, the Word was made flesh in order to reveal the true divine unity and freedom which reigns in the bosom of the deity. He became 'flesh' in order to demonstrate the spiritual mission of the 'flesh,' and to show how everything has come into being and increases and is transfigured through the unity and fecundity of the Trinity... He created it in His image. 'The holy Church is an icon of God, for it brings about among the faithful a unity the same as that which is in God' (St. Maximos the Confessor, *Mystagogy*, ch. 1; PG 91, 668B). . . . The Lord... came to unite us, through Himself, with His Father and our Father... He came 'that they may all be one' (Jn 17:21) . . . He who has really seen the Church has seen the Holy Trinity . . . . The unity of all for which the Church prays is not to be understood as an assembly of parts made up of 'Christian communities,' but as an extension of the trinitarian unity divinely active in the liturgical body of the Church . . . . The mystery of unity, as the Church lives and understands it, is the Kingdom of the Father and the Son and the Holy Spirit."[212]

"There is nothing static in the Divine Liturgy, nothing isolated. Everything lives and moves in harmony within the whole. Everything acquires meaning. Everything is concentrated round one central point. Everything is made known. Its nature and its *raison d'être* are revealed in 'reason-endowed worship,' in the Liturgy of the Word 'through whom all things were made.' . . . it is the blessed Kingdom of the Father and of the

Son and of the Holy Spirit, which receives and sanctifies creation. It is the uncreated grace of the Holy Trinity, which renews creation. The opening blessing of the Divine Liturgy glorifies the thrice-holy Kingdom: 'Blessed is the Kingdom of the Father and of the Son and of the Holy Spirit . . .' In what follows, all we ask for is this Kingdom . . . It is to this that the faithful offer themselves in all and for all. The Divine Liturgy becomes the theological ground on which all things meet. Outside its warmth things are all unrecognizable, frozen and isolated."[213]

A monarch God rules over us, but does not love us and does not plant love within us. A pantheistic essence does not open for us but the perspective of personal annihilation. But our union with the Holy Trinity and among us after the image of the triune unity is not achieved without renouncing our egoism, without our self-offering to God and to our fellow humans. It is Christ who gives us the power for this offering. At the basis of Christ's sacrifice as man is the very eternal self-offering of the Persons of the Holy Trinity. This is why we combine the sign of the cross with the remembrance of the Holy Trinity or with its glorification. We praise the God of love, the God who out of love for us, based on the love of the triune Persons, sent the Son to become man and to sacrifice Himself for us and to remain with us in the state of sacrifice in order to lead us to the unity in love with the Trinity.

"When the witness of the Resurrection writes: 'I, John, your brother... was in the Spirit on the Lord's day . . . then I saw a new heaven and a new earth,' it is as if he were saying to us: 'I, John, your brother *took part in the Liturgy*."[214] We should mention the Apostle John's full saying: "I, John, both your brother and companion in the tribulation and kingdom... was in the Spirit on the Lord's Day" (Rev 1:9–10). The fact that Christians see in the Holy Liturgy the new heaven and the new earth does not take them out of the hardships and sufferings of life on earth. But the Kingdom is present in these. For the Kingdom is together with the cross and we reach it through the cross, whose ultimate foundation is found in the Holy Trinity and in the incarnation of Christ. As long as we are in the body inclined toward sin, the cross takes for us the form of abstentions, of sufferings and hardships. Even these make the Spirit transparent, who strengthens within us the new heaven and the new earth, the heaven and the earth of love. The cross to which the Kingdom is linked belongs not only to the Holy Trinity nor does it actually accompany only the Son who took on our body, but it also accompanies us in this life. This is why we, too, are to share in it. Without the cross nothing can be achieved. The cross means for us abstention from the egoism of sins and repentance for them. It is suffering, but also consolation, because through it we enter into the authentic depth of our being and into the living expanse of the Kingdom of love.

"There reigns everywhere the devout contrition which secretly and inexhaustibly comforts everyone, making them joyful and uniting them as brothers. Human emotionalism is one thing and the devout contrition of the Liturgy quite another. The one causes man skin-deep irritation but torments him physically; the other nails him down but comforts him, revealing our God-like nature in the very depths of our existence . . . . In his unknown depths, man conceals a divine miracle. In the Church, he does not lose heart when he is depressed, nor is he disturbed by petty and inappropriate sentiment when he is joyful. Both sorrow and joy have a liturgical function."[215] The antinomy is always present, soliciting the fortitude of joy in suffering and maintaining the feeling of the complex mystery of existence, apparently contradictory but still unitary.

The love that reigns in the Kingdom of God founded and opened for us by Christ through the cross specifically shows us the fact that this Kingdom is not the Kingdom of three uniform Persons, but of the Father and of the Son and of the Holy Spirit, the perfect sign of union in love. It is not the Kingdom of a despotic ruler, but the Kingdom in which the King is the Father and in which all its citizens are children by adoption or through grace, thus by an act of love and, consequently, siblings of the Son, the Only Begotten from the Father according to essence. This means that the King is the Father of its citizens not in a paternalistic sense, but it is also the Kingdom of His Only Begotten Son and He makes us siblings of this Son, heirs together with Him of the quality as kings in it. "For as many as are led by the Spirit of God, these are sons of God. For you did not receive the spirit of bondage again to fear, but you received the spirit of adoption by whom we cry out, 'Abba, Father.'...and if children, then heirs—heirs of God and joint heirs with Christ, if indeed we suffer with Him, that we may also be glorified together" (Rom 8:14–15, 17).

The Kingdom Christ has brought to us is the kingdom of love because the King is a Father who, having a Son of one essence with Him, wished to also extend the love He has for the Son to other conscious beings, capable of feeling His paternal love and of responding to it, as the theologian Jürgen Moltmann has emphasized recently. The

Father sends His Son to become man, says Moltmann, so that He may regard human persons as His siblings. Thus, "Jesus did not proclaim the kingdom of God *the Lord,* but the kingdom of God *his Father* . . . . This gives the kingdom he proclaimed a new quality... In this kingdom God is not the Lord; he is the merciful Father. In this kingdom there are no servants; there is only God's free children. In this kingdom what is required is not obedience and submission; it is love and free participation . . . . The Lord's Prayer shows this too, ultimately speaking. It is *the Father's* kingdom, *the Father's* will and *the Father's* name for whose coming, fulfillment and hallowing we pray in the fellowship of Jesus."[216] "The liberty of his prayer to the Father reveals the sonship. Through the 'Abba' prayer believers are taken into the fellowship of the Son with the Father . . . . God does not speak like the master or lord who has to be unquestioningly obeyed; God listens to the requests and suggestions of his children like a Father."[217] "Through the sending of the Son, that is to say, the sonship is communicated. . . . By sonship therefore we certainly have to understand the special relationship between Jesus and the One who sent him; but this relationship is no longer merely exclusive; it is now inclusive at the same time."[218]

The Son makes us loving children of the Father not only by the fact that He becomes man and our brother, but also through the fact that He offers Himself completely also as man to the Father and He transmits to us as well this tendency toward offering, giving us through His Holy Spirit the power to offer ourselves as pure sacrifices to the Father out of love.

We become loving children of the Father together with the Only Begotten, because we, too, appropriate His state of sacrifice as man. Through sacrifice He became also as man joint king with the Father, because through sacrifice He has shown also as man His perfect love for the Father. Therefore, only by appropriating His sense of sacrifice, that is of identical love for the Father, do we also become children and joint kings with the incarnate Son. Our love for the Father unites us in the dignity as His children and as heirs of the Kingdom. St. Cyril of Alexandria says: "And Christ is the King of all by nature and participation. For being God by nature He emptied Himself of glory, descending to the form of a bondservant (Php 2:7) and receives the Kingdom, in the form of a man, even though He reigns beforehand and from eternity together with God and the Father and is co-leader and ruler of all."[219] By receiving the power as children from the Only Begotten Son, once He united us with the Father, we have, together with Him, the power to rule over all things together with the Son through the love by which we have attained self-denial.

St. Cyril develops both the idea that in the Son the Father perceives us, too, as children and the idea that He perceives us as children not only because the Son became man, but also because by offering Himself as sacrifice He gives us the power to offer ourselves to the Father as sacrifices together with Him. Like all the Fathers, St. Cyril shows that we cannot manifest our love for the Father except by offering ourselves, too, as sacrifices together with the Son, as St. Paul the Apostle said. Explaining the inscription of the names of the tribes of Israel engraved on the two emerald stones on the garment worn by the high priest of the Old Testament on his shoulders (Ex 28:9–12), St. Cyril says: "And the engraving on the stones is said to be as remembrance of the sons of Israel by the Lord, for the Lord will receive, so to speak, all of them in the person of Aaron. For God and Father perceives us in Christ for remembrance and in Him we have been made known and worthy to be seen and written in the book of God."[220]

About our sacrifice from the power of Christ's sacrifice and our entrance through this before the Father, St. Cyril says: "Thus, He has been slain for our sins, but we also were buried together with Him, suffering death—not the physical one—but putting to death the earthly parts and not living for ourselves but for Christ and through Him for the Father."[221] Or: "For if Christ did not die for us, we would not have been accepted as a sweet fragrance by God the Father. But once He has been perfected [as man] through passions, we follow Him at once as a sanctified gift to God the Father and we offer ourselves as a truly spiritual and blessed sacrifice."[222] Or: "Our Lord Jesus Christ sanctifies us in numerous ways, making us saints and well received. For through Him and in Him we have acceptance [entrance] and we become well pleasing to God the Father. For being under corruption and sin, His death and life are most useful and necessary for salvation and, in addition to this, perfection through His body and blood. For perfection is found in Christ, not in the law."[223]

The Holy Liturgy is the action of our joint offering with Christ, or the union of the community with Christ in the state of sacrifice in order to offer itself as sacrifice together with Him to the Father, so that the Kingdom of the Trinity might be achieved in all. This is not about a sacrifice of physical death, but a renunciation of any egoism and of any interest in our own things.

The priest stands behind the royal doors, next to the holy table, separate from the faithful, but not without a connection with them through prayer, dialogue and various entrances and appearances. However, he remains fully visible after communion. Through this he represents Christ who stands as a slain Lamb before the throne of the Father (Rev 5), interceding for us, with His attention to us, wishing to raise us also to where He is. The priest represents Christ, the High Priest, who entered with His sacrifice into the Holy of Holies in heaven, incessantly interceding for the absolution of our sins through His blood. "Not with the blood of goats and calves, but with His own blood He entered the Most Holy Place once for all . . . . how much more shall the blood of Christ, who through the eternal Spirit offered Himself without spot to God, cleanse your conscience from dead works to serve the living God?" (Heb 9:12–14). "Therefore, brethren, having boldness let us enter the Holiest by the blood of Jesus" (Heb 10:19), adding our sacrifices to the sacrifice offered by the heavenly High Priest represented by the priest. For, by representing Christ, the priest prays in the altar for the faithful, mentioning their names connected with the particles placed as their sacrifices next to the Agnetz that represents the Lamb who stands as an invisible sacrifice on the invisible altar. If God communicates His powers through Christ's humanity as through a central medium, and through this medium strengthened in the experience and help of God is brought the sacrifice and the intercession before God, why would this intercessory role of Christ's humanity not be extended also through the priest's humanity, chosen to be a visible center of the gathering of the faithful?

St. Cyril of Alexandria has extensively studied the necessity of priestly service for our salvation in Christ. Just as Aaron was called by God to serve Moses who represented Christ before the people, so are the priests of the New Law called to serve Christ, the real one. "For the divine disciples were co-workers in a spiritual way of Christ, the High Priest and the Head Captain of all, joining with Him who can fulfill all things, not as to one weak in power, but as those who have been called and well chosen to serve Him, and they have gained from Him power for everything. The divine Paul also testified to this by saying: 'I can do all things through Christ who strengthens me'" (Php 4:13).[224]

Just as the names of the tribes of Israel engraved on the emerald stones from Aaron's shoulders "were memorials for the sons of Israel before the Lord," for the Lord will receive them, so to speak, in the person of Aaron, so does [the Lord] perceive us in the person (the face) of Christ, but also that of the priest in whom Christ is present. If in an invisible way we are recapitulated in Christ, in a visible way we are recapitulated in the priest. If in an invisible way we are "placed near the heart and mind of Christ, in a way felt by us [and by Him] we are placed near the heart and mind of the people." And if Christ is together with the saints,... because He carries before the Father what is ours, "since He always lives to make intercessions" (Heb 7:25) for us, He does this visibly and audibly through the priest. The priest is the location of Christ's descent to us. The priest's conscience, which is not for his own service, but for ours, is imprinted with the conscience of Christ.

In the ordination of certain persons for officiating the sacrifice of Christ for the salvation of the faithful is shown that man cannot do this on his own, but only the one called through the grace from above, which comes through the Apostles from Christ Himself. The priest is chosen by Christ from among the most diligent Christians for the intercessory service of His grace. Christ has taken on a human face distinct from ours. He works even now through the face of another person chosen by Him. "For did not the divine Paul say that those chosen for priesthood should have a name worthy of praise and be respected in all things? So, he says, 'that the man of God may be complete, thoroughly equipped for every good work' (2 Tim 3:17). He also affirmed that the bishop must be spotless and gave many details in this regard."[225]

The Kingdom of the Trinity is the Kingdom of love between the Father and the children adopted by the Son and offered entirely in the Son as a gift to the Father. Thus, it is the Kingdom of total freedom. Freedom is the second feature of the Kingdom of the Trinity in addition to that of unity in love. In fact, these two features are implied in each other.

Commenting on the words: "Your Kingdom come" from the Lord's Prayer, St. Gregory of Nyssa says: "There is one true and perfect power which is above all things and governs the whole universe. But it rules not by violence and tyrannical dictatorship, which enforces the obedience of its subjects through fear and compulsion."[226] God attracts through love, through goodness and through a power in which greatness and meekness are not in opposition.

God does not impose Himself through any kind of force similar to those in nature, nor through the pressure of a force exerted through weapons or human cunning. He does not bring nor hold anyone under His authority against his or her will. He attracts and keeps through the enormous force of His love that extended all the way to the sacrifice of His Son, as well as of a life-giving and inexhaustible power. This is what creates true happiness. The more a mother loves her child, the more she holds him close to her, the more she dedicates herself and the more she sacrifices herself every moment. But she does not have an amount of power and of life which to communicate at the same time with her total sacrifice, while God has eternal life out of which He can grant us everlasting life. The Kingdom of the Trinity is not enforced, but attracts, and unhappy are those who do not want to become its citizens.

On the other hand, St. Gregory of Nyssa says that true virtue is free of any fear and it is not ruled by anything, choosing the good through free will. And the supreme good is not an essence, but the loving supreme Personal Reality. It is this supreme Personal Reality that the virtue of the righteous one chooses freely. For It is good, or rather the goodness is a willed and personal action. The righteous one chooses God as the personal good that is infinitely loving and that stimulates him toward the ever increasing good.

The dispassionate person has broken down the middle wall of separation through full union with Christ, by the fact that Christ's will has become his own will since he no longer lives himself, but it is Christ who lives in him filled with the spirit of sacrifice (Gal 2:20). St. John Climacus says this, and he has in mind not only Ephesians 2:14, but also quotes the word of God from Isaiah 59:2: "Is it not your sins that separate you and Me?"[227]

In this sense, where the Spirit of Lord is, who has strengthened our spirit, a spirit of sacrificing communion, there is freedom; there we feel like children of the heavenly Father (Rom 8:15; 2 Cor 3:17).

Our nature has lost its freedom by freely deviating from communion with God, thus deviating from the supreme Good as Personal Reality, falling under the power of egoism that narrows it and subjugates it more and more, even though it seems that in this way its freedom is affirmed more and more. Proof that this state is a type of freedom that moves in bondage is the fact that it cannot escape this fold of egoism. This diminishes its power and life, keeping it in a spiritual death and finally taking it to physical death. Thus, the human persons living under the bondage of passions and death tend with a weakened will toward the true freedom of the Kingdom in which they will no longer be subjected to any restriction. But we cannot ascend with our weakened will to this Kingdom above which there is no power.

When we, therefore, bless the Kingdom of God we also ask for it to come to us through the power of God. "So if we ask that the Kingdom of God may come to us, the meaning of our request is this: I would be a stranger to corruption and liberated from death; would that I were freed from the shackles of sin and that death no longer lord it over me. Let us no more be tyrannized by evil so that the adversary may not prevail against me and make me his captive through sin . . . when the Kingdom of God comes upon us, all the things that now hold sway will cease to exist... death is undone and corruption is no more when life and incorruption reign in us unopposed."[228]

The power of this Kingdom resides in the Holy Spirit through whom God comes to us. He is the heavenly King whom we ask to abide in us, as does the priest before he starts the Holy Liturgy.

Our liberation through the Holy Spirit—the One who strengthens the spirit in us—from the passions through which we impose by force one upon other, brings about our mystical liberation from the cosmic nature. It will also no longer reign over us through its laws, but we will bend it according to our will. All things will form an empire of freedom and we will communicate with all things above laws. Animals will obey us on account of our love that will pervade them, too. Nature itself "will be delivered from the bondage of corruption into the glorious liberty of the children of God" (Rom 8:21).

Both through the sign of the cross, which the priest makes with the Gospel over the Antimension blessing the Holy Trinity and bringing to mind the good It does for humans, and by replacing the Gospel with the cross during the small entrance, one shows that this Kingdom heralded by the Gospel or by Christ preached through the Gospel is not separated from the cross. This is not because the cross would essentially and involuntarily be part of the Trinity and consequently would impose both the incarnation and the crucifixion of the Son of God, similar to a combination of suffering and happiness that alternate painfully like in the pantheistic systems, or because love would force God to give His Son to death in order to gain the love of humans that He would desperately need. But this is so because only through free love can one overcome the free separation of creation—itself the work of divine freedom—from God, a separation that caused its suffering. This is why He accepts the cross, because only through the cross can He bring the creation to union with Him Who is immortal. And this is done through the Son of God Who, out of the entire Holy Trinity's love for humans, takes on human nature and at the same time accepts its death so as to overcome it within the divinity's fullness of life communicated through love.

God's will to create conscious beings, who through their freedom associated with their creatureliness can fall—a fact that when it happens produces God's mercy and the decision to regain them through His Son's sacrifice—is in conformity with the love among the Triune Persons, but this conformity does not imply that it is necessary for God to act that way. We do not deny God's mercy, which implies even a certain spiritual participation by Him in their pain accepted through His "descent" to them, for this shows the reality and depth of His life. This is why we must not forget that Christ suffered the pain of the cross in a tension of human power through which He overcame pain, as St. Maximos the Confessor says.[229] In this way the death He suffered has conquered the death of nature and with it any subjugation under which human nature was held. Again we have the paradox: His divine participation in human pain through which He conquers pain or He does not allow Himself to be conquered by it. Pain did not entirely break Him, it was not stronger than Him, as certain Protestant theologians maintain, for this would entail that His love forces Him to create human beings and to gain their love through sacrifice. His participation in pain is united in the Spirit with His freedom and power.

The human person can die in two ways: either by persisting in voluntary separation from God, or in the elan of self-renunciation so as to immerse himself in the divinity's plenitude of life; either to be lost and to weaken his life in the stale water that lacks the spiritual oxygen of divine life, or to live by sipping the water of the immortal divine life. In neither of these two cases does he totally come out of the existence that God gave him for eternity. But in the first case he falls into an extremely reduced and narrow participation in existence, in a minimal clinging to God, while in the second case he becomes a participant in the infinite life of God, plunging into the depth of divine life without vanishing as a person. In any case, it also depends on the human person whether he is able to reach this divine life or not. Through his will to believe, the human person discovers God or God comes to meet him by revealing Himself to him. And thus the human person reveals himself in his positive actuality and not in the helplessness of being separated from God. God does not want to reveal Himself to the human person without the latter's contribution, just as the human person cannot reveal himself in his plenitude without discovering God, bringing his own contribution as well. This is a mysterious cooperation between God and the human person in God's revelation to the human person and, hence, that of the human person himself as well as in the human person's participation in the divine life.

But God does not only reveal Himself to the human person who perseveres in the will to believe, but, through the power He gives him from the death suffered by His Son incarnate as man, He also helps him to die to his superficial self that is separated from God.

Here is why the Triune God has made a preoccupation out of the death that entered the existence of His created beings, wishing to conquer their death as separation from God through their death as union with God and with His infinite life. God conquers this death once for all in His Son who became man. From His position as conqueror of death by death, His victory as Lamb slain for us extends until the end of the world to every human person who believes in Him and is united with Him in His death offered to the Father. Thus, the Son extends the Kingdom of freedom among humans until all things will be willingly "subjected" to Him, until He will subject all to the Father through their love, the ultimate source of life (1 Cor 15:24, 27) outside of Him, Himself remaining King over all together with the Father. In this way His Kingdom is extended until the end of the world, out of His position as conqueror of death, as a victory over the egoism within created beings through His sacrifice. This causes Him to remain in a real relationship with our death so as to conquer it through another death, from the power of His death. Therefore, we understand into what kind of death the Son of God as man has transformed our death and how He engages through it those who believe in Him. It is a death as an act of the unmanifested loving power and as a path toward the manifested power of the resurrection. Thus, as Christ continues to remain after the resurrection the slain Lamb, on the one hand He is immersed as man within the Father, and on the other hand He is glorified as the One Who conquered His death as a sacrifice, death as estrangement from God. "Emmanuel's death is sanctified and well accepted before God and the Father after the prototype of sacrifice. This is understood from the fact that the blood is poured [in the Old Law] on the holy altar [where God is] and the altar is anointed with it . . . . Thus, Christ's death progresses toward the divine glory, having as its final goal the glorious resurrection and the conquering of passion, which disappears into non-existence, being overcome by the supreme glory."[230] As liberation from the sins of egoism, the sacrifice is one and the same with sanctification. And since out of Christ's sacrifice we also receive the power to ascend toward God through sacrifice, as a liturgical ascent with Christ, a sacrifice with Him is also an ascent into holiness. St. Cyril of Alexandria always unites sacrifice with sanctification. To the extent to which we empty ourselves of our egoism and of our spiritual death, we conquer death, because we fill ourselves with God and we are thereby sanctified. This is why St. Cyril says that all things are sanctified through the cross: "Our Lord and Savior Jesus Christ sanctifies us in various ways, making us saints [sanctified gifts] and well accepted. For through Him and in Him we have access and we become well-pleasing to God and the Father. For as we are under corruption and in sin, His death and life are most beneficial and absolutely necessary for our salvation."[231] Ultimately, through our sacrifice we manifest our love for God. Thus, love as union with Him is what sanctifies us. In order to give us strength for this sacrifice, Christ remains in a sort of death, as completely immersed full of His love as man in His mutual divinity with the Father, which is also His complete offering to the Father as well as His glorification by the Father, so that out of its power He may give human persons the power to die and to conquer death as separation from God and to be glorified together with Christ.

Thus, out of perfect love for the Father and for human beings, the Son of the Father actualizes for everyone His death as sacrifice in order to conquer our death as separation from God.

This keeps the entire Trinity connected with the death of human beings until the end of the world. Furthermore, since the Trinity will keep human beings in its infinite life through the act of conquering death in the incarnate Son, accomplished with the benevolence of the Father and with the cooperation of the Holy Spirit, it will forever remain connected with the remembrance of Christ's death and there will forever remain in it the force by which it conquered death. For St. Paul says: "Not with the blood of goats and calves, but with His own blood He entered the Most Holy Place once for all, having obtained eternal redemption... But this Man, after He had offered one sacrifice for sins, forever sat down at the right hand of God" (Heb 9:12; 10:12).

Forever the slain Lamb will sit and receive praise alongside the Father, or better said on the throne of the Kingdom that has been established for us sits the Lamb as well: "Blessing and honor and glory and power be to Him who sits on the throne, and to the Lamb, forever and ever" (Rev 5:13). Or: "You are worthy to take the scroll, and to open its seals; For You were slain, and have redeemed us to God by Your blood out of every tribe and tongue and people and nation, and have made us kings and priests to our God; and we shall reign on the earth" (Rev 5:9). The sitting on the throne of the slain Lamb is the foundation of our participation in the Kingdom.

But we also give glory to God in Trinity, Who gave His Son to death for us in order to give us eternal life, and we praise the Kingdom in the Holy Liturgy, learning to do this from the book of Revelation (5:13). When we say that glory is due to the Lamb forever and ever, we show that we will praise Him forever for His kindness toward us manifested through the blood He shed for us, because we will partake forever, thanks to Him, of the happiness in the perfect, eternal life of the Trinity's Kingdom. "And raised us up together, and made us sit together in the heavenly places in Christ Jesus, that in the ages to come He might show the exceeding riches of His grace in His kindness toward us in Christ Jesus" (Eph 2:6–7).

Every time when, making the sign of the cross, we say: "Glory to the Father and to the Son and to the Holy Spirit unto the ages of ages," we show that we glorify the Trinity that remains connected forever with the cross through one of its Persons who was crucified with the assumed body and bears in this eternally living body the signs of the cross, showing that we will be in eternal communion with this Trinity connected with the cross. Even through the word "Amen" we give glory to God in Trinity Who perfected creation through the cross. For in this has been manifested the greatness beyond all imagination of His love toward us. One of the Trinity is in eternal communion with us through the body that He has in common with us, a body that bears the signs of the cross. Our mutual body with that of the triune Person is the means by which we become partakers of the infinity of divine life. And this is proven in its resurrection from death.

The humanity of one of the Persons of the Trinity has reached the climax of overcoming all egoism and of perfect love for God through the cross and, therefore, through that humanity is poured out over us, who have a common body with Him, His love for the Father and for us; through the cross His humanity has become a perfect vessel of divine love. This trace of the cross imprinted on us is never erased from Christ's humanity and thus from our humanity, and it remains *par excellence* the supreme medium for the irradiation of the life of the all-loving Trinity for us and of our love for It. "For [through Christ and through His cross] all the promises of God in Him are Yes, and in Him Amen, to the glory of God through us" (2 Cor 1:20).[232]

Through the cross God has raised Christ's humanity, and through it ours as well, to its perfect freedom not only through His divinity, but also through His humanity's effort to abstain from the desire to escape the suffering for God and also through its effort of self-renunciation, even though this effort has also been supported by the divinity united with humanity.[233] Therefore, through the cross there has been placed the foundation of our liberation from the inferior tendencies so that through the real consequences following the suffering on the cross by Christ's humanity — consequences that irradiate as power for abstention, patience and self-renunciation — our humanity may ascend toward resurrection and eternal life. Thus, when we praise the Father, the Son and the Holy Spirit and the royal freedom promised to us, we make the sign of the cross, imprinting on us the liberating freedom of both Christ's cross and of the Trinity. For we cannot imprint one without the other. Only when we conquer the egoism of passions for inferior pleasures and endure the pains up to the point of self-renunciation out of Christ's power, do we open up ourselves with love toward the loving and life-giving operation of the Holy Trinity and vice versa.

We cannot praise the Trinity without showing and praising the means by which It operates in us, nor can we make the sign of the cross without praising the Trinity and Its life-giving power manifested through the cross. Through the cross of Christ the Holy Trinity has worked and is working in us. This is why when we glorify It we make the sign of the cross. Likewise, when we praise the loving Kingdom of which It makes us a part, we make the sign of the cross through which we open ourselves up to this Kingdom, an opening symbolized by the opening of the royal doors. This is what we do at the beginning of the Holy Liturgy when the priest blesses the Kingdom of the Holy Trinity making with the Gospel, which represents Christ and His saving teaching and works, the sign of the cross over the Antimension, which represents the living memory of His real death toward resurrection. For the placing of Christ in the grave is not the placing in an eternal grave, but His encounter as man with the Father to Whom He totally offered Himself at the end of His death, an offering whose outcome was His resurrection.

In order for God in the Trinity to have been able to conquer death through the cross of the incarnate Son and to establish the Kingdom of God for those liberated from death and raised to eternal life in God, He had to have had this capacity from eternity. The cross must be for the Triune God a possibility from eternity as a means of establishing His Kingdom for human beings. We are to understand this as follows: the Son who is born from eternity from the Father has in Himself the capacity to "descend" not as essence, but as hypostasis, to the possibility of freely uniting human nature with His nature, without His divine nature being changed, but to suffer the death of this human nature caused by its separation from God through freedom, so that He may conquer death by the union of human nature with God. Understood in this way, the cross eternally connected with the Trinity lies in the possibility for the descent of the Son of God as hypostasis to the human nature fallen under the subjugation of death, as well as in the possibility of His ascension anew to the Father, as hypostasis united with this nature. And since this descent to the level of man incarnate of the Virgin Mary is accomplished through the operation of the Holy Spirit over her, the Holy Spirit, too, takes part in this descent up to the point of the cross and in the ascension of the Son become man. Furthermore, since this act is accomplished with the goodwill of the Father, the entire Trinity has the capacity for the cross inscribed in Its existence out of love for humans, since It has the capacity to create them as free beings with bodies.

Through the very fact that the Father has a Son from eternity, He has from eternity the capacity to adopt us, but not through birth from His essence, for one cannot relativize the value of the Son through multiplication, but through His Son's incarnation and—following sin—His cross, through His descent to us with brotherly love up to our death and through His resurrection as man forever. St. Paul says this: "Just as He chose us in Him before the foundation of the world, that we should be holy and without blame before Him in love, having predestined us to adoption as sons by Jesus Christ to Himself, according to the good pleasure of His will" (Eph 1:4–5). Or: God "has saved us and called us with a holy calling, not according to our works, but according to His own purpose and grace which was given to us in Christ Jesus before time began" (1 Tim 1:9). Or: "The mystery which has been hidden from ages and from generations, but now has been revealed to His saints. To them God willed to make known what are the riches of the glory of this mystery among the Gentiles: which is Christ in you, the hope of glory" (Col 1:26–27).

The cross foreseen and chosen by God for His Son before the foundation of the world means God's mercy for us before the foundation of the world.

In this plan of God, established by Him before the ages for us as free beings whom He was going to bring into existence and who, in their freedom, would be able to separate from Him and be subjected to death, was also included the potentiality to bring them back to Him through the descent of His Son all the way to suffering their death so as to conquer it in Himself as man and to ascend again to the Father, still remaining, as incarnate Son, our Brother forever. In this way death would be forever conquered in our body and we would ascend with Him in glory. As such, this plan is the same as the mystery of our love and is of such great value that it is beyond our comprehension. But at the same time in this mystery lies the supreme sense of our creation. In any pantheism, produced by human philosophy, death—or the nonsense of existence—is not conquered. Personal Reality appears in the Gospel as the incomprehensible mystery of a supreme and eternal value. But in the person, understanding the human person, there is also the supreme sense of the entire created existence. The person is the mystery that illumines existence. The possibility of this mystery of such great value that illumines existence can only be given in the quality as person of the supreme existence.

Only because God created the human being as a person capable of conscious or understanding love can He rejoice so much in the human being that He wants to preserve him forever in the dialogue of love with Him. Otherwise creation would have had no sense at all. This is why the Son of God can also become a person of the human nature, because the human being is a person. Otherwise there would be no point to the Son of God's incarnation, and the relationship between God and human beings or between God and creation in general would not have been possible.

Creation would have had no sense. God would have been closed off in Himself, or He would have been one with the world. Neither of these two leaves the possibility of unending love in existence. The human being may be infinitely small as essence vis-à-vis God, but as a person is deemed worthy of being God's eternal partner of love, or all the infinite richness of divine life can consciously fit in the human being. The small infinite comprehends the large infinite or everything; in a way it is also capable of infinity. Thus, when we make the sign of the cross we affirm our connection forever with the Holy Trinity, the supreme source of love, but also our eternal value for the Trinity, once it has been decided that one of the Trinity would become man and would offer His supreme sacrifice for us and would rise again as man forever so as to resurrect us, too, forever, and to contemplate as man together with us the infinite existence in an eternal dialogue of love.

The sacrifice fits into the framework of attaining this goal as a necessary fact realized on the human part as well. It is not enough that God wants to enter into a dialogue with the human person forever. The human person, too, must want this. For God gave him freedom. But because the human person cannot do this on his own, following sin that weakened him, the Son of God takes upon Himself the role that needs to be fulfilled by the human person, Himself becoming man; but this means that in such an achievement He wants humanity to also have a contribution. Christ fulfills this role of the human person through the sacrifice He offers as man. It is a sacrifice that could not be offered without God Himself being active in it, but humanity also remains active in it. It is a sacrifice offered by the Son of God, but with the participation of humanity's will and sentiment.

When someone sacrifices himself, that person gives everything in his possession for what he can receive from the other whom he considers richer than him. Through sacrifice Christ the man offers His human life to God out of the aspiration for quenching His thirst for infinity, to receive in that life this infinity from God to Whom He offers Himself totally. He gives all out of a love which God strengthens and maintains, and thereby He becomes the human instrument through which God can humanly contemplate the entire existence in an eternal dialogue with the human person, and the human person is raised to the capacity of contemplating in a divine form the infinity of existence in this eternal dialogue.

The human person paradoxically unites in him the boundary and the infinity, or the thirst to pass over to infinity above his boundary. Death as a result of sin is the closing off within boundary, while death as offering or as sacrifice is the passing into infinity, but not as something proper to the human person through essence. He who does not want to die, dies by closing himself off within the tormenting limitation of his being. He who accepts death in order to enter infinity, in fact assumes upon himself infinity. In Christ, the human person has through death been filled with eternal life.

The incarnate Son of God has filled human blood with the infinite and all-pure sense perception of divinity, actualizing the infinite value and quenching the thirst for infinity placed through creation in the human person as a medium for knowing the entire existence in human form, or of the being that is in itself for us infinite and existence-creating, in the form of the limited being in itself but participating through grace in the divine infinity. God became man without limiting His nature, and man became god, or has overcome his limit, not through nature but through grace. This in order for God to be able to speak eternally with the human person in the form proper to him and for the human person to be able to understand God through grace.[234] The sign of the cross made over the being of the human person tells us this. We experience this continuously in the Holy Liturgy and we express it through the words: "Let us offer ourselves and each other and all our life unto Christ our God." Through the cross is shown the infinite value in which God has clothed our being. It is the seal of this infinite value that He places on our being. It is the sign of the mutual relationship achieved by the endless love between us and God as well as among ourselves.

St. Paul the Apostle says: "For the word of the cross is foolishness to those who are perishing, but to us who are being saved it is the power of God" (1 Cor 1:18). Truly, those who consider the cross foolishness are perishing forever, showing themselves as servants of nonsense or of egoistical foolishness. Only in the cross is there wisdom or the true sense of existence made eternal through love. For those who pantheistically consider this world as the ultimate reality, in which death is definitive for human beings, succeeded by the successive birth of others, it is foolishness to consider death followed by resurrection. This is why they seek to avoid it as long as possible. But in the end they still succumb to it. Thus, in this affirmation of their cleverness is implied further nonsense. Why should we be born if we have to die definitively? They affirm the nonsense as a thesis of their cleverness. The cross has total value because through it Christ has conquered death, has risen.

For those who believe that above the world there is the immortal God, and that death was conquered by the Son of God who became man so as to eliminate a death that unnaturally entered creation through the fall from God or from love by assuming such a death, a death as reunion with God through the renunciation of self or of the breaking away from God, the cross is not foolishness, but true wisdom. Death willingly accepted, from faith in union through it with God, is avoided out of a false wisdom, but without escaping it. On the contrary, this avoidance out of a pretended wisdom inevitably leads to definitive death, while its acceptance out of faith in union with God through the renunciation of an egoism that has no power to keep the human person alive forever, leads to life. Thus, what to them seems wisdom is in fact foolishness, and what to them seems foolishness is the true wisdom and power of God. St. Paul the Apostle puts it this way: "But we preach Christ crucified, to the Jews a stumbling block and to the Greeks foolishness, but to those who are called, both Jews and Greeks, Christ the power of God and the wisdom of God. Because the foolishness of God is wiser than men, and the weakness of God is stronger than men" (1 Cor 1:23–25). "Has not God made foolish the wisdom of this world?" (1 Cor 1:20). What wisdom is that which affirms the nonsense of definitive death, of existence without sense? What power is that which inevitably ends in definitive death without being able to do anything to avoid it? True wisdom and true power lie in regarding and accepting death as an act of overcoming egoism and an act of union with God, the source of eternal life. In this wisdom one confesses a God who has power even over death, a God whose Kingdom is not subjected to any power nor to the power of death, not a god identical with nature ravaged by death and nonsense. The eternal Kingdom of human beings within the triune communion is founded on the resurrection attained by Christ through the cross. It is the Kingdom of the almighty God who was able to vanquish death once and for all, without always being again overcome by death, the One who was able to enter forever into the created nature in order to conquer death that has entered it through its free separation from God. And at the same time this is the loving God and the God in whom the positive meaning of all is implied. To this omnipotence and love and Kingdom of His, not subjected to any other power and much less to death, omnipotence shown in the apparent weakness of suffering death in Christ, "are due glory and worship unto the ages of ages." In the victory through the cross was revealed that He is "the Lord of glory" (1 Cor 2:8). Only a God different from the world, transcendent to the visible world as His creation, makes out of death an explainable phenomenon that can be defeated.

The generous interest of God's love for us is also shown in the fact that His Kingdom is the Kingdom of the One who freely wanted to be our Father as well. The Father is not a tyrant; the Father does not seek through us anything of His own, for He has everything from eternity. Nor is He forced by His love to create other sons and to make His Son man so as to adopt them. He wants our happiness, but freely. If we praise Him on this account, He does not need our praise for Himself, but He rejoices in it, because in it we express our joy for the happiness of communion with Him. The happiness He wishes for us lies in our free communion of love with Him, in the manifestation of His love for us and in our response to His love as a sign that we feel the joy of His love. He gave His own Son out of love to become man and to die for us. He gave Him to become our Brother and thus, remaining His Father, to also be our Father by grace.

But in being advised to call God "our Father," not "my Father," we are taught to consider ourselves brothers, equally His children and equally Christ's brothers. This is the Kingdom of God: our unity in a perfect love springing from the love of the Holy Trinity; unity filled with all divine good things and with the joy of love and of eternal life, free from any forced domination. All of us are royals in this Kingdom, ruled by no one and ruling over no one, but everyone having everything, everyone having the hearts of all and offering the heart to all.

This is what St. Maximos the Confessor means when he says that in the Kingdom of God we cease to want something contrary to God's will. On the one hand we are free, royals over ourselves together with God; on the other hand we no longer affirm our own will of which we are rather servants. We voluntarily agree to do God's will through which we authentically accomplish ourselves as what we potentially are. This is our submission to the Father of which St. Paul the Apostle speaks (1 Cor 15:27). And when we all appropriate God's will as our will, we all have the same will. This is why in the Lord's Prayer, immediately after the petition "Your Kingdom come" follows "Your will be done." Thus the progress into the Kingdom of the Holy Trinity during the Holy Liturgy is the progress of the faithful into the communion of love with the Holy Trinity and among themselves. "And this will take place because that which is within our power, I mean our free will — through which death made its entry among us, and confirmed at our expense the power of corruption — will have surrendered voluntarily and wholly to God, and perfectly subjected itself to His rule, by eliminating any wish that might contravene His will... 'It is no longer I who live, but Christ who lives in me' [Gal 2:20]. Let not these words disturb you, for I am not implying the destruction of our power of self-determination, but rather affirming our fixed and unchangeable natural disposition, that is, a voluntary surrender of the will, so that from the same source whence we received our being, we should also long to receive being moved."[235]

Since in the Kingdom we all wish for the same that God wishes, as a state produced by love for God and among ourselves, it is the Kingdom of kings among whom there is no combat. St. Maximos says: "This makes it clear that the Kingdom of God the Father belongs to the humble and the meek."[236] Christ's dominion is the yoke of the lowly of heart, so that we also may be humble; it is the yoke of the slain Lamb so that we also may be lambs. This yoke will give us rest (Mt 11:28). Explaining the words: "Take My yoke upon you and learn from Me, for I am gentle and lowly of heart, and you will find rest for your souls" (Mt 11:29), St. Maximos the Confessor says: "The dominion of the heavenly Kingdom is called rest; it is like a dominion over those who are worthy, freed from all servitude."[237]

From all that has been said we can sum up that the Kingdom of the Trinity, into which we are called to enter and to advance as a community through the beginning words of the Holy Liturgy, is a Kingdom of God's mercy and love for humankind, given to us so that we may strengthen our community through mercy and love. But we cannot have God's mercy and love toward us and among ourselves unless we feel the need for it and ask for it. This is why we continuously ask for His mercy: "Lord have mercy." The mercy among ourselves, which drives us to ask for God's mercy for all, is the universal link and the remedy for all our divisions. It strengthens the communion among us as God's Kingdom.

Thus, when we address God in the supplications from the litanies that follow, we expect that each one be fulfilled through His mercy. This is the meaning of the repetition after each supplication of the words: "Lord have mercy." In this way we follow the parable of those who ask for Christ's mercy in the Gospel (Lk 17:13; Mk 10:47), and even more so do those who ceaselessly say the Jesus prayer: "Lord Jesus Christ, the Son of God, have mercy upon me, a sinner." Also following the Gospel, we ask for God's mercy for others as well (Mt 18:15). In this we show that we, too, have compassion for them, or we make ourselves subjects of God's mercy for others. For if we do not have compassion for others, that is if we do not ask for God's mercy for others, neither will God have mercy on us (Mt 18:17; Rom 9:15). These will face perdition without mercy (Mt 21:41). Through this communal supplication for God's mercy we strengthen the unity among us as the Kingdom of love in God.

3. *The Threefold Series of Fervent Supplications (Litanies)*

By announcing and beginning the final union of all in the Kingdom of God and their communion in love whose source is the Holy Trinity, and by calling the faithful into this Kingdom, the Church asks them to prepare for it, giving them its first foretaste in the Holy Liturgy as peace.[238] Through this is shown again that the rule of normal human life and its unfolding toward perfection is not contradiction and struggle, but peace. One understands by peace our peace from passions that tears up the unity within us and among us. For only in this way can we become partakers of the heavenly Kingdom as a Kingdom of perfect harmony within us, among us and between us and God. It is to this peace that are called not only those who are not baptized, but the faithful as well. For one can continuously advance in this peace. This is stated by St. Maximos the Confessor, during whose time the litanies for peace took place after the entrance of the hierarch and the faithful into the church: "The entrance of the people into the church with the bishop represents the conversion of the unfaithful from faithlessness to faith and from sin and error to the recognition of God as well as the passage of the faithful from vice and ignorance to virtue and knowledge . . . by the salutations of peace which are issued from within the sanctuary on the signal of the bishop at each reading are indicated the divine favors imparted by the holy angels. By them God determines the combats of those who fight bravely for the truth against opposing forces by breaking the invisible struggles and by giving peace 'in the destruction of the body' [Rom 6:6] and by giving to the saints the grace of detachment in return for their labors for virtue."[239] The faithful must place their souls in a state of peace from the very beginning of the Holy Liturgy. Only in this way will they be able to concentrate in their mind on God, without disturbance, and will be able to pray together. Nicholas Cabasilas regards peace as the very Kingdom of God.

On the other hand, the final harmony will not be authentic unless it includes all, or most of all. The Church wants all to prepare themselves for this harmony within her bosom and, thus, within the Holy Liturgy as well, even if for practical reasons the faithful gather in smaller groups at the Holy Liturgy around the same Christ, together partaking of Him. The Church, in her intention, embraces the entire human universe and wants all of it to attain unity within the same Christ and within the same true faith which He preached and which represents Him. The Church regards as a mistake the division of Christendom into lesser groups, which lost the unity in the true faith.

Our life on earth covers a path crisscrossed with pains, hardships, diseases and difficult problems that we create for each other. As we advance in age our conscious intensifies by experiencing them. And at life's not too distant end, death is awaiting us. The question rises in our conscience: why all these? The same, increasingly mature conscience realizes that even if there were no hardships and no death in the end, life on earth and this world would not completely satisfy us with everything they offer. We tend toward an infinity of a different order than the material order. This dissatisfaction with this world and the aspiration for an infinity of a different order makes the human person distinct from animals. The human person realizes that the infinity he desires cannot be obtained here.

The same continuously intensified conscience realizes that we cannot escape by ourselves the pains, the dissatisfactions connected with this life and especially death. Only a superficial conscious can dismiss this fact with indifference. There would remain the alternative of either resignation, united with a senseless acceptance, or tragic desperation. But the thirst of the human person for an infinity devoid of imperfections does not leave him in this resignation or lost in hopelessness.

This is why there is faith in the supreme conscious of a God in Trinity, equipped at the same time with supreme power and with infinite mercy that urges It to help us both in easing the hardships tied to this imperfect life, and in sustaining our thirst for a life without shortages and for the fulfillment of its meaning on another plane after passing away from this life. Based on this faith, we ask the supreme conscience of God for mercy and salvation. During the course of the entire Holy Liturgy we ask God to have mercy on us, to ease the hardships of this life and to save us from its imperfection in the realm of infinity.

Our faith in God's ability to grant us these, as well as in His will to grant them to us, are based on the Revelation which tells us that He is a God in Trinity, therefore a God of intrinsic love out of which grows mercy toward us, mercy on account of which He sent His Son into the world to bring us salvation, which we cannot appropriate unless we unite ourselves with Him in carrying the cross and through a life of sacrifice after His example and from His power. For in this way we receive the power to endure the shortcomings of life on earth and thereby to strengthen ourselves, as well as to liberate ourselves of the egoism that heightens the dissatisfactions and shortcomings of life on earth.

Only within a God in Trinity, in which there is a Father and a Son, can there exist a tendency to extend the love for the Father toward the created, conscious persons as well, and to make them partakers of the life given by Him to His Son. Only such a Father is able to will that His Son may become man and may sacrifice Himself for us so as to save us from the narrow life of egoism, division and separation from the source of life which is God Himself. Only from such a God can one expect, and ask for, mercy and salvation.

This is why the Liturgy is replete with the confession of the Trinity, of a Father who sent His Son to become man for the salvation brought by Him through incarnation, cross and resurrection, as the basis for our supplication addressed to God in Trinity to make us partakers of His mercy and of the salvation brought through the Son as adoption.

This supplication for mercy is not a begging unworthy of the human person (Nietzsche), because the things we ask for we cannot give to ourselves no matter how confident we are; then God does not show His mercy in the gestures of a disdainful master, but in His participation at our level in our pain through the cross He assumed and in the value He imparts to us by becoming human like us for eternity. Furthermore, His help does not save us without our contribution from the hardships and shortcomings of this existence, but He makes use of our free and heroic cooperation with Him through our response to His love with our love, which He expects from us in order to save us.

The universality of the Kingdom of God and the preoccupation of all to prepare for attaining it is affirmed by the Church in the Holy Liturgy even from the first litany following the praise of the Kingdom of the Trinity, in which Christ came to gather all persons and all things. We know from the Apostles that "the Kingdom of God is not eating and drinking, but righteousness and peace and joy in the Holy Spirit" (Rom 14:17). The Kingdom of God is peace and where there is no peace, there is neither joy nor righteousness. The true peace includes all and so does true righteousness.

This is why from the very beginning, the three litanies place peace as the foundation for the supplications that follow, which is the main characteristic of the Kingdom of God: *In peace let us pray to the Lord.*

In this exhortation one does not affirm only the necessity for a peace that causes every believer to not be disturbed by any thought about something or someone else, but to concentrate on God alone. For in the following supplications the faithful are encouraged to ask many things for all categories of people. This appeal to the faithful is in the first place for peace and harmony among them. This is also an extended peace, not one that excludes all people and all things. As we are about to pray to God, we are asked to be at peace with one another, to ask from God "with one mouth and one heart" the things we want to receive, as is said later in the Holy Liturgy when we are exhorted to praise God. From the first supplication of the litany until the end of the Liturgy, every supplication is made in the plural; it is a supplication of all together for all and for each one present in prayer as well as for others who are not present. Prayer creates harmony. Each one feels sustained by all in his prayer and before God. In this is also manifested our belonging to the same Kingdom.

This "we" of the liturgical prayer that is addressed to God as to a Thou common for all is not just a coming together of I's, but a mutual interpenetration of personal I's. I am not just adjacent to the others, but I am in them and they are in me. Their word resounds in me, I feel the warmth of their sense perception and faith that warm me as well in my sense perception and faith; they become my own sense perception and faith without ceasing to be their own and without losing the feeling that they are also their own. The other's thought becomes my own without ceasing, in my own conscious, to be his thought. His I moves within my own I and mine in his. We are interior to each other without being intermingled. We form an I comprising many I's in a unity. The "we" that we form is my I, but it is also everyone else's. All are in me and I am in all. My prayer belongs to this unitary and also multiple I and its prayer is my prayer. In it there is the spiritual love among us and the common love for God. Personal love gains an indefinite extent, a warmth and firmness, becoming our love; my love is no longer mine alone, but everybody else's; I no longer feel it only as mine but as that of a an extended multi-personal unity, even though I feel it as mine as well. Everyone is the subject of the unified, extended and endless love of all. Through this extended love I love God, but I love others as well, being united with God through this love as I am united with them, without feeling either separated from or confounded with them. The triune communion is active in our communion.

From the very beginning, all of us present are urged to constitute in a single, multiple "I" of the Liturgy, in a communitarian "I" just like God is, one God in Trinity. God wants us to be intensified through love in a generous unity, lacking all egoism, in which everyone's love for God is strengthened by that of all. He wants us to increasingly advance during the entire time of the Liturgy in this unity up to a culminating unity between us and Christ, and in Him between each other through the partaking of Christ together, so that we may attain the supreme stage of this unity in the Kingdom of the age to come. In the prayer sung in common we experience the pledge of our unity in the Kingdom of the Holy Trinity.

But the peace between those of us who are present cannot be fully achieved if the peace of God in Trinity is not in it. The Apostle taught us that it is God who fills us "with all joy and peace" (Rom 15:13); that God "is a God of peace" (1 Cor 14:33; 2 Cor 13:11; Php 4:9), that "the Lord of peace Himself gives you peace" (2 Th 3:16), etc. Thus, we manifest our will to follow the Apostle's exhortation: "Be at peace among yourselves" (1 Th 5:13). The first Christians also learned from the Apostle that where God's peace is, there is God Himself or Christ (Eph 2:14), who saved them by making peace among them. For He has abolished through the cross the enmity within us and among ourselves (Eph 2:16). Thus, there is a strong connection between the cross and peace. The cross is the foundation of true peace. In the cross of Christ there is our peace. By accepting the cross, we imprint our being in peace and we enter into communion with all. Thus, the peace among us who pray is the extension of the peace of Christ, who dwelled in us and brought us salvation from the sin of being separated from God and of division within and among us. The crucified Christ, peace and salvation are, therefore, one and the same thing, or they are one within the other.

This is why immediately after the first supplication of the litany, we address to Him the following one: "For the peace from above and for the salvation of our souls let us pray to the Lord." The true horizontal peace cannot be separated from the inner peace, which comes from Christ along with salvation.

As we said, Nicholas Cabasilas sees in this "peace from above" the Kingdom of God itself. This was announced by the priest when he began the Holy Liturgy, but now we also must ask for it in a more concrete way. "The 'peace from on high' signifies the righteousness of God, of which St. Paul says 'the peace that passes all understanding (Php 4:7)... And in the same way that the word 'righteousness' implies more than a strict legality, meaning every kind of virtue, so the word 'peace' has a wider implication for it is the fruit of all good and all wisdom. No one is in possession of perfect peace if he lacks any of the virtues."[240]

After we have asked for this inner foundation of peace among us who are present, we are exhorted to ask that this peace be extended beyond those present: to be extended throughout the world. And since this depends even less on our power, we ask God for this peace among all human beings everywhere: "For the peace of the whole world... let us pray to the Lord." Through this, Nicholas Cabasilas says, is shown that God, to whom we pray for the peace of the whole world, is the Creator and Provider of all things. "Especially since Christians know that their God is common Lord of all, and that all things are in his care, since he made them."[241] The glory they give to God is thus all the greater. Then, through the peace given by God to the whole world Christians are assured of a life of peace and of peaceful spiritual growth.

Peace among all humans is, however, considered as a condition for "the welfare of the holy churches of God and for the union of all" (in faith). Peace and unity among persons are offered as a first foundation on which to build the superior unity, manifested in the unity of faith, thus in the stability in unity of Churches, which in its turn sustains the unity among people. The world cannot attain full peace and unity if its natural unity is not strengthened and perfected through the unity of faith or the relationship with God, the One, the Creator, the Provider and its Savior in Christ. The world continuously inclines on its own to fall into all kinds of contradictions and battles, and even the Churches weaken in their unity through the divisions among people. We, therefore, also pray for the stability, or better said for "the good of the Churches" in the right faith, or for the return to it, with the help of the peace among people or as its foundation.

The world can advance toward the Kingdom of God by cultivating from now on harmony and peace, not contradiction, battle and war. The catechumens also receive through these prayers an exhortation to unite themselves with the Church.

When we ask for this peace from God and for the union of the Churches we do not leave this concern for them to God alone, but we show that we also want to work toward that end, following the exhortation of the Apostle: "live peaceably with all men" (Rom 12:17; Heb 12:14); or: "let us pursue the things which make for peace" (Rom 14:19).

Then follows the exhortation to ask God for other goods, some with a general content, others more specific.

First there is a supplication with a general content for the church building and for all those who enter it with faith and fear of God. It is a solidarity with those who pray at any time in this holy building. Then there is another supplication also with a general content for the right-believing Christians all together, affirming the solidarity on a larger scale of the Orthodox faith. Thus the right-believing Christians from all church buildings pray for each other. Thirdly, the community addresses to God a supplication for the bishop of the local diocese, as its archpastor and as representative of the Church in her unity everywhere, through his communion with the other bishops, but also for the priesthood and the diaconate throughout the Church as well as for all the clergy and right-believing people everywhere (Heb 13:17; 1 Th 5:12; 1 Pt 5:5). The Church is a unit organized spiritually and externally, one body, not only because all members have Christ as their unique head, but also because in this body there are some members in positions of responsibility, therefore with special gifts within the community for keeping it in unity in all places and in the same faith throughout generations by officiating the same Mysteries and by preaching the same faith.

One does not forget the exhortation given to the community to also address to God a supplication for the civil authority so that within the order it maintains, the Church may be able to work for the fulfillment of her mission, for strengthening the unity among people in view of the perfect unity in the Kingdom of God. The supernatural needs the natural to lead it to the fulfillment of its true aspirations (Rom 13:1–8). But in addition to the concern for the organized life of the people, the community is urged to also be concerned and thus to pray for the locality in which it exists, and immediately after that for all towns and villages and for those who with faith live in them. The faithful do not live in solitude, but in towns and villages. God is also entreated for these organized localities of people that sustain a communal, national life of union and of mutual responsibility among people as the basis for their growth, or for their entrance into the communion of the Kingdom of God.

But the life of people depends also on seasonable weather, on the abundance of the fruits of the earth and on peaceful times. The liturgical community is urged to pray for these as well, that is for the entire cosmic and spiritual environment. With these, the supplications begin to be specific in their content.

People do not live passively in localities, but they find themselves in various conditions and activities in and outside localities. The liturgical community is urged to think of all those who are in any state or activity: by the seaside, in the air or other kind of travelling, of those who are sick, those who labor in any kind of work, for captives and for their salvation ("Remember the prisoners as if chained with them — those who are mistreated — since you yourselves are in the body also," Heb 13:3).

After all this, the faithful who are present are urged to turn their eyes toward themselves, but without excluding other persons. They are now urged by the priest or the deacon to pray together with them: "For our deliverance from all tribulation, wrath, danger and need." It is a negative supplication. But immediately after it another supplication with a more interior content is added: "Help us, save us, have mercy on us and protect us, O God, by your grace."

These are specific supplications: first for the avoidance of external hardships, then for protection against visible and invisible enemies, for salvation, for the mercy of God and for keeping the faithful in everything that is good and against evil things. The last ones refer both to the external conditions of life and to help for salvation.

All these supplications have been proposed to the liturgical community by the priest or the deacon to be directed toward God together with him. After each one the priest or the deacon has proposed to the faithful present: "Let us pray to the Lord." He proposed to the community these supplications or invited the community to address them to God together with him. In fact the community uttered them silently together with the priest or the deacon and then prays to God after each one: "Lord have mercy." The liturgical community showed that it joins with each supplication uttered by the priest or the deacon through the words spoken by them in a loud voice. In the words: "Lord have mercy" one asks in a special way on behalf of the community what the priest or the deacon has proposed. Or through these words the community directly shows that it prays for everything that the priest or the deacon has proposed to pray for. Everything comes because of God's mercy. In God's mercy is the source of everything we ask, there is the very Kingdom of God, says Nicholas Cabasilas.[242] Through "Lord have mercy" one has responded on behalf of the community to the invitation of the priest or the deacon: "Let us pray to the Lord" for this or that thing. Through the supplication "Help us, save us". . . etc., one has passed from the proposals made by the priest or the deacon to the community to pray together with him to his own direct supplication. For in the previous supplications of the priest or the deacon addressed to the community God remained in the third person.

Expressly through the connection of the community to the priest's or the deacon's proposals, one passes to the prayer addressed directly to God in the second person. Now the priest and the deacon continue with the prayer addressed directly to God together with the community. Still, the priest has a special role, as Nicholas Cabasilas says: "he is appointed to this office and is for this reason placed in front of the people. He is also there as their representative and mediator, so that his prayer may be very efficacious, as the Apostle James says: 'The effective, fervent prayer of a righteous man avails much' (Jam 5:16)."[243] Without the presence of the liturgical community it would be useless for the priest or the deacon to speak in the plural. Hence, neither the Liturgy could be officiated. It would be, therefore, good for all who are present to respond to the invitation of the priest with "Lord have mercy" sung by the choir. Previously, most of these supplications were offered for others. In fact we cannot separate care for ourselves from care for others. God did not create humans as isolated beings, but all are entrusted to all.

Then, after these supplications, the faithful who are present promise, in response to the proposal of the priest or the deacon, to offer themselves and each other to Christ. He who receives something upon request, must also give. Only in this way is the community realized in love between he who receives and he who gives. But only in offering each other to Christ can we help each other toward salvation.

Our life is a gift from God. This is why we are to return it to God as our gift. By granting it to us as conscious and free life, God also made us capable of giving, but He asks us to freely offer it in our turn.

In order to make ourselves a gift to God, we should have gained peace from egoistic passions and peace with others. Only thus have we raised ourselves to the quality or the capacity to offer ourselves, to the status of a gift pleasing to God. For this, our decision to turn our life around as a gift to God comes after we have asked and have received from God not only life, but also peace or freedom from sinful egoism, praying to Him for good things for others.

God rejoices in this gift, even though in the end it is from Him. He rejoices in the will we exercise to live our life granted by Him with the conscious that it comes from Him and with the decision to return it to Him and to use it toward His praise. In this He shows us the value He places on us. However, we also fulfill ourselves completely only by offering ourselves to Him. He who offers himself does not lose himself, but fulfills himself and enters into the plenitude of life, in the flow of life lived together with others. Even more so, he who offers himself to God by consenting to willingly return to the union with Him, is fulfilled to a higher level in Him. He who offers himself, receives himself to a higher degree. If we want that unity, this circuit never ends.

But our fellow humans are also gifts given to us by God. Without them we cannot fulfill our life, nor can we make it fruitful or enrich it. But we must return to God the gift given to us in the persons of our fellow humans for their happiness. Certainly, we cannot return it by force, against their will, but by convincing them to also offer themselves to God, since we speak to them of God's generosity toward them and about the fulfillment that comes to them from offering themselves to God. We cannot offer them to God unless we offer ourselves to them. Only then do they also offer themselves to us, so that by offering ourselves to God we may offer them as well. By offering each other to Christ we do not remain on the outside as some kind of object.

That the others are not passive objects in their offering by us to Christ, but they remain subjects who offer themselves, is seen in the expression showing that we, too, are being offered by them as a gift to Christ: "Let us offer ourselves and each other and all our life unto Christ, our God." The other lets me work upon him because I also let him work upon me. He obeys me because I also obey him. We advance together on this path learning from each other, helping and advising each other as the Apostle says: "Therefore comfort each other and edify one another" (1 Th 5:11). "And let us consider one another in order to stir up love and good works" (Heb 10:24). In this way we grow together and thus the body of Christ grows in harmony, increasingly uniting ourselves among us and with Him through our mutual offerings that are increasingly more complete. For out of the one's self-offering, the other receives the strength to offer himself and causes the first one to offer himself even with a greater offering.

Only because I offer myself to the other in complete freedom, does he also offer himself to me. And by offering myself to him, I offer myself to God through him and vice versa. No subordination is conceivable where the person is constituted or develops through an infinite expropriation of self or through total reference to another.[244] This is how it is in the Trinity, and this is how it must become among us. Where there is love, there is self-offering and freedom. For there are no more egoistic passions that close us off in ourselves. This is why Nicholas Cabasilas says that it is not easy to submit ourselves to God, for this requires abandoning all egoism. This is why for this heroic act we ask for power from the Lord's Mother and from all the saints, or we draw strength from their example. Therefore, we commemorate them before we promise to offer ourselves to each other and to Christ. When all of us offer ourselves to God and to each other we follow the example of the Lord's Mother and of all the saints, but we also unite ourselves with them, strengthening the unity of faith and of our lives in Christ.[245]

Where there is self-offering, there is freedom because there is the Spirit of God not subjected to any bondage. For at the same time He is the Spirit of love: "Now the Lord is the Spirit; and where the Spirit of the Lord is, there is liberty" (2 Cor 3:17). There is such a strong connection between love and liberty that one cannot be understood without the other. It is to this liberty of self-offering out of love that Christ has called us. And we respond to this call when we do not serve the bodily passions, "but through love serve one another" (Gal 5:13). Only because we offer ourselves out of love are we free. However, we must stand strong in this freedom through our own effort as well: "Stand fast therefore in the liberty by which Christ has made us free, and do not be entangled again with a yoke of bondage" (Gal 5:1). This is a liberty that we have only in Christ, for only He was entirely free from passions and permeated with love. With this strength He has conquered death through resurrection. In this liberty of Christ's perfect freedom and total offering and that of each other we will live in the Kingdom of heaven. This is why we are asked at the end of the litanies to prepare ourselves through our offering to Christ and to each other for the Kingdom of the Holy Trinity. Freedom from passions, for which we must fight now, that is the power for offering ourselves to God and to each other in love, will lead us in the life to come to liberation from the corruption and death of the body, which will be completely imbued with the Holy Spirit. This freedom from corruption and death as well as our infusion with the Holy Spirit will be shown in our glory in the life to come. For he who is submitted to a certain domination cannot be glorified. "Because the creation itself also will be delivered from the bondage of corruption into the glorious liberty of the children of God" (Rom 8:21).

In fact when we offer ourselves to each other, we offer ourselves to God. For who, if not God, would place such value on someone so that I may offer myself totally to Him and find happiness in this? A Western theologian rightly says: "As long as one remained at the exterior man, God was situated on the outside and has been placed in the space behind the stars as a stranger, as a distant ruler, as a dominator, as a limit and as a threat; one has made Him an idol whom science does not need, for it only needs a world of materializeable evidence, it feeds on its order in which no other type of explanation is allowed, except the one known through its method. Left to its instinctual determinations, the passional universe remains indifferent for other reasons, if not hostile to this God: hostile to life. We are to search for God, the source of life, in a universe . . . . for which we are to be reborn in order to discover Him in Himself as the source of eternal life . . . . The interpersonal universe of mutual commitment must be reconstructed . . . . Therefore, the more we love, the more we know... Love is indeed the sole key of the spiritual world in which all values reside. We cannot enter, advance and remain in it except through a continuously renewed commitment, through a love more generously offered, and through a self-denial increasingly more profound."[246]

"It is obvious then that truth itself is nothing other than the unspoken perception, through a network of phenomena subjected to determinism, of a Face, a Person, a Light and a Love that illumine our deepest mystery . . . . We are confronted with an inner demand: to always be more and to be or to offer ourselves by making our very self an offering of light and love. Only through the mediation of this self-offering can we encounter the Face worthy to be venerated, that Face awaiting us in the most intimate of our being, that Face that is in the heart of all our sensitivities with their eternity, that Face of the first love that makes us inviolable for ourselves and for others to the extent to which we really become the sanctuary of the infinite Presence."[247]

But this discovery of our own intimacy through the discovery of the other's intimacy and that of God in our encounter with the help of our self-denial begins, on the one hand, through the cross and, on the other hand, it is strengthened in our spirit through the Holy Spirit, who is the power of communication between the Holy Trinity and us, power that liberates us from the prison of the egoistical and superficial I, and realizes the true communion, or the Church, between God and us and among ourselves.

"If our person is constituted as being referred to God and grows according to the measure in which we deny ourselves more in order to offer more fully the space of our love,"[248] then the Lord's Mother received in herself in the utmost manner the Son of God, since she dedicated herself to Him in the utmost manner. "She gives birth to Him through her liberation from her very self, through a contemplation that detaches her from herself before He took His body from hers. Her fertility is not part of the determinism of the species; she surges from the full relation with Him, from this reference that personalizes her through the dedication of her entire being."[249] By achieving in herself supreme dedication to her Son, she unites herself entirely with Him, but this dedication is also extended to us so that, being filled with her tendency for dedication to Him and to us, we too may dedicate ourselves to Him and to her. Thus, she dedicates us to Him since she dedicates herself to us. We draw strength from this to dedicate ourselves and each other to Christ.

The saints do this with us in a lesser degree. The Lord's Mother has raised femininity to the climax since she united the two forms of woman's dedication by fulfilling them: virginity and motherhood. Certainly, she could only unite these two through God; only through Him could she be ever-virgin and mother because she was the Mother of God. Only through Him did she realize to the fullest the two forms of pure feminine affection. She dedicated herself totally to God through virginity and she dedicated herself to God totally as the Mother of His Son without dividing her affection between a husband and this unique Son. The I of her Son has truly become her I, certainly without annulling Him, but maintaining Him as affirmation of His I with the quality of her I. All the feelings of her soul and body were filled with Him. Through this, His Holy Spirit, the Spirit of power and spiritual fire has overcome the bodily processes as the Spirit of freedom from any law, as the Spirit dominating every passion forcefully imposing itself. Through this the feelings of her soul and body were completely filled with Him. Therefore, the Spirit was able to achieve that He Who is the Light and the source of all created material forms could take His soul and body from her soul and body. Thus, He was filled with her pure feelings of her soul and body, or His I was imprinted with her I. This is why, on the one hand, we cannot speak of Christ without speaking of His Mother and, on the other hand, she has enjoyed even on earth a glory of freedom from the bondage of certain laws active in the body, the latter becoming a place and instrument for the works of the Spirit.

This is why we call her: *The Most-Holy* (better said *All-Holy*—Panagia), unlike any other saint; *All-Pure* both in her spiritual and physical sentiments; *Most Blessed by God* in a unique way among women, *Glorified* unlike any other creature, *Our Mistress* unlike, again, any other saint, for the Master's Mother is herself Mistress, having the Lord Jesus as a central I in her I in the sense mentioned above. All these because she is *the Birthgiver of God and Ever-Virgin Mary*.

One more thing needs to be mentioned: we determine the strong relation between Her and "all the saints," through the fact that we do not say: "The Birthgiver of God and all the saints" but "with all the saints." The saints can only be next to her, with her, because she is filled with Christ in a most special way. Their sobornicity as well as that of the whole Church cannot be realized without her or without being alongside her. She is in the most distinct way united with Christ, the head of the Church, in the perfect sense of the word. For she has no other son, nor husband, nor brothers and sisters. This is why she is always presented as holding Him in her arms, or praying to Him, or as He holds the soul of His Mother at her Dormition; it is impossible to conceive of her any other way.

So it is not necessary to always mention "all" the saints with their names. This would not even be possible. It suffices to name her, for "all" are with her. None of them is outside the relation with her.

Just as she offers herself to Christ and as all the saints offer themselves and each other, dedicating themselves together with her and she together with them as the Mother of all, so we too offer ourselves and each other from their power, tending to be ever more in each other and all in Christ. When someone is mentioned in prayers means that that someone is present there. The Lord's Mother and all the saints are with us in our offering of ourselves.

As the priest or the deacon proposes that we offer ourselves to God, we do not respond with "Lord have mercy," but with "To You, O Lord," because now we return our life as a gift to Him in exchange for the mercy we asked for when addressing the previous supplications to Him.

The priest establishes the proposal to offer ourselves to God through the exclamation that follows. For as he now addresses God in the second person he says: *For to You are due all glory, honor and worship to the Father and to the Son and to the Holy Spirit.* Through the gift of our life offered to God, we confess His glory and we offer the worship due to Him for everything He has given us.

At this time the priest recites this prayer silently: "O Lord, our God, whose dominion is incomparable and glory incomprehensible, whose mercy immeasurable and love toward mankind ineffable, do You, O Master, according to Your goodness, look down upon us and upon this holy temple, and show us and those who pray with us the richness of Your mercy and Your goodness."[250]

The exclamations of praise after the litanies date back to the gathering for the liturgical offering in Jerusalem during the time of the Apostles. This can be seen in 1 Peter 4:11, 5:11. In the same place we can also see the blessing: "Peace be to you all" (1 Pt 5:14). These praises are due to God because, on the one hand, He is incomprehensible in His glory and mercy; on the other hand, He fulfills these supplications and for this reason the faithful offer all their lives as a gift to Him.

The liturgical community, by appropriating the conviction about the glory and worship due to God in the Trinity, responds by singing: "Glory to the Father and to the Son and to the Holy Spirit. Bless the Lord, O my soul, and all that is within me bless His holy name. Blessed are You, O Lord" (Ps 102). At the Sunday Liturgy of the royal feasts that are dedicated especially to the saving works of the Lord Jesus, the community remembers in its hymns the Lord's Mother as well, asking for salvation from the Lord Jesus through her prayers, too: "Through the prayers of the Birthgiver of God, O Savior, save us!" One cannot speak of the economy of salvation without mentioning the Birthgiver of God.

In his prayer, the priest praises the mystery of the immeasurable and incomprehensible dominion of God. But His incomprehensible dominion and His immeasurable glory are not opposed to God's incomprehensible mercy and love toward mankind, which give the priest courage to ask God to look down upon this holy temple of His and upon all those who pray together with him in the church. The dominion of God does not operate with tyranny, but with love and mercy. This is why this dominion makes the faithful free, on the one hand, and on the other hand, happy to be in the kingdom of His love. They are free and their own masters, because they are not slaves to passions. Only the passions make people, on the one hand, slaves and, on the other hand, tyrannical masters over others when they can, or masters over themselves and tyrannical masters over others. The Kingdom of God has as its own members human beings purified of passions, delicate beings with a sensibility and sharpness of understanding that grasp the infinitely delicate plan that can only belong to a Person or Trinity of Persons. God's dominion is, therefore, beyond any imagination, since it implies His mercy and love toward human persons. The world He creates can become a world of contradiction and fighting between good and evil. Contradiction and fighting emerged out of its freedom wrongly used through which it broke away from God, from His mercy and freedom. Thus, this world is not part of God's essence, but a creation of His freedom, itself being given freedom without having in itself the source of life and happiness. The God of mercy and of goodness can cure this world of the contradiction and evil in it only if it freely attach itself again to Him, asking for His mercy and power.

By the very fact that the priest stands in an elevated place—that is in the altar, not only in the visible sense, but also in the spiritual sense, namely in a life elevated above passions and into the knowledge of God—one can see that God's dominion and glory is higher than the dominion we pretend to have united with tyranny; for His dominion is united with mercy and love and takes into consideration our freedom. Precisely through this dominion He is the rich source of mercy and compassion, and there is no contradiction between His dominion and His quality as the Father of mercies and compassion.

This is the God experienced in the Liturgy: the apophatic God, ineffable in His mystery, but at the same time experienced in His outpourings of mercy, compassion and help; a God who is absolute master, but precisely because of this He is incomprehensible in His mercy. For if He were limited in His dominion He could not have so much mercy, for He would be afraid that His dominion would be at risk. He is not a God of negative theology, which is also rational, in a sense of being closed off in Himself, nor is He a God who can be wholly contained in creatures through the fact of His outpouring in acts of mercy and power. For even in these outpourings of mercy one can feel the infinity of His mercy and power.

Then follows the second litany, which briefly repeats the supplications from the first litany. There are three beginning litanies to remind us that God is threefold in Persons and that the number three is a symbol of infinity, but an infinity in love because in God there is the infinity of life in love. When there are only two persons, there is only one you and therefore it limits me; when there are three, the community avoids limitation and there is still a community of persons and a communion of love. His mercy is asked three more times or a threefold praise is offered to God so as to show that our supplication and the praise we offer Him aim to increase together with His intimate infinity. This is why for a Christian the number three has a special significance. The perfection without end of every good thing comes from the infinite and intimate Holy Trinity. By repeating three times our supplications and our promise, we intensify more and more our supplication or praise, and we grow increasingly warmer in addressing our supplications and in our promises of our praises offered to the infinite and familiar Trinity, determined to grow into a familiar infinity. We do this every time we offer threefold prayers for something or when we promise something three times. The repetition of the same word especially in a prayer or in a promise of any kind, is not a monotonous replication, but one places an even bolder emphasis on that repetition, if not even a more determined and ceaseless intention, so as to understand the infinite meaning of the spoken word, of the prayer and of the promise made. This is why the Lord Jesus praises the widow who persists in her prayer (Lk 18:5). This is how the Kingdom of heaven is taken, by force (Mt 11:12). Christ also commands us to be persistent in our prayers (Lk 11:9–10). Through endless persistence there is created, maintained and intensified in us the motion to ask something from God or to praise Him, to thank Him and to infinitely offer ourselves to Him. It does not simply create a static habit that gradually lacks power.

The poet Charles Péguy has remarked that he felt "un eternal recommencement" (an eternal new beginning) on the same path he took every morning, stopping every time with another interest in, and another understanding of, the things he viewed in every scene. The same thing occurs in the repetition of the same words and prayers when one pays attention to them.

The threefold appeal to the triune God maintains this feeling of the infinity, because if two Persons would simply make us turn from one to the other, the Holy Spirit as the third Person causes each one of the three to infinitely renew the communion between the two. In the Holy Spirit of God is given the potential attention of the three Persons toward all the subjects that they will create. The Holy Spirit opens to us as well the perspective of infinity in directing our prayer to the Holy Trinity—of which we become aware—by reciting it three times.

Now the promise of the faithful to offer themselves to God is founded on the exclamation: "For Yours is the dominion, and Yours is the kingdom, and the power, and the glory: of the Father, and of the Son, and of the Holy Spirit, now and ever, and unto the ages of ages. Amen." This exclamation establishes the basis of the first one in which it was said that all glory, honor and worship are due to God. At this time it is shown that to God are due glory, honor and worship because in fact He has in Himself the dominion, the power and the glory. Now it is more precisely specified that His dominion was established through the Son, or that it is a Kingdom to which we, too, are called as kings, a Kingdom of love and of freedom from passions.

The faithful say this when they sing the second antiphon in which, after offering glory to the Holy Trinity, they address the incarnate, crucified and risen Son to save them by leading them to the Kingdom of the Trinity. He can do this because He has the same glory which the Father and the Holy Spirit have. This antiphon comprises the confession of the Son's entire work of salvation. The dominion God has in Himself is united not only with His mercy poured out upon human beings, but also with the Son's saving work in which this mercy has reached the highest degree. The mercy that God shows us is now specified as the mercy of salvation through His Son's incarnation for eternity and through His crucifixion for us, through His total sacrifice for us and through the annihilation of the death in us on account of His resurrection:

Only-begotten Son and Immortal Word of God, Who for our salvation did will to be incarnate of the Holy Birthgiver of God and Ever-Virgin Mary, Who without change did become man and was crucified, O Christ our God, trampling down death by death, Who are One of the Holy Trinity, glorified together with the Father and the Holy Spirit, save us!

This hymn sung by the community after the second litany starts with the small doxology dedicated to the Holy Trinity. For to the Trinity is due infinite praise for our liberation from eternal death through the incarnation, crucifixion and resurrection of the Only-begotten Son of the Father. The glorification of the Trinity is not diminished, but It is shown even more brightly in Its infinity through the incarnation as man of the Father's Son, through His crucifixion and resurrection. For in the hymn is shown that all these were done out of freedom ("did will") and out of love ("for our salvation"), not on the basis of an inner and unfree process of the Godhead. By accepting our death, the incarnate Son has trampled it down, because He accepted it without being changed in His almighty Godhead and because He is immortal. He has trampled it down because even though He became man and has suffered our death, He is One of the Holy Trinity. Through His death He has immersed His humanity in the endless life of the Godhead, maintaining in His own hypostasis the awareness of that Godhead; He has immersed it by totally offering Himself as man to the Father and thereby He has been filled with the endless and eternal life of the Godhead lived in a human manner. This is why He is glorified together with the Father and the Holy Spirit, even though He is man at the same time. And in Him we, too, are filled with the same life together with Him, if we adhere to Him.

In the prayer which the priest reads silently at this time, he also asks specifically: the salvation of the right-believing people and their blessing. But since this depends on the sanctification of the faithful in which is implied their glorification, the priest is asking for these as well. The faithful obtain all these in the Church, thereby contributing to the preservation of her fullness. The fact of their remaining as living members in the fullness of the Church is associated with honoring the House of the Lord and with their gathering together in the Church. The priest asks for all these again in the plural, implicating the faithful in his prayer.

In this case, by praising God they receive in exchange His glory through His divine power. Here is the text of this prayer: "O Lord our

God, save Your people and bless Your inheritance. Preserve the fullness of Your Church. Sanctify those who love the beauty of Your house; glorify them in return by Your divine power, and forsake us not who put our hope in You."

The house of the Lord is holy, because the Lord who dwells in it, in the ark of the Holy Eucharist, is holy and still in a state of sacrifice. This is why those who love its holiness and come to encounter and praise the Holy God within it are also sanctified and glorified. "By those who come near Me I shall be sanctified; and before all the congregation I shall be glorified" (Lev 10:3). God is sanctified and praised in those who honor Him through their deeds, and in this they are themselves sanctified and glorified by Him.[251]

In the Old Testament those were sanctified who entered the tent of the covenant or the temple where the sacrifices offered to God were sanctified, and there they were filled with the glory they were offering to God through those sacrifices. All the more those are sanctified who enter the church building where the holiest sacrifice is offered to God, Christ's sacrifice, and the sacrifice of the hearts of those who are united with Him through faith and where God is praised through this supreme sacrifice. Why would they not be sanctified in this house of God by the holiest and most glorious sacrifice offered there to the Father, that house itself being filled with the holiness and glory of the Father who accepts His Son's sacrifice? "For if the blood of bulls and goats and the ashes of a heifer, sprinkling the unclean, sanctifies for the purifying of the flesh, how much more shall the blood of Christ, who through the eternal Spirit offered Himself without spot to God, cleanse your conscience from dead works to serve the living God?" (Heb 9:13–14). The holiness of the church building, which is full of the spiritual fragrance of Christ's all-holy sacrifice and of its power spiritually perceived, is imbued within the minds of those who enter therein and it inclines them toward the same state of sacrifice and, thus, of holiness. Christ who is on the altar in a state of sacrifice as man, or who offers Himself as sacrifice in every Liturgy, being filled with the holiness of the Father and with His glory which He magnifies, spreads this holiness and glory over those who approach Him in the holy place of His presence as sacrifice: "For both He [Christ] who sanctifies and those who are being sanctified are all of one, for which reason He is not ashamed to call them brethren" (Heb 2:11); brethren within the holiness that came from the same Father to Christ as man for the sacrifice He offered to the Father, but also for His unity with the Father according to His divine essence, and to them as to those with whom the Son of God became their Brother through incarnation.

And because they are Christ's brethren and, thus, sons of the heavenly Father according to grace, they are also co-heirs with the Son made man. To be an heir means to become, in union with Christ as man, possessor of all the heavenly Father's good things, reigning together with the Father over all these good things, without Him ceasing to be their supreme possessor and king, or their ultimate source. Therefore, they are a blessed family of the Father. This is why Jesus will tell them at the Last Judgment: "Come, you blessed of my Father, inherit the kingdom prepared for you from the foundation of the world" (Mt 25:34). Even though the good things that will be inherited by those who glorify the Father through faith (Rom 4:16) and are glorified by Him, are endless and eternal, they will be adapted to them as human persons. This is why it is said that this Kingdom is prepared, thus made according to them, from the foundation of the world or from their creation. It is in the inheritance of this Kingdom, or of the eternal life—the plenitude of life—that salvation consists (Heb 1:14; 1 Pt 33:7). This inheritance is a true blessing. And only those who bless others receive this blessing, namely only those who respond with good to those who do evil, with good wishes and good works, will also inherit the blessing or the eternal good things of the Kingdom: "Do not return evil for evil or reviling for reviling, but on the contrary blessing, knowing that you were called to this, that you may inherit a blessing" (1 Pt 3:9). This is what Christ did, blessing those who were crucifying Him. This is the path to the inheritance of the blessing with all the good things prepared for us from the foundation of the world, or for which we have been created, instilling in us the tendency toward them and the desire to attain them and to work in order to elevate ourselves to their height. We are reminded of this call in the Holy Liturgy. And it helps us to advance toward the Kingdom we are called to. Therefore, in a sense we are all "called" through the Liturgy.

Thus, both in the second antiphon sung by the faithful and in the prayer of the priest one has passed from supplication for God's mercy in general and for His blessing, to supplication for salvation in Christ and to the care of the faithful to be preserved in the fullness of the Church as heirs of God's Kingdom and to their glorification in return for the glory that they acknowledge and offer to God.

There follows the third litany of the same brief or concentrated content as the second.

In the third exclamation, which the priest pronounces audibly, the hope for the fulfillment of the supplications from the third litany and for the salvation, sanctification and glorification of the faithful—asked for at the end of the second litany—is founded not only on God's power and holiness, but also on His goodness. God, who in the first exclamation was acknowledged as being due glory and worship and in the second one as having in Himself the dominion, the Kingdom, the power and the glory—of which by saving us He makes us also partakers in Christ—can give all these to us because He is good and the lover of mankind.

"For You are a good God and loves mankind, and unto You we ascribe glory, to the Father, and to the Son, and to the Holy Spirit, now and ever, and unto the ages of ages. Amen!" The glory and the worship due to Him are founded on the dominion, the Kingdom, the power and the glory which He has in Himself. These are a dominion, a Kingdom, a power and a glory of His goodness and love for mankind. It is not a tyrannical dominion or Kingdom that frightens us, or that is deceptively masked in goodness, but a dominion and a Kingdom of the true goodness that attracts us. In goodness is best shown the glory of God, but also the personal or tri-personal characteristic.

On the basis of God's goodness from this exclamation, intensified with "Amen," the liturgical community sings the Beatitudes as the third antiphon, expressing through them the hope of receiving this Kingdom of God's goodness. In them the community remembers the conditions necessary for living in the Kingdom of heaven and, thus, of the very qualities of this Kingdom, conditions and qualities indicated by Christ the Savior Himself. By expressing these conditions, the liturgical community wishes to obtain them and through them the Kingdom of heaven itself, which is asked for even from the beginning of the Beatitudes: "Remember us, O Lord, when You come into Your Kingdom."

This Kingdom belongs to those who are aware of the poverty of earthly life; to those who will be comforted because they grieved yearning for that Kingdom and strived for it; to the meek, not to those seeking power; to those who hungered and thirsted for righteousness or for all goodness and purity; to those who will partake of God's complete mercy because they were compassionate and merciful; to the pure in heart from passions and bad and evil thoughts who through this purity and delicate sensibility will see God in all His purity; to the peacemakers who, on account of this, will be called children of God, the source of all peace and love; to those who were persecuted and mocked because of God and because of these high human values toward which they endeavored without responding to evil with evil. All these show the Kingdom of God as the Kingdom of a humanity that attained the highest degree of human achievement, namely of the finest delicacy, love and attentiveness toward each other. In that Kingdom will shine the light and sweetness of the infinite love made accessible to us by Jesus Christ.

Through these qualities we become like the Son of God who was incarnate for us and was meek and humble in His heart, who was a peacemaker and merciful like no other, who has suffered all kinds of calumnies and persecutions, including death, out of love for God the Father and for us. We will not be adopted, thus we will not be like Him and co-heirs with Him of the Kingdom, if we too do not strive to be like Him. Therefore, when we are persecuted like He was, for Him and for these high levels which we want to attain like Him, it is meet and right to rejoice, knowing that in the end we will also be glorified together with Him; we will even be glorified when suffering persecutions for the sake of good, feeling comforted and grateful in this. There is joy even in the goodness that succeeds in not responding to evil with evil. It is the joy for conquering evil in its own being. The words at the end of the Beatitudes clearly repeats this. St. Peter the Apostle says: "Rejoice to the extent that you partake of Christ's sufferings, that when His glory is revealed, you may also be glad with exceeding joy. If you are reproached for the name of Christ, blessed are you, for the Spirit of glory and of God rests upon you" (1 Pt 4:13–14). These words must have given so much joy to the Christians of the first centuries in their gatherings when they knew that martyrdom for Christ was awaiting them.

It has been said that the Holy Liturgy is christological, as it mystically depicts for us Christ's saving work, leading us to union with Him through Holy Communion.

This opinion is well founded, since the Son of God is the One who became man, has urged us toward and is leading us on the path of life toward perfection, was crucified and rose from the dead so as to lead us to the Kingdom of the Holy Trinity, in the spiritual zone of its love and happiness.

We need to mention that all praises addressed to God in Trinity, or to His Kingdom, end with "Amen," pronounced by the priest when the faithful are not present (at the Proskomedia), or by the community: after a praise addressed by the priest to God in the Trinity (after "Blessed is the Kingdom of the Father," etc., after exclamations), or after each time the priest or a believer pronounces the words, "Glory to the Father and to the Son and to the Holy Spirit, now and ever, and unto the ages of ages." This has been done since the time of St. Irenaeus in the first half of the second century.[252] Through these words one reinforces not just the praise offered to the Holy Trinity for its glory and goodness, but also faith in the eternity of the consequences of the Holy Trinity's saving work, thus a certitude of the eternity of created beings in God, due to the Holy Trinity's ineffable goodness.

However, if the prayers of supplications do not end with praise of the Holy Trinity, they do not end with "Amen." In the Liturgy there are many prayers of supplications recited both by the priest silently and by the faithful. These supplications end with "Lord have mercy."

The Kingdom is praised both when the Holy Liturgy begins and throughout its course, and all the faithful are continuously called in it to enter and to advance in that Kingdom. When the priest comes out with the holy gifts [the small entrance] he prays that the Lord may remember various categories of believers "in His Kingdom." The faithful themselves praise the Kingdom directly, or by praising the Holy Trinity which makes the Kingdom available through the incarnate Son and through the Holy Spirit. The first and second antiphons begin and the Beatitudes end with the praise of the Holy Trinity: "Glory to the Father and to the Son and to the Holy Spirit, now and ever, and unto the ages of ages. Amen." It has been rightly said that Orthodoxy is doxological. But one must emphasize just as much that its doxology is directed toward the Holy Trinity and, through It, toward the Kingdom proper to It. For only in the Holy Trinity or in Its Kingdom is our happiness to be found. Through the praise of the Holy Trinity the faithful learn to forget their egoism and to realize the communion among them from the power of the Holy Trinity's communion or Kingdom. Thus, only the praise of the Trinity elevates the faithful from the limits of their individual I to the contemplation of, and the desire for, the ineffable love of God in Trinity, and thereby to their true perfection in the Kingdom of the Holy Trinity.

We should mention here that various passages from the Psalms serve as Antiphons sung by the liturgical community on regular days, in which the Kingdom of God is indicated, but less clearly. Thus, as the first Antiphon the following is sung: "It is good to give thanks to the Lord and to sing to Your name, O Most High, to proclaim Your mercy in the morning and Your truth at night" (Ps 91:1–2), which announces the coming of the Kingdom. As the second Antiphon the following is sung: "The Lord reigns; He clothed Himself in majesty. The Lord clothed and girded Himself with power" (Ps 92:1). "The second antiphon celebrates that very dominion, glory, and power which came to the Son of God because of his humiliation and poverty."[253] The following is sung as the third Antiphon: "Come, let us greatly rejoice in the Lord; let us shout aloud to God our Savior; let us come before His face with thanksgiving. And let us shout aloud to Him with psalms. For the Lord is a great God, a great King over all the gods; for in His hand are the ends of the earth" (Ps 94:1–4). This also indicates the joy at the meeting of the Son of God who took upon Himself the human face. The Savior "had appeared and made himself manifest."[254] "It is particularly clear that the prophet sang this canticle with the coming of Christ in mind, so full is it of joy and gladness; he is overflowing with this joy himself, and invites others to share in it with him."[255]

The inclusion of the hymn "Only Begotten" after the second Antiphon and of the Beatitudes after the third Antiphon indicates by name Him who opened in Himself the Kingdom of heaven for us and described its features and the features of those who will belong to it.

But not only on regular days, but also on Sundays, passages from the psalms were sung as Antiphons in the olden times, and certain fragments are sung even today. For example, as the first Antiphon stichera from Psalm 102 were sung, and before the hymn "Only Begotten" stichera from Psalm 145 were sung.[256]

The earlier commentators on the Holy Liturgy spoke extensively about this psalm. They explain this by the fact that until the "Small Entrance" or until Christ's coming out to preach, one still lived in the light of the vague knowledge of the Kingdom of God in the Old Testament through prophets, and in a transparent, but not fully clear image of the Kingdom in the child Jesus by those close to Him: the Lord's Mother, St. John the Baptist, etc. "The royal doors are closed immediately after the blessing is given for the beginning of the Holy Liturgy, only the curtain remaining open. This is intended to mean that only the prophets and the patriarchs of the Old Testament, the Holy Virgin and Joseph, the shepherds and the magi—symbolized by the curtain—recognized the Son of God, while the rest of humans—represented by the royal doors—did not recognize the Son of God in the Newly Born, in Jesus."[257] But, as we mentioned before, the lesser manifestation of the Kingdom through the opening not covered by the curtain could also mean a less advanced phase in the ascension of the faithful toward the Kingdom. The replacement of the Antiphons with psalms on regular days also shows that the Kingdom of the Holy Trinity has been fully revealed through Christ's resurrection.

While the faithful sing the Beatitudes, the priest reads silently a prayer in which he offers to God a general thanksgiving for granting him the power to make the "common and united" supplications in the three litanies and entreats Him to fulfill the beneficial supplications of the faithful, but especially to grant them "in this world the knowledge of Your truth, and in the world to come, life everlasting." There is something additional that the priest asks for in this prayer: knowledge of divine truth and eternal life.

4. *The Small Entrance or Christ's Coming Out to Preach and the Praise of God's Holiness*

Toward the end of the praises offered by the faithful to the Kingdom of God through the Beatitudes, the priest prepares himself for the "Small Entrance." As we have seen from St. Maximos the Confessor, during his time at this moment the hierarch entered the church. This custom has been preserved in the Eastern Liturgy until now. But perhaps even then the priest entered a little before for certain preliminary prayers. However, the hierarchical Liturgy starts at this moment.[258] Christ, the true High Priest, comes out now from His hidden life to His visible ministry. The coming out is followed by a still incomplete entrance before the Father with His obedience as man, with the beginning of His saving ministry. It is the "small entrance." The "great entrance" will be the entrance before the Father through His sacrifice.

First the royal doors are opened, an act by which the Kingdom of God is revealed in a more accentuated manner; or Christ the King enters, coming by way of the priest, through the door on the west side. Now the

Kingdom is manifested to the liturgical community in a more emphasized way, the Kingdom which, after having gleamed briefly at the beginning of the Holy Liturgy, remained rather hoped for during the litanies and the Antiphons, recited or sung before the coming out of Christ to preach. Up until now, after the Kingdom of the Holy Trinity, which will come through Christ, was announced (more strongly through St. John the Baptist, the last prophet), the faithful, knowing about it but still not seeing it truly revealed, knock at its door with their supplications so as to prepare themselves to see it, following Christ's advice: "Knock and it will be opened to you" (Mt 7:7). Now Christ comes out in a more visible way, but He also enters through His service as man in the altar next to the Father, showing that He will fulfill His work as service to the Father for human beings.

This is why right after this entrance the hierarch, together with two others, officiates the first hierarchical act within the Holy Liturgy: the ordination of a new hierarch, when this is the case, so that the new hierarch may himself begin the new Liturgy, just as Christ began His service.

If no hierarch is present, the small entrance is done by the priest.

Taking the Gospel from the Holy Table, the priest gives it to the deacon, if he is present, if not, he carries it himself and, together with the deacon, if he is present, they go around the Holy Table and come out through the door on the west side of the altar to the middle of the church. If the hierarch is present, the priest stands next to him with the Gospel. Here he says a prayer asking God to grant that together with their entrance "there may also be an entrance of holy angels con-celebrating with us, and together with us, glorifying Your goodness." It is, thus, a prayer since it speaks of glorifying God by the angels and by the priest, or priests. The prayer concludes with the doxological exclamation from the end of the first litany. The priest and the deacon—the hierarch, too, if he is present—do not represent the angels, but they have the angels alongside them during their entrance. And, certainly, where the angels are together with the ministers on earth, Christ is there as well.

In fact, this entrance has been considered as representing Christ's coming out to preach. Sometimes it was considered that the hierarch himself represents Christ coming out to preach and entering the altar with His face toward the Father from where He would fulfill His preaching and then His sacrifice for the benefit of the world. But the fact that the Gospel is carried not by the hierarch and not even by the priest when the deacon is present, shows that, on the other hand, a distinction is made between Christ, represented by the Gospel, and the hierarch or the priest. The Gospel represents Christ in a more accentuated manner, because it is the bearer of His saving words and deeds that are always current and at work, wherever they are honored or are listened to with faith, He who spoke and fulfilled them and forever fulfills them is Himself seen as being present. Nicholas Cabasilas says: "For the Gospel represents Christ."[259] The entrance with the Gospel is a commemoration of His initial coming out to preach, but also a continuous coming out to teach us.

Christ's presence through His Gospel is also shown by the fact that the deacon, or the priest if he is not present, proceeding to the royal doors and raising the Gospel, says: "Wisdom, attend!" That is: "Stand aright with a pure thought, unchanged and raised up, for this is Christ, the Wisdom of God." Or: "Look at the height where He is. Do not look downwards, but stand aright so that you may look upwards, for Christ's teaching is great and great is the image of human life that He shows us." Nicholas Cabasilas says: "When these are over, the priest, standing in front of the altar, raises the Gospel-book and shows it to the people, thus symbolizing the manifestation of the Lord, when He began to appear to the multitudes."[260] The fact that the Gospel is taken from the Holy Table and is taken back, after exiting through the door on the west side, and placed again on the Holy Table, contradicts the fact that Christ is considered as only now coming out and arriving to preach. Christ who is with us is coming again to us even more fully. In addition to this, every exit presumes that the one who exists was already inside and after an exit there follows another entrance, as St. Gregory of Nyssa says. The entire spiritual ascent is a continuous exit from a condition and an entrance into the same condition at an even higher level. This is why God is asked to bless the "comings out and goings in" of the faithful.

Nicholas Cabasilas presupposes this presence of Christ in the Gospel when he also says that, while the third Antiphon is sung, "the Gospels are brought in; the holy book is carried in by the deacon, or, if he be not present, by the priest himself, surrounded by a procession of acolytes bearing candles and incense."[261] This is how Christ was surrounded by angels when He was baptized in the Jordan. The lit candles also symbolize the light contained in the Gospel.[262]

Fr. Petre Vintilescu says that "the lit candles also symbolize St. John the Baptist as well as other prophets before the Savior who heralded His coming, the Holy Apostles whom He sent before Him to preach in villages two by two."[263] Thus, we would have around Christ all those who preceded Him and those who succeeded Him, announcing Him, namely the whole Church of those who attached themselves to Him by serving Him, but also continuing to work for Him and with Him for our instruction and salvation. The entire past is present in Christian spirituality. The multiple symbols of the moments, the words and acts of the worship are explained precisely from the fact that in Christ, being alive, are condensed the past together with the present and the future anticipated in eternity. This is also explained from the mutual interiority of all those who serve Christ, in Christ and together. However, each time there comes to the forefront a moment, an act or a meaning of this unique totality of moments, of acts or of meanings. In this sense, when the priest takes the Gospel from the Holy Table, he places the cross in its place. There is an inner connection between the Gospel and the cross. The Gospel leads to the cross. But the coming out with the Gospel places in bold relief the fact that initially Christ came out to preach, and the cross will come to the forefront in His life at the end of His preaching by fully shedding light on it and confirming it.

"In Christ everything is already fulfilled, but the full cosmic and universal resound still remains in expectation. Nevertheless, God does not stop His work. He continues His actions in the Mysteries [Sacraments], in the Liturgy. These extend the historical visibility of Christ and, thus, they are the actual interventions of God."[264]

"Time enclosed in a curve bends toward itself, it provokes the anxiety of the absurd's infinite repetitions . . . . Existential time is totally different: each moment can open from the inside toward a totally different dimension. This is the holy or liturgical time. Its participation in the absolutely different One changes its nature. Eternity is neither before nor after time; it is that dimension toward which time can open.

True finality of time is not the final point, but the pleroma. The sacrifice is not reproduced, but it appears in the ever present reality of the Ascension. St. John Chrysostom specifies: 'He [Christ] went up with a sacrifice.'[265] Up there the sacrifice took the proportion of the pleroma that fills the heaven and the earth, time and eternity, and this is why the prayer of the anamnesis can bring to mind the entire economy of salvation, including the Parousia . . . . Events do not melt away, but they remain deposited in God's memory . . . . Through analogy, one can imagine a certain dimension of time in which time meets the future . . . . Through the power of the liturgical mystery time opens up and we are projected onto the plane where eternity intersects with time and in the Liturgy we become real contemporaries with the Biblical events from Genesis until the second coming; we experience them really as eyewitnesses. This is why every reading of the Gospel places us within the event that is being related . . . . At Christmas we participate really at Christ's birth and the risen Christ appears to us really at Easter night and makes us eyewitnesses to the events of Holy Week. Here there is no longer the characteristic of the dead time of repetition . . . . St. John Chrysostom says: 'It is the same Sacrifice that is performed . . . . No time is limited for the performance of this Sacrifice.'[266] And Theodore of Mopsuestia says: 'This is not a new thing, but it is the Liturgy that takes place in heaven and we are with Him who is in heaven. All the holy Suppers of the Church are nothing but one and the same eternal and unique Supper, that of Christ in the upper room.'"[267]

Through every liturgical moment we connect ourselves with all the moments of Christ's life found in eternity, for He Himself lives all of them all over again; but for the need of every moment and of every believer in one moment or another He places in bold relief and re-experiences the work proper for their salvation in that particular moment.

This presence of Christ through the Gospel is shown in the hymn sung by the faithful at this time: "Come, let us worship and fall down before Christ! O Son of God, who rose from the dead, save us who sing unto You, Alleluia!" By saying this, the faithful together with the priest bow down and make the sign of the cross, as before Christ.

Even though this entrance signifies Christ's coming out to preach, the faithful worship Him as the One risen from the dead, because they know that Christ is the one who was crucified and has risen, and at this liturgical time the One who comes out to preach is at the same time the One who is risen. The Liturgy of today, following the Liturgy of the Church from the time of the New Testament, knows Christ after He has accomplished all His saving work; and in the Liturgy He relives for the sake of the faithful, on the one hand, all His saving moments, on the other hand, He relives with particular efficacy what is necessary for the faithful at that moment. Knowing him to be the One who rose and ascended into heaven, being seated at the right hand of the Father, the faithful know that He now relives the beginning of His preaching full of all glory and invisibly surrounded by the heavenly hosts; namely, He gives the Gospel all the light that His preaching obtained after the resurrection. For this act of accompanying Christ by those in the altar and of His being received by the faithful, they all prepared through the prayers of supplication and through the praises addressed until now to God.

After the entrance with the Gospel, the deacon pronounces from the royal doors addressing the faithful: *Let us pray to the Lord*. They respond: *Lord have mercy*. They now ask for God's mercy so as to become worthy to praise His holiness. They have come close to angels who know above all creation God's holiness and they are filled with it. For the Son of God became incarnate and came to us so as to give us, too, the opportunity to know God's holiness, or the purity of His love, making us also saints and thus preparing us for Holy Communion. This takes us from the stage of the supplications addressed to God for our various physical and spiritual needs—as external conditions for holiness—to the stage of the knowledge of God and of the praise of His holiness, without which we cannot partake of holiness nor can we be saved.

Then the deacon, bowing his head toward the priest, says softly: *Bless, Father, the time for the Thrice-Holy hymn*. The time for this hymn calls for it to be blessed and sanctified so that the faithful may feel being imbued through it with God's holiness. And everything is blessed through the priest. He was chosen by God to visibly communicate His blessings as from a unique center, which is not dependent on laity.

Even when the deacon proceeds from the middle of the church with the Gospel, after he presented it to the priest to kiss it, he asks the priest: *Bless, Father, the Holy Entrance*. The entrance is holy in and of itself because it is the entrance of Christ as man before the Father in order that from next to Him He may complete His sanctifying and saving ministry through visible works. Also Christ visibly communicates His holiness through the priest, so that the faithful may renew their conscience that holiness comes neither from him nor from an impersonal ambiance, but from Christ as a distinct Person and source of holiness. All the moments of liturgical time, filled with God's glory and with the sanctifying of His name by the priest and by the faithful, call for this characteristic to be shown. It is imperative to show that they are sanctified only by God made man. Thus, the entire liturgical time becomes a blessed time. Hence, even from the beginning of the Liturgy, when the deacon comes out of the Holy Altar to recite the litanies in front and on behalf of the people, with his face toward God in the altar or in heaven, he asks the priest to bless the beginning time by saying: *It is time to begin the service to the Lord. Bless, Father!* Through Christ eternity enters liturgical time, which is open through Christ to God's personal eternity. Paradoxically, eternity is poured into time and through time we advance into eternity on account of God become man.

In general, the priest's "blessing" is not just a "good word" equivalent to a kind of "good luck," but a word through which God's Spirit irradiates out of Christ when it is pronounced in the name of the Lord and in officiating the saving work of the Church, or of the faith meant to unite human persons in Christ. Since the blessing is a means for the irradiation of Christ's Holy Spirit, it is Christ Himself who blesses through the priest, thereby irradiating from Himself the sanctifying power of His Holy Spirit.

Everything that the priest blesses is invisibly filled with Christ's Holy Spirit. The priest performs the blessing with the sign of the cross, since most of the time it is one and the same with the sign of the cross made over the people or the things that are blessed. This shows once again that the divine power that is poured out through blessing is the power of Christ, who as God incarnate has vanquished death through the cross or through sacrifice; or that the power of the Trinity poured out over those who are blessed (also for their benefit) has been made accessible to us through the cross of Christ, of the Son of God incarnate out of love for us and crucified out of the same love. It is not an impersonal power, stirred up magically. Through the sign of the cross, by which the blessing is performed, was shown to us and is being communicated to us the love of the personal Son of God, who out of love for us went all the way to the cross, and He continues to relive the cross He suffered out of the same love for us. The Holy Spirit pours out His power over us through the fact that Christ, out of Whom He irradiates, sacrificed Himself bodily on the cross, stripping the human body He assumed in the earthly life of its needs. In the marks of the cross left on Christ's body and through which His body was made perfect by rising up again and being deified as beyond any self-preoccupation, is deposited as in an active, living and transparent source all the power of the Holy Spirit that is being poured out at the same time with Christ's love over those who are blessed. The suffering borne patiently by the incarnate Son of God out of the power of His love for us has become the means or the source of the power of divine love irradiating permanently, because it means the freedom from any closing off of God and of His assumed humanity in His internal life. The "good word" of the priest accompanied by the sign of the cross is the "word of the cross" of Christ. In this is all the power of God (1 Cor 1:18), as love directed toward us.

After the entrance into the altar, the deacon asks the priest to specially bless the time of the singing of the thrice-holy hymn, showing that now the cross, through the power of Christ, is meant not only to cleanse the faithful of all the sins of egoism, but also to make them know and praise God's holiness as the culminating stage of purity and of love for humans manifested in the incarnation and the sacrifice of the Son of God. It is the time when He begins to work at our sanctification. That is why the priest says: *For You are holy, O our God, and we offer glory to You, to the Father, and to the Son, and to the Holy Spirit, now and ever...* implicitly showing that he asks for the sanctification from God of the time of these moments.

While in the previous exclamations the power, the glory, the Kingdom, the goodness and also the incomprehensible, apophatic nature of God were praised, now the liturgical community is urged to praise God's holiness. In this way God makes His presence more felt. It is not only the priest who praises this, by asking the community to confirm it, but the liturgical community itself must praise this holiness manifested through Christ, for the entire community ought to be sanctified by this. The time has come for God's holiness, active through Christ, to be praised by the entire liturgical community so that the whole of it may partake of His holiness. For it is the attribute we praise in God that we receive, because we admire it and we open ourselves to it.

But before the liturgical community begins to praise God's holiness, the priest adds the exclamation: *O Lord, save Your faithful people! And hear us! And unto the ages of ages!* Hear us when we also praise Your holiness, or purify us in the praising of your holiness so that You may receive this praise. Only because we partake of the saving work of God, purifying ourselves through faith, can we know and feel within us God's holiness. In addition to this, God's holiness cannot be praised with full conviction except by those who taste the happiness of His salvation, which does not lack holiness. And only the praise offered with all this conviction is heard by God. This praise must be offered three times, as a confession of the triune God, as a gift and symbol of the eternal extension of this praise, a fact that guarantees eternity to those who offer it. This is said by the priest through the words: *And unto the ages of ages.*

In fact, not only do the faithful repeat this hymn three times, but they crown the hymn with the doxology: *Glory to the Father, and to the Son, and to the Holy Spirit, not and ever and unto the ages of ages, Amen,* followed by *Holy Immortal, have mercy on us,* one time. In this way we show directly that only to the Immortal One is due an everlasting praise by those who will not die either, on account of Him. Then the priest urges the liturgical community through the words *Powerfully* to repeat the hymn, thereby also calling upon the heavenly *Powers* to add their praise to that of the community, or as the community senses the praise of the angels in its praise, the chanting of the community could reach the supreme intensity. Thus, the community wills that the praise of God's holiness may not be just an eternal one on its part, but also fulfilled by the praise of all the powers of creation, including that of the angels. For in fact the Seraphim also praise God's holiness unceasingly forever with so much power that because of the power of their voice the upper lintel of the house in which the Lord sits on His high throne engulfed in glory is eternally lifted up (Is 6:1–3); that is of the visible and the invisible Church.

The praise of God's holiness rises up and raises both the angels and human persons to the partaking of it more than the praise of His other attributes. For human beings may conceive of those attributes as worldly and may reinterpret His glory as worldly glory, His Kingdom as a worldly kingdom, and His power as worldly power. But through His holiness God is sensed as being totally on a different plane which is transcendent to all the world categories, *dans ganz Andere*. It represents the mystery of God *par excellence*. It is profoundly apophatic, but at the same time profoundly experienced. One can advance and rise *ad infinitum* in sensing and understanding it. Holiness cannot be converted into an attribute that is narrowed and stained by human understanding, like others, because it is *par excellence* one and the same with the limitless purity of God Who, in order to understand and sense it, asks for an increasingly greater purity from human beings, a purity that can never be reached by the latter. It is a fact expressed by Dionysius the Areopagite in describing the endless ascent of angels. Holiness is thus the mystery that always fills us with a fear and trembling of a different category than the fear and trembling in the world (*Mysterium tremendum*). Accompanied by that other fear, we advance in sensing God's holiness as we feel more and more its inexhaustible infinity and our growth in the endless understanding of His existence. Holiness is exclusively proper to God, it is not proper to a certain extent or a certain way to human beings, as are other of His attributes, which can be experienced together somewhat stained and in various degrees of narrowness. It provides its unstained garment to all the other attributes of God, and to the extent that it can be partaken of by people it can help them as well to experience with a certain purity the other attributes of God and to sense their infinity. The experience of God's holiness by human beings purifies, to the extent that it is experienced, the understanding and the experience of the other attributes of God shared with them. It can be projected upon certain persons, too, but only when they can preserve it unstained by worldly things, that is when they purify themselves of worldly things. It cannot stand together with what is worldly, but it always opposes the worldly things. At the moment you sense it, you distance yourself from the worldly things and you rise above creation into transcendence. And to the extent to which you make progress in it, the worldly sense in you decreases. This is why those who partake of God's holiness awaken in their fellow human beings a sense of holy fear. Holiness is filled with the purity of perfect love.

The saints are, therefore, filled with a purity that they obtain not only through their own efforts, but as a gift from God, given that the purity is united with holiness which is exclusively the gift of God. This is why Isaiah cries out: "Woe is me, for I am pierced to the heart, for being a man and having unclean lips, I dwell in the midst of a people with unclean lips; for I saw the King, the Lord of hosts, with my eyes! Then one of the seraphim was sent to me. He had a live coal in his hand, which he took with tongs from the altar. He touched my mouth, and said: 'Behold, this has touched your lips. Your lawlessness is taken away, and your sin is cleansed'" (Is 6:5–7). How exclusive the holiness proper to God is, being identified with His transcendence, is also shown in the fact that the seraphim themselves cover their faces with two wings, being unable to gaze upon it spiritually, even though they feel its presence and irradiation, while with two wings they fly around it (Is 6:2). God's holiness is experienced not in a static way, but in the vibration of the soul's wings. On the one hand, it fills you with fear, on the other hand, it draws you just like it causes the seraphim to cover their faces, but still they fly around it. They experience it in this vibrating ascent of their spirit.

The experience of God's presence has now become much emphasized in the liturgical community as well, motivating it to express this experience in its enthusiastic singing, similar to that of the angels and united with it. It has become felt to them through Christ who has come out to preach, but from whom the Holy Spirit irradiates, given Christ's purity and innocence as of the reasonable Lamb. Christ preaches a teaching that expresses Him. He is the "Holy of God" who came to human beings with a pure body and thought, filled with God's holiness.

On the other hand, He was able to enter before the Father, able to minister to Him and to offer Himself as sacrifice to Him on the heavenly altar. Christ has brought God's holiness close to us, filling His humanity with it, which is thus all-pure and at the same time close to God through His ministry and sacrifice offered to the Father for us, or for the fulfillment of His will to save us, purifying and sanctifying our humanity if we open ourselves to Him with faith. "And for their sakes I sanctify Myself" (Jn 17:19). "Christ also loved the church and gave Himself for her, that He might sanctify and cleanse her" (Eph 5:26).

But through the coming of the Son of God to us and through His concomitant entrance as man before the Father by His ministry that would end in crucifixion, resurrection and ascension, He clearly revealed to us God as Trinity. This is why we now sing to Him the thrice holy hymn. "Next we praise God himself, the Triune God, as the coming of the Saviour revealed him to us."[268] The teaching about God as Trinity is the first teaching revealed to us by the Savior. Thus, it is the teaching that God is love from eternity. "The hymn which we sing comes to us from the angels, and is taken in part from the book of the sacred psalms of the prophet. It was gathered together by the Christ's Church as dedicated to the Trinity. For the *Hagios* (the Sanctus), which is repeated thrice, is the angelic acclamation; the words 'Strong and immortal God' are those of the blessed David, who exclaims: 'My soul thirsts for the strong and living God.' (Ps 42:2) The Church which is the assembly of those who believe and profess the Trinity and Unity of God, played its part in gathering together these two acclamations, joining them, and adding the ejaculation, 'Have mercy on us;' she wished to show, on the one hand, the harmony of the Old and New Testaments, and on the other, that angels and men form one Church, a single choir, because of the coming of Christ who was of both heaven and earth."[269] Through Christ, the loving and merciful characteristic of God has been put in bold relief.

God's Trinity is manifested not only through the triple repetition of the hymn, but also through the three parts of each repetition. *Holy God* can refer to the Father, "the source of godliness"; *Holy Mighty* can refer to the Son, who through His word has strengthened the heavens and has brought us to a new life, conquering sin and death in human beings, or it can remind us of the words: "The voice of the Lord is strong" (Ps 28:4). Nothing has manifested God's might more than the salvation of human beings through the Son in their deification. *Holy Immortal* can refer to the Holy Spirit, for the Spirit is the one who communicates to us life in Christ (Jn 6:63); He is the life-creating one.

After each praise of the Trinity's holiness, the community of believers asks: *Have mercy on us*. Only because God is holy, thus above the ambiguous, unconscious nature that is subjected to the laws of repetition, can He have mercy. Only the Person can have mercy. What lacks conscience, what is not a Person pure of every egoism, therefore holy, being in eternal communion with other Persons, cannot have perpetual mercy, a mercy that is eternally saving. At this time the faithful do not say in general *Lord have mercy*, but *Have mercy on us*. Even now it is not an individualistic *Lord have mercy* but it is restricted to the present community of those who have decided to partake of God's holiness jointly, and who receive Christ as God, their common Savior, raising them to the state of communion.

During this time the royal doors continue to remain open. For the thrice holy hymn of the faithful people is united with that of the priest in the altar, and both the community of believers and the priest are at the same time united with the angels who also glorify God around the heavenly altar, signified by the church altar. The Kingdom of heaven or of the Holy Trinity comes over those in the church in a way that is more felt concurrently with the knowledge of its holiness, which can only be the holiness of the Trinity. For a single person being unable to have love, cannot have holiness either, being unable to inspire the pure gentleness toward other persons. The community rises to heaven at this time, to the Holy Trinity, surrounded by angels, doing this through the living, transparent and spiritualized veil of Christ's body that became like this through sacrifice (Heb 10:19).

While the faithful continue to sing this hymn, the priest recites silently the prayer in which he asks God to accept the thrice holy hymn and, as the One who is holy and rests among the saints, to sanctify both the souls and the bodies of the faithful, including his own soul and body, so that they may also rest and serve Him with the holiness with which they wish to be filled from Him all the days of their lives. In this supplication the priest includes himself, speaking in the first person. However, his prayer, offered especially by the people, has a meaning. For even though he is one of the "sinners" who offer to God this thrice holy hymn, he still maintains the role of the one who specifically prays for all, including himself. He does not separate himself from others, but is not to be confused with them either. This is the position of the priest during the entire course of the Liturgy: one of all and still distinct from all. This is how Christ was, too: He worked for the deification of all, but since He worked specifically for the deification of His body, He has offered His body as sacrifice so that He may bring the bodies of all into a bond with His. Certainly, the priest is not distinct from the community as Christ is. For he is a sinner, too, and he needs salvation just like the faithful, as Christ did not.

In his special prayer for all, in which he includes himself, the priest signifies Christ and is His visible instrument, united with all and still unconfused with them. He must elevate himself as the representative of all in his prayer. Precisely because of this he can also elevate their prayer, can give it wings, can attract the prayer of all in his prayer, raising it together with his. The leader of an army attracts the soldiers even more precisely because he jumps first into battle and steps up ahead of all. The more he shows himself to be fighting before them and for them, the more they are determined to fight as well. "In the days of His flesh, when He had offered up prayers and supplications, with vehement cries and tears to Him who was able to save Him from death, and was heard because of His godly fear, though He was a Son, yet He learned obedience by the things which He suffered. And having been perfected, He became the author of eternal salvation to all who obey Him" (Heb 5:7–9). This is what Christ does now and this is what the priest does, as His visible instrument, or serving Him in this quality through the grace of priesthood given to him by which Christ's high-priestly work of salvation is officiated. By receiving and continually activating the grace of priesthood, as the operation of Christ the High Priest, the priest must follow the One about whom it has been said: "Therefore, in all things He had to be made like His brethren, that He might be a merciful and faithful High Priest in things pertaining to God, to make propitiation for the sins of the people. For in that He Himself has suffered, being tempted, He is able to aid those who are tempted" (Heb 2:17–18).

Precisely this union with, and distinction of the priest from, the liturgical community of the faithful causes the plural "we" used by him to be understood as referring either to him, or to him and the community. Nicholas Cabasilas refers it to the community by saying: "Before the Trisagion is begun the priest asks God to accept this song of praise and to give grace to those who sing it."[270] However, when he includes himself, he says: "Forgive us every transgression, both voluntary and involuntary." But when, aware of his duty to proceed by the grace of priesthood especially given to him, he says: "Who has vouchsafed unto us, Your humble and unworthy servants, to stand before the glory of Your holy altar [signifying Christ's state before the heavenly altar], You, O Master, accept the thrice-holy hymn from the mouths of us sinners," the boundary between the prayer for himself and for others, in which he includes himself as well, is very fluid. He continuously crosses it, now distinguishing himself from the faithful, now joining their ranks.

It is for the first time when the altar before the face of God is mentioned in the Holy Liturgy. But as of yet one does not speak of Christ's sacrifice that will be offered upon it, but only of the worship and the glory that will be offered to God before this altar.

Also for the first time God is praised not only as holy in Himself, but as the One resting in the saints, making the people, too, saints. This is due to the fact that He has brought everything from non-being into being and has created man after His image and likeness and has adorned him with all gifts; and that He gives to the one who asks wisdom and understanding and does not overlook the one who has sinned, but establishes repentance, as escape from the narrowness and staining of egoism, for salvation and sanctification. Only God who could bring all things into existence, who gave the human person so much honor that He created him after His image and likeness and adorned him with the grace that is poured out from Himself, and who even when the human person sins does not abandon him to forgetfulness, separated from Him, but brings him back to the right path and to a renewed relationship with Him through the repentance implanted in him, can raise the human person up to the point of making him partaker of the most proper attribute of Him, namely holiness, by dwelling with His holiness in him.

In pantheism everything is immanent and subjected to determinism, namely nothing exists beyond the essence of this world lacking freedom, and everything is ambivalent, a mixture of good and evil where purity and holiness do not exist unmixed with evil and sinfulness. Holiness shows God as a pure Person through His freedom; this is not a vague, obscure and impersonal "sacred" mixed with what is sinful.

In this prayer of the priest to God the Birthgiver of God appears also as well as all the saints. For everything that the priest asks in this prayer, is asked "through the prayers of the Birthgiver of God and of all the saints who from the ages have been well-pleasing to You." Once Christ has appeared to preach, it is no longer possible for His Mother and for all the saints, who have been at all times well-pleasing to Him, not to be seen together with Him and also prayed to. For in the reality of their holiness we have the proof that our prayer for our holiness is not without hope of being fulfilled. If God wishes us to pray for each other in this life so that He can see our selfless love among us being strengthened, it is not possible for Him not to wish the prayers of the Mother of God and of His saints for us, or that these would not show their love for us through their prayers to the Lord; for He wants that they all may be gathered together in Him through their love toward Him and among themselves (Eph 1:10). We cannot even conceive that the saints, who have attained so much love for Christ, would not have a boundless love toward us as well, and that love would not urge them to pray for us. Much less can we imagine the Lord's Mother looking indifferently at the work of her Son for our salvation and not showing her love for us, following her Son's example. And we cannot wait passively for their prayers, as a sign of their love, but we also must show that we rejoice in this evidence of their love for us, in their imitation of Christ in this regard as well.

When the Liturgy is officiated by the hierarch, he also enters the altar at the same time with the Gospel or with Christ, for the work of salvation of the gathered faithful. In this case, after the hierarch enters the altar he gives the blessing for the thrice-holy hymn and addresses the first supplication to God for the salvation of the faithful, the right-believing people.

Then he comes out through the royal doors and blesses the people with the trikirion in one hand (three candles), the symbol of the Holy

Trinity, and with the dikirion (two candles) in the other hand, the symbol of Christ, the incarnate Son of God in two natures.

By making the sign of the cross three times from East to West with these candle holders over the faithful present, the hierarch says these words every time: *Lord, Lord, look down from heaven and behold, and visit this vineyard which Your right hand planted, and perfect it* (Ps 79:15-16).

Salvation is conditioned upon perfection. By asking for perfection, the hierarch asks for the salvation of the faithful. He asks that the vineyard in-breathed with soul by God through creation and raised to the level of Church may bring forth fruits pleasing to God, namely good works, because salvation depends on this, and in this is shown that this vineyard walks on the path of perfection.

The three blessings of the hierarch are interspersed among the three parts of the hymn "Holy God." From these three powers of God — holiness, might and immortality—or from the Holy Trinity, comes salvation or perfection, which is shown in the holiness, spiritual might and immortality of the faithful.

Salvation is achieved through cooperation between God and the faithful. The vineyard brings about its role through the ministry of the workers sent into it (hierarch, priest) and through the attributes granted to it by God. But the work of both the ministers and the faithful takes its power from prayer. This is why they are united in the dialogue of prayer.

5. *Christ's Preaching: the Reading of the Epistle and of the Gospel*

After this prayer, the priest also says silently three times "Holy God . . . " Then he goes to the Proskomedia table and at the prompting of the deacon, if he is present, *Command, Master,* and if not he says by himself: *Blessed is He who comes in the name of the Lord*. These are the words with which the Lord was met when He entered Jerusalem. Through the sung praise of God's holiness and through the elevation of souls up to the point of sensing the union with angels, the community has prepared itself for receiving Christ's teaching. Only with elevated minds, purified from unclean thoughts and from sins, and sanctified through closeness to God by praising His holiness, can the faithful understand Christ's teaching, which can lead them to a purer and more enlightened life. Besides, the Epistles of the Apostles are not a theoretical exposition of Christ's saving work, but a glorifying or doxological one. The doxology of "Holy God" is followed by the doxology of the reading of the apostolic Epistles, which represent in a condensed way everything that Christ did and, thus, it is a thanksgiving and praise offered to God at all times for the salvation He gave us. This does not mean that the epistles are less important as teaching. But as we learn from the Apostles about what God did for us in Christ, we learn about an activity worthy of praise and thanksgiving; we learn about the loving God, who is worthy of all praise and glory. This is why the right faith is the right glorification, the unending and undistorted glorification of God, which is Orthodoxy. On any page to which we open an Epistle, we read words or testimonies of glorifying God (Php 4:20; 2:9–11; 1:3; Eph 5:19–20; 3:16; 1:8; 1:3, 6; Gal 1:5, etc.). This is why the pericope from the Epistle is sung, as in fact is the entire Liturgy. Singing gives wings to words. By reading first from the Epistles of the Apostles and then from the Gospels shows that the preaching of the Apostles is needed today for understanding Christ, as it was in the beginning. They gave us the true understanding of Christ and of His saving work. True faith preserved in the Orthodox Church stands on their foundation. We do not go first to the Gospel so as to understand it at our whims. The teaching of the Apostles is the true and complete understanding of Christ's teaching, which remains uninterrupted and permanent in the Church.

Even if at this time the preaching of the Lord begins through the reading of the Epistle, He is still blessed as the One who enters Jerusalem in order to be crucified. Christ's preaching is not separated from His sacrifice. Everything is concentrated and visible, so to speak, in His Person. His preaching will lead Him to the cross and it will be crowned through the cross. This is seen in the Proskomedia. In fact, He "comes in the name of the Lord" to preach, in the name of His heavenly Father who "sent" Him (Jn 17:18). The priest blesses Him with the sign of the cross. For we make the sign of the cross before Christ. In this way we manifest our devotion and gratitude toward Him or toward His goodness and sacrifice for us. It is through the cross that He is the Savior and with this name we praise and portray Him. The blessing we give Him is not like the blessing He gives us, but it is a praise we offer Him. And we praise Him by showing the cross as His decisive action. The cross is His sign of praise, His glory. It will appear preceding Him when He comes to judge the living and the dead. The veneration of His cross will be the basis for our acceptance into His Kingdom. He who disdained His cross, or His sacrifice for us, as the sign of His love unto death, and he who did not make of His cross the power for conquering his egoism and for loving Christ and his fellow human beings, will not be saved. When His cross appears, its light will overwhelm the light of the sun and of the stars. In their stead, there will appear shining forth the sign of the Son of Man (Mt 24:29–30) as the source of the overwhelming light of the meaning of existence, which has an incomprehensible depth. The glories of the world will fall or fade away, so that the cross, the sacrifice of the Son of Man, will show its true glory, eliminating all division caused by egoism and lack of love. Whoever will not receive it with honor and glory as the sign of Christ *par excellence*, he will not receive Christ Himself or the true Christ.

The priest goes to the place behind the Holy Table where the bishop's throne is, which signifies Christ's throne, and says: *Blessed are You on the throne of the glory of Your Kingdom, Who sits upon the Cherubim; always, now and ever, and unto the ages of ages. Amen.* And he stands at the place on the East side of the "High Place." Christ looks invisibly from that "High Place" that is made up of Cherubim, at the teaching about Him in the Church. He teaches, but He teaches through the Apostles and their successors, or through the Church, and He keeps the Church in the true teaching. He teaches, but since He teaches through the Church, He keeps watch over the teaching given about Him. It is the norm and authority of what is being taught. This is the royal throne of His glory, for the Cherubim represent the highest level in His Kingdom, but they are also full of Christ's glory. Christ does not sit on an inanimate throne, but on the throne of the pure and highest minds of creation, the closest to God through understanding and love. God, and especially His incarnate Son, is not separated from creation, but He is within it. He is especially in understanding and loving minds, and especially the Son of God, who has united Himself eternally through incarnation with creation, particularly with the conscious one. Thus, Christ's sitting upon the Cherubim extends to us if we open ourselves to Him through faith. His light, which enlightens to the highest degree the pure minds of angels and the minds purified of every sin of the saints, comes into us bringing with it the capacity of the highest and purest creatures to understand it.

It is from this place that Christ hears His preaching, coming from Him, but transmitted by the Apostles and by the entire tradition of sanctification of the Church, united with its understanding by the pure minds of angels, namely by the hierarchical successors who put into practice His teaching during the course of the entire Tradition, even though, on the other hand, He will always be with them: "Go therefore and make disciples of all the nations.... teaching them.... and lo, I am with you always, even unto the end of the age" (Mt 28:19–20).

After the ending of the thrice-holy hymn the deacon comes to the royal doors, which have remained open since the small entrance so that Christ's teaching is dispensed through them after the first knowledge of God's holiness, and says: *Let us attend!* And the priest says from his place behind the holy table, *Peace be to you all!* If there is no deacon, the priest says both. The word about Christ from the Epistle must be listened to attentively, but also with inner peace of the soul and with a mind of peace for each other. In him who is troubled by worldly thoughts and in him who has evil thoughts about others, the word about Christ cannot work; that person cannot observe all that Christ has commanded (Mt 28:20). Peace is required at prayer, peace is required at listening to the word about Christ so as to bring forth good fruits. Only in this way can one pass from the world to Christ-God. The word about Christ is intended to reconcile all with Him, in the unity of faith and love so that no one remains attached to fleeting things and closed off in one's egoism (Col 1:20). The true teaching brings peace; it is not a theory without a unifying and saving effect.

The community of the faithful responds: *And to your spirit!* It is not only the priest who wishes peace upon the faithful in the church and prays for them, but they also wish peace upon him and pray for him. Prayer works not just from the priest toward the faithful, but also from them toward the priest. For Christ does not remain closed off either in the priest or in the liturgical community. The flux of the prayer carried by the Holy Spirit moves from both sides, thus realizing an increasingly greater unity among those who pray. Only if the priest has peace in the depth of his being, in the spirit in which he is called to meet with God, can the peace wished by him spread over the community of people, as the peace of God. Properly speaking, it is from within God that the peace irradiates from the priest to the community of faithful and vice versa. But it begins to work through the priest. There are priests from whom the community of the faithful feels how the spirit of prayer extends over and within it. From these priests who are concentrated in prayer, peace is also extended over the community. But when the priest is distraught by worldly things and due to lack of concentration, a spirit of distraction is extended over the community of the faithful, which in its turn is felt by the priest as well.

The reader then recites the prokeimenon of the Epistle, or a stichera prescribed from the Psalms, as a sign of the connection between the teaching of the New Testament and that of the Old Testament, or of the unity of God's plan of salvation unfolded throughout history.

The deacon, or the priest if the deacon is not present, says: *Wisdom!* What will be read from the Epistle is the same wisdom of Christ which is also comprised in the Gospel. Or, through those writings the same Christ is proclaimed, the hypostatic Wisdom of God. Just as He is the Word that speaks words, so He is the Wisdom that communicates wisdom. For the true Word speaks the words of wisdom, of the correct understanding and living. Both the wisdom and the word are not separated from the person. So much less from the supreme Person. The very supreme Person is the Wisdom and the Word. The supreme Person is the meaning consciously comprising all meanings in which that Wisdom can express itself. The human being, by his very essence, bears in his image the seal of God's hypostatic Wisdom. With this he understands Christ as Wisdom. Then the reader announces the Epistle of the Apostle from which will be read. As has been said, any pericope of these Epistles represents the entire preaching of the Apostles about Christ. The deacon or the priest again urges the faithful: *Let us be attentive!* It is good to insist upon urging the faithful to be attentive, because the content of what will be read has a divine profundity and is decisive for salvation. During the reading of the Epistle, the deacon, or in his absence, the priest takes the censer, and if the deacon is present he asks the priest to bless the incense; if the deacon is absent, the priest himself blesses the incense with the sign of the cross, saying: *Incense we offer You, O Christ, as an odor of spiritual fragrance. Receive it upon Your heavenly altar and send down in return upon us the gift of Your Holy Spirit.* Through its sweet fragrance, incense is the symbol of pure prayer rising up to God: "Let my prayer be set before You as incense" (Ps 140:2). We should raise to God our prayer as a pure sacrifice so as to understand the Gospel of the all-pure One who offered Himself as sacrifice for us. This is why incense is also the symbol of every sacrifice we offer with a pure heart, the symbol of abandoning the bad smell of our egoism and of our attachment to things on earth. It is especially the symbol of offering ourselves to God in purity from the power of Christ's sacrifice and together with it, such as St. Cyril of Alexandria developed this idea in his work, *Adoration in Spirit and in Truth*.

We must at all times offer ourselves as sacrifices to the Father, like Christ who is forever in a state of sacrifice on the heavenly altar before the Father. This is our "ministry," our permanent latreia together with that of Christ's. "Therefore, brethren, having boldness to enter [permanently] the Holiest by the blood of Jesus, by a new and living way which He consecrated for us, through the veil, that is, His flesh, and having [endlessly] a High Priest over the house of God [built out of living stones, which are us], let us draw near with a true heart in full assurance of faith, having our hearts sprinkled from an evil conscience and our bodies washed with pure water" (Heb 10:19–20). Christ is permanently priest and sacrifice. He permanently washes us through the power of the blood and water that flowed out of His body on the cross, raising us to heaven through this body that became transparent (for it entered through the locked doors). Thus, we permanently can and must fulfill our "ministry" to God according to the words of the Apostle: "How much more shall the blood of Christ, who through the eternal Spirit offered Himself without spot to God, cleanse your conscience from dead works to serve the living God" (Heb 9:14).

Incense symbolizes this offering of our sweet fragrance of sacrifice, purified of sin, to Christ's sacrifice, as it rises together with the latter and from its power; it is offered as a "gift from gift" of the love from God, in Him through the Holy Spirit. The Liturgy is an ever increasing exchange of gifts between us and God, maintained by the cross of Christ. God offers Himself to us in Christ through His cross, by self-renunciation — and we offer ourselves to the Father together with Christ from the power of His cross, which we imprint in our being that has become a living cross, a life in a continuous self-advancement toward God. It is a continuous crescendo of life that increasingly became love which sprouts out of Christ's body, which itself is configured as love toward the Father and toward us through the cross; that body became through the cross a voluntary channel of divine life, foreshadowed by the tree of life in paradise. Our "ministry" lies in being partners of God in this dialogue of love, which we also extend among ourselves.

The deacon, or the priest in the deacon's absence, and in the case when the hierarch is serving, censes the altar and the nave of the church according to the prescribed rule and three times every time in the form of the cross. For only in the spirit of self-overcoming through the cross is our being raised as a sacrifice with a sweet-smelling fragrance to God. The order of censing is this: around the Holy Table, starting from the front and going around it from the right and then the gifts from the Proskomedia. Over there is the living foundation of Christ's sacrifice. Then, coming back behind the Holy Table, the icons on the wall are censed, thus honoring the saints, especially the holy hierarchs from the first centuries of the Church who have served the Holy Liturgy in the altar. Then he comes out through the royal doors and censes first the icon of the Savior on the right, of the Lord's Mother on the left, the other icons from the lower row of the iconostasis ending with the icon of the patron saint. Then the hierarchical throne, the chanters and the faithful in the church. This is the censing before the reading of the Gospel. It prepares the faithful for receiving Christ, elevates their thoughts toward Him as in a prayer. Then he enters the Holy Altar, censes again the Holy Table, the gifts from the Proskomedia and the High Place, places the censor in its place and the deacon receives the Gospel from the priest. While the deacon censes, or if he is absent, the priest after finishing censing asks silently that Christ illumine the hearts of those in the church with "the pure light" of His divinity and to open the eyes of their minds to the understanding of His Gospel teachings. He is asking not only to awaken in them the natural light of the mind, but the light that radiates from Christ Himself, which places Him in their spiritual sight. God cannot be known if He does not make Himself known, evident. He is light and from Him radiates the light that makes Him known as light. The priest asks for this light not only for the faithful as if he had it. In this case he could ask that they would share in it as he does. But he says: "Illumine our hearts, O Master, the lover of mankind, with the pure light of Your divine knowledge and open the eyes of our mind to the understanding of Your Gospel teachings." If it were only about a theoretical knowledge of the dogmas about God, the priest would have that knowledge, as the faithful do not. It is, therefore, about a knowledge coming from the shining forth of the light of God, who becomes Himself light in the priest and in the faithful. It is about a deeper understanding and a more powerful sense perception of Christ as Person, as God made man: "In Your light, we shall see the light."

From asking God's help for various needs, and from praising and sensing of His holiness, the community of faithful has stepped up to a new level: that of asking for the light of knowledge of the incarnate God who is Himself light and the supreme source of light; it is the light as Person that came to us, or the supreme Person as light and as the source of all light. For in general the person is identical with the light generating light, a reduced and unclear light if the person is created, but an unending and all-pure light if it is God the Word. One can see here that from listening to the words of the Epistle about Light or about Christ, the liturgical community is elevated to receiving the very words of Christ, or of Christ Himself as the incarnate divine Person who spreads the light within their hearts and minds, which strengthens their unity even more. For it is Christ Himself who now states His words through the deacon or the priest and it is His light and power that come through His words that enrich their life. "For You, O Christ God, are the light of our souls." He is the complete meaning of the entire human existence, in contrast to any pantheistic philosophy.

As has been said, the word of Christ and His power do not have the purpose of bringing about only a theoretical understanding of Him in the hearts and souls of the faithful, but also of strengthening their will to receive His commandments which require the overcoming of bodily passions and a spiritual living stimulated by love. For the words of Christ that interpret Him show us a model to be followed and at the same time they are commandments. The light of Christ is united with the purity of His life; the Word is united with His Holy Spirit, therefore it is life and holiness, or rather it is life because it is holiness. Where Christ is, there is spiritual or loving life as well. In it is the true light, the harmony of the order that drives away disorder and strengthens the inner peace as well as the interpersonal communion from the Spirit of the divine communion (2 Cor 13:14). One now asks not only for peace and help for one own's life, but for an interpersonal life in communion, contrary to the one dominated by bodily passions, closed off in egoism and lacking the light and the generous unity between persons.

The prayer of the priest said by himself during the entire course of the Liturgy, in parallel with the sung supplications or praises of the faithful people, does not separate him from the community of the faithful, but it presents him as one chosen to pray to God for the community in a higher place (in the altar). His elevation to a deeper intimacy with God and, thus, to the finding of his own intimacy, does not take him out of the intimacy with the liturgical community, but it gives him a position of initiative in the realization of this ascent of the community, thus symbolizing Christ who entered and remains in the heavenly Holy of Holies before the supreme altar and who comes to us through His body as in a thin, spiritual membrane made transparent through the cross and, consequently, through the divine light which His Holy Spirit irradiates.

This is how Moses entered the higher place, and Aaron the Holy of Holies to pray for the people. The prayer that penetrates more intimately to God is said during one's own self-concentration. This elevation of the priest to a higher spiritual level did not cease in the New Testament. But now the type of Moses has been replaced with the reality of the fully efficient Mediator. Thus, the sensible image of the Mediator did not cease, either. God Himself has invested this living image of the Mediator with power of representation.

Coming out through the royal doors, through the doors of the supreme King, the deacon asks from the priest who is at his usual place facing the faithful: *Bless, Father, him who proclaims the good tidings of the holy Apostle and Evangelist (N)*. Even if Christ's power works in him who proclaims His words, it works in him to the extent of his spiritual vibration to this power. Christ does not annul the human person's power, but He increases it to the extent to which he wants to put it into practice through his faith. In the human person's faith his power encounters Christ's in a single experienced conviction which works upon the faithful all the more as it is more firmly and more warmly felt. This is why the priest responds to the deacon that God Himself may, through his blessing in which the power of God also encounters his conviction that God works through him, *enable him with great power,*[271] *to proclaim the good tidings, to the fulfillment of the Gospel of His beloved Son, our Lord Jesus Christ*. Only if the Gospel of the Son of God is proclaimed with great power, will the Gospel attain "fulfillment," that is, the believers, by being filled with faith, will lead their life to perfection or will be able to benefit from the salvation proclaimed by Christ through the Gospel, through the cross and the resurrection that will crown it.

The deacon responds: *Amen. Let it be unto me according to your word, Master!* Just as the Virgin received with faith the promise that the power of the Most High would overshadow her and she would bear the Son of God, so does the deacon receive with faith the priest's assurance about the power to make it possible for Christ Himself to be spiritually born, through the word of Christ read by him, in the hearts of the listeners, so that they may feel that He is the one who speaks His words in their hearts. Then, the priest, or if there is a deacon present, says: *Wisdom! Let us attend. Let us listen to the Holy Gospel*. At the small entrance with the Gospel, he only says: *Wisdom. Let us attend!* At this time Christ, the Wisdom of God (1 Cor 1:24), or His saving teaching (Jam 3:17; 2 Pt 3:15) is manifested not only by raising the Gospel, but also by speaking to us. This is why we are asked to listen to it, standing upright with both the mind and the body, unbent from the right thinking and living and not distracted by other thoughts. Christ, or His teaching, does not lead us on crooked paths, to disorder, to untruth or to nonsense, but He enlightens us with the true wisdom through which we attain the full, eternal life. "Let us therefore hear the Gospel, just as if we were listening to the Lord Himself present; nor let us say, O happy they who were able to see Him! because there were many of them who saw, and also killed Him; and there are many among us who have not seen Him, and yet have believed."[272]

Nicholas Cabasilas says that through the word "Stand up" we are given an exhortation to make an effort in following very attentively what is being said and done, not with indolence and indifference. "The first sign of this fervor and devotion is the uprightness of our bodies."[273] Thus, we show that we are ready to begin the fulfillment of the heavenly King's commandments.

The priest continues: *Peace be to you all*. Only in a mind undisturbed by thoughts foreign to the Gospel can the divine word enter and work upon the soul. Only in a state of the soul undisturbed by worldly and evil thoughts, by hatred, unpleasant memories and ungodly worries, can the word of the Gospel penetrate deeply and can make the human person concentrate totally and fruitfully on its content. It is especially essential that this word be heard as the word of the incarnate Son of God through which God wants to adopt us. The Gospel must be for us the evidence of God the Father's love, who sent His Son as man into the world so as to make us, too, His children. How can we not abandon for the love of God the Father and of His Son all attachments to the fleeting things that do not guarantee us life?

Then the deacon announces the Gospel from which he will read and after the prompting of the priest or of another deacon, *Let us be attentive*, he reads the appointed pericope. The pericopes are established in such a way that during the course of an ecclesiastical year those who come regularly to church may know the important moments of Christ's life and all His saving works, as well as His essential teachings which are directions for the life that leads us to resurrection. From every pericope one can fully know Christ, the incarnate Son of God and His saving work. This is why it is wrong to say that the Church has kept the Gospel hidden from the people. For it is read accompanied by the glory offered to God and, therefore, hymned, awakening festive feelings in souls or, rather, the sense perception of the ineffable mystery of the content of Christ's words and deeds in which the spiritual presence and pulsation of His Person is felt. "There where the word ceases, the ineffable is indicated and singing leads the human person beyond limit, into the apophatic."[274] The Gospel is not read critically, coldly, inquisitively, with inclinations to doubt what is being read, but with the feeling that we are elevated into another zone; it is read in a spirit of praise, doxologically, in a festive joy for what God has given and is giving us. Once we know that His disciples had died to the last one, confessing that they had seen Him risen, and once there is no teaching of Christ in the Gospel that has been touched in its height by another teaching, and furthermore, once it raises our minds to a life higher than any life that we might live with our own powers, what would be the point to doubt Christ's divinity and not glorify Him for all He has taught us and for all He has shown us in His Person, as well as for all He has done for us by becoming incarnate, being crucified and having ascended into heaven as "the First Born" into eternal and all-happy life for us? Once we are united, through the word of the Gospel, with Christ-God who utters that word, what else do we still seek?

After the deacon finishes the reading of the pericope of the Gospel, the priest says: *Peace be unto you who have proclaimed the good tidings*, namely you who have read the Gospel, have evangelized and have made known the good tidings of salvation, or of eternal life in Christ. The priest told the reader of the Epistle only *Peace be to you, reader*, or *to you who have read*. The laity can also speak in church about Christ. But only at the urging of the priest to the faithful to be attentive to the one who speaks. The very word of Christ is read in the church only by the priest or the deacon with the blessing of the priest, because Christ is presented to the faithful by the person of the priest as a person sent from God, through the grace received from above, as Christ was sent by the Father (Jn 15:21). The priest does not say at this time *Peace be to you all*, but only *Peace be unto you who have read*, or *to you who have evangelized*, so that he may continue to speak about Christ or to proclaim the word of Christ even afterwards through his own being filled with the peace of Christ, and to further have an influence upon the faithful, to further manifest his conviction that he has read the very word about Christ or of Christ. If he does not prove himself in his life as a man of peace, how would the faithful who have heard the word he read about Christ or of Christ remain convinced that he believes in this word and that he believes in the saving divinity of Christ? The word read about Christ or of Christ, from the power of Christ, is followed by the word from the power of the community, which sings after the reading of the Epistle: *Alleluia*, or *Praise the Lord God*, and after the reading of the Gospel this praise is addressed directly to God: *Glory to You, O Lord, glory to You*. The teaching given to us by the incarnate Son of God or the presentation of His saving works, with the eternal love of God for us manifested in them, is a doxological opportunity for praising God.

Coming then with the raised Gospel to the royal doors, the deacon gives it to the priest, who kisses it and raises it in his turn, blessing the people with it in the form of the cross and with the icon of the resurrection on the front cover. The cross and the resurrection form one whole. The cross led to resurrection, and through the resurrection Christ's work for us has been crowned. The power of the crucified and risen Christ works even now upon us, causing us to accept His cross that leads us to resurrection. Christ Himself, who has been crucified and has risen for us, is blessing us through the priest. Then the priest places the Gospel on the Holy Table above the antimension that has the burial of Christ painted on it. We pass now from the Liturgy of teaching to the Liturgy of Christ's sacrifice, or this is now in the forefront; the sacrifice is no longer implied in the teaching, hidden in the teaching, as it has been during the time of Christ's preaching activity. The antimension still remains folded. At the Lord's entrance into Jerusalem, it was not clearly evident that He would be crucified. The teaching was the preparation for sacrifice and resurrection.

6. *The Litany After the Reading of the Gospel and the Prayers for the Deceased and for the Catechumens*

a) The antimension, with the mystery of Christ's victorious death, will not be opened until after the departure of the catechumens. At this time, a final litany for them and for the faithful who remain will be offered, a series of fervent supplications for God's mercy and His help for the general necessities of life.

The community of the faithful shows persistence in these supplications in the fact they say the words "Lord have mercy" not once, like in the supplications from the beginning litanies, but three times, actually once after the first and the second supplications, and three times after the others. This shows that the supplications have become more ardent; the community had resolved to insist until God hears and fulfills them, like the widow from the Gospel about whose persistence the Savior said: "And shall God not avenge His own elect who cry out day and night to Him, though He bears long with them?" (Lk 18:7). The catechumens and those who cannot yet partake of the Eucharist due to certain grave sins, have special reasons to cry our persistently when asking for God's mercy. They are assured by the Savior, by His enduring patience, by the fact that God will make them worthy to pass from the state they are in to another state in which they may partake. An example of persistence in asking God's mercy is given in Orthodoxy by the unceasing prayer of Jesus, attained not only by monks, but also by certain faithful: "Lord Jesus Christ, the Son of God, have mercy on me, a sinner." This is why even those who can partake feel often the urge to prolong more persistently their prayer in which they ask for God's mercy. He creates within them, through the continuous repetition of the supplication for God's mercy, a state of continuous desire for this mercy, namely the permanent sense perception of the need for His mercy, an imprint of this need in their being.

Since the catechumens are still in the church together with the faithful, the priest or the deacon, if he is present, begins this litany with the words: *Let us all say from our whole soul and from our whole mind, let us say*. Even the repetition of the words *let us say* indicates the recommendation to persist in prayer. Then there follow two supplications addressed to God in the second person in which mercy for the priest, or the deacon, as well as for the faithful people is fervently asked for. In the first supplication all make a persistent appeal to God to hear their prayer and to have mercy on them, showing their hope in Him as "the God of our fathers." In the mercy shown to their fathers, they have the basis for the hope that God will also have mercy on them. In the first supplication the priest asks for mercy once and the faithful respond, or they also address God, with *Lord have mercy* once. *O Lord Almighty, the God of our fathers, we pray You hear us and have mercy.* From the start, at this time one asks for mercy, not for peace. One asks from God the mercy that gives not only the peace on earth, but also salvation or the eternal life through the sacrifice of His Son. God's great mercy was needed to make His Son man and for the Son to be crucified for us, thus liberating us from the eternal death brought about by sin. In fact, the entire Liturgy is, at base, an alternation between the supplications for God's mercy and the praise we offer Him for the salvation He made us a part of through the sacrifice of His Son. God's mercy comes in the form of many blessings, but it culminates in the offering of Christ's body and blood to conquer our death. And our praise grows continuously after each of God's increased gifts, the praise being accompanied on our part by an even greater dedication. In the beginning litanies, one asks only once for mercy, among other good things, in the last supplication: *help us, save us, have mercy on us,* etc. At this time mercy is asked for right from the beginning.

In the third supplication, mercy is asked for twice, namely fervently: *Have mercy on us, O God, according to Your great mercy, we pray You, hear us and have mercy.* The faithful people respond with *Lord, have mercy* three times. In the following three supplications, even though mercy is not mentioned, it is presumed, as in the entire litany, and the faithful respond with the same *Lord, have mercy* three times. Mercy is asked for the bishop, for the civil authorities, for priests, monks, *for all our brethren in Christ,* even for the founders of the church and *for all our fathers and brethren, the Orthodox departed this life before us who, here and in all the world lie asleep in the Lord.* The entire, universal ecclesiastical community—those living on earth and those who have departed this life—is embraced with generosity and in a spirit of solidarity.

Then one asks again for God's mercy and, in connection with it, for the *remission and forgiveness of the sins of the servants of God: members, supporters and benefactors of this holy church.* Mercy is placed at the forefront. Only after it are also mentioned: life, peace, health, forgiveness of sins, salvation and visitation.

Then mercy is asked for *those who bring offerings and do good works in this holy and all-venerable church, for those who labor and those who sing* to God in it and *for the people here present who await from You great and abundant mercy.* All the faithful people ask and wait for mercy. This litany may be called a litany of mercy.

In the exclamation God is called merciful, as He was not called in the previous ones: *For You are a merciful God and loves mankind, and we send up glory to You: to the Father, and to the Son, and to the Holy Spirit, now and ever, and unto the ages of ages. Amen.* We do not send up glory to a God before whom we tremble as before an almighty ruler, but to a merciful God to whom is due the greatest admiration and the most profound praise. From the knowledge and sense perception of God's immensity and holiness, through which He still remains to some extent unapproachable, we ascended to the knowledge of God as merciful and, thus, as the One who lowers Himself by descending to us from His immensity and His holiness that is unapproachable and untouched by us. He is a great God because He becomes human. This fact is manifested in the incarnation of His Son, in His crucifixion for us, in His resurrection, in His union with us through the Eucharist and in our being raised next to Him forever.

In the prayer which the priest recites at this time he says again: *O Lord, accept this fervent supplication from Your servants and have mercy on us according to the multitude of Your mercy.*

God's mercy has been revealed in its richness and greatness after God's descent to us through His Son made man was known from the reading of the Epistle and the Gospel; but it will be fully made known to us after the Son accepts death for us. Thus, this litany of mercy begins to make known to us Christ's sacrifice and the Eucharist that follows.

God's mercy is not only an exterior act of granting what He is asked by those who are in need of what they ask. If it were only that, it would not move us so much. When someone throws a coin to a beggar, passing quickly by him so as not to be bothered by his suffering appearance, that someone does not yet show his soulful participation in the beggar's suffering. His mercy still remains much reduced. Only when he stops compassionately by the one who is suffering, when he speaks to him, when he commits to a more permanent involvement, and when he brings him so close to himself that he becomes like the beggar and the beggar becomes like him, that is when mercy has reached the truly amazing dimensions that are worthy of all admiration. This is what the Son of God has done for us. He became like us and we became like Him, as He entered into an eternal communion with us, making us kings like Him, we who are nothing before Him, but who are in great suffering on account of our own fault of not remaining close to Him. This is why to His act of mercy must correspond a deep feeling of mercy in Himself. The God of the Liturgy is not a God of a cold rationality, but of a merciful sensitivity, of a participation in the pain of those who suffer terribly in the state of deep and senseless decadence in which they are. The Son of God was incarnate not only to teach us, but to also die for us.

All who are inferior to Him—and all created beings are infinitely inferior to Him—are deeply unhappy when they separate themselves from Him. He suffers for them not because He lacks the good things which they lack. God's mercy is not an exterior gesture combined with inner indifference, but an inner participation in the pain of those He has mercy upon. There is a deep mystery in this ability of God to participate in the pains of His created beings. Perhaps what could help us in the understanding of this mystery is the fact that in the suffering of His created beings through their separation from God is reflected His will to have created them for communion with Him, and thus the purpose of their creation remains unfulfilled due to their refusal to remain in this communion. But it is precisely God's participation in the suffering of His created beings that prompts Him to grant them what they are lacking, namely to offer Himself, and if they want to receive Him, in this way He may heal their spiritual and physical pains. This is what God established His relationship with His created beings should be; not a relationship between someone insensitive to their pains, who has only a theoretical, rational knowledge of their concrete life with the shortages that might occur in it, and these created beings who suffer from their lack of communion with God, but a living, touching and vibrant relationship on both sides. God's mercy is the mystery of a living God, not of a God frozen in His insensitivity. The inner-principle of this mystery is superior to the reason that can be understood through a theoretical speculation about a monotonous God who lacks life and conscience. There is in this mystery the rationality of love that unites on the inside, not just on the outside, the parts capable of love. It is "the reason beyond reason," as St. Maximos the Confessor says, understood not as a law of abstract, schematic thinking, but as the one hypostasized in the triune communion and in the Son of God as a Person with a plenitude of life that is above any person's contents of life. It lies at the basis of the act through which God created the world, sustains it and leads it to happiness in His bosom. It is the inner-principle of a God whose Son was incarnate and was crucified out of mercy for human beings, experiencing as the divine hypostasis of the human nature all the fears and agonies of death. That inner-principle contains not only mercy, but an abundance of mercy, which means the wealth of feeling which is not lived as a force that rules over Him against His will.

We ask for His mercy, which means that it depends on His will to grant it to us, namely to participate in our pain. If God were not capable of it, we would ask for it in vain; but also if His will were not in this mercy, we would again ask for it in vain, for in this case we could not ask Him to experience interiorly His mercy toward us, or He would experience it against His will. The more we ask for it, the more we show that we need even more the mercy of a personal God and all the more does He have mercy on us, conscious of the need we have of His mercy.

A God of mercy is a different God than the one of rational legality, intransigent. He is a different God than the one of overbearing glory, of inflexible justice to which he himself is subjected, of ruling impossible to be softened, of a reigning that rules over him and he does not control, of a kind of reigning that cannot be the object of the greatest glory because it is not united with his will. The God of mercy is the God of love who is more powerful than any reigning and power, of firmness in delicacy, of the glory pertaining to the goodness that descends to those who suffer. We have emptied the glory, power, righteousness and heartless reigning from this content of the heart, of this quality that is above all others; instead, we have imbued ourselves with admiration for rigid glory, for heartless reigning, without freedom, and for the arrogance of being distant. We gave those qualities a rigid content through the sin of egoism, lessening our character of a free person and giving ourselves a half-objective characteristic. And we projected all these upon God, without understanding how a God can be glorified in mercy, strong in love and dominant in the free beating of the heart at the pain of created beings.

A God of mercy is a God of freedom, a personal God in the full sense of the word, and the world He created is His free creation called to His full freedom, a world gifted to certain beings whom He can help to rid themselves, if they want, of limitations and to enjoy the happiness of communion even with God Himself. His relationship with the world is a relationship of life, not a relationship of dead repetition, as in the pantheistic world—the construction of the most schematic, abstract philosophical systems. The human person asks mercy from God because he knows that He can help him and wants to help him, and about himself he knows that he can be helped, not being subjected to certain implacable laws. He knows that through His mercy God does not humiliate him, because He suffers with him. This is why the personages of the Greek tragedies experienced the tragic totally, because they moved within a philosophical, pantheistic horizon, having nobody to ask mercy from and being unable to escape the implacable, fatal laws of an essence that lacked freedom and was subjected to certain inflexible laws that recurred identically. To ask for mercy does not mean to be humiliated, but to be considered as a being created by a God capable of mercy, by a free God so as to grow through free love in communion with Him. In the Christian conception, the human being is seen at the level of partner with God. Between the human being and God there exist certain relationships that are in some sense human, or they could become human and they are among human persons. And whoever thinks that he humiliates himself by asking for mercy, neither does he have mercy, thinking that he might humiliate those to whom he shows mercy. In this case, the relationship among humans become purely exterior and, thus, full of severity and also of incapacity. These relationships become poor, rigid, schematic and subjected to certain general laws as among objects, even when they are called relationships of equality and justice. The "super-man" of Nietzsche, through his arrogance and cruelty, is much more inferior to the complex man, rich in his spiritual content, and with a powerful will and mercy. Likewise, the merciful God is infinitely more worthy of glory than an unconscious essence governed by monotonous laws. He is mighty because He also has a will.

In this mercy and love of God above all understanding is given the force that keeps the human beings in inner unity, that causes the outside world to serve this unity. In God's mercy is also given His capacity to achieve the perfect, but unconfused, inner unity between God and human beings and also, through them, between God and cosmic nature. It is not rigid laws that are the foundation of unity, but God's love; and the unity among all things is not destined to remain at the level of these laws, but it becomes an inner unity in which humanity and the cosmos are spiritually transfigured by God. The laws with their severity came about as a minimum form of unity, as its extreme form, without freedom, after the conscious created beings began to use their liberty in an egoistic way for the weakening of the unity among them. The inner-principle that keeps all things in unity has God's mercy as its foundation, but in mercy the inner-principle attains a superior form and a superior power to maintain unity among all things. "His excellence covered the heavens" (Hab 3:3).

b) Before releasing the catechumens, a litany for the departed is sometimes offered, which is also founded on God's mercy. Mercy cannot be limited only to those who are still in this life. When we ask for God's mercy for us living, we think to ask it even for our loved ones who have fallen asleep in the Lord. We think of them at the Proskomedia as well, but also in other supplications in the Liturgy. At this time, however, they are accorded a special litany.

Why would the litany for the forgiveness of those departed from among the relatives of the catechumens be postponed until after their baptism? What guilt do the departed have that some of their relatives are not yet baptized or others cannot receive Holy Communion because of certain grave sins? The desire to be in communion with their departed who will be forgiven may encourage them to be baptized sooner, or to prepare more quickly for Holy Communion through repentance of the sins prohibiting them from this.

The first supplication of this litany coincides with the third one from the litany of fervent supplications presented above: *Have mercy on us, O God, according to Your great mercy, we pray You, hear us and have mercy*. In its first part this supplication is taken from Psalm 50, in which David asked God for the mercy of forgiveness for his sin of adultery and of Uriah's murder. Having to ask for the forgiveness of our departed, we first pray for the forgiveness of our sins. For how could we expect God to listen to our prayer for the forgiveness of our departed when we ourselves are stained by sins and are in need of God's mercy and forgiveness? The mercy we are asking from God for our departed is at the same time God's mercy toward us. For we cannot be completely at peace when we know that our departed are in need of God's forgiveness and we can do something about this through our prayers. But if we did not ask first for God's mercy for ourselves, it would mean that we considered ourselves better than those for whom we pray and that we pride ourselves in comparison to them before God and before our conscience, thinking that we do not need His mercy. In this way our prayer would be heard by God even less. We ask for God's mercy so that we can pray for others.

Only after the priest offers on our behalf and his own behalf this supplication to God, and the community of faithful responds with *Lord have mercy* three times, he then offers also on our and his behalf the supplications proper for the departed, with the mention of what is expected for them from God's mercy. First he prays for the repose of their souls, mentioning them by name, and for the forgiveness of their sins, both voluntary and involuntary. The souls of the departed cannot have rest as long as they are tormented by the memory of the sins committed and do not receive from God a sign of forgiveness of those sins. And one asks not only for the forgiveness of the voluntary sins, but also for the involuntary sins, because they did not activate the power of their given will to avoid sin. Further on, the priest prays for the souls of the departed to be established where the righteous repose. Namely, he asks for them to share in the repose enjoyed by the righteous, in the repose of the communion with them. No one can rest in his own self, in his solitude, until he is received into the communion of the righteous and, through them, into communion with God. He who is left outside this communion has reasons to believe that this is happening to him because he is unworthy of that communion, and because he is incapable of communicating truly and intimately with God and with others. Only the rest in this communion gives the departed the full guarantee that they have been forgiven, which can calm their conscience. Furthermore, only in the cradle of the love of others one can rest "in the bosom of Abraham" where all the saints are and where each one rejoices in the comforting of others. For this rest is not a static rest, but a communication of attentions and consolations. "The bosom of Abraham" as the ancestor of Christ as man, is Christ Himself, says St. Athanasius.

Additionally, the priest asks for God's mercy so that through this mercy God may grant them the Kingdom of heaven and the forgiveness of sins. It is good that before we want to ask for anything else, we should ask first for God's mercy, or after every supplication we offer, we should show that we await its fulfillment through God's mercy. At this time one specifies that the rest one asks for the departed is not a negative state, of inactivity, but a joy for the Kingdom of heaven, which is the communion of all, full of all spiritual good things: knowledge of the loving God, attentive perfect brotherhood, glory from God and from all, about which everyone rejoices, and perfect spiritual richness. This rest is life, but a life without the activity full of worries for the body and for the fleeting things of this world. It is a life in which we taste, feel and assimilate all the spiritual good things that pour forth from God and from the communion with the fellow human persons with whom we are united in God.

We cannot partake of all these until we are forgiven of sins. For the unforgiven sins perturb our conscience, stop us from looking with clear and confident eyes at those who are in the Kingdom of love, and disturb the full communion which is the essence of the Kingdom of heaven. When we have the departed in mind, we place the strongest accent on asking for the forgiveness of their sins, because they can no longer do anything to obtain this forgiveness; they can no longer cleanse through good deeds the path from their souls to the souls of those they trespassed against. Neither do they have the possibility of showing their mercy to those they wronged who, because of them, have probably suffered ongoing consequences, nor do these have any more need of their acts of mercy.

Does not this state of their inability awaken in us our mercy even more than the state of those still alive? If we need God's mercy, how much more do they need it? This is why we pray for the departed, asking first God's mercy for us. God's mercy for us moves all the more our mercy for the departed, who are in some sense tied up in their inability. The most authentic human vibration moves in our mercy for them, as for certain fellow human beings who are suffering. In a certain way they are in the pit of an extreme lessening of existence. In our mercy for them the most sensible chord of our humanity is activated.

This is why we ascribe the supplication for the forgiveness of their sins to Christ, the immortal King and our God, for in His quality as King of existence, which is the same as the King of nations, He can offer them forgiveness as liberation from the limited existence, from the existential pit, in which they are. Christ is the immortal King also as man through His resurrection from the dead; His humanity has been filled in this perfect union with God with all the fullness of life, which as such is also immortal. He also experiences as man His mercy for His brethren. By forgiving their sins, Christ raises them to communion with Him, to joy in Him for His fullness of life, hence of immortality, too. United with an essence, you either melt into it, or you grow bored (Origen). A person's love, especially God's, lasts forever and is forever new; it gives you eternal rest.

To this threefold supplication, the community of faithful responds not with one, indefinite *Lord have mercy*, but with *Grant this, O Lord,* namely *pour out, O Lord, upon them the boundless richness of the Kingdom and of immortal life and rest in it.*

The priest concludes these supplications with a prayer in which is shown in even more detail what he has asked from God for the faithful. He asks God to rest the souls of His departed servants, whom he mentions by name, *in a place of light, in a place of green pastures, in a place of rest, from where all pain, sorrow and sighing have fled away.* He asks this by addressing Christ with the words: *O God of spirits and of all bodies, who trampled down death, and overthrew the devil, and bestowed life on Your world.* "The place of light" is the spiritual zone of the total and comprehensive understanding of existence, of its meaning, which irradiates from the sun-Christ; "the place of green pastures" is the spiritual zone of the life that is forever fresh and indefatigable or evergreen, because it never diminishes; "the place of rest from where all pain, sorrow and sighing have fled away" is the plenary living, without flaws and without feeling any shortage. These last words are from Revelation 21:4. The expression "the place of green pasture" is a reference to the tree of life whose leaves "were for the healing of the nations" (Rev 22:2) and which is always green because is near the river and the water of life (Rev 22:1). And the expression "the place of light" is based on Revelation 21:23 where it says that the future city of nations "had no need of the sun or of the moon to shine in it, for the glory of God illuminated it. The Lamb is its light." The Lamb's meekness and spirit of sacrifice will reveal and maintain the true meaning of existence. They will engulf and transfigure not only the interpersonal life of human persons, but also the material cosmos, as a means of communication among them, which loses its aspect of wall between them and of reason for fighting.

The emptiness of death or of the extreme shortage of existence will be cured by the ever-flowing, always fresh and new water of life. Those who will be seated near it will drink from it and will rest in the green pastures nourished by it, near the tree of life and in the light of the full and unlimited understanding that will irradiate from the plenitude of life and of meaning as well as from the meekness of the Lamb and of His love, which He proved by allowing Himself to be pierced for us and reliving eternally this love which went all the way to sacrifice.

This full life cannot be given except by Him who trampled down death, which was diminishing and killing life; He who conquered the devil that pulled the conscious being away from God, the source of life; He who forever granted the world eternal life contained in His humanity; He who has done all these as One who is more powerful than all the spirits, being their Creator, but also more powerful than the body which He was, thus, able to assume, to free from death and to fill with life forever.

But in order to be able to rest in the light and love of the Lamb and in the ever-fresh greenery of the Tree of Life, the departed need the forgiveness of all sins. For the memory of any unforgiven sin is like a thorn that pesters their being, not allowing the full joy of life. This is why one asks for the forgiveness of all sins committed either in word, or deed, or even in thought. For any sin has troubled others and can keep them in distress, just as it troubles and continues to trouble those who committed it, disturbing and, thus, lessening the life of those who committed it and those against whom it was committed until it is forgiven, and also weakening the unifying love that sustains the happiness in the heavenly Kingdom. Nothing that is impure can enter this Kingdom of love whose source is the Trinity.

In the exclamation, the priest affirms even more directly the faith that Christ Himself is *the resurrection, the life, and the repose of His servants*. He is "the place of light," the place of green pastures," and "the place of rest" from where neither pain, nor sorrow, nor sighing come. Because from Him there come only sweetness, joy and happiness since He is only love and comfort. He is the water and the tree of life, He is the Lamb who does not chase away people like a beast, but gathers all near His throne of glory, the glory of the love and of the sacrifice forever relived for human beings. The Person of Christ is light, life and rest. His Person is the light of total and endless meaning. Out of that Person springs eternal and loving life, always new and undiminished. With His love He gives us rest, with His steady meekness He drives away from us every fretfulness and fear. We do not say only that "in You is the resurrection, the life and the repose," but *You are the resurrection, the life and the repose of Your departed servants*, or "You as a Person are the resurrection, the life and the repose." His Person is the supreme mystery that makes us happy, that Person itself is life, light, joy and rest for other persons. And even if we are "servants" of Christ, this Master becomes our life and does not seek to make use of our life. He became a meek and sacrificed Lamb at our disposal, so that we may consume Him and become like Him, uniting ourselves fully with Him. To Him is due glory, not to some impersonal realms The supreme communion of the triune Persons is the river and the water of our life, is the love between us.

For You are the resurrection, the life and the repose of Your servants [names] who have fallen asleep, O Christ our God, and unto You we ascribe glory, together with Your Father who is without beginning, and Your All-Holy, Good and Life-giving Spirit. Christ is our resurrection, life and rest, because He is united according to essence with the Father who is without beginning and with the life-creating Spirit. If the Father has no beginning, He has no end either, and He communicates this life without end not only to His Son through His birth before the ages, but also to those whom He adopts on account of the fact that they unite themselves with His Only Begotten Son become man. But it is not an impersonal life without beginning that makes others happy, but a person who is the Father *par excellence* of existence. An impersonal life would not give life out of love, and happiness at the same time, to a Son; it would not give life to a Son who is similarly conscious from eternity, therefore capable from eternity of experiencing this happiness, but to a form of existence of a life equally impersonal, or temporarily personal. The personal Son is the life of those in whom He dwells, because He is also united according to essence with the life, namely with the supreme personal Spirit who is the giver of life in freedom, or giver of life out of love to persons aware of this gift, not irradiating unwillingly other forms of unfree and unconscious life, or free and conscious only in passing. The Spirit is the supreme person opening for us the immortal life, the One who purifies us from the sins of egoism; He brings us the élan of untiring life in communion.

Only to such a personal or tripersonal God one can offer glory and thanksgiving. Only He can rejoice in the glory offered to Him, being conscious of this act of ours through which we acknowledge Him as full of glory and we rejoice in Him.

The departed are the servants of Christ, for they are the created beings of a free God and precisely because of that He can also save them. But even though they are servants, Christ becomes their resurrection and life, uniting Himself with them. Thus, He becomes equal with them. They are servants through creation, but brothers through His union with them. They are servants worthy of infinity, because they are raised to eternal life in God through the Son of God's infinitely valuable sacrifice. The servant is valued to the extent that he offers himself. Each servant is valued separately. This is why each one is commemorated by name, not all together like an anonymous mass. By asking all these things for our departed loved ones, we intensify our thoughts about them and desire for them, better said the desire to be united with Christ in whom we have all those things. When we ask gifts from God for others, we also receive them, because we value and want them as goods of great value.

In conclusion, the priest asks from Christ not just rest for the departed, but *eternal rest* and *memory eternal. Grant eternal repose to the souls of Your servants who have fallen asleep, O Lord, and make their memory eternal.* And those present respond to the triune God by also asking for *memory eternal*, in remembrance of Christ's cross through which life came to all who believe in the saving love of the Son of God, who sacrificed Himself for human beings. This can be asked only from a God who is a Father without beginning and without end, and from His Son begotten from eternity and without end, who gave through the resurrection of the body He assumed the same eternal life, without end, extending this life also to those who adhere to Him with faith; and also from the good and life-giving Spirit, hence the Spirit who could not negate His goodness by giving a transitory life, Himself being eternal and life-creating.

But this eternal life is given by God to those who open themselves through faith to His Son, risen as man for eternity, only if He thinks eternally of each of them by name. For to remember someone means to send toward that person a current of life. And to constantly and eternally remember a person means to send toward that person an uninterrupted and eternal current of life. To remember eternally, therefore, means to eternally keep in existence the one remembered. The more frequently you remember someone, the more familiar he becomes and the more you imprint his living image in your existence.

The frequent commemoration of someone, together with the will to commemorate him eternally, is the sign of a love that tends to last eternally. You become accustomed to think of him permanently, since you can no longer exist without remembering him. There is no love that does not want to be eternal and, thus, there is no subsisting being that would not want to remain immortal, but imprinted upon the remembrance of those commemorated and, thus, united with him. As Gabriel Marcel demonstrated so well, "love is a power that immortalizes; to say: 'I love you' means to say: you will not die."[275] But this love, on the one hand, carries a current of life toward the loved one, and on the other, it nourishes itself from faith in the immortal One. So the eternally existing and eternally loving One, that is God, deigns to eternally keep someone in His memory and, therefore, alive. God cannot let the one He thinks of with love disappear into nothingness. We, too, by asking most frequently for the remembrance of our loved ones, we can convince God that, out of mercy and love for us, He may extend His mercy and love even to those we ask Him to remember. Aside from this, by remembering them most frequently, we can keep them almost ceaselessly in our memory, increasing our love for them. And only if we, too, will exist eternally will we be able to also keep them eternally in our memory, asking God to remember them eternally. Thus, when we ask for "memory eternal" from God for our loved ones, we confess that we will also last eternally through God, and we ask Him for that so that we may be able to rejoice eternally in their existence and in the love between us and them.

To remember someone eternally means to keep his name unforgotten in our memory and, in a way, in our own being and, through the name, to keep him connected to our being. When the pronounced name is not directed toward a void, but toward someone, and that someone feels noticed through the name pronounced by someone else, he also feels moved, that is reinforced in his life by the one mentioning his name.

The person is the being remembered by other persons and remembers especially other persons. This is why that person has a name. My name is me for others. For me I am "I." A person does not want to and cannot forget eternally another person and does not want to be forgotten eternally. This shows that persons are destined to exist eternally. Thus, neither can God, if He exists eternally, forget persons forever. Only animals and things are forgotten. God will forget forever those who did not do His will and did not repent for that. The fact that we ask Him to remember our loved ones eternally means that we ask for a remembrance that gives them happiness. In a way, God knows even those who did not believe in Him and did not do His will. In this way He keeps them, too, in existence, but not in happiness, but in a diminished and unhappy existence. He says to them: "Depart from Me," not "vanish." He knows them, but does not think of them. This means that not one person disappears completely. Precisely the fact that we can never forget the evil we commit against another person if that person does not forgive us, is proof that we want to be forgiven at a certain time by the person we offended and that he maintains an eternal existence for our conscience, but that we too have an eternal existence not forgotten by that person.

But only God can keep someone in His memory eternally, and we can do that only when united with God. For only God exists eternally by Himself, while we can exist eternally only united with God. When we want to remember someone eternally, we consequently evince that we want to live forever, which is not possible except through God. Thus we manifest our faith in the eternal existence of the personal God and of ours in Him.

The priest asks not only God to remember the departed, but he also expresses the desire that the living may remember them as well "from generation to generation;" *Their memory from generation to generation*. Parents will transmit to their children the commemoration of their parents and so on. If their names cannot be specifically recalled, the duty is passed from one generation to the succeeding one to commemorate them at least with the general title of "ancestors." We have the duty to keep the commemoration of our predecessors, of our parents, siblings, and ancestors with the intention of seeing all of them again and to be with all of them in the Kingdom of heaven as a living and not forgotten presence of the entire past, of the entire history of what the human beings had the best in them This remembrance gives eternal value to the good achievements in history. Nothing will be lost in forgetfulness, everything will be relived and deepened eternally in its significance in eternal life. By commemorating the ancestors, we evince our gratitude to those through whom God had brought us into existence.

But once the successors of the first or second generations have commemorated the predecessors and have asked God to remember them by name, and the "ancestors" in general remain distinct forever in God's memory by their name—for the successors from the first and second generations will pray to God to keep them eternally in His memory by their names—the successors of the following generations offer to God only the supplication to not forget those for whom their predecessors had prayed to keep them in His memory by name.

The supplication addressed to God to eternally remember the departed by name affirms the faith in the eternal existence of every person through the eternal remembrance of that person by God. The eternal identity of every person is strongly affirmed, and this eternal identity cannot be sustained except by the personal God, Himself eternally identical. Only an identical person values persons in their identity. For keeping other persons in the memory of a person and, thus, faith in their eternal existence, depends on one's own identity. A human person who keeps remembering others shows that it will remain eternally identical and, thus, affirms the truly personal eternity of God, who cannot exist without mercy and without eternal love for the persons He created.

When we ask God to eternally remember certain persons, we show not only the eternal value of those persons and our will to love them forever, but also our responsibility for their happy eternity; we think of how they will look at us eternally if we did not do everything possible for their assurance of, or increase in, eternal happiness. This is why it is said in *The Life of St. Pachomius* that when the soul leaves the body it is first met by its relatives.

Nature does not maintain similar individualities, for it is indifferent to them and those individualities are not aware of the value of their existence; nature only maintains the identical species on the basis of certain laws to which it is subjected against its will.

Theories of incarnation have an ambiguous and unclear position regarding persons, in conformity with their ambiguous doctrine regarding the personal characteristic of the fundamental essence of reality. Reincarnated individualities are not conscious of their identity, because they do not have such an identity. These theories cannot clearly tell us what is maintained of the former incarnations of an individuality. Is an identical "I" maintained? But then, why is it not self-conscious of all its reincarnations? Most of the time, those theories affirm reincarnations not only within the frame of the same species, but they are extended beyond the boundary of the human species, to animals, or in superior beings, up to their melting in the fundamental essence in order to begin again the streak of reincarnations starting from the most strictly material ones.

We do not see here a clear distinction between the fundamental essence and nature; everything is subjected to a cyclical law of eternal manifestation of the fundamental essence in some transitory individualities, identical as species or in their general essence, but not as persons.

The persons meant to remain eternal cannot be but the free creations of a personal God, not the non-free emanations of an essence subjected to the same laws.

How can the adherent to such a theory ask, and who can he ask, for "memory eternal" of the loved ones? Can he still ask for the remembrance of those persons by name when at the same time with their new reincarnations their names are also changed? The permanence of the name indicates the permanence of the person. Only the persons asking for memory eternal of a person by name affirm that person's eternal value in its own identity. And only the persistence of persons explains and establishes the love between them. Plants do not have proper names, nor are animals distinguished by name in the frame of their species by a large community, but mostly by one or two persons who keep them in a special proximity. They do not present themselves to other people by their own initiative, much less among themselves. This is why they are not meant to respond to just anyone when called by name.

The human being awakens very early to his conscious identity by being conscious of the name with which he is called. This is why some theologians have said that his very creation by God is also his coming into existence through his being called by name by another person, namely by the supreme, creating Person. A basis for this could be seen in the fact that it is possible for the child to respond in his own self to being called by name even before he can talk, once he hears several times that he is called by a certain name meant for him.

c) After the litanies for the departed, there follows the departure of the catechumens that takes place after a final prayer for them. In the first five or six centuries those leaving were the two classes of catechumens (or the called), namely those who still had to complete the course for instruction in the teaching of the Church together with those nearing baptism, and the three classes of penitents. In the current text of the Byzantine Liturgies one finds only the prayers for the first two categories of catechumens. But the prayer for those who were going to be baptized at Easter has been preserved only in the Liturgy of the Pre-Sanctified Gifts: "Those for illumination (baptism), approach. Those for illumination, pray." "The purpose for the catechumens' participation in the Liturgy being restricted to their instruction into the truths of faith and Christian life, there was no longer any reason for them to remain in the church for the mystery of the Holy Sacrifice."[276]

Fr. Petre Vintilescu finds that this ritual for the departure of the catechumens no longer makes any sense: "The fact is that this ritual does not correspond to any reality of the present ecclesiastical life, it remains not only incomprehensible for the faithful, but also with no purpose for the officiants who are required to pray (silently) that God may deem worthy of the sacrament of Baptism a non-existent category of attendees whom they previously urged to pray and then to bow their heads while exiting the church. Therefore, even if sentimental considerations were made in favor of keeping this ritual at the end of the Liturgy of the catechumens, still one cannot deny its anachronistic feature and, regarding it as meaningless, its current presence in the Holy Liturgy is nothing more than the effect of a norm or automatic process of a so called 'liturgical hereditary succession.'"[277]

But this would mean that we should also eliminate the name "the Liturgy of the catechumens" or of "those who are called."

We think that not only historical considerations plead for keeping in the Liturgy these prayers for the departure of the catechumens, but also those based on entirely objective realities. The catechumens are becoming nowadays a real category. There are again persons who have not been baptized as children but, living among faithful who frequently attend church, they also attend the Liturgy, which can determine them in time to be baptized. Also, the number of those indifferent at various levels has increased and when sometimes attending the Liturgy they may rekindle their faith, but they are not ready for Holy Communion. Certainly, they are not asked through these words to actually exit the church at this moment, because it is good that they should know what is being officiated in the Holy Liturgy until the end. But from this moment they begin to have an inner separation from those who understand and receive in their hearts what continues to be officiated.

In a certain way these "called" "exit" the flow of the liturgical life that leads the faithful to union with Christ through the Holy Eucharist, even though in another way they remain and watch or, up to a point that can become more accentuated, they can be part of that flow.

Besides, the words "Catechumens, depart" may resound as a warning to a great part of all the participants in the Holy Liturgy.

Many may ask themselves: is it good to remain in this state of unworthiness and partake of the Lord's body and blood? Have I really made enough progress that in reality I am not one of those separated from the ones most advanced in Christ? The awakened conscience in them that they are still part of the category of those who must exit, or that they are not worthy to partake, may determine them to enter the core of the liturgical mystery. "Certain biblical texts make reference to the importance given always to entrances. He who knows to enter and to exit 'worthily' is capable of holding in his hands his destiny and that of the world."[278] Not being conscious that you are not worthy to be somewhere, means not being able to feel deficiencies and therefore to strive to overcome them.

Thus, in a certain sense, every participant in the Holy Liturgy may feel being "called" or being "urged" to "exit" the pretense of being a complete believer. On the other hand, all who are baptized and are not banned by their spiritual father from Holy Communion, may advance toward that goal, and the others may only attend until the end of the Holy Liturgy, feeling that they are only "called" and therefore compelled to "exit" the category of those who are prepared to receive Holy Communion. Thus, some are only in a state of being "called," others of being "believers-called" and others of being "believers," but subjectively, even the latter may feel like "believers-called." God has endless heights. Even those united with Him feel called to ascend even higher, or still incapable of ascending higher, as St. Gregory of Nyssa showed. In a way, even the believers may feel as if in a state of catechumens, in a broad sense, in the teaching phase.

In the final prayer for the catechumens, first these are urged to pray: *Catechumens, pray to the Lord*. Then, addressing the faithful, the priest invites them to pray together with him for the catechumens. The prayer for the catechumens cannot have a full effect if the faithful do not also pray for them: *Let us, the faithful, pray for the catechumens*. This could be also understood in the case when only the faithful are present in church, in the sense that the faithful pray for themselves as the ones still being in one way on a level from the phase of the catechumenate, and in another way in the phase of faith. First the priest asks that *the Lord may have mercy on them* (the catechumens). Then he asks God to specify His mercy, first *that He may teach them the word of truth*; then *that He may reveal to them the Gospel of righteousness*. These are the things especially necessary for the catechumens. "The word of truth" is the content of teaching in the field of knowledge; "The Gospel of righteousness" is the herald that shows us how Christ "became for us righteousness" (1 Cor 1:30), planting in us His righteousness so that we may live a life comprised of all the virtues.

Although the faithful have previously heard both "the word of truth" and "the Gospel of righteousness," they have not sufficiently understood the meaning of the teaching, nor has the righteousness that Christ brought us been made evident in their hearts and they have not advanced far enough on the path of its assimilation. Much less have the catechumens understood them. This is why there follow the four supplications for the catechumens along with the unfolding of the four parts of the antimension. This means that before they leave from among the faithful—who will advance in experiencing the mystery of our salvation accomplished on the cross through Christ's resurrection and ascension and, eventually, through their partaking of His body and blood after the transformation of the bread and wine into them through the descent of the Holy Spirit—the catechumens are given a word and a sign of this Mystery, but they are not taken all the way or up to a true experience of the true revelation of the Gospel of righteousness.

Concurrently with the words: "catechumens pray to the Lord" the part on the northern side of the antimension is unfolded; then at the words: "let us the faithful pray for the catechumens that the Lord may have mercy on them" the part on the southern side of the antimension is unfolded. Thus, there begins the preparation for the revelation of the scene of the Lord's burial, which has not yet been fully revealed. Only at the words: "that He may teach them the word of the truth" the part from the western side of the antimension is unfolded, and at the words: "that He may reveal to them the Gospel of righteousness" the very scene of the Lord's burial is revealed, showing to the catechumens, too, as in a gleam of light, His crucifixion and burial for our salvation. In this is comprised "the word of truth" or the true meaning of our existence, destined to obtain salvation from death and its perfection, through adoption by God, due to the Lord's incarnation, crucifixion and resurrection. For out of the Lord's tomb His life has risen as the source of our life made perfect; united with His tomb, our tomb will also be transformed into a place of passing toward the life in Christ, after He has transformed His tomb from a place of decay or of passing toward the extremely diminished existence of our being into a chamber of risen life and of a new sprouting of our life from the divine life, which nothing can destroy and out of which our life is renewed.

The Lord's tomb, in which the catechumens will enter and from which they will be renewed in their souls for their existence on earth and for the one after the death of the body—and at the end of the present image of the world, will also be renewed in their body—is Baptism. This is why while they are in church the Lord's tomb is revealed to them as an appeal for their death with Christ through Baptism. For through Baptism the catechumens will be united with Christ or with His universal body, which is the Church, with the mystical body of Christ constituted by all those who died with Christ through Baptism, thus being raised to His everlasting life. This is why after the antimension has been fully unfolded, as the image of the Lord's tomb, while the priest using the sponge collects in the center of the antimension all the nearly invisible particles, like those who are not yet gathered into Christ through burial with the Lord, that is through Baptism, he says: "that He may unite them with His holy, catholic, and apostolic Church." The death of life as such, not out of disgust for life, but through the will to sacrifice it for Christ so as to live with Him, is the reason for union in the unique, communitarian body of Christ. For he who lives with Christ, lives together with Him on behalf of all who are part of the same body.

The priest concludes these supplications for the catechumens with the one that ends the other supplications. In them he prays God to make them share in the end, through His grace, in His same good things, but in a somewhat changed order, for at this time he asks first for His salvation and mercy for them and then for protection (from enemies, temptations), and not the other way around as in the supplications for all at the beginning of the Liturgy. The catechumens first need both salvation and mercy: *Help them, save them, have mercy on them, and keep them, O God, by Your grace*. After this, the priest invites the catechumens to bow their heads to the Lord: *Catechumens, bow your heads to the Lord*. This is the gesture by which the human being awaits the outpouring of heavenly gifts on him. It is the gesture by which he manifests the conscience that he needs God's gifts from above and that he is not entirely outside of God's mercy and of partaking of His gifts, even if he is not yet baptized. It is a gesture of humility before God. He who stands upright shows that he expects nothing from others and has everything by himself. By making this gesture of bowing the head before God, the catechumens enforce it with the words: *To You, O Lord*, that is we are Yours, even if we are not yet baptized. We bow to You and it is from You that we await salvation and all that is necessary. To bow before God does not mean to look down or to turn away from the things on high, but to manifest the conscience that we await for everything from the One on high, that we are not on the supreme level of existence and that our life on earth does not come from us, nor do we expect eternal life to come from us.

While the catechumens continue to bow their heads, the priest prays silently to God for them, addressing Him in the second person, thus in a more intimate manner; addressing God who dwells on high, therefore He is in fact higher than they and higher than everything, but still looks toward the humble and has even proved that He has so much attention for the human race that He sent His own Son for its salvation, humbling Himself and teaching us to be humble, showing us that humility is the channel through which flow from God the gifts of divine life. Thus, the priest prays God to look toward the catechumens who have bowed their heads before Him and to make them worthy of five good things: *Make them worthy, in due time, of the second birth through water, of the forgiveness of sins and the robe of incorruption; unite them to Your holy, catholic and apostolic Church and number them with Your chosen flock.*

The priest concludes this prayer with the exclamation in which he asks from God that even those who are not yet baptized may be able to praise God for the gifts they have received and which are included in their salvation, like those who are baptized: *That they also, together with us, may glorify and praise Your all-honorable and majestic name of the Father and of the Son and of the Holy Spirit, now and ever and unto the ages of ages. Amen.* Those who knowingly glorify God in Trinity, they glorify Him because they experience the joy of being in communion with the communion of love of the supreme Persons. He who glorifies God has joy in himself. To every good thing that God gives to human beings, they respond with His glorification, because they taste the sweetness of this good thing. And this is the gift they return to God, regardless of what this gift might be. Those to whom God grants serenity, return to Him the serenity they enjoy. Those to whom God grants the gift of prayer, return to Him the prayer that primarily gives them calm. Those who are saved will eternally and ever increasingly glorify God in Trinity, offering themselves entirely and perfectly to Him, once they have been granted the perfect life.

"May it always and in all things be our aim to glorify God."[279] And St. Paul says: "Do all to the glory of God" (1 Cor 10:31). St. John Chrysostom, when he gave up his soul to the Lord in a ruined church in wintertime as he was taken into exile by the imperial guard, said: "Glory to You, O Lord, for all things, glory to You."

At the same time with the words: "of the Father and of the Son and of the Holy Spirit" the priest makes the sign of the cross with the sponge over the Holy Antimension. This sign shows that the reason both the catechumens and the faithful have for glorifying the Trinity is in the cross accepted for us by the Son of God, a cross that is linked to the Trinity itself. It is in this that, in fact, the Trinity has been revealed in the plenitude of its love. For if the Son of God had not come into the world and had not offered the supreme sacrifice to the Father through the body He assumed and had not made, thereby, His body a means of the Holy Spirit's descent upon us, we would not have known the Trinity's love for us. The sponge reminds us of the exhausting suffering of the Lord on the cross, but it also means the expunging of our sins through the cross as well as our gathering in the Lord's tomb or in His blood with the love present therein and spread through its shedding, which unites us all with Him and among ourselves.

At this time the deacon invites the catechumens to leave: *Catechumens, depart!* If this invitation is not addressed to those not baptized, it is addressed to the conscience of those who are not prepared for Holy Communion, or live a life of sin, to consider themselves different from those who live the life of true believers. But even the best believers or those most advanced in living their life according to Christ can consider themselves as being in this state. The repetition of this invitation two more times may be a remnant from the first centuries when several categories of catechumens or penitents were departing successively. Nowadays it can be addressed to those who are on various levels in their church life: first to those weighed down with heavy sins, second to those with menial sins, and third to those who are not satisfied with the state in which they find themselves, regardless of how advanced they may seem to those who know them. The fourth invitation to leave addressed to the catechumens is even more categorical by its negative form: *That no catechumen remain.* It is a persistent invitation to search the conscience, which causes even those who seem to be without stain to examine themselves if somehow they are not as stainless as they seem and if it might be necessary to come out of that state.

Another meaning of this invitation could be given by the Greek word προελθετε, which essentially means "come forward," "depart ahead," that is not simply "depart." The invitation in this sense could be addressed today not to those not baptized, but to those who have not yet decided to fully join the faithful: come spiritually among the faithful, come to their front rows.

But the words *Catechumens depart* could have nowadays a prophetic sense. Through them the Church can express the duty to raise herself to a future when more intense mission is done and there will be more catechumens.[280] The word can also have an eschatological sense, by expressing the fact that those who remain in a state of being catechumens (or called) but do not decide to have a true Christian life, will be invited at the last judgment of God to depart from among those who will remain in the Kingdom of heaven as believers (Mt 25:12). Thus, one could bring again into bold relief the eschatological horizon or perspective of the Holy Liturgy.

In any case, it is also good for the litany for the catechumens to be kept for the reason that initially in the Christian gatherings for worship, the offering of the Eucharistic sacrifice was preceded by serious preaching and the Church should take up again this practice. It is necessary to return to what is said in Acts 2:42: "And they continued steadfastly in the apostles' doctrine and fellowship in the breaking of bread and in prayers."

Our time and the Apostolic tradition demand that we not reduce the Holy Liturgy either to the offering of Christ's sacrifice only and to the partaking of it or to "continue steadfastly in the apostles' doctrine," but to give equal importance to both parts.

CHAPTER THREE

THE LITURGY OF THE FAITHFUL OR OF THE SACRIFICE AND OF HOLY COMMUNION

1. The Litanies for the Faithful and the Two Prayers of the Priest as Preparation for the Offering and the Transformation of the Gifts of the Faithful into the Unbloody Sacrifice

a. The First Litany and Prayer for the Faithful

The Liturgy of the faithful starts with two litanies similar to those from the beginning of the Holy Liturgy of the catechumens, anticipating another entrance of Christ, the one leading to sacrifice at the end of His preaching activity. The first one, however, is similar to one of the two short litanies from the beginning of the Liturgy of the catechumens, since one considers sufficient the supplications with a more horizontal content from the litany at the beginning of the Liturgy, from where those who remain to participate at the officiating of the Mystery of the Holy Sacrifice have advanced. It begins with an invitation to prayer addressed to the faithful: *As many as are faithful, again and again in peace let us pray to the Lord.* For even if we do not see ourselves as on the summit of Christian living, we are considered as faithful, but as faithful still in need of asking God for peace, salvation, mercy and protection against temptations, by His grace.

One no longer repeats the promise of offering ourselves and each other, with the remembrance of the Birthgiver of God and of all the saints as examples. But the priest announces now that he will offer supplications, prayers and sacrifices for the faithful and in which they are themselves represented. This litany is partly enlarged in the second one, for if the first litany is restricted only to the faithful, the second one shows that they do not forget about the world and about all those who pray in that church.

The first litany which is made up of only two supplications, namely the one mentioned above and this one: *Help us, save us, have mercy on us and protect us, O God, by Your grace*, concludes with an exclamation that is identical with the one from the first of the three litanies at the beginning of the Holy Liturgy: *For unto You are due all glory, honor and worship*, etc. But the glory, honor and worship to God must now be viewed at a different level, just as the peace with which the faithful pray and the salvation, mercy and protection have gained a more profound meaning.

To be able to view at this level the glory, honor and worship due to God, a distinctive wisdom is needed. This is why before this exclamation the faithful are asked for and they are promised from God: *Wisdom*.

But before this exclamation, the priest first reads the prayer for the faithful. In it he thanks God that He has made him worthy to stand before His holy altar. He first spoke of this worthiness during the singing of the hymn *Holy God*, but without mentioning the sacrifice. At that time he only confessed that God is holy and that is why the angels cannot approach Him, either, except by offering Him due worship. For this approach, repentance and forgiveness of sins are required.

At this time, after he has previously asked to be blessed so that he can approach God as he is about to begin the action of the sacrifice itself, the priest declares that he finds himself before the Holy Altar in order to fall down before God's compassion and to pray for his sins and for the people's sins of ignorance. One intensifies the conscience of sinfulness as the prospective imminent offering of the sacrifice appears, which must be done in total purity. For historically, Christ also approached His sacrifice after He had come near to the end of His preaching. And He offered Himself as an efficient sacrifice being pure of every sin. Only in this way was it possible for His sacrifice to have the proper effect of our salvation. Having now to offer to Christ the sacrifice on behalf of the people, the priest asks for the forgiveness of his sins and those of the people so that he may be worthy to offer *prayers, supplications and bloodless sacrifices for the people*. By the words *bloodless sacrifices* we believe that one understands both gifts of bread and wine brought by the people and by the priest on behalf of the people, and Christ's body and blood into which they will be transformed. The latter understanding is seen also in the expression uttered by the priest before entering the altar when he says: *O Lord, stretch forth Your hand from Your holy dwelling place on high, and strengthen me . . . . that standing uncondemned before Your awesome throne, I may offer the bloodless sacrifice*. Then also from the expression recited in the prayer before the entrance with the holy gifts, when the priest certainly refers to the Holy Eucharist: *But because of Your inexpressible and immeasurable love for mankind, You did become man, yet without change or alteration, and as Master of all, did become our High Priest and granted us the ministry of this liturgical and bloodless sacrifice*. Also the identical expression from the beginning of the Eucharistic epiklesis (the calling upon the Holy Spirit) refers to the sacrifice in these words: *Furthermore we offer You this spiritual and bloodless sacrifice, and we call on You, and we pray to You . . . . send down Your Holy Spirit upon us and upon these gifts here offered, and make this bread the precious body of Your Christ, and that which is in this chalice the precious blood of Your Christ*.

The expression *bloodless* is certainly meant for this sacrifice to be opposite to the bloody sacrifices in the Old Testament and those of the pagans. But it does not mean only a thanksgiving and self-offering brought to God through words, as some Catholic theologians have surmised.[281] As Odo Casel, a Catholic theologian himself, responded, even though the Eucharist as a thanksgiving sacrifice offered to God on behalf of the people consists of words as well, still the words are accompanied by more concrete gifts, namely the bread and the wine that will be transformed into a gift of an even higher thanksgiving, that is into the sacrifice of Christ's body and blood offered by Him in our name and for us. For only having been transformed into the Lord's body and blood, out of His power and will to offer Himself as gift, do the bread and the wine receive the characteristic of full sacrifice. But being offered toward this transformation, they have from the start the potential characteristic as Christ's sacrifice, which becomes real through His will and power.

First, according to Odo Casel, thanksgiving or the Eucharist or the sacrifice consists of returning to God the gifts received from Him. "Because God is *agape*, love freely offered, He has called creatures to life . . . . But He gifted them with love so that they may return to Him their love in freedom. This returning of love is nothing else but love—the Eucharist (thanksgiving). Properly speaking, this returning as gift of the gifts received is sacrifice. This is why Christ's sacrifice, which we mystically celebrate, bears the name of Eucharist."[282] Properly speaking, this is the maximum fulfillment of the meaning of sacrifice, the supreme thanksgiving. This is also the greatest gift offered to God, not by us, but by the incarnate Christ on our behalf.

Odo Casel uses texts from both the New Testament and the first Christian writers to support his idea that "the bloodless sacrifice" consists not only of thanksgiving through words, but also of the concrete gifts which we are returning to God, specifically the bread and wine that represent in anticipation our life on earth, namely our body and blood, and as such they were chosen by God for their transformation into His body and blood, offered by Christ as a sacrifice of thanksgiving (as Eucharist) to the Father. Christ's sacrifice implies in it our sacrifices, but these are raised to the supreme level of Christ's sacrifice as the supreme fulfillment of the sacrifice.

On the basis of texts from the Didache of the Twelve Apostles (end of the first century), and from Justin, Irenaeus and Clement (second century), Odo Casel concludes: "I am more and more convinced that in ancient Christianity one cannot speak only of a sacrifice of natural gifts. Certainly, there is an offering of bread and wine for the Eucharist, as well as of other gifts for agape feasts and for giving to the poor; but the Eucharist was not seen in this, not even partially. The sacrifice proper of the Eucharist is the mystery of Christ's death. If the bread and wine are simply brought forth beforehand and then are accompanied by hymns and prayers, this is only a preparatory action for the Eucharist, or an anticipation of the true sacrifice that follows after that."[283] "The Lord chose as elements for His Mystery a simple and wonderfully profound symbolism. The symbolism of bread is easy for all to understand, because it is the most appropriate means for nourishing and strengthening natural life."[284]

Therefore, we can say that the bread and wine are also considered, on the one hand, as the bloodless and reasonable sacrifice by the fact that they potentially have in them our reasonable body organically united with the blood in one whole, in which they will be naturally transformed; on the other hand, they are considered as the body and blood of Christ, similar to ours, in which they will be mystically transformed, without Christ repeating the shedding of His blood. Better said, they are a natural condition met by us for celebrating the mystery beyond reason of the Eucharist, in which is perfected in a culminating way "the reasonable Sacrifice" as the sacrifice of Christ's reasonable body, all the more reasonable as it is the body of the divine Word from which come all the words manifested in created things, but especially in reasonable human persons. Being the sacrifice of the reasonable body, it is the sacrifice of the supreme conscious Person, infinitely different in value from the sacrifices of unreasonable animals, because they are unconscious and they do not sacrifice themselves willingly. By transforming the bread and wine offered by the faithful into His body and blood, Christ shows that He had offered as His own sacrifice the body taken from us as potential sacrifice, so that by giving it to us as actualized sacrifice we may also become actual sacrifices.

Thus, the priest's words "bloodless sacrifice" could refer to one whole in which there may be contained both the bread and the wine offered by the faithful, and the body and blood which Christ intends to offer to God, through their transformation, joining us as well through prayers to His act of sacrifice. The Lord's sacrifice of body and blood is also a bloodless sacrifice, because the risen Lord no longer sheds His blood anew in the Eucharist, but on the other hand He relives in His eternity as a continuous present the breaking of the body and the shedding of the blood on the cross for us. What took place once in someone's life remains in a way permanent, even if not repeated, or precisely because it has an eternal value, it is not repeated. Odo Casel says: "Death no longer has dominion over him (Rom 6:9). But God gave us the possibility of presenting ourselves, to make present in worship the sacrifice offered once on Golgotha, the sacrifice eternally valid. This representation in the present of the death as sacrifice through symbolic acts is what we call Mystery. It is the mystical counter-image of the sacrifice accomplished once in history two thousand years ago."[285] That sacrifice has been imprinted in Him as an eternal state. We partake of His transfigured blood, but in this state of sacrifice.

This present representation of Christ's death is not understood only as a subjective act of ours, but as having its basis in a continuous reliving by Christ, alive and transfigured, of His disposition from the moment of the sacrifice on the cross for us, a reliving in which there is both an identity and a distinction between what has been done or suffered once by a person and the present reliving of that. Christ is in a continuous offering of Himself to the Father for us so that He may offer Himself to us in this state, in order to attract us as well into this offering of His. But to relive does not mean to repeat. He relives so intensely the breaking of the body and the shedding of the blood that they cannot remain inefficient in Him; and our partaking of Him in this reliving of His is also efficient in us as our "co-reliving" of His experience through the efficient remembrance of the shedding of His blood, without this being a real shedding of His blood at the moment of our partaking. The eucharistic sacrifice, as bloodless representation of the sacrifice on the cross, does not exclude the happiness in which Christ lives, but on the contrary, it includes it.

But because those for whom the priest is praying at this time are believers and members of the Church, he asks for them or knows that they will be given the power of the Holy Spirit through the eucharistic sacrifice, so as in the testimony of a pure conscience to call at all times and in every place upon the name of God and that He may hear them with mercy and goodness. Thus, the priest no longer asks for them to receive gifts from God (such as the forgiveness of sins), but also the power to bring their gifts themselves. But the power to give, which shows them to be on a higher level, must also be received from God.

By eliminating the bloody sacrifices, even as symbols of His sacrifice, the Son of God wanted to raise humanity from the inferior sense perceptions sustained by the slaughter and eating of animals. At least in worship there should not appear meat of slaughtered animals. In this way the spiritual view of humankind is directed toward the higher life of the age to come, which some anticipate even now through continuous fasting or even through fasting at certain times.

Christ has ended and surpassed the bloody sacrifices of animals, not only because He is an infinitely more precious sacrifice, since consciously and in full freedom He gave His own life to God as the most precious life, but also because He did not take His own life, which is a gift of God, and was not slain by His executioners with the conscious that they offer a sacrifice to God so that they might have merit for His death. With the first fact He fulfilled every need for new sacrifices, and with the second, He had stopped the human persons from slaying their fellow human beings with the excuse that they did so in order to offer a sacrifice to God. To be sure, people continue to kill others. And some of those slain for being confessors of God are martyrs and sacrifices (Mt 24:9; Rev 6:9) from the power of Christ's sacrifice. But those who slay them gain no praise for that, because they do not slay them to offer a sacrifice to God.

But while the killing of people, with the excuse that those killed are offered as sacrifice to God, is forbidden, the killing of animals is permitted. However, Christ did not indicate animal meat as an image of His sacrificed body, so that one may not consider that His sacrifice did not end the sacrifice of animals or that His slaying was not entirely condemnable. So, the killing of animals is permitted not because their meat would be an image of the sacrifice offered to God, but because they fulfill a need for natural food. Hence a higher spiritual level is indicated, toward which those who wish may be able to aspire even through their food.

Therefore, the insistence in the Holy Liturgy on the expression "bloodless sacrifice" has this meaning as well. On the other hand, Christ has as His symbol just as telling not only the lamb, who suffers slaying in silence, but also the bread. He is the bread that nourishes us spiritually, just as the Lamb who suffered to be sacrificed for us fills us with His meekness ready for sacrifice. On the invisible plane, He prefers to be considered as a Lamb who has feelings, which bread does not have; but on the visible plane, He wants to be represented through the bloodless bread that nourishes us.

The power to offer yourself is also a gift from God, for through this you have escaped from the narrow prison of egoism and entered into the infinite expansiveness of God's life in which the Holy Spirit, or the Spirit of love, breathes. This is why in this prayer one asks first for the Holy Spirit who causes the one in whom He dwells to be unceasingly animated by God's love and, consequently, to call upon God at all times and in all places, filled with the feeling of His goodness.

Thus, the priest begins to speak at this time about the offering of the sacrifice and about the descent of the Holy Spirit upon the faithful.

But the priest asks in this prayer to be brought into the altar not only the gifts of bread and wine that have been prepared at the Proskomedia to be transformed into Christ's sacrifice, but he also offers "prayers and supplications for all people." These are in the first place the prayers that the priest will offer for the transformation of the gifts into the bloodless sacrifice of Christ. For this sacrifice cannot be accomplished without prayers. In the second place, just as the priest offers on behalf of the people the gifts of bread and wine in view of their transformation, so will he offer on behalf of the people their prayers and supplications that have accompanied the gifts he offers. It is in the tradition of the Orthodox Church that the faithful bring prayer lists with their loved ones, living and departed, to be commemorated by the priests at the Proskomedia, taking out particles for them and placing them in front of the Agnetz that will be transformed into the Lord's body. These particles placed at the time of mentioning their names represent their persons, and in some sense they even make these persons present. The prayer lists brought by the faithful for them show that they also pray for those on the list. These prayer lists are usually accompanied by lit candles, which shows that they ask for the life brought by Christ through resurrection, that they are not left in the darkness of eternal death that lacks all meaning. Some of those commemorated at the Proskomedia are remembered by the priest during the Great Entrance so that the faithful may also think of them. But the priest offers supplications not only for those named in the prayer lists, but also for all the faithful who participate at the Holy Liturgy as well as for those who live everywhere. The priest appropriates all the supplications and prayers of the faithful, adding his own, at certain moments of the Liturgy, so that all may be brought near Christ's sacrifice and that they may be beneficial to all.

b. The Second Litany and Prayer for the Faithful

When only the priest serves, he recites the second litany identical with the first. If the deacon is present, he says: *Again and again in peace, let us pray to the Lord* and before *Help us, save us...* he inserts four more supplications from the first litany from the beginning of the Holy Liturgy of the catechumens: *For the peace from above . . .* , etc.; *For the peace of the whole world . . .* , etc.; *For this holy church . . .* , etc.; *For our deliverance . . .* , etc. These are supplications of a more general content which the deacon recites so that the priest may have time to say silently the second prayer for the faithful. Thus, one takes a step further toward the next liturgical act. The priest asks for himself and for those who pray together with him to be cleansed from every defilement of flesh and spirit and to be able to stand innocent and uncondemned by God and by their conscience before His holy altar, not only to offer the bloodless sacrifice, but also to partake innocent and uncondemned of His holy Mysteries and thereby to partake of "His heavenly Kingdom." Thus the perspective of Holy Communion and, in connection with it, of the Kingdom of the Holy Trinity is opened: "Time centered in Christ finds now its eschatological dimension."[286]

Approaching the partaking of Christ must coincide with "growth in life, in faith and spiritual understanding." This is why the priest prays for these as well. "Spiritual understanding" is the understanding enlightened by the Holy Spirit. The Holy Spirit will transform the gifts into the body and blood of Christ, but He will also give the faithful the capacity to understand, to see spiritually this Mystery and its deep, salvific meaning. The Holy Spirit asked for in the previous prayer is now viewed in the effect of His operation upon the faithful.

The exclamation that ends the priest's second and last litany as well as the prayer is not an exact repetition of the exclamation of the second litany from the beginning of the Liturgy, in which one acknowledged that to God belongs the dominion, the Kingdom and the glory, but it is a praise united with the supplication that both the priest and the faithful *may be always guarded by His might*, that they may not be attracted by temptations or adversary powers, so that they can ascribe to Him glory unto the ages of ages. God's dominion is not only praised now, but also asked for. For happy are those who will always be under this dominion of the triune love, therefore of the freedom, whose glory beyond any glory of worldly dominion will be known through the Spirit and praised as a glory that has become their own.

To understand the happiness whose foretaste the faithful begin to have from the looming in the horizon of the loving dominion under which they will be accepted to live, one asks again on their behalf from the Holy Spirit: *Wisdom!*

This supplication to the Holy Spirit and the depiction of His activity in the second prayer for the faithful is made directly in the Liturgy of St. Basil the Great: "O God, . . . Who has set us, Your humble and sinful and unworthy servants, to serve at Your holy altar before Your holy glory, by the power of Your Holy Spirit strengthen us for this service; and grant speech to our lips so that we may call down the grace of Your Holy Spirit upon the gifts that are about to be offered." We have here another proof that the bloodless sacrifice, mentioned in the corresponding prayer from the Liturgy of St. John Chrysostom, refers to the eucharistic sacrifice, but this is produced through the transformation of the gifts of bread and wine. For here is announced both the transformation of the gifts by the Holy Spirit, and the connection of this activity with the word to be uttered by the priest. It is a word that must be uttered with faith, filled with the power of the Holy Spirit. It is Christ Himself, the Word of the Father and the source of all words, who is active in this word. Thus, the Holy Spirit will work not in a purely exterior way upon the gifts, but through the strengthening of the priest "for this service" and by uttering the word of calling upon the Holy Spirit. The external things are not done except through the intermediation of the interior ones; there is no fixed boundary between them.

We think it proper to complete here the connection mentioned above between the Lamb and the Bread as symbol of the Word. The Word in itself implies the characteristic of both Bread and Lamb. The Bread nourishes us, He sacrifices Himself out of mercy for us and rules over us with the meekness of the Lamb so that He may offer Himself to us as Bread. If the Word did not exist, the Bread and the Lamb would not exist either. This is why only in His quality as Word does He give, through the Spirit, power to the priest's word and is the bread transformed into the heavenly Bread or the Lamb who bears the marks of being pierced. And since the word is so essential in offering the sacrifice, or He who offers Himself to us in the Mystery is visibly shown to us as Bread and the invisible One works as Lamb, the Eucharist can be called a bloodless and reasonable sacrifice, especially since the prototype of the Lamb in the invisible plane is no longer sacrificed at every Eucharist, but only relives the feeling of the sacrifice that was imprinted forever in Him. Also our word of thanksgiving, filled with the divine Word, can be called a sacrifice offered to the Father in a less complete sense: a sacrifice of praise. For us the Word is especially Bread, although He is also Lamb; for the Father He is especially Lamb and Word.

At this time the community begins to sing the Cherubic hymn. The first part is sung until the entrance with the Holy Gifts: *We, who mystically represent the Cherubim, singing to the life-creating Trinity the thrice-holy hymn, let us now lay aside all earthly care.*

After the entrance with the Holy Gospel, the faithful sang the thrice holy hymn of the Seraphim, but without saying explicitly that it was in honor of the Holy Trinity, for Christ had not yet fully revealed it through His preaching. At this time the community declares that it offers this hymn to the Holy Trinity, albeit without naming explicitly the three Persons. Moreover, it now affirms the consciousness that it must lay aside all earthly care. Christ will now reveal Himself as the One going to the saving sacrifice, even as the sacrificed One who goes toward burial and resurrection. The mystery is much greater. It is for this act of Christ that the Holy Trinity is praised by both the Cherubim and the faithful who represent them. In the Old Testament the Seraphim did not have before them the fulfilled mystery of Christ. This is why the enthusiasm with which "Holy God" was sung then is replaced by serene singing, the expression of deeply contemplative wonder before the ineffable love of the Holy Trinity. The liturgical community was not aware during the singing of the thrice-holy hymn that it represented the Cherubim; only the priest, carrying the Gospel containing the word of Christ not yet explained through preaching, prayed that his entrance, or the act of preaching, might be accompanied by that of the angels.

2. *The Prayer of the Priest in Which He Asks Directly to Be Deemed Worthy of Offering Christ Himself as Sacrifice*

During this time, standing before the Holy Table, the priest reads silently a prayer in which he asks Christ to "cleanse his soul and heart from evil thoughts" and, by the power of the Holy Spirit, to deem him who is clothed with the grace of priesthood worthy to stand before the Holy Table and to sacrifice His holy and all-pure Body and His precious Blood. The more he is aware of his unworthiness, the more he asks Christ to deem him worthy, or vice versa: You make me worthy, as a priest, but I cannot be passive in the worthiness You grant me, or I cannot receive it without asking You for it and opening myself to it. This is the paradox expressed in this prayer.

Secondly, the priest knows that he who is clothed with the grace of priesthood is the one who sacrifices Christ, but at the same time he knows that it is Christ who sacrifices Himself as the One Who became for all of us the High Priest we need. The paradox is shown in the fact that, although Christ is our High Priest and as such He offered Himself as a unique and all-efficient sacrifice, He gave the priest the visible and holy service of this liturgical and bloodless sacrifice, namely He made him a conscious organ through which He Himself bloodlessly actualizes the sacrifice on Golgotha so that the faithful may partake of it through the visible species. If there is a need for visible species for the actualization of the sacrifice on behalf of the faithful endowed with eyes, mouth and in general with a visible body, surely there is a need for a person as a visible organ to offer the prayers by which through these visible species the invisible sacrifice of Christ is actualized in time. The priest trembles at the responsibility given to him, but also at Christ's presence working through him.

Thus, Christ has not now abandoned His high-priestly service, but He makes use of the priest as visible organ of this service. The priest says this toward the end of the prayer. For even though he refers to the gifts which he asks to be deemed worthy to offer to Christ, these gifts are meant to be transformed into the holy body and blood of Christ through Christ Himself. Therefore, these gifts and the priest himself involves Christ Himself not just as symbols of Christ, but as having in relation with them Christ who will work upon the gifts through the priest. The priest says this with these words: "Accept the offering of these gifts by me, Your sinful and unworthy servant. For You are He who offers and is offered"; that is You who are offered by me, the sinful one, although on the other hand You offer Yourself; You who receive Yourself as sacrificed and who offer Yourself (by sacrificing Yourself).

Then the priest censes the altar and the church so that all may receive with all purity Christ who comes toward sacrifice, as they received Him when He came to teach through the Gospel.

The King of kings ought to be met by the faithful present in church with the sweet-smelling fragrance of their thoughts and senses.

3. The Great Entrance

Returning to the Holy Altar after censing, the priest makes three bows before the Holy Table, saying every time: *O God, cleanse me, a sinner, and have mercy on me*. Through these words, as through Psalm 50 recited during censing, he asks with special fervor to be cleansed so as to be deemed worthy of carrying the gifts that will be transformed into the body and blood of Christ. He then kisses the Holy Table and the Holy Antimension on which Christ will be placed, under the species of the holy gifts, or as a tomb in which He will descend in order to rise again from it; he also kisses the Holy Cross on which Christ offered Himself as a saving sacrifice. Then he turns and makes a bow in front of the royal doors toward the faithful, on the one hand blessing them in order to worthily meet Christ under the species of the holy gifts, and on the other hand in order to ask for forgiveness from all: "Therefore, if you bring your gift to the altar, and there remember that your brother has something against you, leave your gift there before the altar, and go your way. First be reconciled to your brother, and then come and offer your gift"

(Mt 5:23-24). How will the Lord receive our gift, which He first offered to us, so that our union with Him may be accomplished at an even higher level, if we are alienated from our fellow human beings, when God wants all to be united with Him through sacrificial love? The priest then goes to the Proskomedia where the gifts have been previously covered.

The glory of the Son of God was covered right from the incarnation and remained covered to the highest degree during the time of His progression toward crucifixion and burial and at the entrance into Jerusalem, although those close to Him sensed even in His humility His true quality as King. But even now, in the Holy Liturgy, when His entrance into Jerusalem from that time is extended as entrance into the altar from above, He enters as a humble King, as an "invisible" King for those who see with worldly eyes, but for those who see with spiritual eyes He enters as the King who will be asked to remember us in His heavenly Kingdom. Only the aer covering the paten and the chalice is taken, that is the cosmic nature under which He was covered like any man who is born into the world and is dependent on it. In some way it shows at this moment His quality as the Son of man who goes toward sacrifice since His body and blood are especially represented under the covers of the gifts. By covering His glory through incarnation, the Son of God had shown us that the closer He comes as man for those who can see, the farther He can be as God for those who do not have spiritual eyes to see. Generally, by being born as man, the Word of God is covered by His creation, by the "aer" of the cosmos, revealing at this time, when He is about to enter before the altar of sacrifice, the quality as the One who will offer Himself as sacrifice for the people. He covered Himself because He does not want to obtain a forced recognition and gratitude from us. How would He in this case make effective His descent out of love up to sacrifice? Nonetheless, the believers glorify Him precisely for this descent, for they see His glory precisely in this deep humility of His out of love.

As he approaches the Table of oblation, the priest bows three times, by which he manifests the intention of his infinite bowing and also its direction toward the Holy Trinity. Through the kiss he shows that this God who was laid in the manger for us, no matter how glorified, is a God who rejoices in being loved by us for our benefit. But while kissing Him, the priest does not forget to ask for his cleansing and for His mercy, because His love for us and ours for Him requires from us an ever growing cleansing so that love may also grow. This why he says: *O God, cleanse me, a sinner, and have mercy on me.* The deacon does the same, if he is present, then he addresses the priest: *Lift up, Master!* The priest takes the aer or the large cover and places it on the deacon's shoulders, and if he is not present, on his own shoulders like the shroud carried by Joseph of Arimathea in which Christ was wrapped at burial, or like the cross of Christ carried by Simon from Cyrene. Then he gives the paten to the deacon to carry above his head, saying the words: *Lift up your hands to the Holy Place and bless the Lord.* Through sacrifice Christ directed His way toward heaven, toward His Father. He was crucified on the peak of Golgotha, or the place of the skull, so that He can be seen by all in this condition. The peak of creation is the human person, the head; the Lord sacrificed Himself so that the human person's conscience, manifested through the head, may recognize that. If the deacon is not present, the priest takes both the paten and the chalice, holding them raised to his forehead. Christ fills the mind of the priest with the word of preaching and with the act and meaning of the sacrifice. "The peace of God, which surpasses all understanding, will guard your hearts and minds through Christ Jesus" (Php 4:7). He wants us to always have in our mind the sacrifice of our salvation. In this is also shown the glory to which Christ ascended through sacrifice.

When the priest comes out through the door on the northern side of the altar the liturgical community stops singing at the end of the first part of the hymn with the words: *Let us lay aside all earthly care.* Through these words the community prepared for seeing and receiving the King covered, or invisible, or hidden in His inscrutable mystery, who comes out and enters with His sacrifice or toward the actualization of His sacrifice; He departs from us and enters before the Father. Or He raises His sacrifice to the Father from us and for us. At this time the community observes in silent awe the great Mystery: the King who appears entering for us into Jerusalem, covered with humility, to sacrifice Himself, being led to Golgotha and toward burial; and at the present time, He lies down before the Father on the altar from above, for spiritual vision, as the risen One, but in a state of eternal sacrifice. He walks toward a Golgotha of compassion and toward a tomb into which He wants to attract our old life as well as toward the perpetuity of the state of sacrifice in heaven for us, escorted and glorified invisibly by the heavenly hosts for this sacrifice offered out of endless love. The descent up to the point of the cross and the ascension in glory but still in a state of sacrifice do not contradict each other; the first intensifies the glory, which on account of the love He manifested no one surpasses, or is far beyond any comprehension. The King of all sacrifices Himself, showing us the true authority which He thereby gains over the souls as the most authentic King. He sacrifices Himself even though He is greater than any worldly king, or precisely because of this, or further yet, in order to show what the quality as true King consists of. The disciples and those close to Him have felt this while on earth, and they enter together with Him, in the person of the priest (or even of the deacon) filled with all humility at that pinnacle with Him, in the name of the faithful who understand with their spiritual understanding this paradox of the quality as King of Him who sacrifices Himself. Those who are spiritually advanced, even in the disorder born out of the unbelief of those who are used to seeing and recognizing God only in acts of worldly power, see the great power of God who raises the world out of chaos only through love and in view of an eternal and happy love in the Kingdom of the Holy Trinity. They see that Christ is the true King who raises them through sacrifice to the happy existence of eternal life. Even those who welcomed Jesus when He entered Jerusalem before He was crucified felt that under His humility was hidden His quality as supreme King. Moreover, "all the city was moved" (Mt 21:10) when He entered Jerusalem with all His humility manifested in His sitting on a donkey. This is why in the Gospel of St. John it is said: "Fear not, daughter of Zion; Behold, your King is coming, sitting on a donkey's colt" (Jn 12:15). This is a rendition of the prophet Zechariah's words that speak even more explicitly about the meekness of this supreme King, recommending not only being unafraid of Him, but joy in Him: "Rejoice greatly, O daughter of Zion [the Church of the New Testament]! Proclaim it aloud, O daughter of Jerusalem! Behold, your King comes to you; He is righteous and saving. He is gentle and mounted upon a donkey, even a young foal" (Zec 9:9).

Even when Jesus gave up His spirit on the cross, accepting the last powerlessness of the human being, all the earth quaked and was covered with darkness (Mt 27:51; Lk 23:44). This means that if for those who through their advanced spiritual level are able to see God in Christ's supreme meekness and mercy, He is the King to whom they offer sincere glory, on the contrary, for those who think that God cannot be seen except through a power like that in the world, when this is not seen they promote chaos in the world with the idea that there is no God. They are used to offering glory only to those who forcefully manifest their power over them. But God does not need such a flattering glory combined with hidden slandering.

After we have laid aside "all earthly care" we concentrate entirely on His glory that goes along with His love for us all the way to His sacrifice. Why should we care any longer about our ephemeral concerns when we have the assurance of this eternal love of Christ the King? The spiritual experience of His glory that is intensified even on Golgotha but much more in heaven, even though He remains in a state of sacrifice, finds a more telling expression in the Cherubic hymn from Great Saturday: "Let all mortal flesh keep silence, and stand with fear and trembling; and let it take no thought for any earthly thing. For the King of Kings and Lord of Lords draws near to be sacrificed and given food for the faithful. Before Him go the choirs of angels with all the principalities and powers, the many-eyed cherubim and the six-winged seraphim, which cover their faces as they sing this hymn: Alleluia, alleluia, alleluia" (Praise the Lord God).

The priest gives expression to the conscience that He who goes toward crucifixion to be remembered, or is crucified and in this quality ascends to or is found on the holy altar on high as a loving sacrifice for our sins, when—in line with the example of the thief on the right hand of Christ—he asks on behalf of all those who believe in Him to be remembered in His heavenly Kingdom where Christ ascends now with His sacrifice. The faithful give the same expression to the same conscience by reinforcing through "Amen" the conviction that Christ, carried by the priest in his hands in the form of the gifts, is the King who enters for us as a sacrifice into the Kingdom of heaven, properly speaking establishing on our behalf that Kingdom foreseen before the ages. Before praising the invisible King, as it continues to sing the Cherubic hymn, the liturgical community asks Him for the salvation of all those in the church and especially for the loved ones, living and departed, both for those present and for those absent. It will ask Him who will ascend to or is found with His sacrifice on the holy altar on high that they may be remembered in His Kingdom, namely that they may be placed next to Him. Just as the thief on the right side is certain of both Christ's imminent entrance into the Kingdom on high, in which He returns as man because as God He has it from eternity, and of His saving death for all, asking Him to be remembered, to take him, too, into that Kingdom by remembering him: *Lord, remember me when You come into Your Kingdom* (Lk 23:42), so are those in the church certain of both Christ's imminent entrance, or of Christ the King, the invisible One, being on the right hand of the Father in a state of sacrifice for us, as well as of His power to bring them to the true life, they who may end their life at any moment, and all the loved ones who believe in Him, either living or departed, if they are remembered by the all-eminent King in order to raise them closer to Him.

Even though the faithful have laid aside all earthly care, they have not laid aside their responsibility to offer their prayers for the salvation of all and the care for their salvation. It is precisely in this that the concentration of all their trust in Christ is shown, the invisible King who offers Himself unceasingly as a sacrifice for all. They praise Him first through these supplications before praising Him through the content of the hymn.

Through these commemorations the consciousness of the sobornicity of the Church acquires in each of its members a new reinforcement. Those on earth are oriented toward eternity, but they want to have with them all both living and departed; they feel attached to those departed as having the duty to ask for them to be remembered by Christ, thus fulfilling on their part the responsibility for them. But they pray not only for the commemoration of the departed, but for all those who are present or absent. We all should want and should ask to be together in Christ's Kingdom. We are not persons excluding others. This would show our lack of love, which does not fulfill the condition required for being part of the Kingdom of eternal love. We are all responsible for one another. The permanent sacrifice of Christ initiated on Golgotha connects all of us because it was offered for all. If Christ did not restrict the purpose of His sacrifice, neither must we restrict it through a sort of egoism, either individual or collective.

First we pray for the commemoration of the hierarch through whom Christ's grace is communicated to us, coming from the Apostles and which he has in communion with all bishops, thus with the entire Church. In this is shown that we want to remain in the unity of faith, the correct one, of the Apostolic Church. We can only be saved in this faith. Separation from it is the same as the separation from Christ, from the unity of those who recognize Him in His truth, just as the Apostles knew Him. It is not only the hierarch and the priest who pray for the faithful they shepherd, but the faithful pray for them as well. The blood flows not only from the heart to the parts of the body, but also vice versa. This is how the unity and the life of the body is maintained.

We pray especially for the commemoration of the founders and benefactors of the church building in which we found ourselves. This gives those of us in a parish the practical possibility of maintaining our unity in faith by receiving the Mysteries and strengthening it through the Holy Liturgy. But we also pray for the founders and benefactors of the holy churches of God everywhere. Thus we affirm in every way the consciousness that our salvation is effected within the universal framework of the Church and that we all have the duty to pray for all. At the same time we affirm that this universalism is maintained not only through our prayers for others, but also through sacrifice. Wherever there is no sacrifice, egoism is strengthened and crumbles the universal unity of the Church, the unity of God's creation.

We also pray for the commemoration of those who "have brought these holy gifts and those for whom they were brought." The gifts that will be transformed into the body and blood of the Lord, as well as the highest gifts of which all will partake by being united with Him, also come from Him. Just like the prayers of one for another, they are signs and means of unifying love. Those who have brought the gifts have done so out of love for unity. By praying for their commemoration, we respond to them with our love and with the will to be in unity with them in Christ's Kingdom.

The priest concludes the commemorations with the supplication for the commemoration of those present, who out of love give priority to the prayers for all others: *And all of you, faithful Christians, may the Lord our God remember in His Kingdom, always now and ever, and unto the ages of ages.* Those present are happy that they first prayed for all others. This makes them more worthy of being remembered themselves by God.

The priest proceeds with the chalice and the paten toward the altar through the royal doors. If the deacon is present, he has already entered the altar with the paten after the supplication he offered at the beginning of the entrance: "May the Lord God remember all of you, faithful Christians, in His Kingdom." It is the priest's duty to commemorate certain categories or persons of the faithful. In the altar, standing at the right of the Holy Table, the deacon waits for the priest with the paten at the top of his head. He stands just as the angel stood, in bright vestments, near the tomb from which the Lord rose. The historical events condensed in the person of Christ and in an eternal present, draw attention toward them and work simultaneously over the faithful.

After the priest has finished the commemorations, the community of the faithful continues the Cherubic hymn, regarding itself, after the promise to lay aside all earthly care, worthy to receive the King of all: *That we may receive the King of all, Who is invisibly escorted by the angelic hosts; Alleluia, Alleluia, Alleluia.*

At this time when the priest arrives in the altar he places the chalice upon the antimension on the Holy Table. He does the same with the paten taken from the deacon. He places Christ, regarded as crucified and the spilled blood from the body, in the tomb signifying Joseph from Arimathea, something recalled through the words: *The noble Joseph, when he had taken down Your Most Pure Body from the wood* [of the cross], *wrapped it in clean linen with the spices* (Jn 19:40), *and placed it in a new tomb* (Mt 27:60).

While saying this, the priest takes off the covers from the chalice and the paten and covers both with the aer taken from the deacon's shoulder. In the tomb Christ was even more covered by the elements of nature because He was no longer living and no longer manifested His soul full of divinity in His eyes, but, on the other hand, His state of sacrifice was even more visible. This covering with the aer also indicates the undressing of Christ's dead body, His anointing with spices and His wrapping in linen. This is what has been seen. It is a new level of kenosis (of lowering). He who is undressed by others is in the ultimate degree of His lack of power. Through this sacrifice Christ not only offers Himself, but He lets Himself be offered by others in this state, although those who crucified Him did not do it with the intention of offering a sacrifice. But the priest undresses Him with this thought, as Joseph and Nicodemus also did it and by this they caused the act of Christ's sacrifice be accomplished. Without the participation of the priest and of the faithful, without the participation of the people at the accomplishment of Christ's sacrifice, this however cannot be fulfilled.

Then the priest says what has not been seen, or has been seen only in part: *In the tomb with the body, in hades with the soul as God; in paradise with the thief, and on the Throne with the Father and the Spirit was Thou, O Christ, fulfilling all things, O Thou who are boundless.* Even before Christ, no one stayed entirely in the tomb. Everyone went deeper with the soul, but to the depth of extreme lessening of his life. Persons remain within the frame of existence established by God through creation. But because they have willingly separated themselves from Him they remain only in the plane of created existence, and no longer being in communication with the source of life, even though they continue to be sustained in existence by the power of God, they do not enjoy the communication of His very life.

By going with the soul to that deep place separated from the communion of life with God, and because He had in Himself divinity itself, Christ took life itself there, not letting the soul united with Him, as God, to fall into this extremely lessened degree of life separated from God. He went to the hell of the extreme lessening of life, hence into the hell filled with darkness taking there the life and the light which He imparted to all those who believed during life on earth in the divine promise of His incarnation. Christ has shattered the bolts of hell, He has broken the gates of the prison from which no one could come out, with His life that entered there to those who were taken there awaiting trustfully the promised coming of the Son of God Who was united with the human nature (1 Pt 3:19–20). Being filled with His life, these were thus moved to paradise, that is within the ambiance of His divine life and light. The first who was filled with the life and light of Christ, with the paradise radiating from Him, was the thief on the right side, who left this life united with Him in faith, his death immediately following Christ's death (Jn 19:33), transforming his death from a path to hell into a path to paradise.

From Christ's soul there poured out the divine life and light because at the same time He was as God on the throne of power that, together with the Father and the Spirit, filled all things, being boundless. His divine hypostasis does not separate itself after the incarnation from His human nature. He lives even on the throne of the supreme dominion as the One not separated from His humanity. This is why the priest does not say: "Your body was in the tomb," but He addresses Christ Himself as the divine hypostasis, saying: "In the tomb [were] with the body," and he also says to Him: "In hades [were] with the soul as God, in paradise with the thief and on the Throne . . . was Thou, O Christ God." In Greek this fact is emphasized even more clearly with the words, "in the tomb [were] bodily" (σωματικῶς).

Christ Himself knew that He was in the tomb with His body. Mystically, as He was living in heaven, as bearer of His humanity He lived as being present in the body placed in the tomb, joined with this body. In fact, even the human soul knows this when the body is dead. Sometimes, the saints remain joined with the body through a special grace. All the more did Christ's divine hypostasis, even His soul, seeing His body in the tomb, know it as being joined with Him and He felt connected with it. The paradox was combined: the death of the body with the conscious of the hypostasis, and Christ's soul with this body belonging to Him. The divine hypostasis was not only in His soul, but also in His body, or rather these were held in connection with Him, Who was on the throne of dominion over all things. Moreover, His body, although being in the tomb, was presented to the Father as sacrifice, and the soul was also living the sacrificial state of the body.

Death had carried Christ not only as God, but also as man before the Father. Death as sacrifice had carried Him also as man into the plenitude of the divine life, while death carries him who dies in sin into the ultimate depth of the lessening of created life. This is why Christ's tomb is a "new" tomb in the preeminent sense, because His human body, too, placed in the tomb is a new body. And even though Christ's body is not omnipresent, Christ as God, Who lives also as man, is omnipresent and His divine life extends everywhere, imprinted with human feeling, through His love become brotherly love, in the proper sense of the word, vis-à-vis human persons.

Being the hypostasis of the body in the tomb, thus also man who presented His body as sacrifice to the Father, even if this body is in the tomb, He brings it back to life, returning to it not only the life from before, but a human life perfectly overwhelmed by the divine life. He assumed a mortal human life so as to raise it through sacrifice to immortal life. He lowered Himself, receiving a mortal life in order to renew it from within by accepting the sacrifice or the union with God through sacrifice. And in this was manifested His love for us and at the same time the will that we may accept our sacrifice together with Him, which He willed. The life of His body has been strengthened, renewed and enriched forever from the source of godhead.

Precisely because the divine hypostasis is not separated from His body in the tomb, but with the cooperation of the will of His assumed human nature, accepts the sacrifice, His "new" tomb is the tomb from which life comes out, as life-bearer and the source of our life, even more splendid and more radiant than any royal chamber. Because in it dwells united with His body, even before He brings it back to life, the King of kings Who is high above paradise.

The acceptance of the sacrifice and the union with God in a single hypostasis are the facts that make this tomb a "new" tomb, but also a different kind of tomb for every mortal human being who is united with Christ through faith. Every believer will come out at the end of the world from his/her tomb as Christ came out, but even until then their souls are with the life received from Christ. "O Death, where is your sting?" (1 Cor 15:55). Where is your power? "Death no longer has dominion over Him" (Rom 6:9). In fact, the pure sacrifice naturally encounters God and life in Him. It means the human person's self-overcoming, it is immersion in God. The human person's aspiration toward God being infinite, it reaches God. But only the humanity borne by God is capable of a pure and total sacrifice, without reservations, in which the human person retains nothing for himself. God then also comes to meet the raising of the sacrifice toward Him, or He helps it to rise to Him. Only in Jesus Christ did the perfect encounter between God and the sacrifice take place, and this is why only that sacrifice was a total, all-pure and perfect one.

Thus where the sacrifice is, there is God. But where the sacrifice is, there is also death.[287] Therefore, where death is as sacrifice, as total submission of life not kept for oneself, God is there, and especially in Christ's death as sacrifice. As real as His death was, just as perfect was His sacrifice and just as present was God in it. Death does not escape God's presence when it is received as sacrifice. If God is oftentimes present in the relics of saints and martyrs, all the more was He present in the human body He assumed, not letting it to decay. His body was even more immersed in God through death, not in the lessening of existence, not in a state of decay. His tomb was the palace of God. This is why it was and is the source of life, and this is why there is no contradiction between its qualities as throne, as palace, and as tomb of the Holy Table.

And precisely because God was present in the dead body of the Lord, the myrrh-bearing women and Joseph and Nicodemus had a special reason to wash it, to anoint it and to honor it. The Son of God Himself has honored it and destined it for eternity as His perfect dwelling. But He brought it to this state by the fact that He caused it to become a sacrifice. It is precisely in the fact that only through the body one can offer a sacrifice to God, is the honor to which the body is destined shown.

But at this time Jesus's soul filled with the entire divinity, since it also suffered the sacrifice of His body or it also participated in this sacrifice, was in hades, not in order to suffer the pains of hades, but to fill it with the light of His divinity. In hades one no longer offers sacrifice, but one suffers for not having sacrificed oneself. This is why in Orthodoxy the resurrection is depicted as beginning in hades. And in order to make clear that He really died, Christ resurrects His body only on the third day. It was only natural that the life and light of the resurrection be extended into the visible plane of bodies, after they erupted in hades through His soul and established paradise through the soul. Through Christ's soul life comes from the ultimate depth of divinity into the tomb where the body was.

Through the total love manifested in it, the sacrifice is so full of power, especially as it is not overshadowed by any doubt or reservation, that God's glory is revealed in it more than in acts of power similar to those of nature, even if the latter are of a more potent degree or in contrast to the normal acts of nature.

If the miracles or the more evident interventions of God in the decisive moments of our life can be contested through various explanations, God's revelation through Christ's sacrifice is made evident in the most difficult mode to contest His loving power beyond any natural power. It is precisely the sacrifice that covers God for those who do not have eyes to see the supreme power of the spirit. This is why "the cross of God" or His sacrifice for us could be considered by pagans as "folly," having been used to seeing the power of the gods in natural phenomena, and in modern times this gave birth to the "death of God" theology. But those who have spiritual eyes sing to God who accepted the cross and death: "Glory to your long-suffering, O Lord!"

This shows that sacrifice, or the death of the body as sacrifice, begins to be conquered in the soul full of God's power, but also united with the body. This is why Christ's resurrection also began with God's operation in the soul that descended into hades so that from there it could also come into His body, which did not lack the presence of godhead in it.

After the priest has expressed these things, he takes the censer from the deacon and censes the holy gifts three times, saying: "Do good, O God, in Your good pleasure to Zion and may the walls of Jerusalem be built." And the deacon responds: "Then You shall be pleased with the sacrifices of righteousness, with burnt offerings and whole burnt offerings; then they shall offer bulls on Your altar!" Through these words it is shown that the prophecies and the expectations of those in the Old Testament referring to the complete sacrifice have been fulfilled. The sacrifices of bulls at the temple which David expected to be built indicated another future sacrifice, the supreme sacrifice, the sacrifice of justice, the sacrifice of the true whole burnt offering that will be brought to God on behalf of the people. This sacrifice has been offered when Zion was built or when the human body has been rebuilt without sin — just as it was in the beginning — through the fact that it has been assumed by the Son of God, and thereby the Church was built, being made up of the bodies of all those who adhere to Christ. At this time there are being placed on the altar of God, alongside the sacrifice of the Lamb of God, not bulls with no conscience, but a conscious sacrifice.

Then the priest asks the deacon to remember him as well. His priority in grace obligates him to the priority in humility. The deacon responds: *May the Lord God remember your priesthood in His Kingdom.* After he has commemorated everyone, the priest could not let himself not be commemorated. He could not remain alone outside the Kingdom of eternal love which can be reached through the participation in Christ's sacrifice and through the commemoration of all including himself. In his turn, the deacon asks the priest: *Pray for me, Father.* And the priest asks God on behalf of the deacon the highest gift, the coming of the Holy Spirit upon him as promise of the Kingdom: *May the Holy Spirit descend upon you, and the power of the Most High may overshadow you.* The Spirit will give the deacon's soul the power to give spiritual birth to Christ in him, the sacrificed and the risen Christ, just as He gave the Lord's Mother the power to give birth to Christ with the body from her body. The Spirit will give the deacon the power to give spiritual birth to Christ in the faithful and to show Him to them through the litanies he chants in their midst.

At the gift of this prayer, the deacon returns to the priest the gift of the same prayer, with the awareness that where the Spirit is, there appears the communion of exchange, and that the Spirit does not operate without the cooperation of the people: *May the same Spirit serve together with us all the days of our life.* It is now that the deacon asks the priest to commemorate him, which de does. Thus all the commemorations conclude with the commemoration of the deacon, with the commemoration of the humblest servant of the Church, just as perhaps were commemorated, in the early times of the Church, the deacons who worked at the agape meals. But the last commemoration in time is not the last one in its outcome. The servants on the lowest level serve all, but in the end all those who are served remember them. And the general thanksgiving is crowned with the thanksgiving offered to them.

All the principal acts of the Holy Liturgy are introduced and followed by litanies. The small entrance, "Holy God," the reading of the Epistle and of the Gospel have been introduced by litanies and were concluded with one. The departure of the catechumens was anticipated by a litany. The Great Entrance, the entrance into the spiritual coming of Christ who sacrificed Himself, was introduced with two litanies. But it must also be followed by a litany, as was the reading of the Gospel.

4. *The Litany and Prayer of the Priest before the Creed*

The Great Entrance is followed by another litany. This litany is meant to prepare the faithful for the confession of faith in the Creed and for the transformation of the gifts into the body and blood of the Lord. This is why it has certain characteristics appropriate for this purpose. First it begins with these words: *Let us complete our prayer to the Lord*, namely let us complete our preparatory prayers for the act of transformation. (At Matins the last litany begins with the words: *Let us complete our morning prayer to the Lord*, and at Vespers with the words: *Let us complete our evening prayer to the Lord.*) It does not begin with the supplication for peace because the community has concluded the petitionary prayers. The "completion of the prayer" is also its degree of being perfected. The litany after the Gospel began with the appeal: *Let us say with our whole soul and with our whole mind, let us say*. This time it begins with the appeal to raise the prayer to its perfection, to completely dedicate ourselves to it so that, through it, we may show ourselves to be at the peak of the state that caused us to bring the gifts which represent us and which will be transformed into the Lord's body and blood. This is why the second supplication of this litany refers to the gifts: *For the precious gifts here offered, let us pray to the Lord*. We pray that the Lord may receive and consider them worthy of being transformed into His body and blood. Thus, we no longer ask something for ourselves, but we offer our gift to God. But our gift is made perfect through God's operation as well. And the gifts will be considered worthy of being transformed into the supreme gift that will be returned to us, providing we offer them with our whole heart or with the heart purified of thoughts foreign to

God, providing we offer them not with indifference or in ways not corresponding to God's will; this is why this supplication refers to both the gifts and to us.

From the standard litanies only two supplications are taken that have a more spiritual content: *For this holy church... That we may be delivered.... Help us, save us....* Then follows a series of supplications referring to more specified spiritual goods. The faithful respond to them not with *Lord have mercy*, but with *Grant this, O Lord*. Through these one asks for more specific goods, such as: *that the whole day be perfect and sinless, an angel of peace and faithful guardian of our souls and bodies, mercy and forgiveness of our sins, all that is good and useful for our souls and peace in the world, that we may spend the remaining time of our life in peace and repentance*. This is an entire program for the personal life and for the world. For through such a program is established not only a pure living and peace in the world, but the believer also prepares himself for a Christian end of his life and for the fearful judgment of Christ. Such an end and a good account at that judgment are asked for especially in the last supplication, which again shows the eschatological opening of the Liturgy through Christ's sacrifice and through the partaking of it by the faithful. This is our ultimate goal to which Christ's sacrifice takes us. We ask even at present, at every Liturgy, that the end of our life may not shake our faith, our hope for the life to come, and that we may not commit out of fear of death any act that might prevent us from reaching that goal. We do not boast with our lack of interest for the pains that will come in the days or moments before death. For the Christian does not boast about human powers, he is not foolhardy, being aware of human weaknesses and limitations. This is why he asks to be protected from too severe a pain, and even if they occur he will support them with God's help, which he asks for well before death. The pains will be abated precisely by the conscience that God is with him.

The believer thinks of those pains with fear also for the reason that they may push him toward acts and words that may prevent him from gaining eternal happiness. He could utter words and commit acts of hopelessness, of doubt in God or in His providence, of betrayal of Him. He fears the shame such words and acts might bring, not so much upon him as upon his Christian faith or upon Christianity in general, proving himself as lacking the strengthening power during great pains.

Through the last supplication one looks beyond the end of life on earth: *A good account at the fearful judgment seat of Christ*. The believer fears this judgment the most. The thought of this judgment is a guiding power toward good for the entire life on earth. The pains of death are transient, no matter how great. But the judgment of Christ upon the believer will have eternal effects. For him this judgment is fearful. It is not "Sein zum Tode," not the permanent knowledge of this life's end into non-being, that makes the Christian the most sensitive. This happens only to those who do not believe in the eternal continuation of the human being's personal life, of this superior value vis-à-vis all the world values. And not even to all of these. For most of them become accustomed to not thinking about this end, or are used to not giving any importance to it. After all, if death annihilates me completely, what importance is there in rising up from an impersonal, irresponsible living that lacks the conscience of personal self-value?

Only the permanent thought about "the fearful judgment" of Christ, fearful on account of its eternal effects consciously experienced, can truly sensitize the human conscience, it can lift up the human being from the worn-out and semi-personal behavior, from the decline from person into species. And only faith in eternal life, conditioned by living in the sensibility of conscience, can foster and give meaning to it.

Thus only Christianity, with its true opening toward real eschatology, toward an eternal living beyond life on earth, and only this personal and eternal eschatological characteristic—which is the true eschatology—is the basis for fearing the judgment of Christ and gives power for the realization of human capabilities, constituting the most efficient factor of sensitizing humanity, or of actualizing all its noble capacities. The theories on incarnation have no knowledge of such a personal, eternal and true eschatological characteristic. According to these theories eternity will not be mine as a person and this is why it does not concern me. Other and still other consciences will live in the same monotonous and relative plane of existence and keep returning to the same levels, not settling eternally in an unending happiness or unhappiness. Other impersonal or transient personal individualities will live in relative and monotonous repetitions. Thus, they will neither suffer eternal unhappiness (hades), nor will they rejoice eternally in a certain plenitude of life.

"The good account" at this judgment is not a lawyerly trick to find excuses for the evil works done, for the lived unchristian life. In this respect the Romanian words "good account" seem more appropriate than the Greek words "good defense" (καλη απολογια). The good account is the account of the good works, or of the acknowledgment full of repentance of one's own sinfulness. Thus, the believer asks God during life on earth for the strength to prepare himself for this "good account," or that God may give him repentance when he will be before Christ the Judge, and not to continue the habit of finding a false justification. But the spirit of repentance grows in him in this life. The believer exhorted by this supplication has even at present an experience as if being before Christ's judgment, being continuously sensitized, transcending this earthly life. He takes strength from this presence—experienced with anticipation—before Christ's judgment so that he may regulate all his life in such a way as to be able to give a good account when he actually finds himself before Christ the Judge. He lives even now in the eschatological perspective. Thus he asks to live in the present in view of this "good account," leading a life as someone destined to a responsibility. He must always live as one called to account for his deeds, for his words, as a responsible being. His eternal existence is dependent on the fulfillment of his responsibility. Eschatology opens with the presentation before a supreme forum in front of which the way in which the human person lived as a responsible being will be examined. The Liturgy is not a simple announcement of Eschatology, but in it Eschatology is experienced in anticipation, as normative for the entire life here on earth. This is how the faithful prepare themselves at the Holy Liturgy for the most complete encounter with Christ in Holy Communion. This encounter will be followed with another one in which will be verified the believer's fulfillment of his responsibility, of which he becomes more aware through Holy Communion.

These supplications are concluded like those in the litanies from the beginning of the Holy Liturgy, with the commemoration of the all-holy Birthgiver of God and of all the saints and with the promise of the faithful to offer themselves according to their example and through their prayers, as well as each other to Christ. Only in this way do they do everything on their part to prepare themselves in view of such an end and of the supreme verification of their responsibility's fulfillment at Christ's judgment.

But all the things asked for, as well as such an end and such a response, depend first of all on Christ's compassion. This is why all this is asked in the exclamation addressed to the Father, based on the compassion of His Son who became man and was crucified out of love for us: *Through the compassions of Your only-begotten Son, with Whom You art blessed together with Your all-holy, good and life-giving Spirit, now and ever and unto ages of ages. Amen!* The ultimate hope is being placed in the compassion, in the tender and merciful feelings of the Son of God who became man and sacrificed Himself for us, remaining man and in a state of sacrifice for us, showing His closeness to and mercy for us through this quality as man, which He maintains, and through the state of sacrifice in which He remains. One also places hope in the goodness of the Holy Spirit, who will give us strength to fulfill our responsibilities in this life so that we may be found at the supreme judgment as having fulfilled them.

The final, "completing" litanies from Vespers and Matins, in which are mentioned only the goodness and mercy of the Holy Trinity in general, are not ended like this one. Only a God from whom one Person, namely the beloved Son of the Father, became man, sacrificed Himself for us and remains man forever, having acquired the quality as Son as well as man, has been manifested to be a God of mercy until the end, guaranteeing for us, too, an eternal, happy life partaking of His love. It is only from Him that we can ask for mercy, forgiveness and the strength for an account He shall deem good at the supreme judgment.

Before this exclamation, the priest reads silently a prayer in which he prays to God—the Pantokrator (the All-Sustainer) who alone is holy and who receives the sacrifice of praise from those who call upon Him—to receive his prayer and that of the faithful, although they are sinners, and to bear it to His holy altar. He continues: *Deem us worthy to offer unto You gifts and spiritual sacrifices for our sins and for the transgressions committed in ignorance by the people. Count us worthy to find grace in Your sight, that our sacrifice may be well pleasing to You and that the good Spirit of Your grace may dwell upon us, upon these gifts here offered and upon all Your people.*

The eucharistic role of the Spirit is here specified. In the presence of the offered gifts, the Church prays to the Father to send the Holy Spirit upon the gifts and upon the people.[288]

Better said, the priest prays that he and the faithful may be made worthy to find grace before God so that the gifts offered now by them, as a sacrifice of theirs ("our sacrifice") may be well accepted and, consequently, the Holy Spirit may dwell upon him, upon the gifts when he invokes Him, and upon all the people present there. This is an anticipation and preparation of the Epiklesis (invocation of the Holy Spirit) and of the transformation of the gifts into the body and blood of the Lord through the Holy Spirit.

Properly speaking, the distinction is made between gifts and spiritual sacrifices, or the sacrifice of praise, which is a prayer addressed by the priest to God for his forgiveness and for the forgiveness of sins committed in ignorance by the people. The gifts without the prayer for the forgiveness of sins would convey nothing and would not be well pleasing to God. The priest asks that especially this prayer may be borne by Christ as a sacrifice of praise upon His altar from above. St. Cyril of Alexandria has extensively developed the necessity for us to add our sacrifices to Christ's sacrifice found on the altar from above, or that Christ may add our sacrifices to His sacrifice, purifying our sacrifices with the purity of His sacrifice. He calls our sacrifices "spiritual" because he sees in them, just like the prayer from the Liturgy, purification from sins by asking it from God and through repentance: "That is why we were instructed to say in the prayer: 'And forgive us our trespasses,' or 'Cleanse me from hidden sins' (Ps 18:13). This is the spiritual sacrifice with a sweet fragrance to God, for our salvation . . . . Thus, in the old law the goat is the sacrifice for sins, and now our sacrifice, of those who approach God in spirit and in truth, is repentance and asking for forgiveness."[289] And about the connection between our gifts and Christ's self-sacrifice offered together upon the altar on high, St. Cyril of Alexandria also says: "Being One and the Same, Christ is offered as sacrifice by the succeeding worshipers . . . . The daily offering of gifts (in the Old Testament) signifies the uninterrupted and unending of Christ's sacrifice every day as well as the offering of gifts by those made righteous through faith. For there will always be worshipers and the offering of gifts will never cease. And Christ will be offered by us and for us, being mystically sacrificed in the holy tabernacles (churches). He is our primary gift above all things. For He had offered Himself as sacrifice to God the Father, not for Himself, but for us who are under the yoke and guilt of sin. According to His likeness we are also sanctified sacrifices, as those who died to sin . . . . And we live for God the life of holiness and piety."[290]

One is to observe the alternation between considering Christ as our gift and considering our gifts, or our very persons, as such gifts, as well as the alternation between Christ's self-offering and Him being offered by us. We believe that this alternation also occurs in this prayer. It says that Christ offers Himself for us, but not with a saving effect if we do not also offer Him and if we do not thereby make Him "our sacrifice." This is our identification with Christ, but also our distinction from Him, which is shown in the fact that the gifts of bread and wine are ours, but they also become Christ's body and blood. The same thing is shown in the fact that the petitionary sacrifice for the forgiveness of our sins is at the same time a sacrifice of praise to God and is united with Christ's sacrifice. For through this supplication we acknowledge and praise His forgiving goodness manifested toward us through Christ's sacrifice. We see this in the Epistle to the Hebrews 13:15: "Therefore by Him let us continually offer the sacrifice of praise to God, that is, the fruit of our lips, giving thanks to His name."

As our distinct gift is shown especially in the supplications for our forgiveness and purification, the priest insists in this prayer on asking expressly for the forgiveness of his sins and those committed in ignorance by the people. In his humility, he considers the sins of the people lesser than his own, given that they are committed "in ignorance," while he cannot invoke this excuse for his own, because he was supposed to know and to overcome his ignorance.

In this prayer we have the same combination of the act of offering these sacrifices of ours by Christ and the act of Him being offered by us through the priest, something that is affirmed in reference to Christ's sacrifice in the prayer said during the singing of the Cherubic hymn. This combination is also frequently affirmed by St. Cyril of Alexandria: "Christ adds our sacrifices to His sacrifice." However, we cannot remain passive in this adding by Him of our sacrifices to His sacrifice, but we also must offer them, or we should offer ourselves through them. Moreover, even Christ is offered not only by Himself, but also by us. Or Christ, Who cleanses our sins through His pure sacrifice, does not cleanse us as some kind of passive objects, but as those who also make the effort to cleanse ourselves through the power of His sacrifice by identifying our sacrifice with His, or making His sacrifice our own; that is, by being filled with the feeling with which He offers Himself to the Father.

The deep meaning contained in this is also shown on the lower level of the relationships between us. Our communion is shown not only in the fact of sacrificing ourselves for each other, but also in the fact of sacrificing ourselves together with another when he sacrifices himself for us and for others. Only in this way is his feeling of offering himself for us imprinted in us.

Then follows the exclamation mentioned above, after which the priest addresses the people with the words: *Peace be to you all*. He wishes for them a state of peace superior to the one from the beginning litanies, or from before the reading of the Gospel, because they want to jointly recite the confession of faith. It is a peace that also comprises love in it, because the unity in faith cannot be upheld without love. This is why the faithful respond: *And to your spirit*, wishing that the same peace full of love, which the priest wishes for them as a factor of unity for them, to be in him as well, so that their faith may be common not only between them, but also between them and the priest as the one who has the principal role in maintaining the unity of faith among the people.

5. *The Love Among the Faithful and the Recitation of the Creed*

The need for love among faithful as well as between them and the priest, or the deacon if he is present (and also among priests if there are more than one), as it is based on the common faith in the God of love and as the foundation of the faith in common, inherited from the Apostles through the preceding generations with which we are connected through the same love, is proclaimed by the priest or the deacon with these words: *Let us love one another that with one mind we may confess*. It is not just about the love among lay believers, but also that between them and the priest. The priest is not the master of the faithful, but a servant obliged to love them. And the love among all of us is requested by God not only as something without importance for Him, but first of all because otherwise we cannot all confess Him in one mind. If we do not all confess Him in one mind, our faith in Him is not strengthened through the conviction and warmth we mutually communicate to each other. Without the love of others for me and without my love for them, both my faith and theirs weakens. This on account of the fact that one criticizes another out of envy when someone's faith is strongly affirmed, finding certain insincere motives in the strength of this affirmation. The members of a certain group of divided people undermine reciprocally their faith in God. This is why God sees in the love among us the premise of the strong faith in Him. Certainly, the relation is also vice versa: from the strong faith in Him, jointly affirmed, the love among us grows. In the end we are the ones who benefit. God wants this unity realized among us and between us and Him (Jn 17:11). In this way we advance in the Kingdom of the Holy Trinity, which is love.

In fact, the Holy Liturgy shows us this connection between the love among us and the confession of faith. In essence, our faith contains God in Trinity. But the triune God is a God of love. And if He is a God of love, He is the source of all love, thus also of our love for Him and of the love among us. By confessing God in Trinity, we praise and glorify the love within Him and its reflection toward us as His created beings. This praise and glorification would not be sincere if we did not endeavor to receive its reflection within us. Or if we did not feel the value of love, which can only come from God in Trinity, we would not praise and admire the Holy Trinity with all our strength, nor would we endeavor to advance in it. Thus, by confessing our faith in the triune God we do not consider God as a theoretical truth, but we confess our faith in a God of love in Himself and the source of the love within us. This makes us also manifest our love for a loving God and to express our experience of this love that comes from Him.

One can add that, in addition to the connection between love and the confession of a triune God of love, there is also a connection between love and knowledge. This connection consists in the fact that he who loves opens himself up to the one he knows and the latter enters the inner being of the former. Thus, the love between the two is also a knowledge of each other through their mutual communication.

The liturgical community affirms the connection of love between us and the Holy Trinity by responding to the deacon's appeal to love one another so that in one mind we may confess. Only if we love one another are we able to confess in one mind: *The Father, the Son and the Holy Spirit, the Trinity one in essence and undivided.* Only in this way can we realize the unity without melting into each other, similar to the Holy Trinity.

Therefore, the priest confesses the connection between love among us and the loving confession of the Holy Trinity as the source of love. Both these loves (among us and between us and the triune God) are necessary for the confession of God. At bottom, to confess God in Trinity is to confess love as supreme truth not just theoretically, but also as life-creating and preserving. God can only be such a truth. Only he who experiences the everlasting love, experiences God and vice versa. To say: *I believe in You, O Lord,* means to say: *I love You, Lord; I love You because You are love; You are my refuge, because in the love for You I have life; You are He* who brought me to life, sustains me in it, leads me toward the plenitude of life and its eternity. Otherwise, I submerge myself into death.

This is why the priest recites the words from Psalm 18 (17):1: *I will love You, O Lord, my strength. The Lord is my rock and my fortress and my deliverer.* I will love is the equivalent of I will believe. Or my faith in You is the basis for my love for You. For through Your love, You are my strength and my refuge and my deliverer. To a god of impersonal essence I cannot confess either faith or love. But our God is worthy of love because He showed me His love by sending His Son to become man and to sacrifice Himself for me, something He could not have done if He did not have love in Himself. In this way He became strength for me, which liberates me from the slavery of sinful egoism, and He became an unshaken foundation of my personal, eternal existence by delivering me from the fatal power of laws that without a personal God in Trinity would lead me to decomposition and would not give me any power to overcome egoism.

The priest and the faithful have advanced from feeling holiness and then God's mercy after the reading of the Gospel to feeling His love, and thus they became able to understand and to confess God in Trinity with all their conviction.

But feeling this love of God in Trinity will give them the possibility of rising higher, to the understanding of Christ's sacrifice, of the Son of God become man out of love for us as the basis for the transformation of bread and wine into His body and blood to be partaken of by them, and thereby the doors of the eternal Kingdom of the Holy Trinity's love may be open to them.

At this time the priest kisses the paten, the chalice and the edge of the Holy Table. The kiss is the most expressive act of love.[291] The priest shows through this kiss as well that he loves God who gave His Son for us, thus he confesses Him as the God of love. But the chalice and the paten are still covered, because the moment of Christ's presence before us in the image of bread and wine has not yet come. Through the three kisses the priest indicates his confession of the Holy Trinity, but by kissing the paten, the chalice and the Holy Table he manifests his love directed toward the sacrificed Christ and toward the sacrificial altar on high where He is in a state of permanent sacrifice, showing His love for us before the Father. By kissing the Holy Table the priest shows that Christ will, through the transformation, make Himself present in the most intensive way also on this Holy Table, which is the Table of the Church since it is located in one of the places of Christ's universal Church. The priest responds with his love in the name of the faithful to Christ's love for us manifested before the Father and about to be shown also on that particular Holy Table.

If there are two or more priests present, they exchange the kiss of peace, showing the link between the love among them and the joint confession of faith in Christ, a confession made in one mind, thus showing the presence of Christ's love in their love and unity. The first among priests says to the second, while he offers the kiss of peace: *Christ is in our midst*. He unites us in love, in unity, through His love. The love of the Trinity for us, which has also filled us with love for It and among ourselves through the incarnation and sacrifice of the Son, has been manifested in Christ, who shows that He remains eternally in the state of sacrifice for us through these covered images upon the Holy Table; thus, His sacrifice also fills us mystically with love.

Confessing the same faith, the other priest says that Christ is in their midst, not simply repeating the same words, but through his own contribution that shows him as a person: *He is and ever shall be*. We are united not only for this moment through Christ's presence and through His love poured out within us and by confessing Him, but also in the future without a determining end. The first priest continues this thought in his own way, concluding the discovering of their unity as the Spirit concludes the unity between the Father and the Son: *Always, now and ever, and unto the ages of ages. Amen*. Christ will be among us not only in an undetermined future, but eternally, and our union in Him will be eternal as well as our communal confession of Him and, therefore, through our love for Him. In the olden times the faithful also exchanged the kiss of peace.

In certain churches in Transylvania the younger faithful still kiss the hands of the older ones and the latter embrace the former. This is done by men with men and by women with women. It is the kiss of peace, following the priest's words: *Peace be to you all*.

St. Cyril of Jerusalem says about this kiss, which during his time followed the instruction of the deacon: "Receive one another; and let us kiss one another. Think not that this kiss is of the same character with those given in public by common friends. It is not such: but this kiss blends souls one with another, and courts entire forgiveness for them. The kiss therefore is the sign that our souls are mingled together, and banish all remembrance of wrongs. For this cause Christ said, *If thou art offering thy gift at the altar, and there rememberest that thy brother hath aught against thee, leave there thy gift upon the altar, and go thy way; first be reconciled to thy brother, and then come and offer thy gift* (Mt 5:23)."292

Blessed Augustine says in his turn: "After that it is said: Peace be to you all, and the Christians exchange the holy kiss. This is the sign of peace [of reconciliation]. Let there be in the hearts what the lips say" (PL 38, 1101A). And in deepening the meaning of this act, Theodore of Mopsuestia says: "They all give each other the peace and by this kiss they make a sort of confession of the unity and love among themselves." It is a unity received through Baptism, which they confess while approaching the Holy Eucharist. "Through Baptism we in fact received the new birth by which we were reunited in a unity of nature; we receive its nourishment again when we receive the same body and the same blood. All of us, though many, make up one body because we partake of the same bread. Thus, before we approach the Holy Mysteries, it is proper for us to offer the peace through which we manifest our unity and love for one another. It is not proper for those who make up one ecclesial body to hate a brother in the faith."293 Commenting on this text, Danielou says: "There appears here a new sign of the Mystery: it is the sign of unity among the members of Christ's body. And the kiss of peace appears as the sign of that unity."294 What the priests said to each other while exchanging the kiss, *Christ is in our midst* and *He is and ever shall be*, is valid for the faithful, too. They make up one body only because Christ is among them. This is why they can be one body only in Christ. The words *Christ is in our midst* are based on what St. Paul the Apostle said in 1 Timothy 2:5: "For there is one God and one Mediator between God and men, the Man Christ Jesus." Wherever Christ is between two or more people "the middle wall of separation" is broken down, the wall of arrogance, envy and distrust. In Christ human persons encounter each other and together in God. If two separated persons can be reconciled by another, all the more does Christ bring them to unity in Himself, who loves both or all of them equally, since by offering Himself for others "He has abolished in His flesh the enmity." By uniting them in Him in "one new man from the two," He thus makes peace, "reconciling them both to God." In this sense Christ "is our peace" (Eph 2:14–16).

Then the priest from inside the altar, or if the deacon is present from his place in front of the people, says: *The doors, the doors, with wisdom let us be attentive!*[295] One of the believers, or all together recite the Niceno-Constantinopolitan Creed, which is the Creed common to the entire Church.

An interpretation of the expression "The doors, the doors" appropriate for today's faithful as well as for those of all times, an interpretation in which the words "with wisdom let us be attentive" can be included, is that of St. Maximos the Confessor: "The closing of the doors which takes place after the sacred reading of the holy Gospel and the dismissal of the catechumens signifies the passing from material things which will come about after the terrible separation and even more terrible judgment and the entrance of those who are worthy into the spiritual world, that is, into the nuptial chamber of Christ, as well as the complete extinction in our senses of deceptive activity."[296]

In the Armenian Liturgy the old practice has been maintained until today. The deacon says: "Receive one another with the kiss of peace and let those who are not worthy of partaking of these Holy Mysteries leave and pray outside." And all the faithful receive one another with this kiss, saying: "Christ is in our midst." The people sing a brief hymn that sums up the infinitely rich meaning of what takes place in this moment: "The Church has become one body and our mutual kiss is the sign of this union; enmity has departed and love has pervaded everywhere."[297] This expresses the feeling that Christ has come even closer to the liturgical community. He sends out the rays of His presence, which will be complete from the moment of the transformation of the gifts.

St. Cyril of Alexandria places the expression "The doors, the doors" in connection with the commandment of the Old Testament to remain inside until morning after eating the Paschal lamb (Ex 12:21–23). This is why St. Cyril considers the invitation as referring to the entire Christian life after Holy Communion. St. Cyril says that in the Old Testament the doorposts were struck with the blood of the lamb so that death would not enter into the house where those who ate the lamb were, so neither should one's thoughts depart from God: "By asking that those who ate the lamb should stay inside the doors, the law shows that it is necessary and useful for those who became worthy to partake of Christ to lead their life in unshaken and steadfast holiness so that they may not perish together with the Egyptians by exiting the house."[298]

Through the words: "The doors, the doors, with wisdom let us be attentive" the faithful are told, according to St. Maximos the Confessor:

Think of the doors that will be closed to those who will be excluded at the last judgment from the happiness of living with Christ. This will happen to those who did not close the doors of their senses to the passions triggered by transitory things. Be attentive, with wisdom, to Christ's saving truth contained in the Creed. Guard the senses of your senses, close them now so that you may not suffer from the closing before you of the doors to the heavenly Kingdom. Thus, these words continue to prepare the faithful for the eschatological perspective. That happiness, which means our salvation as persons from destruction through nature, has been brought to us by Christ through His incarnation and sacrifice. We advance toward that happiness by confessing the Creed. All that it comprised assures us of that eternal happiness, or of the salvation from destruction through death, or of the eternal suffering in the existence reduced to the maximum degree.

The Creed is the evidence of God's love for us and our confession of Him; it is the recognition of this evidence of His love. And our joint confession of Him is the manifestation of our love for each other based on His love for us. It is a manifestation of the sobornicity of the Church in the right faith, based on the joint confession of God's love for us and of our love for Him and for each other, especially since it is recited in all churches, in conformity with the decision of Patriarch Timothy of Constantinople (512–518), as a sign of the Orthodox Christians against heresies.[299]

But the confession of our love for God is united with our confession of everything He has done for us through the incarnate Son and of our firm hope in the eternal life that He guaranteed for us through His incarnation for eternity, through His sacrifice as an unending operation, through His resurrection, ascension and sitting as man at the right hand of the Father.

In amazement we confess our faith in the awe-inspiring love of God for us manifested in the fact that the very Son of God, who is of one essence with the Father, became man for us and for our salvation, was crucified and rose again in order to guarantee for us as well the resurrection and the life of the age to come.

By jointly confessing the Creed, the faithful prepare themselves to receive the same Christ through Holy Communion, just as they prepare themselves by confessing the same Creed to receive Him in the Mystery of Baptism, or to receive Him again in the Mystery of Confession or, finally, those who will receive the grace of hierarchy. They know that in the Eucharist they will have the ultimate and supreme act of the Son's coming to them and they show, through the Creed, the basis of this coming and the happiness prepared in this way for them in the Kingdom of the Holy Trinity, confessing all that the Trinity has done for them out of love. In the Creed they confess that God is not a blind force without any knowledge of the human beings, but a Father full of love for a unique Son, who, wishing to show His fatherly love for other children as well, creates human persons and sends His only begotten Son to become man, to be crucified for us, to rise again and to eternally remain man united with us who are also resurrected through His power. In the love of God as Father and of God as Son is founded the love for us. And this is all the greater as the Father makes us in the likeness of His Son, making Him like us. The conscious love for every human person lies at the basis of salvation, not a blind law of repetition. In that love is the meaning and the totality of the fundamental meanings of existence, concentrated in the Creed, not in the laws of eternal and monotonous repetition that lead nowhere.

The mystery of God's love for us, the mystery of this amazing value placed by God on each of us, the mystery of the blessings He assured for us, is so great that we will never cease to go deeper in its happiness and meaning as well as in the thanksgiving and praise offered to God for it.

This is why St. Maximos the Confessor sees in the joint recitation of the Creed, after the exchange of the kiss of peace, the sign of eternal thanksgiving and praise offered to God by us in unity and as one. Through the eschatological orientation of confessing the Creed we emphasize this orientation confessed in the last supplication of the previous litany: *A good account before the fearful judgment seat of Christ, let ask of the Lord*. We will be able to give this good account if we have held strongly the confession of the Creed.

St. Maximos the Confessor presents this eschatological orientation of confessing the Creed with these words: "The profession by all of the divine symbol of faith signifies the mystical thanksgiving to perdure through all eternity for the marvelous principles and modes by which we were saved by God's all-wise Providence on our behalf. Through it those who are worthy are confirmed as grateful for the divine favors, for otherwise they would have no other way of returning anything at all for the numberless divine blessings toward them."[300]

The Christian Creed comprises two fundamental paradoxes. If God Himself is an infinite ocean which our reason cannot comprehend, all the more endless for our understanding are the inner-principles and paradoxical modes by which we were saved. Thus, at the basis of salvation is the paradox of the unity of being and the personal distinction between the Father and the Son. This is why it can be said that this is the primal and the most fundamental inner-principle of existence or of supra-existence and the basis of our salvation. A divinity that is only a unity of essence or only a plurality of separated persons would not be truly rational. It would lack the conscience of the will to love, which is the most fundamental inner-principle of existence. So, this inner-principle is paradoxical. Only in it is unity combined with knowledge and love.

But the paradoxical inner-principle of supra-existence also constitutes the foundation of creation and salvation. Only such an existence is able to make a free creation come to life. Without love it would not be possible for God to create the world as a field of free manifestation for persons after His image. All the less would salvation be possible, uniting the world with Him and deifying it. If He decided to create it, it is natural that He wanted to strongly unite Himself with it when it separated itself from Him through sin. Thus the incarnation of the Son of God is rational, too, precisely through its paradoxical characteristic, just as the unity of the divine being in the Trinity of Persons is rational and paradoxical. Coming out of the paradox means coming out of the rational.

If Christ was not of one essence with the Father, and also with us [according to humanity], He would not be able to raise us up to the level of the infinite life of the divinity; and even if only a unity of essence existed in God, He could not have saved us as conscious persons and we would be lost in the great unconsciousness of the all-encompassing essence. Only by existing as divine being, and also being a distinct Person, and only by becoming man and remaining God, was Christ able to save us, deifying us as persons for eternity.

But who could ever understand completely the inner-principle of the paradox of the unity of being and the personal distinction between the Father and the Son?

And who could understand the second, through which our salvation was in fact achieved, and which is the union of divinity with humanity in the Person of the Son? If the Son of God had remained only God, we would not have been able to unite ourselves with Him without being engulfed in Him, therefore He could not have made us partakers of His infinite life. But also, even if by becoming man He would have ceased to be God—through a pantheistic evolution—He could not have raised us above the human condition and that of our death as persons. The Son of God's real humanization, without the change of His divinity, could not have been achieved through a union between a divine person and a human one, thus remaining two persons. There would have continued to remain in existence the boundary between God and man. Neither could have this union been achieved by one human person assuming the divine nature. In this case the initiative of salvation would have been man's and man would have directed the entire saving action. Man would have been proven to be greater than God. But then he would no longer have had need for salvation. Or that would have meant an ascending evolution of man to the level of divinity. The entire divine essence would have become man's, therefore divinity no longer existing in eternal Persons so as to guarantee the eternity of human persons. Only through the fact that a divine Person had assumed human nature, which generally subsists in distinct individuals, was the One and the Same able to also become man, without ceasing to be God. And only in this way, by remaining a Person distinct from us, can He unite us with Him and deify us.

But who can completely understand the inner-principle of this paradox: one person in two natures? And the basis of this paradoxical inner-principle is the love that unites without confounding. The love that is at the basis of the first paradox also explains the love that is at the basis of the second.

But the inner-principle of the second paradox requires additional explanations: how can a divine Person unite finite human nature with its infinite divine nature without annulling it? The response must admit that in the divine nature there is something not entirely contrary to the human nature; and in the human nature there is something that makes it not incapable of the divine Person's manifestation in it. Who can completely understand these truths? Thus, the inner-principle of the incarnation refers not only to the basis and motive of the incarnation, which is the love within the Holy Trinity, but also to its possibility. And the possibility has its basis also in love. In this we are shown that love can do anything. The infinite Person protects the finite human nature and makes it its medium of manifestation. The infinite Person can make the finite humanity its own nature also through love, by which it created it with the possibility of responding to the divine love and making it shine forth from within, and also with the possibility of opening itself up by knowing the divine infinite and at least suggesting, if not exactly conveying, this infinite. Between the infinite God and humanness there is no contradiction by which they would mutually exclude each other, but a possibility for union without annulment or confusion, for humanness is not purely and simply finite, but a finite open to the infinite, just as the divine is not closed up within its infinity, but open to the finite and capable of filling up the finite with its infinity. Between the divine and humanness there is no contradiction by which they cancel each other or which may entail confusion, just as there is no contradiction in God between the unity of being and the Trinity of Persons, but on the contrary, one calls for the other because true unity, which is also love, calls at the same time for the enduring existence of persons who love each other. In all pantheisms there is a battle among all so that in the end they all dissolve in essence. Christianity affirms both the unity and the enduring existence of persons. Christianity is *par excellence* paradoxical in its core, not just on the surface. In paradox there exist simultaneously the unity and the distinction of persons, as well as the unity and the distinction between the divine and humanness, without separation and without fusion. Everything is paradoxical: the world and the life of the person. Cardinal Nicholaus Cusanus, who was sent in the fifteenth century on a delegation to Constantinople, having come in contact with this paradoxical thought of the Holy Fathers, called the paradox *coincidentia opositorum*. It is in this that the inner-principle of the entire existence consists, from God to the created being. The ultimate possibility of the inner-principle of existence is given in God, in whom everything exists, some actually (the being and the three Persons) and others potentially (the uncreated God and the potential of the relationship with created beings). The paradox is full of meaning because it makes both love and freedom possible.

 Here appears the paradoxical inner-principle of the mode of incarnation. It consists in the unity so strong between the Son of God and the human nature that He became both man and the Person of our nature. The question arises: How did He experience before resurrection His humanity, so strongly united with Him, but still maintaining its weaknesses and pains, and how does He experience it after resurrection? And how does His humanity experience the depths or the infinite horizons (heavens) of the Hypostasis's divinity, which also became its Hypostasis, before resurrection and lasted after resurrection as well?

From the inner-principle of the two fundamental paradoxes there follow others. For example, the paradoxical inner-principle of the fact that God, the source of life, can accept death in the human nature of which He becomes bearer. "Thou who art the Life wast laid in a tomb," as we sing at the Lamentation service. This leads to the conquering of death. This is why "your tomb (O, Christ) is the source of resurrection." We have here, properly speaking, two paradoxical inner-principles: how can the immortal One accept death in His human nature? And why was death necessary in order to conquer death? How can death co-exist with the infinite life in the incarnate divine Hypostasis? And why is death necessary for our salvation from death? How is death trampled down by death? How does a dead person rise again? The paradoxical inner-principles proper to Christ's death are presented also as the union of certain aspects, both distinct and opposed, while He was dead: He is in the tomb with the body, in hades with the soul, and as God on the throne together with the Father, fulfilling all things as the one who is boundless.

The inner-principle of the last paradoxes, or the answer to the questions they raise, lies in the fact that no personal created being can completely die, once brought into existence by God and being under the ray of His attention. Here is shown again His eternal concern for the created human persons. He who dies by being separated from God, dies because in the inner-principle of his spirit, the roots of the inner-principle or of the unitary complex of his body's inner-principles are weakened, as his very spirit has been weakened through the separation from God. But as spirit, he is still maintained in existence through a certain power of God. And in the one who dies to God, because he wants to completely offer himself to Him, even though in his spirit the roots of the inner-principle or the unitary complex of his body's inner-principles are also weakened, the inner-principle of his very spirit remains strong, or is strengthened even more through the union with God. In this way the strength of his body's inner-principle can be renewed.

The most united with the Father was Christ, not only as God, but also through His soul. And through His human soul the Son of God united with it was able to reinforce and super-inforce in it the roots of the complex of His body's inner-principles so that in this way He might resurrect

His body. For God also has power over matter, which through the endurance of God's union with the body did not begin to decay.

Those united with Christ who die to God, when at the end of the world's actual image God will strengthen in their souls the rational roots of their bodies, will also rise with the bodies, giving material form through the power of Christ's risen body to these inner-principles in a new body, according to the likeness of Christ's body. But since all will then have to receive their bodies again, the power to give material form will be extended out of Christ's body also to the rational roots of the bodies of those separated from God, having received through the same power the material form in new bodies. But they will not be engulfed in Christ's Spirit, because Christ has not dwelled in their souls, either. Thus, these bodies will be new only in that they will not be the bodies from life on earth, or identical with those, and they will not be new in a spiritual sense. All these inner-principles, although fully founded on the one hand in a particular reason, maintain on the other hand never-ending depths. In both cases one attains resurrection only through death. And this is why Christ has trampled down death only by death. For having gone through sin, the body must die in order to be brought back to a life without death. These paradoxes are shown as paradoxes of love and, therefore, as rational paradoxes. Even in the bodies resurrected for the state of unhappiness, there remains a trace of God's love, as much as the persons of those bodies could not refuse to receive it. In them neither death or life will ever reach a definitive victory.

But the paradoxical inner-principle of the union between the immortal Son and His death and resurrection with the body has its own paradoxical mode. This mode consists in the immortal One experiencing His death with the body, just like experiencing the resurrection and the infinite life in His body, even though this union occurs in a limited body. If the saint experiences the awareness of his body in the grave (sometimes even the power of grace in it) without sensing it as a medium for pleasures and pains, and the power of grace also pours out over his relics, all the more does Christ experience with His soul and divinity the connection with His body, without the latter being a medium for the senses. But the mode of this paradoxical experience of His dead body and of His resurrected body, though enduring in the humanity of its senses, remains a theme never completely understood.

Returning to the expression "The doors, the doors," it can also have this meaning: "Open the doors of your minds so as to understand the saving content of the Creed."

While the community confesses the Creed, the priest (or the priests, if there are more) also recites the Creed softly and lifts the aer from the holy paten and chalice, gently raising it up and down above them. Cosmic nature no longer covers Christ who sacrifices Himself, thus showing His saving power, but it trembles out of fear around Him. God's love manifested in the incarnate and sacrificed Christ is also known at the time of confessing what He has done for us through this uncovered showing of Christ's sacrifice and resurrection. Their uncovered showing places in a state of trembling the entire creation, including the angelic one, which brings to memory the quake which occurred at the Lord's crucifixion and resurrection, when the angel rolled back the stone from the tomb (Mt 27:51; 28:2). This is why after the fifth article of the Creed ("And on the third day He rose again according to the Scriptures") the priest stops raising the aer up and down. The resurrection was God's most wonderful and loving act toward us. In it the economy of salvation has reached the climax, based on the love of God in Trinity. When all these were made known through Christ, they shook the angelic hosts and the cosmic elements.

The aer is then laid down on the side and the holy gifts remain uncovered. Through His death as sacrifice offered to the Father, Christ has come close to the Father also as man, but He became strongly efficient in us as well through His Holy Spirit, no longer being covered by the cosmos that thickened His body as a consequence of the general thickening of creation brought about by sin. He is no longer subjected to the conditions of life in the actual image of creation. The moment of the supreme kenosis is at the same time the moment of coming out of kenosis. He tramples down death by death, and through death He passes to resurrection and to a revelation of the divinity made evident to us through the Holy Spirit at a superior level. However, after resurrection and especially after ascension, Christ remains as a sacrifice before the Father, but also at our service. By reciting the Creed we show that we have been raised to the knowledge of His saving economy, which is confirmed by the gifts remaining uncovered, or through Christ's efficiency in the state of sacrifice until the end of the ages. The recitation of the Creed ends with the assurance of eternal life for us, resulting from the Son of God's incarnation, crucifixion and resurrection for us. In this is shown the fullness of God's love for us. By confessing our faith in that eternal life, we confess God's perfect and eternal love for us.

6. Anamnesis as Preparation for the Presentation of the Gifts to God and for Their Sanctification

a. Introduction to the Anamnesis that Prepares the Gifts for the Transformation

Through the confession of faith the faithful have opened themselves up to God's love that will be shown to them in the partaking of Christ's body and blood, which He will share with them. For one cannot reach the eternal Kingdom of the Trinity without frequent communion with the sacrificed Christ, in which way we also become children of the Father, like Him. Thus, the incarnate Son communicates to us through His state of sacrifice His love for the Father, so that we may also appropriate it. But one reaches communion by offering one's gifts to God so that they may be transformed into Christ's body and blood, found upon the heavenly altar in order to be given to the faithful as well. Through these gifts the faithful first offer themselves to God in order to become partakers of His sacrifice; then they will sacrifice themselves together with Christ through their gifts transformed into His sacrifice.

Before the anaphora, the deacon or, if he is absent, the priest directs from the royal doors the faithful to be attentive to what follows: *Let us stand aright, let us stand with fear, let us be attentive, that we may offer the holy sacrifice in peace!* The entire liturgical community officiates "the holy offering" (the anaphora). This consists in the gifts which, by offering them, as they are potentially the same with the Lord's body and blood, we offer Christ Himself, therefore they can also be called "holy sacrifice," as in the Romanian translation. On the one hand, Christ receives them, on the other hand He transforms them into His body and blood, thus offering Himself together with us. Therefore, the "offering" of the gifts will result in the "mercy of peace," or the mercy of God's reconciliation with us through their transformation into Christ's body and blood. But both the gifts offered and Christ's sacrifice into which they will be transformed are a sacrifice of praise to God. By so answering, the faithful do not simply repeat what the priest said, but they complete his words.

Still, the words "the sacrifice of praise" show that before the Symbol of faith was introduced in the Liturgy, they immediately repeated the same words which the priest used previously in his prayer, which in olden times was probably recited in a loud voice.

Fr. Prof. Petre Vintilescu, based on the separate use of the words *mercy* and *peace* in certain old liturgical codices, considers that the faithful of old promised to offer to God their mercy and peace toward their neighbors around the Eucharistic transformation.[301] But this would not justify the instruction of the priest to offer "the offering" with fear. The mercy expected from God must certainly have as a consequence our mercy toward human persons.[302] In this sense one can also see in the words "the mercy of peace" the meaning noted by Fr. Vintilescu.

We note that the words mercy and peace reproduce the verse from the Epistle of St. Jude: "Mercy, peace, and love be multiplied to you" (Jude 1:2).

In fact, from the first litanies of the Holy Liturgy when the faithful say to God "Lord, have mercy" for every supplication on behalf of anyone, they show that not only do they expect God's mercy for others as well, but they also show their mercy toward them. Only the one who has mercy toward another person can pray to God to pour out His mercy over that person. In this sense, throughout the entire course of the Holy Liturgy the faithful ask not only for God's mercy for themselves and for others, but they also express their mercy and, thus, their love for others. In this way they prepare themselves to enter the Kingdom of the Holy Trinity's eternal love. The faithful offer to God this mercy of theirs toward others with even more power around the transformation of the bread and wine into the Lord's body and blood for their communion, as the supreme evidence and consequence of God's mercy toward them. The explanation given by P. Vintilescu is confirmed by the same connection between doing good (Heb 13:16) and "the sacrifice of praise" (Heb 13:15). These acts of doing good, or this mercy toward the neighbor, which the Lord considers as the true praise offered to Him, through His care manifested toward His created beings, is thus considered in Hebrew 13:16 as a sacrifice of praise offered by us to God. For doing good to others is a sacrifice, but it is a sacrifice offered out of the power given to us by God, therefore a praise to God for the power He granted us to do good. But we really offer ourselves to God by extending the fruit of our lips that we offer Him into our self-sacrifice toward His precious created beings, our fellow human beings. By doing good to others, we reinforce the praise we offer Him through words, since we appreciate the worth of God's created beings through our acts of love. We praise God for the value He has placed through creation on His conscious created beings, but we also increase their value and ours, or we develop them and ourselves toward good or in the direction toward God. We praise God by developing our tendency for good He placed in us, or our likeness with Him, but also awakening in this way the tendency for good which God placed in others.

We can sacrifice ourselves, or praise God in this way only from the power of Christ's sacrifice. Here are the words of Hebrews 13:15–16, in which all these meanings are comprised: "Therefore by Him let us continually offer the sacrifice of praise to God, that is, the fruit of our lips, giving thanks to His name. But do not forget to do good and to share, for with such sacrifices God is well pleased." We offered a sacrifice of praise to God by confessing His works in the Creed; let us continue to do this through works. Therefore, let us also commit to His praise through the real sacrifice of doing good and by partaking of His sacrifice.

It is true that the Lord Christ seems to place mercy opposite sacrifice when He says: "I desire mercy and not sacrifice" (Mt 11:13). But the sacrifices He does not desire are the bloody ones. Was it not mercy that prompted Him to go all the way up to the sacrifice on the cross? Also, is not the mercy for those suffering physically and spiritually, the mercy that breaks the heart in pain for them, a true sacrifice? Is not that mercy united with the desire for peace and brotherhood with them? Does it not bring peace in the soul, liberating it from the pangs of indifference?

But our heart open to the union with others through mercy also receives God's mercy, which reconciles us with Him through the sacrifice offered by Christ for God's praise and love. We cannot be united with God unless we also have mercy. He who is merciful can only be united with him who is merciful. Christ offers Himself as sacrifice for those who offer themselves to others out of mercy. He has the greatest mercy for human beings, because He said: "But when He saw the multitudes, He was moved with compassion for them, because they were weary and scattered, like sheep having no shepherd" (Mt 9:36). But the Father is also merciful. "Therefore be merciful, just as your Father is merciful" (Lk 6:36). God is merciful. He is "the source of mercies." But no matter how merciful He is, as well as His Son who sacrificed Himself for us out of mercy, if we do not open our heart with mercy for others, neither are we able to receive His mercy. A hardened, hostile and envious heart cannot feel mercy, which comes not only from a human person, but primarily from God. This is why it has been said: "Blessed are the merciful, for they will obtain mercy" (Mt 5:7), namely, they will feel God's mercy.

One can see from this that the reference of the words: "A mercy of peace, a sacrifice of praise" to Christ's sacrifice cannot be excluded, a sacrifice that will be offered by the priest together with the faithful, asking for the transformation of the offered gifts. This reference corresponds more directly with the priest's instruction: *Let us stand aright, let us stand with fear, let us be attentive, that we may offer the holy sacrifice in peace.* For to offer the King of all made man as sacrifice fills us with fear more than the sacrifice of mercy and praise offered by us and from us. This fact immerses us into the incomprehensible abysses of the mystery of God's love, who places Himself at our service by becoming man so as to sacrifice Himself for us. He is the "mysterium tremendum," the mystery that makes us tremble, but not a "mysterium tremendum" that makes us flee from it, or which can destroy through its blind impersonality, but one that on the one hand makes us marvel at, and on the other hand fills us with gratitude and endless love through the personal love which it shows us. It awakens in us not the fear of disappearing by approaching it, but the fear of the child to look at the immense pain mixed with love in a mother's eyes, who dies by throwing herself in front of a car to save him, her child, from death. It awakens our fear in us when we acknowledge our unworthiness as we approach this mystery, but it does not stop us from approaching it.

St. John Chrysostom shows the principal reference of the "offering" not to our mercy for fellow human beings, but to Christ's sacrifice, when he reminds us that the angels themselves have this fear at the heavenly Liturgy: "Angels, too, fall down in adoration before their Lord."[303] And this ambiance full of mystery, which is proper to the heavenly Liturgy, also pervades the visible Liturgy. This is why St. John Chrysostom says that the moment of the transformation of the gifts is "filled with holy fear and trembling."[304]

It is with fear that we offer our gifts because in a way we think of our unworthiness and impurity when we approach God with them, since they are offered to be transformed into the very body and blood of God made man. St. Cyril of Alexandria says that only through our pure sacrifice can we enter before the Father. But it cannot be pure unless Christ attaches it to His sacrifice. But the thought arises: is it so impure that Christ does not want to attach it to His sacrifice?

By offering Himself for us out of mercy, Christ has reconciled us with the Father. This is why at this time the royal doors are opened, as they were opened at the beginning of the Holy Liturgy at the reading of the Epistle and the Gospel. All these have shown increased outpourings of the divine love, or of the promise of the Kingdom of the Holy Trinity, upon the faithful. The doors are opened so as to proclaim the even more abundant outpouring of the Kingdom, or of the Holy Trinity's eternal love, upon them. They are opened especially to proclaim to the faithful the grace and the love of the Holy Trinity that will be poured out upon them through the common offering of the gifts that will be transformed, through the descent of the Holy Spirit upon them, into the Lord's body and blood.

For when the priest turns toward the faithful and blesses them with the cross—from upon which Christ out of His mercy brought and brings us peace, salvation and all blessing, as the One who sacrificed Himself and remains in a state of sacrifice for us, giving us, too, the power to offer our sacrifice represented by the gifts—says: *The grace of our Lord Jesus Christ, the love of God the Father, and the communion of the Holy Spirit be with all of you.* The royal doors are opened in order to communicate to the faithful concurrently with the grace of our Lord Jesus Christ the love of God the Father, who will make them sons through the partaking of His Son, and the descent of the Holy Spirit upon all together, as power to strengthen the communion among them so that they may jointly offer their gifts or themselves.

Any gift or sacrifice of the faithful is anticipated and facilitated by the gift of God. At this time is shown that the gift announced by the community will be facilitated by God through the grace granted to them and through the fellowship of the Holy Spirit, who in a short time will transform their gifts into Christ's body and blood.

St. Paul summarized the gifts coming to us from God in 2 Corinthians 13:13. This is why the priest repeats them exactly. The Holy Trinity is present in the entire Liturgy, as structure and supreme source of love that is at the basis of the Son of God's incarnation, of His sacrifice and resurrection for our reconciliation with the Father, for our salvation, adoption and resurrection. When one speaks about Christ, when one actualizes His saving actions, He is seen as one of the Trinity. Everything that He did in the past and is actualized in the Liturgy has its foundation and explanation in the Holy Trinity, in the fact that He is one of the loving Trinity. Making the sign of Christ's cross means praising the Trinity. The entire Liturgy is filled with the Trinity, as irradiating source of Its love and mercy, therefore of Its saving action. This is why the entire Liturgy is filled with the Trinity commemorated and called upon while making the sign of the cross.

The Holy Trinity is praised in all of the priest's exclamations, in the hymn "Holy God," in the Cherubic hymn; it is the Holy Trinity that the priest addresses in his silent prayers, It is confessed by the liturgical community before reciting the Creed and, largely, in the Creed itself.

But only at this time, after the Creed, does the priest proclaim to the faithful the outpouring of the Trinity's gifts upon them. Before this, the dominion, glory and goodness of the Trinity were praised, or the Father was praised as without beginning and the good and life-creating Spirit, or Christ who was incarnate, crucified and risen for us. Now it is wished upon the liturgical community to have the love of the Father, the grace of Christ and the communion of the Holy Spirit, which also means the wish of the three Persons that these gifts may be offered to the faithful.

The Father is the supreme source of love. This is why He is called Father, having from eternity a Unique Son whom He loves and who, being the fruit and the eternal destination of the Father's love, naturally responds to Him with His love, which in fact has its source in the Father. Here the faithful are told that the Father pours out His love toward them as well. He wanted His Son to become man and to take upon Himself the human face so that in Him the Father may love us as well as He loves His Son, that is to also make us His children, Himself becoming our Father through the grace of Christ.

But this means that the Father's love is poured out upon us because we clothe ourselves with the grace bestowed upon us from the Son's body, who makes us like Him if we, too, endeavor for that. Only through the incarnate Son has grace been made possible for us. St. Cyril of Alexandria says: "Christ is in the Lord's presence, namely in the Father's eyes. For when He became like us, He entered the Holy of Holies through the highest and most perfect tabernacle, namely in heaven, so that He may 'appear in the presence of God for us' (Heb 9:24). For He presents Himself and us within Him before the Father, since we fell from before His face and eyes on account of Adam's disobedience and of the sin that dominated everywhere. Thus, in Christ we have obtained the access and the courage to enter the Holy of Holies, as the wise Paul told us (Eph 2:18). For as we arose and sat on the highest places in Christ, in the same manner within Him we reached the presence of the Father."[305] "And after Emmanuel has risen from the dead, the new fruit of humanity in incorruptibility, He ascended into heaven so as to appear 'in the presence of God for us' (Heb 9:24), not presenting Himself in His sight, because He is forever together with Him and as God is never without the Father, but rather presenting us within Himself in the Father's sight, as we were outside of His face and under His wrath on account of Adam's disobedience and of the sin that forcefully dominated over us. Thus, in Christ we gain the possibility of coming into the presence of God. For as of now He makes us worthy of His sight as the ones who are sanctified."[306]

But the Father's love is poured out upon us through the grace of Christ so as to make us one in love. In Christ the Holy Spirit unites us. St. Paul tells us this when he says: "For in Him we have access in the same Spirit" (Heb 2:18). This shows us how important in the thought of St. Paul is our union in the Holy Trinity. And only if we all have in common the same Spirit of Christ can we be one in the Trinity through Christ.

For the Holy Spirit, being truly holy and having the power to sanctify us, does not allow Himself to be partaken of more by one than another, but has the power to purify everyone from the egoism that separates and divides. He becomes in everyone that partakes of Him an individual "I" but also a common "I," or better said as the one who makes us consider ourselves as a perfect unitary "we," although each of us feels his own "I" in this "we," but as an "I" fully convergent and equal with that of the others, sustained and strengthened by others, all at once increasing and strengthening that of the others, thus each one of us being an "I" of all. One's own "I" is not annulled by that of the others, but elevated to the capacity to be united with the "I" of the Spirit, therefore united with the "I's" of others in this unique "I" of the Spirit. This has also the meaning of a sacrifice of ours offered to God the Father together with Christ, a sacrifice that is not separated from our repentance for our previous egoism.[307] "Thus He was pierced for our sins, but we were also buried together with Him, suffering death, not the bodily one, but destroying the bodily members on earth, no longer living for the world, but rather for Christ and, through Him, for the Father."[308]

The faithful will attain this unity in Christ and through Him in the Trinity through His Spirit by partaking of Christ's body and blood full of His Spirit. The proclamation by the priest of the Trinity's dwelling in the faithful, through the words pronounced now, opens their sight toward the approaching Holy Communion.

The community responds to the priest with their desire for him to also be with the Holy Trinity: *And with your spirit.* It is not only the priest who prays for the community, but the community also prays for him, although he has the initiative by specifying the content of things asked for. He directs the unitary spiritual movement of the liturgical community, not standing outside of it, but united spiritually with it and also being moved by it.

The priest then invites the faithful to lift up their hearts together with him: *Let us lift up our hearts.* Let us lift them up so as to offer our gifts for the mystery of their transformation into the Lord's body and blood of which we will partake. And we lift them up toward the heights of the love of the Holy Trinity who offers us the sacrificed Son for communion. Each one preserves his heart unconfused with that of the others, although united with theirs in the same upward movement. The unity and the non-mixing are expressed paradoxically. Shortly thereafter the priest will say: *And grant us that with one mouth and one heart we may glorify,* etc.

The Trinity descends to those who elevate themselves toward It. The movement of convergence and encounter is made on both sides. The Trinity offers Itself to those who offer themselves to It, or who open themselves up to It by elevating themselves. The Trinity descends toward those who have elevated themselves toward It with "the sacrifice of praise," beseeching It to receive that sacrifice. But when the faithful feel Its descent they elevate themselves even more toward It so that It may approach the act of the transformation of the gifts into the Lord's body and blood which will be given to them for communion. It is an unending dialogue of approaching steps, of those who will never end the path of union. It is unending, but it culminates in the partaking of the Lord that will continue eternally at increasingly higher levels.

St. Cyril of Jerusalem says: "After this the Priest cries aloud, 'Lift up your hearts.' For truly ought we in that most awful hour to have our heart on high with God, and not below, thinking of earth and earthly things. In effect therefore the Priest bids all in that hour to dismiss all cares of this life, or household anxieties, and to have their heart in heaven with the merciful God. Then ye answer, 'We lift them up unto the Lord:' assenting to it, by your avowal. But let no one come here, who could say with his mouth, 'We lift up our hearts unto the Lord,' but in his thoughts have his mind concerned with the cares of this life. At all times, rather, God should be in our memory; but if this is impossible by reason of human infirmity, in that hour above all this should be our earnest endeavour."[309]

The community responds: *We lift them up unto the Lord*. This "up" to which the priest invited them is personal, not an idea, it is not an impersonal value. Ideas and values do not float within themselves, like clouds in the air. They are experienced and incorporated by persons. Better said, they are forms of spiritual movement of one person toward another, thus also the states of relation and superior quality which they have thereby attained. *We lift them up unto the Lord* means that we have our hearts directed toward the Lord, we have our love directed toward God in Trinity. Our hearts are offered to the Trinity in which love is so perfect that the Trinity could be called "Lord" or "God" in the singular.

That "up" is signified by the cross which the priest raises at the same time with the invitation: *Let us lift up our hearts*. It is the height of Him who lowered Himself all the way to enduring the cross out of love for us and who will again descend to us as sacrifice under the form of bread and wine. We should ascend on the vertical line of the cross and of humility, on the vertical line of renouncing our egoism which under the appearance of ascension lowers us, while the cross exalts us even if it seems to lower us. Only in this way can we benefit from His descent to us as sacrifice in Holy Communion. While ascending we see even more the greatness of the loving and saving acts of the Trinity which descends to us all the way to our partaking of the incarnate Son in the Eucharist. The lifting up of our hearts must also be done in humility. By seeing the height through God's descent to us we cannot but thank Him. This is why the priest continues by saying: *Let us give thanks to the Lord*, while he turns toward the icon of the Savior on the right side of the royal doors and crosses himself. It is to Him, first of all, that thanksgiving is due, because He descended to us, or rather He was all-exalted on account of the cross endured for us. But the Trinity is transparent through Him. In Him the entire Trinity descended to us, has worked and is working for us. Our thanksgiving consists in the worship we offer through Christ to the Trinity, making—as we do every time we commemorate the Trinity—the sign of the cross by which one of the Trinity, together with the cooperation of the other two, has saved us and lifts us continuously toward It through the cross and through humility. When you thank someone for his sacrifice for you, you bow before him. You offer thanksgiving to the giver and bow before him, especially when the giving goes all the way to sacrificing his life. This is how one shows appreciation to the offerer and to the gift itself.

In the instruction of the priest: *Let us give thanks to the Lord*, he reminds the people about the "thanksgiving" by which the Lord Christ transformed at the Mystical Supper the bread and wine into His body and blood, thus he prepares them for the same act that will now take place and associates himself with that thanksgiving of the Lord Christ. In fact, the priest has first used the word "thanksgiving" at the beginning of the first prayer for the faithful when he announced for the first time the sacrifice he was about to offer.

But the faithful do not consider themselves worthy to do the same thing as Christ, so they let the priest offer this "thanksgiving." They are content to just offer worship to the Holy Trinity, whose love has made possible the Holy Eucharist at the Mystical Supper and will also do the same now: *It is meet and right to worship the Father, and the Son, and the Holy Spirit: the Trinity, One in essence, and undivided.*

b. The Two Parts of the Anamnesis

Pavel Florensky made the remark that any prayer of supplication has four parts: a) an address to God; b) mentioning past acts of God as basis for the things asked for; c) the supplication itself; d) praise to God.

Thus at this time, before petitioning through epiklesis (calling upon the Holy Spirit) the transformation of the gifts, the priest recalls what God has done before. This is the anamnesis, which in this case has two parts. They will end with: *Take, eat...* and *Drink of this...* Then follows the presentation or the raising of the gifts of bread and wine and then the calling upon the Holy Spirit for their transformation, or the epiklesis.

The liturgists use to call the entire prayer from the first part of the anamnesis until the end of epiklesis, anaphora. But in a strict sense, the anaphora begins only with the words: *Thine own of Thine own, we offer unto Thee, in behalf of all and for all* and ends with the words: *Furthermore we offer unto Thee this rational worship* [sacrifice]. The supplication or the epiklesis begins with the following words: *And we ask and pray . . . send down Thine Holy Spirit...*

Here is the content of the two parts of the anamnesis:

In the first part, which begins with the words: *It is meet and right to hymn Thee,* the priest shows in the form of praise (to hymn) that, even though God is above all our words and thoughts, out of love for us He has, by dispensation, brought us out of non-existence into existence, and when we fell He raised us up again and did no longer abandon us, but He has brought us up to heaven through His Son and through the Holy Spirit, and has endowed us with the Kingdom which is to come. *For all these things we give thanks to Thee, and to Thy Only-begotten Son, and to Thy Holy Spirit.* Not only for these, but also *for all things of which we know and of which we do not know, whether manifest or unseen.* In this part of the prayer the priest declares that the thanksgiving offered to God is as greater as greater is the height from which He descended and remains in that state with us. There is no connection of essence with us that would have indebted God to do all those things for us. In describing this glory of God the Father, which can be done schematically, glory which He has in common with the Son and the Holy Spirit, the prayer finds the occasion to insist on His apophatic character, boundless and incomprehensible by thought. The positive description of God's glory is mixed with the evidence of the impossibility of describing it, or is rather a description of the impossibility of describing it. He is not only the One about whom something or something more cannot be thought of (Anselm of Canterbury), but also the One who surpasses any thought and understanding.[310] Every thought, understanding and word stop at His feet. But our thought wishes to rise up to an existence that it can no longer understand. It is forced from within to think of the existence of the reality beyond its comprehension. Only that reality can fulfill existence. There must exist something that exceeds our thought and our power of comprehending. Without that something, nothing can exist. There must exist something beyond us and all our things, therefore beyond our own thinking. What we can comprehend is limited, or we set limits by the very need to comprehend; thus what we can comprehend is more restricted than our thinking or our spirit. We feel and experience this. But who created our soul? Because we realize that it did not come into existence by itself. There must, therefore, be a thinking that has thought us through and is thinking us through and of which we can think; a thinking that has programmed us and created us in conformity with this program, just as everything we do in a rational way must be programmed by us. Just as only through our quality as thinking created beings can we somewhat comprehend spiritually everything that can be comprehended, so only a thinking being, which we cannot comprehend, can comprehend us, too.

So the fact that we cannot comprehend that being does not mean that we have no relationship with it. Our own conscience feels this relationship. "Out of the depths I have cried to You, O Lord" (Ps 129:1). For "the heart is deep" (Ps 43:7). He who thought us and thinks us, created us and sustains us in conformity with His thinking, has planted in us the consciousness of our dependence on Him. Our depth is connected with His infinite depth and through Him we feel the presence of His depth. Here we find the first feature of our quality as image of God.

We know about this infinite, thinking and creating depth as about what comprehends us, not about what we can comprehend. In a certain way, we cannot comprehend ourselves, either. But we know that our incomprehensibility hangs on an infinitely deeper incomprehensibility than our own incomprehensibility. Still, He comprehends us as we cannot comprehend ourselves. For someone must be able to comprehend us. Otherwise we could not have been brought into existence. Our very own existence would have no explanation: "For the Spirit searches all things" (1 Cor 2:10).

In the accent placed on the fact of God's incomprehensibility, but as an experienced fact, not simply thought out, lies the experienced apophaticism of the Holy Fathers, in contrast with the rational negative theology of Western scholasticism that stops at the intellectual negations of the understood affirmative attributes of things and stressed to the maximum.

I feel enveloped by His comprehension, not as an object, but as a subject by a supreme Subject. I feel enveloped by a Subject endowed with will and conscience, but as one who am also preserved as a subject endowed with will and conscience. I have His conscience in the fact of my being comprehended by Him. I feel enveloped by a Subject who did not only wish to think me through, but also to bring me from nonexistence into existence and wants to maintain me in intimate communion with Him by granting or communicating to me everything that He has. Therefore, I feel enveloped by a Subject full of love toward me or toward all of us. But this love is as much less understood by me as it belongs to a Subject who has no need of me, is infinitely higher than me and does not depend on me to exist, as I depend on Him. I do know of Him not only through a cold apophaticism of thought, but I experience Him as an apophatic reality whose loving warmth I feel enveloping me. I feel Him as much more apophatic as I know that He descended to me out of love. Lo, how the apophatic does not mean to know nothing about God, but to have the experience of some of His acts that make the glory even less understood, and we can express these two things through our thoughts.

If I cannot exist by myself, it is only from Him that I can have my very own existence. But His capacity to grant me existence itself, or to bring me into existence out of nothing, makes Him even less comprehended in His power and places into an even bolder relief His love toward me that cannot be comprehended. He was able to grant us existence itself because He has an existence that is not presupposed to have been brought into existence out of nothing by someone else. For in this case He would have been forced by someone else to also bring me into existence, so in my bringing into existence there would be no complete love manifested. I would not be the product of a love unmixed with necessity, therefore with powerlessness, neither would I be called to a response full of thanksgiving, through a similarly unforced love. He is by Himself existent and similarly forever undiminished or not grown into existence, not owing to other superior powers, "eternally existing and being the same." It is such a perfect existence that it has its origin from no one else and does not require to be sustained by anyone else. It is the existence *par excellence*, which has no power above It, thus doing everything out of love and without any constraint, while we have our existence from Him and through Him, but not out of a necessity to which It might be subjected, but out of pure love and as such we are created with the quality as being able to also respond with a love not subjected to necessity.

But God is an apophatic (incomprehensible) Subject precisely because He cannot be explained through certain laws that can be defined. He is an apophatic Subject to whom, since He created us out of pure love, we feel indebted to thank Him also with love for our very existence, with everything connected to it, namely also for the fact that we must think of Him as the One who cannot be comprehended with the thought. He is an apophatic Subject to whom we must sing, whom we must worship and praise precisely because of His descent from such an incomprehensible height.

Moreover, we have to thank Him also for the fact that we are able to thank Him and to praise Him, that we are aware of the unfathomable gifts He has given us, and for the fact that we can give material form to our gratitude in our gifts which have their ultimate origin also from Him. We thank Him not only for the fact that we have these gifts from Him, but also for the fact that through them we are able to approach Him, that He is willing to accept them from us, thereby showing the value He accords us.

But the greatest gift we can offer Him and which is also from Him is the sacrifice of His incarnate Son. He took upon Himself our body and blood so as to offer them in our name to His Father and thus to sanctify us, too, who unite ourselves with Him in the sacrifice He offers, also offering us as sacrifice together with Him, both through His act and through our act. The special value we enjoy from Him is that He did not establish for the sacrifice of His incarnate Son to be offered by angels, but by us. Because He wanted His Son to unite us with Him, not only according to the spirit, but also according to the body in order to sanctify not only the created spirits, but also the created beings bearing bodies and through them the entire material world.

The entire anamnesis of God's works for us is united with thanksgiving, especially the anamnesis of Christ's sacrifice. But also the thanksgiving we offer Him through the sacrifice of His body, and of our bodies that will be united with His sacrificed body, makes possible the Mystery of the Eucharist, the mystery of our union with the Father through the sacrifice of His Son's body united with our bodies thus raised in this way to the state of sacrifice. This is why this sacrifice of ours is called "Eucharist," namely thanksgiving, and this thanksgiving or Eucharist is one and the same with our highest sacrifice, with the sacrifice of His body taken from us and offered by ourselves through the priest, by which His Son shows that He wants it to be our sacrifice as well. *We thank Thee also for this Liturgy which Thou art pleased to accept from our hands, although before Thee are standing thousands of archangels and tens of thousands of angels, the many-eyed cherubim and the six-winged seraphim who in flying soar high.*

But we offer thanksgiving to the Father not only because, being unutterably high, He is willing to accept us to offer on our behalf His Son as sacrifice, but also because we are made worthy to be united with His Son: "We are nothing and less than nothing, and He who is all and more than all draws near, and becomes permanently one with us: one soul, one body. He gives His soul and body, the whole of His divinity and humanity to us."[311]

We are all the more overwhelmed by God's glory as the moment in which He will unite Himself with us is so much closer.

This beginning prayer of the anaphora from the Liturgy of St. John Chrysostom is an abridged version of the more extended prayer from the Liturgy of St. Basil the Great, which seems to be his own.[312]

In this prayer one insists upon the Son's feature as coessential with the Father and upon the role of the Holy Spirit in the sanctification and strengthening of creation. It comprises a true trinitarian theology in its orientation toward creation, as St. Basil the Great developed it. We must know before we partake of Christ's body and blood, into which the gifts of bread and wine have been transformed, who are the Father, the Son and the Holy Spirit, or better said that each of them is true God. If the Son was not God "He would not have led us up to heaven."[313] The Son Himself, who is not only of one essence with the Father but also the first and unique Person born of the Father, would not have presented us in Himself as unconfound persons to the One who is the supreme origin of persons. The Son is "the living Word," the rational Word, "Wisdom before all ages," Who stands at the beginning of ages imprinting on them an intelligent order, not produced by them, "Life, sanctification, power, the true light" that does not lead us astray, but enlightens all and sustains life in them, preparing them for eternal life. He is apophatic or unutterable, not darkness, but the bosom of all light, and thus of all conscience. Through Him "the Spirit of truth has been revealed," the Spirit who makes known within us the truth of all things and of God Himself, the source of truth or of the true reality, "the gift of adoption, the promise of future inheritance, the beginning of eternal blessings, the life-giving power, the source of sanctification," "by which all rational and intelligible creation being strengthened" can serve and raise hymns of glory to God together with angels who are also rational and intelligible beings.

God is apophatic (unutterable), but He enters into relationship with us through His Son, who takes upon Himself our body and sacrifices Himself for us, and through His Spirit He becomes known to us and enlightens us within, sanctifies us, strengthens us for the good and fills us with the life and the feeling of the Son for the Father. The more He descends, the greater He is; and the more He descends, the harder He is for us to comprehend, although we have a life-giving experience of His presence. His apophaticism fills us, too, so much so that we become incomprehensible ourselves, revealing this incomprehensibility of ours to the extent to which we are increasingly filled with Him, we experience Him more and, on the other hand, we become more aware of ourselves and of the mystery of our being. Having been created as miracles, when the miracle of our being has been covered up or become banal, it is the Holy Spirit who enlightens and deepens it again in the infinity of divine light. Our depth is unlocked and enlightened again by the divine depth penetrating it, infinitely extending at the same time its mystery.

The priest concludes the first part of the anaphora, after he speaks at the end about angels who praise God's glory, specifying with a loud voice what their praise consists of: *Singing the triumphant hymn, shouting aloud, crying out and proclaiming*.

While he is saying these words, the priest takes the star from the paten, makes with it the sign of the cross over the gifts, kisses it and places it on the top part of the Holy Antimension. The incarnate and sacrificed Son of God is now prefigured in the bread even more fully, thus as the One worthy of all praise. As the act of transformation approaches, or the act of the Son of God's self-offering as sacrifice to the Father so as to offer Himself in this state to those who participate at the Holy Liturgy, the cosmos no longer covers the glory or the great humility in which the slain Lamb is in heaven. He comes directly close to us. The distance between the Agnetz on the visible altar and the Lamb on the heavenly altar is eliminated. If the awed angels seeing this shout aloud their praise, the priest cannot continue to pray softly, but says with a loud voice: *Singing the triumphant hymn, shouting aloud, crying out and proclaiming*.

Signifying the angels and joining them, the faithful continue these words by singing the thrice-holy hymn of the Seraphim: *Holy, holy, holy is the Lord Sabbaoth! Heaven and earth are full of Thy glory*. The recitation of the word holy three times refers to the Holy Trinity as well, but it also means the endless hymn, proper to God's infinite holiness, an infinity sung by the angels "with unceasing voices" (Liturgy of St. Basil). As the angels "soar high in flying" while singing this hymn, namely they rise increasingly higher in their knowledge, awed contemplation of God and fervent enthusiasm (Dionysius the Areopagite, *The Angelic Hierarchy*), so do the faithful. Perhaps the ascending movement of angels, with their bodiless spirits, has an even richer meaning. Our soul is more fixed and weighed down in its movement. In the pure spirit of angels is the light joy, unrestricted by anything belonging to the body, and their enthusiasm is lived as a fluidity weighed down by nothing.

The faithful no longer say *of His glory* but *of Thy glory*, because in Christ God has entered into a direct dialogue with human beings, assuming their nature. The Son of God who came close to them through incarnation is still full of the same divine glory. Furthermore, God reveals Himself to us in an even more ineffable way in His incarnation, given that in it His love manifested toward human persons is even more incomprehensible and at the same time more overwhelming, being activated from a greater approach toward them. This height has been shown all the more overwhelming in its greatness the more humble it became. This is why the faithful continue the angelic hymn with words that pay attention to the Son of God's incarnation, praising the One who comes in the name of the Lord. Christ who enters Jerusalem and also comes in the Eucharist, both times in deep humility, is one and the same with the God praised by the Seraphim. God from on high comes now like the King who establishes all the more complete dominion as He now comes in a state of ineffable humility and of perfect sacrifice into the souls that receive Him, and this is why they receive Him as their King (Mt 21:9–10; Ps 117:26). Christ is "God who has revealed Himself to us."

This hymn is called "the triumphant hymn" because in it one praises the Son of God's victory through sacrifice over the devil and accepting those who were liberated from under its domination. This is the greatest victory. During the singing of this hymn, the deacon standing at the right side slowly moves the aer over the holy gifts, symbolizing the movement full of deep veneration of the Seraphim's wings around the King on high who stands as a slain Lamb and to Whom the faithful offer their hymn, completing the one in the Old Testament together with the praise of His saving activity: "Then I looked, and I heard the voice of many angels around the throne, the living creatures, and the elders; and the number of them was ten thousand times ten thousand, and thousands of thousands, saying with a loud voice: 'Worthy is the Lamb who was slain to receive power and riches and wisdom, and strength and honor and glory and blessing!' And every creature which is in heaven and on the earth and under the earth and such as are in the sea, and all that are in them, I heard saying: 'Blessing and honor and glory and power be to Him who sits on the throne, and to the Lamb, forever and ever'" (Rev 5:11–13).

In the singing of those in church resounds the praise of the entire visible creation joined to the praise of the invisible creation. Everyone and all things praise the sacrificed Lamb as the true King who rules over us all the more as He is the incarnation of meekness and of the spirit of sacrifice. All things move or stand in awe before Him, just as all danced before King Solomon.

In a way even in the singing of the inanimate creation there is a sense of the singing of the billions of beings, visible and invisible. The singing of all is strengthened by the joint singing of all. All grow together in knowledge and in enthusiasm. The visible beings are not simple objects manipulated by the invisible ones from which they gain nothing except a dexterity in their manifestation, but the former actively and consciously communicate to the latter through love their own mode of comprehension and of joy. The warmth everyone puts into their voice, joined to that of those around them, is due to sensing the praise of the invisible spirits whose presence is efficient. How the angels who have no physical voice sing is difficult to understand, but the spirits can manifest their praise and love in a different way, and they can also be sensed in a different way.

In church all are in all and in all things because the King of all is here. The singing in church comprises inaudibly in its spiritual waves all and all things. This is why Christ's sacrifice should be offered only in church and only in church are the sacrifices of all united with it, being filled with a maximum intensity. "For at all times and without ceasing, from the beginning until the end, in Christ we spread the sweet fragrance through all virtue in the holy tabernacle, that is in the church. Because the smoke that rises from the Lamb in the morning and evening is again an image of the one who rises on our account and in our favor toward the Father with a sweet-smelling fragrance, and brings together with Him the life of those who believed in Him."[314] We should also mention that the words: *Singing the triumphant hymn, shouting aloud, crying out and proclaiming* are not a fourfold pleonasm. Each one means something on its own: the melody is united with the rising of the mind and with expressing the meaning of what is sung. The faithful conclude with the words: *Hosanna in the highest. Blessed is He who comes in the name of the Lord.*

The Lord comes from above so as to offer Himself to us with His body and blood that have passed through death and are triumphant over death. This is the fulfillment of what was foreseen at the Lord's entrance into Jerusalem. He comes as a conqueror of death, in His humanity, by suffering death so that He may conquer it in us as well. This is why the angels sing a triumphant hymn and the faithful join them. This conquest of death through the cross gave Christ the possibility of now offering Himself to us toward resurrection in the form of bread and wine that will be transformed. This is why the priest removes the star from the paten where the Agnetz is, showing it uncovered after he has made with it the sign of the cross over the paten. This has been to some extent the addressing part of the anaphora.

About the thrice holy hymn of the Seraphim who eternally encircle the Trinity, St. John Chrysostom says: "Think by whose side you are standing . . . . It is with the Cherubim. Think of those with whom you are joining to form the choir. . . . Let him transfer entirely to heaven and let him stand next to the very throne of glory and raise his all holy hymn to the God of glory and majesty."[315] The same idea is found at St. Cyril of Jerusalem: "We make mention also of the Seraphim, whom Esaias in the Holy Spirit saw standing around the throne of God . . . crying *Holy, Holy, Holy, is the Lord of Sabaoth*. For the reason of our reciting this confession of God, delivered down to us from the Seraphim, is this, that so we may be partakers with the hosts of the world above in the Hymn of praise."[316] Theodore of Mopsuestia shows the connection between the thrice holy hymn and the feeling of fear and respect of the community, saying: "We use the fearful words of the invisible powers in order to show the great mercy that has been abundantly poured out upon us. Fear fills our conscience throughout the course of the Liturgy, both before we cry 'Holy" and after that."[317]

By declaring that we lift up our hearts to the Lord and by praising Him through the thrice holy hymn we are near the sacrifice. "We are no longer on earth, but in a certain way we are transferred to heaven."[318] But we do not forget that the Triune God to whom we have lifted ourselves fills the entire heaven and earth with His glory and that the Son of God came down from on high to us through the incarnation and He continues to come to us through His sacrifice. The heaven is connected with the earth through the Son of God's sacrifice for us, or continuously renews this connection with us through His sacrifice. We are not in a heaven separated from the earth. The heavenly Liturgy is extended in the Church.

At this time the priest reads silently the second prayer, or the second part of the anamnesis, addressing the Father. He tells Him softly that, together with the angels, he also, like those in the church, praise with their whole being His holiness, that of His Son and of the Holy Spirit. The reason is that it is no longer a glory far away from us, but a love manifested in the saving economy of His Son, especially in His sacrifice. Thus he prepares the transition to the calling upon the Holy Spirit, while the community unites the hymn of the Seraphim in the Old Testament with that of the angels who praise the slain Lamb: "For You have loved Your world so much, that You gave Your only-begotten Son, that all who believe in Him should not perish, but have eternal life." It is His love that lies at the foundation of existence, not the processes of nature. It gives out of its infinity always new gifts, new, conscious and eternal life. Love implies the impenetrable depth of the free Person, while the processes of nature make everything blindly, monotonously and flatly. The nature becomes hardened within rigid laws only when the Spirit fades. But the whole depth of love culminates in sacrifice. God's love opens the doors of the Kingdom of heaven for the conscious creatures. Love does not let them disappear in the avalanche of nature's processes, but raises them together with a nature made flexible, into the bosom of the immortal One above nature. Technology is only a sign of nature's flexibility. But since it does not actualize the flexibility of nature through the spirit, it leaves the human person subjected to a great extent to its processes.

Out of love the only-begotten Son, not made—thus the One who does not die, just as the Father does not die, and He is only-begotten, not one made out of many that are made and unmade—fills with His life, not subjected to making and unmaking, all those who believe in Him and are united with Him. And He gives us this life by the fact that, after He has fulfilled everything concerning us, on the night when He gave Himself up for the life of the world, but not to remain in death because He was also God, He established the Eucharist in which He gives us His body and blood that are filled with the immortality of divinity, in the form of bread and wine. Love leads Him all the way to death, but it does not keep in death the One who accepted death because of it. Love is stronger than death and conquers it forever. And the evidence and power of this love that went all the way to death the Son left us in the moment prior to death in the Eucharist, giving us the proof of victory that would be obtained over death. He has not terminated His relationship with us at the time of His death accepted out of love for us, but continues to maintain it by communicating Himself to us as the One who bears life in Himself as a consequence of this death out of love and of this sacrifice.

Jesus goes all the way to death out of love, showing that He does not stop at some point, but He remains unceasingly in His love, thus instituting in the sacrifice out of love the mystery of His continuing offering as the One sacrificed, that is concurrently as the One eternally alive through His sacrifice. And as evidence that He in fact will remain like that, "taking the bread with His holy, pure and blameless hands, giving thanks and blessing, sanctifying and breaking it" He gave it as His body to His disciples, as guarantee that He will not remain in death, that He will not be overcome by death, but will triumph over His death through His love for those whom He wants to be immortal, passing over to eternal life so as to pass them over as well.

By giving thanks He shows that the bread, but also the body into which it will be transformed, He has from the Father; consequently, He also blesses it in this way, but especially through the act of sanctifying He returns it to the Father after He has transformed it into His own body. Then through the breaking, showing that in His body in the form of bread are permanently imprinted the signs of His sacrifice, makes of the offering of the bread transformed into the body an even more complete offering. In general, he who blesses triggers the act of God's passing over to the one who is blessed, or in what he blesses. Here He who blesses is God and it is He who decides to place Himself in the form of the bread.

Even before death, Christ bears in Himself the intense feeling of His sacrifice for us. Through the intense feeling of the sacrifice and through the Spirit in Him, He transfigures His body profoundly and through it the ontological foundation of the bread, leaving it as bread only on the surface for its organic connection with the entire cosmos before the end. But the profound transfiguration of the bread anticipates the future age when the bodies spiritualized by Christ's body will place their seal on all spiritualized things, and they will be seen through all things as bodies united with Christ as source of the power of resurrection and transfiguration of all. At that time men will no longer feed themselves from the inanimate things of the cosmos, but through all things will be given them the divine nourishment of Christ's body. Their inner-principles will be fully gathered in the cognizant reason of man, or of men in communion, and through all of them the incarnate Logos will nourish the cognizant reason.

The Eucharist has in it an eschatological and universal opening. And Christ's transfiguring power comes from His sacrifice. He who sacrifices Himself out of love overwhelms everything through love. His body immerses itself within the inaccessible depth of His divinity out of which there pours through Him the transfiguring love and life over all. The greatest love and offering of life is experienced as coming from the permanent state of sacrifice of the Son of God's body. It is a continuous overflowing of life over all who are loved when they want to receive this life. The permanent state of sacrifice is a permanent state of the life of resurrection poured out by Christ into human beings, never-ending, overflowing and always new by its infinite depth. Through it Christ's humanity is deepened in God for eternity by His eternal self-renunciation. In the sacrifice of love, in the permanent state of sacrifice out of love, Christ lives consciously with His body in the ocean of love and infinite life. The loving God, become an inner ocean of the One who sacrificed Himself as man, remaining in a permanent state of sacrifice, floods with His life, transfigures and gives eternal life to all who want to receive it, renewing, transfiguring and uniting fully with Him the cosmos connected to Him as well.

In the Holy Liturgy of St. Basil the Great the second part of the anamnesis is more developed. Especially the teaching on the nature of man created by God is developed, his fall and the perpetual care of God in order to prepare him for a new and superior ascent to Him through all the acts of Christ's economy. It is a detailed exposition of faith, such as is not in the previous prayers of the priest and not even in the Symbol of faith. We realize that by reading it with a loud voice in olden times, the conscience of those present about matters of faith was sustained.

Still, this exposition, too, has a doxological form, one of praise of God's acts, of glorifying Him. In these acts of praising and glorifying God, there are no simple declarations of human sentiments and beliefs.

But let us ponder upon a few of the themes from the content of the second part of St. Basil the Great's anamnesis. In it one does not only say that God brought us from non-existence into existence, as in St. John Chrysostom's anamnesis, but one also shows that He created man by taking up dust and honoring him with His image, then He promised him life without death "through the keeping of the commandments" and the inheritance of eternal blessings. Then one describes at length God's care for the human person up to the sending of His Son, "Who, being the radiance of Thy glory and the image of Thy Person, and upholding all things by the word of His power. . . . He was God before ages, yet He appeared on earth and lived among men, becoming incarnate of the Holy Virgin; He emptied Himself, taking the form of a servant, being likened to the body of our lowliness (Php 2:7), that He might liken us to the image of His glory. For as by man sin entered into the world, and by sin death, so it pleased Thine Only-begotten Son . . . , Who was born of a woman... to condemn sin in His flesh, so that those who were dead in Adam might be made alive in Thy Christ Himself . . . . He gave Himself as a ransom to death, in which we were held captive, sold under sin. Descending through the Cross into hell—that He might fill all things with Himself—He loosened the pangs of death. He arose on the third day, having made for all flesh a path to the resurrection, since it was not possible for the Author of Life to be a victim of corruption. So He became the first fruits of those who have fallen asleep, the first-born of the dead, that He might be Himself truly the first in all things. Ascending into Heaven, He sat down at the right hand of Thy majesty on high, and He will come to render to every man according to his works."[319]

We have here not only the teaching about God in Trinity, but also an essential teaching about man and a very detailed one about Christ's incarnation and work of salvation. Almost every word of the exposition can be identified in the New Testament.

The prayer concludes with the explicit affirmation that the Lord has instituted the Eucharist so as to leave us the remembrances, certainly operational, of His Passions. For continuing to address the Father, like he does in the entire prayer, the priest says: "And as memorials of His saving Passion, He has left us these things, which we have set forth according to His command. For when He was about to go forth to His voluntary and ever-memorable and Life-creating death—in the night in which He gave Himself up for the life of the world—He took bread into His holy and pure hands, and having shown it to Thee, the God the Father, having given thanks, blessed and hallowed it, and broken it"[320] then he says with a loud voice: *He gave to His Holy disciples and Apostles saying: Take, eat, this is My body which is broken for you for the forgiveness of sins.*

Thus the "recollections" of His saving Passions represent the promise according to which He transforms even now the bread and wine, through whose forms His body sacrificed in the past is given to us. This body that is being given to us sacrificed is a living remembrance, by extension, of His passions on Golgotha. The soldier who bears in his body the wounds he suffered and communicates with us through this body that feels the living memory of the moment in which he suffered these wounds, relives this moment with all his pain, but also with that love for us with which he experienced that moment.

In the anaphora (anamnesis) of St. Basil the Great is specified that "these" which are left as memorials, or as having to be transformed into the prolonged recollection of His Passion, are "set forth before the Father" as was placed the sacrifice on Golgotha before the Father, but now "we set them forth" (I as the priest together with the faithful) before the Father, or Christ placed them and we place them visibly, by which we also engage ourselves in this act. That this offering is directed by Christ in a visible way through us toward the Father, as He did visibly at the Mystical Supper, is mentioned in this prayer even more clearly through the words: "Taking the bread, showing it to Thee, God the Father."

At the time these words were spoken, the transformation of the bread into the Lord's sacrificed body took place at the Mystical Supper. It was still bread, but bread about to be imminently transformed into His body. The showing, the thanksgiving, the blessing were still referring to the bread. The principle "A is not B" loses its validity here. Here the principle "A=B" is valid. The bread offered as gift to God by Christ is His sacrificed body. For He identifies Himself with it. He transfigures and transforms it through His body. For just as our self-sacrifice is not separated from that of Christ, so is the visible form of the bread not separated from His body. The union of the bread, which represents us, with Christ who blesses it is so strong that one can no longer speak of it and of Christ as two distinct things, but to speak of the bread now means to speak of Christ's body found in the form of the bread. St. Cyril of Alexandria says: "The daily offering of gifts (in the Old Testament) signifies the uninterrupted and unending celebration of Christ's sacrifice every day as well as the offering of gifts by those made righteous through faith (in Christ). For there will always be worshipers and the offering of gifts will never cease. And Christ will be offered by us and for us, being mystically sacrificed in the holy tabernacles (churches). He is our primary gift above all things. For He offered Himself as sacrifice to God the Father, not for Himself, but for us who are under the yoke and guilt of sin. According to His likeness we are also sanctified sacrifices, as those who have died to sin, as sin has been destroyed in us and we live for God the life of holiness and piety."[321]

He who loves another so much that he dies offering himself as sacrifice for the other can no longer distinguish himself from the other. I am he, he is I. Sin separates, love identifies but without confusion. For in the fact that one feels identified with the other persists the happy consciousness of being one with the other, therefore not alone.

Through thanksgiving and blessing the bread has been placed by Christ in a strong connection with God the Father, thus it has been filled with the divine Spirit who is also the Spirit irradiating from Christ. The sanctification carries this even further. For sanctification is the same as the sacrifice and as such the transformation is accomplished through it. The sanctification as an act of the Spirit creates the presence of a divine power over what is being sacrificed,[322] a more accentuated presence than the blessing. And because in the bread that Christ holds in His hands the entire Spirit of Christ is poured out, Christ Himself is intimately united with the bread; the transformation has brought then and brings even now not only a presence of power, but has given and gives the very quality of His body to the bread, which through the breaking shows the sacrifice or the accomplished transformation.

Certainly, the transformation of bread and wine into the body and blood of Christ at the Mystical Supper, and on its basis in every Liturgy, is an unfathomable mystery in its comprehension and in the mode of its being accomplished. For mystery is not only God's mode of being, but also every work of His upon creation.

The mystery of the transformation is based on a special connection between body and bread and also on a profound and mystical relation between the divine Word and His animate human body into which the bread is transformed. But it is also based on the fact that the bread is thus the most proper gift that we can offer to God, having concentrated in it our work and especially representing our body or our life on earth. In bread God's gift encounters our gift for Him, especially in the bread we offer to be transformed into Christ's body. Air is only God's gift to us, but not our gift to Him, because we contribute nothing to it. Water is almost the same where it is found plentifully. Only in arid places can it also be our gift offered to God since we offer it to our fellow human beings. Vegetables are also close to being only God's gift. Meat is the same, since we do not labor to produce it but we take it ready made from the animals we slaughter. A certain contribution of ours is shown only in feeding the animals. Apart from bread, only wine requires a special effort on our part. In bread our persistent work is shown.

As we said, bread also has a special relation with our body. It is the nourishment, *par excellence*, of our body, being the essential element for its sustenance.

God has placed bread in a special relation with our body. The inner-principle of bread naturally assimilates into the inner-principle of our body. But since the soul manifests itself through the body, or since within the inner-principle of the soul is implied the inner-principle of the body, in the very reason of earthly existence of the soul, and thus of the human subject, the inner-principle of bread is implied.

But the implication of bread in the human subject exteriorized through the body means in the last instance its implication in the relation between the human subject and the divine Word. The human subject is the image of the divine Logos as subject. But in this image, potentially found in the Logos, bread is potentially implied. Only because the human subject is the image of the divine Logos, can the latter become man and take upon Himself the human body, which needs bread. Thus, in the incarnate Logos is shown the actualization of the essential relation between bread and body.

The incarnate Word can assimilate in Himself the inner-principle of bread, but as inner-principle connected or correlated with the body which He assumed, thus He can absorb it in His body, actualizing this correlation. We do not fully understand now what the quality of the human being, endowed with a body, as the image of the Word means, upon which St. Basil the Great insists in this prayer, an image which the Word re-establishes in Himself through incarnation.

But it is certain that the human person, as the image of the Logos in his normality, must imply a living relation, an intimate communication between the subject of the Word and the human person bearing a body, and through this also a possibility for the Word to assume the body and to speak through it to the human person, to make use of the body as the human person does and vice versa. Therefore, the bread, too, intimately connected with the human body, enters into an actualized relation with the incarnate divine Word as with its primordial Subject. Its inner-principle is fully assimilated within the inner-principle of His body. This fact is realized in Him only by eating, as well as through the Holy Spirit Who causes Christ's body and through it the hypostasis of the Word to assimilate the inner-principle of the bread to the point of absorption, setting the foundation of the mystery (sacrament) of Eucharist. In the body assumed by the Word, or under His cover transparent through the resurrection, is implied the solidarity not only with the bread that became spiritualized, but also with the matter of the cosmos that will be resurrected and transfigured.

With His transfigured body Christ can enter and show Himself through all things, but He still allows them to remain in their present form. He could in some way keep the form of the bread transparent, but He does not do that because He wants to allow for the latitude of faith. But when we will all rise again and the entire matter will become transparent through resurrection, all of us will show ourselves transparent through all, from the power of Christ's omnitransparent divine body. All things will be His body, but also ours since we partake of His body. We will live as subjects mutually interior in Christ and all of us will be one body, Christ's body, without the annulment of our bodies. Nothing will hinder us from full communion.

But the transparency of the body and of matter for subjects is not the result of some physical process, but of an extreme sensibility and delicacy of the subjects. And this delicacy is due to the death of any kind of egoism, to everyone's mutual sacrificing for the other and of all to Christ, from the power of the inexhaustible sacrifice of Christ as man, through His body. Only sacrifice rarefies the bodies through their subjects as spiritual substrata extremely sensitized and makes them transparent. The brightness and the glory of the Kingdom bear the sign of the cross. The cross led to perfection the commitment of conscious created beings among themselves and in Christ, and it remains eternally implied in their delicacy or perfection which makes the commitment possible. The cross or the sacrifice have their foundation in the need experienced by created beings to mutually give of themselves.

The priest concludes the second part of the anamnesis with the words uttered in a loud voice: *Take, eat, this is My body* . . . . and *Drink of this all of you, this is My blood* . . . . These are the words with which Christ offered the bread and the wine transformed into His body and blood to the Apostles. Through these words both the priest and the liturgical community are assured that at the Mystical Supper a transformation did indeed take place and thus Christ's power will accomplish even now this transformation.

The community receives this assurance by responding: *Amen*, "this is so," "we are assured that this happened and this will also happen now."

The Savior assures the disciples that even then His body was broken in the form of bread for the forgiveness of sins; or it was broken at the moment when the bread was being broken. Jesus was living His death before it happened in a visible way. And in His decision to die for others He goes out of Himself into those who open themselves to His love, to the triune, endless love, in the form of bread. "When through love He is voluntarily offered to death in order to save His friends, there comes into the world [into them] a ray of the triple brightness."[323] Love carries with it the one who bears it into those who are loved. For the one who loves and therefore for Christ, the source of supreme love, the dimension of space and the succession of time, then and now, here and there, no longer exist.[324] For He is both before the disciples and in the form of bread since He is beyond space and time. All boundaries of things become transversal.

The Lord's body which the disciples ate and which we eat today is so overwhelmed by the Holy Spirit and so transfigured by the state of sacrifice that its consumption is like a spiritual absorption due to the Spirit in it. Still, the body retains its structure of senses. But by their purity these are spiritualized, producing this effect in our body, too, to the maximum, on a plane we cannot perceive. In Christ who offers Himself, the boundary between the soul and therefore also between the Spirit within it and the body is overwhelmed by Christ's soul and by the Spirit within Him is overcome. Thus, Christ's body becomes an organ bearing the spirit and through it bearing Christ's Spirit, being realized in a unity between His body and spirit as well as the Holy Spirit in Him, a unity also realized in the saints. Commenting on a passage from St. Gregory of Nazianzus about the duality overcome by the saints, St. Maximos the Confessor says: "In saying that the saints 'passed beyond the material dyad on account of the unity perceived in the Trinity,' I take it that Gregory means that they 'passed beyond matter and form, out of which bodies are made,' or that they 'passed through flesh and matter,' as he says, 'and were united with God and mingled with that most pure light,' by which he means that they set aside the soul's relationship to the flesh, and through the flesh to matter—or to speak more generally, in setting aside the natural bond that sensation has with sensible objects, they nobly took hold of desire for the divine alone, 'on account of the unity,' as I said, 'perceived in the Trinity.' Knowing that the soul lies between God and matter, with the potentialities to be united to either—I mean the intellect's potential for union with God, and sense perception's potential to unite with matter—they completely swept aside sense perception along with what is perceived through it, by means of the relevant activity of their disposition, while by means of the intellect alone they ineffably assimilated the soul to God."[325] Perhaps this, too, is another aspect of Christ's death of the body so that by partaking of Him we may also appropriate this death of the body in order to intensify our relationship with God to the maximum. But this death of the body is not manifested in its being devoid of life, but in its being filled with and overwhelmed by the life of the spirit which is filled with the divine Spirit.

Jesus lived this overwhelming state of the body, or of the death of the body, through His Holy Spirit out of love for God the Father and for us even at the Mystical Supper, and with this state of maximum spiritual sense perception He penetrated the bread's inner-principle all the way to its absorption into the inner-principle of His body.

In the Holy Liturgy it is said that Christ placed His body in this state of sacrifice and gave it to His disciples and will give it in the future to all who believe in Him "for the forgiveness of their sins." The words "for the forgiveness of sins" are found only in the Gospel of St. Matthew, but they refer not to His body, but to His blood (Mt 26:28). In the Gospel of St. Mark nothing is specified about the purpose of the disciples' partaking of His body, but only about the blood that is shed for many (Mk 14:22–24). In the Gospel of St. Luke it is said about the partaking of the body that "is given for you; do this in remembrance of Me" (Lk 22:19–20). St. Paul the Apostle writes that the Lord said after the disciples' partaking of the body and the blood: "Do this in remembrance of Me." And St. Paul himself says: "For as often as you eat this bread and drink this cup, you proclaim the Lord's death till He comes" (1 Cor 11:23–26).

In the second part of the anamnesis of St. Basil's Liturgy he does not speak of the Lord's incarnation, crucifixion and resurrection as having as their purpose "the forgiveness of sins," but to bring the knowledge of truth and "the resurrection from the dead" of each body, for through death "He condemned sin in the flesh" (Rom 8:3). Through this one emphasizes more the ontological aspect of salvation brought about by

Christ. By offering to the disciples His body for eating and His blood for drinking, the Lord, in the Gospel of St. Matthew, sets the purpose for partaking of them as "the remission of sins" (Mt 26:27).

So, while in the anaphora of St. Basil we have an ontological interpretation of Christ's work of salvation, in the sense of renewal and resurrection of the human nature first in Him and then in all who adhere to Him, in the Lord's words "Take, eat" there seems to be seen the purpose of His death in obtaining the forgiveness of sins.

In fact these two purposes must be seen in an inner unity. Salvation does not consist only of the forgiveness of sins, but after the elimination of their obstacle between the human being and God, the first is raised to the new and immortal life in God. This is the reason for their interchange. We see this interchange also in the New Testament. The Savior teaches us in the prayer "Our Father" to ask: "And forgive us our trespasses," showing as the condition for this forgiveness the forgiveness of "those who trespass against us" (Mt 6:12, 14–15). He gives this double instruction also in Mk 11:25–26. The Savior Himself forgives sins (Mt 9:2; Mk 2:5, 10; Lk 5:20, 24; 7:48; Mt 12:31; Mk 3:28; Lk 12:10). He assures the sinful woman of God's forgiveness of sins (Lk 7:47–48). The Apostles also write about the forgiveness of sins by God or by Christ (Eph 4:32; Col 3:13; Jam 5:15; 1 Jn 1:9; 2:12).

But in the New Testament the Lord also speaks of the new life given out of love to those who return to God. The Prodigal Son is not only forgiven by his father, but also embraced and clothed in the bright garment and honored with a great feast. Certain virtues are asked from those who believe, which elevate their humanity considerably even now (the Beatitudes). They are asked to be the light of the world, to love others as themselves. They are asked to be perfect as their Father in heaven is. They are asked for acts of mercy (Mt 24). Those who receive the word of God with a pure heart increase it a hundredfold; it brings forth a new life even now (Jn 5:25).

St. Paul the Apostle tells those who receive Christ: "For through Him we both have access by one Spirit to the Father . . . Now, therefore, you are no longer strangers and foreigners, but fellow citizens with the saints and members of the household of God" (Eph 2:18–19). He tells them that they are "a holy temple of God" (Eph 2:21). He wishes for them that Christ would grant them "according to the riches of His glory, to be strengthened with might through His Spirit in the inner man" (Eph 3:16). About himself he says: "I have been crucified with Christ; it is no longer I who lives, but Christ lives in me" (Gal 2:20). Or: "For it is God who commanded light to shine out in darkness, who has shone in our hearts to give the light of the knowledge of the glory of God in the face of Jesus Christ [with whom we are united]. But we have this treasure in earthen vessels, that the excellence of the power may be of God and not of us . . . always carrying about in the body the dying of the Lord Jesus, that the life of Jesus also may be manifested in our body" (2 Cor 4:6–7, 10).

About the forgiveness of sins through Christ's sacrifice, and also about our new life through this sacrifice, St. Cyril of Alexandria also speaks, but in such a way that even in Christ's death for our sins he sees the means by which we also die to them.

St. Cyril speaks about both these aspects in the same sentence when he says: "Thus He was slain for our sins, but we were also buried together with Him, suffering death, not the physical one, but destroying the bodily organs on earth and not living for the world, but rather for Christ and through Him for the Father."[326] He describes the same connection between the two, saying: "He has brought us in Himself into the sight of the Father, especially us who were out of the Father's sight and under His wrath on account of Adam's disobedience and of the sin that was forcefully dominating over us. Therefore, in Christ we gain the possibility of coming before God, because He now deems us worthy of His sight as the ones who are sanctified."[327]

St. Cyril speaks incomparably more about the transforming effect produced in the human person by Christ's saving work. Thus, he says: "Now I think that every believer is a dwelling and a temple of God, having Christ dwelling in Him."[328] Or: "As I said, we approach the Father through the Son, and the Son is the Mediator who unites us through Him [with the Father] and raises us to the heights far above nature."[329]

As can be seen, in contrast to Protestantism, which sees an opposition between the forgiveness of sins and the human person's purification or the new life, and considers that we receive only the first through Christ while we are on earth, the New Testament and the Eastern Holy Fathers see both of these combined.

St. Basil unites both of them in the anaphora of his Liturgy, saying in its second part that Christ was "likened to the body of our lowliness, that He might liken us to the image of His glory," and saying at the end that Christ offers His body and blood to the Apostles "for the forgiveness of sins."

How are these two reconciled? So that we may understand the reconciliation between them, we must see that the one who forgives softens his heart toward the one who is forgiven; better said, his heart softens even before the act of forgiveness, and the one who is forgiven also feels his heart being softened. He feels how a wave of mercy and love comes to him from the one who forgives, which transforms him as well.

Sacrifice is the expression of a person's capacity for tender emotion in relation to another person, and Christ's sacrifice seeks the renewal of our humanity by being stamped by God's love for us that goes all the way to sacrifice. The Son of God imprints Himself in us in His state of sacrifice precisely in order to make us experience His sacrifice for us, or His sense perception capable of sacrifice for us, and so that we, too, may respond with our sacrifice, or with renouncing our pride under the imprint of His love that extends all the way to sacrifice for us.

The heart of him who loves, of him who has mercy toward the one who suffers for the weakness produced by his sins, is burning with another suffering for that one. This means that he wants to sacrifice himself for him. But the one to whom Christ wants to show forgiveness through His sacrifice must open himself up to this forgiveness that goes all the way to sacrifice for him. And this means for him to also renounce his egoism, his pride, through the love that goes all the way to sacrifice, thus also supporting the suffering of the One who sacrificed Himself for his sake. Christ's sacrifice to the Father is, therefore, a sacrifice for us. It is a sacrifice that should move us toward sacrifice. The affection of the Father and of the Son for us, manifested in the Son's sacrifice, is meant to move us, too, to be affectionate. But in order to offer Himself as sacrifice for us, the Son had to become man. And by offering Himself as sacrifice for us He also shows as God His love for us and the love of the One representing us as man before God, which is meant to awaken our love as well. The Holy Scripture presents the union of these two loves in this way: "For God so loved the world that He gave His only begotten Son, that whoever believes in Him should not perish but have everlasting life" (Jn 3:16). Or: "He who did not spare His own Son, but delivered Him up for us all, how shall He not with Him also freely give us all things?" (Rom 8:32). He also gave us the adoption. Or this is the greatest blessing God gave us. But by receiving adoption as the Father's love we as children also love Him. On the other hand, we cannot receive this adoption unless we also die with Christ to our egoistic passions: "And if children, then heirs—heirs of God and joint heirs with Christ [the first man among us who offered Himself as sacrifice], if indeed we suffer with Him, that we may also be glorified together" (Rom 8:17). Only he who loves God up to the death of his egoism, being united with Him, receives His life in himself and thus he is filled with His glory.

It is in this sense that the Son offered Himself as sacrifice for the forgiveness of our sins, as forms of our egoism, in order to make us die to this egoism. He wished to show us God's forgiveness through the sacrifice He offered for us in the body He assumed and to continuously give us communion through this sacrificed body. But He also wished to show God His sacrificial love as man and to make us, too, imbue ourselves with this love for God and for us up to sacrifice, a love which once received predisposes us to this sacrificial feeling of Christ for God in which His love as God for us has also been shown. Christ as man has shown us through His sacrifice for us all of man's self-renunciation so that we, too, may receive power to renounce our pride, to love God up to sacrifice, responding to God's love which offered His Son as sacrifice for us.

If Christ's body received by the Apostles had purified their physical senses and had imprinted upon them the feelings (the sense perceptions) of sacrifice of His soul filled with the Holy Spirit, His blood was poured into their blood with the warmth of His pure love for God, thus giving to their senses and thoughts the orientation toward God, filled with the enthusiasm of the love for Him up to sacrifice and hence the power to penetrate increasingly deeper into the infinity of love of God and for God, experienced through His blood.

But what happened then with the Apostles, it will also happen now with us in this Holy Liturgy when we partake of the Lord's body and blood. By remembering Christ's saving commandment to do this in remembrance of Him, by eating this bread and drinking this blood we will proclaim in our being His very death and resurrection as a living recollection. The Mystical Supper will be celebrated for us, too. By remembering Christ's entire saving work from back then and of its continuation until the end of the world, it will in fact also be celebrated now. For He was alive not only then, but He is also alive now. He is more alive than any human being on earth through the state of resurrection in which He is. The remembrance of that work is one and the same with our opening toward it. Remembering someone who bears in himself all his deeds is like my introduction in his being, and vice versa. All the more does this happen with Christ who from His supra-spatial heaven and all the more intensely present extends His work anywhere He finds an open heart.

However, Christ asks us not only to remember what He did at the Mystical Supper and all His past work, but also "to do" now what He did then in order to give all the efficiency to the remembrance. To remember His deed through our deed. Only in this way what happened then, happens now. Only by showing my willingness to actualize His deed imprinted in me does He also participate in its actualization. When I remember with my being a good deed of my mother, actualizing her dynamism imprinted in me, I show that this dynamism is also sustained in me by her.

"Do this in remembrance of Me." This means that Christ gives us not only the commandment to commemorate what He did at the Mystical Supper, but also the power to do this. This is why we can do this. But we receive this power by calling upon His Holy Spirit for the accomplishment of this deed.

c. The Offering of the Gifts of Bread and Wine (the Anaphora)

But the first thing we need to do is to offer the bread and wine to Christ, as they were offered by the disciples at the Mystical Supper, so that He may transform them into His body and blood in order to return them to us as such. *Thine own of Thine own, we offer to Thee, on behalf of all, and for all.* These are the words of the priest by whom they are offered. And the priest connects this offering to the anamnesis, saying: *Remembering, therefore, . . . the cross, the tomb, the third day resurrection,* etc., but also the commandment to do what He did at the Mystical Supper.

And through this offering we give Him in a concentrated way all that sustains our life, we offer ourselves to Him. Christ's self-offering will come as a response to the gift of our self-offering. We give Him the earthly bread so that He may give Himself to us as heavenly bread in which He has transformed the bread we gave Him. Theodore of Mopsuestia says: "Just as in order to exist in this life we take as nourishment the bread capable of maintaining life in us, because God gave it this power, in the same way we receive immortality by eating the mystical bread, for even if bread does not have in itself such a nature, when it received the Holy Spirit it became capable of bringing to immortality those who eat it."[330]

We give Christ the bread meant to be transformed into our earthly body so that He may return to us the bread transformed into His risen body. "A gift passed on as gift leads up to Paradise."[331] This is the circuit of love. Actually, in the gift of bread and wine we offer and through which we offer ourselves, on the basis of His appeal, there is a reinforcement of our propensity to offer ourselves and the very offering of our being is prefigured, but also His will to offer Himself as man and to offer all creation to the Father. Thus, He, too, offers Himself in these gifts or through the act of our offering. By offering ourselves we also offer Him as well; or He offers Himself through our offering. All things are from Him, not only in their quality as gifts given to us, but also in their quality as gifts which we offer. Our propensity to offer ourselves is the propensity planted in us by Him. When He created us and gave us all things He also placed in us the propensity to offer them and to offer ourselves, just like His will to offer them and to offer Himself together with us.

But we do this not only to fulfill His commandment, but also out of our propensity to offer ourselves together with Him and out of gratitude for what God gave and promised us as well as out of the desire to open ourselves to the ocean of His mercy and love, who offers to us for them and through them His slain body and His outpoured blood. "We do not know what to do. We can find nothing of our own to give Him as an offering of thanks, . . . That is why we take everything that is His own and offer it with gratitude: 'Bringing before Thee Thine own of Thine own, in all and for all.'"[332]

When the deacon, or the priest in his absence, says these words he takes the diskos with his right hand and the chalice with his left hand, lifts them up and makes the sign of the cross with them over the Holy Antimension, for by offering all things, and through them ourselves, to God we thereby leave ourselves behind, that is we accept the cross. And we take the power for this from the power of the One crucified and buried for us, represented by the Holy Antimension.

The role in this offering is divided between the priest and the faithful. This is why the priest uses the plural when he says: *Thine own of Thine own, we offer to Thee, on behalf of all, and for all*. Concomitantly with this, the priest lifts up or "shows" the bread and the wine to the Father. But the blessing, the thanksgiving, and the prayer for them, which is another part of what Christ did at the Mystical Supper, is done by the community through the hymn: *We praise Thee, we bless Thee, we give thanks unto Thee, O Lord, and we pray unto Thee, O our God.* But it is the priest who lifts them up. There is solidarity between him and the community.

In fact, by offering the bread and the wine to the Father, Christ did not offer simple bread and wine, but the bread and the wine that prefigured and were potentially His body and blood. In the same way, the priest and the faithful do not offer simple bread and wine, but those that prefigure and are potentially not only their life or their body and blood, but Christ's body and blood that endured the cross and bears its marks. Precisely from this moment on, the priest begins to fulfill Christ's priestly work from the Mystical Supper. But the liturgical community is associated with him because the lay believers also partake to a certain degree of Christ's priesthood, but only in solidarity with the officiating priest and with the sacred gestures he makes in the liturgical solidarity of the community. Here the role of the lay believers as priests of the cosmos is revealed, a role they fulfill by offering everything they receive from God, not to lose them, but to receive them at an even higher level. Their work for the preparation of the things received from God, like the bread and wine, is also included in this quality of theirs as priests of the cosmos before God.

Both in the sense referring to bread and wine as well as in the sense referring to the very body and blood of Christ, who is virtually implied in them, these offered gifts represent the entire creation which, having been received from God, is returned to Him after a work of fulfillment of the human persons through and upon them in order to be raised to the level of deification into the body of Christ. In the words: *Thine own of Thine own* one says that the gifts offered to God by the human person are from those first offered by God to the human person. "Of all" means that in the bread and wine, or in the very body and blood of Christ, are concentrated and raised up all of God's gifts for the human person and of the human person to God: the earth in all of its aspects, the water, the air, the light and the warmth of the sun, but also the power given to the human person to have been endeavored in making use of them for the preparation of these gifts, the conscious and voluntary effort which is, in part, also from God.

It is possible that the Greek words κατα παντα could rather mean "in all" and not "of all." In this case one would emphasize that the gifts offered to God are offered totally, that we have detached ourselves completely from them. "For all" could mean that they are offered both on behalf of all and for the sanctification or for the benefit of all. The latter meaning is even more proper when referred to the body and blood of Christ.

These words determined Archimandrite Vasileios from the Holy Mountain to make these deep reflections: "This total liturgical offering given in return to the Lord who is eternally slaughtered—an act of thanksgiving and freedom—forms the center of the mystery, the source of the sanctification of man and of the precious gifts. This offering strips us of everything: we are lost (Mt 16:25). We cease to exist. We die. At the same time, this is the moment when we are born into life; we partake in divine life through offering everything, through becoming an offering of thanksgiving. So the loss of our life is at the same time the emergence of our existence into a world 'new and uncompounded': and when we have reached that world, we are truly human beings... With this experience of 'bringing before Thee, in all and for all' we are already partaking in the new life that consists in offering, in self-emptying. In that life everything exists in a different way, everything interpenetrates: all experiences are contained there. Man is contained; he is stretched to the point of being lost, and comes to himself in the one thing which is all. He finds the Lord who is Alpha and Omega. We call to remembrance everything that has come to pass and will come to pass in the future. It is all present, blended together in the light of His countenance and the sweetness of His beauty. Eternity is contained in a moment. In one holy pearl there is the whole of Paradise—there is Christ . . . . The Holy Spirit takes over and fills the space left empty by the offering, the act of humiliation and thanksgiving."[333]

In this way we prepare ourselves, through the offering of what we have, to receive within us Christ who is all, through His body and blood in the form of bread and wine. For once they were offered by us, the bread and wine were emptied of what we regard as sustaining us naturally. In the space we emptied, which we no longer seek to fill with bread that represents the whole universe concentrated in them of which we think we need, Christ will enter who will transform them, in concentrations of all things, into His body and blood. As "heavenly bread," He will be all our bread. We will carry together with Christ His body and blood in which, however, there are also our body and blood which Christ took into His body and blood and transfigured them in their foundation after the image of His body and blood. St. Symeon the

New Theologian describes in this way this dwelling of Christ in the one who empties himself:

> And being made one with Him, I am transported above to the heavens.
> That this is true and certain I know,
> But where then is my body, this I do not know.
> I know that He who remains immovable descends.
> I know that He who is invisible appears to me.
> I know that He who is separated from all creation
> takes me within Himself and hides me in His arms.
> And I am completely outside of the whole world.
> But I, so mortal, so insignificant in the world, contemplate in myself
> completely the Creator of the world.
> And I know that I will not die
> because I am inside of life,
> and that I have the entire life that completely flows out from within me.
> Each member of our body will be in the whole Christ; . . .
> and each part is He, the whole Christ.[334]

The fact that by offering all things to God He alone takes their place in me is also described by Kallistos Kataphygiotes: "For that supernatural and hidden and mysterious One above essence is infinite and inaccessible to any intellect. And It does not allow the contemplating intellect to turn its contemplation anywhere else, to the extent that it has participated in the purification and divine aid proper to it. Henceforth the intellect does not fall away from this divine contemplation and exceedingly beautiful splendor and infinitude unless it is drawn away by the influence of some passion or preoccupation, or else by the natural mutability to which it is susceptible."[335] Only those things that are not subsistent give man the illusion that he is self-existent.

This One to whom our being opens itself up when it offers all things to God, being liberated from all, is Christ who is experienced in the transcendence of His body through which all the lights, all the meanings and benefits of love flow out of the divine spring. It is from Christ-God that His body became a transparent and unimpeded transmitter of these lights, meanings and good things. "As the intellect casts its sightless gaze [this is why the Lord's body and blood overwhelmed with light are concealed within the form of the bread and wine] on the exceedingly divine, unique, transcendently principal and most-supreme Hiddenness, a reception comes to the intellect from It—also without sight. It is unified and unique, full of exceedingly beautiful, effulgent, and ineffable splendor, and it overwhelms the intellect with wonder and amazement in silence, after having prepossessed the heart with spiritual energy and sweet joy. This reception becomes for the intellect noetic illumination, enlightenment, and subsequently, divine eros and radiant joy. . . . Contemplatives contemplate God as the unified One in His formless form, His immaterial, incomposite beauty far surpassing nature, and His supremely simple countenance: garlanded about with infinite goods, resplendent with innumerable beauties, brilliantly flashing forth luminous rays of beauty to every intellect; an ineffable and indescribable wealth, a generous and infinitely ever-flowing abundance of things good and beautiful, a treasury of glory—inexhaustible, unfathomable, unfailing—filling intellects deprived of sight with the most abundant delight."[336]

This is what we receive in exchange for what we offer. This is why the community of people gives thanks to God and praises Him: *We praise Thee* . . . . Not only do praise and thanksgiving accompany the offering by the community of the gifts given by God, but it also extends into the encounter and the witnessing alongside their transformation into the supreme gift of the Lord's body and blood.

The offering (at the same time with the ascending toward God) of our whole life to God is so connected with the immediate transformation of the gifts into the Lord's body and blood through the invocation of the Holy Spirit, or through epiklesis, that Archimandrite Vasileios says that it is the inner epiklesis. In any case, both the offering of our gifts and the invocation of the Holy Spirit are expressed by the priest in the plural, and the community of people continues, during the invocation of the Holy Spirit, its hymn of praise, thanksgiving and prayer toward God, the Holy Spirit by whom Christ transformed the bread and wine at the Mystical Supper, and on the other hand, the priest invokes the Holy Spirit to descend not only "upon these holy gifts" but first "upon us" (upon the priest and the community).

This also shows the intimate connection between the offered gifts and the life of those who offer them, as well as, on the one hand, between them and the people and, on the other hand, between them and Christ who offers Himself and is continuously offered to the Father. All are spiritually interpenetrated. To a certain extent, this makes the transformation comprehensible.

d. Epiklesis (the Invocation of the Holy Spirit) and the Transformation of the Gifts into the Body and blood of Christ in a State of Sacrifice

After this preparation for receiving Christ by offering everything we have, through the bread and wine raised toward God, that has Christ prefigured in them as gift for us (through incarnation) and as gift for God the Father (through crucifixion), the priest invokes the Holy Spirit so that they may be transformed into Christ's body and blood as supreme gifts sacrificed by Him to the Father for us, as well as gifts offered again to us at the supreme level.

As we said, before the invocation of the Holy Spirit to descend upon the gifts at the time of their transformation, the priest invokes the Spirit to come upon him and upon the present ecclesiastical community so that His invocation may be heeded. We would not invoke Him if He did not give us the power to invoke Him. We would not entreat the Holy Spirit properly if He did not give us the power to entreat Him (Rom 8:26). We would not want to have Him if we did not previously have Him. And this alternation of the gift given by God and the invocation of the gift originates in our being created with the need to entreat Him for an ever greater gift, up to the gift of His Son, incarnate and crucified for us. And the Person of the Trinity who brings Its gift in our conscience and instructs us to ask for it more and more, as the One who cleanses us from cares and gives us the élan for God, is the Holy Spirit. The Holy Spirit is the divine Person who makes our conscience sensitive and ardent for God, forgetting about ourselves.

And as evidence that the Spirit whom the priest will invoke for the transformation of the gifts is not a spirit without any connection with the Son, he first prays to the Son to renew unto him and unto the faithful the Spirit given to the Apostles and through them to the Church at Pentecost at the ninth hour (the third as it was considered at that time), at the hour when the light and warmth of the sun are stronger. This moment of the Holy Liturgy is a renewed Pentecost in which one acknowledges that the Holy Spirit will not be given again to the faithful without an effort on their behalf of renewal through prayer. All good things are asked from

God, but for all of them one's own effort is required: *O Lord, who at the third hour* (Acts 2:15) *did send Thy Holy Spirit upon Thine Apostles, do not take Him away from us, O Good One, but renew Him unto us who pray unto Thee!* The priest repeats this petition three times, because the number three represents the infinity of the petition and the infinity of the gift, as a perfect number, which is so by the fact that it represents the Holy Trinity, as multiplicity which does not annul the unity. He intercalates between the three petitions the stichera from Psalm 50: *Create in me a pure heart, O God, and renew a right spirit within me* and *Cast me not away from Thy presence, and take not Thy Holy Spirit from me!* We cannot ask for the Spirit without asking for purity as well.

Prof. Petre Vintilescu agrees with the opinion of some liturgists that this troparion was included in the Liturgy rather late (fifteenth–sixteenth centuries, while others think it was added in the twelfth–thirteenth centuries). However, he also accords it a significant role, saying: "As seen in the above text, the officiating priests first pray that the Holy Spirit may not only not be taken away from them so that they may not be deprived of Him, but to be renewed unto them, to be restored in them, namely that their souls may be re-animated through Him, investing them with power, like the Apostles were on the day of Pentecost. During the service, the officiating priests have prayed several times that God might cleanse them with the power of the Holy Spirit of every stain of the body and soul so as to be worthy to officiate without any spot at His holy altar. But at this moment they need more than ever that breathing of God's Spirit so that He may move its flame within the depth of their being in order to burn up the tar of their sins and to burn up all uncleanliness. This is why they persist in a heightened élan of the spirit by reciting three times the prayer from the troparion of the third hour."[337]

Convinced that being strengthened by the Spirit, petitioned through this troparion, he can effectively invoke the descent of the Spirit upon the gifts, the priest proceeds to the eucharistic epiklesis itself, namely to the invocation of the Spirit, from the power of the Spirit asked for beforehand, for this culminating work of His.

In Romanian the Greek word ετι, which at the beginning of the other litanies is translated with "again," is here translated with "furthermore" [încă]. According to Prof. Vintilescu this word shows that it is not only about a presentation of the gifts of bread and wine, but even if it is also about them, as can be seen below through the invocation of the Holy

Spirit for their transformation, it is also about something more. "The text of the epiklesis is more simplified in the Liturgy of St. John Chrysostom, through which the adverb 'furthermore,' with which the prayer of the epiklesis begins, one underlines the idea that the eucharistic sacrifice is not limited to the material symbols of bread and wine, but 'furthermore [additionally] we offer unto Thee this reasonable and bloodless sacrifice, and we call on Thee, we pray unto Thee and humbly supplicate Thee: *Send Thy Holy Spirit upon us and upon these gifts here offered, and make this bread the precious body of Thy Christ. And that which is in this chalice the precious* [pure] *blood of Thy Christ, transforming them by Thy Holy Spirit.*'"[338]

We should mention that if the adverb "furthermore" refers to something extra, it should be placed before the words "we call on Thee... send Thy Holy Spirit upon these gifts."

It would seem that the Greek adverb ετι should be translated with "furthermore" [*încă*][339] in the sense of "additionally" with the following meaning: additionally we also offer these gifts, which through the descent of the Holy Spirit will be transformed into the reasonable sacrifice. This would strongly connect the offered gifts with the reasonable sacrifice that will be accomplished, in the sense that the words "furthermore we offer" show our act of offering, thus continuing the anaphora, and the following words, "we call on Thee, and we pray unto Thee" show the transition to the prayer of petitioning the Holy Spirit or to epiklesis. Our gift and God's response through its transformation, or the anaphora and the epiklesis, become thus strongly united. Otherwise the adverb "furthermore" [*încă*] would not have much sense. The words "furthermore we offer Thee" specify what has been offered through the words: "Thine own of Thine own." They are gifts to be transformed into the reasonable sacrifice, otherwise what was sought through the offering expressed by the words "Thine own of Thine own" would remain unspecified.

Through the words *reasonable sacrifice* one expresses both the offering of the gifts of bread and wine as the sacrifice of our body, and the offering of the Lord's body and blood. For both are reasonable bodies. But one also expresses the fact that the offering is accompanied by the words of prayer.

Although it would follow from the text of the epiklesis that the gifts are transformed at the moment in which, at the supplication of the priest when he makes the sign of the cross upon them, the Holy Spirit descends upon them, still, if we consider the text of the epiklesis as a whole, or if we take into consideration the intention with which the priest begins reciting that text, one can say that the Spirit begins to respond through His work to the priest's prayer at the beginning of this prayer and makes His move toward the gifts for which He is petitioned from the first words of this supplication. This is why it can be said that the gifts are, from the first words of the supplication for the Holy Spirit recited by the priest, in the process of transition from bread and wine to the Lord's body and blood, especially that they prefigure even from the Proskomedia the Lord's sacrificed body and His outpoured blood, as they are proximate to Him and under a certain diffusion of His power. Thus, as they are, on the one hand, gifts of bread and wine, and on the other hand, as they are in the process of transition to the reasonable sacrifice, the priest can call them from the first words of the epiklesis "reasonable and bloodless sacrifice." Fr. Petre Vintilescu, who made the expression "reasonable sacrifice" the subject of a special study, declares: "There remains no doubt regarding the application of the expression 'reasonable sacrifice' from the text of the epiklesis at the sacred eucharistic sacrifice, through the fact that the prayer of the diptychs from the Liturgy of St. John Chrysostom begins immediately after the epiklesis with the remark that this 'reasonable service' is offered "for those who have fallen asleep in the faith."[340] The same is said in the third prayer after the transformation: *Furthermore we offer this reasonable and bloodless sacrifice for the whole world*, etc.

But since the Holy Spirit, who transforms the bread and wine into the sacrificed body and blood of Christ, descends through the priest's prayer accompanied by that of the community, it can be said that the expression "reasonable service" (sacrifice) also refers to the prayer of the priest and of the community. The community offers not only the bread and wine, thus all that it has, to God, but it also offers itself so that the bread and wine will make the transition to the state of Christ's body and blood. But the community also offers itself through prayer. To the extent to which we offer up everything we have, they are more undoubtedly transformed into the body and blood of Christ wholly ascended. Fr. Pavel Florensky draws the conclusion from this that first I as a created being, fallen into unrighteousness, offer myself as sacrifice to God, accepting my fallen state before Him. But through this prayer my fallen state is taken by the Lamb of God upon Himself. This is why in the Liturgy "the reasonable sacrifice" is first understood as the sacrifice of the human person[341] and then that of Christ.[342] But perhaps one should specify that first there was Christ's sacrifice on Golgotha, then my sacrifice through prayer, word and life represented by the bread, and then the eucharistic sacrifice. All are also "reasonable sacrifices" united among them, but more strongly the last two.

Before the gifts that have imprinted on them the sacrifice on Golgotha, and also knowing the Mystical Supper and Christ's commandment to do this in remembrance of Him, the priest and the community are moved by the word of the prayer toward petitioning the Holy Spirit for the transformation of the gifts.

The following reflections of Florensky can be useful for the understanding of Christ's sacrifice as "reasonable sacrifice" *par excellence*, the priest's prayer and that of the community having their contribution to their presence on the altar, so that subsequently from Christ's sacrifice on the altar the believer, too, can again receive power to become a more superior "reasonable sacrifice."

Here is a passage from Florensky's reflections in which he refers to the person who through faith and prayer becomes a "reasonable sacrifice" to God, but which must be applied exceptionally to Christ. He first gives the following biblical quotations: "Be well pleased with the freewill offerings of my mouth, O Lord" (Ps 118:108). "Return, O Israel, to the Lord your God, for you became weak through your wrongdoings. Take with you words and turn to the Lord your God. Speak to Him, that you may not receive the reward of unrighteousness, but that you may receive good things. We will render in return the fruit of our lips" (Hos 14:2-3). Then he continues: "The word of my lips is the prayer as a sacrifice and source of the entire sacrifice, because any other sacrifice becomes sacrifice through the prayer of supplication, regardless of the deeds through which our mystical slaying is done and becomes visible. Any sacrifice is an image of our creatureliness that is annulled through the unrighteousness into which it fell before God. The slain Lamb is me, my being, and He became thus because in reality I have brought myself as sacrifice before God, but I pass over the incorporation of this spiritual act to the Lamb through active prayer, and only then does He become slain, sacrificed. And any other sacrifice is me, but since I offer myself mystically and actually as sacrifice, this act also takes shape in a material form."[343] And about the role of prayer as word he says: "The word is not an addition to human nature, it is not an accidental characteristic of the human person, but a constitutive feature. Moreover, it is the very being of the human person, since through the word he has discovered himself in his spiritual energy, has become existent for others and for himself. One cannot say 'the person and his word.' The word is the person himself, but within the aspect of his revelation and activity. And the person's activity . . . is essentially reasonable . . . . We speak through our actions . . . ." And for the materialization of the word of prayer as sacrifice in the body, Florensky quotes St. Paul from Rom 12:1: "'I beseech you therefore, brethren, by the mercies of God, that you present your bodies a living sacrifice, holy, acceptable to God, which is your reasonable service.' The service the human person offers to God, expressed by the Apostle through the words 'reasonable service,' means the created being's orientation toward the Creator. The Apostle speaks only about the human person's body, and because his spirit is compelled to be oriented by itself toward this offering of his as sacrifice. But he does this only because he does it with the body. Therefore, this living, holy and well-pleasing sacrifice to God is the 'reasonable sacrifice.' The believer speaks through his body; by offering himself as sacrifice, he confesses through his body the One to whom he offers himself . . . . It is not to the service through the body that the Apostle calls, but to the service through the spiritualized body. This is the reasonable service. When the intellect becomes similar to the present age, namely to the unreasonable creation, to the elements, then the human person separates himself from the Word with the body as well, because it no longer speaks to the body about the Word [or with the Word], it no longer confesses God."[344]

One can continue Florensky's reflections: by his being the human person is a reasonable word, since the word is the person in his revealing work. But he reveals himself not only through his words, but also through his deeds, which he thinks through just as he does with the words. Therefore, deeds are words, too. But since through these words and deeds he reveals himself to others, the person as word involves other persons. And he does not only involve them, but he cooperates with them, improves their life or is obligated to cooperate with them through his words and deeds. Through the words of his lips and through his deeds, the human person is thus called to offer himself to others. By doing this he strengthens himself in good and attains perfection. But the human person can also alter the function of the word, either the function of the word of his mouth or of the word as deed. Under the pretext of cooperating with others, he can make use of others for himself. It is a word that captures, a deed that grabs, a lying word, a word through which, on the one hand, he acknowledges that he should be oriented toward others and that he needs them, but, on the other hand, that he is exclusively oriented toward himself. The deeds of this kind of person are the same. And thus he not only isolates himself, but he also becomes corrupt.

But if before other fellow human beings the person can hide through word, he cannot hide before God. When he believes in God the human person cannot use his word except with sincerity both before God and before his fellow humans. The sincere word before God is the word as prayer. Through the word as prayer the person acknowledges God as almighty, as the One from whom he has everything, whom he must praise and to whom he must sincerely give thanks. For He is the only one who can give him the help he needs in the situation in which he finds himself and thus from whom he is entitled to ask for this help. Through the sincere word he offers himself to God and to his neighbors and objectifies himself. He enhances his life by offering up his life.

God is for the human person not only the One to speak to with sincerity, returning to the true use of the word as a means of self-discovery, in his limitations and dependence, but also the One before whom he feels the unconditional need to respond to His appeal to reveal Himself; and not only for God to reveal Himself, but also for him to attain perfection through the help given and the gift asked for, persevering in good works and humility, which are not necessary for God as they are for his neighbors and for himself. Through faith in God the human person thus restores his word and deeds before his fellow humans as well, and he also restores himself in this way, since he offers himself through them to God and to his fellow human beings.

Before his fellow human beings, the human person can foster insincerity, lie, but before God he cannot, except if he no longer acknowledges His existence. But in this way, as he is not offering himself, the human person does not truly accomplish himself. When he acknowledges God's existence, he feels Him as the absolute partner in his word. The human person should surrender himself to God sincerely through word and deed, responding to His call. This means that the human person cannot be maintained as a sincere reasonable being (and only under these conditions is he truly reasonable, or revealing of the self) except through

God. The human person reestablishes himself as a true reasonable word by encountering the Word of God, or the reasonable God. The human person is created as a reasonable word in order to respond to God, or to the supreme reasonable Word. Only in this way one maintains and develops what has been created—a reasonable word.

The human person is created as a reasonable word after the image of the supreme reasonable Word and is maintained as such in relationship with that Word. Even when he uses the word in a dishonest way, namely to falsify the function of the word, he still must respond to the appeal or to the question of others. He can lie to God, when his faith has weakened, but he must respond to Him either directly, or to others who speak to him who are also sent by God. The first use of the word in a dishonest way we see with Adam and Eve after their fall into sin.

But how can the Son of God be reasonable Word, thus being an example for the human person? We have the answer to this question in the fact that in God there are three Persons. In God there is a Father of the Word and a Son born as reasonable Word, Who responds to the Father but Who also has His subsistence as such from the Father. The Father is not sent by the Son to become man and as such to be in the state of the one praying to the Father. As reasonable beings, who ask anything from the Father and responsibly fulfill what the Father asks from us, we are, properly speaking, created like the Son and the Word of God. And as He is the image of the Father, we are "in the image" of the Father, namely similar to the Son. This is why it is the Son who becomes man and not the Father.

We maintain or reestablish ourselves as reasonable words when we preserve unaltered the relationship with the divine Son who is the Word, who is obedient to the Father and responds to Him positively, fulfilling His will. We speak sincerely in prayers to the Father, or we can also appeal to Him, but only being strengthened by the Son or together with the Son, or remaining in His image, or further yet, reestablishing this image after the Son reestablished it in Himself as man. The Son teaches us how to pray to the Father. And, in fact what we ask, in the last analysis we ask from the Father and it is to Him that we respond, as the Son responded to Him all the way to sacrifice. Certainly, when we say "Father" we understand that He is the Father of a Son, but we do not always name the Son. We surely pray to the Son, too, but not without remembering that He is the Son of the Father, and through Him we know that our prayer reaches the Father. In fact, we cannot attain to the Father except through the Son (Jn 14:6). But we must attain to the Father. The words of the Son given to human persons are the words of the Father (Jn 14:10), the commandments of the Son are the commandments of the Father: "If you keep My commandments, you will abide in My love, just as I have kept My Father's commandments and abide in His love" (Jn 15:10).

One could say that Jesus Christ as man had the words from the Father and kept as man the Father's commandments, and also as man was asking the Father. But it is not without significance that it is not the Father who becomes man to bring the words of the Son, to fulfill the Son's commandments and to ask from the Son, but it is the Son who becomes man in this humility before the Father and in view of His surrender as sacrifice to the Father. It is not the Father who comes to offer Himself as sacrifice to the Son, but it is the Son who comes to offer Himself as sacrifice to the Father.

Not only while He was on earth did the incarnate Son pray to the Father for us, but also after He ascended and sits at His right hand: "But He, because He continues forever, has an unchangeable priesthood. Therefore He is also able to save to the uttermost those who come to God through Him, since He always lives to make intercession for them" (Heb 7:24–25).

He remains forever the High Priest over us. He cannot remain passive before the act of the transformation of bread and wine into His body and blood. If at the Mystical Supper He transformed the bread and wine into His body and blood, "giving thanks [to the Father] and blessing," why would He not do the same now? In any case He speaks even now, offering Himself as reasonable sacrifice also in this sense, or showing that He wishes that the bread and wine be transformed into His sacrificed body and blood that disclose His state of reasonable sacrifice joined by His manifested will.

Without a word of praise and blessing to the Father, of thanks offered to Him by the Son in our behalf, He could not place Himself at our disposal in a state of saving sacrifice for us. The priest and the community could not effectively pray for the transformation of bread and wine into His body and blood without their prayer being strengthened by the manifestation of His will that this transformation be accomplished, a manifestation which is also a word. We see the priest's prayer in the epiklesis. But that prayer is not separated from the word of the High Priest, Christ.

The prayer of the faithful is sung at this time as a praise and blessing to God, as thanks offered to Him, just as the Lord did at the Mystical Supper and as, in a certain way, He is doing now without being absent from the prayer of the faithful. The Lord cannot forget that He also did this at the Mystical Supper, and this means that He continues even now this praise, blessing and thanks offered to the Father for us and together with us for our salvation. His praise, blessing and thanks offered as man to the Father for us and together with us is a condition for the transformation of the gifts offered by us into His body and blood for our benefit. This, in fact, is also said in the prayer recited by the priest before the Great Entrance with the gifts, that Christ is not only "offered," but He also "offers" Himself to the Father. And how would He offer Himself without showing the Father His will to be accepted by the Father on behalf of the faithful? The community gives thanks to the Father and blesses Him because He gave the Son as man and, in this quality, as a sacrifice offered to the Father on its behalf, a sacrifice of which, since it is offered to the Father, it partakes as from a sacrifice thus sanctified. This thanks and blessing was offered first by the Son as man to the Father at the Mystical Supper, and it is natural that He would not forget about it now, but in remembering it even now He may also associate with it the priest and the community present there.

In fact the Savior Himself told the disciples that He would pray for us: "And I will pray the Father, and He will give you another Helper, that He may abide with you forever" (Jn 14:16). St. Cyril of Alexandria said plainly that "we have an intercessor to the Father, Jesus Christ who is redemption for our sins and for the sins of the whole world."[345]

In fact, if the Spirit prays with us with ineffable groans, coming on the other hand as a response to our prayer (Rom 8:11, 15), why would the Son not work for us before the Father? On the other hand, in His very presentation as a continuous sacrifice for us His petition is implied. By asking the Father to send the Spirit, it is Christ Himself who sends Him (Jn 15:26). In the Holy Trinity everything is done jointly. This is why Christ is also active in the Eucharist. The priest's "part is but to open his mouth, while God worketh all; . . . Christ even now is present, even now operates."[346] If the words were to belong only to the human person, they would not have any power. How often do we feel the lack of power and of capacity to express the mysteries of life through our words? But in the words recited by the priest at the Holy Liturgy it is Christ Himself who opens up the mystical horizons through those words and brings into them His divine power.

In addition to this, Archbishop Alexei rightly observes that when the priest speaks in the plural at the epiklesis (as in all liturgical prayers), he speaks in the name of the Church, of the mystical body of Christ.[347] This is why Christ speaks through him.

On the other hand, since Christ unites His petition with the priest's prayer in asking for the Holy Spirit in the epiklesis, and since both the priest's prayer and Christ's petition united with it is a "reasonable sacrifice," this expression could be meant to indicate the petition of both. Thus, Christ places Himself at the disposal of the priest and of the community to be presented to the Father as a sacrifice for them and with them. However, in His prayer, therefore in His sacrifice, Christ unites Himself with the priest and the community without confusion. Otherwise, one would not know who offers the sacrifice for whom. By accepting His offering as sacrifice, Christ does this willingly so that He may unite His petition with the prayer of the priest and of the community. Both the priest and the community can say not only "we pray," but also "we bring Your incarnate Son together-praying with us." This enduring distinction allows the priest to say in the second part of the epiklesis: *And make this bread the precious body of Your Christ, and that which is in this chalice, the precious blood of Your Christ, transforming them by Your Holy Spirit.* Something occurs here similar to what took place at the nativity of the Son of God as man.

The prayer of the priest and of the community has reached the supreme efficiency as service or "reasonable sacrifice" through the union with the petition of the incarnate Word, namely with the supreme reasonable worship. This is added to the prayer of the priest and that of the community, invoked by both the priest and the community. A more accentuated expression to the awareness of this union was given in the epiklesis of an old Liturgy, that of Serapion of Thmuis, which was a petition to the Father to send the Word for the transformation of bread and wine into His body and blood: "O Lord of truth, may Your Holy Word come upon this bread so that it may be transformed into the body of the Word and over this chalice so that [the wine] may become the blood of truth."[348]

The fact that it has been thought that the bread and wine are transformed into the Word's body and blood also through the prayer addressed to Him we find in St. Justin the Martyr and St. Irenaeus. The first says: "As Jesus Christ our Savior, having been made flesh by the Word of God, . . . so likewise have we been taught that the food which is blessed by the prayer of His word . . . is the flesh and blood of that Jesus who was made flesh."[349] And St. Irenaeus says: "For as the bread, when it receives the invocation of God, is no longer common bread, but the Eucharist."[350] Archbishop Alexei affirms that the Alexandrian school considered the Eucharist as being "consecrated through the Word, while the Antiochian school, through the Spirit: in the Alexandrian school the Spirit as the third Person of the Trinity remains in shadow."[351]

We note that it is true that in the Alexandrian school the emphasis has been placed on the role of the Word in the Eucharist until Cyril of Alexandria inclusively, because this school made out of this a means of defense of the Word's divinity, while the Antiochian school regarded Christ-man offered as sacrifice as being made a sacrifice through the Spirit. But following the emphasis on the importance of the equality between the Spirit and the Son at the Second Ecumenical Council, the roles of the Word and of the Holy Spirit have been combined in the Eucharist, a fact made evident in the epiklesis of St. Basil the Great's Liturgy and that of St. John Chrysostom. Actually, in the connection that the Alexandrian school makes between the incarnation of the Word and the transformation of bread and wine into His body and blood, a work of the Spirit is also implied in the latter, as it is implied in the first. St. Cyril says that we are accepted with our sacrifices together with Christ sacrificed "in the Spirit." Thus, Christ, too, is in the Spirit, in the eucharistic sacrifice. "Through Christ we have been accepted as we offer in the Spirit our gifts to God the Father."[352]

Precisely because there is a supreme encounter between the reasonable service of the human person and the reasonable service of the Word through the Spirit, the prayer of the epiklesis has its supreme efficiency. The transformation is effected with the will of the Father through the Word and through the Spirit.

There are also other reasons for this efficiency: asked by the priest and by the liturgical community, Christ petitions the Father together with them to transform the bread and wine into His body and blood, but He also works this out Himself in order to offer them, on the one hand, to the Father for them and, on the other hand, in order to return them to the faithful as they were thus transformed, because these gifts have become His through the words: *Thine own of Thine own, we offer to Thee, on behalf of all, and for all.* But the community has offered them through the priest so that He may assimilate them completely and may return them as His body and blood, after He has Himself offered them to the Father and has, through the petition and the action asked for by the priest and the community, effected their transformation through the Spirit. His petition to the Father is at the same time action, but an action not only of him who asks, but also of the One being asked. So, in a certain way Christ continues to be interested in the gifts offered to Him by the community. They are somehow common to the community and to Christ. Being asked by the community, He petitions the Father together with the community to transform them through the Holy Spirit into His body and blood—and thereby He Himself contributes to their transformation—in order to offer them as His sacrifice, and as the gift of the community, to the Father and also to return them to the community.

> When we entrust to Him our whole life and hope, this is the inner, "practical" invocation of the grace of the Holy Spirit. At the moment of the *epiklesis*, our offering to God in all and for all brings grace to us, being in itself our entreaty, prayer and supplication to the Father to send down the Holy Spirit.
>
> We understand that the epiklesis is not simply said aloud by the priest, but is accomplished by the whole body of the Church: it is a rite of invocation, an act of supplication for the changing of the bread and wine into the Body and Blood of Christ and for the sanctification of the faithful: for remission of sins, the communion of the Holy Spirit, the fullness of the Kingdom of Heaven, boldness toward God, and deliverance from the judgment and condemnation that result from partaking unworthily. So the fact of the changing and sanctifying of the precious gifts and of the faithful is experienced consciously and with our whole physical being. In the attitude of thanksgiving that comes naturally to him, the whole man, the whole liturgical community, and through it the whole of creation, becomes a prayer, an entreaty and a supplication, enjoying the descent of the Holy Spirit and the grace of Pentecost, and "the whole of creation is made new and divine" (Kathisma at Matins, September 8).[353]

In the very fact that, together with the community and thus with the whole Church and entreated by it, Christ asks the Father through the priest for the transformation of the bread and wine into His body and blood through the Holy Spirit, He shows that He has intimately appropriated them, although He considers them as gifts of the community. He is proven as preserving a special connection with the community and with the priest or the bishop physically present.

But where Christ is, as Subject who, together with and for the community, asks for this transformation as "a Minister of the sanctuary and of the true tabernacle" (Heb 8:2), there is His body also, which is, on the one hand, risen and wholly become light, on the other hand He bears in Himself the marks of the nails, the living memory of the sacrifice on Golgotha, thus standing at the right hand of the Father like a Lamb who has been slain (Rev 5:6). At the petition of Christ and the priest's prayer, the Holy Spirit, with whom the body of Christ is filled, also enters the bread and wine which Christ made His own, thus making them perfectly Christ's own. In this way His own body and blood, which have imprinted on them the state of sacrifice, are perfectly imprinted into the bread and wine, making them, too, His sacrificed body and blood.

Nicholas Cabasilas declares that the very receiving of our gifts by Christ means their transformation into His body and blood: "What does he do in receiving them? He sanctifies them into his own Body and Blood; for it is the true nature of receiving to appropriate a thing to oneself, so that it becomes in a sense oneself."[354] And Prof. Ene Braniste explains the fact that in this way the liturgical sacrifice is accomplished, identical with the one on Golgotha without being a repetition of it: "Different from the reality of the cross as regards the temporal framework or its external or phenomenal appearance, the Liturgy is—in its essence—identical with that reality. Certainly for us, corporeal and temporary beings subjected to the limits of time and space, the historical reality of the cross took place in time only once, and consequently the Liturgy appears either as a *commemoration* or as a periodical *repetition or reproduction* of a past event consummated over two thousand years ago. However, for God who is above time and space the sacrifice on the cross is a permanent, uninterrupted and present fact, actual with the saving eternal power or, to use an imperfect comparison, it is like an eternally flowing river into which flow, from place to place and from time to time, other streams of the sacrifices offered in the Liturgy on earth."[355] But this means that in

Christ is eternally perpetuated the living experience of the state of sacrifice paradoxically united with His state of resurrection and into this state are raised, through the transformation into His body and blood, the bread and the wine as our gifts in order for us to share in His sacrifice by partaking of them.

But in their appearance the bread and wine remain bread and wine so that, through eating and drinking, Christ's body and blood may become accessible. In their distinct forms on the surface, His body and blood are present from the plane that surpassed space and time. In general the gifts being offered as sacrifices to God are filled with His holiness and with His power. And they are appropriated so totally by Christ, or they are so much filled with the Holy Spirit, that they become Christ's very body and blood.

In the epiklesis from the Liturgy of St. Basil the Great it is not said: *And make this bread the precious body of Your Christ, and that which is in this chalice the precious blood of Your Christ*, but *May the Holy Spirit come upon us and upon these gifts here offered to bless, to sanctify and to show: this bread to be the precious body of our Lord and God and Savior Jesus Christ, and that which is in this chalice the precious blood of our Lord and God and Savior Jesus Christ shed for the life of the world.*

Sanctifying means their being received by the Father as a sacrifice. Everything that is sacrificed to God is sanctified. This puts an end to the many discussions on the moment in which Christ becomes sacrifice in the Eucharist. The answer is: the moment of the transformation. Properly speaking, it is the coming of Christ eternally in the state of the One sacrificed in the form of bread and wine.

And the *showing* is not just a subjective phenomenon, although it is that, too.

The person we love shows his image in an object he used at other times in a place that person used to be. But Christ shows Himself objectively in the bread and wine of which He said at the Mystical Supper that they are His body and blood. It is in this way that He first shows Himself as sacrifice to the Father. But by showing them to us, too, He shows them to our physical eyes and also to the spiritual eyes of faith. He who truly believes "sees" Christ's body in the bread and His blood in the wine of Holy Communion. They are transported into Christ's plane of light that envelops His risen body. In order for us to "see" Christ's body and blood in the bread and wine, we ask that the Holy Spirit may come not only upon the gifts offered, but also "upon us." It is only in the Spirit that we "see" spiritually, we "see" what is in the realm of the Spirit. But faith is required for this "vision." If up until now Christ has been sensed as presenting them, together with us, to the Father, thus asking Him at the same time for their transformation through the Spirit, He is now "seen," He is sensed in His Body and blood. One passes over to the foundation of reality, to the foundation of the image of bread and wine, which is the divine Logos, who came and established Himself at the foundation of creation through His body and blood transfigured through resurrection. Through incarnation the Son has descended to us; through sacrifice He ascends together with us to the Father. Then He returns the precious gifts to us so that by partaking of Him we may also ascend together with Him to the Father. This is now a new descent of Christ to us in a state of sacrifice. This is at the same time a total renunciation of His own self, thus an immersion or an ascension out of love into the Father. By remaining in a continuous state of sacrifice for us at the right hand of the Father, He "descends" in the Liturgy to us in a state of sacrifice, since, at our and His appeal, the Father transforms through the Spirit, for us, the bread and wine into His sacrificed body and blood so that He may also raise us who partake of Him to the place where He is. This is a renewed act of love for us, but also for the Father together with us, done for us. His "descent" to us in an act of special living experience for us of His state of sacrifice has begun at the moment of His petition united with the priest's prayer, which is expressed in the words: "Furthermore we offer unto Thee this reasonable service [this common prayer of the priest, of the community and of Christ] . . . send Thy Holy Spirit upon us and upon these gifts here offered . . . . And make this bread the precious body of Thy Christ . . . ." His love for the Father and implicitly for us brings Him in a special way to us. He offers Himself now to the Father especially for us. He has asked together with us for the Spirit for this special offering of His on our behalf in order to attract us, too, into it.

In the Trinity of whom One bears our humanity, the mutual love is not static, but in motion from one person to another. The incarnate Son does not remain motionless in His state of sacrifice, as man, before the Father, nor does the Father remain motionless in contemplating that state of sacrifice, but there takes place a continuous and special reference by the Son of His act of presenting Himself as sacrifice to the Father for every believer and liturgical community every time the believer or the liturgical community wishes to present Him, in unity with Him, to the Father. And every time the sacrifice offered by the Son to the Father, in which is also implied a prayer, takes into consideration the sins of those in the community who need His sacrifice, and the Father accepts it for these sins. Their partaking of it brings them the power to sacrifice themselves, too, thus overcoming their sinful egoism in the act of co-sacrificing. In a way, the Son suffers in His sacrifice offered every time to the Father the sinful weakening of the believers, helping them to overcome it through the compassionate sacrifice.

Christ is now no longer only in the state of the One who offers Himself through the priest as representative of the community or of the hierarch—who offers Himself through the priest who offers Him—but also as the One offered as sacrifice for the sins of the liturgical community present, as well as for the release from its egoism and weakening, even though now in His passivity He is also active because He willingly lets Himself be placed in this state. He accepts passivity so as to make us even more compassionate. Precisely in this way His sacrifice has the greatest efficiency. But it is in this state of sacrifice relived especially for a community that Christ allowed Himself to be placed and has placed Himself through the transformation of our gifts. Thus, in His sacrificed body and blood we are also incorporated, represented through the gifts we have offered and transformed through the Spirit asked for from the Father by Him and by us. He has allowed Himself to be placed in this state of sacrifice especially by us, but in His turn He took us with Him or has especially raised us into His state of sacrifice. In His body and blood is, thus, implied especially the liturgical community present. This is an additional reason why the priest, as representative of the community united with it, prayed together with Christ: "Send Thy Holy Spirit upon us and upon these gifts here offered, and make this bread the precious body of Thy Christ." In this body we, too, will be included.

By offering ourselves as sacrifice together with Christ, we have immersed ourselves, through the transformation of our gifts accomplished by the Holy Spirit, in Christ so that we may immerse ourselves together with Christ in the Father in order to be healed of our egoism that takes a different form each time in each person.

But the meaning of the sacrifice is not only to be offered to God, notwithstanding its meaning of self-renunciation of the one offering himself and the immersion in God, becoming sensible of Him. But it also implies an inverse motion. From the One who accepts the sacrifice there begins a wave of thanks and compassion toward the one who offered himself as sacrifice. He who received the gift feels the impulse to offer himself in his turn to the one who has offered the gift or the sacrifice. This is the dialogue of perfect love through sacrifice, which is for us a means of healing from the egoism that has been manifested into everyone's own sins. The Son who has been offered to the Father as a sacrifice by the community in its loving propensity for the Father, but also under the influence of His loving propensity for the community, wishes to imprint even more into it the loving propensity of His state of sacrifice for the Father and for the community; and the Father wishes to show His thanks not only to the Son, who has been offered and has allowed Himself to be offered as sacrifice for the community, but also for the community that has offered to Him the Son as sacrifice and has offered itself together with Him, the sacrificed countenance of His Son being thus imprinted in the members of the community so that the Father may show His love for them as for those who have imprinted in themselves the countenance and, therefore, the sense perception of His sacrificed Son.

The depth of the Father's love in which we immersed ourselves through the sacrifice of the Son in which our sacrifice was also implied, does not remain passive before our act of love attached to the Son's love, but it is poured out in its turn into us as the Father's love. And the Son who has assimilated into His body our bodies represented by our gifts, since we attached them to Him out of love, responds to us by coming in a real way with His body and blood into our body and blood, so as to cleanse them even more of egoistic tendencies and to make them similar to His body full of His love for the Father and for us.

Thus, it is only through Holy Communion that there comes to a conclusion the truly ontological circuit of the dialogue of love between the Father, the Son and us, through the sacrifice of His Son.

Through the sacrifice of His Son we submit ourselves to the Father, laying aside the features of our egoism, uniting ourselves with that sacrifice; by partaking of it, the Son offers Himself to us more fully with His love for the Father and for us so that we may be able to resume at other Liturgies, on a higher level, this mutual offering.

From the strong connection between the reliving by Christ of His state of sacrifice for the community that offers Him as sacrifice through the priest, offering Himself at the same time, and the concrete needs of those for whom He is offered and for whom He offers Himself, as well as from the remembrance of the sins and needs immediately after the transformation, it follows that Christ offers Himself as sacrifice exactly at the moment of the transformation of the gifts into His body and blood. He presents Himself in that moment as the sacrifice suited for the sins and needs that weigh down the members of the community at that time.

The Eastern Fathers affirm the real transformation of the bread and wine through the work of the Spirit. St. Cyril of Jerusalem says: "Consider therefore the Bread and the Wine not as bare elements, for they are, according to the Lord's declarations, the Body and Blood of Christ."[356] And about the moment in which the transformation takes place he says: "Then having sanctified ourselves by these spiritual Hymns, we beseech the merciful God to send forth His Holy Spirit upon the gifts lying before Him; that He may make the Bread the Body of Christ, and the Wine the Blood of Christ; for whatsoever the Holy Ghost touched, is surely sanctified and changed."[357] First the faithful had to be sanctified through their elevation to the ranks of angels whom they joined in singing the thrice holy hymn and blessing the One who came and continues to come to unite heaven and earth, so that when His Spirit is petitioned to come upon the faithful, and also upon the gifts, He may transform them, sanctifying them as He sanctified the faithful. Theodore of Mopsuestia declares: "When the priest says that the bread and the wine are the body and blood of Christ, he indicates what they became through the coming of the Holy Spirit."[358]

"What has been made evident on the altar, is not only the body and blood of Christ, but His very sacrifice, that is the mystery of His Passions, Resurrection and Ascension, the Eucharist being its anamnesis, its efficient memorial," says Jean Danielou. He bases this on the following words of Theodore of Mopsuestia: "Every time when Christ's sacrifice is offered, the Lord's death, His resurrection, His ascension and the forgiveness of sins are signified."[359] And Danielou continues: "To signify does not mean here only to remember. But the word intends to mean that the offered sacrifice is not a new sacrifice, but Christ's unique sacrifice made present. This teaching has been given value especially by the Antiochian Fathers. I give two more examples. In a eucharistic catechesis inserted in the commentary on the Epistle to the Hebrews, St. John Chrysostom, after reminding that the sacrifices of pagans were repeated because they were inefficient, shows that Christ's sacrifice is efficient and, therefore, unique: 'What then? Do not we offer every day? We offer indeed, but making a remembrance of His death, and this [remembrance] is one and not many. How is it one, and not many? Inasmuch as that [Sacrifice] was once for all offered, [and] carried into the Holy of Holies. This is a figure of that [sacrifice] and this remembrance of that. For we always offer the same, not one sheep now and tomorrow another, but always the same thing: so that the sacrifice is one . . . . Christ is one everywhere, being complete here and complete there also, one Body. As then while offered in many places, He is one body and not many bodies; so also [He is] one sacrifice . . . . It is not another sacrifice, as the High Priest, but we offer always the same, or rather we perform a remembrance of a Sacrifice.'[360] One can see in this passage the force of the anamnesis to make present, not in memory, but in reality, under the sacramental species, Christ's unique sacrifice."[361] The intense reliving of a past event in my life is a relived experience of the respective event. By reliving His sacrifice for us through the Spirit of His love for us, at the supplication we addressed to Him through the Spirit for Whom we ask Him and to Whom we open ourselves up, Christ makes His sacrifice present in the form of bread and wine that we offer to Him so that He may assimilate our gifts into His sacrifice or to unite them with that sacrifice. St. Cyril of Alexandria says that we cannot present ourselves before the Father except in a state of pure sacrifice, and we cannot enter before Him in a state of pure sacrifice except by being united with His incarnate Son in His state of pure sacrifice.

Theodore of Mopsuestia places in bold relief not only the identity of the sacrifice on the altar with the one on Golgotha through anamnesis, but also with the one being continuously offered in heaven. In fact, if Christ did not continuously relive in heaven His sacrifice for us, neither would He be present in this state on the altars of visible churches. Here are Theodore of Mopsuestia's words in this sense: "Even though we remember our Lord's death when we eat and drink, it is clear that in Liturgy . . . the sacrifice we offer is a sort of an image of the Liturgy taking place in heaven . . . . Thus, every time when the Liturgy of this fearful sacrifice is offered . . . we must think that we are with the One in heaven. In our mind the vision of the heavenly reality takes shape through faith, considering that Christ Himself—who is in heaven, who died for us, rose again and ascended into heaven—has been slain and is now present here through the means of these images."[362] Danielou says: "This means that Christ's sacrifice subsists in three different modes. The same priestly activity that took place at a given moment in history, which is eternally present in heaven, subsists now in the sacramental images. Christ's priestly activity is, in its substance, the action by which creation attains its final goal, because God is glorified through it. It is the same activity which through a unique privilege is done in time to subsist eternally and which the Mystery makes present at all times and in all places."[363]

In Christ, who offers Himself to the Father and of whom we partake in our churches at various times and in various places, and in the life to come we will partake "more truly" of Him, creation reaches its perfection, because it offers itself in Christ to God, being filled with God as having overcome any separation from Him, any imperfection, making visible how God's glory fills not only heaven, but also the earth, as we sing in the thrice holy hymn before the transformation.

This is why the Holy Liturgy is creation's ascent toward its perfection and toward the glorifying of the Trinity through the sacrifice of the Son of God made man and by partaking of it. The Son of God's descent through His incarnation as an immortal man and through His eternal offering to the Father together with us is the condition for the perfection of the created being and for the glorifying by him of God. The sacrifice unites forever the heaven with the earth. In the slain Lamb God is united with the human person. And He sits on the throne forever.

The Mystery of the transformation of bread and wine into the Lord's body and blood is so great that after the Holy Fathers, who following the words of the Lord, affirmed it with all their conviction, the theology after them dared not make any other effort of deepening its comprehension, or when in more recent times had tried to understand it more, it dissolved the mystery by reducing the presence of the Lord's body and blood to a spiritual presence.

We believe that expanding on two ideas affirmed in the Christian tradition could contribute to the understanding of this great Mystery, which must be preserved in its real meaning: the one as a symbol and the one as inner experience of the state of sacrifice.

a) According to the tradition of the Holy Fathers, all visible realities are symbols of the invisible ones. The material bread is the symbol of the heavenly bread, which is Christ. But the Holy Fathers do not separate the symbols from what they symbolize, but the visible symbol has as its foundation the invisible reality which it symbolizes. And between the material symbol and the highest spiritual reality which it symbolizes a series of steps are intercalated. For example, the spiritual bread could be any good word; more so a word of faith in Christ.

The presence even in the material image of spiritual realities with the symbolized steps makes itself felt, for example, in the fact that the material bread strengthens not only our body, but also the soul or our spiritual life. And also vice versa, a good word strengthens not only the soul, but also its body. This fact can facilitate a certain understanding of the overwhelming of the bread and wine in the Eucharist by Christ's body and blood, as bread and wine from a superior level, but not separated from the bread and wine on the lowest material level.

On the other hand, Christ's body and blood after the resurrection have been raised to the superior content implied in them as body and blood, overwhelmed by spirit to such an extent that the body has been raised to incorruptibility and the blood is no longer poured out of them as from the body before the resurrection. Furthermore, the body has been so raised to the photonic state which constitutes the essence of the entire matter that it can enter through locked doors.

The bread and Christ's body became so close to each other, through the activity of His body upon the bread, that the bread is perfectly absorbed into Christ's luminous body and Christ's body has raised the bread to the level of a luminous part assimilated into His body, a part potentially implied in Christ's body.

b) Any bearer of a body bears it not only as a material structure of his own, subject to sense perception through the senses reduced to their external function or to the dissection and analysis operated with instruments that lack a conscious sensibility. This is not a living body, but a dead body. The living body cannot be known by the scientist either, except by making use of his humanity, experiencing in himself what the other is communicating through his eyes and words, similar to what he feels and what he can use as a means of understanding what the other is communicating. For the bearer of the body experiences in it its states and motions and everything happening to it as phenomena perceived externally as a spiritual content. All these create a content indefinitely rich in senses and inner thoughts. And these are not closed off in the individual I, but they are communicated outwardly. More of them are even triggered through the body by the things outside. The most vibrant experiences are triggered by outer persons through the means of the body and it is toward them that they irradiate or perceive them with the most dynamic interest.

Some persons manifest through their experiences an egoistic life to make use of others, or to despise everything that comes from others. They want to be closed off in themselves. But they cannot be closed tightly in themselves vis-à-vis others, but on the one hand they remain closed to others, and on the other hand they make others uncomfortable. They are experienced by others as "rejectors." On the contrary, other persons direct all their thoughts and feelings full of compassion toward others, or they open themselves up joyfully to the thoughts and feelings of others. These are people who dedicate themselves to others, or are welcoming toward others. They dedicate themselves or welcome others through the body. They do this not to seek physical pleasures, but through generous spiritual communication.

There are persons who live the experiences of others more than their own, or they dedicate themselves more to them. A mother experiences more than anyone else the pains and joys of her children, or she strengthens with her words and deeds more than anyone the souls and bodies of her children. Their pains are really felt as her pains and she dedicates herself to them to such an extent that she forgets entirely about her interests and even about her existence.

But our pains, our weaknesses as consequences of our sins are experienced by Jesus Christ in the highest degree. He also gives us all His affection for the Father and all the strengthening hope coming from the state of His risen body. These He gives us through His body. These we must feel when we partake of His body and blood. He assimilates our vision into His vision in order to cleanse us from envy and from the passions of egoism; He assimilates our hearing into His hearing in order to cleanse it from the tendency to despise and to doubt what others tell us. He became our subject in us and His body has been united with our body, without annulling us. But we also must open ourselves up to Him in our thoughts and feelings and this equates with our being dedicated to Him with the determination to become a dwelling place for Him Who wants to dwell in us. This is why we repeat so often during the Holy Liturgy, before we receive Him within us, the words: *Let us offer ourselves and one another, and our whole life to Christ our God*. This is why He said: "If anyone loves Me, he will keep My word; and My Father will love him, and We will come to him and make our home with him" (Jn 14:23). If we do not do this, we partake "in an unworthy manner" and we eat "judgment" to ourselves, because by doing this we increase our insensitivity, "not discerning the Lord's body" (1 Cor 11:27, 29) with His feelings of love with which He comes to us. St. Symeon the New Theologian describes like no one else this action of Christ's appropriating the feelings of all of us through their cleansing and our feelings' appropriating of Christ as their subject, without us being annulled.

This presence of Christ in us, as a participant in our inner life, being its guide and the One who purifies it and who strengthens and comforts us, we must feel when we receive in a worthy manner His body and blood filled with love for us, this being equivalent with self-sacrifice and when we receive Him as body and blood that became the bread and wine of our eternal life, filled with all the content of His love for us. As body and blood that are presented to us not without significance in the form of bread and wine which we eat for our strengthening, His body and blood that are communicated to us, fill us in a real way through the form of bread and wine with all their feelings, without ceasing to be outside of us as well. They come so intimately in us that there takes place their consumption by us, producing in us an elevated spiritual life. This is why they are given to us in the form of bread and wine, in this way being manifested the fact of eating His body and drinking His blood as true food and drink that sustains not just our physical life, but also the spiritual one, being both cleansed and elevated by them.

There exists between those who love each other a phenomenon of mutual internalization, not only through feelings and thoughts, but also through bodies, the spiritualized bodies, yet not being separated. Christ becomes interior to us through His body and blood filled with the Holy Spirit.

7. The Supplications Addressed to God after the Transformation

What has been said above shows us why immediately after the transformation the priest says in his prayer: *That they may be to those who partake thereof for the awakening of the soul, for forgiveness of sins, for communion with the Holy Spirit, for fulfillment of the Kingdom of Heaven, for boldness toward Thee, and not unto judgment or condemnation.*

From connecting the forgiveness of sins with the awakening of the soul, one can see that it is not about specified sins, because for these one must obtain beforehand the forgiveness through confession. But it is about certain fleeting mistakes and thoughts that escape our ability to perceive, to express exactly and to remember distinctly, or about inappropriate thoughts that appeared after confession and which could bring about judgment or condemnation. It is about the volition to always ascend higher from the state we are in which never satisfies us.

Those who will partake of the sacrifice being offered are also promised certain greater blessings. In the first place we ask for a state of "the soul's watchfulness as uninterrupted as possible." It is not about the awakening of the soul from the sleep of indifference, but of a state of continuous watchfulness (εις νηψιν ψιχης) so that we may not be disturbed by thoughts, concerns or tempting passions. It is this that St. Peter the Apostle speaks of: "Be sober, be vigilant; because your adversary the devil walks about like a roaring lion, seeking whom he may devour" (1 Pt 5:8). Then one asks for the steady communion of the Holy Spirit of which St. Paul the Apostle speaks (2 Cor 13:14). One also asks for the "fulfillment of the Kingdom of Heaven" as the Kingdom of love which may comprise all people, if possible, but especially those who are partaking. This could also mean the plenitude of union between the faithful and Christ. "And He put all things together under His feet, and gave Him to be head over all things to the church, which is His body, the fullness of Him who fills all in all" (Eph 1:22–23). Finally, one asks for the "boldness" before God. St. Paul speaks of this boldness/confidence (2 Cor 3:4) and it is the saints' state of the soul, who are emboldened while on earth to approach God, as children approach their father, and to ask Him for everything that is necessary for them and for others with full confidence that they will receive. He who is united with Christ has become the Father's son according to grace, and this is why he has the continuous watchfulness and the communion of the Holy Spirit as well as the boldness before God.

After this general indication of the blessings expected from the partaking of the Lord's body and blood, the priest continues with the specific commemoration of those for whom Christ's sacrifice is for glory and of those living and departed who benefit from it. But none of these are told that the glory and the benefit will come through partaking, but that Christ's sacrifice offered in the Liturgy will be for the glory of the saints and for the benefit of other believers remembered, living or departed.

First the priest announces that he offers the reasonable sacrifice for those who have fallen asleep in the faith, and specifically in the their order in the history of salvation: forefathers (Adam and Eve, not forefathers in the sense of our related ancestors), fathers (the first descendants of Adam and Eve), patriarchs, prophets, preachers (who succeeded the Apostles), evangelists, martyrs, confessors, ascetics. We want all to be united in Christ. These are commemorated silently. Then with a loud voice so that all faithful may hear and praise her, the priest commemorates the Birthgiver of God as above all: *Especially for our most holy, most pure, most blessed and glorious Lady, the Birthgiver of God, and Ever-Virgin Mary.*

Although one does not begin the commemoration with the words "in honor of" as at the Proskomedia, this can be seen in the fact that the faithful respond with the hymn of praise for the Birthgiver of God: *It is truly meet*. The commemoration of other saints concludes, as at the Proskomedia, with the words: *by whose prayers visit us, O God*. One can see here that the purpose of the eucharistic sacrifice is not to bring them the forgiveness of sins, watchfulness, the fulfillment of the Kingdom of Heaven and boldness before God, because they already have all these, but at every eucharistic sacrifice they receive an increase in glory and this is why we are also given a greater confidence in their prayers for us.

The perfect sacrifice which Christ offers to the Father for us places in an even greater light the glory of His Mother who gave birth to Him, and the glory which the saints received through the fact that they benefited by obtaining power from her so that they may also sacrifice themselves as well as encouragement to pray even more for us, disregarding themselves. "For I consider that the sufferings of this present time are not worthy to be compared with the glory which shall be revealed to us" (Rom 8:18). On account of Christ's sacrifice, strengthening their faith and transmitting it to other generations together with the examples of their abstinences and labors for Christ, the saints have assured the efficiency of Christ's saving work through the eucharistic sacrifice until today. Thus, their confidence in the saving power of Christ's sacrifice is again confirmed every time. And because of this they are glorified.

St. Paul the Apostle says: "And if children, then heirs—heirs of God and joint heirs with Christ, if indeed we suffer with Him that we may also be glorified together" (Rom 8:17). Or "For our light affliction, which is but for a moment, is working for us a more exceeding and eternal weight of glory" (2 Cor 4:17). And again: "But we all, with unveiled face, beholding as in a mirror the glory of the Lord, are being transformed into the same image from glory to glory, just as by the Spirit of the Lord" (2 Cor 3:18). St. Peter the Apostle says: "Beloved . . . . rejoice to the extent that you partake of Christ's sufferings, but when His glory is revealed, you may also be glad with exceeding joy. If you are reproached for the name of Christ, blessed are you, for the Spirit of glory and of God rests upon you" (1 Pt 4:13-14). The saints have believed in Christ's sacrifice and have appropriated this state of His. This is why even at the present time they continue to be glorified. Let us emulate their example.

St. Peter the Apostle says especially to the priests who shepherd souls with the love of Christ: "The elders who are among you I exhort, I who am a fellow elder and a witness of the sufferings of Christ, and also a partaker of the glory that will be revealed: shepherd the flock of God . . . not by compulsion but willingly . . . and when the Chief Shepherd appears, you will receive the crown of glory that does not fade away" (1 Pt 5:1-2, 4).

If by becoming partakers of Christ's sacrificial passion when they were on earth, transmitting the knowledge of its power to others who succeeded them in time, they have attained joy and glory, will their joy not increase when seeing how through Christ's eucharistic sacrifice many other souls are saved, and also will their glory not increase through the acknowledging by others of the importance of their faith in Christ? Likewise, Christ Himself by granting salvation through His sacrifice, received with conviction by others also due to the faith of the saints, will He not make more evident in their own eyes their glory? But their progression from glory to glory, of which St. Paul the Apostle speaks, also consists in a joint activity of theirs for the salvation of others through their prayers, an activity begun out of their compassion for others, just like Christ's sacrifice, as a joint-sacrifice of theirs or a generous disregard for themselves in view of this salvation.

Everyone who follows the saints in faith will receive perfection (Heb 11:39-40). This is why it is natural for the saints to rejoice about all whom they see ensuring their eternal happiness by honoring Christ's sacrifice, because in this way the saints themselves approach their full happiness according to the measure of their being sensitive of others. And in the faith of those who follow their example over time, the saints see the fructification of the spiritual seed they have planted.

After the commemoration of the Lord's Mother, the priest commemorates silently St. John the Baptist, again the Apostles, the saint of the day and all the saints after Christ, saying: *by whose prayers visit us, O God*. The entire heaven prays for us, offering the sacrifice of all the saints' prayer to Christ's sacrifice that polarizes around it and in it their prayer like a spiritual magnet. The saints have not ceased to exist and to have a role in our life; they are alive and continue to be of help on the path to the eternal Kingdom, together with Christ and from the power of His sacrifice.

And the Lord's Mother is surrounded by the choir of all the saints, being in their midst, alongside Christ who renews again and again the experience and the offering of the sacrifice in order to train those who believe in Him in their offering as sacrifices full of sensibility for others.

After he has commemorated the saints in order to ask for their prayers as from those who stand near Christ who presents His sacrifice to the Father for us, the priest continues with the commemoration of those who have not reached holiness but have fallen asleep in the hope of the resurrection and eternal life. The priest does not ask them for prayers, like he does from the various categories of saints, but he prays God to remember them and to rest them where the light of His countenance shines: *Remember, O Lord, all those who have fallen asleep in the hope of the resurrection and of eternal life; grant them rest, O our God, in a place where the light of Thy countenance shines*. The very remembrance of them by God is their rest in the attention or in the light of Christ's countenance, who saves them from the torment of darkness or of the non-sense of an unhappy existence and emptied of substance through their being forgotten by all others. Their being forgotten by God, reflected in their being forgotten by all, deprives them of the communication of life which no one has only by himself. These are in need of the prayers of the Church, attached as a sacrifice to Christ's sacrifice. It is again evident in this that the eucharistic sacrifice is beneficial also for those who do not partake of it at that particular Liturgy. The Church presents the offering of the sacrificed Christ also for those who have fallen asleep in the faith but who have not yet attained holiness. The eucharistic sacrifice requires that we keep them in solidarity with us on the path to the heavenly Kingdom, except in the case when they left the Church and are still on earth.

Then one proceeds to the prayers for those on earth. Christ wishes to be of benefit to all who are in the Church through the permanent resumption of the offering of His eucharistic sacrifice. It is the spiritual bond of the Church's sobornicity and an exhortation to everyone's love, always repeatedly addressed to all present at the Liturgy.

The priest first prays God to remember the categories of officiating clergy of the Church: Orthodox bishops who teach rightly the word of truth, the priesthood, the deaconate and the monastics. Without their service the Church could not be preserved, nor could the saving work of Christ be officiated. The Church receives power from the continued sacrifice of Christ in order to pray for her own existence. The Church exists through Christ's sacrifice which is continually renewed due to the existence of bishops and priests. But she also exists through her willingness to value in her own prayers the power that irradiates from Christ's ever-active sacrifice. The life of the Church, as a way of continuing the saving work of the Holy Trinity and of Christ, is sustained through a dialogue of sacrifice as a form of love between God and the human community.

Then the priest, using again the expression "furthermore we offer Thee this reasonable service (sacrifice)," broadens his attention by declaring that he offers it *for the whole inhabited world, for the Holy, Catholic and Apostolic Church, for those who live in chastity and purity of life*.

This shows that the priest's previous prayers to God for the remembrance of the living and the departed were also based on Christ being offered as sacrifice at the Holy Liturgy. Additionally he declares that he offers this "reasonable sacrifice" for the civil authorities. But here he specifies that this sacrifice is offered for "their peaceful governing" with the purpose that "in their tranquility," namely in the public tranquility they maintain, *we may live a peaceful and quiet life, in all reverence and purity*. The life of the faithful according to God's will is the purpose for which Christ offers in the Liturgy His sacrifice to the Father.

Next, the priest shows in a concrete way that he offers this "reasonable sacrifice . . . for the salvation and forgiveness of the sins of the servants of God" and he mentions the names of the living. Then, "for the forgiveness and repose of the departed servants of God (names) in a place of light . . .", repeating the prayer for the departed.

The priest says all this silently, while the hymn of praise to the Theotokos is sung. It is from Her that the prayer is extended like a wave, like an omophorion, joined to the priest's prayer for those mentioned. Then with a loud voice the priest asks God to first of all remember the ruling hierarch of the local Church and to grant him length of days, honor and health so that he may teach rightly the word of truth.

The faithful respond with *Remember all Thy people*, thus including all those commemorated by the priest alongside the hierarch. According to the Greek Liturgy book these words are spoken aloud by the deacon before the royal doors with the addition: *And all whom everyone keeps in their thoughts, and all the people.*

At this time the priest silently asks God to remember all categories of faithful who are in various situations. His prayer concludes with the words: *And send Thy mercies upon us all.* God's mercy is the source of all that is needed for everyone. The Church includes all in her prayers; Christ sacrificed Himself for all and He unceasingly presents His sacrifice to the Father from the midst of the liturgical community, He extends to all the waves of His mercy which animates the community and causes it to express, as its response, its will that all may benefit from Christ's sacrifice. The community wants God's mercy to be extended to all, because His Son has been offered as sacrifice for all.

The priest concludes this prayer with the petition to God to extend His will for unity of all in the universal Church up to the gift granted to them to glorify and praise the name of God in Trinity with one mouth and one heart, as one body. God has one name, even though in Him there are three Persons, or this name is triune. The faithful praise and hymn this name with one mouth and with one heart, as one body, even though there are many persons. They wish that there may exist among them a unity which may be likened through love to the unity of the three divine Persons. Just as God, even though triple in Persons, has one name, so it is meet for us, too, to attain to one heart and to one mouth, to one sense perception expressed in the same words of praise. The unconfused unity of the Trinity is the model to which must correspond the unconfused unity of the faithful, or of the Church in which the faithful constitute a multiple unity.

One should also retain from this exclamation of the priest the fact that he asks from God the strength that he and the rest of us *may glorify and praise Thy all-honorable and majestic name of the Father and of the*

Son and of the Holy Spirit. Wherever the name of God is mentioned, God Himself is present. Any prayer addressed to God implies God's presence in the prayer itself and in those who recite it. Sergius Bulgakov has put in bold relief the fact that any prayer is nourished by the calling upon God's name. He remarked in a special way that the name given to God by the human person is not the product of that person, but a sense perception of God's energy in itself, which determines the human person to give that energy, or to the divine Subject manifested through that energy, an adequate name. In this way the human person elevates the word used as a name for God above its meaning relating to things or actions in the world, but still this name makes use of the names given to certain energies of things and actions in the world, since the latter have God as their ultimate cause or their active and conscious support. Consequently, any praise offered to God, or to a name of His, is an experience of God who is present and active through all things and actions in the world, but as being above all and comprising all.

"Prayer becomes the prayer of God; it receives its objective meaning as the union of a human being with God precisely through God's presence in the prayer itself, the transcendent-immanent abiding of the Name of God in it. The Name of God is the ontological foundation of prayer, its substance, power, and justification." The very name of God spoken or thought of with reverence is a concentrated prayer. "Therefore, in its essence, prayer is the invoked Name of God. But as the Name of God contains divine energy, gives God's presence, then one can say, although with imprecision, that practically and energetically the Name of God is God. More accurately, God's Power, which is indivisible from the Essence of God and is in this sense God himself, is present in it."[364] Or "Always and everywhere, where in invoking we name Him, we also have His presence in the Name, and it already depends on us, on the transparency of our soul, how we will feel this presence."[365]

God gives the revelation of His presence or energy, and the human person, by sensing this presence or energy, gives it a name as adequate as possible, taking a word relating to the energy of things in the world, but elevating it from the significance proper to them as self-sustaining energies of things. The name of God conveys cataphatically-apophatically God's presence or energy as direct cause present in all things and sustaining of all, but above the word borrowed by the human person from the world, applied to God, and it becomes transparent for God and proper to Him, without exhausting God in all of His mysterious depth.[366] But Bulgakov makes the distinction between the multiple names given to God as names of His attributes and God's "proper name."

The words we use for God's attributes or for His names, such as: Good, Almighty, All-Sustaining, etc., are sacred by the fact that they are used for God, but they also maintain their meaning received from created things but infinitely expanded. The "proper name" given to God causes to appear in the first instance God's mystery, going almost totally beyond their meaning borrowed from the things in the world. For the proper name refers to God's Subject, which has no relation to created things sustained by Him. At most, this name has a relation with the human subject. But this is in itself an unfathomable mystery.

"The difference between Names of God and the Name of God as such is connected with the fact that their independent, verbal, predicative meaning lives in them, whereas here it is completely absorbed by the name, it exists only as a name. In both cases the grace and power of God are present, . . . But in the first case we have only a gracious hallowing of an element—namely of a word; we have, so to say, a holy word, similar to how we have holy water, holy blessed bread, . . . the element nevertheless keeps its proper nature . . . . In the second case, when we have, as it were, the proper Name of God, God's I, the proper nature of the word, its 'inner form,' or significance, seemingly evaporates. Yahweh is the Name of God not at all because it signifies *who is*, for the attribute of being still does not express the essence of God in any exclusive sense, it stands here alongside other attributes or names. This word makes the exclusive presence of God's power in it the Name of God . . . . However, once the revelation has occurred, and the Lord has proclaimed, 'I am Yahweh,' the independent meaning of the word *who is* completely dissolves and becomes only a verbal form for containing the Name of God, for containing what is a super word for human language while being a word that humans accommodate. One can say that the proper meaning of the word *who is* no longer has that meaning that it had in the moment of choosing this word for the Name. After this, it becomes transparent glass and only lets the rays through but does not reflect them."[367]

Bulgakov's observations need to be correlated with new specifications in order to make more evident the distinction between the Name and other words used to indicate God. The name is given only to the human being and to God, in their quality as persons, capable of using the word. Only the human being can speak, because he is a person. And the human being speaks to another human being, because the latter is also a person. Only persons are capable of dialogue, because only they can transmit their thought to each other. Only persons can use words. They imply an addresser and an addressee, as persons, while the content of words forms the world of objects as well as the thoughts, feelings, deeds of persons, which in general are also connected to objects. All are communicated by a person to another person who receives them. The nonexistence of a recipient makes the word, just like the letter, impossible. The words are common, but not in the sense of a "we" that speaks them as a multitude united in a single subject, but in the sense of a mutual addressing and reception. When they are recited or sung by a group of faithful as "we," this "we" still has a *You* who receives them, namely God.

But there is another way in which one can see that the words mutually addressed by human persons have the personal God as their ultimate origin and as both supreme addresser and addressee. When human beings mutually address and receive words, they show that their things, thoughts, feelings and actions are to be expressed as being addressed by one person to another. All of them are not to be possessed by an indistinct *we*, but mutually communicated and received by persons. I offer all of them continually to others and I receive them from others. I relate through all to others and others relate to me. Through all I offer myself voluntarily to others and others offer themselves to me. All our life is made up of acts of continuous mutual offering and sacrificing, thus uniting ourselves ever more, but also affirming each other. These are limited self-offerings and affirmations.

But I would like the other to offer me greater things than the ones he offers me and I would like to hold him in his absolute self-offering. However, I see that he cannot do that and in his self-offering I have neither the absolute nor the unlimited and eternal life. I would like to see the world transformed by my fellow human beings in my favor to a greater extent, or even to feel that they offer it to me as the ones producing it. But I see that it is not my fellow human being who gives me the most essential things, but they are given both to me and to him. The intellect itself is not given to me by others, nor did I give it to myself, but I realize that it is given to me. Corresponding to this, neither do we create words out of nothing, but they represent the expression of sense perceptions found in the things given to us.

But if we do not give each other from ourselves the things themselves and the intellect that discovers their meanings, but we give each other only certain transformations and discoveries of them, I am forced to admit that there is someone who addressed them to us so that we may receive and use them, acknowledging their existence as not coming from us. If things and our mind that thinks them are created for all in order to, as persons, mutually address and receive them—but we do not have the power to mutually address them except after we slightly transform them—I am forced to admit that there is a person who gives them to me, giving at the same time existence to the world and to me. The almighty Person can address to us the world and the words, as the author of their very essence or existence, after He has created us as persons capable of receiving them. There must exist an almighty Person, an unlimited offerer of the world, which He created so as to address it to us to be used and to maintain it as always intended for us for this purpose. The very fact that we are able to express everything in words shows that everything is addressed to us, since we are capable of receiving and repeating the words. For only the supreme Person can address words as primary, ontological and sonorous incarnations. Only that Person can address words from the beginning and these words can only be addressed to persons. The world is thus created by a supreme Person for other persons who are also created by that supreme Person.

It is with that Person that we are in the fundamental dialogue that lies at the basis of every inter-human dialogue. We are to ask for many things from others, but only what they can give us, thus what we can ask from them is also limited; we are to thank others, but the thanksgiving addressed to them is not for all things. We are to praise others for what they have accomplished for us and for others. But the praise offered to them must be measured according to the much too small amount they could do.

But this tendency to ask, to thank and to praise through words in an absolute manner cannot be without sense. We want to receive everything and to offer ourselves totally in an absolute manner. For this there must exist an absolute addressee and an absolute addresser who raises us, too, to the level of partners with absolute wishes. We sense that there is someone from whom everything comes, who sustains all and to whom we must offer thanks for everything.

And He who gives us everything, He to Whom we offer thanks for everything, He Whom we praise for everything, He Who offers Himself to us in the fullness of His almightiness and to Whom we can offer ourselves in an absolute manner, must be a person like us but capable of giving us everything and on whom we depend totally. He addresses Himself through all things to the human person and can create and maintain all things for this purpose. He is thus the supreme Person, the supreme I who comprises all things, but above all things. He can thus make us His partners, even though He is absolute, as the original and endless source of all things, and we are created. He is an I like the human I, related to but distinct from the human I. The human I can make use of all things, can address himself to God through all things, being able to encompass all and to communicate through all things with God, but he cannot create and sustain. Therefore, the human I can see God through all things.

But God's proper name indicates especially God as the supreme conscious Subject above all the things He gives us, but having in Himself as potentialities all created things which He could and can sustain infinitely, since He has infinity in Himself from eternity. In Him there are the inner reasons of all things, as He Himself is above all uncreated and created reasons, knowable and knowing, just like the name of the human person, too, indicates the human, conscious I, incomprehensible neither by the self nor by other human I's, but only by the divine I, although the human I's are able to communicate through words. The human I can sense the presence of the divine I and can speak unceasingly about Him, but the human I cannot totally comprehend the divine I eternally and cannot express Him explicitly through any name. The divine I and the human I are in a dialogical relationship, due to the good will of the divine I, telling each other many things, but the words to each other never being exhaustive. The human I can produce words ad infinitum when interpreting the meaning communicated by the divine I through the created world by His uncreated energies, but the words of the human I can never be sufficient for comprehending the divine I completely and properly.

As a person being addressed, I found myself being able to engage in the dialogical relationship with the supreme Person, initially addressing me out of His good will. The supreme Person also granted me the quality of being able to address Him. But I address the supreme Person only after I had been created and thereby being able to address Him. Because the supreme and original Person that does the addressing wants me to be in a dialogue with Him in which I may not be only a recipient, but also one who can address, capable of initiatives even vis-à-vis the supreme Person. Thus He endowed me with the capacity of voluntary growth, with the conscience that I can ask and receive from Him even more things along the line of what I received, that I can understand not only the incarnate words given to me through creation, but also other words increasingly deeper and richer and to sense, both as addressee and addresser, the supreme Person ad infinitum in the mystery of His unfathomable presence, and to express this sense perception in the praises I offer Him. Only in this dialogue in which I am also active am I able to advance, on the one hand, into the infinite depth of the supreme Person, but on the other hand, I am not confounded in Him.

My active and proper role in the dialogue with the absolute I is manifested specifically in prayer. The prayer, therefore, makes a complete person, but dependent on the supreme I. Otherwise I would remain an object adorned with all kinds of ornaments, but incapable of rising to the role of being a true partner of God and also dependent on Him.

Along the line of what has been said about persons as both addressees and addressers, and about God as the addresser and supreme Person who also allows Himself to be addressed, one can go a step further in distinguishing the person, a bearer of a proper name, from the objects that only have common names.

It is not at random that God names Himself to Moses as: "I am Who I am," giving the people the task of elevating Him above the usual meaning of the general word "is," to immerse it in mystery, as Bulgakov says. Only the person can say "I am," because only the person is conscious of his existence; objects cannot say about themselves that they are, because they cannot speak. And this is why neither are they in the fuller mode in which persons are. Furthermore, conscious persons, even if they can say that the objects are, they can also say that they *have* them, while about any person I can only say that he *is*. The person *is*, the object is owned. The object does not have meaning except for the fact that it is owned by a person. The persons consciously handle the objects, while the objects cannot consciously handle persons. The objects have a "is" handled without their will, the persons do not.³⁶⁸

The sense perception of one own's existence is an immeasurable plus of existence. The existence that senses itself has an acuity, a powerfully imposing presence, it is an existence of an incomprehensibly superior degree. It is a complete and true existence. Hence it can also say *I*. Between the word *is* and *I* there is an organic relation. There is a mutual implication between their meanings. Another person's existence is sensed by me as having the same acuity and as having a power to exert pressure, thus being for me an active hindrance or wall, a power to make my existence easier or to make it grow. I feel someone else's existence much more intensely when I am in the I-you dialogue with that person. That person acts and reacts consciously to my existence. We handle the objects together, we offer them to each other transformed or not, or we talk about them using words. The objects acquire a much greater importance when they are handled by two or more persons, when they form the medium of communication or of mutual giving or receiving. We *are*, but the objects we *own*. We hold a dialogue between us about them, but we cannot hold a dialogue with them. Strictly speaking, I do not use my name when speaking with another person, but I simply say *I*. I can call the other by name, but I never discard the pronoun *you, to you, yours*. I use the name more when I speak about a third person so as to distinguish him from other persons. When I speak directly to you, I have distinguished you by this very fact from other persons. My communication with you is more direct when I say *you, to you, yours*.

In any case, even if I call you by name, I cannot detach myself from the forms of the second person pronouns. If I do not say *you*, I at least say *thou*.³⁶⁹ I fully sense my independent existence in myself when saying *I*, and similarly the existence of the other person with whom I speak when I say *you* or *thou*. The name is only a substitution, thus a completion, which at first indicated a specific characteristic of *you*. You are Theodore (the gift of God) as an independent *I* or *you*. Through *I*, *you*, and *he* applied to the person, I express the experience as an active center of the person. The proper name substitutes this experience. When the person is far off, it is necessary to express that person through a name. I can no longer identify that person through a *you* experienced here. But I experience myself differently when saying *I* than I experience you. When saying *I*, I live my existence as mine, which is distinct from the experience of existence as yours.

When speaking in the first person, God says not only: "My name is the One who is," but also "I am Who I am." Additionally it would be almost a pleonasm if God did not want to distinguish Himself from the human being who says *I* or *I am*. By adding the words *Who is*, God shows that He is the only One who exists in a perfect and true mode. Through the very pronoun *I* that someone says about oneself, one says that one is; it is sufficient to say *I* to show that *I am*. But God says about Himself: *I am Who I am*, showing that He has not only the conscience that He exists among others who exist, but that He exists *par excellence*. He is uniquely the One who exists truly. He is the primordial existence of everything that exists, the source of all existences.

He gave an existence to all incomparably reduced than His: to objects, an existence with no other purpose than to be possessed and mutually shared, without their knowledge, by persons; to persons He gave an existence much more real, but having need of objects that are possessed and shared among them so as to manifest themselves to each other as well as to manifest their mutual interest, having the need to mutually communicate themselves. The more what they communicate is formed of objects, the more they make use of words. Moreover, God gave the persons all things He created as transferable objects between them as well as words for deciphering. But created persons have the objects as gifts from Him, not as being produced by them. If all the things in the world as objects could be ours in a limited way, they must totally belong by their very essence to a supreme Person. By manifesting through them our love among ourselves, or by communicating ourselves through them to each other, we manifest and communicate ourselves within God's love for all of us, we sustain our love among ourselves from His love.

How did God create the human being as person, an I as partner of dialogue with Him, also giving him a name?

What sometimes occurs between the human person and an animal to whom he is sentimentally attached, helps us to slightly understand this mystery. When a human person is attached to a domestic animal and thereby also gives it a name, the latter responds through a manifestation of a feeling to the calling, caressing, or the command of the master. It awakens in it a sort of half an I. But the human person cannot go so far with the degree of his affection and power as to determine the appearance of a proper I in the animal attached to him. Neither can he give the animal the power to call him by name, as the human person addresses God, even if this name is a pronoun, given the mystery of the divine Subject as well as that of the human subject. God was able to do this through the "breathing" of His almighty Spirit full of supreme love, through the breathing of His life into man, or through the setting of the human person in a special ontological relation with Him.

By creating each person as an I, God has placed us in dialogical dependence on Him, as our You. For there cannot exist an I except as an addresser and as an addressee of a you and, in the last instance, of the divine You. In order to distinguish each of our you's, God has also given a name to each one of us.

Thus He has become Himself our You, our supreme You. So He has placed Himself in a dialogical relationship with us. And in His quality as almighty addresser and as addressee from whom we ask for everything, He gave and gives us all things as objects of His dialogue with us, as His gifts to us, so that we may return them to Him. But He has given and also gives us many other superior, uncreated energies in order to elevate our life and to fill the created world with a divine content. However, He Himself as You remains indescribable for us, thus showing Himself as our model, or us as His image. The name refers precisely to this subject at the basis of every self-offering and of every dialogue, just as the pronoun I or you.

To God we can give any name taken from the attributes in the world, especially from the human person's good attributes amplified to the maximum through the experience of His uncreated energies meant to elevate the attributes of things and of human beings. Because it is from Him that everything comes. All things have their source in Him, but to Him we say more properly *He who is*. But we cannot use any name, not even *He who is*, if we do not link it to the pronoun *You* or *to You* by which we affirm God's mystery, just as through this pronoun we affirm our mystery as persons, still elevating the mystery of the divine pronoun infinitely above the mystery of the human pronoun, as a mystery from which the human mystery derives its existence. In this pronoun: *You, to You* we feel most directly His supreme presence and existence on which everything depends.

But God is not a single Person, but a Trinity of Persons. Similar to this, He has three names in addition to the one name God. In the case of human beings, the name of each person refers to a subject manifesting himself as another in the dialogue with other persons. In the case of God, the name of each Person also refers to a subject manifesting Himself as being another in the dialogue between Him and us. But since the divine subjects are not fractionized in their modes of acting well, but each one has in Himself all possible good modes, they cannot be distinguished through names that would show a certain fractionization, but through names that show each one in relation with the others and as having in Himself the infinite goodness and life, yet one manifesting Himself as supreme Father, the other as supreme Son of the supreme Father and the Holy Spirit as the supreme Spirit giver of life. Each one implies the others and through each one we see the others. One is the Father *par excellence*, but we cannot think of Him as Father without thinking of the Son. We cannot be in relationship with Him as Father if we are not in relationship with His Son. Still, this name distinguishes the Father from every other human or divine person. Another Person is the Son *par excellence*. This name distinguishes Him from every other human or divine person, but we cannot think of the Son without thinking of the Father. The Holy Spirit is likewise the name of a Person distinct from every other human or divine person. But we cannot think of the Holy Spirit without thinking of the Father and the Son. And by having the Holy Spirit we are in relationship with the Father and the Son. Human beings are not distinguished from all through one or another of their names, but only from some of them. The divine Persons are distinguished not only among themselves, but from any other human person through these names. The human person is not distinguished through the proper name from all other persons. Additionally, the name does nothing except to distinguish him from other persons, but it does not also characterize him. However, the names Father, Son and Holy Spirit not only distinguish the divine Persons from other persons, but they also show their unique characteristic. From the Father comes all fatherhood, from the Son comes all sonship. When we say Father, or Son, or Holy Spirit we know that we do not name except the unique Father *par excellence*, the unique Son *par excellence*, and the unique Holy Spirit, and all together as the Unique God. This is why the priest can say: *And grant us that with one mouth and one heart we may glorify and praise*

Thine all honorable and majestic name, of the Father, and of the Son, and of the Holy Spirit, now and ever, and unto the ages of ages. Amen! The persons bearing these names will procure supreme happiness for us, because one is our Father without diminishing, His Son is our perfect Brother and the Holy Spirit is our cathartic Spirit purifying us from every sinful egoism as well as our unifier through love with the Father and with the Son and among ourselves. And they will grant us this happiness unto the ages of ages, for by existing from eternity they can make us happy for eternity. They will grant us the happiness of union with Them and among ourselves in the Kingdom of the Holy Trinity or of the eternal love. This is why we praise Them now with one mouth and one heart, sensing even now the unity which They have begun, as one God, to accomplish among us. But this happiness will be granted to us through the mercy of the Savior Jesus Christ. This is why, by continuing the supplication, the priest addresses the faithful, saying while he blesses them with the sign of the cross—like the one by which Christ has saved us: *And may the mercies of our great God and Savior Jesus Christ be with you all.* He has asked for God's mercy or announced it in the litany after the reading of the Holy Gospel in which Christ showed how merciful He is with us, and he asks for it and recalls it again at this time when, through the transformation of the bread and wine into the body and blood of the One sacrificed in order to be given to us, He showed us even more how merciful He is. One asks and recalls with more certainty the mercy of the One who showed that He is disposed to give what is asked. But the incarnate Son of God had shown that He wants to give us even His life so as to save us. This is why one asks and one announces in a certain manner (as stated in the Greek text) the mercy of the incarnate Son who has sacrificed Himself for us. One announces or one wishes upon those present the mercy of the One who has shown through the transformation of the bread and wine into His body and blood that He is at their disposal to unite Himself with them and thereby to lead them to the resurrection in which He is with His body. Through the incarnation the Son took a new name, the name of Savior: Jesus Christ. This new name will be written on the city of the new Jerusalem, of the Kingdom of those saved and united with the Holy Trinity (Rev 3:12). It is in this name that we will be saved. His mercy, which will be manifested also in the fact that He will be given to us in Holy Communion, is announced or wished upon the faithful.

Through the prayers recited after the transformation of the gifts the priest petitioned God's mercy for various categories of people on the basis of the sacrifice offered at that particular Liturgy for and by His Son. At this time he asks that all together may share in God's mercy, but in the first place for those present in church and, thus, on their behalf; he asks that God's mercies of all kinds may be extended to all. All praise God as a single body; it is upon all that God's mercies may come as upon one body. These mercies have been shown as being available through Christ's sacrifice. This is why His sacrifice is a sacrifice of mercy. And through His mercy coming upon all from His sacrifice, Christ wants to bring all to a multi-personal unity similar to the Holy Trinity. For the lack of unity produces suffering, because it is the result of sin, of pride, of greed and of disagreements.

Salvation is the same as bringing all people to unity, and the force by which God wants to bring them to unity is His mercy for all manifested in His sacrifice for all. One cannot understand Christ's sacrifice without His mercy. The permanence of His state of sacrifice before the Father is the permanence of His mercy, which also keeps the Father in this disposition toward mercy, and it comes within souls through the Holy Spirit. The healthy life of humankind is measured by its unity. And its health and unity cannot be restored and sustained without the sacrifice by the mercy of the Holy Trinity, meant to sow in the faithful, too, the mercy for each other and the disposition for sacrifice.[370]

Through the sacrifice on Golgotha Jesus Christ has become a Savior for us in general. By offering His sacrifice to the Father in the Liturgy being officiated He is Savior for those present. Only at this point in the Liturgy is Jesus Christ named Savior: *the Savior* and *the Great God*. This is the moment to mention this, because the state of sacrifice in which Christ is on the altar shows that He is the Savior *par excellence*. But this humble and generous state of sacrifice on the altar is not opposed to the fact that at the same time He is God, even "the Great God," not lesser than God, although He is incarnate and sacrificed. This is precisely the condition for which He is the "Savior" through His sacrifice as man. As non-incarnate God, He would not have become a Savior for us, nor would we have truly known Him as "the Great God." Through His sacrifice His true divine glory has been manifested, by which He was able to save us. A god who cannot save us, who cannot act so as to prevent the appearance [into existence] of humans and then their disappearance [from existence] altogether is not great, or not even God.

We have seen that Father, Son and Holy Spirit are the most proper names of the triune Persons, that distinguish them from all created persons and among themselves, but they also indicate each one's proper and unique meaning.

But the Son did not remain Son only within the Trinity. He also became Jesus Christ and the Savior through His incarnation, sacrifice and resurrection. These are two names that express His special relation with human persons. He became man, but He maintained His uniqueness since He also remained "the Great God." He has a unique name. By taking the name Jesus Christ He took a name similar to human beings. But this name belongs only to Him in all humankind, we cannot find it repeated among other human beings. For this very name translated in Romanian means Savior, Messiah, or the Savior anointed as eternal King. It is only in Him that we are saved and have eternal life as heirs of the eternal Kingdom. "Nor is there salvation in any other, for there is no other name under heaven given among men by which we must be saved" (Acts 4:12). It is only through Him that mercy has been manifested and that God's mercy will be eternally manifested toward men.

"According to Paul, Jesus' name is not only *a* name above all names, it is *the* name above every name. It is not only a way to God, a name for salvation; it is the only name that 'salvation is.' Jesus and the life he gives are one, He and God have the same name."[371]

The Orthodox bishop Kallistos Ware has collected in a book many texts from the writings of the spiritual Fathers on the power of Jesus Christ's name. Here are two of them: "'The Name of the Son of God is great and boundless, and upholds the entire universe.'"[372] "In the words of two Elders of Gaza, St. Barsanuphius and St. John (sixth century), 'The remembrance of the Name of God utterly destroys all that is evil.'"[373] "'Flog your enemies with the Name of Jesus', says St. John Climacus, 'for there is no weapon more powerful in heaven or on earth.'"[374] And Kallistos Ware himself says: "The power and glory of God is *numen praesens*, God with us, *Emmanuel*. Attentively and deliberately to invoke God's Name is to place oneself in his presence, to open oneself to his energy."[375]

This is why from ancient times the Eastern Church has practiced the prayer: "Lord Jesus Christ, the Son of God, have mercy on me, a sinner."

Perhaps these words of the priest from the Liturgy refer to this prayer. And it is possible that upon hearing these words the faithful pondered on this prayer. And in the early Church by the name Christ one indicated: "Jesus Christ, the Son of God, the Savior" (ιχθυς).

Conscious of the deep mercy for human beings, which lies at the basis of the sacrifice offered now by Christ to the Father, the priest wishes that this saving mercy of Christ, which is also the Father's, be poured out upon all. This is why the people respond to the supplications of the litany that follows with: *Lord have mercy.*

But first the faithful respond to the priest's wish that God's mercies be with all of them with the words: *And with your spirit.*

Sometimes the priest finds himself speaking in the singular in the dialogue of prayer with God, but very seldom. Even then he does not feel that he is alone, but together with the community. This is why many times he addresses God with "we," showing that he speaks on behalf of all the faithful in the church and for all.

Therefore, in his dialogue with God he directs his attention to them. At other times he is in dialogue with the faithful, like here: *And may the mercies of our great God and Savior Jesus Christ be with you all.* And the faithful respond: *And with your spirit.* In this case, the priest's dialogue with the community also includes God. The dialogue always keeps all three parts connected: God, the priest, the community. Never is the priest's direction of his attention toward God or toward the community lacking. The dialogue always takes place among the three. God, even if He holds the position of He, is above, being the source of power and of mercy. The prayer is directed to Him, and the community, even when it holds the third place, is the main object of the priest's care and of God's. And the priest is in the middle, between God and the community as main characters he is in one way God's servant, and of the community in another. But most of the time he is the addresser, either by himself or with the community, and God is the addressee. But the priest is the addresser on account of his responsibility for the community.

At this time he draws the curtain over the royal doors, as he did after the words: *Let us give thanks to the Lord,* thus indicating the incomprehensible mystery of the Lord's body and blood's presence on the Holy Table, as it was seen earlier at the mystery of the transformation.

Then the priest continues with the litany in which he asks from God what is necessary for the preparation of those who will partake, but also for various favors specified on behalf of those who will not partake. The faithful respond to all these supplications with: *Lord have mercy.*

In the first supplication, after the fulfillment of the duty to commemorate all the saints is proclaimed, for glorifying them through the transformation of the gifts, the community is urged by the deacon, or by the priest if the deacon is not present, to again pray to the Lord in peace. The peace asked for now is certainly one on a another level. It is the peace of those who are standing before the sacrificed Lord.

Then the community is encouraged to pray together with the priest and the deacon *for the precious gifts which have been offered and sanctified*. They were first offered to God, then they were sanctified, namely they were transformed into the Lord's body and blood. This is a supplication that the transformed gifts may be beneficial to those who will partake of them and also those who will not.

In the third supplication, after it has been established that God "has received them onto His holy, heavenly and spiritual altar as an offering of sweet spiritual fragrance," He is asked that in return for the gifts transformed into the Lord's body and blood, He may send down upon the priest and upon the faithful "the divine grace and the gift of the Holy Spirit." The Holy Table upon which the gifts have been transformed is the visible image of the heavenly altar. The gifts have been transformed precisely at the moment in which they were received upon that altar.

This "spiritual or reasonable altar" is none other than Christ. He is both the High Priest, the Sacrifice and the Altar. "He is the Altar, He is the incense and the High Priest" and He is also "the blood for the forgiveness of sins."[376] St. Cyril sees Him signified by the mercy seat (cover) set upon the ark of the covenant from the Holy of Holies guarded by a cherubim on each side. From above this mercy seat God spoke to Moses and made Himself known to him (Ex 25:17–22). The image has been fulfilled in Christ. He is the true altar, or the cover (mercy seat) upon which He offers Himself, both the High Priest and the sacrifice of a sweet fragrance offered to the Father. This is why St. Paul and St. John the Evangelist, by applying to Christ the words "the altar of reconciliation" or "the altar of redemption" from the Old Testament, name Him both sacrifice and redeemer. For them the sacrifice and the altar are in Christ one and the same thing. This understanding by the Apostles, as High Priest, as Sacrifice and as Altar, is taken up by St. Cyril of Alexandria when he writes: "And we say that the Redeemer [the mercy seat—ιλαστη'ριον], if understood spiritually, is the One who became man for us. God set Him forth as redeemer for the faith in His blood 'to demonstrate His righteousness' (Rom 3:25), as St. Paul says. And also John, the wisest disciple, writes: 'My little children, these things I write to you, so that you may not sin. And if anyone sins, we have an Advocate with the Father, Jesus Christ the righteous. And He Himself is the propitiation for our sins, and not for ours only but also for the whole world' (1 Jn 2:1–2). For through Him there is redemption, all prayer and all supplication for the good things. 'Until now you have asked nothing in My name. Ask, and you will receive' (Jn 16:24)."[377]

St. Cyril of Alexandria goes on to say that in Christ, who is up there before the Father, as High Priest, as Sacrifice and as Altar, are our gifts as well, or ourselves, and that He raises us, too, to the height He ascended as man through sacrifice, since He is also God: "So He is the Redeemer. For through Him the Father is merciful to us and in Him our prayer reaches its mark and through Him we draw near to the Father, as we are accepted in no other way. This is why He says: 'No one comes to the Father except through Me' (Jn 14:6)."[378] Therefore, even though the Word, God's Only-begotten, became like us descending to humanity through kenosis, and to the possibility of our partaking of Him, it is still proper for Him to also abide, through His essence, in the divine glory and to be at the heights above creation, as He was before incarnation. This is why the Cherubim stand around the Redeemer (altar, sacrifice, Christ the High Priest). They cover Him with their wings, are turned toward Him and keep their gaze fixed on Him. The clear proof that they stand on guard is that they stand at both the right and left hands. And the fact that the Cherubim are forever looking toward the Redeemer shows the proclivity of the Powers on high to never be satisfied in their desire to see God.

The loftier God is, the more amazing and greater His sacrifice for us as well as the value conferred upon us.

But the state of sacrifice before the Father for us shows a new relation, extremely intimate, of Christ as man with the Father, as well as His relation as God with us. It is a supreme relation of the Father's love with and honor for Christ also as man. This is why it can be said that the Altar on high is supported by the Father, that Christ's sacrifice permeates the Father with its fragrance. The reasonable altar is the spiritual "place" before the Father, it is the heavenly Father's bosom. It is in His intimacy that the sacrificed humanity of the Son was received; or the

Son sacrificed His humanity by immersing Himself within the loving bosom of the Father. When I sacrifice myself for someone else, I find in him something similar to a table upon which I set this sacrifice and from which he who receives it nourishes his joy and mercy. This table in the one I sacrifice myself for is personal. Even if it is the person of the other, still that person is not outside of me. The one I sacrifice myself for is different from me, but in my state of sacrifice the union between him and me is accomplished. In this sacrifice we encounter each other: I as the one who offer myself and he as the one receiving me. But we also unite with us even those for whom I offer myself as sacrifice. The Son and the Father have become "our God" through the sacrifice of the Son. They have become for us an intimate God.

Where Christ's sacrifice is there is not only Christ, nor is there only the Father or only the Holy Spirit, but all three of them. To use an image, it is the weeping of the Son sacrificed as man for us in the bosom of the Father. It is the maximum entrance of the humanity appropriated by the Son into the Father's intimacy through sacrifice. It is our Brother who weeps for us in the Father's bosom. As long as humanity appropriated by the Son was not sacrificed, it was not fully pervaded by divinity, because it had not been perfectly offered to the Father. But the incarnate and sacrificed Son represents us. He enters before the Father suffering and sacrificing Himself for us. He enters through mercy before the One who is mercy. And in His sacrifice is also our sacrifice represented by our gifts. His mercy for us, that causes Him to sacrifice Himself, and the Father's mercy for Him as man and for us are united. Christ's humanity raised to the Father in a sacrificed state makes the Father full of compassion for us. This compassion is poured out over Christ's humanity and upon us through the Spirit of the Father. St. Paul the Apostle says: "For through Him we both have access by one Spirit to the Father" (Eph 2:18). St. Cyril of Alexandria developed at length this idea of St. Paul that we do not have access to the Father except through the Son's sacrifice to which we join our sacrifice. In this way Christ's sacrifice effected not only Christ's encounter with the Father, but also ours: "For Christ sacrificed Himself because of us and for our benefit and He climbed up on the altar as a Lamb with a sweet smelling fragrance for God."[379] "Therefore, in Christ we gain the possibility of coming before God. For He deems us worthy of gazing upon Him even now, as the ones who are sanctified [namely sacrificed]."[380] "In Christ we have gained the courage for and the access to the Holy of Holies, as the wise Paul told us . . . . For in Him we arrived before the Father."[381] "Thus Jesus necessarily climbs up with us [onto the divine altar]. Because we draw near the Father, as we said, through the Son and He is the Mediator who unites us with Him and raises us to the heights above nature."[382] The Son is both sacrifice and altar. But He is both of these before the Father. It is to this height that our humanity rises. If we ascend to the Father with our sacrifice united with Christ's sacrifice, one cannot dilute the reality of the eucharistic transformation or of the presence of Christ's body and blood in the Eucharist.

The Russian Archbishop Alexei and another Russian theologian, Vitalie Borovoi, adopt Bulgakov's theory that the transformation of bread and wine into Christ's body and blood means only a connection between the bread and wine with His body and blood in such a way that he who eats the bread and drinks the blood surely makes the transition (ascends) to His body and blood. Bulgakov says: "The transformation means not a transformation of one matter into another within the framework of the material world, but the union of two worlds, of two domains of existence that are metaphysically separated from each other. The transformation in this sense cannot be an object of perception through the senses that relates to this world. This is why this transformation, which is totally invisible to the bodily eyes and totally inaccessible to physical sense perception, cannot be but the object of faith."[383]

Bulgakov understands the "transformation" only as a transformation of the use of bread and wine as a means of transition (passing over, ascent) to Christ's body and blood, as a "trans-value." But we think it worth considering that Christ's body and blood penetrate through the Holy Spirit in them so much into the eucharistic bread and wine that they become the latter's invisible foundation and content. If the transition from them to Christ's body and blood is necessarily effected, it is impossible for them not to have a transforming effect on the bread and wine, albeit not physical or chemical. If the holy water has within it a supra-essential power, although physically and chemically it remains the same water, even more so does this occur with the eucharistic bread and wine. There is not just the power of Christ's body and blood in them (or of the Spirit in them, as Archbishop Alexei says in conformity with Calvinism), but the very body and blood of Christ who, in this sense, transformed the eucharistic bread and wine.

This transformation takes place on the invisible plane and in an invisible and incomprehensible manner. On the surface the presence of the Word's body full of light and fire, into which the ontological foundation of the bread was transformed, remains covered by the image of bread in solidarity with this world. But the bread and wine do not remain outside the influence of Christ's body and blood. They can no longer be considered as simply bread and wine. They no longer have in themselves their independent foundation. The bread has rediscovered its foundation in Christ's body full of light, just as in the life to come the foundations of all will be found in His transfigured and luminous body. The inner principles (reasons) of created beings coming from the supreme Reason are again being immersed in It, as St. Maximos the Confessor says.[384] By taking within us the images of bread and wine, we take within us Christ's body and blood in which they have found their foundation. This fact anticipates our partaking of Christ through all things in the age to come when the inner principles of all things will be united with their models found in the divine Logos and in His body, thus with Himself. The working divine power of the Holy Spirit from within His body is so great that Christ's body has no need to assimilate as nourishment the bread and wine in order to transform them, but it incorporates them at once into His body and blood, or it acts so that His body and blood may be extended into the bread and wine and so that only their images remain, distinct from Christ, still preserving in Him their foundations or proper inner principles (reasons).

We do not partake of a static body and blood, but a body activating to overwhelm, to assimilate the bread and wine; or through the images of bread and wine we partake of Christ's body and blood in their action of articulating and unifying the bread and wine in them. The hypostasis of the Word, bearing His resurrected body and blood, begins to become—by receiving the bread and wine incorporated in His body and blood more and more like the hypostasis of the human body and blood—the central hypostasis of all those who partake of them. This is why many faithful partake of them more often, thus giving Christ the opportunity to become more and more the central Hypostasis of all who partake.

This understanding of the transformation gives us the possibility of understanding the expression "reasonable sacrifice" applied to both our sacrifice and to that of Christ. Our body can transform the bread into our body. But we offer the bread as our potential body to the Father through

Christ. And God the Word acts so that our potential body may be transformed into His sacrificed body through His word of prayer to the Father united with the priest's word. If the divine Word becomes body, all the more does He transform into His body our bread which is potentially part of our body.

In this sense the transformation itself is an act of sacrifice, of reasonable sacrifice and of sacrifice of Christ's body, with which we have already united ourselves through words and through our gifts of bread and wine. For Christ who sacrifices Himself comes into the words of our body and into our gifts, transforming them at the invisible level into His body, but allowing them to remain at our visible level with their image of bread and wine as our gifts representing the sacrifice of our body in union with the sacrifice of Christ's body.

This is the reason why the Lord's bloodless sacrifice is also called reasonable sacrifice, which also includes our sacrifice, for any gift of the Lord to the Father for us and to ourselves includes our gift as well, which the Lord offers to the Father so that it may be returned to us. And this gift is the very word of the Lord and of us. This is also based on the fact that His fundamental gift to the Father and to us is Himself as the incarnate Word and us as reasonable words. He shows therefore His sacrifice through the images of bread and wine, and our sacrifice through the bread and wine that we brought forth as potentialities of our body in order to transform them into His body and blood, through which He offers Himself to the Father and then He offers Himself to us. Our gift of bread and wine, as our potential body, transformed into His body and blood, becomes His sacrifice.

Our body is a means of our subject's manifestation as image of the divine Word. It is a thickened, materialized means. But it contains in itself the necessity and capacity to transform the bread and wine into itself. Essentially, the body is bread and the bread is body. But this capacity of the body to transform the bread into itself is implied in our subject as image of the Word. It is only because and only as long as we can speak is the bread our potential body and is the body the bread that reaches the end of its destination. Thus, properly speaking, the human word, as image of the divine Word, implies in itself the bread, or is destined to transform the bread into the body. But this is so because its foundation is the divine Word.

This is what also occurs with the body taken by God's Word. He becomes incarnate and, as the Word making use of His body, He transforms the bread into His body. In Him there is the ultimate power destined to transform the bread into the body, for He has in Himself the inner principles of all and sustains or spiritually nourishes all. This Mystery could not take place if at the basis of existence was not the supreme reasonable Person, Who makes use of the body as a means for His appearance and activity and who is Himself an indefinite complexity of words in material form and a means of expressing them.

But if for the body subjected to the actual conditions of creation the transformation is accomplished by being consumed, in the resurrected body the Word is so overwhelming that His body has become light and Spirit, but a light and a Spirit of great richness and meaning that can penetrate into all things and can appropriate all. As such, He especially transforms the bread into His body through His light of infinite, all-encompassing and transforming meaning. If we still see the bread as usual bread, it is so as to be given us the possibility of living outwardly in the conditions of the world's actual image.

Thus, the eucharistic transformation is the guarantee and the starting-point of the age to come, when all things will belong to the Lord's body, when He will be seen through all things, when they will be so transparent for Him that it will be possible to name them His body; when all will be spiritually transparent for Him and through all we will partake of His body.

Therefore, the troparia before Holy Communion so greatly emphasize the fact that Christ's body in the Eucharist is light and fire, as it is said of His resurrected body in the hymns from the Bright Week. So, it is not about a transformation similar to chemical transformations in the present world. It is about a transformation through the Spirit, Who made Christ's body light and fire, radiant and transparent, maintaining it in this state.

The sacrifice of His humanity offered by Christ to His Father fills the Father with its sweet-smelling fragrance, namely with the joy to see that humanity is foreign to any egoistic capacity that hides its thoughts, and that it is perfectly gifted to Him.[385] The mercy of Christ for people—which causes Him to offer Himself as sacrifice showing us His humanity raised over any egoism, overcoming any boundary without being annulled, filling the Father also with mercy for the Son as man, the Father who suffers for the human beings for whom the Son become man suffers—causes the Father to pour out over them His grace or benevolence, operating in them for the conquering of their opacity. And not only the grace of mercy, but also the grace of the Holy Spirit, as the Spirit of communion with them, Who actualizes and increases their power to communicate in this ambiance of divine love.

It has been said that Christ suffers together with us until the end of the world.[386] Nicholas Cabasilas also says: "So He determined to preserve in His body the signs of His death and always to have with Him the marks of the wounds which were once inflicted on Him when He was crucified. Thus it might be evident in the distant future that He had been crucified and pierced in His side for the sake of His servants, and together with His ineffable splendour He might regard these too as an ornament for a King."[387] But wounds are wounds. They reverberate or are lived also in Christ's unique soul and hypostasis. This is why His glory as King bears the undeleted mark of the crucifixion, having the eternal value of His sacrifice and the penetrating power of His mercy for us.

This co-suffering of Christ with us is directed especially toward a community at the moments when the gifts are brought forth at the Liturgy in which the community participates and associates its gifts to Christ's offering, praying the Father together with Christ to transform them through the Holy Spirit into His sacrificed body and blood. It is then that the Lamb forever slain on the heavenly altar is attracted toward a specific community; it is then that the human beings for whom He suffers put on the concrete faces of those who participate at the offering of His sacrifice, associating to it their sacrifice, or making His sacrifice efficient in their propensity for sacrifice present in their gifts.

In this way in Christ's sacrifice for us, with which our sacrifices have been united, the image of our history is reflected. For whenever human persons are subjected to various temptations, they struggle against other trials, pray for the forgiveness of other sins, or for the forgiveness of the same sins committed in different circumstances and under different temptations. The tribulations of history described in the Book of Revelation are all felt by the slain Lamb in His wounds; He leads humans in history through His sacrifice toward conquering them by associating their sacrifice to His as well as toward the ultimate, eternal rest and happiness as the ultimate goal.

When will He accomplish this work? When He will make us perfect in Himself. As long as we are not subject to the Father, neither will He as man be subject to Him (1 Cor 15:28), that is He will not have reached the fullness of joy and rest. He has no need of subjecting us to the Father for Himself, but for us in whom His work is not yet finished. This is why St. Paul said that it will be then when He will be subject to Him (1 Cor 15:28). Since all of us are His body and are called His members, as long as there are still some of us who want to be subjected, but are not yet completely subjected, He Himself is not yet subjected. This is why He as man still suffers for us, still feels in Himself as a lack of fulfillment our state of incomplete subjection, of incomplete sense perception of the Father as Father; He is in pain because we do not love the Father as He loves Him and does everything to move us so as to love the Father as He does.[388]

On the basis of His sacrifice before the Father, of His exhortation He gave us through this to ask in His name from the Father everything that is beneficial to us (Jn 16:24), there follows the series of supplications identical with those from the litany after the Great Entrance until the words: *That the end of our life . . .* inclusively. To the first supplications the faithful respond with "Lord have mercy," and then with "Grant this, O Lord."

Then in the supplication *Asking for the unity of the faith and the communion of the Holy Spirit* is included the promise to make this gift bear fruit by our mutual offering to Christ: *Let us commit ourselves and one another and our whole life to Christ our God.* This promise is identical with the one from the litanies at the beginning of the Holy Liturgy, but it is no longer linked to the remembrance of the most holy Birthgiver of God and of all the saints, but to the supplication for union in faith and for the communion of the Holy Spirit. In approaching the partaking of Christ and thereby the receiving of the Holy Spirit, it is proper for everyone to expect from these the power to offer each other and their life to Christ, especially since the two [partaking of Christ and receiving the Holy Spirit] bring about a deeper union in faith. But also inversely: the union in faith and the communion of the Holy Spirit cannot take place if those who ask for them do not strive to commit themselves and each other to Christ. Neither the Spirit of Christ nor the unity in faith are fully given to us through Holy Communion if we do not fully commit ourselves and each other to Christ. The unity of faith, too, is a gift of the Holy Spirit, but the Holy Spirit does not enter into those who do not want to commit themselves to Christ, or He has not entered into those who do not manifest themselves as having committed themselves and each other to Christ and thus having torn down the prison of their egoism. For the Holy Spirit is the Spirit of communion. Where He is there takes place the communication from one to another. We must offer ourselves to Christ and to each other so that He, too, may offer Himself to us or may offer His Holy Spirit to us. One cannot offer oneself to Christ if one does not offer oneself to others, or vice versa. It is not enough to offer myself to Christ so as to accomplish or to increase the union in faith with others and to receive the Holy Spirit. Comfortableness or egoism does not take me to the union in faith or to its growth and to the unity in Spirit with others. I ought to offer others to Christ, but not through an effort whose purpose is to impose on them my opinion, but by proving Christ's presence in my entire being through the generosity of my self-offering to Christ and to them. Christ must gain others by His love manifested through me. I cannot offer others to Christ except by offering myself to Him and to them. I must approach to receive Christ's sacrifice with my self-sacrifice, with forsaking my egoism, in other words Christ's sacrifice is truly received when its result is my self-sacrifice, the abandonment of my egoism.

While the deacon recites loudly these supplications, the priest reads silently a prayer in which he asks from God that we may partake with a pure conscience of the heavenly and fearful Mysteries of Christ for the forgiveness of sins, for receiving the Holy Spirit, for inheritance of the heavenly Kingdom, and for boldness before God. This makes the transition to the preparation for Holy Communion and to the manifestation of its effects.

Christ is present with His body and blood here, on this table, but beyond the visibility of this presence is its invisible reality, is the reasonable, heavenly altar, is Christ Himself as reasonable sacrifice for the reconciliation before the Father. Spacelessness has entered space. Through what I see here I am raised above the heavens. Through the boundary of the immanent I penetrate into the supreme transcendence. Our sacrifice has become His sacrifice before the Father, or it has been transformed into His sacrifice so as to be given to us full of the Father's Spirit. The Son's Father as God has been filled with His parental affection also toward Christ as man, and through Him toward all of us who unite ourselves through faith with the Son and thereby appropriate upon our countenance the spiritual features of the Son's countenance. The Son's sacrifice is accepted as our sacrifice, His love as our love, without leaving us outside of Him, but receiving us within Him with our sacrifice and love purified and strengthened by His sacrifice and love. Thus we become heirs of the Father's Kingdom like His Son or together with Him and united with Him. By uniting ourselves with the sacrificed Son we appropriate the Son's love for the Father, we are filled with the boldness of sons before the Father, but we also feel the Father's love for us together with His Son become man. This is why we pray Him to deem us worthy to partake as His children of His Son's body and blood, to deem us worthy as being regarded as His children. In this way we become co-heirs with the Son of His Kingdom, of the Kingdom of love which has been shown to us at the beginning of the Holy Liturgy as a distant promise, but now as standing at the door of our being to enter within us concomitantly with the partaking of His Son's body and blood filled with the Holy Spirit, thus filled with love for the Father. By becoming sons united with the Son we receive the boldness of sons before the Father. But only if we partake "with a pure conscience." Otherwise we will partake "unto judgment and condemnation." Because we will not be united in love with the Son, but we will approach Him as severe Judge, as fire causing painful scorches in our conscience. The pure conscience will give us the boldness of the innocent child before the Father, which drives away fear, or maintains a loving but not dreadful fear. Much has been written about the "boldness" of saints before the Father. This is linked to the sentiment that God is their Father. St. Isidore says: "The partaking of God and of the Mysteries has been called communion (comuncatio), because it grants us union with Christ and it helps us to have His Kingdom in common with Him."[389]

This is why, after the priest has asked on behalf of the faithful the unity of faith and the promise has been given to offer themselves and each other as sacrifice to the Father together with the sacrificed Son, they dare to ask through the priest: *And deem us worthy, O Master, that with boldness and without condemnation we may dare to call Thee, the heavenly God, Father, and to say*. The impure person who calls God his Father makes Him the Father of evil, says St. Gregory of Nyssa in his commentary on the Lord's Prayer.[390] In this case addressing God with the word "Father" is done toward condemnation. This is why by praying God to deem us worthy to call Him Father, we ask Him to make us pure. The faithful respond to this supplication of the priest by reciting the prayer "Our Father." In the dialogue between the priest and the faithful, they do not simply repeat what the priest says, but they complete it.

If He deems us worthy to call Him Father, it means that He also deems us worthy to unite our body and blood with His Son's body and blood. Or by the very fact that we are deemed worthy to receive with purity His Son's precious body and blood, which are entirely sacrificed to the Father for us and accepted by Him in a spiritual sweet-smelling fragrance, we also become pleasing to the Father; in this case the Father's love for the Son's humanity sacrificed for Him is extended to us as well. In Christ Jesus "we have boldness and access with confidence through faith in Him" (Eph 3:12). "He who has the Son has life; he who does not have the Son of God does not have life.... Now this is the confidence that we have in Him, that if we ask anything according to His will, He hears us" (Jn 5:12, 14). If we are united with the Son through faith and through keeping His commandments, we have boldness before His Father just as before our Father. In this case we can say: "If our heart does not condemn us, we have confidence toward God. And whatever we ask we receive from Him, because we keep His commandments and do those things that are pleasing in His sight" (Jn 3:21–22). And if we now have boldness, we will have boldness also when He appears at the second coming, because we will await Him as our brother. "And now, little children, abide in Him, that when He appears we may have confidence and not be ashamed before Him at His coming" (Jn 2:28).

As we said, if we were filled with the filth of sins, we would insult God by calling Him Father and would cause His name to be blasphemed by people. For they would say: "Look to what kind of people is God a Father." This is why between calling God Father and hallowing His name through our behavior, which fulfills His will, there is a strong connection.

By loving Him as Father, we wish that His loving Kingdom may come. If we sensed Him as a severe, heavy-handed master, we would not wish for the coming of His Kingdom. But sensing Him as Father, we want His Kingdom as a Kingdom of true freedom, as a Kingdom in which we are not subjects and slaves, but children and co-rulers with His Son. By asking for His Kingdom to come to us, we show that it is love that we love. This is why concurrently with calling Him our Father, we also ask for the forgiveness of our sins and for the avoidance of other sins so that the Kingdom of love may be realized between Him and us and among ourselves. If He is our Father, we have the courage to ask Him to forgive us, but we also avoid offending Him through our sins. He has shown us through the incarnation of His Son that He wants to be our Father and, therefore, to forgive us. It is now up to us to behave like His children and to be all equal in this Kingdom. This is why we call Him our Father, not my Father. This is why we do not want to be exclusively children of this Kingdom so that we boast in front of others, condemning them, and thereby intending to exclude them from the Kingdom of God and from the dignity as His children. In this way we would exclude ourselves. But we also want to forgive the trespasses of others, considering them just as worthy of that Kingdom in which love dominates. For we do not grant ourselves the worth as children of that Kingdom, but we have it from God who wants to be our Father. This is why we do not have a greater right to that Kingdom than others. We want to have them, too, as brothers in that Kingdom, because this is how the Father wants all of us.

We conclude the preparation for the partaking of the body and blood of the heavenly Father's Son, Who became man, accepted death in the body for us and has vanquished it for us through the resurrection, by praying the Father to accept us, too, as children through the union with His Son, thus to deem us worthy so that we, too, may call Him, the heavenly God, "Father." We ask Him to make us worthy to call Him "Father" with the boldness of children, He Himself giving us this boldness through the love He shows us. For we have the boldness to call our father on earth "father" when we see him encouraging us through all kinds of loving manifestations. We ask Him to make us worthy so that we may not condemn ourselves by calling Him "Father" when we are stained with all kinds of evil tendencies and deeds. For in this case we, so deserving of blame, would offend Him by boastfully calling Him our "Father." This would make all those who hear us calling Him "Father" to regard God as one related to us who are so worthy of disdain.

But before we ask God to call Him "Father," we ask Him for "the unity of the faith and the communion of the Holy Spirit." If we are not united in faith, we cannot have the same God as common Father. And if we have Him as common Father, He wants us to be united in faith in Him. And if we want to unite ourselves with His same unique Son so that we may become His brothers and sisters, we all must believe that the one with whom we unite ourselves through communion is truly His Son made man. And if we all unite ourselves with the same unique Son of the heavenly Father, His Holy Spirit—who, by eternally proceeding from the Father is eternally resting, as the personified love of the Father, upon His

Son—will also rest upon us. And only by receiving the eternal Son's Spirit upon and within us will we, too, have the courage to say to the heavenly Father filled with the boldness of love, "Abba, Father" (Rom 8:15).

We have the Spirit and are advancing in various degrees in Him even before we partake of the Son's body and blood, for otherwise the Father would not accept us to partake of His Son. But we receive more fully the Spirit who rests upon the Son when we partake of the Son's body and blood and thus we will also become sons and daughters. And since in the Holy Liturgy we advance in the Spirit in various degrees, in the same way we advance into the union with the Father and His incarnate Son during the Holy Liturgy so that we may reach the highest degree of the union with the Father and of the communion with the Holy Spirit through the partaking of Christ's body and blood, the only begotten Son of the Father, upon whom the Spirit of the Father's love rests.

We also reached a degree of union with the Holy Trinity, and also among ourselves through the love among us, when we confessed our faith in the Trinity before the recitation of the Creed and before the beginning of the prayers that lead to the transformation of the gifts into the Lord's body and blood. But only when we partake of them will we have reached the highest degree of union with the Holy Trinity and among ourselves.

In fact the entire Holy Liturgy is a progress into union with the Holy Trinity and among ourselves, on the one hand through the blessings we all receive through the priest, and on the other through the common prayers of one for the other during the Liturgy. This is why everything is expressed in the Holy Liturgy in the plural: "We, who mystically represent the Cherubim," "We praise Thee," "Our Father."

The Holy Liturgy is the service that accomplishes the union or the communion between us and God, and of the union, communion and brotherhood among the believers. This is why it would be proper that all hymns be sung in common so that also in this way the faithful may advance into a greater union and communion.

But the true union among us and between us and the Holy Trinity is most easily strengthened neither by our exclusive will nor by being helped by the conscience that we are made up of a unique, unconscious essence—for in this case we could consider that the union among us might be accomplished even without our effort—but being helped by a personal God and by the conscience that we are nonetheless brought into existence by a supreme Father, Who wants to take us to the eternal happiness of perfect love between us and Him as well as among ourselves; it is toward this end that He grants us the Spirit of His love and gives us the possibility of partaking of His Son's body and blood.

This is what we ask when we pray the Father to cause His Kingdom to come, the Kingdom of love, in which the King is our Father and His Son is our brother.

But, as free beings we must also contribute to the establishing and strengthening of this Kingdom of love. And in the most general way we contribute by freeing ourselves from all egoistic passions, a liberation that is equal with our sanctification. We show this in our life through which we cause the name of the heavenly Father to be hallowed by us, namely to be respected by us and by all those who see us. On the other hand, we ask for this kind of life from Him. In this way we confess that He is the source of holiness, asking that by our participation in it His name may be hallowed both by us and by all who see us. We ask for the power to make His holiness visible through our sanctification granted by Him. We ask Him that we may be able to offer to Him His own of His own.

We also ask for the coming of His Kingdom. And we, too, contribute to its coming by doing His will. Properly speaking, in this way we show our sanctification as a testimony to His holiness granted to us.

In the Kingdom of the Father, as the Kingdom of love, no one wants to do his own will, but the will of others and above all the will of the Father who is the common Father of all. In fact this is His will: that everyone does selflessly the selfless will of others.

After these supplications which refer directly to what we want to be accomplished for the Father, and indirectly for us, there follow the supplications which refer to what we want to be accomplished directly for us: forgiveness of our sins and the power to forgive others, as well as our protection from being tempted to commit other sins. These are additional ways of overcoming our egoism and of growing in love, which is to rule in the Kingdom of the heavenly Father.

The first of these supplications refers to the bread that is "essential" for our being. It cannot be exclusively the material bread. This supplication cannot be excluded from the context of other supplications in the prayer, which all refer to our preparation for the heavenly Kingdom. It must refer directly to "the bread that came down from heaven" and which "gives life to the world" or to Jesus Christ (Jn 6:33, 35). For He is "the resurrection and the life" (Jn 11:25). We must ask for Christ every day. If for one day we forget to ask for Him, we weaken our life. This is why we say: "Give us this day our essential (daily) bread," or rather also today. We ask Him not only once for the future. We must always have the awareness that we need Him.

Through this supplication we prepare ourselves in the Holy Liturgy for the imminent partaking of Christ.

Since we partake of Christ's body in the form of bread for the body, this supplication can also refer to this bread. But we must always see this as an image of Christ's body, which helps us to sustain our life on earth so as to prepare ourselves for the eternal life. This is what Christians do when they make the sign of the cross over the bread when they begin to cut it (to "sacrifice" it). We cannot attain to the bread for eternal existence if we do not have the bread for the existence on earth.

The prayer "Our Father" concludes with acknowledging that the eternal Kingdom of love, which we ask for and which we will attain through the union with Christ in Holy Communion, lies in the power of the Holy Trinity.

The exclamation of the priest: *For Thine is the Kingdom, and the power, and the glory of the Father, and of the Son, and of the Holy Spirit, now and ever, and unto ages of ages* expresses not only the eternity of this Kingdom, of the communion of the Holy Trinity and of the Holy Trinity with us, but also that, although it is a Kingdom in which God will be a Father and a Brother to us and we will have the same Spirit as They do, it is still a kingdom of power and of glory and that it is not established by us. Love is not contrary to power and glory, but only where there is perfect love is there also the greatest power and glory. Love is stronger than anything. Nothing can conquer love, it endures all things. And the love of this Kingdom is unconquered because it is sustained in all by God and because it comes from God, not from us.

After the priest again offers peace to the faithful, the full peace of the unity that is willed and loved, so that they may partake in love of the Lord's body and blood, he asks them: *Bow your heads to the Lord*. The faithful respond directly to God: *To You, O Lord*. They must not forget after they were given the boldness to call God, Father, that He is nonetheless almighty and it is out of His benevolence that He became their Father. This is why, while they keep their heads bowed, the priest offers on their behalf thanksgiving to God because He has deemed them worthy to call Him Father, although He is the invisible

King and He created everything with His immeasurable power. On this occasion he affirms again the union between God's power and mercy. Only through the union among them has God brought all things into existence and He makes the people, through the incarnation and sacrifice of His Son, His sons and daughters, uniting them with Him. The priest asks this King and Father, full of immeasurable power and inexpressible mercy, to look down from heaven upon those who have bowed their heads before Him. *For they have bowed them not unto flesh and blood, but unto Thee, the awesome God.* They have bowed them not unto a certain dominion that relies on the power of flesh and blood, which is not a true power, nor did they bow them unto a certain flesh and blood full of passions, but unto God, Who even though He became Father, is still God fearful to all other kinds of power. The priest is asking this God—who even though He is their loving Father, He nevertheless maintains the immeasurable power through which He overcomes all burdens that those who want to be His sons and daughters might encounter and be led astray by—to make the partaking of the gifts set forth be for benefit according to the individual need of each: to travel with those who travel, to heal the sick. For He is "the physician of our souls and bodies."

This is why the Lord's body and blood worthily received are the most effective medicine, just as for those who receive them unworthily they are toward condemnation and sickness, according to the words of St. Paul the Apostle (1 Cor 11:29-30). Medicine taken without the proper prescription makes the sick even sicker and sometimes causes them death. "For this reason many are weak and sick among you and many sleep" (1 Cor 11:30). The greater God's love, the more evil is the one who opposes Him and the more contrary he becomes to that love, increasing his propensity toward disorder, which leads him to spiritual death. This is why God is fearful to those who oppose Him. He who partakes unworthily is like the one who tears the Lord's body with the teeth of a wild beast, or he eats it carelessly.

In the proclamation at the end of this prayer of the priest, one sets in the forefront the Son's grace, mercies and love for mankind, although the priest addresses the Father, who is blessed together with the Son and with His all-holy, good and life-giving Spirit. The Son is brought to the forefront because His body and blood represent the special means of grace and the special sign of His mercies. And through them the Father's

Spirit will be shown as operating in an accentuated manner, as the good and life-giving Spirit.

As a consequence of this proclamation, the priest addresses especially Jesus Christ by saying: "O Lord Jesus Christ our God, hear us from Thy holy dwelling place and from the throne of the glory of Thy Kingdom and come to sanctify us; Thou who sittest together with the Father and are also invisibly present among us. And make us worthy that Thy most pure Body and precious Blood be given to us by Thy mighty hand and through us to all Thy people." At this time it is no longer the Father or the Spirit who give us Christ, but He offers Himself to us through the priest's hand.

Both from this prayer and from the following words of the priest: *The Lamb of God is broken* . . . as well as from the words from the priest's prayer before the Great Entrance: *The One who offers and the One who offers Yourself* or *The precious and most pure Body and Blood . . . is given to me . . . is given to you . . . . The servant of God (N) partakes*, therefore not "I commune you," is seen that the priest is not a substitute for Christ who would be absent, but only a medium, a visible organ through whom Christ Himself operates. The priest is a mystery in the Church. Between him and Christ there is a spiritual relationship, not a juridical one.[391]

Christ Himself continuously lives His death for us on the basis of its experience on the cross, both in the moment of His preparation to offer Himself to us and in the moment when He is given to us. He "breaks" Himself through the action of the priest over the visible Agnetz; it is not the priest who breaks Him. Christ's death as passage to resurrection fills the entire Liturgy. This indicates to us that he who dies for others, does not die completely. And particularly Christ, who is God and as one who had no sin dies exclusively for others, does not die. Those for whom someone dies, even if he is a man, keep him in their conscience, and this is not just a subjective retention, but it means a certain retention as an objective reality. All the more is this true when both one and the other are rooted in the foundation of life, that is in God. This occurred and is fully occurring with Christ, because He is the only one who dies exclusively for others, without being subjected to the necessity of death for some guilt of His own, a guilt that causes the disintegration of the human body through the weakening of the soul.

By dying exclusively for us, He had only us perfectly in Himself, He was concentrated exclusively on us. And not only in His quality as man without sin, but also as the Son of God, willing to gather all of us as His brothers and sisters in Him as man, as well as the inner principles incorporated in Him as the Word of God. When the human person seeks to gather in himself through all his actions as many as possible, thereby giving of himself, he abides in them. But it is Christ who gathers them in Himself most fully through His death. This is why He remains in them through death. But the need to remain in them so that they also may remain in Him, makes His death a passage toward resurrection. This also happens to human persons only if they believe in the immortal God. If they do not believe, when they die, those whom they have in their conscience also die. By embracing all even to the point of self-forgetting manifested in the death exclusively for them so as to offer Himself to them with His life, with His total love, Christ thereby rises again as an extension of His act of self-offering, as a source of eternal life. By filling all with His love and by living to the supreme intensity the responsibility for their life, He cannot remain dead. In the elan of His endless responsibility for others, or of His boundless mercy for their state as subjected to death (therefore reduced to the ultimate limit of life) is given the force of vanquishing death accepted for them. In Christ's conscience to have all in Himself both as man and as God, as their life, is given the power to rise again so as to guarantee their life through Him. Love is a power stronger than death, a power that conquers death.

Although He is in a state of sacrifice, although He prays and suffers together with us, Christ as risen and full of the Spirit is at the same time in His holy dwelling place and on the throne of glory as King. His dwelling place is the communion with the Father who cannot change. His Kingdom that has been opened to us in Him and is expanding is the Kingdom of love in which all the souls of the departed in faith rejoice; it is the Kingdom of mercy with which He seeks and helps all those who strive on earth to advance in it. He is up there as almighty God and as man who is not dominated by any passion, but has offered once and for all the pure sacrifice; but He is also down here with us through His mercy and love, offering to us the partaking of His sacrificed body. The sitting at the right hand of the Father is a co-sitting on the same throne of glory not only as His only begotten Son, but also as the man who offered Himself perfectly to the Father through His sacrifice, remaining at the same time with us through His humanity and through the same sacrifice, remaining close to us spiritually and ready to give Himself to us with His sacrificed body as well. He is almighty both up there for Himself and near to us with His mercy. As almighty as He is in Himself, so is He full of His mercy for us. He is almighty because He is all-merciful. He is all-merciful because He is almighty. The unfathomable depth of His mercy is equal to His immeasurable power. Power is manifested in mercy. True and unlimited power is shown in immeasurable mercy. His mercy is granted to all without stinginess, but it depends on us to benefit from it. For it respects our freedom. But the suffering that comes from refusing it maintains His mercy. And by receiving His mercy we do not become weak, but we become strong. Only the unmerciful one is weak.

His unbent mercy is like a strong hand that offers the communion of His blameless body and His most pure blood so as to overwhelm in our body and blood the sinful tendencies, and to plant in them the propensity to sacrifice ourselves with the help of the strength of His mercy that we received from Him. Not being offered as sacrifice, but by offering Himself as sacrifice, Christ is not given in a state of passivity, but He offers Himself to us. Mercy is always active. Only the active sacrifice is a complete sacrifice. Only an offering through one's own act is a complete offering. His body is given to us by His own hand. This is a mystery that remains now covered for many. But the mind raised through purification to mystical visions "sees clearly the cup in the Lord's hand, filled with the wine of unmixed mixture (between the power of divinity and the purity of His humanity), contemplates most evidently the pouring from one to another and knows clearly that His love was not emptied out (Ps 74:9). For the depth of the divine outpouring and, so to speak, the depth of richness and the fullness of grace are revealed to none of us, deserted in this life, even if deemed worthy of the highest step in the ascent toward God and of the greatest deification. For completion and perfection are reserved for all in the age to come."[392] Divinity poured out through mercy in the boundaries of the Lord's body is inexhaustible. The human body has in itself the possibility of being a means of communicating divinity endlessly, which means that its sense perception, too, can be filled endlessly with the power of divine mercy and to transmit it.

This prayer of the priest concludes with the words: "And through us to all Thy people." These words can have two meanings: a) and cause that through us Your body and blood may be given to all Your people. And this does not mean that through the visible hand of the body Christ does not Himself also give His body to the faithful; b) it can also mean that in a sense the faithful who do not partake also benefit from the priest's partaking; they do not remain entirely without any sense in the church until the end of the Holy Liturgy, which implies at least the priest's partaking. If the priest did not partake, the Holy Liturgy could not be officiated from which all faithful receive a certain benefit. One cannot dispute the fact that the faithful who do not partake, but live their life among the others, contribute to the betterment of everyone's life, or they represent at least a barrier that prevents the communal spiritual life from its total collapse. Such a contribution makes all the more, without a doubt, the regular officiating of the Holy Liturgy be conditioned by at least the priest's partaking. But this should not determine one believer or another to consider himself satisfied with the benefit resulting from simple attendance at the Liturgy. Christ does the maximum for us offering Himself as sacrifice; we should also do the maximum we can, by receiving Him in purity.

8. *The Preparation of the Holy Gifts for Holy Communion*

After this prayer the priest makes three prostrations before the Holy Table, saying the words: *O God, cleanse me, a sinner*. Then either the priest or the deacon when asking the community through the words: *Let us be attentive* to focus their attention on what follows, takes with both hands from the diskos the holy Body, raises it making the sign of the cross and says: *Holy things for the Holy*, namely the holy things will be given to the saints, or to the pure ones. St. John Chrysostom says: "They who share this blood stand with Angels and Archangels and the Powers that are above, clothed in Christ's own kingly robe [once they become co-rulers with Him], and having the armor of the Spirit [they feel the angelic powers around them looking upon them with respect]. Nay, I have not as yet said any great thing: they are clothed with the King Himself. Now as this is a great and wonderful thing, so if thou approach it with pureness, thou approachest for salvation; but if with an evil conscience, for punishment and vengeance. 'For,' It saith, 'he that eateth and drinketh unworthily' of the Lord, 'eateth and drinketh judgment to himself' (1 Cor 11:29); since they who defile the kingly purple are punished equally with those who rend it, it is not unreasonable that they who receive the Body with unclean thoughts should suffer the same punishment as those who rent it with the nails."[393]

Only the soul worn out and rude is devoid of the sense perception capable of grasping the merciful purity and gracefulness of the King who is offering Himself in a state of sacrifice. But this indifferent or denigrating rudeness has in itself the consequences of lacking superior joy and, ultimately, a self-disgust.

When the priest announces: *Holy things for the Holy*, the community responds in humility: *One is Holy! One is the Lord Jesus Christ, to the glory of God the Father! Amen.* There is no other holy among human beings except Jesus Christ, because only He sanctified Himself as man through the perfect sacrifice to the glory of the Father, not to mention the fact that He is also God. From Him and through Him comes all holiness. But being the only Holy one, He is also the only Lord over all passions as well as over all created beings. We unite ourselves with the uniquely holy Person, or the source of holiness among human persons, not with certain holy substances (impersonal body and blood). The Lord Himself said: "And for their sakes I sanctify Myself, that they also may be sanctified by the truth" (Jn 17:19), namely in Himself, for He is the Man in whom was poured out all divine holiness to the glory of God. In commenting on these words St. Cyril of Alexandria says: "For He offers Himself for His Church in a sweet fragrance to God and the Father. This is why He also said: 'For their sakes I sanctify Myself' (Jn 17:19). 'I sanctify Myself' He said instead of 'I offer Myself and I surrender as a blameless offering to the Father.' For it is said that what is surrendered (dedicated) to the Father is sanctified, according to the words: 'It is a snare for a man to quickly sanctify something of his own things as holy' (Pr 20:25)."[394] He who offers himself as sacrifice overcomes the obscene, rude and devious egoism. He glorifies God.

While the faithful sing "One is Holy," the priest says: *The Lamb of God is broken and distributed, Who is broken but not divided; Who is forever eaten, yet never consumed, but sanctifies those who partake thereof.* There appears again the symbol of the Lamb from the Proskomedia. It is the symbol of the slain Lamb who accepted with all meekness the slaying for us and thus offers Himself to us so as to make us, too, spiritual lambs for one another and sanctified for God by receiving His state of sacrifice. While saying these words the priest divides the holy Body into four parts, setting the part on which IS is written on the top side (east) of the paten, the one with the initials HS on the bottom side (west), the part with the initials NI on the left side (north), and the part with the letters KA on the right side (south). In this is seen His state of sacrifice.

The Lamb offers Himself whole to the Father in a state of sacrifice, and to us who live limited by space, therefore physically separated, he is given broken, but invisibly He is undivided. He is given whole to us, but in a state of inner spiritual brokenness out of mercy for us. This is why the four parts that were still joined by the crust are now separated. IS is no longer in continuity with HS, but they are separated. NI and KA, representing His state of glory which He attained through the cross, are also separated. He is victorious and glorified, but still full of mercy for us and in a state of sacrifice. The four parts are placed in the form of the cross, comprising within that framework the entire universe so as to place on everything the seal of His cross, to imprint on them the cross as a means of salvation. Through His incarnation Jesus Christ connects the heaven with the earth, perfecting this connection through the cross. He descends and climbs up on the vertical part between the two, raising with Him the earth to heaven after He had descended on earth. And through His activity upon the horizontal creation He inundates it with divinity through the cross that opened up His body bloodlessly, thus making the vertical of His Person bearing the cross the spine around which the entire creation is gathered and ascends to heaven. The cross is Christ Himself who conquers through His sacrifice the sin within creation or its separation from God.

The separated manifestation of the slain Lamb, or of Christ's body, expresses more emphatically the fact that the cross imprinted in the body produces in it channels through which the spiritual life hidden there pours out and through them this life is given to us, too. Through the cross we pass from what is created and visible to what is not created, or what is not created passes to us through what is created and made transparent through the cross.

The Lamb of God is broken, but in each of His parts He is whole. For He is alive and full of divinity. In any part of a living organism there is the whole organism, together with what is beyond what is seen. Each part is determined by the whole. All the more does this occur in the whole body that belongs to Christ's unique hypostasis and is filled wholly in its resurrected state with His same unique Spirit. The body of the Lamb, always eaten in the form of one of its particles, remains whole in Him. Christ maintains His body united with our bodies, at once distinct from ours, although we all have eaten it, made it interior to our bodies and made it our own. The sun is received by all, it fills the life of all with its warmth and light, but it does not cease to exist in itself. We are many. But in all there is the same, unique Christ, uniting us too. And the same Christ continues to also exist in Himself as an infinite reserve of life, which is not from us. A mother is spiritually whole in every one of her children during pregnancy and afterwards, without having been divided; and she remains whole in herself as a reserve of love distinct from them. Love overwhelms space and separations, manifesting itself as an infinite reserve, yet making a distinction between the one who loves and those who receive it. Space remains as a form extended outwards so as to guarantee the unconfused existence of persons in their love. By partaking of Christ's body that was sanctified through sacrifice, He also sanctifies us, entering within us full of His Spirit of sacrifice and immersed in the light of the Father.

Beyond the dividing spatial prolongation, there is the inner unity among persons. All the more does Christ's great love overwhelm this space showing it as an extended form outward. By partaking of Christ's body that was sanctified through sacrifice, He also sanctifies us, entering within us full of His sense perception of sacrifice. Immersed in the Father's light through His sacrifice, which itself unites us as we appropriate it, and through the renunciation of a separate existence for Himself, His body imprints itself in our bodies with all the holy and pure light of divinity with which it is filled and which also makes it a body of light, a body made sensible at maximum and overwhelmed by the expansive gracefulness of the divine mercy.

Then as he takes the part IS and making with it the sign of the cross over the chalice, the priest puts it inside saying: *The fullness of the chalice of faith of the Holy Spirit.* The wine in the chalice is identified with Christ's blood, but it is not separated from His body or from His Person. The blood is not totally separated from Christ's body, although it is distinct from the body. It shows its specific fullness in its being concretized in the body. Thus, Christ will remain not only with His blood unspent through communion, but also with the body. The particle IS that was pierced with the spear is placed in the blood, showing in this way the side from which came out blood and water. The union between body and blood is a communicating union. Out of blood the body is made. From the pierced body there flows blood. Jesus represents *par excellence* the unifying hypostasis. He maintains both the body and the blood in unity, but unconfused.

After this warm water is brought, which the priest blesses, saying: *Blessed is the warmth of Thy saints, always now and ever and unto the ages of ages. Amen.* The he pours it into the chalice, saying: *The warmth of faith full of Holy Spirit. Amen.* Those who commune as "saints," as believers and cleansed of sins, bring with them the warmth of faith. But they do not have this warmth of faith without the operation of the Holy Spirit in them. Christ offers us His blood, but we are to receive it with the warmth of faith. And our faith itself with which we receive Christ's blood is the fruit of our cooperation with the Holy Spirit. This is why at the epiklesis the Holy Spirit is called upon to come not only upon these gifts, but also "upon us." We bring to Christ our faith and this is how we partake of Him. But not just our personal faith, but that of all the saints from all ages. Christ is not isolated. Christ, too, has a joy, a warmth when we bring our faith as we partake of Him. There is a certain union with Him which begins from the moment when we approach to partake of Him.

9. *Holy Communion for Eternal Life*

The priest then partakes of the part with the name HS, and the faithful of the parts with the names NI and KA. But both the priest and the faithful partake of "Christ's body and blood" in the form of these separate parts. Hence, the name of Christ is also mentioned when the faithful partake.

However, the fact that the priest partakes with the part HS and the faithful with NI and KA shows a certain distinction between him and the faithful. Through the priest's partaking with the part HS is shown not only that he partakes of Christ who came down for His activity in the Church, but also that the priest is sent by Christ to visibly fulfill his mission in Christ's service, while the partaking of the faithful with the parts NI and KA shows their partaking of Christ's victorious work against sin and against the death of their own person, but also of Christ's power to make them victorious in the world.

Having to commune the laity as being sent by Christ to the people, the priest must partake first, not through someone else, but by himself. Because one cannot commune others if one does not first partake. And he mentions his own name, saying "I," namely in the first person.

If the hierarch is present and he communes the priest, or the deacon being communed by the priest or by the hierarch, both the priest and the deacon are indicated in the second person. In this way the priest or the deacon are distinguished from the laity even when they receive communion from the hierarch. For the hierarch says: *To you is given* . . . . This again shows that the priest is sent for his mission by Christ, the same as when the priest or the hierarch says when partaking: *To me is given* . . . . Only the lay person is not indicated in the first or second person, but only in the third person: *The servant of God (N) partakes* . . . . Still, the priest realizes that there is a direct relation between Christ and the lay person who has taken communion, a relation before which the priest somehow remains outside, even though he serves as a visible instrument of Christ for offering communion to the lay person. The lay person does not feel directly touched by the hierarch as the priest does who, in fact, is sent in the name of Christ. When the hierarch or the priest says "I" or "To me is given" they feel directly, without any intermediary, that they are touched by Christ with a view to a certain mission. But the lay person, too, is put in a direct relation with Christ by his or her name being mentioned. He is self-aware and has the duty to show Christ as being active in him, for him and for motivating others as well as for promoting the communion of love with others in Christ.

Even though the name of every person is also given to many others, each person's name is connected to certain circumstances of his own and together with these to certain thoughts and feelings with their own seal that make that person unique. A person's name Nicholas common to other persons becomes that person's own by the fact that it is a Nicholas born from a specific father and mother, in a certain year and certain place, that he lived in his own specific circumstances experienced as being proper to him. And through his name his unique "I" is distinguished. By being received in Christ with his unique identity, he is received eternally as a person unconfused with others, because Christ has His attention set on him in a special way as He endures forever with this attention toward him. Thus, when a person is indicated at the moment of communion with his unique identity, that person's eternal preservation in Christ is also indicated. Christ cannot forget nor can He allow someone to perish, someone in whom He has dwelled or with whom He united Himself out of love.

The priest takes the part HS, or a portion from it, and says: *The precious and most holy body of our Lord and God and Savior Jesus Christ is given unto me, the priest (N) for the forgiveness of sins and for eternal life*. If a deacon is present, the priest gives him a portion from the part HS saying: *The precious and most holy body . . . is given unto you, deacon (N) . . . .* If the hierarch is officiating he gives a portion from the part HS to the priest and to the deacon, saying the same words.

In every mystery (sacrament) one indicates by name the person who receives it. In this way one underlines the value of that person, his identity and uniqueness unconfused on mass. Certainly, someone's person is strengthened only in relationship with another person, not with objects. In the case of Mysteries, indicating by name the receiving person implies his entrance into relationship with Christ's Person (Holy Communion, Confession, Ordination, Holy Unction), with the Holy Spirit (Confirmation or Anointing with Holy Chrism), with the Holy Trinity, but also especially with Christ (Baptism, Marriage).

When Holy Communion is received by the deacon, priest or bishop their office is also indicated. When it is received by the other faithful their profession is not mentioned as it is not a serving profession of the Church, or a relationship with Christ through their profession. This fact, like the fact that the priest or the bishop give to themselves the Lord's body and blood, does not mean that they wish to put themselves in bold relief. That would be contrary to humility which requires denying the person's own self. But, as the indication by name of every believer in each Mystery means the awakening of his responsibility before Christ, or before the Holy Trinity, so the priest's or the bishop's self-indication by name, together with indicating the position as priest or bishop, puts in bold relief their responsibility in their quality as instruments of Christ's work for the salvation of the faithful.

We have seen that no one mentions his or her name when in dialogue with others, but simply "I." Here the priest or the hierarch makes an exception, because there is no one else to commune him. Here the "I" indicates the responsibility full of trembling which the priest or the hierarch acknowledges before Christ, just as Samuel felt when he heard God calling him by name. In fact, the priest or the hierarch places himself in the position of the third person when he says: "The precious body is given to me . . . ," without ceasing to play the role of the first person as well.

In addition to what has been said regarding the indication of the name, we note that this is further necessary also because all who receive Christ's body incorporate themselves, on the other hand, into Him equally, forming one single body of Christ, or the Church. But the indication of the name emphasizes the fact that those who incorporate themselves into the body of Christ are not confounded, but each one maintains the personal identity and, therefore, the responsibility in the body of Christ. Each one is called to fulfill in the body of Christ the role of a special member. St. Paul the Apostle has said this and the Holy Fathers of the Church have developed this theme. St. Paul the Apostle says: "For as the body is one and has many members, but all the members of that one body, being many, are one body, so also is Christ . . . . And if there were all one member, where would the body be?" (1 Cor 12:12, 19).

In Christ's body one has the role of seeing eye, another of hearing ear so as to thereby fulfill his duty, another of active hand, another of leg that runs to the help of others. Thus, the indication of the name does not imply a right to selfish affirmation, but the calling to the fulfillment of a service in conformity with one's own proper characteristics. When a believer hears his or her name upon receiving a Mystery, he not only has only the satisfaction of being taken into consideration, but also the trembling of one being called to the fulfillment of a responsibility according to his gifts. For only when everyone fulfills his or her proper service do they serve others and contribute to the harmony of the whole body of Christ or of the Church. And only in service is there shown that someone is useful to the body or to others, and this is why only through service does he or she grow spiritually. Someone's glory lies only in service. When someone's name is mentioned upon receiving Holy Communion, Christ not only assures him of His special attention, but He also gives him a special responsibility, proper to his capacity, with his unique self.

St. Maximos the Confessor goes even further, saying that everyone receives from the body of Christ what is proper to him or to his status. One can say that everyone receives the whole body of Christ but actualizes in himself those activities or powers of Christ's body that are more fitting to his characteristics, ascending on his own path, but in solidarity with others, from level to level. And the priest has the role of harmonizing these works of the whole Christ.

By interpreting the words from St. Gregory of Nazianzus's oration on Pascha, St. Maximos the Confessor says:

> For *Jesus*, the Word of God, who *has passed through the heavens*, and who is *beyond all of the heavens*, always raises up those who follow Him in their practice and contemplations, so that they are

taken from inferior things to superior ones, and, to put it simply, *time will fail me to tell* of the divine ascents and revelations of the saints, in their transformation *from glory to glory*, through the moment when *each one* of them receives the divinization that is most fitting *to his proper order*.

... that great teacher exhorts and invites all through his teaching to partake of the spiritual food of the Lamb who was slain on our behalf, counseling us to maintain the Lamb's members distinctly and usefully in their unbroken and unconfused organization, lest we be condemned for breaking and tearing asunder the harmonious arrangement of the divine body—either because we eat of the flesh of the Lamb and Word overconfidently, if such eating be beyond our ability, or profanely, if it be averse to our ability—but let each of us, according to his ability, rank, and the grace of the Spirit that has been given to him, partake of the divine Word in conformity with the meaning of each of His parts.

For example, the head shall be partaken of by whosoever possesses, from indemonstrable first principles, a faith ... for it is on the basis of such faith that the whole body of the virtues and knowledge *is knit together and grows with* spiritual *growth* ... The eyes shall be partaken of by whosoever beholds creation spiritually, and blamelessly gathers together all the principles pertaining to sensation and intellect for the singular fulfillment of the glory of God.[395]

Sergius Bulgakov finds another basis for indicating the name of the one receiving Holy Communion. He says that if Christ unites all of us in Him, He also unites the names of all. From this one deduces, we think, that he who partakes declares to agree to belong to Christ together with all, not individually, to respond to the appeal of all who call him by name.

Bulgakov says: "The name of Jesus is the Name of God, but also a human name. The Lord is the absolute, perfect, heavenly Human Being; in Him, the whole fullness of the Godhead dwells bodily, but also in Him, the whole fullness of humanity is included in a heavenly way. In Him, everything that is proper to the human being as positive power has its foundation and belongs to Him (except sin). It is necessary to understand not allegorically but entirely realistically and ontologically those speeches of the Savior where He identifies Himself with every person. This signifies the union of everyone in Christ, made real in a single communion, and in this sense the Church is the Body of Christ. But this unity is necessarily spread to the name in which the substantial core of personhood is expressed. It would be against nature and incomprehensible if humans, who are united to him in everything, should be separated from Him in this essential thing. In other words, this means that all the diverse, endlessly fragmenting names, in their essence, dynamically, form one Name, or rather, are able to enter into it, to partake of it, to become one with it, with its rays existing indivisibly from the sun. If Christ lives, rather, can live and wants to live in each one of the faithful ('behold I stand at the door and knock, that they will open'), this indwelling of the Savior does not signify the depersonalization or dissolution of personhood but its higher, singularly true manifestation in gracious enlightenment. In each of them, the bright Countenance of Christ must be reflected or each of them must find themselves in it and through this see their own countenance. All names meet or proceed substantially and dynamically from the Name of Jesus, for we cannot imagine anything inherent in the human being and lying outside of Christ except the dark region of sin, of non-being, of satanic evil .... The most sweet Name of Jesus also lies inscribed on the whole of humanity through the Son of Man and belongs to all of it. All of us, despite our unworthiness, participate in this great and holy Name; in a certain sense we bear it, we partake of it. Let them not say that this is daring or blasphemy, for is it not a measure of the love and condescension of God? Will the Lord, when he gives His Very Self, His Body and Blood, in the sacrament of the Eucharist, deprive us of the gracious power of His Holy Name? Let it not be so. Since the Lord took on Himself everything human (except sin), which is why each human being can have Him as their personal Savior and Redeemer, so all human names, the essential nuclei of all individualities are united in Him, in His most holy Name, as their center. If the Lord in whom everyone finds themselves is all-individuality, then the Name of Jesus is the *all-name*, the Name of all names .... But true humanity forms the church and is the church."[396] This is why the Church bears the name of Christ, is the Christian Church or Christendom. And all who belong to Christ are called Christians, having the same name, which does not annul everyone's distinct name, but unites all in a common name.

We would like to add a few observations so as to explain even more the connection between all names as basis for their union in bearing the name of Jesus: human beings are distinguished not only by name, but they are also connected through them, just as they are connected through words, or in an even more intimate way. Through the name they give themselves they are connected in a unity of mutual responsibility and of familiarity, which is precisely why they are not confounded, because each one is necessary for the other with his or her specificity. When you call someone by name, you feel that you have reached a deeper intimacy with him and you have discovered in him something that responds to a certain need of yours. To say his name means in general to caress him, to have courage before him, you feel that he allows you to be in a special familiarity with him, to reveal something of yourself and to actualize it. Moreover, when I call someone by name he feels obligated to respond. Through the name he is connected to me. Through his name uttered by me I manifest not only my intimacy with him, but together we manifest ourselves as belonging to each other in a special way and as having a special responsibility for each other. All the more when we call frequently Jesus by name do we feel how we increase our familiarity with Him. And through the name that we feel was given to us at Baptism through Christ Himself, we also feel Him eager to be familiar with us. In the name He gives us in the Mysteries we feel at once called by Him to a responsibility toward Him, we feel in a dialogic unity with Him.

Returning to what Bulgakov said we note, however, that in this general name of Christ the personal names are not lost, but everyone maintains his or her proper name, which Christ Himself gave them through the Mysteries. We are all connected in the name of Jesus, but also distinguish ourselves from each other and before Him through the name He gave us. This very name connects us even more to Him, or it unites us with Him and in Him. The name of every believer is contained in the all-encompassing name of Jesus, but in a dialogic manner, and it is because of this that it does not disappear. And the very name Jesus does not become for us a simply general name, but it is the name of a Person distinct from us, even if this Person embraces all persons. All children of a father bear their family name and feel connected through the father's name that became their name common with him and among them. But since we also have a proper name we maintain ourselves as distinct persons but, precisely because of this, with a responsibility before the father and among ourselves in a mutual attention of compassion, as the ones who, on the one hand, bear the same name, but on the other hand, different names that also connect us to each other. I introduce myself through my name as a distinct person to another person, I draw his attention into a communication with him, I extend the bridge between me and that person. This is why especially other persons use my name signaling my existence and presence, feeling the need to enter into relationship with me, to solicit my help, and to assure me of their help. We, human beings, use God's name signaling His presence everywhere His name His uttered, feeling the duty to honor His name and feeling protected and helped by Him when we say His name. We feel Christ exceptionally close to us when we call Him by name. It is in Him that we sense our salvation.

Generally, by mentioning the name of a human person those who do this signal the precious existence and a certain presence of that person somewhere, and this in fact brings into those who mention the name a certain power from that person in the place where his name is mentioned. But the human being wants to rejoice in God's attention and presence, in His power coming to him. This is why the human person mentions God's name so as to rejoice in His help and to avoid evil things. This is why we ask that God may also mention our loved ones unto the ages of ages, that God may thereby be attentive to them and to preserve them alive and happy unto the ages of ages.

When taking or giving the Lord's body and blood, the priest also mentions the purpose for partaking of them: *Unto remission of sins and unto eternal life*. In other Mysteries one mentions their special purpose. Or the purpose of each Mystery is implied in its characteristic: in the Mystery of Confession the priest says that he unbinds him who confessed and repents of his sins; the purpose of the Mystery of Marriage is comprised in the words: *The servant of God (N) is crowned for the servant of God (N)*. Two equal persons are united, equal in value and of an eternal value in love and respect as well as in the responsibility for each other, because they are within the ray of God's care and power, but not persons as objects or as two instinctively impersonal forces. And so on in every Mystery.

At Holy Communion the special purpose is especially indicated: "Unto remission of sins and unto eternal life." "The remission of sins" is the condition strictly necessary in order to attain eternal life. The awareness of sinfulness is overwhelming in him who approaches Holy Communion as a result of being conscious of the glory of the One we approach. In all the prayers before Holy Communion one expresses the consciousness of this sinfulness, one confesses repentance for sins asking to be forgiven for them. In these moments we experience the supreme sensitiveness for our sinfulness before Him who offers Himself to us. This is why, even if we have received the forgiveness of sins in the Mystery of Repentance before Holy Communion, we experience at once with our ontological smallness the inability to be entirely pure, to escape by ourselves our egoistic deterioration, without the state of sacrifice that Christ imprints on us.

In this way a spiritual sensitiveness of the Christian is sought. Baptism has brought the forgiveness of original sin and of the personal sins from before Baptism (if Baptism is received by an adult). But through Baptism a person is also accorded the strengthening of faith as a deterrent against future sins. For faith as an almost constant thinking of God maintains in the human person the fear of sinning. But human nature is left with a weakness due to the habit of sinning. Scholastic theology calls this habit concupiscence and considers it devoid of the sinful characteristic. The Eastern Fathers see this weakness in passion and anger. They are not totally extinguished, or entirely oriented toward wanting the good things and toward the reaction against evil things (repulsion toward sin, fortitude in meekness and humility). The process of diminishing the sinful aspect of passion and anger and of being strengthened in what is good is a long one. This process ends in the state of sinlessness and of total love. Until that end very useful to us is the fear of sin, repentance for all sins, greater ones first and then the smaller ones committed beforehand, even if we have received forgiveness for them. The greater our fear of sinning and the more often we repent and confess the sins we have committed, the more we weaken the tendency toward sin, or the orientation of our passion and anger toward sin. It is the sacrificed Christ of whom we partake that strengthens us in this state. He raises us to a new level of power from the one to which Baptism and Repentance raised us. Christ Himself with His power of sacrifice dwells in us as life in a spirit of sacrifice, contrary to passion and anger in which our egoism, or our weakness and deterioration, is manifested. Christ with whom we unite ourselves helps to reduce at maximum the weakness of our habit to sin, which manifests itself in new sins which we barely notice. The training of a lion is done gradually; all the more gradually is the human person's transition from the state of a wolf to that of a lamb. This is why at the outset of Christian life one is given not only Baptism and Confirmation, as powers for good, but also Holy Communion. And during life on earth one makes a constant progress toward sinlessness and pure sensitiveness through Confession and Communion. In this sense the Liturgy, as the order of Holy Communion, is a continuous ascent in Christian life.

Hence the step toward the ultimate purpose of Holy Communion, which is eternal life through union with the sacrificed and risen Christ, is the forgiveness of sins no matter how small or indescribable. Or since Christ unites Himself with us, He gives us through this forgiveness, on the one hand, the highest strengthening against sins and, on the other hand, the guarantee of eternal life as maximum attention toward God and fellow human beings. "He who has the Son has life; he who does not have the Son of God does not have life" (1 Jn 5:12). The Son is the life born of the Father, which is never weakened through indifference and is put at our disposal. The Father Himself bore witness to this. And he who believes in the Father has received this witness of the Father and has its confirmation in himself by the fact that he has received the Son with His maximum love as life. "He who believes in the Son of God has the witness in himself. . . . And this is the testimony: that God has given us eternal life, and this life is in His Son" (1 Jn 5:10–11).

The fact that the body which partakes of Christ, although it dies, will nonetheless rise again to a deified life, is based on the intimate connection that exists between body and soul that lasts even after the death of the body. For the fact that Christ's body remains not only in the body of the one partaking of it, but it also penetrates into his soul, is based on this connection. On the other hand, due to this connection, through Christ's body the divine life penetrates into us, therefore a spiritual life, and this penetrates into our soul as well. St. John of Damascus says: "It is Christ's body and blood entering into the composition of our soul and body without being consumed, without being corrupted, without passing into the privy—God forbid!—but into our substance for our sustenance, a bulwark against every sort of harm and a purifier from all uncleanliness . . . . since the flesh of the Lord was conceived of the life-giving Spirit, it is itself life-giving spirit—for 'that which is born of the Spirit is spirit' [Jn 3:6]. I say this not to detract from the nature of the body, but because I wish to show its life-giving and divine character."[397]

Any sense perception in the body becomes also a sense perception of the soul, and any sense perception in the soul is imprinted in the body. Pure sense perceptions in the soul sanctify the body and vice versa.

This is why the living body of the Lord, full of pure sense perceptions and of divine life, in which are reflected His sense perceptions and the life of His soul and thereby the divine life, imprints in the one who partakes of Him through His body the purity and the divine life from the Lord's soul manifested also in His body. In fact, do we not experience in our soul, even through a warm touching of our hand by a fellow human being, the warmth of his spiritual friendship?

Many of the prayers before Holy Communion affirm this penetration of the human and divine spiritual life of the Lord through His body into the soul of him who partakes. Some even speak of a dwelling of the Holy Trinity in the soul of him who partakes of the Lord's body. For where the divine work is, there are also the Persons whose work it is: "May I be sanctified in soul and body, O Master! May I be enlightened! May I be saved! May I become Thy dwelling through communion of the Sacred Mysteries, having Thee living in me with the Father and the Spirit, O Most-Merciful Benefactor!"[398]

The Lord's body has become most emphatically a conveyor of the streams of divine life through the cross imprinted in Him. Moreover, the cross has rendered it sensitive and delicate, making it a transparent and communicating membrane through which His spiritual life is seen and transmitted. The accusation against Him has contributed even more to His body becoming sensitive and delicate. This sensitivity is continually experienced by Christ through His mercy for us: "Taste and see that the Lord is good; the Lord Who of old became like us for us and Who, having once offered Himself as an Offering to His Father, is forever immolated, sanctifying those who partake of Him."[399] As we experience a wolf as evil when it produces in us the sensation of being mauled or eaten, so do we feel the kind Lamb, who is permanently slain spiritually for us and offers Himself to us wholly for spiritual nourishment, as producing in our soul sweet and pure sense perceptions that strengthen our life.

We believe that the meaning of Christ's body as conveyor, and of our body as receiver of sense perception and thus as superior understanding, is based on the fact that the body is a materialized word of the divine Word and a materialized sense perception of the divine Spirit. For we believe that this is the distinction between the divine Word and the divine Spirit. The Word or the Reason (inner principle, understanding, wisdom) and sense perception are strongly united in the Holy Trinity and both come forth from the Father as a full manifestation of His. Together they create the beings as materialized inner principles (reasons) or materialized words and sense perceptions. Such a materialized reason and sense perception is the body, too, meant to be a means of communicating the thoughts (words) and sense perceptions of the soul, a conformity existing between body and soul. It is the Word Who through His conscience and will makes the reasons and sense perceptions of the soul conscious, making them at once to activate in one way or another.

When the soul is pure in its thinking and sense perception, it also makes the body pure in the words and sense perceptions through which the soul communicates itself, and vice versa. In any case, the body is nothing but a vibrating membrane of thoughts and sense perceptions that have a certain unity with those of the soul.

Christ's body has been imprinted the most in His sense perceptions by the pure thoughts and sense perceptions of His soul, and in both of them there has been manifested most fully the word of the Word and the sense perception of the Spirit after which His soul and body have been created. These pure thoughts and sense perceptions, imprinted with the divine Word and with the Holy Spirit, are communicated through Christ's body to those who partake of Him.

If biology and medicine do not see anything but a body composed of material elements and in which material processes occur, the human person lives in his inner being a rich spiritual life, produced or occasioned by the body, which does not mean that there exists no subject who receives and renders conscious these sense perceptions produced by the body. We receive Christ's body together with the spiritual life lived inwardly by Him.

This affirmation of the positive effects of Holy Communion upon the body and soul is expressed in the following prayer: "Sanctify my mind, soul, heart, and body, O Savior! O Master, grant that I may draw near, uncondemned, to the dread Mysteries!"[400] On the one hand, they are dreadful if they are received with indifference and in a state of sin; on the other hand, they are full of spiritual delight if they are received with faith and in a state of purity. And their operation is all the more positive as it is accompanied by our prayer. Their effects upon both the body and soul are expressed in the following prayer: "O God and Word of God, may the burning Coal of Thy Body be a light in my darkness, and may Thy Blood be the cleansing of my defiled soul!"[401] The living body of the Lord has this cleansing effect upon the soul, even though it is spiritually broken out of mercy for me, because it is the body of the Word's Person. In His body given to me His mercy is felt; His blood comes into me full of the sense perception of mercy that the Word has for me. His very mercy and His love are distributed to me through His body always spiritually broken for me. Someone's living body is only a means of communicating his spiritual sense perceptions. All the more is the body of the divine Word, in which He continually experiences His brokenness out of mercy for us with a sense perception beyond any human sense perception. Through His body given to me I feel the Word vibrating out of His love for me, or communicating this love to me as a word of the supreme Word.

In one of their Centuries, Kallistos and Ignatios go so far in affirming the penetration of Christ's body with divinity that they consider that "the flesh of the Lord is *a life-giving spirit* because it was conceived through the *Life-Giving Spirit*, and *that which is born of the Spirit is spirit* (Jn 3:6)."[402] From conception there are imprinted in the body being conceived the sense perceptions of those from which they are conceived, sense perceptions expressed through words of a certain kind. From the time of Christ's conception by the Spirit the divine sense perceptions of the Spirit were imprinted in His body, overwhelming the human ones; sense perceptions of God's mercy for humans for whose salvation His Son deigned to become man in order to translate Himself into human words as Word full of mercy for us; sense perceptions that would be manifested also in accepting death on the cross for human beings.

Continuing this idea, Kallistos and Ignatios quote from St. Makarios of Egypt where he affirms that the divine Spirit is so mingled with Christ's blood that he who drinks it absorbs the Holy Spirit who imbues Himself perfectly in the soul: "Just as wine is diffused into all the body parts of him who drinks it, and the wine becomes part of him, and he part of the wine, likewise the Spirit of Divinity is poured into him who drinks the Blood of Christ; the Spirit is mingled with the perfect soul, and the soul with Him . . . . Furthermore, through the bread of the Eucharist, those who receive communion in truth are granted to become participants in the Holy Spirit, and those worthy souls are made capable of living forever. Again, just as the life of the body is not self-sustaining, but is sustained by matter external to it—from the earth—so God has been pleased to provide the soul with food, drink, and clothing not from its own nature, but from His divinity—from His own Spirit and Light, which are the true life of the soul."[403]

Again, the body and blood are thought of as means of communicating the spiritual sense perceptions overwhelmed in Christ by the divine ones. We have here the recurrent affirmation of the ineffable mystery of the fact that those through which someone touches or nourishes the body carries with them his sense perceptions into his soul. A spiritual I encounters another spiritual I through the material means by which they communicate. The material things have in them the capacity to be, as instruments, at the service of the sense perceptions of a person who addresses through them another person. The material things are overwhelmed by the spiritual ones, and the human spiritual things are overwhelmed by the divine spiritual ones. For the material ones are not purely material, they do not serve as a living body without having in them the powers of the soul and a rationality rooted in the person's reason (inner principle). Just as the wine is mingled with the human blood, but it gives to the latter its warmth, so is the divine Spirit mingled within the human person's soul, but the Spirit gives the soul an enthusiasm, a life, that could not come from itself. And the Spirit is mingled within the human soul through the mediation of certain gestures, material things or words—which are not purely material—that touch the sense perceptions of the body.

What St. Makarios says can also be used for the power of the soul that partakes of Christ to someday resurrect its body to an eternal life deriving from the divine Spirit found in the soul and which He maintains. As the natural body does not have natural life from itself, but from the power of the soul that organizes it and preserves it organized and alive in conformity to it, making use of the earth and what the earth produces, so the risen body will not have its resurrected life from the natural soul, but from the soul full of the Spirit found in itself. It could be said that in a way the body has the roots of its rational formation in the soul which makes use of the earth in order to constitute the concrete body. These roots are the soul's functions: a spiritual vision, a spiritual volition, a spiritual sense perception. They form out of the earth material organs, giving birth to the body. These functions, actualized during life on earth, the soul preserves gathered in their roots even when they lose their material organs. Through them, the soul, strengthened by the incarnate and risen Word and by the Holy Spirit, will again be able to develop the complexity of material organs, or the body from a transfigured earth, or a transfigured body from its functions transfigured by the risen body of the Word and by the Holy Spirit found in the soul. These functions can be considered as roots of the body, because they have in them the distinction and the capacity to be in a concrete relationship with the material world through their formation and development in material organs through which they can express themselves and to enter into a relationship with the material world, as the spiritual functions of angels do not have. In this way one can say that the body is potentially comprised in the soul, that there is no soul that does not have in itself the body as an undeveloped potentiality. This is how is explained the extension in the soul's thinking and sense perception of every external activity of the body and vice versa, of every activity and sense perception in the soul over the body. When a human being is born, there is no interval between the soul's coming into existence and the beginning of formation, through it, of the body. After the death of the body, the soul can continue to exist with its functions which form the body and which have ceased this activity of theirs. However, the functions of the souls that have Christ in them are nourished with a different content. Only those who do not have Christ are without a luminous content, or they are in "darkness," in a total disorder of thinking and sense perception and at war with all.[404]

St. Maximos the Confessor presents the following argument for the endurance in the soul after the death of the body of this structure capable of being extended in concrete organs, or of forming such organs: "Above all, the soul is rational [λογική] and intellectual [νοερά] either through itself or through the body. If it is through itself, or its own essence/being, that it is rational and intellectual, then it is certainly also self-constitutive [αὐθυποστάτος]. If it is self-constitutive by nature through itself and in accordance with itself, and is also active through the body, then it is naturally intelligent and makes use of reason, never at all ceasing from its intellective faculties that belong to it by nature. For whatever belongs in any way to an existing nature cannot be taken away from it, so long as it subsists. The soul, therefore, being forever, from when it came to be, and subsisting through God, who thus fashioned it, is eternally intelligent, making use of reason, and capable of knowledge, both on its own and together with the body, through itself and through its own nature. No reason could be discovered for attaching the soul to what belongs to it, other than through the body, after it has been deprived of this and alienated from it. If the soul is rational and intelligent through the body, then, first of all, the body would be more honourable than the soul that has come into being through it. Then it also possesses intelligence and rationality from it [sc. the body], for it has come into being out of it. For if, apart from the body, the soul cannot in any way understand or reason, then it is certainly from [the body] that understanding and reason belong to [the soul]. If the soul possesses understanding and reason from the body, it cannot possess these faculties apart from the body, according to what they say, nor certainly will it be self-constitutive. For how, without the body, could it have on its own account that which characterizes it? If it is not self-constitutive, it is clearly not an essence [ουσία]. Not being self-constitutive, it will be an accident, existing naturally only in the body that subsists. After that is dissolved, it can exist in no way at all. And there will be nothing more for those who lack understanding in this way, having been deprived of the immortality of the soul, that is, of the vain labours of the Epicureans and Aristotelians, and likewise for those who affect nobility by subjecting themselves to them."[405]

Affirming the deprivation of a new content of the soul that is dead outside the communion with Christ, St. Maximos also declares that the soul, at its exit from the body, will not take with it from the time of its living with the body anything but the conscious always filled with the qualms for all the evil things committed. This is why everything that the soul takes with it will forever remain the same, absent of progress, in an endless monotony and as a cause of incessant regret.

As for the light which the souls have when they exist in the body in communion with Christ, it can be said that it replaces plentifully the nourishment of the soul's functions while occupied with the things in the world, since in the risen Christ will appear as transparent all the inner principles (reasons) of created things and of human faces, which are united in Christ, and the remembrance of the things known during the life in the body is not associated with regrets, but with the joy of seeing them. In fact, it is for this that the Word of God became incarnate and was able to become incarnate: so that He can give and was able to give in Himself, as the angels cannot, existence to a soul that can activate its functions for the formation of the body with maximum benefit for the profound knowledge of, and love for, the things and persons in the world on the basis of the fact that the Word has in

Himself as God all their inner principles. And through crucifixion and resurrection He has passed beyond the thick cover placed over created things and over human faces so that He may reveal them at maximum in the unending light of His Person. He has done this in our favor so that we too may see them in Him, to a certain extent in this earthly life, and to a greater extent in the life of the soul after death and, finally, to the maximum extent, after the resurrection of all in the risen Christ, when all things and all persons will become transparent in the transparent Christ.

This light intensified at maximum, in which all things are seen in Christ, increases at maximum in our soul the power of grasping the functions of the human soul. This is why one speaks so much of Christ, of whom we partake, as of light. We receive this potency of our spiritual functions through Holy Communion at the same time with the power of these functions to reactivate themselves in the organs of a risen, transparent and imperishable body at the universal resurrection.

All the more is this so as after the universal resurrection all will be gathered and illumined in Christ, being united with their inner principles found in Him. If a parent has on his face characteristics proper to the faces of all his children, and the more he loves them, appropriating their pains and joys, the more he lives them in himself and reflects their faces in his face, all the more does Christ have in Himself characteristics that remind of the faces of all human beings, especially when on their faces are reflected faith in Him and a life after His example. And when a person utters Christ's name with thought and sense perception concentrated on Him, he thinks of all those whose faces he feels reflected in His face. And vice versa, that person sees Christ in all, especially in the humble and the needy, as He Himself was, in conformity with what He said: "Inasmuch as you did it to one of the least of these My brethren, you did it to Me" (Mt 25:40). And when He says "to one" Jesus thinks with a delicate feeling of everyone. This is why when someone partakes of Christ he thinks that he enters into communion with all and he also thinks of his responsibility for all.

The consciousness that the eternal life which we receive through the partaking of Christ is conditioned on the purification as much as possible from the egoism of sins—and this depends on our profound repentance for them and on the petition to be forgiven, because without this forgiveness the partaking is toward our condemnation—is so powerful that both the priest and the faithful ask for this fervently before Communion. The entire canon read by the priest on the evening and morning before officiating the Holy Liturgy, composed of psalms, hymns and twelve prayers (in the Greek Liturgy book there are only nine prayers) from various Fathers, represents a confession of his own sins accompanied by a profound repentance and the petition to be forgiven as well as to be worthy of partaking. The same sentiments are also expressed in the three prayers read by the priest and recited along with him by the faithful immediately before partaking.

"Accept the repentance of me, a sinner," says the priest in the prayer of St. Basil the Great, the first of the twelve prayers. Or "I have sinned, O Lord, I have sinned before Heaven and before Thy face and I am not worthy to look upon the height of Thy Glory," the priest says again, repeating the words of the Prodigal Son who returns after a long separation from his father. The priest says these words here with all the more sense perception as he asks to be accepted by the all-exalted One in glory.

The act of approaching the sacred Body and Blood for partaking of them is full of a fear similar to the one with which he will approach the judgment seat at the end of the world: "Just as I stand before Your fearful and undissembling judgment seat, O Christ God, answering the questions regarding the evils I have committed, so I stand now, before the coming of my day of judgment, before You and Your fearful and holy angels at Your altar, and being prompted by the testimony of my conscious I lay forth my evil deeds and transgressions and expose them openly . . . . What evil have I not committed? . . . . I have stained and defiled all my senses down to the depth of my being . . . . Do not put Your servant on trial" (the fourth prayer belonging to St. Symeon Metaphrastes, missing in the Greek Liturgikon).

The entire Holy Liturgy, from beginning to end, is full of supplications for God's mercy, which is manifested both in His Son's sacrifice for us and in the Son's benevolence to be partaken of by us, even though we are so small and so far from perfection. And this makes us approach Holy Communion with fear, asking God not to condemn us for partaking unworthily.

Both the priest and the believer are dominated by contradictory sentiments at the moment when they want to approach Holy Communion. Simplification would lead them to despair or to a certain indifference. Neither of these would help them to overcome themselves through sensibility. On the one hand, they experience the feeling of unworthiness and fear, produced by the awareness of their hollowness, but especially of their sinfulness, which makes them hesitate to approach the Holy Mysteries; on the other hand, they experience a great desire to be united with Christ, to experience His goodness and this desire prompts them to approach the Holy Mysteries. What makes them decide to approach is the trust in Christ's mercy. But the feelings of fear and unworthiness do not leave them even when they have decided to approach. The struggle between fear and the desire to approach does not cease even in the moment when they partake. On the contrary, the fear is so much greater as the priest or the believer is closer to the chalice. Even in the moment of Holy Communion and afterwards both their fear and happiness, trembling and joy and the sweetness of the Body received are mixed. For in these moments both the sense perception of the glory of the One they partake of and the happiness that they are united with the Almighty One reach their climax; in this moment they completely feel His mercy, which extends to the end, in the fact that He offers Himself to them, such insignificant beings. The fear is amplified by the fact that even now they cannot free themselves entirely from thoughts that are inconsistent with the greatness of the One they receive. In them is united the fear with the fear or with the feeling of not having enough fear. There is a paradox in the fear to approach and the desire to approach. There is also a paradox in the union between fear and the sentiment that one cannot distance oneself from sinful thoughts. I am afraid to approach because I am a sinner; but neither does the fear weaken the sinful thoughts, nor do the sinful thoughts wear out my fear. The fear does not raise me above the sinful thoughts, and the sinful thoughts do not weaken my fear. The fear should raise me up to a state proper to the gravity of the moment's solemnity. But I still remain in the indifference of improper thoughts: "I stand before the doors of Thy temple, and I forsake not my wicked thoughts" (the prayer of St. John of Damascus). On the one hand, the base thoughts accentuate even more the feeling of unworthiness and of fear, on the other hand, they wear it out. Additionally, I increase my desire to partake that, perhaps, I may be raised up from this state. But in spite of the appearance of not being raised to a new level of sensibility, this still takes place. By flogging myself, I ascend. I ascend through the fear of unworthiness, but also through the trust in God's mercy.

Over all these sentiments of sinfulness there hovers the trust in Christ's mercy: "Receive me, O Christ God, as Thou did receive the sinful woman and the woman with the flow of blood . . . . burning up the iniquity of my sins." But His mercy does not make me insensitive to my sins.

The encounter between the human person and God, the union with Him cannot but have the form of paradox. Experiencing the paradox is much more accentuated in Christianity, where the Son of God comes so close to us and unites Himself with us through His body and blood, but still remaining God at the same time. In paradox the human person experiences both the self-conscience and the conscience of God united with him, God remaining neither distant from nor confused with him. The paradox is the sign of union with God, specifically with the God who came as man close to the human person, as well as the sign of one's own person remaining unconfused. Only in this way can the human person truly experience the happiness of his encounter with God. In paradox we have a state that is extraordinarily complex, rich, happy and conscious in happiness, which cannot be offered either by the melting of the person in the great pantheistic essence, or by faith in a God who does not become incarnate and remains separated and distant from man. Everything is a paradox in existence; all things are in a relation, but unmixed.

Dominated by the consciousness of our inability to reach the perfect end of purity, our path toward perfection never ends. We want to always ascend into a constant and endless sensibleness: when humility is profound, "then this is the perfection of humility," says St. Isaac the Syrian.[406] Nothing is higher than humility. And St. John Chrysostom says: "I know that none of us is exempt from faults, no one can boast that he might have a pure heart. Awful is not so much as not having a pure heart, as in the absence of that we will not run to the One who could cleanse it . . . . Who as of old was more sinful than the publican? However, he only had to say: 'God, be merciful to me a sinner' (Lk 18:13) and he went down from the temple justified rather than the pharisee. What power was in these words? None in the words; all the power is found in the warmth with which they were spoken or, rather, not in this warmth, but before anything else, in God's goodness."[407] That is, trusting in it. The paradox maintains a continuous tension in the soul. I always want to rise above my condition, to be even more within God whom I know as infinitely more than what I have so far received from Him. The human person wants to be more than he is, to receive more than he has from the endless love of the One endless in love, although he knows that he cannot be always more on his own. For this would mean that he is himself infinite. If the human person is sad when he thinks that he exists only through his own powers, when he knows that he can always receive more from the infinite God, he is not unhappy on account of this, because he knows that he will always receive more. And knowing that only through God he can make progress, he is always humble.

The human person is a contradictory being, but thereby not unhappy when he thinks that he is in a relationship with God; he is happy when he senses God's greatness and when he advances in it, but also conscious of the inability to lift himself up through his own powers from monotony, banality, platitude, the muck of sin, perfidy, envy, arrogance and the slavery of passions.

Fear of God is not a sentiment through which the human person lives out his smallness before a fundamentally unconscious essence, but a means of knowledge, of existential perception of the greatness of a God consciously interested in the person's life and capable of helping him to grow in existence. In fear we are impressed not only by a great God, but also by a God who is consciously asking us to live in conformity with His will, not for His sake, but so as to raise us to the possibility of a pure and free communication with Him as well as to receive His divine life increasingly free from failings. The human person knows God to a greater and more vivid extent through his fear than through speculative reason by which he thinks that he disposes of himself on his own, or that a blind and unconscious law disposes of him. In this speculation there is no personal relationship between man and God. Man's characteristic as person is annulled, or it cannot be valued except for a short while and mostly in an imaginary way. Through Christian fear man's entire being enters into contact with God's conscious greatness and he trembles. But this underlines his personal responsibility and thus his characteristic as person. Only this fear has a saving effect, a beneficial effect upon man's being as person; only this fear is not paralyzing and does not produce resignation. It is produced by the very work of God as a mystery of His love that does not cause trembling through His greatness and benevolence toward us.

Nicolai Hartmann evidenced the trans-subjective reality of the objects of knowledge by the fact that knowledge is bathed in emotional states, which we do not produce. And we experience these states by touching the reality of known things (*Modus der Betroffenheit*); we experience a "harshness of reality" (*Die Härte des Realen*).[408] But only a personal God produces in us emotions of maximal responsibility with a deeply transforming power on the vertical of good with the collaboration of our will. Only the fear of a personal God has this emotional characteristic in the highest degree, but of responsibility at the same time, without annulling our freedom. It unites in itself the characteristic of medium for the knowledge of God's greatness with that of a medium for experiencing one's own sinfulness and the need to improve through the activity of the will. Only a personal God fosters us as persons. All these are at once known and experienced intensely only in the fear of God. St. John Chrysostom insisted specifically on the knowledge of God through fear.[409] But he united the knowledge of God through fear with the knowledge of Him through love. Through both of them we receive power to reform ourselves. This is why in the Liturgy that bears his name, when the priest exits through the royal doors with the chalice containing the Holy Mysteries he calls the faithful to Holy Communion with the words: *With the fear of God, with faith and with love draw near*. Without the faith in a personal God the fear would not be united with love. By knowing through faith that in the chalice there is the body and blood of the Lord who sacrificed Himself for them and offers Himself to them through love, the faithful are filled with love but also with fear because they know their unworthiness. But the priest still urges them to approach, overcoming their fear through love. The fact that the fear of God is united with the consciousness of sin proves even more that this fear is connected in our being with the relationship with a personal God, that it manifests our inalienable responsibility before God, a responsibility never completely fulfilled. And sin is shown as unforgettable especially by the fact that through it we have neglected our duties before our fellows, God's created beings. God created us imprinted with a responsibility for one another in view of mutual help and love, to abandon egoism, to promote love among ourselves, conscious that we all are God's beloved created beings. He created us with this duty because we are conscious beings, capable of showing mutual love through actions, and thus contributing to our spiritual growth toward our increasingly greater likeness and union with God.

If we partake of the Lord with such repentance and fear, He will strengthen us to continue on the path of our repentance and to attain forgiveness at the last judgment and eternal life. It is these sentiments that must accompany us all the more while approaching the Lord's body and blood, as He was crucified and offers Himself to us in a state of sacrifice out of love for us, willing to lead us to this union with Him through love. He wants to unite all of us in Him so that we may find all happiness in Him and in the union among ourselves, and we are very far from this state.

This moral distance between Him and us raises us to the consciousness of our unworthiness, for we have done almost nothing to follow His example. By approaching His mercy that went all the way to sacrifice for us, which He endures in its sense perception, we realize how far we are from the example of His mercy and sacrifice.

If we do not approach with this sentiment, it means that we are in an extreme feebleness, closed off in indifference and insensitivity. And this very thing means our condemnation, our fall from true humanity, a state of callousness that does not lack torment and deadly boredom.

In this sense, the Lord who offers Himself to us with the warmth of His endless love for us becomes a burning or tormenting fire for us. This is why St. Isaac the Syrian and St. Maximos the Confessor say that God's love itself will be a fire that will burn us in the life to come. For our eternal torment will be part of the loveless state in which we immersed ourselves. It will be an eternally burning torment, because the feebleness has become impossible to get rid of. We will live an eternal regret, and also the inability to escape the state we created for ourselves through our continual indifference toward others. The callousness and the torment will be paradoxically connected, as well as the freedom and the inability.

On the other hand, the fact of never being able to forget the non-fulfillment of our duties toward others, at the same time with the eternity of our feebleness, shows the unconditional and eternal value of other persons, or the foundation of their value in God's love for them. Any sin toward another person is a sin toward God, therefore a huge sin that needs His forgiveness.

And if we do not obtain forgiveness here, we will have to give an account in the eternal realm. Here is why we have a reason to repent while still on earth when our sense perception has not been totally exhausted and to ask for the forgiveness of sins we committed. This is why we approach the Lord's body and blood with repentance and with the fear with which we will approach the last judgment. The very fact of not feeling the need to ask for forgiveness is a sign of feebleness.

Here is the sense that the repentance with which we approach the partaking of Christ does have. This is why the fear we have when we approach the Lord's body and blood is also a fear so that we may not approach hardened in sins and, therefore, a fear of not receiving forgiveness for them, the liberation from the feebleness they have produced. This is why it is also a fear accompanied by fervent prayer for forgiveness. The greater this fear, the greater the sensibility that cannot stand the evil committed, sensibility that tends toward good, thus toward Christ's power so that we may do the good. We have here a great paradox: in the deep fear of Christ there is the deep desire for Him. St. John Chrysostom considers fear of God as a sign of the conscience to stay near the unutterable divine greatness. We can add that this fear is so much greater as the consciousness of our sinfulness is greater. "This is why we are bidden at that sacred moment to stand straight up. For to stand straight up is merely to stand in a manner which befits one who is a mere human being to stand before God, that is, 'with fear and trembling' [Phil 2:12], with a soul that is sober and vigilant."[410]

When St. John Chrysostom describes the fear with which the Seraphim look at God's glory he explains it only from seeing this glory. But the fact that the proof for this fear is taken from the prophet Isaiah who, when sharing in this vision he weeps for his sinfulness, shows that St. John Chrysostom also sees the awareness of our sinfulness present in the fear with which we, human beings, approach God's greatness. St. John says about the Seraphim: "Why, tell me, do they [the Seraphim] stretch forth their wings and cover their faces? For what other reason than that they cannot endure the sparkling flashes nor the lightning which shines from the throne? . . . . Even though the Seraphim are closer to God's essence than we men are, they still cannot look upon it just because they are closer."[411] On the contrary, the closer they are, the more they realize their inability to look upon God. The closer someone sees someone else's goodness, the more disgusted is he by his own wretchedness. "The blind man does not know that the sun's rays are unapproachable as does the man who can see. So we do not know the incomprehensibility of God in the same way as these powers do. The difference between a blind man and a man with sight is as great as the difference between us men and the powers above."[412] It feels as if we hear the words of St. Gregory of Nyssa in *The Life of Moses*: the higher he was ascending in knowledge, the higher he was ascending in the consciousness that he did not know. One affirms here as well the same experienced apophaticism of the knowledge of God. In addition, Isaiah presents sinfulness as cause for man's fear before the divine glory: "So I said, Woe is me, because I am pierced to the heart, for being a man and having unclean lips, I dwell in the midst of a people with unclean lips; for I saw the King, the Lord of hosts, with my own eyes!" (Is 6:5).

This is why St. John Chrysostom sees in the Liturgy as reason for fear not only God's glory, but also the sinfulness of the one looking at it. This because in the Eucharist the boundless God descends to us in an incomprehensible way for our sins, and in this descent through the body to bodily beings His glory appears even more amazing. God does not avoid taking on the body and suffering the cross in order to descend to us for our sins, but, on the contrary, precisely those things cause Him to descend to us. Precisely these cause Him to show even more His mercy for us. And this is what makes His mercy even more amazing, and therefore His greatness capable of such mercy even less understood. God's kenosis for my sins fills me up, on account of that, with an even greater fear. I ask myself: what if God descended in vain since I continue to remain in my sins? What if He sacrificed Himself and offers Himself to me in vain since I remain indifferent? Would not my condemnation be so much greater?

Additionally, in the union between the fear of approaching God and the awareness of sinfulness there is hidden another important significance. The feeling of sinfulness when approaching God shows the personal characteristic of God against whom we have sinned and also the value of our fellow human beings in His eyes, whom we have defrauded perhaps forever through our sins. If God was not personal and did not give human beings such a value, He would not take cognizance of our sins. So, the fear of God for our sins is not one of an impersonal essence, a fear of drowning in it, but the fear of being repudiated by the personal God, of being deprived forever of the life in communion with Him, of the happiness of His love superior to all loves and of a different order than them, the only one that can give me full happiness of which I can never be satisfied. Not taking seriously God as a person implies not taking seriously the value of the human person, regardless of how much one affirms his importance as supreme value. The human being as a person of eternal value exists and is accomplished only in union with God and in responsibility before Him. How could one take seriously the consequences of sins for him who commits them, or against whom he commits them, when the human being, either sinful or not, is a transitory speck of nature, issued from nature and destined to be again lost in nature? Is not, then, this human being a great contradiction when, on the one hand, he laughs at sin and, on the other hand, emphasizes with such force and passion the value of the human person and his will to be accomplished?

Only when sin is taken seriously is the real value of the human person implied, since there is also implied faith in the personal God and the fact that God takes the human person seriously, as well as his real growth toward the capacity of communion with Him in love.

Thus God does not inspire fear as an impersonal ocean does, which swallows us in both cases: when we sin and when we do not sin, but through the personal mystery of the One who has in Himself the ocean of power and life. A person, even a human one, is to us more incomprehensible than any impersonal ocean, even though that person is the only one in true contiguity. But the uncreated Person—who created and sustains everything, who is capable of so much love that He wants to make human persons His children, partakers of eternal happiness, and toward this end He sends His Son to become man like them, to sacrifice Himself for them, to rise again for them and to unite Himself with them for eternity, offering Himself to them for this purpose through Holy Communion—is infinitely more incomprehensible than the human person, although He became as man close to us.

The believer does not manifest his fear and repentance, sustained by the consciousness of his sinfulness, before an essence that does not take cognizance of this fear and repentance, but before a personal God. He does not address himself with his confession of sins and with the willingness for change to an essence devoid of conscience and subjected to certain implacable laws, but to a supreme, free conscience: "It is before You only that I have sinned." Only from that conscience can he ask for and receive forgiveness. The abyss that causes him dizziness is borne by this conscience that manifests this abyss variedly according to His will. This conscience can cause the sinner to dread this abyss or it can deprive the human person of absorbing from it. Only the life intensity of a reaction of a conscience bearing such an abyss of power can stimulate and sustain in the human person the unutterable and unquenched fear at the same time with the assurance given that it is also all-merciful. Being assured of the love and mercy of such an almighty God, who wants to assure us when we follow His will of the eternal life in communion with Him, the fear of Him is mixed with the supplication for His mercy and with our love for Him; through this fear our being, on the one hand, is overwhelmed by Him, on the other hand, is attracted by Him as toward the One who can offer eternal life in loving union with Him. It is not the fear that drives away the servant from his master who wants to waste him, but of a God who, being the Son of a Father, became our brother so as to make us too children of the Father. It is the fear of not losing the love of the Father, and thus of not losing ourselves. That very fear maintains in us the sensibility which connects us to Him and does not make us indifferent. In this fear is mixed our love for Him and our will to approach Him more and more as we increasingly become more purified and more worthy of Him.

The priest urges the faithful to all these when he calls them to approach Holy Communion. One expresses here a strong sentiment of Christ's presence, who Himself is calling us to union with Him, showing us how much He loves us and willing to offer Himself to us in a state of sacrifice. In the Holy Liturgy we are not alone with our sentiments as in neo-Protestant gatherings. In a paradoxical way the priest asks the faithful to have fear, but still to approach with love.

In the ancient pagan religions the human being experienced, when offering sacrifices, only a sentiment of strong, unclear fear (*Angst, Mysterium tremendum*). On the one hand, he confused heaven with nature; on the other hand, nature itself also had something personal with the destructive phenomena taking place in it. This is why the idol was depicted as half human, half animal, or in a monstrous image. It was not integrally a person, capable of a purely voluntary and loving action. Through sacrifice the deity had to be tamed in its unrestrained tendency, but on the other hand it could not be tamed because it was subjected to certain laws above it. By its nature it demanded blood. And he who was offering the sacrifice was pressed to commit some cruel act, like shedding blood. He had to satisfy the god's appetite for blood, which on the other hand, was imposed upon him by an inner law. Rising above the inner tendencies to which nature is subjected, or the altered nature, was not demanded, in the sense of being liberated from them or of overcoming them, as in Christianity. Also in the Mosaic religion the idea of a God to fear is not totally eliminated, nor is it in Islam where Allah demands bringing into submission by force those who do not accept it. Christianity rose to the idea of the God of love. Christianity does not want the human person to shed blood in order to offer sacrifice. When the believer brings offerings to God, or when he brings himself as offering, he shows that he loves Him above all, because out of love for humankind God Himself gave His Son to be sacrificed. The fear of the human person is the fear of approaching God in a state of moral impurity, of unworthiness, of egoism. This is not a less deep fear, but it is an ennobling fear.

Through the right faith in God, who is an eternally loving Father, to whom His own Son offers Himself as sacrifice on behalf of humans, His sacrifice being caused by the sinfulness of human beings, we are helped to pass over to His love. It is a love mixed with fear for our sins, a fear so much greater as we are called to union with His sacrificed Son; the greater the One who unites Himself with us in His state of sacrifice and the greater the love He shows us, the greater our fear of approaching unworthily, all the more do we make use of fear in order to ennoble ourselves. It is not about a paralyzing fear, a fear of being resigned, but a fear that generates in us the power to become better, because this fear is mixed with the attraction of love. A child respects his father, but he also loves him.

All these spiritual motions and sensations are briefly expressed in the three prayers which the priest reads for himself after he has taken in his hand the part HS, and for the faithful those read before he gives them Holy Communion with the spoon. One of the prayers is the twelfth read by the priest the morning before he starts officiating the Holy Liturgy. Both he and the faithful who pray along with him ask to be made partakers together with the Apostles of the Supper of which they were made partakers. Thus, they ask that the content of that Supper be actualized, that Christ may be invisibly given to them for food and drink, just as He was given to the Apostles at the Mystical Supper. All the faithful in every time experience what does not vanish with time. The risen Christ is partaken of unceasingly, for the power irradiating from Him is the power of His love that continually actualizes His sacrifice. It is with this power that He crushes the chains which diminish through the egoism of sins the life of the faithful: "The believer, the pilgrim, is a guest at the Wedding. He is inside, and sees the whole world from the inside. History is interpreted differently: the events of divine Economy are not past and closed, but present and active. They embrace us, they save us . . . . This is the consolation of the faithful in every place and time: the door of the Mystical Supper has not been closed. The refreshment of Pentecost is not passed... And each day at the Liturgy the faithful dare to ask the Lord, 'At Thy Mystical Supper, O Son of God, receive me *today* as a communicant.' The faithful do not know the Lord and His saints through recollection or by looking back into history... Being baptized into the joy of the new creation, they enter into the iconographic and liturgical world where they find the Lord and the saints alive. They come into immediate contact and communion with life . . . . What unites people and things in the liturgical and iconographic world is not bodily sensation . . . . For the world of the icon, distance in space and the passing of time do not exist."[413]

No distance in space and time can separate the risen Christ from those whom He loves. Time and space do not separate from Christ those who believe in Christ either, or from those who continue to be alive in Him even after their physical death.

The Mystical Supper is extended in the chamber full of light and joy of Christ's wedding banquet with more and more souls, with other brides and wedding guests who are added to the previous brides and wedding guests.

Being called by Christ to the Mystical Supper and to the wedding banquet of love, we should therefore approach clothed in the garment of love, unstained by the sins of egoism, evil thoughts contrary to love, like Judas with his countenance darkened or with a pretended light. This is why the believer promises to not neglect this love by betraying Christ to His enemies, namely to make a pact with them by renouncing Him. "I will not speak to Your enemies of Your Mystery" cannot mean keeping a secret about the teaching on the Eucharistic sacrifice, but the renunciation of Christ and mocking Him by him who participated at His banquet of love when he is among His enemies, while he behaves like a believer when among believers. Nothing can weaken faith more than this insincerity or duplicity. Christ rejoices more in him who did not pretend to be His disciple, but evidently acted as a thief, and in the moment when Christ was mocked he had the courage to be on His side and to confess Him. Christ will rejoice more in the one who approached the partaking of Him after a life similar to that of the thief, but full of courage in his confession and with supplication for the forgiveness of his sins. While the former has never experienced intensely the divine power of Christ, the latter has experienced it deeply in the moment when he returned to Him. His sincerity fills him with light.

Before this prayer, one recited the confession of faith in Christ, the Son of the living God, who came into the world to save the sinners, among whom the one who partakes considers himself to be the first; thus, a confession of his faith in Christ as the Son of God and as Savior, as well as of his acknowledgment as the greatest sinner. It is not a theoretical confession of faith, but a confession placed in connection with his own sinfulness. He is the humble publican, not the arrogant Pharisee. Additionally, one confesses the faith that in the form of bread and wine there is the very body and blood of Christ, and the believer prays that Christ may remember him when He comes into His Kingdom.

The third prayer before Holy Communion is based on the words of St. Paul the Apostle (1 Cor 11:29–32). Following St. Paul the Apostle, the priest and the believer pray that this communion may be not unto judgment nor unto condemnation, but unto the healing of not only the soul but also of the body. When the soul is strengthened and harmonized in its thoughts and senses, this has a strengthening effect on the body as well. But when someone partakes with indifference, this state of insensitivity has a negative effect even on the body, depriving it of the strengthening pull of the soul. If he is now indifferent, how much more indifferent will he be for the rest of his life?

In the Greek Liturgikon, in addition to the three prayers mentioned above, the priest is required to recite the following prayers before Holy Communion:

> Behold, I draw near to Holy Communion. O Creator, do not burn me as I partake, because You are a fire which consumes the unworthy. Instead, cleanse me from every stain.

Christ purifies with His body and blood those who willingly separate themselves from sin. Everything is accomplished through the cooperation between the human person and Christ. Tension meets tension. Christ does not operate upon the human person as upon a log. This is why Christ burns him who remains identified with sin together with his sin; He burns him through the sufferings he will have to endure on account of his indifference. The feebleness and self-disgust will appear all the more connected with that person insofar as he showed himself even more insensitive toward receiving in his own body Christ's body and blood. The presence of a pure person always produces irritation in the one with a rude attitude. Insensibility when approaching the good things is paradoxically united with a tormenting sensibility of regret, followed by disgust for such a life, by the intense experience of its nonsense of which the human person cannot get rid in the life to come.

The priest expresses in the following prayer the positive effects, which go beyond the forgiveness of sins up to the deification and the nourishment of the soul with everything that the good things of Christ's wedding banquet have to offer, but also the negative effect of burning through torments of the unworthy ones:

> Shudder, O man, as you behold the divine Blood. Because it is a burning coal that burns the unworthy. It is the body of God and it deifies and nourishes me. It is the Spirit of God that wondrously nourishes my mind.

In another prayer one states that Christ's fire burns sins. He who loves, sins no more. He who does not respond to love, suffers from self-disgust. Christ attracts through the longing for Him, which He awakens in the one who wants to partake of Him, and His love produces real change in that person. For the love showed to someone makes him good. Love fills him with sweet delight that makes him praise with exaltation the two modes of Christ's presence: purifying and giver of new sensations.

> You attracted me near You with desire, O Christ, and You have changed me with Your divine love; do burn away with the invisible fire my sins, and make me worthy to be filled with Your divine joy, so that with lips of joy I may magnify both Your first and second coming.

Through Holy Communion, an act of supreme love, a great change is produced in us. It is not only Christ who, through it, enters the depths of our being, filling them with the tenderness and goodness of His love, but we also enter the banquet from His wedding chamber, in the warm intimacy with Him; the soul has reached the state of a bride and of a wedding guest, just as Christ is experienced as both groom and chamber and as host who nourishes with the sweetness of His own body the entire being of the believer, as in an intimate and loving perichoresis. In the moment of entering that intimacy, the soul is overwhelmed with both the happiness of entering and with the fear of not having the garment according to the beauty and purity of the "place" in which it enters. For in the latter case he knows that he will be burned by "the immaterial fire." Christ is the "immaterial fire" or the spiritual warmth of love that cleanses the sins of the one who unites himself in faith with Him, but it burns with its torments the one who despises what is taking place. The love you do not respond to ends up tormenting you through the feebleness of your insensibility.

"Into the splendor of Your saints, how shall I, the unworthy, enter? For if I should dare to enter into the bridal chamber, my robe will betray me, and I will be bound and cast out by the angels. Cleanse my soul from uncleanliness, O Lord, and save me, for You are the lover of mankind." No one is perfectly pure. But the important thing is for someone to not seek to enter into Christ's intimacy with indifference, but praying to be cleansed by Christ Himself with the immaterial fire of His love.

Holy Communion is the guarantee of the fully evident wedding chamber in the life to come, of the endless Mystical Supper, of the happy feast of love and of the unceasing full communion.

Love cannot be expressed except in poetry, in poetic images, in hymns and songs. All the more does "The Song of Songs" express the love between the soul and Christ. When St. Symeon the New Theologian wrote "The Hymns of Divine Love" he had certainly started from the expression "You transformed me with Your divine love" from the hymn before Holy Communion quoted above. In Christ's love the soul feels an unutterable tenderness. The transformation produced by Christ's love in the soul into which Christ comes—in a total offering of Himself, in His will to perfectly unite His body and blood with the believer's body and blood—causes that soul to see the entire creation transfigured, just as the soul in love generally sees it. The entire creation is seen as participating at the wedding of the soul with God, as in the Romanian poem *Miorița* (*The Ewe*). It is not for nothing that the Anglican theologian A. M. Allchin titled one of his books in which he describes the transfiguration of the world at the end drawing on St. Maximos the Confessor, St. Symeon the New Theologian and also on certain English poets (Edwin Muir, David Jones, T. S. Elliot): *The World Is a Wedding*, London, 1978. The author describes in his book the life of God in the life of man, the life of the human spirit transformed and renewed by receiving God's Spirit.

The wedding chamber in the life to come is made up neither of the darkened rooms from *Walhala*, where armed cavaliers hold parties, nor of the paradise of bodily pleasures through the plentiful *houris* at the disposal of all, but the source of the banquet, the light and the joy in it is Christ's self-offering, who sustains the love of all for Him and among themselves. Where there is love, as the product of sacrifice and self-offering, there is also joy. The divine depths, made accessible in Christ to human persons, are not the depths of endless emptiness, but the depths of love, of the wealth of spiritual gifts and of endless revelations (meanings). The depth is not in contradiction with love, light and joy. For the depths in all of their infinity are the depths of the Person. This is why they are depths of life in its plenitude. All good things consist of the personal God's sense perceptions of love toward us.

This is why, as we mentioned above, only the sound of hymns is appropriate to express the bright good things of Christ's divine depths into which we enter through the partaking of His body and blood as means of those depths. This is why every Irmos before Holy Communion is a true hymn.

But just as Holy Communion can be a guarantee of eternal happiness, it can also be a gurantee of eternal damnation. For the Lord will come in "flaming fire taking vengeance on those who do not know God, and on those who do not obey the gospel of our Lord Jesus Christ. These shall be punished with everlasting destruction from the presence of the Lord and from the glory of His power, when He comes, in that Day, to be glorified in His saints and to be admired among all those who believe" (2 Th 1:8–10).

After he has partaken of the part HS, the priest also partakes of the Lord's blood, drinking from the chalice. As no one partakes of the part IS, thus showing that Jesus Christ remains as unconsumed hypostasis in the believers, so no one drinks the entire content of the chalice, showing that Christ remains with His blood as His own inexhaustible Person. He is united with us and distinct from us. This is the mystery of love.

After he has drunk from the Holy Chalice and with the cloth wiped his lips and the part of the chalice he touched while drinking, the priest says: *Lo! This has touched my lips, taking away my transgressions and cleansing my sins*. And then, after he has given the deacon a portion from the part HS and also given him to drink from the chalice, the priest tells him: *Lo! This has touched your lips . . . .* The wiping of lips implies the cleansing of the entire being: through lips we express sin, for through lips we express our thoughts that accompany or anticipate sin. Sin extends as a nectar through every limb. So does cleansing. One cannot be clean in one limb if one is not clean in all of them.

After the deacon has partaken, or if he is not present, then the priest puts the parts NI and KA in the chalice (he cuts them into smaller pieces for the faithful who are going to partake), then he recites three prayers of praise. The first one praises Christ's resurrection together with His cross: *Having beheld the resurrection of Christ, let us worship the holy Lord Jesus, the only sinless one. We venerate Your Cross, O Christ, and we praise and glorify Your holy resurrection. For You are our God and we know no other than You, and we call upon Your name. Come, all the faithful, let us venerate the holy resurrection of Christ. For, behold, through the Cross joy has come to all the world. By always blessing the Lord, we praise His resurrection; for by enduring the Cross for us, He destroyed death by death.*

Through partaking, one has seen the resurrection of Christ which He attained through the cross. This is why both of them are praised. Thus, His name is the name of the One who had conquered death and is eternally alive, therefore of the One who guarantees our resurrection as well. This is why when we call upon His name, we know that we will also rise again. If Christ did not rise again so as to remain eternally alive, the partaking of His body and blood would not have continually taken place, nor will it continually take place. A body that remained dead would have been totally decomposed. The Apostles gathered together with the first Christians to partake of Christ's body because they had seen Him risen. They were saying: "Having beheld the resurrection of Christ, we can partake of Him." And these words have been repeated by the succeeding Christians until today.

Thus, in Holy Communion we have the evidence transmitted by the Church from the Apostles until today that they had seen His resurrection. The cross of Christ, His crucifixion, has thus been proven to be the cross, or the crucifixion, of the incarnate Lord, Who could not be held by death. The death through the cross, or through crucifixion, has thus been accepted by Christ so as to be conquered by the One who was not only man. This is why we also praise His cross. Without Him accepting the cross, the resurrection, or the conquering of death, would not have taken place; without resurrection, the cross would not have been proven to be the cross of the incarnate God. Through the cross, resurrection has come or "joy to all the world." Both were necessary. This is why the Apostles were right to first affirm seeing the resurrection as basis for the veneration of the cross: "After we have seen Your resurrection, we have reason to venerate Your cross. Now we see that through the cross salvation has come to all the world." Through the death on the cross He destroyed death. And the Holy Communion practiced by the Church from the time of the Apostles is a living testimony, continually maintained by the Church, to the resurrection of Christ after accepting the cross. It is a testimony to the central core of the fact of our salvation in Christ. This is why St. Paul said: "For as often as you eat this bread and drink this cup, you proclaim the Lord's death till He comes" (1 Cor 11:26). The proclamation through the Holy Communion of Christ risen with the body from the death which He suffered with the purpose of trampling down death, is also a testimony to the faith that He, being alive, will come for the second time in order to raise us all. This is why in the words of St. Paul the following words are also implied: "Proclaim not the death of him who remained dead, but the death of Him who rose again and this is why He will be able to come and in fact will come again." Through Holy Communion we practically proclaim the death and the resurrection of the Lord, and not only these, but also His future coming for our resurrection. We proclaim them not only because this is what we want to believe, but because this belief is based on the testimony of the Apostles that came from them to us through Holy Communion. The Apostles did not preach the resurrection of Christ only by word, but they have given testimony to it through the Holy Communion which they had practiced from the beginning, immediately after the foundation of the Church. Thus, in Holy Communion we receive the risen body of the Lord, not a remembrance of the Supper.

St. Paul the Apostle brings to the forefront the proclamation of death, because if Christ did not die, He would not offer Himself to us as a sacrificed body and as spilled blood. Similarly, if He did not die, neither would He have risen. On the other hand, Christ would not offer Himself to us in a state of sacrificed body, but at the same time alive and life-giving, if He only died and did not rise again.

Through the death and resurrection of Christ, the remembrance and living extension of which remained for us in the Eucharist from the Apostles, we know that He is the true God, and we know no other than Him. For as long as death lasted with no exception in the world, faith in God and in His love for us did not have an irrefutable foundation. A death that would have endured unconquered by anyone would have been an argument difficult to refute against the existence of God. And a god who does not find a means to conquer death from within it, is not a true God. For such a god has no love for human beings, nor does he have power to liberate them from death. He is a god (deity) subjected to an inner necessity, thus not a true God, lacking freedom, power and love. Only a God in Whom there is a Father and a Son is a God of eternal love and only from this love can there be explained the goodwill of the Father to send His Son, with eternal life in Him, to become man and to conquer, as man, death from within it by accepting it so as to free the human persons from death and to make them, too, through the union with His Son, His eternal children through grace. Any other god is not a true God.

But the "beholding" of the resurrection of which this hymn speaks is not only a "beholding" of the Apostles transmitted to us, but also a certain present "beholding" which those who partake share in. He who surely believes in the resurrection of Christ, on the basis of the testimony received from the Apostles, also "beholds" as present the risen Christ through the images of bread and wine, on the basis of the assurance given to the Apostles by the Savior. And if He is present and has transformed the bread and wine into His body and blood, it is impossible that He does not act upon our sense perception to make it detect His presence, if our sense perception has been refined through its liberation from the callousness (rudeness) produced by sin and from exclusively accepting material things. In fact, one has asked through the epiklesis the coming of the Holy Spirit not only upon the gifts for their transformation, but also "upon us." The Spirit has come upon us not to "transform" us from something into something else, but to "change" us, as we have seen in a supplication of one prayer before Communion; to change us by raising us to a higher level where we can "behold" or "sense" in the image of bread and wine the Lord's body and blood (νοερα αισθηοιξ = spiritual sensing or perception).

Then the priest recites the prayer: *Shine, shine, O New Jerusalem, for the glory of Lord has risen over You. Dance now for joy and exult, O Zion, and you, O pure Birthgiver of God, rejoice in the resurrection of your offspring.*

The light of the resurrection has spread over the entire creation and in the first place over all of humankind, virtually changing it into a new Jerusalem, in the becoming Kingdom of the Holy Trinity where the God of peace dwells. The resurrection has now actually changed creation in its ripening through the transformation of bread and wine, transfigured by the Spirit, into the human body of Christ. This is why one speaks so much of the resurrection of Christ while partaking of Him. The light of His resurrected body penetrates into the bodies of those who partake and through them into creation. The human person's partaking of this body full of light, of the true meaning and purpose of the body, realizing a true wedding between Christ and humanity, attracts the entire creation even more into the light and joy of this wedding. In fact, the risen body of Christ is the risen or transfigured ripening of the entire creation upon which the true meaning and purpose of its existence is projected. The resurrection of Christ gives assurance of our resurrection as human beings, it begins the transfiguration of the entire matter showing its true meaning and purpose. For the matter of Christ's risen body is a part of the matter of cosmos in which it acts as dough toward its general transfiguration. The resurrection renders transparent the meanings of matter, causes it to become bright and to reveal these meanings. The human person discovers the fullness of meaning in words (reasons) incorporated in creation.

But the highest representation of creation, and especially of humanity, is the Birthgiver of God. Upon her is spread first of all and in the most intensive degree the light of her Son and Bridegroom's risen body, as she is the created being closest to Him. She rejoices the most in the resurrection for eternity of her divine Son's body, conceived and created in her body and blood. In her joy is concentrated as in a ripening the joy of the entire humanity and creation, because she is the first created being non-hypostasized in God who has risen. In her person she is the true Zion toward which were directed all the hopes of history with all its hardships and wanderings, and who assures all people that they will also rise again. She is the true Israel, who sees all the made promises fulfilled. "She is the 'people of God' bearing fruit through God's gracious power."[414] She is the creation that responds to God's call, to His gift, which culminates with the gift of Himself, with her gift of herself. In her there has been illuminated the full meaning of the human body and of creation with which the body stays connected.

In the first prayer after Holy Communion the Lord's resurrection and cross have been praised; in the second prayer, taken from the Katavasia of Pascha, the light spread from them upon creation has been praised as its full meaning, conditioned by its purity brought about in it by the incarnation and resurrection of the Word.

In the third prayer, also taken from the Katavasia, Christ is seen as the One in whom creation "passes over" into another plane, in the sacred plane of eternity. The received Communion opens up the perspective of the truer partaking in the age to come: *O Christ, the Great and most Holy Pascha! O Wisdom and Word and Power of God! Grant that we may partake of You more truly in the never-ending day of Your Kingdom.* Pascha means "passing." For the Jews it was the passing from the Egyptian slavery to freedom, the crossing over the Red Sea. That passing was done due to the sacrifice of the lamb. Through it the divine power of passing from the Egyptian slavery to freedom was communicated to Israel. For God said to Israel through Moses: "Thus it shall be, when your children say to you, 'What does this service mean?' that you shall say, 'This is the Paschal sacrifice of the Lord, who passed over the houses of the children of Israel in Egypt when He struck the Egyptians and delivered our households" (Ex 12:26-27).

But the passing from the slavery of sin to the perfect freedom of the Spirit and the salvation from eternal death has been done through the sacrifice of the reasonable Lamb. Moreover, it is in Him that the passing of humanity to the divine life and from death to the life of the resurrection is accomplished. It is the passing from the limited human plane to the divine plane, to the infinite transcendent plane of perfect freedom. Through Christ's sacrifice on the cross and through resurrection there is accomplished in Him and through Him, for all who are united with Him, the passing from life toward death or bearing of death, to the eternal and narrowless life of the resurrection, to the divine life. Those of us who partake of Him here, accomplish in part and in anticipation this passing and thus we will be able to partake of Him more truly in the life to come, becoming partakers of His unending life, bearers of a reasonable body entirely revealing unending meaning. At that time Christ's body will shine so intensely through everything that day and night will no longer alternate, and the entire existence will be illuminated by an eternal day, by an unending revelation of meaning and of the endless love of Christ-God, Who is in the very center of creation as the transmitting medium of the endless light.

By calling Christ Pascha the priest remembers that He is the reasonable Lamb, conscious and full of mercy, Who sacrificed Himself and did not remain in death but has conquered death, passing to the immortal life and liberating all from death forever. It is of this Lamb, sacrificed and at the same time eternally alive, that we will partake eternally, perfectly imprinting Him as living sacrifice in our being, so as to become for each other forever lambs fully reasonable and conscious, like Him, lambs full of all meekness in our wills unshaken by any hardship, devoid of any quarrel and of any will toward foolish dominion. Several odes from the Katavasia of the resurrection call Christ Pascha or "Passover" because He is the Man who has passed over to the state of God, yet remaining man, who has passed from the life subjected to death and decay to the eternal life of the resurrection in order to bring us in Him to this state. Other odes call Him a yearling Lamb, like the one in the Old Testament, namely Lamb in the fullness of youth, not old or weakened in vigor: "Christ is the New Pascha, the living sacrificial Victim, the Lamb of God Who takes away the sin of the world. Christ, our blessed Crown, like a yearling Lamb, of His own good will sacrificed Himself for all, a Pascha of purification, and as the glorious Sun of Righteousness, He has shone upon us again from the grave." Christ is "the living sacrifice" because He sacrifices Himself and remains alive unto the ages of ages, being at the same time in a state of sacrifice. He is not the sacrifice that dies as in the Old Testament. Christ is "Pascha the Redeemer," "the Pascha that has opened the gates of Paradise to us," namely that has brought us to Paradise, Christ Himself passing there as our ripening. He is "the spotless Pascha," for He has brought His humanity and ours to a life that will never fall into corruption, being kept in its living integrity by the Spirit of Christ. He is the true Pascha, not just an imagination, because He has passed from death to the true life since He came forth from the tomb. It is the most radical passage that one can think of. "It is the Day of Resurrection! Let us be radiant, O people! Pascha! The Lord's Pascha! For Christ our God has brought us from death to life, and from earth unto heaven." In Christ we have the radical transcending, the rising from the world of determinism into the plenitude and freedom of perfect life. He did not make us a part of a certain relative passing from one state to another within the framework of the same world that ends in death, but He has passed us beyond the life closed off in death. Here we only have the pledge of "passing." We will have the perfect passing at the resurrection; at that time we will pass to "the Kingdom without evening" of Christ where we will partake more truly of Him.

In the human person's propensity to sacrifice himself for another person is shown his propensity to pass from this world subjected to death, for he gives his fellow human being an absolute value which the latter cannot have from himself, but from a Person who is infinitely above him and the only one who can explain the existence of the human person that has such great value. But this propensity manifests the dynamics of his fundamental structure as reasonable lamb called to sacrifice, toward leaving this life for the absolute one, out of love for the persons regarded as having an absolute value. This structure has been fully actualized by Christ as man, thereby showing that He is God and also perfect man. In fact humanity cannot be perfectly actualized except by the one who is also God and offers Himself as perfect sacrifice for human beings, giving them an absolute value. Christ showed Himself perfect in His sacrifice through His innocence. For he who lacks innocence does not sacrifice himself fully, because he is dominated more or less by the egoism of sin. Precisely the innocence of the reasonable Lamb has in itself the conquering power over death. For in innocence there is also the total opening of humanity toward God. The one who is stained and diminished through egoism dies spiritually and thereby is closed off within himself, becomes rigid and separated from God, the source of fluid and infinite life. This kind of person becomes incapable of transcending himself. He closes himself off to the real and truly living transcendence. And the consequence of death or extreme spiritual weakening is the decomposition of the body, the components of which have become hardened, sclerotic, and their interpenetration weakened. Christ with His body was not necessarily subjected to death, although He has taken our body that could also die. His death in the body was not the inevitable consequence of spiritual death, because He was entirely without sin and open to God's personal and boundless transcendence that gives life. His death was a totally benevolent sacrifice, not the product of some necessity. He has assumed our death, taking a body capable of dying as a consequence of a certain hardening produced by our sin, but which He could surpass. He retained, out of love for us, His inner power that could bring His body to immortal transfiguration. His death was totally benevolent, a death as sacrifice. He accepted death so as to conquer it, having in Himself the power to conqer it. For being innocent in His soul, He had the strength to also conquer it, or better said He was able to receive the divine power in His soul so much that He could thereby conquer death, having no hardening in Himself.

By taking our body capable of dying and by withholding His inner power that could avoid death, He manifested solidarity with us, even in His inner self, without thereby losing His innocence, but also manifesting it in this way. By making Himself sin for us and having become a curse for us, He has nevertheless not become sinful Himself (2 Cor 5:21; Gal 3:13). On the contrary, this has accentuated even more His innocence by increasing His love and transcending or His self-forgetting. He has suffered even in His soul on account of our sin, for He considered it as His own, without Himself becoming sinful. He has made out of the cross (out of the suffering for us) a path from God to us in order to also become for us a path from us to Him. He who suffers for another takes that one into himself so as to cleanse him. The cross is the means of union out of love between him who loves and the beloved. But since the suffering of the Son is also assumed by the Father and the Spirit, the cross is also the path of the Trinity toward us and our path toward the Trinity. It is the means of union of the Holy Trinity with us and of our union with the Holy Trinity. It is the bridge of love between the Holy Trinity and us. This is why through the cross there comes the Holy Spirit of divine sense perception over us and over things so as to implant in us the sense perception toward God, or to sanctify us and the things as we offer them with a sacred sense perception to God. A mother suffers more than her child for the crime he has committed and she feels guilty for that crime, accepting as deserved the punishment for it, and still she does not become sinful herself through this, but even more innocent. And her sense perception of suffering love is also poured out over the child, softening him and uniting him with her.

We also receive the power of the spotless and therefore deeply sensitive Lamb, Who has conquered death, through our union with Him in frequent Holy Communion. For by accepting in His body our mortal bodies as His own members, He experiences together with us the death of our bodies so as to conquer it, but we are also filled with His suffering sense perception for us. He dies with us, but He is at the same time alive. Through both He brings each one of us from death to life, or He makes this passing together with us by descending with us into death so as to raise us from death to the true, full and immortal life.

The priest has recited these troparia while placing the broken parts NI and KA in the chalice as well as those of the Birthgiver of God and of all the saints, thus showing Christ's victory over death. Then, while placing the particles for the living and departed in the chalice, he says the words: *Wash away, O Lord, by Your precious Blood the sins of all those remembered here through the intercessions of all Your saints.*

In Christ's blood a solidarity is established between the Birthgiver of God and the saints, on the one hand, and on the other hand, between them and sinners, living and departed, commemorated while taking out the particles, the former praying for the latter and thus accomplishing a sort of union with them in the blood of Christ. Even if the living commemorated do not partake, they also benefit from the Lord's sacrifice, not only through the prayer of the priest and of those who presented prayer lists for them, namely through the prayer of the Church, but also through the prayers of the Birthgiver of God and of the saints. The solidarity or sobornicity among them indicated by the placing of their particles on the same paten around the Agnetz that will be transformed into the Lord's body, becomes even more accentuated by introducing the particles of all into the unconsumed blood of Christ as an infinite reserve of life. The blood is the organism's principle of life. Christ's blood, in which there is also the power of the Holy Spirit, is all the more the principle of the unitary life of all who are introduced into it through their particles. They are not received as concrete persons in the Lord's blood, as are those who partake, but their names are received in it, united with the particles representing them.

One should mention that the other particles, aside from the parts NI and KA, are not placed at this time in the chalice, unless there is no one about to partake, so that there is no risk of giving someone to partake of one of these particles. If there are faithful who are going to partake, these particles will be placed in the chalice after they have partaken.

After the parts NI and KA [and all others] have been placed in the chalice, the priest places the folded aer on the paten, then the star and the cover for the paten. He also covers the chalice with its cover. These have to be safeguarded against other uses. In the chalice there is still Christ's blood left over after the communion of the faithful. Christ has now retreated with His blood into the heavenly altar.

Then the priest reads silently the thanksgiving prayer to God for deeming him worthy to partake of *His heavenly and immortal Mysteries*, asking for strengthening in the fear of Him, guidance and guarding of his life through the prayers of the Birthgiver of God and of all His saints. "Fear" must further keep him in obedience to the One Whom he received in himself, or Who willingly united Himself with him. Fear must preserve in him the love for Christ, the unceasing thought of Him; to prevent him from ignoring the One Who deigned to again dwell in him. "Fear" is a means of guarding and refining his sensibility, of the consciousness of such a great presence in him. For someone to willingly unite himself with you does not mean to weaken your sensibility toward him, to forget the respect and appreciation due to him. All the more should this not be forgotten in the case of Christ's union with us.

Then the deacon, or if he is absent the priest, coming with the chalice to the royal doors and raising it, says to the people: *With the fear of God, with faith and with love draw near*. If the deacon is present he does this after receiving the chalice from the priest. St. Paul the Apostle also unites faith with love, and both of them with the divine grace, when he says: "And the grace of our Lord was exceedingly abundant, with faith and love which are in Christ Jesus" (1 Tim 1:14). Christian life begins with faith and advances to love, which is endless. And it is not only faith that sustains the progress of the Christian to love, but also the fear of God. Especially when the human person is close to God, fear dominates him so as to not approach being unworthy. It is the fear before the inexpressible greatness and Christ's holiness, but also the fear of insulting through his indifference Christ's great love for him, love that makes Christ let Himself be partaken of with His body and blood. He who does not have this fear, does not live truly the closeness to God. In a state of carelessness God is not felt. God, especially in His quality as Son, incarnate and crucified for us, is the center of an inexpressible sensibility and source of sensitiveness for us, the means for the human person's ascent to the climax of sensibility and tenderness. We should be afraid to insult, through our insensibility, the sensibility of the One sacrificed for us.

But this fear must not prevent the believer from approaching Christ in this supreme degree, the One who approaches us with the sensibility of the One sacrificed for us. Still, when approaching, the believer should not forget the fear. And he cannot maintain the fear without faith. For faith in His divinity and willingness to save us, through His body sacrificed out of mercy for us and given to us with love, will give the believer boldness to approach with the whole fear he holds. And this boldness will be stirred even more through love. St. John the Apostle said: "There is no fear in love" (1 Jn 4:18). But here he speaks of the fear of beginners, the one without love, not of the perfect fear. Of this it has been said: "The fear of the Lord is clean, enduring forever" (Ps 19:9). Or: "Oh, fear the Lord, you His saints!" (Ps 34:9). Or: "Blessed is every one who fears the Lord, who walks in His ways" (Ps 128:1). When you are in a sensible spiritual state before God's infinite and mystical goodness, you cannot distinguish fear from love. In the sensibility toward another person, love and timidity, concern for not offending him and love form a totality.

Who can say that he knows fully the divine mystery and does not tremble before His greatness? Who can say that he fulfills so completely God's will that he would not fear of being united unworthily—he who is imperfect—with the perfect One? God wants us advanced to an unending sensibility, just like Him Who was incarnate for us, sacrificed Himself and offers Himself to us in a state of sacrifice and of a compassionate vibration for us. Can anyone think that he has reached this climax of sensibility which He wants us to attain? I love our God because He is good, because He offers Himself to me sacrificed, out of compassion and inexpressible love for me and to unite Himself with me. He who approaches Christ in order to receive His body sacrificed for him out of compassionate love and given to him out of the same love, does not approach with an indifferent or unilateral state in his soul, but with one full of various sense perceptions, each one more impressed by the greatness of God's love.

While the faithful behold the Holy chalice through which Christ comes to them so as to offer Himself to them, they respond: *Blessed is He who comes in the name of the Lord; God is the Lord and has revealed Himself to us.* On the one hand, Christ comes as the One who became man, but also as the Son of the Father, in the name of God, sent by the Father to save us. How can we not bless Him who deigned to come to us, becoming human like us, sacrificing Himself out of compassion for us and ready to unite Himself with our suffering through His compassion? On the other hand, He who comes is simultaneously God who has shown Himself to us in a human body and with a human face. Both these two qualities, and even more so their combination, fill us with awe and cause us to thank and to bless Him. This is how the multitudes met Him at the entrance into Jerusalem: as the very God who came to them, but in a humility that is beyond any imagination. God comes now into the Jerusalem of our being, He is God descended to us, into our being that is too small, unworthy and far from the perfect sensibility which God wants us to attain. These are prophetic words from Psalm 117:26–27. "Work out your salvation with fear and trembling" (Php 2:12). St. Paul the Apostle told his addressees, explaining further: "that you may become blameless and harmless, children of God without fault in the midst of a crooked and perverse generation, among whom you shine as lights in the world" (Php 2:15). If God has made us His children, making His Son man who unites Himself with us, how much sensibility does He show us and with how much sensibility should we respond to Him!

This fear with which we should approach Him is a sense perception full of this sensibility. Through it we prove that we sense God's sensibility toward us, which fills us with awe, but also attracts us. It is a sense perception superior to a cold, distant knowledge that remains insensitive to God's love.

Then the priest offers communion to those who want to receive, after they have recited the three prayers before partaking.

The faithful are given communion from the Holy chalice, the priest taking with the spoon wine and a small particle from the parts NI and KA that were soaked in it, showing that they are given the power to overcome the sins of their insensitivity and the temptations to sin as well as the spiritual and eternal death that comes from sins. But they are also given the strong propensity toward sacrifice. The same blood of Christ, pure from every egoistic and improper sense perception and full of the elan of compassionate love, will flow in their veins, triggering in them corresponding sense perceptions. But Christ will remain as divine hypostasis, incarnate, sacrificed and risen, as a reserve of power and of infinite love for our eternal life. He is not confounded with us, although He experiences His blood flowing in our veins as guarantee of our resurrection. Through partaking, the faithful are united with the incarnate Son, thus becoming themselves children, or if they have partaken in the past they increase their status as children of the Father and brethren of the Son of God who became man for them. Thus they have become heirs of the Father's Kingdom, members of the Kingdom of the Holy Trinity. This is the highest level human persons can attain. Nicholas Cabasilas says: "It is impossible to conceive of anything more blessed than this. It is therefore the final Mystery as well, since it is not possible to go beyond it or to add anything to it . . . . After the Eucharist then, there is nowhere further to go. There we must stand, and try to examine the means by which we may preserve the treasure to the end . . . . So we dwell in Him and are indwelt and become one spirit with Him. The soul and the body and all their faculties forthwith become spiritual, for our souls, our bodies and blood, are united with His."[415]

We became one with the incarnate Son, according to His deified human nature; when the Father beholds Him He sees us in Him, and while beholding each one of us He beholds Him. But we can advance in our status as children. For love has no end. Thereby we became heirs of the Father's Kingdom together with His Son. And we can also advance eternally into experiencing the happiness in that Kingdom.

After all who want to partake have done so, the priest blesses the people with the Holy chalice in the form of the cross, saying: *O God, save Your people and bless Your inheritance*. Through the fact that they have received in their bodies the body of the Son of God made man for them, and in their blood they received His blood sacrificed to the Father as man who perfectly submitted Himself to Him, they too became children of the Father and heirs of His Kingdom, together with His Son, as they have totally submitted themselves to Him out of love. They have become His people forever, who through the sacrifice of His Son became members of the Holy Trinity's eternal Kingdom.

Those who became God's heirs by the fact that Christ has entered with His love within the depths of their being, or by the fact that they have entered into the light and the everlasting personal life of Christ who became their brother, respond: *We have seen the true light, we have received the heavenly Spirit, we have found the true faith, worshiping the undivided Trinity who has saved us*. The supplications of the priest and the responding hymns of the community have referred up until now to the future and to certain goods received from God. Now, through Christ's union with them, everything has been received. Now the community has surpassed hope. Now it lives in love. The mercy they had asked from Him through the recurring litanies has been given to them abundantly. By receiving Christ's body and blood "we have seen the true light." His risen body has brought the light within us. For by guaranteeing us the eternal life of the resurrection, He has given meaning to our life. We know what we live for. We know that we, too, will rise again. We know that death will not put a definitive end to our life, emptying it of all meaning. The hardships of life, pains, death that awaits us are all transitory and no longer do they place a non-sensical veil over our life. We know that precisely through them, if we endure them patiently, we go to the life without end, as Christ did as man, as they strengthen us in spirit. And everything came to us through Christ, the Father's Son incarnate, crucified and risen, sensitive and spiritualized through obedient patience and thus filled with Holy Spirit. Through Him is communicated to us the Father's love and the power of patience and of faith in this love. The entire Trinity has saved us with Its love, pouring out Its love over us and within us through Christ. The faith in the Trinity is the true and saving faith, because it is the faith in the God of communitarian, conscious love that is also poured out over us by His will. This is why we worship the Trinity. We do not come out of, nor do we get lost in, an unconscious essence or in the individualism of general unhappiness. We do not worship an unconscious and unfree essence that does not know about this worship nor can it rejoice in it. We do not climb down from humanity. Worshiping is a relation between persons, it is a relation from our person to the Persons of the Holy Trinity. If the Trinity did not exist, the ultimate reality would consist of an essence and of laws. Everything would be inexplicable, dark. Everything would make an unconscious mockery out of the human person. Knowledge would be reduced to the knowledge without light of certain monotonous laws, closed off in the blind immanence beyond which there is nothing.

Only the personal Trinity, superior to laws, opens up for us the perspective of a new knowledge, of an understanding of existence, of the "light," of personal fulfillment in communion. Even a human person is a source and a thirst for knowledge and of unending illumination, always new, of the existence for us, of the existence of that person who seeks meaning and who finds to a certain degree a meaning as that very person has a meaning in his value experienced in a conscious way. But a person has all this in communion with another one or with other persons.

While scientific knowledge knows only the laws of the material, opaque substance of the outer body and its contacts with the opaque material plane of the world, personal inner experience of the body by the conscious person and of its contacts with the material world, and especially with other persons, brings about a knowledge and a life for which everything is transparent and infinitely complex, the body itself and its contacts with the world having a role in making existence transparent as well as a role in communicating its knowledge. The body is thus revealed to the person as an occasion for and as a vehicle of spiritual life, as its means, which comprises light in it. The body itself causes a much richer thinking, freer and always new. But through communication the person knows not only his own body as occasion for and vehicle of spiritual life, but also the body of others that also promotes and communicates spiritual life.

In this way we know the Son of God's compassion for us lived through His body as well as our relation with Him through the partaking of Him. And thus we know the love of the Trinity for us. We know that we advance in grasping the meaning of existence up to the supreme climax. This has been opened to us through the Spirit Whom we received from Christ and Who, on the one hand, is heavenly, above all immanent existence, and on the other hand, He gives us a supreme light which explains the immanent existence. Thus, the Liturgy is the medium of our experiencing and knowing the personal divine love, as the supreme meaning, or the plenary, "true light" of existence.

But the knowledge given to us by the Trinity of divine Persons is not obtained by force, but with the prayer addressed to the Trinity's freedom to reveal itself, just as we obtain the knowledge of a human person through our appeal to that person to communicate himself to us. For that person is not an object, but freedom. The most amazing descent of the Trinity to us was the incarnation and the sacrifice of the Father's Son for us. The Holy Liturgy is the continuous extension of the Trinity's descent to us through the sacrifice of the Son, a descent that is a response to our prayer with the purpose of raising us to union with the Trinity in love. This light is given to us especially through the Son's body sacrificed for us, which is full of the entire sense perception of love for us and of all light.

In this sense, Christ's body and blood have filled us, too, with light. Through them we have seen the light, we have seen the sacrifice of complete love lived by the Son of God for us through the body and we have felt it within us. We have seen the value of every human person's existence. We have seen that the sense of existence and its plenitude lies in the Son of God's sacrifice out of love for us so as to bear fruit in our sacrifice out of love for others. The sacrifice of the incarnate Son of God opens up for us the ascent toward our perfection in God through sacrifice, since through it He descended to us and has perfected our humanity which He assumed. It is not a sacrifice imposed by the big one upon the small one, but the sacrifice of the big one for the small one and, in the last analysis, the sacrifice of the very Son of God for us.

For this sacrifice and, together with it, His complete descent to us gives us, too, the power of sacrifice through which we ascend to God and of the sacrifice through which we descend to others, which, on the other hand, is in itself an ascension. In the union of the Son of God, incarnate and sacrificed for us and descended to us in this state, we have seen the value we have in the eyes of God, who takes upon Himself our body so as to unite it, full of His divinity and purity, with our body so frail, and to fill it with the power of the resurrection in order to raise it to the supreme light. His sense perception of sacrifice stimulates our sense perception of sacrifice and is united with it. Into our hands have penetrated the hand of Christ, in our eyes the eyes of Christ, in our sense perception Christ's sense perception full of love for mankind. We live the sensible life lived by Him in His body as ours and vice versa. We no longer have in us an earthly spirit, but Christ's "heavenly Spirit." This is why we understand, we see, we sense the true light, one with the eternal life, which is Christ Himself, as He has said (Jn 8:12). His Spirit opens up for us the immortal life not subjected to the laws of corruption; He opens us up to the immortal life of Christ as man and to His all-pure sense perception. By partaking of Christ, we have proven that our faith is the true one, that the Trinity has saved us from eternal death through the love manifested in the sacrifice of Christ and in His union with us. Our faith is no longer from hearing. We have verified the faith through experience, through the fear and love awakened in us, born from the encounter with Christ in His Spirit. Diadochos of Photiki says: "But he who only believes and does not love, lacks even the faith he thinks he has; for he believes merely with a certain superficiality of intellect and is not energized by the full force of love's glory."[416]

The true faith is the experience of God's love for us, of the infinity of God in Trinity. It is the experience of the love of a God who is a Father that sends His Son to become man, out of love for human persons, to also extend His love as a Father to human beings. By knowing this Trinity, we cannot but worship It. Because only this can be the true God. A monopersonal God cannot be a true God, since he lacks love. In the pantheistic religions in which the world is confounded with God and in which everything unfolds according to certain necessary and narrow laws, there again cannot be a God of love, of unending life and, thus, of salvation for human persons from death. We can worship only a God in Trinity, because He alone was able to save us as persons, wishing for us to be in love with Him and to know His infinity forever. Only such a God can receive us in the Kingdom of His supreme freedom. And only a God in the Trinity of Persons is able to rejoice in our worship.

10. Praises, Thanksgivings and the New Supplications Addressed to God after Holy Communion

If the Holy Liturgy begins with the blessing of the Kingdom of the Father and of the Son and of the Holy Spirit, and thus with the invitation to advance in it, after we have entered into it through Baptism, it ends with the act of Communion through which, by being fully united with the Son incarnate, crucified and risen, we have become new children of the heavenly Father and brothers and sisters of His Son as well as bearers of the Holy Spirit. Thus we have become members of the Kingdom where God is not a despotic ruler and where we are subjected in a worldly sense, but children of the Father and brothers and sisters of the Son, united with Him in the same Spirit in which They are united. The Reformed theologian Jürgen Moltmann has developed the idea that God created human beings because He has from eternity a Son and wants to extend His love for His Son to other children through His incarnation, establishing a Kingdom in which He is Father and human beings are His children or brothers and sisters of His Son. It is an idea he took from St. Athanasius the Great. But full union with the incarnate Son and our full adoption by the Father is achieved only through our partaking of the sacrificed body and blood of His Son, or offered to the Father. The union with Christ through Holy Communion is the final act of salvation. This union, as a perfect union, was the final act of Christ's life among His disciples and He asked that this act be continued after His death, resurrection and ascension in order to unite those who believe with Him in the state of His sacrifice, resurrection and ascension so that they may share with Him in these states of His.

By receiving within us the body and blood of God's incarnate Son with the sense perceptions found in them, our faces are imprinted with His countenance. As St. Cyril of Alexandria says, the Father beholds in our faces the face of His Son incarnate and sacrificed for His glory, as we are united through Holy Communion with His risen Son. Thus, our adoption does not mean a simply juridical new relation, but becomes an ontological reality, for we are now members of the Son's body, incarnate and sacrificed to the Father out of love. The ontological characteristic of this filial relation does not exclude its acceptance and growth through our will as well. For, as St. Cyril of Alexandra also says, no one can enter into the Father's presence except in a state of pure sacrifice, and we cannot appropriate this state except in His Son.

The words of St. Paul the Apostle: "For as often as you eat this bread and drink this cup, you proclaim the Lord's death till He comes" (1 Cor 11:26) should be therefore understood not only as a theoretical proclamation, but through our very life in the sense that we manifest in ourselves the power to sacrifice ourselves to the Father together with Him, a power received along with the blood of Christ who gave up His life. We ought to proclaim Christ's death by showing ourselves capable of offering ourselves to the Father and to our fellow human beings together with Him, giving up any form of sin in which is shown our egoism and the eternal deprivation of our existence. This is why St. Paul warns against partaking in an unworthy manner (1 Cor 11:27).

Thus becoming new persons, the Eucharist acts in us as a germ of the resurrection into incorruption. Theodore of Mopsuestia says: "To partake of the Father means to commemorate [the anamnesis that makes real again] the Lord's death, which procures for us the resurrection and the joy of immortality; because it is proper for us, who have, through the Lord's death, received a mystical birth [in Baptism], to receive after that death the nourishment of the Mystery of immortality. By partaking of the Mystery we achieve in that form the anamnesis of His passion through which we will obtain the future blessings and the forgiveness of sins."[417] We appropriate the Lord's death in a sort of death of our own which, if it is not bloody, must at least be spiritual so as to unite ourselves with Him in giving up the old and narrow life of egoism. In this way we belong to the Father together with His Son. For this is what it means to forget our old selves and to die to the dead life, reduced to the extreme; it means to offer ourselves to the Father together with His Son so as to have together with Him the infinite and immortal life. "For through Him we both have access by one Spirit to the Father" (Eph 2:18). Our sacrifice with Christ and the divine adoption, and thus the eternal life, belong together because they take us out of the narrowness of the egoistic existence, receiving endless life from the source without beginning or end of the life which is the Father. "But now in Christ Jesus you who once were far off have been brought near by the blood of Christ" (Eph 2:13). Evidently, this blood has to become our own in order for us to approach the Father together with His Son. The text has a eucharistic meaning. Christ's blood has been shed so as to be communicated to us. After the descent of the Holy Spirit, constitutive to the Church through the Eucharist, Christ's blood has become the blood of those who attach themselves to Christ, as a means of union with Him. Christ's blood has been shed on the cross in perfect generosity in order to be given to us full of this generosity. In this quality it is loved by the Father as blood that comprises and manifests in it His Son's will to offer Himself as man to the Father, but also to offer Himself to us out of love so as to produce in our blood, too, this will to offer ourselves with total devotion to the Father and with all generosity to our fellow human beings. United with this generosity of Christ's offering of His blood is also given to us the immortal life, since through this we have also offered ourselves to the Father and have opened ourselves up to His life without beginning and without end.

The shedding of blood for someone means the offering of one's own life for that someone. Christ's blood was offered to the Father and has also been offered to us simultaneously with the immortal life received in it from the Father, or from His divinity.

Christ's blood has so much power not only because in Him there is His own immortal life and that of the Father's divinity, but also because in Him there is His Holy Spirit as well, the life-giving Spirit. The Spirit is the immortal and tireless life on the spiritual plane, filling Christ's blood, and through it ours as well, with this life. Where Christ's blood is, there is also His Holy Spirit, the giver of life. Where His blood is, pure of all egoism that closes off and narrows down, there is also the Holy Spirit of great and generous communion and of the life that this communion gives to everyone. In the paschal hymns of Pseudo-Chrysostom, in which can be seen the influence of St. Cyril of Alexandria (*Adoration in Spirit and in Truth*, PG 68), it is said: "There is no other way to escape the destroying angel except the blood of God, which He shed out of love for us. Through this blood we receive the Holy Spirit. In fact, the Spirit and the blood are related, if through the blood which is co-natural we receive the Spirit who is not co-natural with us, and death's access to our souls is closed. This is the power of the blood" (PG 59, 727A). The blood is a symbol of the Spirit and therefore they are related, because in blood the expansion of life is also manifested.

Thus when we all unite ourselves with Christ through Holy Communion in order to offer ourselves together with Him to the Father, we all unite ourselves not only with Christ, but also with the Father in the Spirit. But we also unite each other among ourselves. For where there is the common sacrifice nourished from the central Sacrifice offered by the Highest Priest, to Whom we attach ourselves, there is the Father as receiver of that sacrifice; and there is the holy dwelling of God, overshadowed by the Spirit, a dwelling made up of all of us.

In this unity we thus build ourselves as a house of the Holy Trinity: "Jesus Christ Himself being the cornerstone, in whom the whole building, being fitted together, grows into a holy temple in the Lord, in whom you also are being built together for a dwelling place of God in the Spirit" (Eph 2:20–22).

This is the Kingdom of the Holy Trinity: an intimate divine household that comprises all of us. The Liturgy takes us ever deeper into it through Christ's sacrifice out of love, which generates in us love and sacrifice.

By taking the human nature into His divine hypostasis, the Son of God has activated in it the potentialities of human nature that hypostasizes itself in all His brothers according to humanity, although it remains His nature as His own hypostasis. No human person can activate his nature's potentialities except in communication with the human nature hypostasized in other fellow human beings. But the lack of unimpeded communication, which is not achieved except through complete love, hinders in others the unimpeded fulfillment of the positive hypostasized potentialities, actualized in others, and does not communicate his own to others, fully actualized as union with those of others. But Christ appropriates out of love and actualizes the positive potentialities of human nature in all. In Him the unity of human nature is experienced in a real way. He loves this nature's potentialities, present and positively actualized by every hypostasis. For nature, although it is one and the same in all human hypostases, is present in each hypostasis especially with certain potentials, and it actualizes them to a certain extent due to special circumstances in which it receives its concrete existence in various hypostases, which in their turn influence hereditarily the variety of potentialities in which this nature come to existence in other and other hypostases.

In the love among human persons there is also manifested everyone's need to actualize in him its potentialities in communication and union with its potentialities hypostasized and actualized in others.

Through His love, to which His sacrifice pertains as its culminating manifestation, Christ opens up the nature in Him for its potentialities to be received and actualized in all human beings. Thus, when we receive His body and blood through Holy Communion we feel the potentialities and aspirations of the nature in us taken to their full and appropriate fulfillment. Christ, too, having in Him our potentialities already fulfilled, lives them as His own when He dwells in us, or we in Him. In this sense St. Symeon the New Theologian can say:

> We become members of Christ—and Christ becomes our members,
> Christ becomes my hand, Christ, my miserable foot;
> And I, unhappy one, am Christ's hand, Christ's foot!
> I move my hand, and my hand is the whole Christ . . .
> I move my foot, and behold it shines like That—one![418]

In this sense we can understand the words of St. Paul the Apostle that we are members of Christ, namely each one of us living with our sense perception as one member all that Christ is as fulfillment of integral reality at a supreme level (1 Cor 12:12; Rom 12:5), but also these words of the same Apostle: "It is no longer I who live, but Christ lives in me" (Gal 2:20). This is so because out of love for Him "I have been crucified with Christ . . . who loved me and gave Himself for me" (Gal 2:20).

Also in this sense we can understand Christ's words that he who has fed the hungry and visited the sick has done it to Him (Mt 25:35, 40). But this does not annul the persons. For each one being a member in Christ's body has his own gift, although he lives in his own way everything that is in Christ. Christ lives all of them, not as one member, but as the one who has all members as His own, the actualized potentials of all members. Both of these occur because one and the same Spirit of Christ "works all these things" (1 Cor 12:11). So Christ has the potentials of the entire human nature actualized in Him and every member, by receiving Him, experiences them as in his own body, or as in his own nature, but in a manner proper to himself as a distinct member. But Christ senses every one in whom He is received, or makes his abode in Him, as belonging to His [human] nature or to His integral body.

But if a certain person does not want to receive Christ in himself with the potentials of his nature more or less actualized in him, that person makes Christ to not see the fruit of their actualization in him. Consequently, this leaves part of humanity not actualized according to the will of the Son of God, who took upon Himself our nature in order to positively actualize the potentials of the entire humanity in all persons. Thus, Christ cannot gather all in Him so that all may fully make use of the actualized potentials of all in Him, because not all human beings want that. These do not, therefore, get to feel as being members in His body or to rejoice in the actualized potentials of all those rightfully gathered in Him so that, thereby, they may actualize their own potentials with the help of those gathered in Christ.

This is what Christ wants: that all human potentials may be positively actualized in every human person through the gathering of all in Him and through everyone's effort to be in the fullest communication with all in Him, and first of all with Christ Himself.

But many remain forever with their potentials not actualized at all, or wrongly actualized through their refusal to receive Christ in them or to unite themselves with Him and in Him with all others.

Certainly, Christ in this way does not lack any part of His happiness, for the sustaining divinity of His love has actualized in Him to the optimum degree everything that is human. And this is what will happen in the end to those who unite themselves with Christ, as they live integrally their humanity conforming with their quality as distinct members. But those who in any way do not want to make use of the actualization of the human potentials in them remain in suffering, because they do not want to place themselves in communication with the human potentials in all and with those integrally actualized in Christ by gathering them in Him. Christ will continue to work until the end of the world to convince as many as possible to fulfill this desire of His. But He does this out of love for them, not because He would need the integral human realization of all.

As we recognize the movement of those who gather together in Christ in order to actualize the various potentials of their nature, from Christ's integral and fully realized humanity united through Christ with the Father and strengthened at maximum through the Spirit, we observe that in this way what happens to the humanity of human persons is in fact what has been fulfilled from eternity in the Holy Trinity with the common nature of the divine Persons. Just as in the Holy Trinity each Person has as actualized and as His own the powers of all three divine Persons from eternity, so will each human person be able in Christ to have the potentials of all human persons, or of the entire human nature, actualized and thus proper to them. In this is shown in a more complete way the presence of the Holy Trinity in human beings. The unity existing in the Holy Trinity from eternity is a goal for the unity toward which we move in Christ. This is at the same time an ascent equivalent with the increasingly complete permeation of it by God in Trinity. In Christ, human happiness consists thus of the perfected unity of all human persons in the joy of experiencing all human potentials actualized for all in Christ. Having in Himself as His own all the potentials of divine nature actualized from eternity, together with the Father and the Holy Spirit, Christ imprints His unity according to divinity with the Father and the Holy Spirit upon the unity according to humanity with the human beings gathered in Him.

But the progress in the unity of those gathered in Christ for the unity equal to that of the Holy Trinity and fully pervaded by It is an infinite path, because their unity can never be identical with that of the Holy Trinity. And this progress means not only a progress in love, but also an infinite progress in knowledge. To this progress toward that never-attained goal corresponds the human person's endless aspiration for knowledge and love, as well as the consciousness that both he and his fellow human being can communicate eternally more and more the proper mode of knowing the reality above them, thus advancing toward the never-attained unity of the Holy Trinity. In this is implied the consciousness of the immortality of the person who loves and who is loved.

We also mention that living the integral humanity by Christ and the progress toward this experience by every human person also means for those gathered in Him and for their continuous progress in Him a progress in knowing the entire creation—at once with the progress in the knowledge of the Holy Trinity—and of its roots in the Holy Trinity. For through this progress one achieves the actualization of the integral human potentials through the knowledge of creation by every human person in his own mode and through the synthesis of everyone's mode.

But since the human person knows creation through the body, one asks the question: is not the progress in knowing the world to some extent interrupted while the soul remains separated from the body from the time of death to the time of the resurrection? The answer to this question can be that during this time the soul advances in the direct knowledge of Christ who is in the transfigured body and also, through this, in the Holy Trinity as well as in the roots of creation in God, so that the human person may be prepared to resume, after the resurrection of the body, the knowledge of creation transfigured or transparent for the divine light, or knowing it in the inner principles deepened into the infinite light of Christ and, thus, of the Holy Trinity. But the person is helped in this by the fact that he feels God's presence close to him, on account of the love manifested by the living through their prayers. Only those who died without faith in Christ, and without gaining in any way the love of his fellow human beings, will sink into the darkness or into the void of the ego totally closed off in itself. For the person can communicate from within to others ad infinitum, and can receive communications from another person ad infinitum, only as long as he remains a receptacle and a conscious communicator of the Holy Trinity's infinity of love and existence as well as of the depth of creation in its infinity.

In the communication between persons lies the life of the person. And not only between two persons, but among as many as possible. This is the community with a characteristic of the greatest possible communication among the persons who constitute it.

This community is necessary for everyone's life. But at the same time everyone feels that neither the community nor the purely human community can offer the plenitude of life. Only the communion among themselves, or their community having in its center a Man, who is also God, guarantees them eternity and communicates to them the plenitude of life, or gradually drives away insufficiencies from their community and communion. This is Christ. "And of His fullness we have all received, and grace for grace" (Jn 1:16). In Him there is the plenitude for us not only because He is God, but also because He is God made man. He communicates to us the divine plenitude through His humanity or in a human form. This because in Him the hypostasis of humanity is the Son of God and as such has filled the humanity He took upon Himself with the entire divine plenitude in human form.

The Church teaching tells us that hypostasis is the nature's mode of existence. Human nature is shown in as many concrete modes of existence as there are persons. But the human hypostasis is not only the nature's mode of existence, but every human hypostasis is a proper mode, distinct from the concrete existence of nature through themselves, but also according to the circumstances and conditions in which every time the general nature receives its concrete existence. John is different than Peter, although they have the same nature, says St. Basil the Great. There is a paradox in the fact that every hypostasis is the entire nature's mode of concrete existence, and still these modes are not entirely uniform. This imposes upon the human hypostases or persons the necessity for communion. Nature lives the need to experience the plenitude and the unity within the communion of hypostases. Nevertheless, they cannot achieve this plenitude only by themselves. This is also because the sin of egoism places obstacles on the path of achieving full unity among them.

In Christ the human nature does not exist concretely as a self-hypostasis, but it receives its concrete existence in the hypostasis of the Son of God. Thus, its concrete mode of existence in Him is characterized by an integrity of humanity, corresponding to the fact that the Son of God is the model and the origin of all human hypostases, in Whom they are to gather together. In Christ is not given the communion of the entire humanity, for as man He is also distinct from others, offering us a proper way of the nature's concrete existence, as St. Theodore the Studite has developed this idea. But what distinguishes Him as distinct man is His human integrity or plenitude. As such, He is totally open to other human persons who easily find themselves in Him, being able to live the most perfect communion not only with Him, but also with all other persons, because each one sees everyone else as having in Christ a corresponding aspect and being able to grow in Him toward full spiritual beauty. And all persons find their integrity, complete realization and spiritual beauty in Him.

This is how the Kingdom of the Holy Trinity and of love is realized in Christ. And the Holy Liturgy is the anticipated experience of this Kingdom. This experience is extended in the enduring community of the Church.

In this sense, the Trinity is the one that saves the world through the incarnate Logos, after It had created it through the non-incarnate Logos. In the entire Liturgy the entire Trinity is transparent and active through

Christ. The waves of love in the Trinity are poured out through Christ upon the liturgical community, strengthening the communion among believers, since through Him love raises the community ever higher into the Trinity. One does not talk about Christ without thinking of the Trinity, because He is One of the Trinity, not separated from It. We do not advance in Christ without advancing in the Holy Trinity and thereby in the communion among ourselves, in the Kingdom of the Holy Trinity.

Neither the melting into an impersonal essence, nor the submission to a unipersonal god-despot who keeps us separated and in a struggle to dominate one over another, is the goal the human heart pursues, but the eternal communion among ourselves endlessly imbibed from the eternal spring of communion which is the Holy Trinity.

If the happiness of persons is found in communion, and for communion is required from everyone the overcoming of egoism or a perfection in pure love and in tolerance, there is no other direction toward perfection and happiness except the one moving toward union with the Holy Trinity.

This ever intimate gathering of all in Christ and everyone's fulfillment through Him and through all persons means an advance into a communion that becomes increasingly deeper. And there is no loftier goal for human beings or more desired by them except the Holy Trinity, on the path on which they grow eternally in the increasingly happy spiritual life toward their ever greater fulfillment as human beings.

For the thirst for communion in human beings and the power that sustains the advance toward it must have a source in which there exists perfectly from eternity this happy communion, a source that has the power to attract human beings toward that communion. Because somewhere there must exist from eternity a perfect state of communion as source and goal of the human beings' longing for communion.

This is the Holy Trinity. It is the perfect communion from eternity. In It there is the force of spiritual attraction toward communion of conscious beings and It gave them the constitution that never feels happy except in the achievement of communion. Its force of attraction is perfectly experienced in the Holy Liturgy, and this experience is extended into the life of the faithful as church community, meant to extend the Trinity's force of attraction into the entire human society so as to make it perfect as communion.

This is why we hymn the Holy Trinity in the Holy Liturgy so often and so full of enthusiasm and of happiness; the Holy Trinity makes us foretaste the joy of perfect communion and to feel even now happy about this foretaste. This is why we glorify so often the Trinity in our everyday life through the words: "Glory to the Father and to the Son and to the Holy Spirit, now and ever and unto the ages of ages," making the sign of the cross, which is the power given to us by the Trinity to come out of the narrow bounds of egoism and to enter through offering and sacrifice into the endless joy of communion with the Trinity and with our fellow human beings that is ever deepened and expanded.

The priest returns with the chalice to the Holy Table and places in it all the particles for the saints, for the living and the dead, that are on the paten. Then he covers it, censes it three times saying to himself: *Be exalted, O God, above the heavens, and let Your glory be over all the earth.* You descended to transform the bread and the wine into the incarnate Son's body and blood so as to offer Yourself in the form of bread and wine to those who wanted. Now You ascend again, taking with You also those who united themselves with You and filling them with Your glory which extends over all the earth. He who descended and sacrificed Himself out of love ascends taking with Him also those who partake of His Spirit of sacrifice. He who was incarnate, accepted death on the cross, and then offered to us His sacrificed body, is exalted by the Father so that at His name every knee should bow, not only of those on earth, but also of those in heaven, as to the One who is above heaven or angels (Php 2:10). The slain Lamb receives praise from all creation in heaven and on earth (Rev 5:13). The fact that He descends to human beings reveals even more the greatness of His love, which the angelic hosts praise with an even greater comprehension and wonder. Eternal glory is due only to the One who, being the Most High, descends out of love up to self-sacrifice. All praises for different reasons are transitory. They are praises mixed with insincerity, or praises at a lower level. Ascension and total glorification above heaven is received only into the sacrificial whole love of the One above all. The Son of God is glorified not only because He is God, but also because being God He has become for us, the most insignificant conscious beings, sacrificial Lamb. Only the One who is above all can give us the example of a sacrificial love above all.

Then the priest, while holding in his left hand the Holy paten with its cover and with his right hand the Holy chalice above the Holy paten, says silently: *Blessed is our God,* and then turning toward the people continues with a loud voice: *Always, now and ever and unto the ages of ages.*

Through the words: *Blessed is our God* the priest expresses the inaudible praise with which the angelic powers meet Christ's ascension, the praise of heaven above which He ascends. The words: *Now and ever, and unto the ages of ages* are linked to *Be exalted, O God, above the heavens, and let Your glory be over all the earth*. But they are also an assurance given to the people that, although He goes out of sight, Christ still remains with the people. And this is why it is meet to bless Him forever. For only by blessing Him forever, the community will partake of Him eternally, and vice versa.

Christ who ascends does not separate Himself from the people and He will never separate Himself. He ascends so as to ascend us too. He will continue to work for our salvation through His sacrifice. He assures the people of this by showing the chalice with His blood, in which He is as hypostasis (I.S.). Close to us there remain the Birthgiver of God and all the saints, whose particles are in the chalice. By assuring the people of this through the words: *Now and ever and unto the ages of ages*, the priest essentially repeats the promise God Himself gave to the disciples when He ascended into heaven: "And lo, I am with you always, even to the end of the age" (Mt 28:20). But the priest links these words to: *Blessed is our God* uttered silently earlier, because the created being cannot speak of Christ's presence and permanent work without blessing Him or without realizing that He is praised by the entire creation; praised not as a master who is careless toward us, but as a Lamb who continues to work for our salvation through His sacrifice, leading us also to a similar state as lambs that sacrifice themselves together with Him.

Knowing that Christ is in the covered chalice, the faithful know that He is with them invisibly in a state of sacrifice. And in the raised chalice they see His ascension and thank Him once again for He has deemed them worthy to partake of Him and that thereby He will raise them as well. Since the faithful have been raised to union with Him in the realm of the eternal Kingdom they still remain, on the other hand, in the world, and because just as they prepared themselves for receiving Him so as to further strengthen themselves in the union with Him and in the holiness He communicated to them through their cooperation, they present to God, together with their praise, another supplication for the future: *Let our mouths be filled with Thy praise, O Lord, that we may sing of Thy glory; for Thou has made us worthy to partake of Thy Holy, Divine, Immortal and Life-creating Mysteries. Keep us in Thy holiness, that all the day we may meditate upon Thy righteousness. Alleluia! Alleluia! Alleluia!* The divine, and immortal, and life-creating Mysteries of Christ, or His body and blood, do not operate without the cooperation of those who have partaken of them, namely without endeavoring to appropriate the righteousness of Christ and to praise His glory. On the other hand, in order to do this they need Christ's help. This is why they say: if You remain always with us, help us to grow every day in our endeavor toward Your righteousness, in the endeavor for the holiness and purity that are found in the body and blood of which we have partaken; or in comprehending the righteousness, goodness and salvation You brought us.

Then the priest takes the Holy chalice together with the paten to the table of the Preparation (Proskomedia). Christ remains with the faithful, but only invisibly. With His body and blood, in the form of bread and wine, He will come to the next Holy Liturgy, also from the place He came before, namely through a kind of mystical re-experience of His birth and crucifixion for us. The priest then censes at that place the Holy chalice, after which he recites before the altar the final litany of thanksgiving with two supplications for the future: one for mercy and protection from God, and the other for help to live every day without sin, united again with the promise of the faithful to offer themselves and each other, from the power of Christ's sacrifice which they received, to Christ-God.

The thanksgiving is expressed in this way: *Let us attend! Having partaken of the Divine, Holy, Most Pure, Immortal, Heavenly, Life-creating, and Awesome Mysteries of Christ, let us worthily give thanks to the Lord.*

Let us attend, with attention fixed on God and on ourselves after we have received Christ's body and blood, Mysteries full of holiness, glory and power to live righteously, Mysteries that are heavenly, immortal and life-creating. The Mysteries we have received within us are so great that to sit indifferently afterward, to not strive to live righteously, would mean to not have any benefit from them, to disdain receiving them. How can we benefit toward immortality from the power given to us by the Lord's body and blood if we allow ourselves to become prey to slothfulness? How can we allow the life-creating Spirit in them to strengthen our life if we do not make any effort? Let us, therefore, keep our spirit focused on the thought of what we have received and on the duty we have to make use of the power given to us through them for a life of righteousness and holiness. And let us give thanks to the Lord for deeming us worthy to unite Himself with us. But how can we thank Him sitting, or standing carelessly, or not thinking of our duty to also cultivate through our effort the purity and righteousness whose power was given to us through them?

At this time the priest has folded the antimension, starting from the eastern side and continuing with the western side, then the southern and northern sides. Then, making the sign of the cross with the Gospel over the folded antimension, he recites the exclamation: *For You are our sanctification and to You we ascribe glory, to the Father, and to the Son, and to the Holy Spirit, now and ever, and unto the ages of ages.* Christ has come from the East to work in the world. It is there that He will retreat at the end of the world and the world with Him and in Him.

The Holy Liturgy began with the sign of the cross and it ends the same way. In the Gospel there is the all-encompassing word and saving power of Christ Who leads those who believe to the eternal Kingdom; it is Christ Himself Who remained with us through words, our unfolding salvation and life with its eternal perspective. It is the manifestation of the Kingdom of the Holy Trinity given to us as a guarantee and it leads us into the Trinity. But the Gospel is united with the cross. For Christ Himself has saved us through the cross. What would a Christ without the cross have brought us, without the descent to the sacrifice on the cross for us? Nothing more than any other man: care for the self, the will to accumulate, to dominate, the disposition of those found under the slavery full of discord in the world. It was through the cross of self-offering that Christ has overcome sin and death in the world and has raised the world into the Holy Trinity. The cross has brought the victory of the Spirit and of the liberty perfectly lived in love. Through the cross we also ascend to the eternal Kingdom of love and of liberation from the passions of egoism. The cross is the means of transcending this relative and monotonous world, subjected to spiritual and physical death, as a life in individualistic isolation. Through the cross of Christ the Kingdom of freedom and love, in union with the Holy Trinity, has been promised at the beginning of the Liturgy to all who believe in Christ, as to the children of the Father and siblings of the incarnate Son, full of the Holy Spirit.

At this time, what has been promised through the Gospel of Christ, or through Christ Himself through His cross, was given to us into our being as a guarantee. Christ sacrificed on the cross united Himself with us in Holy Communion. We offer glory to the Holy Trinity that undertook our salvation through One of Its own, made man, crucified, risen and ascended for us. We have become heirs of the Kingdom. But we became Its heirs because we have been filled with the holiness of Christ's body and blood and because we became like Him and we united ourselves with Him, the sacrificed One. For the human person cannot sanctify himself, cannot cleanse himself from the ugly egoism of sin except through sacrifice. Only through sacrifice can he open himself up to the holiness of the Holy Trinity, or to the perfect love of the three Persons among them and toward us.

Now the priest addresses on behalf of the faithful, thus together with them, the Holy Trinity directly as a single You. For the three Persons appear to us so united that we can address them with a single You.

When a mother says I while carrying her child in her womb she also includes her child in this I. Or we address her in the singular, even though she carries in her another I, distinct from hers. And even after that, she lives everything pertaining to her children as of her own I. Or she feels his veins as her own and the accusations or insults leveled against him as if they are leveled against her. But she does this as she feels ever deeper the existence of her child as her own existence. There is no contradiction in someone considering himself an I of the beloved and simultaneously feeling his own existence full of cares, afflictions, difficulties and also of joys. This is the mystery of both unity and not being blended into one experienced by those who love each other; it is the mystery of mercy that identifies the lover with the beloved without blending them into one.

This mystery of love and of mercy explains also the appropriation by the incarnate Son of God of our sins and the suffering He endured for us. But this mercy and suffering of the Son cannot but be also assumed by the Father and the Holy Spirit. This is why we connect the cross with the Holy Trinity. And this is why we can address the Holy Trinity in the singular, saying "You, Lord." This perfect unity of supreme love, in which there is also the potential of Its mercy for us, is the very holiness of the Trinity. And Its holiness has become our sanctification through the incarnate and crucified Son offered to us in a state of sacrifice. For by appropriating this state we also achieve this mystical unity among us. The Trinity has become first the sanctification of Christ the man, Who offered Himself to It as sacrifice. And through the sacrificed and sanctified Christ partaken of by us, the holiness of the Trinity has also become our sanctification. The one fully sanctified as man through sacrifice, through complete overcoming of the self by coming to us, has given us His holiness as a gift and as power for us to also sacrifice ourselves to the Father and to our fellow human beings and thereby to also appropriate sanctification for us. Our participation in the Kingdom of the Trinity is dependent on the sanctification we achieve. And this comes to us from the Trinity that is so perfect a communion that it can be viewed as a single I. This is why we say: "You are our sanctification," since You lead to our perfection and communion with You and among ourselves, as it is within You. Sanctification cannot be thought of as a quality in itself, impersonal. Neither can it be thought of as a quality of an isolated individual, inconsiderate toward others.

This is why our sanctification is neither a product of some essence or of some individual "deity," nor of some impersonal value in us, awakened in isolation. But "You are our sanctification." Your presence in us, O Triune God, with Your holiness united with Your love produces our sanctification. Only the union with the pure One, that is with the One full of perfect love for another, also makes me pure. For purity is shown in my personal relation with another who also lives in a selfless relation with another. Purity is not the quality of a solitary life. This is why the Trinity is the supreme purity and by entering into relation with us It also makes us pure or saints. Thus the Kingdom of the Trinity is the Kingdom of holiness.

For the Kingdom as freedom in the loving communion cannot exist without purity, without holiness. Only those pure in their relations, in their intentions for each other, do not use their freedom to mutually enslave each other. Truly masters over themselves, allowing others to also be masters over them, they live as free partners in a perfect loving communion.

O Lord, at the beginning of the Holy Liturgy we blessed Your Kingdom, wishing that You may make us Its members. Lo, You made us Its members, since You sanctified us through the union with us of Your Son sacrificed as man, thereby strengthening us in our liberation from the egoistic passions and strengthening each other in this freedom through the sacrifice of each other gained from the sacrifice of Your Son.

The liturgical or joint ascent toward the Kingdom through the union with the sacrificed Christ, and through our being pervaded by His Spirit full of the sacrificial sense perception, has reached the end.

The priest has concluded the work of preparing and offering of the sacrifice and of the faithful's partaking of it, after their own preparation. Thus there ended the movement of transcending their community beyond the life attached to the successive cares of a monotonous existence. They ascended into the spiritual air from where they take power to live as masters in this world, not enslaved to passions and not feuding with each other, but in complete love among themselves. At this time the priest comes out into the middle of the faithful and recites with a loud voice a prayer that sums up once more all the supplications during the Liturgy, according to St. Germanos, the Patriarch of Constantinople, who calls it "the seal of all petitions and the recapitulation in order . . . of all that has been asked through prayers."[419] Whatever spiritual height one has reached, one does not stop there, but starts again with other supplications toward other heights opening ahead, asking for the same good things at a higher level.

The priest begins this prayer with the words: *Let us depart in peace*. It is the first prayer for the dismissal of the faithful. They respond: *In the name of the Lord*. We will depart in the name of the Lord. We will go forth with the Lord also in our life after the Holy Liturgy. The first litany began with the supplication for peace. The faithful must maintain the peace in which God has come to them and extend it toward other people as well, so it is proper that they should take it with them in their life outside the Holy Liturgy. The faithful respond that they will endeavor for that with the Lord's help.

Then the priest recites the prayer in which he asks from God salvation, sanctification, blessing, protection against evil and sins, peace for all those who hope in Him. He ends with the supplication for peace for the world, for churches, and for all the people. No one can pray without the peace of the soul, without the thought of peace for those he wronged or who have wronged him. Peace is asked for in the most fervent way even at the end of the Liturgy. Peace should be now the fruit of union with the sacrificed Lord, the sign that the faithful have appropriated Christ's spirit of sacrifice. Where there is peace there is the sign that passions are overcome, that love conquers, and that pride and egoism are overcome. Christ was born as man so as to bring peace and goodwill upon earth, and it was toward that end that He sacrificed Himself. And He continues to offer Himself to us in the state of sacrifice so that we may increasingly appropriate this state of sacrifice, for the peace that surpasses all understanding, that is above all passions and unites in it all virtues. Where Christ truly is, there is also peace (Php 4:7). We will not prove that we have received Christ within us if we are not full of peace in our relations with others.

The faithful respond by praising the Giver of all good things asked for in the prayer behind the Ambon through the second verse from Psalm 113: *Blessed be the name of the Lord, henceforth and forevermore*, so that they may meet the condition for being themselves blessed by God: *O Lord, who bless those who bless You*. Again, there is here an exchange of gifts between God and us. At this time the priest (with the deacon, if he is present) goes to the Table of Proskomedia and asks Christ—who is *the fulfillment of the Law and the prophets*, and *who has fulfilled all the dispensation of the Father*, taking the believers to the union with Him and in Him up to the Kingdom of the Holy Trinity—*to fill our hearts with joy and gladness*. All fulfillment has been accomplished and is being accomplished in Christ. The Law and the prophets looked for the fulfillment of salvation brought by Him, after His incarnation as man, after His crucifixion and resurrection, after His union with the faithful through His body and blood, and after their adoption through His union with them. Thus, there has been accomplished the oikonomia established by the Father who wanted to extend His fatherly love for His only-begotten Son to human persons as well. Christ is asked to carry on this work until its final fulfillment, filling our hearts with joy and gladness. For only the union with God in Christ can fill the hearts of human beings with true and unending joy and gladness. In this union the ultimate fulfillment of God's saving activity is shown. Or in it is shown interiorly the fulfillment of this activity. The faithful have now found the true and unending joy. The heavenly Kingdom is experienced as joy and gladness in the Holy Spirit, absent of any pain and sorrow.

Union with God is not our disappearance into some emptiness or into an impersonal essence, a loss of one's personal conscience, but it is the most intense and unperturbed joy and gladness. For this union is a supreme state of love. And where there is love there is joy and gladness. It is not a state of submission under a God who dominates us without uniting Himself with us that awaits us, but a union in love with the heavenly Father who became our Father through the incarnation of His Son as man and through His union with us toward everlasting life.

As the faithful finish the hymn: *Blessed be the name of the Lord, now and forevermore* as thanksgiving offered to God for everything, the priest prays that the faithful may also have the blessing of the Lord. Every gift from God should be followed by the gift of the faithful, and vice versa. And the blessing asked from God comes through the evident blessing given by the priest from the royal doors: *May the blessing of the Lord be upon you, with His grace and love toward mankind always, now and ever, and unto the ages of ages. Amen!* What greater blessing than love could we have from God? This is also His greatest gift. These words represent the application of the first words from the prayer behind the Ambon: *O Lord, who bless those who bless You.* The faithful must leave the church with this final blessing of God.

In the practice of blessing at worship there is a great confidence in the power of the word. The benevolent word is bearer of a beneficial power, just as in the cursing, malicious word there is a paralyzing and distorting power that weakens human impetuses. It is enough for someone to be assured of the good word of God for all kinds of power to come upon the one who is blessed, even if God is not directly heard, but He is heard confirming the good word of the priest. At this time the blessing of the Lord brings about His grace and love for human persons. It is enough that a person addresses to another the good word of God (a blessing) so that God may come into his being, awakening in him first good feelings of thanksgiving, and then powers for everything that is good.

Then follows the priest's dismissal proper, as the final prayer for dismissing the faithful. He begins with the glory offered to Christ. The priest addresses Christ in the second person, bowing at the same time before the icon of Christ on the right side of the royal doors. In this way one shows that Christ is present there. The faithful respond glorifying the Holy Trinity, without addressing It directly. The priest is in direct communication with Christ whose priesthood he represents. He offers glory to Christ as to the One who is the hope of salvation of all. Without the incarnate Christ, without His cross, we would have no hope of escaping as persons from the power of nature, or of who knows what impersonal essence, of escaping an existence closed off in cares, in monotony and in definitive death: *Glory to You, Christ God, our hope, glory to You.* The word glory is pronounced twice, because one insists on offering glory to Christ as God and man.

The faithful respond by connecting the glory of Christ to the glory of the Holy Trinity. If Christ was not One of the Trinity, and also Man, He would not be the hope of our salvation. Thus the basis for offering Him glory would be lacking. The Father is the glory of the Son and vice versa. Through His sacrifice the Son glorifies as man, too, the Father, and the Father also glorifies the Son as man for His sacrifice.

After the glory offered to Christ, the priest takes up the last supplication addressed to Him to have mercy on us and to save us. Now he no longer addresses Him directly, but he aligns himself with the faithful and expresses together with them the wish that Christ may have mercy on them and save them. In support of his supplication and that of the faithful he adds the prayers of Christ's Mother, of the Holy Apostles, of the saint commemorated that day, of St. John Chrysostom, the author of the Holy Liturgy, and of all the saints.

Mercy and salvation are asked from Christ, because through Him mercy and salvation come to us from the Father, as we feel them in our souls through the Spirit. The priest asks for mercy and salvation from Christ who rose from the dead and has, thus, proved Himself to be the true God. The faithful know that they are blessed by Christ Who conquered death and is alive now and forever. The perspective of resurrection and eternal life is being opened to them as well. They find themselves to be in relation with this Christ alive and victorious over death. This is why Christ is our hope. We do not care about death.

The faithful are then anointed, a fact that shows the receiving of the uncreated operation of the Holy Spirit in them. They are anointed on the forehead because all decisions for their deeds are taken in the mind. In the Orthodox Liturgy, in the Orthodox worship, the faithful are in a real communication with God; they do not manifest certain purely subjective feelings, like in the neo-Protestant gatherings.

The faithful then exit the church assured not only of Christ's mercy and saving work and strengthened by the activity of the Holy Spirit, but also assured by the prayers of the Lord's Mother and of all the saints to Christ. Just as they were accompanied all the time in the church by their prayers, so will they be accompanied even after they depart from the church. And as they strengthened their communion during the Holy Liturgy, they will also promote it after the Liturgy.[420] God thought from the beginning that man should not be alone. God did not create individuals without a relation between them, in the exclusive relation with Him. But He created man as a being in communion so as to be strengthened through others and to strengthen others. God Himself wanted to work through the mutual love of created beings, or rather to see His love bearing fruit in the love among them, in the help given to each other not only on the material level, but also on the spiritual one. It is in this that they experience the heavenly Kingdom as promise. As they become accustomed in the Liturgy to overcome their reasons for doubt, to forgive themselves for the mistakes committed, and to rejoice together, they prepare themselves to live in full love among themselves in the heavenly Kingdom, but before that they begin to live in this love during their everyday life. The individual's affirmation that he does not need anyone's help, but only God's help, hides in itself a great pride and sterility. In the prayers for each other the Holy Spirit, the Spirit of communion, works in a more evident manner than in the prayers of the isolated individual for himself. Even in prayer, or especially in prayer, we must surpass our own ego. We do this by thinking of our own sins with regret. The saints, devoid of all pride, cannot but pray for us, cannot themselves but be filled with Christ's extremely sensitive mercy toward us. If we feel the need to pray for others, all the more do they feel the propensity to pray for us. The thirst for an ever greater love, never satisfied, will be satisfied only in the life to come in experiencing its infinity. Christ is not isolated. How can He, who attracts to His love through the love He manifests toward all, be isolated? He is surrounded by all those who love and glorify Him, by all those who overcame their egoism and pray for others. You are closer to Christ when you pray for others than when you pray only for yourself. For it is then that you show that you have partaken of Christ's love for others, and you show the true sensibility which is the sensibility purified of any egoism. Christ is surrounded by the saints who pray for us, as well as by the holy angels, in His presence with us at the Holy Liturgy and afterwards. We have this assurance in the words of St. Paul the Apostle: "Now, therefore, you are no longer strangers and foreigners, but fellow citizens with the saints and members of the household of God" (Eph 2:19). For we are fellow citizens of the Kingdom of the Father, and of the Son, and of the Holy Spirit, once we have partaken of Holy Communion, and we will unite ourselves more and more with Christ, the Father's Son made man for us.

CONCLUSIONS

In every Holy Liturgy we advance toward the Kingdom of the Holy Trinity, which will last eternally and in which the King is our Father and the Son of the King is our Brother, and we are united with them in the Holy Spirit. We advance in it and we live more and more in its spiritual ambiance. It is the Kingdom of full communion in love, in which no one is a servant and no one is a master, but all are brothers in the Lord Jesus Christ and children of the Father of the supreme goodness and power, liberated from all the egoistic passions that divide us.

And the One Who leads us toward that Kingdom, through teaching, example and self-giving power is our Lord Jesus Christ, One of the Trinity Who became one of us for eternity, offered Himself as sacrifice for us out of love, has risen and ascended into heaven with the body and sits at the right hand of the Father on the throne of the eternal Kingdom. But He is also united with us through His body sacrificed and risen for us so that He may raise us, too, through the sacrificing of our egoism, toward the resurrection and sitting alongside Him in the Kingdom of eternal love.

Thus, our Lord Jesus Christ becomes for us, in the Holy Liturgy, "path" toward Him, which is the eternal "life," not overshadowed by any shortcoming. He leads us and He attracts us toward the Kingdom of love, of which we will partake together with Him, and it is in Him that we live in the Holy Liturgy as guarantee of this Kingdom. For by living in Him and advancing in Him, we live by being surrounded by the Father's love and we feel connected to Him through the Holy Spirit.

This is why the culminating moment in the Holy Liturgy is the union with the Lord Jesus Christ through the partaking of His body and blood, in which all His love for us and for the Father is communicated to us in order to fill us, too, with His love for the Father.

In this way, His body places in our body and, through it, in our soul the seed of resurrection and eternal life, nourished by endless love. For everything done on earth in our body through our soul has repercussions in our soul, being imprinted in it as in a root of the body. This is why the resurrected body of the Lord Jesus Christ received in our body extends its effect into our soul, if we receive the Lord's body with faith, so that from there it may be able to manifest on the day of the second coming the power for reconstituting our resurrected body.

It was for the value of the human person as a being constituted of soul and body that the Son of God took our body, so that by raising it from death He might make us, too, share in the resurrection with the body. Nobody has made so evident the value of the human body as instrument of the soul as the Lord Jesus Christ. He showed that in the human body it is God Who works and manifests Himself through the soul and that the body can be raised up to the most amazing spiritualization, namely to the state of maximum transparence of the Son of God Who, as the divine hypostasis, has also become the hypostasis of the body, making visible through it the infinite richness and complexity of God's spirituality in an unfathomable beauty and subtlety.

Even the suffering of the body can be felt by the divine hypostasis as evidence of His love for men and of self-offering to God. The Son of God accepts the suffering in the body in order to show us that He can feel our pain in His body. But the intimacy that He achieves between Himself and our body is shown even more in the fact that He can resurrect His body, making it a perfect organ for communicating the divine life. And through His body He can resurrect our bodies as well.

Thus, precisely through His body we reach not only the communion with the Son of God as divine hypostasis, but also the filial relation with the Father through the union with Him as Son, advancing through the Holy Spirit in the spiritualization of our being and toward our resurrection with the body.

Since we all unite ourselves with the same Christ through His body, precisely through this we also advance in the union or the communion among ourselves, thus preparing ourselves for the eternal Kingdom of the Holy Trinity as the Kingdom of love.

In this way the Church is maintained as Christ's mystical body and as the anticipated Kingdom of the Holy Trinity. This is why the Church cannot be conceived of without the Liturgy.

In this way the Liturgy gives us the power to live our life strengthened and warmed up by the love among ourselves, capable of helping each other and other persons as true brothers and sisters.

Thus, together with the hope of the resurrection and of eternal life, the Liturgy also gives us the power to fraternize. It is the holy and efficient service of the resurrection and of becoming brothers and sisters in Christ, the Son of God, the One Who was incarnate, crucified and risen for us.

If the human person is the being who asks about himself, and the fundamental question is: will I be able to conquer death?, the Liturgy gives him the affirmative answer together with the remedy that begins even during its course to strengthen him for conquering death. The Liturgy gives him the answer that he will rise again, as well as the guarantee of the resurrection through the union with Christ, who has as God conquered death in the human body He assumed. No pantheist ideology and no other religion give the human person this assurance and this beginning of the fulfillment of this fundamental need to go beyond death and to live eternally as an irreplaceable person in his spiritual-physical wholeness. This guarantee has been given to us by Christ's Gospel and by the Holy Fathers who understood salvation as victory over death through the resurrection with Christ, having at the same time regarded the eternal life of the resurrection as the Kingdom of love among people nourished from the love of the Holy Trinity.

The Liturgy is this assurance of the Gospel at work. It is the laboratory of the resurrection and the school of learning love among people. It is the manifestation of the communal joy that we will rise again and all of us will be together forever, with our parents, brothers and sisters and our children, communicating through our luminous bodies.

This is why the Holy Liturgy begins with the blessing of the Holy Trinity and ends with the supplication for mercy and salvation from the risen Christ.

NOTES

1. Dumitru Staniloae, *Orthodox Spirituality*, translated from the original Romanian by Archimandrite Jerome (Newville) and Otilia Kloos (St. Tikhon Seminary Press, 2003).

2. *Mystagogia*, PG 91, 657–717, ch. II–IV, 669–672. English translation: *Maximus Confessor, Selected Writings*, translation and Introduction by George C. Berthold (Paulist Press, 1985), p. 181–225.

3. On the church building signifying the faithful's journey toward the East, or toward God, see: Dr. Wilhelm Nyssen, *Bildgesang der Erde* (Trier: Paulinus Verlag, 1977); translated into Romanian by Dumitru Staniloae and Lidia Staniloae under the title *Pamânt cântând în imagini* [*Earth Singing in Images*] (Bucharest, 1978).

4. St. Maximos does not, therefore, shy away from naming the cosmos not only an imitation of the church building as its image, but even the Church: "This is like another sort of Church not of human construction which is wisely revealed in this church which is humanly made, and it has for its sanctuary the higher world assigned to the powers above, and for its nave the lower world which is reserved to those who share the life of sense." *Mystagogia*, PG 91, 669; ET = p. 188.

5. St. Maximos applies to this interpretation—of the three aspects of the church—the image described by Ezekiel (1:15-16) about the chariot of God carried by interpenetrating wheels (*Mystagogia*, PG 91, 669C; ET = p. 189). Dionysius the Areopagite explains this image this way: "Those Godlike wheels of fire 'revolve' about themselves in their ceaseless movement around the Good, and they 'reveal' since they expose hidden things, and lift up the mind from below and carry the most exalted enlightenments down to the lowliest." *The Celestial Hierarchy*, XV, 9. ET = Pseudo-Dionysius, *The Complete Works*, translated by Colm Luibheid (Paulist Press, 1987), p. 190.

6. St. Maximus the Confessor, *Mystagogia*, PG 91, 660A; ET = p. 188.

7. St. Maximus the Confessor, *Mystagogia*, PG 91, 660A; ET = p. 188.

8. Alexander Schmemann says about the duty of the priests to love the laity: "The priesthood reveals the humility, not the pride of the Church, for it reveals the complete dependence of the Church on Christ's love—that is, on His unique and perfect priesthood. It is not 'priesthood' that the priest receives in his ordination, but the gift of Christ's love, that love which made Christ the only Priest and which fills with this unique priesthood the ministry of those whom He sends to His people." *For the Life of the World: Sacraments and Orthodoxy* (St. Vladimir's Seminary Press, 1973), p. 94.

9. Kallistos Angelikoudes, Chapters on Prayer, ch. 40, in *The Philokalia*, Volume V (Virgin Mary of Australia and Oceania, 2020), p. 165.

10. St. Maximos the Confessor also says the same in *Ambigua*, PG 91, 1081C.

11. Kallistos Kataphygiotes, *On Union with God and the Contemplative Life*, 17, in *Philokalia*, Volume V, p. 229-230.

12. Schmemann, *For the Life of the World*, p. 92-93: "Man was created priest of the world, the one who offers the world to God in a sacrifice of love and praise and who, through this eternal eucharist, bestows the divine love upon the world . . . . Christ is the one true priest because He is the one true and perfect man . . . . Christ revealed the essence of priesthood to be love and therefore priesthood to be the essence of life." We consider inappropriate Schmemann's comment on the priest as "man" who has a "creative relation to the 'womanhood' of the created world" (p. 92). Creation is an "object," not a woman. And a woman is not an object.

13. St. Maximus the Confessor, *Mystagogia*, PG 91, 660A; ET = p. 188.

14. Abba Dorotheus describes in this way the conditioning of the union with God of the union between created, conscious beings: "Imagine a circle with its center and radii or rays going out from its center . . . . Suppose now that this circle is the world, the very center of the circle, God, and the lines (radii) going from the center to the circumference or from the circumference to the center are the paths of men's lives. Then here we see the same. In so far as the saints move inwards within the circle towards its center, wishing to come near to God, then, in the degree of their penetration, they come closer both to God and to one another; moreover, inasmuch as they come nearer to one another, they come nearer to God. It is the same with drawing away. When they draw away from God, they withdraw from one another, and as they withdraw from one another, so they draw away from God . . . and inasmuch as we are united with our neighbours, so we become united with God." St. Abba Dorotheus, Directions on Spiritual Training, in Early Fathers from the *Philokalia*, translated by E. Kadloubovsky and G.E.H. Palmer (Faber and Faber Limited, 1981), p. 164-165.

15. St. Cyril of Alexandria, *Adoration in Spirit and in Truth*, Book XVII, PG 68.

16. St. Cyril of Alexandria, *Adoration in Spirit and in Truth*, Book XVII, PG 68.

17. St. Mark the Ascetic, *Response to Those Who Doubt the Holy Baptism*, PG 65, 996.

18. St. Mark the Ascetic, *Response to Those Who Doubt the Holy Baptism*, PG 65, 996.

19. St. Maximos the Confessor, *Four Hundred Texts on Love, Third Century*, 43, in *The Philokalia*, vol. II (London: Faber and Faber, 1981), p. 89.

20. St. Maximos the Confessor, *Four Hundred Texts on Love*, in *Philokalia*, vol. II, p. 89.

21. St. Maximos the Confessor, *Four Hundred Texts on Love*, in *Philokalia*, vol. II, p. 90.

22. Kallistos Kataphygiotes, *On Union with God and the Contemplative Life*, in *Philokalia*, Volume V, p. 260.

23. Kallistos Angelikoudes, *Chapters on Prayer*, ch. 55, in *Philokalia*, Volume V, p. 185.

24. St. Symeon the New Theologian, *Hymns of Divine Love*, Hymn 1, translated by George A. Maloney, S.J. (Dimension Books, 1975), p. 11–12.

25. St. Symeon the New Theologian, *Hymns of Divine Love*, Hymn 23, p. 120.

26. *Concordance des Saintes Ecritures*, 2nd ed. (Lausanne: Societé Biblique Auxliaire de Canton de Vaud, 1965), p. 649.

27. Hieromonk Grigoriou, *Η θεια λειτουργια τηζ Ευχαριστιαξ του Θεου* (Athens, 1971), p. 85.

28. See also Fr. Petre Vintilescu, *Încercări de istoria liturghiei* [*Studies in the History of the Liturgy*] (Bucharest, 1930), p. 2.

29. Clement, *First Epistle to the Corinthians*, ch. XLI, 1.

30. Clement, *First Epistle to the Corinthians*, ch. XL, 5, 5; L. Bouyer, *La spiritualité du Nouveau Testament et des pères* (Paris: Aubier, 1960), p. 221, considers that Clement of Rome was the first to apply the word liturgy, as a public service done by an individual for a community, to Christian worship, which was officiated with great order. But from what Clement said results that he took the data from the Apostles and probably even the name. It seems that we owe to Clement the sense which Christianity will apply to the word *liturgy*. In fact, by using it in the traditional Greek sense as public service done by an individual for the community, he first applied this sense to the Christian worship. And Bouyer quotes from Clement: "Since these are now very clear things for us who penetrated with our sight the depths of divine gnosis, we must do everything in an orderly way that the Master commanded us to fulfill at established times. For He commanded us to offer the gifts and to officiate the liturgies not at random and without order, but at the established times and hours. He has Himself established by His sovereign decision in what places and by what officiants must be done, so that all things may be done with holi-

ness according to His good pleasure and be well pleasing to His will. So, those who present their gifts at the established times are well accepted and happy... To the Hierarch special liturgies [sacred services] have been assigned; to the priests distinct places have been designated" (1 Cor. XL).

31. At the Judaic Paschal meal that took place in the evening, when the first glass of red wine was poured, the saying was: "Blessed is our God. Blessed are you, the King of universe, the one who created the fruit of the vine" (P. Vintilescu, *Încercări de istoria liturghiei* [*Studies in the History of the Liturgy*], p. 21). The name of King is also given in the book of Revelation 15:3 ("King of the saints"). This name is also implied in other passages of Revelation where mention is made of the One who sits on the throne (4:2–3) and of His kingdom (11:17; 12:10).

32. Odo Casel, *Das christliche Opfermysterium* (Verlag, Styria, Graz, 1968), pp. 272ff.

33. St. Symeon of Thessalonica, *Tratat asupa tuturor dogmelor credinţei noastr ortodoxe* [*Treatise on All the Dogmas of Our Orthodox Faith*] (Bucharest, 1865), p. 120.

34. St. Germanos of Constantinople, *On the Divine Liturgy*, translated by Paul Meyendorff (St. Vladimir's Seminary Press, 1984), p. 57, 59.

35. Archimandrite Vasileios, *Hymn of Entry: Liturgy and Life in the Orthodox Church*, translated by Elizabeth Briere (St. Vladimir's Seminary Press, 1984), p. 68.

36. At P. Evdokimov, *The Art of the Icon: A Theology of Beauty*, translated by Fr. Steven Bigham (Oakwood Publications, 1990), p. 145–146.

37. Evdokimov, *The Art of the Icon*, p. 145–146.

38. Evdokimov, *The Art of the Icon*, p. 146.

39. Evdokimov, *The Art of the Icon*, p. 146.

40. Rudolf Otto, *The Idea of the Holy*, translated by John W. Harvey (Oxford University Press, 1923), p. 19ff. The Catholic theologian Heribert Mühlen saw the greatest weakness of Otto's concept of sacred in its dreadful characteristic. But from what Mühlen wants to replace the meaning given by Otto to the sense of sacred with, it can be seen that he considers as sacred the feeling that God eludes us as an infinitely distant transcendence. So neither for him is the "sacred" an experience of God's power: "it is critically to be observed in Otto's analyses that he subordinates the experience of the numinous to a certain internal, religious organ and that, according to his conception, only certain men have this organ [is not this an effect of Calvin's predestination?]... Aside from this, Otto connects these experiences only to feeling, which, in his exposition, takes on the characteristic of a 'subjective' abstraction. This is why his critics accused him, not unjustly, of a subjectivism hard to refute. It is difficult to observe at him the fact that this experience can also be produced through material incorporations, thus from the outside as well." Mühlen himself, by attributing a fascination to the sacred, declares that what fascinates or

attracts man is what eludes him: "What fascinates man attracts him, since it eludes him, or differently put, it attracts him because it eludes him into the incomprehensible/ boundlessness." Heribert Mühlen, *Entsakralisierung* [*Desacralization*] (Paderborn, 1971), p. 14.

41. Mühlen, *Entsakralisierung*, p. 14.

42. Archimandrite Vasileios, *Hymn of Entry*, p. 63.

43. At H. I. Schulz, *Die byzantinische Liturgie*, Sophia 5 (Freiburg im Breisgau, 1964), p. 64.

44. Oskar Wulff, "Das Raumerlebnis des Naos im Spiegel der Ekfrasis," *Byzantinische Zeitschrift* 30 (1929):, p. 531–539. On page 535 he quotes from Homily 18 of St. Gregory of Nazianzus.

45. Procopius, *On Justinian's Buildings*, Corpus Scriptorum Historiae Byzantinae 45, I, 179.

46. Procopius, *On Justinian's Buildings*, I, 175.

47. Procopius, *On Justinian's Buildings*, I, 179.

48. Archimandrite Vasileios, *Hymn of Entry*, p. 64.

49. Evdokimov, *The Art of the Icon*, p. 147.

50. Schulz, *Die byzantinische Liturgie*, p. 126.

51. Wulff, "Das Raumerlebnis des Naos im Spiegel der Ekfrasis," p. 531.

52. Wulff, "Das Raumerlebnis des Naos im Spiegel der Ekfrasis," p. 530.

53. Wulff, "Das Raumerlebnis des Naos im Spiegel der Ekfrasis," p. 530.

54. Evdokimov, *The Art of the Icon*, p. 149–150.

55. Schulz, *Die byzantinische Liturgie*, p. 67–68.

56. Archim. Grigoriou, *Η θεια λειτουργια τηζ Ευχαριστιαξ του Θεου*, p. 85.

57. Evdokimov, *The Art of the Icon*, p. 156–157.

58. Nyssen, *Earth Singing in Images*, p. 26.

59. Nyssen, *Earth Singing in Images*, p. 25–27.

60. Archimandrite Vasileios, *Hymn of Entry*, p. 68.

61. St. Maximos the Confessor, *Mystagogia*, ch. 1; PG 91, 665.

62. Archim. Giorgos, the abbot of Grigoriou Monastery in Mount Athos, "Man as Liturgical Being," *Ο Οσιοζ Γρηγοριοζ*, no. 4 (1979), p. 34.

63. St. Maximos the Confessor, *Mystagogia*, ch. 1; PG 91, 685C.

64. St. Symeon of Thessalonica, *Treatise on All the Dogmas*, p. 253.

65. Archimandrite Vasileios, *Hymn of Entry*, p. 37.

66. Ephraim der Syrer, *Lobgesang der Erde*, Introduction and translation into German by Edmund Beck (Freiburg im Br.: Lambertus Verlag, 1967), p. 32, 33.

67. Georg Bernhard Langemeyer, OFM, "Die Weise der Gegebwart Christi im liturgischen Geschehen," in *Martyria, Liturgia, Diakonia*, ed. Otto Semmelroth (Matthias-Grünewald-Verlag, 1968), p. 301.

68. Archimandrite Vasileios, *Hymn of Entry*, 81, 82: "Once man has participated in the Liturgy, he has an inner vision of the world . . . worldly space

is transfigured; perspective, which puts man in the position of an outside observer, no longer exists. The believer, the pilgrim, is a guest at the Wedding. He is inside, and sees the whole world from the inside. History is interpreted differently: the events of divine Economy are not past and closed, but present and active."

69. St. John Chrysostom, *Homily 82 on the Gospel of St. Matthew*, ET = NPNF, First Series, 10:496.

70. St. Symeon of Thessalonica, *Treatise on All the Dogmas*, p. 110, ch. 101.

71. St. Symeon of Thessalonica, *Treatise on All the Dogmas*, p. 111, ch. 103. Archim. Giorgos, "Man as Liturgical Being," p. 33, writes: "Each hierarch and priest who officiates at the earthly altar exercises Christ's priesthood in the church; he does not have his own priesthood, but participates in the unique priesthood of Christ."

72. St. Germanos of Constantinople, *On the Divine Liturgy*, p. 59, 61.

73. St. Germanos of Constantinople, *On the Divine Liturgy*, p. 59.

74. St. Symeon of Thessalonica, *Treatise on All the Dogmas*, p. 111, ch. 103.

75. St. Symeon of Thessalonica, *Treatise on All the Dogmas*, p. 111, ch. 106.

76. St. Symeon of Thessalonica, *Treatise on All the Dogmas*, p. 112, ch. 106.

77. St. Symeon of Thessalonica, *Treatise on All the Dogmas*, p. 112, ch. 107.

78. Mansi, *Amplissima Collectio Conciliorum*, vol. 11, p. 977–980.

79. Schulz, *Die byzantinische Liturgie*, p. 151. He quotes from Mansi, *Amplissima Collectio Conciliorum*, vol. 13, col. 265, BC.

80. Ephraim der Syrer, *Lobgesang der Erde*, p. 66.

81. Dr. Wilhelm Nyssen, *Das frühchristliche Byzanz* [*The Beginnings of Byzantine Iconography*], translated into Romanian by Dumitru Staniloae and Lidia Staniloae under the title *Începuturile picturii bizantine* (Bucharest, 1975), p. 82.

82. G. Millet, "La vision de Pierre d'Alexandrie," in *Mélanges Charles Diehl*, II (Paris: Leroux, 1930) p. 99–115, 107, at Schulz, *Die byzantinische Liturgie*, p. 145–146.

83. St. Symeon of Thessalonica, *Treatise on All the Dogmas*, p. 113, ch. 111.

84. St. Symeon of Thessalonica, *Treatise on All the Dogmas*, p. 114, ch. 115.

85. St. Symeon of Thessalonica, *Treatise on All the Dogmas*, p. 115, 116.

86. Archim. Elias Mastroianopoulos, "Εκκλησια και Ευχαριστια," Ανα πλασιζ (May–June 1967), p. 183.

87. On this work of Christ among people everywhere, see: Walter Kasper, "Wort und Sacrament," in *Martyria, Liturgia, Diakonia*, ed. Otto Semmelroth (Matthias-Grünewald-Verlag, 1968), p. 350ff.

88. Olivier Clement, *Le visage interieur* [*The Inner Vision*] (Paris: Stock, 1978).

89. Source unidentified.

90. St. Theodore the Studite, *On the Holy Icons*, translated by Catherine P. Roth (Crestwood, NY: St. Vladimir's Seminary Press, 1981), 9.109.

91. St. Theodore the Studite, *On the Holy Icons*, p. 109–110.
92. St. Theodore the Studite, *On the Holy Icons*, p. 110.
93. St. Theodore the Studite, *Epistle 16*, PG 99, 1502–1504.
94. *The Great Book of Needs*, vol. 2 (South Canaan, PA: St. Tikhon's Seminary Press, 2000), p. 217.
95. *The Great Book of Needs*, p. 217.
96. *Homily on Barlaam the Martyr*, 17, 3, at Nyssen, *The Beginnings of Byzantine Iconography*, p. 44. See in this work other texts from the Holy Fathers on the educational role of icons, p. 44–47.
97. St. Gregory of Nyssa, *On the Divinity of the Son and of the Holy Spirit*, PG 46, 572CD. Also *The Homilies on St. Theodore*.
98. At Nyssen, *The Beginnings of Byzantine Iconography*, p. 48.
99. Evdokimov, *The Art of the Icon*, p. 178.
100. St. John of Damascus, *On the Divine Images*, I, I, 16 at Evdokimov, *The Art of the Icon*, p. 178.
101. Evdokimov, *The Art of the Icon*, p. 179.
102. At Schulz, *Die byzantinische Liturgie*, p. 96, note 11.
103. Schulz, *Die byzantinische Liturgie*, p. 96.
104. Evdokimov, *The Art of the Icon*, p. 209.
105. "The icon is sanctified by God's name and by the name of his friends [the saints], and that is why it receives the grace of God." St. John of Damascus, *First Discourse on the Icons*, PG 94, 1300.
106. Clement, *La visage interieur*, p. 46: "In an icon a person opens up, communicates, enters in a relation with us and instructs us in his relation with God."
107. Evdokimov, *The Art of the Icon*, p. 236.
108. P. Florensky, "L'icône," *Contacts* 88, no. 4 (1974), p. 325.
109. Florensky, "L'icône," p. 324.
110. Evdokimov, *The Art of the Icon*, p. 206.
111. Evdokimov, *The Art of the Icon*, p. 207.
112. Bernard Philberth, *Der Dreieine, Anfang un Sein: Die Struktur der Schöpfung* (Stein am Rein: Christiana-Verlag, 1971), p. 21–24.
113. Clement, *Le visage interieur*, p. 52.
114. Hieromonk Simion Grigoriatis, *According to the Image and Likeness of God* (1978; in Greek), p. 64.
115. Hieromonk Simion Grigoriatis, *According to the Image and Likeness of God*, p. 65.
116. Hieromonk Simion Grigoriatis, *According to the Image and Likeness of God*, p. 130–132.
117. Hieromonk Simion Grigoriatis, *According to the Image and Likeness of God*, p. 132–134.
118. Clement, *Le visage interieur*, p. 54.

119. Gregory Palamas, *The Triads*, edited with an Introduction by John Meyendorff, translated by Nicholas Gendle (Paulist Press, 1983), p. 55.

120. Clement, *Le visage interieur*, p. 58.

121. Clement, *Le visage interieur*, p. 59.

122. Clement, *Le visage interieur*, p. 61.

123. Photius, *Ekfrasis*, George Kodinos, Excelta, Corpus Scriptorum Historiae Byzantinae 16, 199, at Schulz, *Die byzantinische Liturgie*, p. 101 and note 23 on the same page.

124. E. Giordani, "Das mittelbyzantinische Ausschmuckungssystem als Ausdruck einer hieratischen Bildprogramms," *Jahrbuch der osterreichischen byzantinischen Gesellschaft* 1 (1951), p. 125, at Schulz, Die byzantinische Liturgie, p. 110. A more detailed description of the iconographic themes in the Orthodox Church, with variation in certain aspects in many churches, can be found at I.D. Stefanescu, *L'illustration des Liturgies dans l'art de Byzance et de L'Orient* (Brussels: Institut de Philologie et d'Histoire, 1936).

125. Schulz, *Die byzantinische Liturgie*, p. 105.

126. Schulz, *Die byzantinische Liturgie*, p. 169.

127. Schulz, *Die byzantinische Liturgie*, p. 170.

128. Schulz, *Die byzantinische Liturgie*, p. 133.

129. Schulz, *Die byzantinische Liturgie*, p. 134.

130. Archimandrite Vasileios, *Hymn of Entry*, p. 81.

131. Archimandrite Vasileios, *Hymn of Entry*, p. 82-83.

132. Archimandrite Vasileios, *Hymn of Entry*, p. 83-84.

133. Tomás Spidlík, *The Spirituality of the Christian East*, translated by Dr. Anthony P. Gythiel (Cistercian Publications, 1986), p. 3.

134. Archimandrite Vasileios, *Hymn of Entry*, p. 84.

135. Archimandrite Vasileios, *Hymn of Entry*, p. 84.

136. Archimandrite Vasileios, *Hymn of Entry*, p. 84-85.

137. Schulz, *Die byzantinische Liturgie*, p. 171.

138. Demetrios Constantelos, "A Note on Christos Philantropos in Byzantine Iconography," *The Orthodox Theological Review*, Brookline 2 (1978), p. 159-162.

139. N. Ozoline, "L'icône: Antologie et complémentarité de l'image par rapport au geste et á la parole de liturgie," in *Gestes et paroles dans les diverses familles liturgiques* (Rome: Centro Liturgico Vincenziano, 1978), p. 167.

140. *Constitutio Liturgica* of the Second Vatican Council, art. 7, enumerates the stages of Christ's presence in worship: the presence in the liturgical sacrifice, the presence in sacraments, the presence in word and in the Holy Scripture when it is read in the church and, finally, the presence in the community that prays and sings. J. Langeling, ed., *Die Konstitution der zweiten Vatikanischen Konzils über die heilige Liturgie* (Münster: Regensberg, 1964), p. 28.

NOTES   495

141. Romano Guardini, *Vom Geist der Liturgie* (Freiburg im Br.: Herder, 1922), p. 30–31.
142. Boris Bobrinskoy, "Αγιαστικαι Πραξειξ," in *Θρησκευτικ'η και 'Ηθικη' 'Εγκυκλοπαιδεια'*, vol. 1 (Athens, 1962), col. 238–242.
143. Fairy von Lilienfeld, "Evlogia und evlogein im gottesdienstlichen Handlen der orthodoxen Kirke," in *Archiv für Liturgiewissenschaft*, vol. 20–21 (Regensburg, 1978–1979), p. 19.
144. Von Lilienfeld, "Evlogia und evlogein," p. 20.
145. Pavel Florensky, "Slovesnie slujenie," *Jurnal Moskovskoi Patriarhii* [*Journal of the Moscow Patriarchate*] 4 (1977), p. 63–75.
146. *The Great Book of Needs*, vol. 4 (South Canaan, PA: St. Tikhon's Seminary Press, 1999), p. 369.
147. Florensky sees this framework also in the Old Testament and even in non-Christian religions; what is new in Christianity is Christ and the Holy Trinity. "Slovesnie slujenie," p. 64–66.
148. Florensky, "Slovesnie slujenie," p. 75.
149. Florensky, "Slovesnie slujenie," p. 67–68.
150. Langemeyer, "Die Weise der Gegebwart Christi," p. 290.
151. Langemeyer, "Die Weise der Gegebwart Christi," p. 291.
152. Langemeyer, "Die Weise der Gegebwart Christi," p. 291.
153. Langemeyer, "Die Weise der Gegebwart Christi," p. 290.
154. St. John Chrysostom, *On the Incomprehensible Nature of God*, translated by Paul W. Harkins, Fathers of the Church 72 (The Catholic University of America Press, 1984), p. 111.
155. Iōannēs Phountoulēs, *Ο λογοζ του θεου εν τη θεια λατρεια* (Thessalonica, 1965), p. 7–8.
156. Phountoulēs, *Ο λογοζ του θεου εν τη θεια λατρεια*, p. 13.
157. St. Symeon of Thessalonica, *Dialogue against Heresies*, 154, PG 155, 173D. These texts are taken from Phountoulēs, *Ο λογοζ του θεου εν τη θεια λατρεια*, p. 14.
158. Phountoulēs, *Ο λογοζ του θεου εν τη θεια λατρεια*, p. 14.
159. Phountoulēs, *Ο λογοζ του θεου εν τη θεια λατρεια*, p. 14–15.
160. Phountoulēs, *Ο λογοζ του θεου εν τη θεια λατρεια*, p. 16.
161. Phountoulēs, *Ο λογοζ του θεου εν τη θεια λατρεια*, p. 16.
162. Phountoulēs, *Ο λογοζ του θεου εν τη θεια λατρεια*, p. 17.
163. St. Cyril of Jerusalem, *The Catechetical Lectures*, Lecture XXIII, V, 7, PG 33, 1116A. ET = NPNF, Second Series, 7:154.
164. Phountoulēs, *Ο λογοζ του θεου εν τη θεια λατρεια*, p. 19.
165. Phountoulēs, *Ο λογοζ του θεου εν τη θεια λατρεια*, p. 19.
166. Nicholas Cabasilas, *A Commentary on the Divine Liturgy*, PG 150, 429B. ET = J.M Hussey and P.A. McNulty (St. Vladimir's Seminary Press, 1977), p. 71.
167. Phountoulēs, *Ο λογοζ του θεου εν τη θεια λατρεια*, p. 20.
168. Langemeyer, "Die Weise der Gegebwart Christi," p. 303.

169. Langemeyer, "Die Weise der Gegebwart Christi," p. 302.

170. In Augustine's writings one can find the expression "verbum visibile" (In John. 80.3, PL 35, 1840). We say that all created works are visible words of God. Schöngnen came up through analogy with the expression "sacramentum audibile," in *Symbol und Wirklichkeit im Kultmysterium* (Bonn: P. Hanstein, 1940), p. 20, at Kasper, "Wort und Sacrament," p. 200, note 43.

171. J. Betz, "Wort und Sakrament," in *Werkuüdigung und Glaube* (Freiburg im Br., 1958), p. 91.

172. Kasper, "Wort und Sacrament," p. 280.

173. Kasper, "Wort und Sacrament," p. 283-284.

174. This is why the affirmation coming from the Catholic and Protestant influence, that participation at the Liturgy is useless for those who do not partake, does not correspond to the truth.

175. On this, see Karl Kristian Felmy, "Kleine Beiträge und Misszellen zur Liturgik: Der Christusknabe auf den Diskos," *Jahrbuch für Liturgik und Hymnologie* (1979), p. 95-96.

176. Robert F. Taft, *The Great Entrance: A History of the Transfer of Gifts and Other Pre-anaphral Rites*, 4th edition (Rome: Pontificio Istituto Orientale, 2004).

177. PG 65, 156-160. *Romanian Paterikon*, 1930, p. 52-54.

178. Felmy, "Kleine Beiträge und Misszellen zur Liturgik," p. 101.

179. Nyssen, *The Beginnings of Byzantine Iconography*, p. 82.

180. St. Irenaeus, *Demonstration of the Apostolic Preaching*, at Nyssen, *The Beginnings of Byzantine Iconography*, p. 84.

181. Ephraim der Syrer, *Lobgesang der Wüste*, Sophia collection (Freiburg in Br.: Lambertus Verlag, 1967), p. 29-31.

182. The pilgrim Paula said in the fourth century: "Blessed are you, Bethlehem, the 'House of Bread,' where the Bread that came down from heaven was born."

183. Ephraim der Syrer, *Lobgesang der Wüste*, p. 31.

184. PG 100, 1, 201-1, 204, at Felmy, "Kleine Beiträge und Misszellen zur Liturgik," p. 100.

185. Nicholas Cabasilas, *A Commentary on the Divine Liturgy*, PG 150, 425CD; ET = p. 70.

186. Ene Braniste, trans., *Explicarea sfintei liturghii după Nicolae Cabasila* [*Explanation of the Holy Liturgy according to Nicholas Cabasilas*] (Bucharest: Tipografia Cărților Bisericești, 1943), p. 199.

187. Nicholas Cabasilas, *A Commentary on the Divine Liturgy*, p. 27.

188. Nicholas Cabasilas says: "The bread therefore remains bread and has received no more than the capacity to be offered to God. This is why it typifies the Lord's body in his early years, for, as we have already pointed out, he himself was an offering from his birth onwards. This is why the priest relates, and represents over the bread, the miracles accomplished in him when he was

but new-born and still lying in the manger . . . the priest covers the gifts, that is the bread and the chalice, with fine veils . . . Thus the power of the Incarnate God was veiled up to the time of his miracles and the witness from heaven." *A Commentary on the Divine Liturgy*, p. 41.

189. Patriarch Germanos of Constantinople says: "The prosphora which is also called bread and blessing and promise, out of which is cut the Lord's body, prefigures the All-pure Virgin who, according to the good will of the Father and the accord of the Son, the Word, and after the indwelling of the divine Spirit, when receiving in herself the Only Begotten Son and Word of God, has given birth to the perfect God and the perfect man" (*Theoria mystica*, PG 98, 397CD).

190. Ιερατικον, Edition of the Holy Synod of the Church of Greece, 1971, p. 64.

191. In the Greek Ιερατικον cited above, on page 65 the word προβατον is used for the first cut, which can be translated as sheep, and for the second cut is used the word αμνοξ. This order reproduces exactly the order from the text in the Septuagint Isaiah 53:7. In the Romanian text the order has been reversed. But the word προβατον also has the meaning of lamb. Thus one combines the remembrance of the birth when Jesus is the younger Lamb destined to be sacrificed with the remembrance of the older Lamb who will be crucified.

192. Ephraim der Syrer, *Lobgesang der Wüste*, p. 10–11.

193. Ephraim der Syrer, *Lobgesang der Wüste*, p. 45.

194. Ephraim der Syrer, *Lobgesang der Wüste*, p. 45.

195. Ephraim der Syrer, *Lobgesang der Wüste*, p. 47.

196. Ephraim der Syrer, *Lobgesang der Wüste*, p. 48.

197. St. Symeon of Thessalonica, *Treatise on All the Dogmas*, p. 97.

198. Nicholas Cabasilas, *A Commentary on the Divine Liturgy*, p. 37: "In the same way that this bread has been separated from other and similar loaves in order that it may be consecrated to God and used in the Holy Sacrifice, so the Lord was set apart from the mass of mankind, whose nature his love had brought him to share. 'He is brought as a lamb to the slaughter,' and in this way 'he was cut off out of the land of the living'" (Is 53:7–8).

199. In Greek "union" is said, meaning that the two natures of the Lord are united, not mixed.

200. Cabasilas, *A Commentary on the Divine Liturgy*, p. 25.

201. Fr. Petre Vintilescu first explains with a text from Nicholas Cabasilas (*A Commentary on the Divine Liturgy*, p. 40) the words of the priest when taking out the particles: "in memory of the Lord, for the glory of his Blessed Mother, and in honor of the saints. 'We give thanks to thee,' says the Church, 'that by thy death thou hast opened for us the gates of life, that from us thou didst choose a mother, that we have as ambassadors our fellow-men, and that thou hast allowed to members of our human family such freedom of access to thee.'" Then he continues: "Once the saints have been united with Christ

and were sanctified through Him, thus finding themselves around the divine glory, they can help us through their intercessions to be united with them. Offering particles for their honor and commemoration is toward our benefit and support, similar to the commemorations done in front of their icons." *Liturghierul explicat* [*The Liturgy Book Explained*] (Bucharest: Editura Institutului Biblic si de Misiune Ortodoxa, 1972), p. 125.

202. Sergii Bulgakov, *Philosophy of the Name*, translated, annotated, and with an Introduction by Thomas Allan Smith (Northern Illinois University Press, 2022), p. 193–195.

203. Nicholas Cabasilas, *A Commentary on the Divine Liturgy*, p. 31.

204. Nicholas Cabasilas, *A Commentary on the Divine Liturgy*, p. 32–33.

205. Cabasilas, *A Commentary on the Divine Liturgy*, p. 41.

206. St. Maximos the Confessor, *Mystagogia*, PG 91, 708B; ET = p. 200–201.

207. St. Athanasius, *Against the Arians*, NPNF, Second Series, 4:333.

208. St. Gregory of Nyssa, *The Lord's Prayer*, translated and annotated by Hilda C. Graef, *Ancient Christian Writers* 18 (Newman Press, 1978), p. 52.

209. Clement of Alexandria, *The Instructor*, ANF 2:295.

210. At Odo Casel, "Die Doxologie und des Amen der Gemeinde," in *Das chrisliche Opfermmysterium*, 561.

211. Blaise Pascal, *Pensées*, ch. "Pensées sur la mort" (Flammarion, 1976), p. 283–284.

212. Archimandrite Vasileios, *Hymn of Entry*, p. 41–43, 45, 48.

213. Archimandrite Vasileios, *Hymn of Entry*, p. 66–67.

214. Archimandrite Vasileios, *Hymn of Entry*, p. 67.

215. Archimandrite Vasileios, *Hymn of Entry*, p. 77.

216. Jürgen Moltman, *The Trinity and the Kingdom* (Minneapolis, MN: Fortress Press, 1993), p. 70–71.

217. Moltman, *The Trinity and the Kingdom*, p. 73.

218. Moltman, *The Trinity and the Kingdom*, p. 72.

219. St. Cyril of Alexandria, *Adoration in Spirit and in Truth*, Book XI, PG 68.

220. St. Cyril of Alexandria, *Adoration in Spirit and in Truth*, Book XI, PG 68.

221. St. Cyril of Alexandria, *Adoration in Spirit and in Truth*, Book XVII.

222. St. Cyril of Alexandria, *Adoration in Spirit and in Truth*, Book XVII.

223. St. Cyril of Alexandria, *Adoration in Spirit and in Truth*, Book XI.

224. St. Cyril of Alexandria, *Adoration in Spirit and in Truth*, Book XI.

225. Source unidentified. (tr. note)

226. St. Gregory of Nyssa, *The Lord's Prayer*, p. 51.

227. John Climacus, *The Ladder of Divine Ascent*, The Classics of Western Spirituality (Paulist Press, 1982), p. 285.

228. St. Gregory of Nyssa, *The Lord's Prayer*, p. 51–52.

229. St. Maximos the Confessor, *On Difficulties in Sacred Scripture: The Responses to Thalassios*, Question 21, translated by Fr. Maximos Constas (The Catholic University of America Press, 2018), p. 143ff.

230. St. Cyril of Alexandria, *Adoration in Spirit and in Truth*, Book XI.

231. St. Cyril of Alexandria, *Adoration in Spirit and in Truth*, Book XI.

232. *Concordance des Saintes Ecritures* (Lausanne, 1965), p. 357 translates: "Amen is pronounced by us for the glory of God."

233. St. Maximos the Confessor, *On Difficulties in Sacred Scripture*, Question 21, p. 147: "So the Lord 'stripped off the principalities and authorities' at the time of His first experience of temptations in the desert, thereby healing the whole of human nature of the passibility associated with pleasure. He 'stripped them off' yet again at the time of His death, likewise removing from our nature the passibility associated with pain."

234. St. Maximos the Confessor says about the human person joined to Christ: "And finally, in addition to all this, had man united created nature with the uncreated through love . . . he would have shown them to be one and the same by the state of grace, the whole man wholly pervading the whole God, and becoming everything that God is, without, however, identity in essence, and receiving the whole of God instead of himself, and obtaining as a kind of prize for his ascent to God the absolutely unique God, who is the goal of the motion of things that are carried along to Him, and the limit (itself limitless and infinite) of every definition, order, and law, whether of mind, intellect, or nature." On *Difficulties in the Church Fathers: The Ambigua*, ed. and trans. Nicholas Constas (Harvard University Press, 2014), Volume II, p. 109.

235. St. Maximos the Confessor, *The Ambigua*, Volume I, p. 89–90.

236. St. Maximos the Confessor, *Explanation of the Lord's Prayer*, PG 90, 871, 910.

237. St. Maximos the Confessor, *Explanation of the Lord's Prayer*, PG 90, 871, 910.

238. Stanley Harakas says: "The faithful experience a foretaste of that Eternal Kingdom through Liturgical Experience." *Living the Liturgy* (Light and Life Publishing Co., 1974), p. 27.

239. St. Maximus the Confessor, *The Church's Mystagogy*, in *Selected Writings, The Classics of Western Spirituality* (Paulist Press, 1985), p. 198–199.

240. Nicholas Cabasilas, *A Commentary on the Divine Liturgy*, p. 45.

241. Nicholas Cabasilas, *A Commentary on the Divine Liturgy*, p. 46.

242. Nicholas Cabasilas, *A Commentary on the Divine Liturgy*, p. 48.

243. Nicholas Cabasilas, *A Commentary on the Divine Liturgy*, p. 45.

244. Maurice Zundel, *Je suis un autre* (Desclée de Brouwer, 1971), p. 85.

245. Nicholas Cabasilas, *A Commentary on the Divine Liturgy*, p. 49.

246. Zundel, *Je est un autre*, p. 28–29.

247. Zundel, *Je est un autre*, p. 30–31.

248. Zundel, *Je est un autre*, p. 85. Zundel says that the human person, as well as the divine one, is constituted as a reference to God. We would say that reference pertains to person. For in order to be referred, it must exist. Or existence and reference are together and at the same time, not one without the other.

249. Zundel, *Je est un autre*, p. 106.

250. In the Greek Liturgy Book this prayer is placed before the exclamation. This is a custom that has its meaning. Placing the prayer after the exclamation is also good, as it is in the Romanian Liturgy Book, because it gives the priest time to recite his prayer during the singing of the first antiphon by the people. It needs to be found out what Liturgy Book was followed, Greek or Slavonic, when this order was first established in the Romanian Liturgy Book.

251. Nicholas Cabasilas, *A Commentary on the Divine Liturgy*, p. 48.

252. St. Irenaeus, *Against Heresies*, Book I, Chap. 3, 1; ET = ANF, 1:319.

253. Nicholas Cabasilas, *A Commentary on the Divine Liturgy*, p. 55.

254. Nicholas Cabasilas, *A Commentary on the Divine Liturgy*, p. 59.

255. Nicholas Cabasilas, *A Commentary on the Divine Liturgy*, p. 57.

256. Fr. Petre Vintilescu, *The Liturgy Book Explained*, p. 163.

257. Fr. Petre Vintilescu, *The Liturgy Book Explained*, p. 172.

258. Fr. Petre Vintilescu, *The Liturgy Book Explained*, p. 170: "In the olden times the Liturgy began once the bishop came into the church and entered the altar. As this always represents the Savior in the person of the bishop, his coming into the church and his entrance into his service could symbolize the beginning of the Son of God's activity in the world. Soon, however, the number of churches increased, so it was impossible for the representative par excellence of the Savior to participate liturgically, namely of the bishop who now had to officiate in the cathedral of his see; in these new conditions of church life the need or the fact for the representation of the Savior was fittingly resolved through the simple, solemn power of the Gospel, even more so that at that time, as it is today, the bishop was met by the clergy with the Gospel when he came into the church. Therefore, what has been done then in the presence of the bishop could be continued even in his absence." Fr. Petre Vintilescu says that it is difficult to point out the era in which this was added to the old beginning of the Liturgy. It is placed at the beginning of the seventh century (*The Liturgy Book Explained*, p. 195).

But if very early on the bishop was met by the priest, once the priests began to appear at the episcopal church, they must have been even then present in the church before the coming of the bishop, and it is possible that they were not waiting silently, but were reciting certain preliminary prayers to keep the faithful occupied (the litanies and the antiphons).

259. Nicholas Cabasilas, *A Commentary on the Divine Liturgy*, p. 59.

260. Nicholas Cabasilas, *A Commentary on the Divine Liturgy*, p. 59.

261. Nicholas Cabasilas, *A Commentary on the Divine Liturgy*, p. 51, 52.

262. Fr. Peter Vintilescu, *The Liturgy Book Explained*, p. 171.
263. Fr. Petre Vintilescu, *The Liturgy Book Explained*, p. 171.
264. Paul Evdokimov, *La prière de l'église de l'Orient* (Paris: Salvator, Mulhouse, 1966), p. 59.
265. St. John Chrysostom, *Homily on Hebrews*, XVII, ET = NPNF, Second Series, 16:447.
266. St. John Chrysostom, *Homilies on Timothy*, ET = NPNF, Second Series, 13:425.
267. Evdokimov, *La prière de l'église de l'Orient*, p. 52–54.
268. Nicholas Cabasilas, *A Commentary on the Divine Liturgy*, p. 59.
269. Nicholas Cabasilas, *A Commentary on the Divine Liturgy*, p. 59.
270. Nicholas Cabasilas, *A Commentary on the Divine Liturgy*, p. 60.
271. The Greek text says: "enable you to proclaim the good tidings with great power." This is good, too, for to the extent to which the human person offers more power from himself, he is enabled by God. Still, the Romanian text is better, for "the great power comes from God."
272. Blessed Augustine, *Lectures or Tractates on the Gospel According to St. John*, Tractate XXX, NPNF, Second Series, 7:186.
273. Nicholas Cabasilas, *A Commentary on the Divine Liturgy*, p. 61.
274. Evdokimov, *La prière de l'église de l'Orient*, p. 34.
275. At Evdokimov, *La prière de l'église de l'Orient*, p. 50.
276. Fr. Peter Vintilescu, *The Liturgy Book Explained*, p. 194.
277. Fr. Peter Vintilescu, *The Liturgy Book Explained*, p. 195.
278. Evdokimov, *La prière de l'église de l'Orient*, p. 59.
279. Nicholas Cabasilas, *A Commentary on the Divine Liturgy*, p. 64.
280. Fr. Staniloae wrote this book during the communist regime when the Church was forbidden to evangelize outside liturgical services. His words were indeed prophetic (tr. note).
281. P. S. Renz, *Geschichte des Messopferbegirffes* (1909), vol. I, p. 254. P. Wieland, Mensa und Confessio (1906), vol. I, p. 51. For both these authors, see Casel, Das christliche Opfermysterium, p. 104–105.
282. Casel, *Das christliche Opfermysterium*, p. 99.
283. Casel, *Das christliche Opfermysterium*, p. 126.
284. Casel, *Das christliche Opfermysterium*, p. 128.
285. Casel, *Das christliche Opfermysterium*, p. 101.
286. Evdokimov, *La prière de l'église de l'Orient*, p. 170 where he quotes from St. Symeon of Thessalonica who says: "The moment when the catechumens depart and the faithful remain indicates the end of time."
287. Blaise Pascal, *Pensées*, p. 283–284: "We know that life, and especially the life of Christians, is a continuous sacrifice, which cannot end except in death; we know that Jesus Christ by coming into the world considered Himself and has offered Himself to God as a complete holocaust and as a true gift of sacrifice; that His birth, His life, His death, His resurrection, His ascen-

sion, His eternal sitting at the right hand of His Father and His presence in the Eucharist are but one single and unique sacrifice; we know that what took place in Christ must take place in all His members; Let us, therefore, regard life as a sacrifice and think that the accidents of our life have no significance in the spirit of Christians except to the measure in which they interrupt or complete this sacrifice. We do not call evil except what makes the gift of sacrifice destined to God a victim of the devil, but we call good what makes out of the victim which in Adam became a victim of the devil, a victim of God... If we do not cross over to God through the Mediator Christ, we find nothing in ourselves except true afflictions or condemnable pleasures. But if we view all things in Christ, we will find complete consolation, complete contentment and our complete spiritual growth. Let us, therefore, view death in Christ and not outside of Him. Without Jesus Christ it is horrible, detestable, it is a horror of nature. In Jesus Christ death is worth loving, it is sacred, it is the joy of the believer. Everything in Christ is sweet, even death. This is why He suffered and died so as to sanctify death and suffering... so as to sanctify in Him all things, except sin."

288. Evdokimov, *La prière de l'église de l'Orient*, p. 176.
289. St. Cyril of Alexandria, *Adoration in Spirit and in Truth*, Book X.
290. St. Cyril of Alexandria, *Adoration in Spirit and in Truth*, Book X.
291. During the first centuries all the faithful exchanged the kiss of peace, men with men and women with women, under the supervision of deacons. *Constitutions of the Holy Apostles*, Book II, Section VII, ANF 7:422.
292. St. Cyril of Jerusalem, *The Catechetical Lectures*, Lecture XXIII, NPNF, Second Series, 7:153.
293. Jean Danielou, *Les homelies catéchétiques de Teodor de Mopsuestia*, Cité de Vatican, 1949; Hom. XV, 40..
294. Jean Danielou, *L'ésprit de la Liturgie*, ed. Cerf, Paris, 1952, 1952, p. 182.
295. P. Vintilescu considers that in olden times this expression was limited to the words: "The doors, the doors," by which the deacons were probably made aware to guard the doors to the entrance of the church. The expression "With wisdom let us be attentive" was added later on.
296. St. Maximus the Confessor, *The Church's Mystagogy*, p. 201.
297. At Evdokimov, *La prière de l'église de l'Orient*, p. 178.
298. St. Cyril of Alexandria, *Adoration in Spirit and in Truth*, Book XVII.
299. Fr. Petre Vintilescu, *The Liturgy Book Explained*, p. 117.
300. St. Maximus the Confessor, *The Church's Mystagogy*, p. 202.
301. Fr. Petre Vintilescu, *The Liturgy Book Explained*, p. 223.
302. Fr. Petre Vintilescu, *The Liturgy Book Explained*, p. 223.
303. St. John Chrysostom, *On the Incomprehensible Nature of God*, PG 48, 707B; ET = p. 113.
304. St. John Chrysostom, *On the Incomprehensible Nature of God*, PG 48, 733C; ET = p. 129.

305. St. Cyril of Alexandria, *Adoration in Spirit and in Truth*, Book X.
306. St. Cyril of Alexandria, *Adoration in Spirit and in Truth*, Book XVII.
307. St. Cyril of Alexandria, *Adoration in Spirit and in Truth*, Book X.
308. St. Cyril of Alexandria, *Adoration in Spirit and in Truth*, Book XVII.
309. St. Cyril of Jerusalem, *The Catechetical Lectures*, Lecture XXIII, NPNF, Second Series, 7:153–154.
310. Karl Jaspers also speaks of an existence beyond what can be thought of. But he gives no indication about the conscious interest which that existence might have for us. He is content to simply remark the impossibility of our thinking of it: "Thinking . . . wishes that thinking might attain non-thinking" (*Philosophy*, vol. III [Berlin: Metaphisics, 1932], p. 39). "Thus I can neither think of this absolute being, nor can I pretend that I want to think of it. This being is transcendence, if I cannot understand it, but I have to rise toward it in a thought, which becomes a non-thought" (p. 38). "It is conceivable that there exists something that is inconceivable" (p. 26–27).
311. Archimandrite Vasileios, *Hymn of Entry*, p. 64.
312. Prof. Ene Braniste, "St. Basil the Great in Christian Worship," in *St. Basil the Great* (Bucharest, 1980), p. 245.
313. Archimandrite Vasileios, *Hymn of Entry*, p. 64.
314. St. Cyril of Alexandria, *Adoration in Spirit and in Truth*, Book XVII.
315. St. John Chrysostom, *On the Incomprehensible Nature of God*, p. 132–133 (slightly different in Romanian; tr. note).
316. St. Cyril of Jerusalem, *The Catechetical Lectures*, Lecture XXIII, NPNF, Second Series, 7:154.
317. Jean Danielou, *Les homelies catéchétiques de Teodor de Mopsuestia*, Cité de Vatican, 1949; Hom. XVI, 9.
318. Jean Danielou, *L'ésprit de la Liturgie*, ed. Cerf, Paris, 1952, 1952, p. 183.
319. From the *Liturgy of St. Basil the Great*.
320. From the *Liturgy of St. Basil the Great*.
321. St. Cyril of Alexandria, *Adoration in Spirit and in Truth*, Book X.
322. St. Cyril of Alexandria, *Adoration in Spirit and in Truth*, Book XVII.
323. Archimandrite Vasileios, *Hymn of Entry*, p. 93.
324. Archimandrite Vasileios, *Hymn of Entry*, p. 71.
325. St. Maximos the Confessor, *The Ambigua*, Volume I, p. 321.
326. St. Cyril of Alexandria, *Adoration in Spirit and in Truth*, Book XVII.
327. St. Cyril of Alexandria, *Adoration in Spirit and in Truth*, Book XVII.
328. St. Cyril of Alexandria, *Adoration in Spirit and in Truth*, Book X.
329. St. Cyril of Alexandria, *Adoration in Spirit and in Truth*, Book X.
330. Danielou, *Les homelies catéchétiques de Teodor de Mopsuestia*, Cité de Vatican, 1949; Hom. XV, 12.
331. Romanian saying.
332. Archimandrite Vasileios, *Hymn of Entry*, p. 59.
333. Archimandrite Vasileios, *Hymn of Entry*, p. 59–60.

334. St. Symeon the New Theologian, *Hymns of Divine Love*, Hymns 13 and 15, p. 46, 54.

335. Kallistos Kataphygiotes, *On Union with God and the Contemplative Life*, in *Philokalia*, Volume V, p. 253.

336. Kallistos Kataphygiotes, *On Union with God and the Contemplative Life*, in Philokalia, Volume V, p. 255, 256–257.

337. Fr. Petre Vintilescu, *The Liturgy Book Explained*, p. 244–246.

338. Fr. Petre Vintilescu, *The Liturgy Book Explained*, p. 241. St. Basil the Great says that the epiklesis is so old that no one knows who among the saints wrote it (*On the Holy Spirit*, ch. 27, NPNF, Second Series, 8:41). And Pseudo-Proclus (+446) of Constantinople regards the epiklesis as coming from the Apostles who, before they scattered into the world, spent most of the time officiating the Holy Liturgy and offering prayers, waiting for the descent of the Holy Spirit to transform the bread and wine mixed with water into the body and blood of our Lord Jesus Christ (*Treatise on the Tradition of the Divine Liturgy*, PG 65, 849). At Fr. Petre Vintilescu, *The Liturgy Book Explained*, p. 241, note 730–731.

339. The Romanian adverb *încă* has more than one meaning: sunt încă aici = I am *still* here; încă o dată = one more time; încă ne rugăm pentru ... = *furthermore* we pray for.... It is this last meaning that Fr. Staniloae wants to give in this instance to *încă* (ετι) used at the beginning of the epiklesis prayer (*furthermore we offer unto Thee*) instead of *iară* (again), used at the beginning of the small litanies, but also used at the beginning of this prayer in some English translations. He makes the case that with this meaning the connection between the act of offering and the sacrifice itself is made, as they are strongly united. (tr. note)

340. Fr. Petre Vintilescu, *The Liturgy Book Explained*, p. 243–244, note 740 where he quotes from his study: *The Expression 'Reasonable Sacrifice' from the Romanian Liturgy Book* (Bucharest, 1935; extract from *Studii Teologice*, VII, 1938, 1939).

341. Florensky, "Slovesnie slujenie," 63–75.

342. H. Androutsos, *Dogmatica* [*Dogmatics*], Romanian translation (Sibiu, 1930), p. 394, also says that in the Holy Liturgy the expression "reasonable sacrifice" refers sometimes to our spiritual sacrifices, prayers of praise and thanksgiving, and inner purification.

343. Florensky, "Slovesnie slujenie," p. 74–75.

344. Florensky, "Slovesnie slujenie," p. 74–75.

345. St. Cyril of Alexandria, *Adoration in Spirit and in Truth*, Book IX.

346. St. John Chrysostom, *Homilies on Timothy*, NPNF, First Series, 13:483.

347. Archbishop Alexei, "Einführung und Erläuterung zu euharistichen Texten in der russichen ortodoxen Texten und der evangelischen Kirche in Deutschland," in *Das Opfer Christi und das Opfer der Christen*. In: *Das Arnoldsheimer Gespräch über die Bedeutung des Opfers am heiligen Abendmahl*

(Verlag Otto Lambeck, 1979), p. 119. ["Introduction to and Explanation of the Eucharistic Texts in the Russian Orthodox Texts and those of the Evangelical Church in Germany," in *The Sacrifice of Christ and the Sacrifice of Christians*, in T*he Conversations from Arnoldsheim on the Meaning of Sacrifice in the Holy Eucharist* (Verlag Otto Lambeck, 1979), p. 119.]

348. At Fr. Petre Vintilescu, T*he Liturgy Book Explained*, p. 241, note 278.

349. St. Justin, *First Apology*, ANF, 1:185.

350. St. Irenaeus, *Against Heresies*, Book IV; ET = ANF, 1:486.

351. Archbishop Alexei, "Einführung und Erlaüterung."

352. St. Cyril of Alexandria, *Adoration in Spirit and in Truth*, Book XI.

353. Archimandrite Vasileios, *Hymn of Entry*, p. 62.

354. Nicholas Cabasilas, *A Commentary on the Divine Liturgy*, p. 111.

355. Prof. Ene Braniste, "St. Basil the Great in Christian Worship," in *St. Basil the Great* (Bucharest, 1980), p. 94.

356. St. Cyril of Jerusalem, *The Catechetical Lectures*, Lecture XXIII, NPNF, Second Series, 7:152.

357. St. Cyril of Jerusalem, *The Catechetical Lectures*, Lecture XXIII, NPNF, Second Series, 7:154.

358. At Jean Danielou, *Les homelies catéchétiques de Teodor de Mopsuestia*, Cité de Vatican, 1949; Hom. XVI, 12.

359. Jean Danielou, *Les homelies catéchetiques de Teodor de Mopsuestia*, Cite de Vatican, 1949, Hom. XVI , 452 B.

360. St. John Chrysostom, *Homilies on Hebrews*, NPNF, First Series, 13:449.

361. Jean Danielou, *L'ésprit de la Liturgie*, ed. Cerf, Paris, 1952, 1952, p. 183.

362. At Jean Danielou, *Les homelies catéchetiques de Teodor de Mopsuestia*, Cite de Vatican, 1949, Hom. XV, 14 and 20.

363. Jean Danielou, *L'ésprit de la Liturgie*, ed. Cerf, Paris, 1952, 1952, p. 180.

364. Bulgakov, *Philosophy of the Name*, p. 232.

365. Bulgakov, *Philosophy of the Name*, p. 233.

366. Bulgakov, *Philosophy of the Name*, p. 199.

367. Bulgakov, *Philosophy of the Name*, p. 210–211.

368. Thinkers such as Gabriel Marcel, in *Etre et avoir*, and Michel Sora, in *Du dialog intérieur*, have insisted upon this distinction.

369. The Romanian pronouns *dumneata* (you, the second person singular), or *dumneavoastră* (thou, the second person both singular and plural) are commonly used when politely addressing another person or persons, usually older or occupying an important position, as a way of showing respect to that particular person or persons. For example, a student would never address his or her professor with *tu* (you), but always with *dumneavoastră* (thou). The same is true when someone addresses a priest, a bishop or any person or persons in high office. Even though the English version (*thou*) is archaic, it is still used in ecclesiastical discourse when one refers to God. (tr. note)

370. *In Leviticum*, PG 12, 749: Origen speaks even of Christ's weeping for all until all will be saved. Perhaps this shows his idea that the Son is lesser than the Father. Maybe this is why he can only see the state of Christ's continued kenosis, not the one of glory as well.

371. Robert T. Osborn, "What is in a Name?," *St. Vladimir's Seminary Quarterly* 12, no. 2 (1968), p. 81.

372. Similitudes, ix, 14, in Kallistos Ware, *The Power of the Name*, Fairacres Publications 43 (SLG Press, 2022), p. 14.

373. Ware, *The Power of the Name*, p. 16. Questions and Answers, ed. Sotirios Schoinas (Volos, 1960), para. 693; translated by L. Reginault and P. Lemaire (Solesmes, 1972), para. 692.

374. Ware, *The Power of the Name*, p. 16. Ladder, 21 (PG 88, 945C).

375. Ware, *The Power of the Name*, p. 14.

376. St. Cyril of Alexandria, *Adoration in Spirit and in Truth*, Book IX.

377. St. Cyril of Alexandria, *Adoration in Spirit and in Truth*, Book IX.

378. St. Cyril of Alexandria, *Adoration in Spirit and in Truth*, Book IX.

379. St. Cyril of Alexandria, *Adoration in Spirit and in Truth*, Book XIII.

380. St. Cyril of Alexandria, *Adoration in Spirit and in Truth*, Book XVII.

381. St. Cyril of Alexandria, *Adoration in Spirit and in Truth*, Book X.

382. St. Cyril of Alexandria, *Adoration in Spirit and in Truth*, Book X.

383. Sergei Bulgakov, *The Eucharistic Dogma*, at V. Borovoi, "Das Opfer Christi nach der Heilegen Schrift," in *Das Opfer Christi und das Opfer der Christen* [*The Sacrifice of Christ and the Sacrifice of Christians*], p. 136.

384. St. Maximos the Confessor, Ambiguum 7, *The Ambigua*, Volume I, p. 107–109. St. Gregory Nazianzen, *The Second Theological Oration*, NPNF, Second Series, 7:294.

385. H. I. Schultz expresses thus St. John Chrysostom's teaching: "Precisely in those places from Chrysostom's Liturgy in which the believers and the priest seem to unite themselves in a unitary subject, they want to make ever clearer that the celebration of the Eucharist as sacrifice is, in the last analysis, a place of experiencing the unique sacrifice that reconciles all." *Liturgischer Vollzug und sacramentale Wirchlichkeit des Euharistischen Opfers* [*Liturgical Celebration and the Sacramental Reality of the Eucharistic Sacrifice*], Extracta ex. Vol. XVI, fasc. 1, 1980, from *Orientalia Christiana Periodica*, Rome, 1980, p. 16).

386. Origen, *In Leviticum*, hom. VII, PG 12, 480, says again that Christ weeps.

387. Nicholas Cabasilas, *The Life in Christ*, translated from the Greek by Carmino J. deCatanzaro (St. Vladimir's Seminary Press, 1974), p. 164.

388. Origen, *In Leviticum*, hom. VII, PG 12, 480, says that Jesus will not be subjected to the Father until all are subjected. It is here where perhaps his apokatastasis appears, or the idea that all will be saved.

389. Source unidentified (tr. note).

390. St. Gregory of Nyssa, *The Lord's Prayer*, p. 39–40.

391. Kallistos the Patriarch, *Chapters on Prayer*, Romanian Philokalia, vol. VIII, p. 328-329. E = St. Kallistos Angelikoudes, *Chapters on Prayer*, ch. 55, in *Philokalia*, vol. V, p. 184-185.

392. Kallistos the Patriarch, *Chapters on Prayer*, Romanian Philokalia, vol. VIII, p. 328.

393. St. John Chrysostom, *Homilies on St. John*, 46, NPNF, First Series, 14:167.

394. St. Cyril of Alexandria, *Adoration in Spirit and in Truth*, Book X.

395. St. Maximos the Confessor, *The Ambigua*, Volume I, p. 217-219.

396. Bulgakov, *Philosophy of the Name*, p. 224-226.

397. St. John of Damascus, *On the Orthodox Faith*, Book IV, Fathers of the Church 37, translated by Frederic H. Chase, Jr. (Washington, DC: The Catholic University of America Press, 1958), p. 360.

398. *Canon and Prayers in Preparation for Holy Communion*, Ode 9.

399. *Canon and Prayers in Preparation for Holy Communion*, Ode 9.

400. *Canon and Prayers in Preparation for Holy Communion*, Ode 6.

401. *Canon and Prayers in Preparation for Holy Communion*, Ode 5.

402. *Philokalia*, Volume V, p. 121.

403. *Philokalia*, Volume V, p. 122.

404. Joseph Ratzinger, speaking about the intimate relationship between spirit and body, says: "The cavalier divorce of 'biology' and theology omits precisely man from consideration; it becomes a self-contradiction insofar as the initial, essential point of the whole matter lies precisely in the affirmation that in all that concerns man the biological is also human and especially in what concerns the divinely-human *nothing* is 'merely biological.' Banishment of the corporeal, or sexual, into pure biology, all the talk about the 'merely biological,' is consequently the exact antithesis of what faith intends. For faith tells us of the spirituality of the biological as well as the corporeality of the spiritual and divine . . . the God become flesh." *Daughter Zion*, translated by John M. McDermott, SJ, (San Francisco: Ignatius Press, 1983), p. 52-53.

405. St. Maximos the Confessor, From Epistle 7 to John Cubicularius: *On the fact that even after death the soul has a rational activity and it does not abandon any of its natural faculties*, PG 91, 436-437.

My thanks and appreciation to Fr. Andrew Louth who translated this text from the original Greek in Migne. As an expert on St. Maximos, Fr. Andrew states: "It seems certain that the Migne reading of the correspondent is wrong: it is Jordanes the presbyter (the recipient of *epp.* 6 and 8)." (tr. note)

406. *The Ascetical Homilies of Saint Isaac the Syrian*, translated by The Holy Transfiguration Monastery (Boston, MA: 1984), p. 385.

407. St. John Chrysostom, *Homily VI on Hosea*, 3.

408. Nicolai Hartmann, *Zum Problem der Realitätsgegebenheit* [*On the Problem of the Givenness of Reality*] (Berlin: Pan-Verlagsgesellschaft, 1931).

409. St. John Chrysostom, *On the Incomprehensible Nature of God*.

410. St. John Chrysostom, *On the Incomprehensible Nature of God*, p. 133.
411. St. John Chrysostom, *On the Incomprehensible Nature of God*, p. 101–102.
412. St. John Chrysostom, *On the Incomprehensible Nature of God*, p. 102.
413. Archimandrite Vasileios, *Hymn of Entry*, p. 82–83.
414. Ratzinger, *Daughter Zion*, p. 43.
415. Cabasilas, *The Life in Christ*, p. 114, 116.
416. *The Philokalia*, vol. I (London: Faber and Faber, 1979), p. 258.
417. Theodore of Mopsuestia, *Homily XV, 7*, at Jean Danielou, *Les homelies catéchetiques de Teodor de Mopsuestia*, Cite de Vatican, 1949.
418. St. Symeon the New Theologian, *Hymns of Divine Love*, Hymn 15, p. 54.
419. St. Germanos of Constantinople, *Ecclesiastical History and Mystical Contemplation*, PG 98, 452.
420. Ion Bria, "The Liturgy after the Liturgy," *International Review of Mission 57*, no. 265 (Jan. 1978), p. 90: "The Liturgy *means* public and collective action and therefore there is a sense in which the Christian is a creator of community."

Alexander Schmemann dealt with the importance of the Liturgy for the sanctification of time and of life in *Liturgy and Life* (New York: Dept. of Religious Education, Orthodox Church in America, 1974). And Jean Corbeau, at the end of an interpretation of the Liturgy as irradiation of the Holy Trinity's compassionate love, or as a river of life that flows from the Holy Trinity, declares: "The more the Liturgy deifies us, the more our life becomes the work of God.... The Liturgy dilates the Church within the human space of divine compassion.... It penetrates our nature, our activity, all of our realities." *Liturgie de source* (Paris: Cerf, 1980), p. 197.

Very beneficial for the Orthodox faithful is the clear explanation of the Liturgy by His Grace Vasile, Bishop of Oradea, Romania, in the volume: *Predici Liturgice* [*Liturgical Sermons*] (Oradea, 1973). Many suggestions from it were used in this book.

www.ingramcontent.com/pod-product-compliance
Lightning Source LLC
Chambersburg PA
CBHW041732300426
44116CB00019B/2957